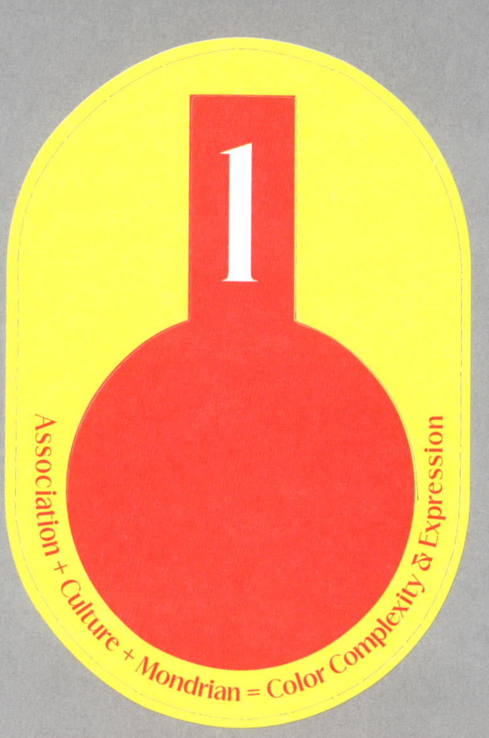

2
Origin
+
De Stijl
+
Bauhaus
=
Simplicity
&
Subjective Expressionism

3
Adventure + Innovation +
Open Mind + Broad Color = Revolution

4
Theory
+
Technique
+
Tunnel
=
Territory

5
Figures
+
Styles
=
Definite
+
Dynamic
+
Desire

THE COLOR TRIO:
PLAY WITH RED, YELLOW, AND BLUE

sendpoints

CONTENTS

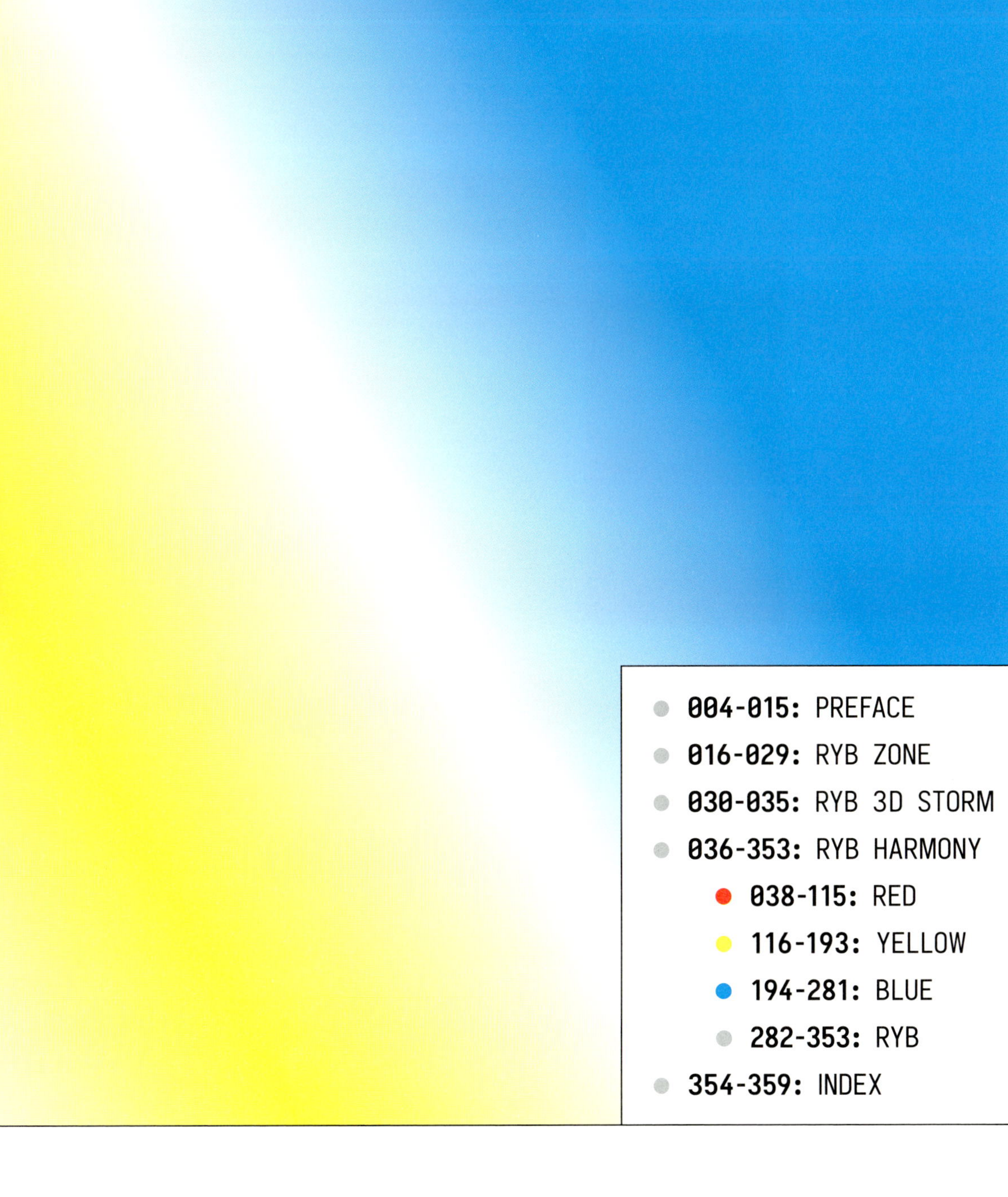

PREFACE

	Association + Culture + Mondrian	Origin + D
Color Complexity & Expression		
Simplicity + Subjective Expressionism		
Revolution		

0

tijl + Bauhaus

Adventure + Innovation + Open Mind + Broad Color

THE IMPACT OF RED, YELLOW, AND BLUE IN DESIGN

Association + Culture + Mondrian = Color Complexity & Expression

● Into the mysterious world of color, there was once a fascinating journey of exploration, a story of "red, yellow, and blue," originated in the times when the transmission of knowledge used to be asymmetric. ● At that time, art and science seemed to be separated yet still interwined in some way. An art major might say mockingly, "those who study art are not good at math and science." Meanwhile an engineering major would be unfamiliar with painting. By then, the principles of color, including optics and color discrimination mechanisms, remained underexplored. However, in this intricate scenario, a miraculous turn took place in 1725, when a German painter named Christopher Le Brun, inspired by Isaac Newton, proposed the "three primary colors" based on his artistic experience. This is now known as the "RYB color model." His discovery not only revealed the mystery of how these three colors made up the majority of colors, but also penned a pivotal stroke in history. ● Once rare and precious cinnabar and blue ultramarine pigments became the eternal primary in painters' eyes, and therefore the trio of "red, yellow, and blue" ushered in a new era. After years of exploration and accumulation, many painters, deeply rooted in their experience and creativity, regarded "red, yellow, and blue" as the cornerstone of color. The concept of color in the field of fine arts painting was then gradually taking shape, providing people with endless creative inspirations. ● At the same time, due to the rapid development of technology in the printing industry, many artists are also devoted to the new trail. In 1906, for the first time, The Eagle Printing Ink Company employed the CMYK color model in printing. Then in 1920 came out Johannes Itten's *The Art of Color*[1]. It turned out that even before Eden revealed the mystery of color, the industry had long mastered the CMYK color model and applied it to many fields.

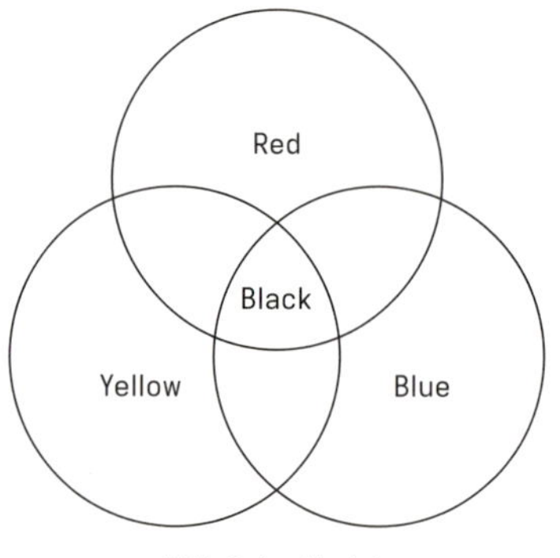

RYB Color Model

Association

• Once we see a color, we tend to associate it with something else, triggering new emotions. Red, yellow, and blue, known as the "three primary colors," shape the base of our visual perception. This implies that everything we see can be broken down into these three colors, a concept that has both confused and fascinated many great thinkers and scientists. It remains a recurring theme in contemporary art and phenomenology—a rich and complex world composed of seemingly simple color elements. • From a pioneering historical point of view, it is not difficult to find that "red, yellow, and blue" is a unique visual language in color expression. The three colors are, first and foremost, natural phenomena as well as having associative attributes. You might say that yellow is optimistic, red is associated with passion or anger, and so on. In this sense, different emotions are subtly associated to distinguish between the perceptions of colors and the truthfulness of colors. Physiologically speaking, color is only a reflection of the human visual and physiological structure of the world. The color in the eyes of humans does not necessarily represent what is real in this world. But this does not prevent people from using various languages to describe the colors in their sight, and using different colors to unveil the world in their minds.

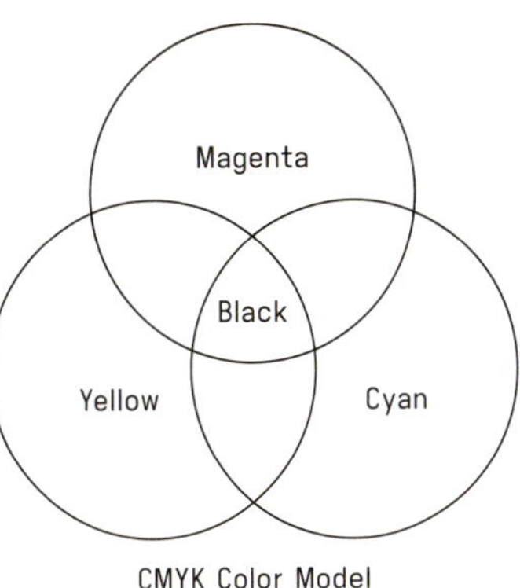

CMYK Color Model

Culture

• The concept of association arises from sociocultural construction. The semantic complexity of colors becomes apparent when their context varies. In 1969, anthropologist Brent Berlin[2] and linguist Paul Kay[3] published the book *Basic Color Terms: Their Universality and Evolution*. Their research shows that while there are differences in how different cultures classify colors, the vast majority of cultures tend to divide colors into certain basic categories, which usually include black, white, and several intermediate colors ranging from black to white. However, the aesthetic or emotional connotation of color can vary from culture to culture. For example, Western culture associates black with death; but in the ancient East, black was called "xuan (玄)" and was a symbol of supremacy and power. Yellow, in ancient China, was regarded as the color of royalty, representing dignity and majesty. In Western cultures, yellow sometimes indicates a warning or danger. Colors symbolize profound meanings in various cultures, abundantly emobodying the

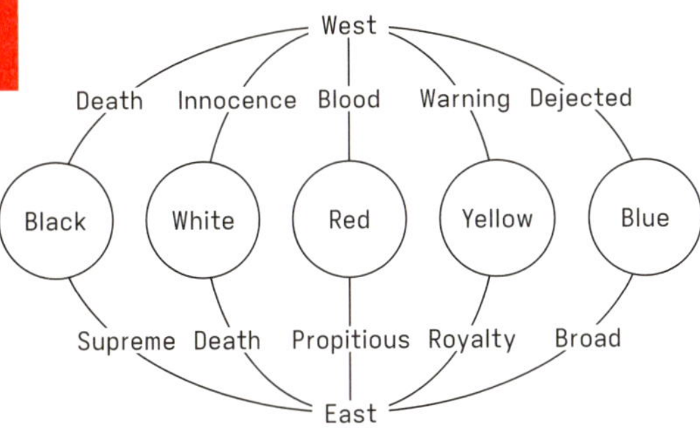

images of nations, regions, and religions. To summarize, cultures enrich colors with multifaceted connotations and associations.

Mondrian

● Piet Mondrian's well-known artwork *Composition with Red, Blue, and Yellow* shows his minimalist exploration of form and color, as well as an exploration of opponent relations, asymmetry, and the plane of pure color. Mondrian saw the painting as a contrasting harmony, symbolizing the balance and tension of dynamic forces. Mondrian viewed his black lines not as outlines but as the plane of the pigment itself. The horizontal black plane at the bottom right of the canvas appears as a contemplative touch at the edge. [1] Mondrian eliminated the illusion of depth and became obsessed with the figure-in-the-foreground concept. As a painter, Mondrain, adept at reason, revealed the universal connections beneath the surface, which is what a physicist usually does to simulate the simple order of the universe via mathematical models. Asymmetrically, he positioned the red, yellow, and blue primary colors as a counterbalance to the dominance of white paint, creating harmonized tension. Meanwhile, a large red square in the upper right corner is in balance with the small blue square in the lower left. What's more, when you see the painting from different angles, you can discern how many variations this color scheme might have been—Mondrian used different shades of black and white, some of which are slightly brighter or darker. ● Up close, these varying lines and textures create a surprising contrast and harmony in this abstract work of art. Through the arrangement of color elements, Mondrian is constructing a visual symphony, showcasing the potential for rich and complex visual expression using simple elements. Even the traces of the artist's brushstrokes stand in stark contrast to what might have otherwise been a rigid geometric composition, forming a balance between his pursuit of universal truth and an intensional intimate touch of personal experience. ● In the realm of red, yellow, and blue, the complexity of color is contemplated, and the significance of inclusive simplicity is expressed, encompassing the personal, social, cultural, and artistic dimensions.

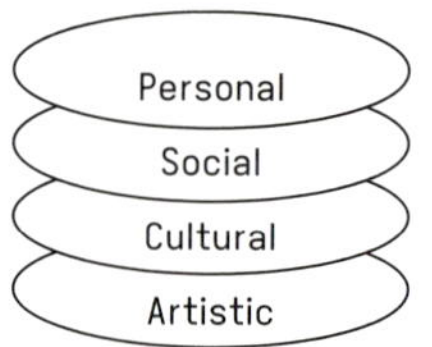

Color Complexity & Expression

● The complexity and expression of color are bound by associative perception and sociocultural construction, providing artists with a solid foundation. However, artists never cease to innovate and explore, revealing their infinite expression with color. Color transcends simple visual perceptions, evolving into a rich and diverse artistic language used to convey ideas, sentiments, and culture. In contemporary art, color complexity has solidified its presence. The prevalence of digital art enhances colors with diversity and richness, while various media's graphic design conducts bolder color experiments. In contemporary art, color serves not only as a visual delight but also as an important medium for exploring identity, emotional expression, and social concerns.

Origin + De Stijl + Bauhaus = Simplicity + Subjective Expressionism

Origin ● In the RYB color model, the three primary colors can be mixed to reproduce various hues. In the formulation of this concept, color complexity becomes perceptibly noticeable within its otherwise absolute simplicity. This complexity emerges from its origin's potential in deduction and mastery. In 1921, the avant-garde Russian artist Aleksandr Rodchenko held an exhibition in Moscow alongside four fellow Constructivism artists. Boldly, Rodchenko created a triptych for the exhibition: pure red, pure yellow, and pure blue. These three canvases, each covered with a primary pigment, represent the first monochrome non-obejctive paintings in modern art. Rodchenko did not describe his work as a tribute to painting, nor did he frame it as a condensed essence of all colors. Instead, he saw it as a celebration of the "material origins" of the art form. Rodchenko returned to the essence of the three primary colors to explain his intentions: "I reduced painting to its logical conclusion and exhibited three canvases: red, blue, and yellow. I affirmed: it's all over."

De Stijl ● Of course, this is not the end of the story. The art of painting continues to evolve, and the three primary colors have always existed, even gaining more symbolic and political significance. When Rochinko declared them to symbolize "the end of painting," Dutch painters Theo van Doesburg and Mondrian saw in the three colors a utopian vision of human harmony. They considered the three primary colors essential to their artistic innovation movement—De Stijl, or "the style" in Dutch, sometimes referred to as "Neoplasticism" or "Elementarism." ● Neoplasticism sought abstraction and simplification in art from its inception. The artists worked together to simplify images into bare elements: plane, line, and rectangle, which later became the pillars of art. Additionally, the use of color was reduced to the three prime colors of red, yellow, and blue and the three achromatic colors of black, white, and gray. ● The Neoplasticism movement was both an opposition to the proliferation of Art Deco, prevalent at the time, and a rejection of excessive ornamentation and intricate composition. De Stijl artists emphasize the basics where people find common ground. ● The political significance of the Neoplasticism movement also lies in its attempt to rebuild the fragmented postwar society through the exploration of new art forms and modes of expression. Art can transcend national boundaries and cultural gaps, becoming a unified language that conveys the common emotions and ideas of mankind. Artists believe that through simplified and abstract art forms, basic geometric shapes, and pure colors, a concept of social unity and harmony will be conveyed. Thereafter, the artistic legacy left by the avant-garde Neoplasticism movement started to have a profound impact on contemporary art and design.

The Bauhaus

● The red, yellow, and blue primary colors also found their place in the Bauhaus School. The founder of the school, Walter Gropius, is widely regarded as one of the pioneers of modern architecture. He believed that artistic innovation should produce simple, rational, and, above all, comprehensible designs. Ever since he incorporated the clear and expressive strength of primary colors into design. ● Color composition, as one of the core courses at the Bauhaus School, laid a solid foundation for the curriculum. Although the Bauhaus style often appears to have a strong industrial trait, it doesn't feature "normcore[4]." Instead, it prominently and boldly utilizes color, especially the three primary colors. Wassily Kandinsky, the leading teacher at the Bauhaus School and the pioneer of abstract painting, believed that only the perceptual combination of structure and color can give birth to real design, with red, yellow, and blue being the most important colors. In this sense, Bauhaus's household slogan "Less is more" made itself loud and clear, originally a theory developed by Mies van der Rohe, the third principal in the history of the Bauhaus. ● The Bauhaus' pursuit of simplicity was a statement of defiance, an attempt to reject the embrace of error-prone and ostentatious handmade ornaments preferred by the previous Art Deco movement. The slogan "less is more" is one of the most important influences that Bauhaus left on modern design. Today's popular design makers, including IKEA, MUJI, and others, all have Bauhaus blood. Even any form of minimalism you can name is a tribute to the Bauhaus, such as normcore and basic designs.

LESS IS MORE

Simplicity + Subjective Expressionism

● The *Red and Blue Chair*, with its highly symbolic cubist characteristics, is one of the most famous representative works of De Stijl, created by the Dutch furniture designer Gerrit Thomas Rietveld. Previously, the Arts and Crafts movement, Art Nouveau movement, and Art Deco movement valued the decorative function of design in different ways, namely the naturalistic style, complex decorations, nature-imitating motifs, exquisite crafts, and traditional manual techniques. ● In terms of design style, Neoplasticism, favoring abstraction, rejects naturalistic shapes and motifs. It forges a pure and universal aesthetic concept through geometric forms and pure colors, emphasizing the functionality and universality of design. It completely demolishes the characteristics of traditional architecture, furniture, product design, painting, and sculpture, and builds up its basic monomer complex. The three primary colors of red, yellow, and blue are also simplified and condensed into "elements." ● In 2017, Constance Rubini, then director of the Museum of Decorative Arts and Design in Bordeaux, France, used red, yellow, and blue to curate the exhibition *Oh Couleurs! Design Through the Lens of Color*. The exhibition explored the historical relationship between objects and color, which is both simple and complex. "Primary colors are straightforward and direct—that is why they are sometimes chosen to transmit their identification to objects," says Rubini. "The hue then loses its own nature and is instead conflated with its function: the yellow mailboxes in France, or the red telephone booths in England. Sometimes the primary color is pure presence; it then seeks to escape from any predefined symbolic value. It is the color that gives life and energy to objects." ● Perhaps no one recognized the "Subjective Expressionism" of color more aggressively than the German-born American artist, poet, and printmaker Josef Albers. In his view, color is a subjective and expressive medium because it is not a real phenomenon in visual perception but an artistic representation through personal interpretation and emotional expression. It serves as a token of emotional truth and freedom of expression, not the reappearance of objects. From 1963 to 1976, Albers devoted himself entirely to the study of this subject, comprehensively and systematically exploring the art, physics, and psychology of color as a discipline rather than just a theoretical field. Arbers wrote in his book *The Interaction of Color* (1971), "In visual perception, a color is almost never seen as it really is—as it physically is. This fact makes color the most relative medium in art." ● Through a series of visual experiments and color contrasts, Albers showed how colors interact and interplay with each other. He emphasized the expressive force and interrelationship of colors, aiming to guide readers to experience complicated emotions and expressions in the world of colors. Through the use and combination of different colors, such as red, yellow, and blue, color is no longer a simple lump but an artistic medium full of vitality and emotional resonance.

⑤

Adventure + Innovation + Open Mind + Broad Color = Revolution

Adventure

● The COVID-19 pandemic over the past three years has caused a widespread stagnation that has fundamentally changed our daily lives, both physically and spiritually. For example, once vibrant art spaces were forced to close, making it challenging for designers to draw inspiration. This pose is a significant challenge for all designers, risking them to be trapped into rigidity instead of self-renewal and growth. ● However, against this backdrop, the contemporary art exhibition Kassel Documenta is set to return in June 2022. Notably, for the first time, the exhibition has entrusted the curatorial position to an art group from Asia. Ruangrupa, established in 2000 and based in Indoesia, translates to "room form" (in Indonesian, ruang means room and rupa means form). Beyond traditional artists, the team includes trailblazers from the circles of technology, sociology, and politics. ● Describing how ruangrupa operates, *The New York Times* stated, "Trying to capture ruangrupa's body of work is like trying to pin down smoke." Ade Darmawan, one of the founders of ruangrupa, commented, "It's like they are taking revenge on this mythical space, trying to hurt it." For a long time, the notions of "breakthrough" or "breaking" have been inherently intimidating—people subconsciously perceive them as difficult and complicated, often delaying taking action before fully prepared. However, artists clearly do not share this sentiment. "Trying to hurt it" has served as an exciting manifesto in art critique over the last two years. It neither embraces stagnation nor settles for breakthroughs but strives to elevate it to the next level. ● For the time being, we may reflect on past achievements and draw inspiration from former art pioneers. We carefully examine the "hurts" in art creation that they casually made without a meticulously planned process, yet their impact was powerful. It is these designers who turned a blind eye to conventional rules but always understood how to bend their tricks, starting anew with simple rules.

Innovation

● In 1929, the Uruguayan artist Joaquin Torres-Garcia, the Dutch artist Mondrian, the Belgian artist and critic Michel Seuphor, and the Spanish artist Pierre Daura co-founded the art group Cercle et Carre (Circle and Square). This group worked with pure geometry as its main focus, even idealizing it, completely rejecting the old rules of painting that emphasized natural features and figurative presence. Their attitude was to find balance, unity, and equality among the simple elements of form, plane, color, etc. that make up a work of art. Cercle et Carre's work encompasses almost all the trends of modernism: Cubism, Futurism, Dada, Constructivism, and Neoplasticism. ● The establishment of Cercle et Carre marks the subversion and breakthrough of the traditions. With an innovative spirit beyond the past, they dared to challenge existing ideas and rules, opening up a new realm of art. Cercle et Carre, transcending time, continued to influence the evolution of art history. The abstract geometric language they created laid a solid foundation for the later development of modern art. Many modern artists have been inspired by Cercle et Carre in their creations, applying geometric forms and pure colors to their own works, forming their distinctive artistic styles. This artistic revolution provided a new creative paradigm and way of thinking for later artists, inspiring countless creators.

Open mind + Broad color

● Experimenting with simple rules to achieve a breakthrough gives more room for open thinking. The three primary colors in the history of design are also a kind of "breakthrough" gained through the re-adaptation of the simple color rules. In traditional color matching practices, analogous or complementary colors are often used until the emergence of the three primary colors, which adopt the principle of contrast. According to Brenda Danilowitz, curator of the works of Joseph Albers, "The idea that red, yellow, and blue are considered 'primary colors' is based on the fact that when red, yellow, and blue pigments are mixed, they produce a series of detailed, nuanced colors, while they themselves are pure and unmixed." ● The three primary colors of red, yellow, and blue were later widely used in modernist design and art movements. Since then, designers have shucked off the bondage of traditional colors and boldly tried new color combinations and palettes while actively exploring the emotional expression of

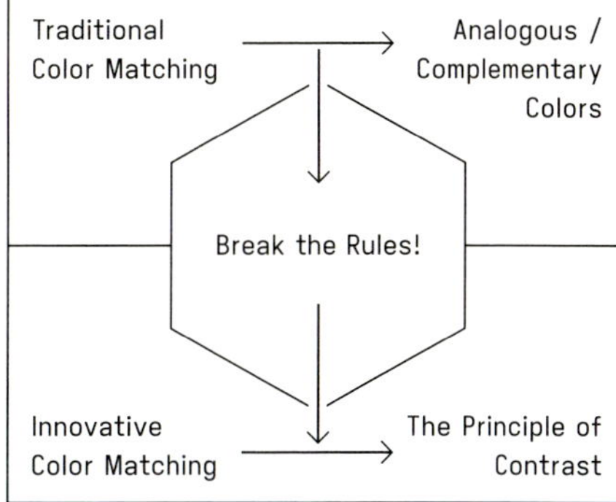

colors. They believe that color is not only a physical phenomenon but also a carrier of emotions and images. For these artists, the three primary colors are elements full of vitality and inner feelings. Through the smart use and the combination of these primary colors, they convey their innermost emotions and sentiments, allowing audiences to resonate when appreciate their works.

Revolution

● The design revolution is a continuous journey of exploration and innovation. In this process, artists constantly break through traditions, dare to challenge conventions, and explore new possibilities with an open mind. They are not satisfied with the limited creative paradigm but are willing to try new ways of expression and creative methods. ● The never-ending creative evolution continues to challenge established frameworks and boundaries. This innovative spirit will drive designers to explore new aesthetic concepts, materials, techniques, and expressions. Artists will constantly see the real world in a new light and express their understanding of and reflection on society, culture, and the environment through artistic creation. In the ever-expanding field of design, diversity and vitality will become the main themes of the future. ● Creators from different cultures and backgrounds will inspire each other and make crossovers to bring more possibilities to design.

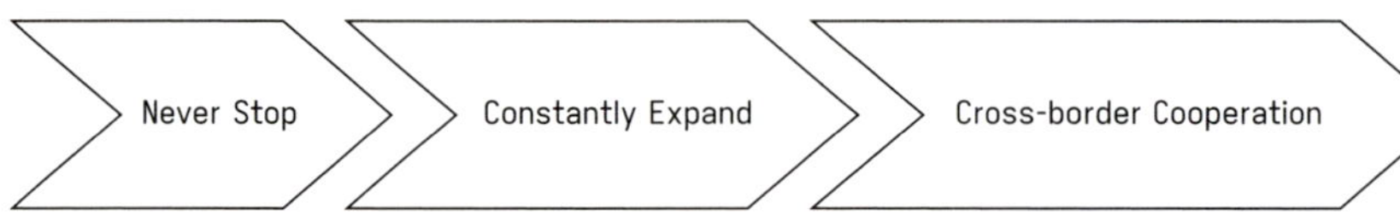

1. *The Art of Color* proposes the 12-hue Color Circle.

2. Overton Brent Berlin, born in 1936, is an American anthropologist.

3. Paul Kay, born in 1934, is an emeritus professor of linguistics at the University of California, Berkeley, United States.

4. Normcore: a unisex fashion trend characterized by unpretentious, average-looking clothing.

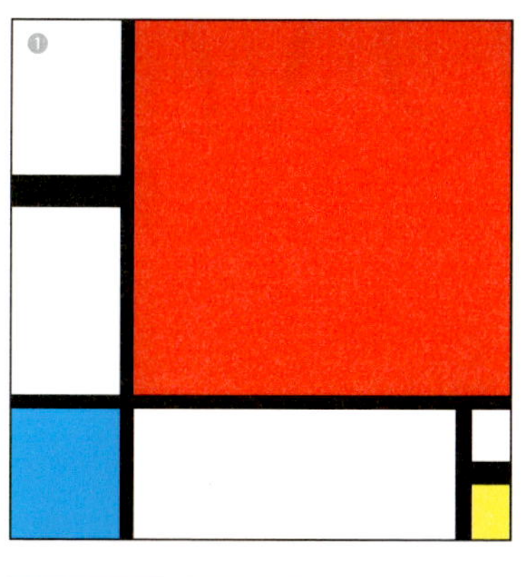

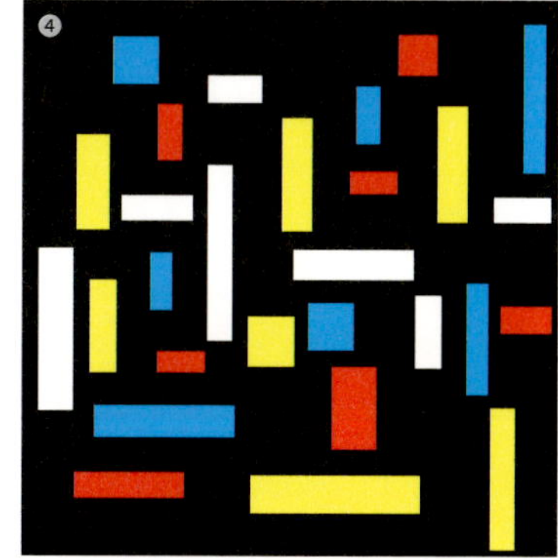

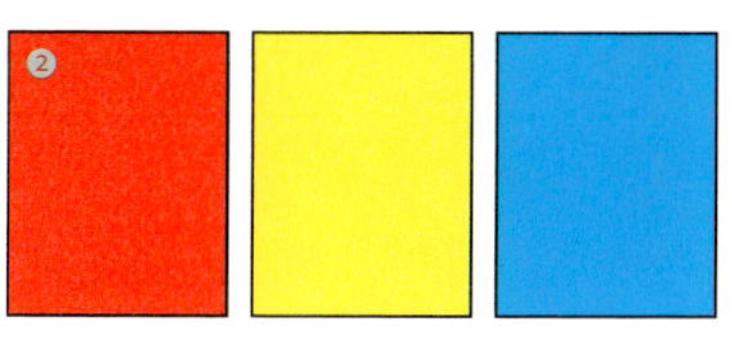

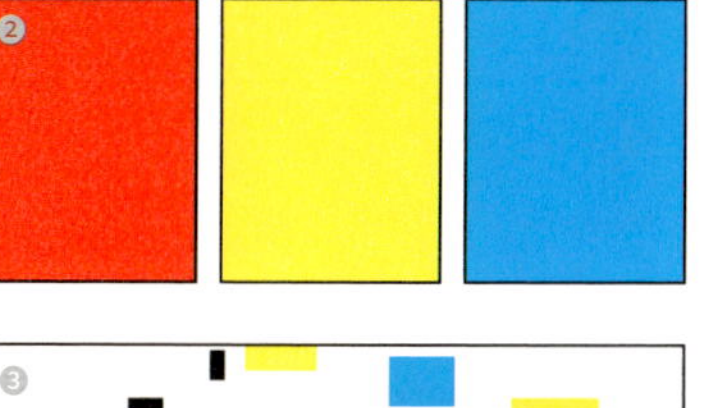

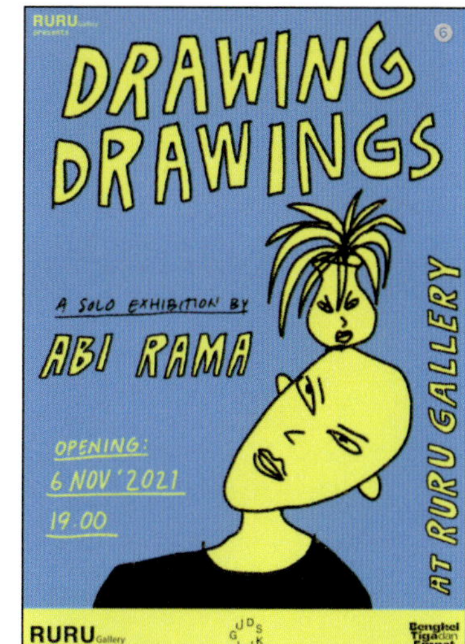

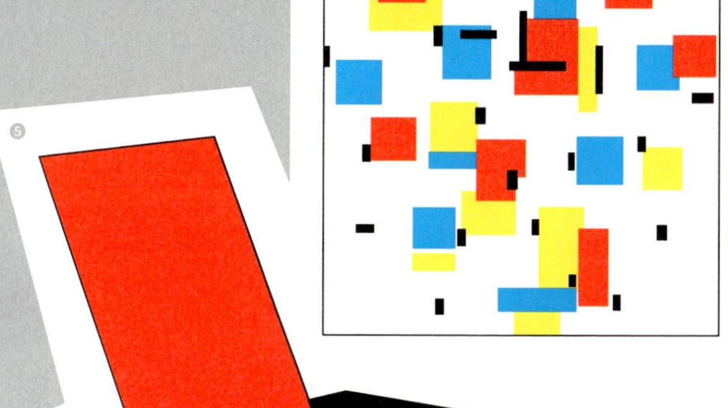

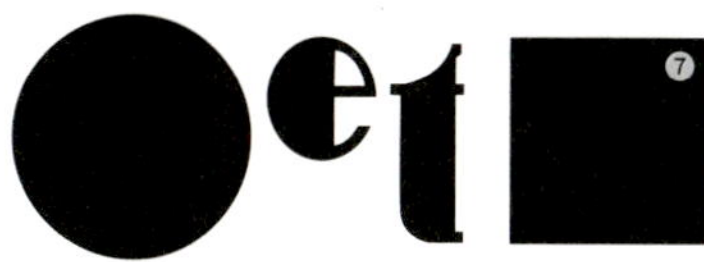

❶ *Composition with Red, Blue, and Yellow*, Piet Mondrain, 1930.

❷ *The Death of Painting*, Alexander Rodchenko, 1921.

❸ *Composition in colour A*, Piet Mondrain, 1917.

❹ *Composition VII (The Three Graces)*, Theo van Doesburg, 1917.

❺ *The Red and Blue Chair*, Gerrit Thomas Rietveld, 1917.

❻ *A Solo Exhibition by Abi Rama – Drawing Drawings*, Ruangrupa, 2021.

❼ Logo for "Cercle et Carré", Pierre Daura, 1929.

RYB ZONE

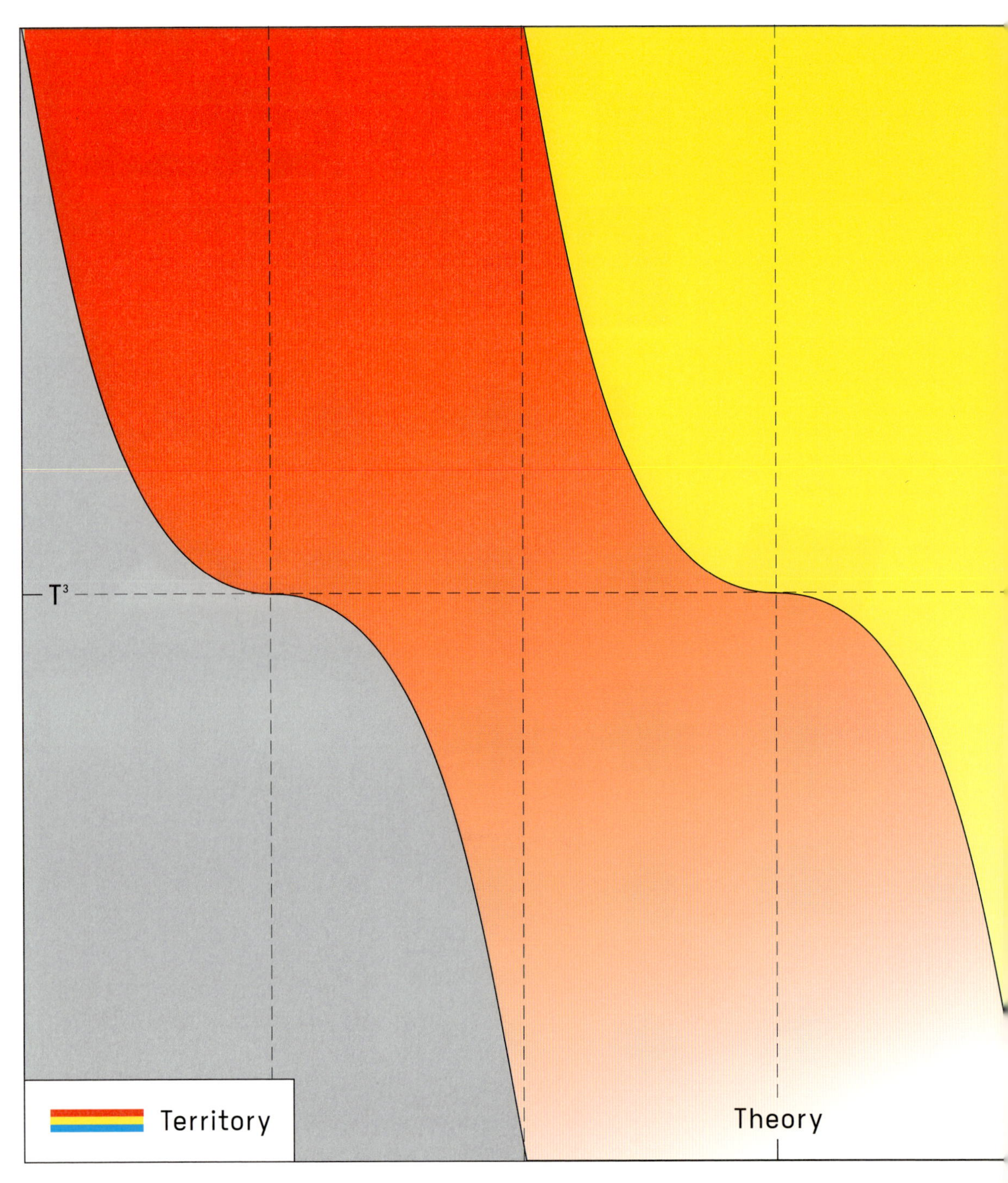

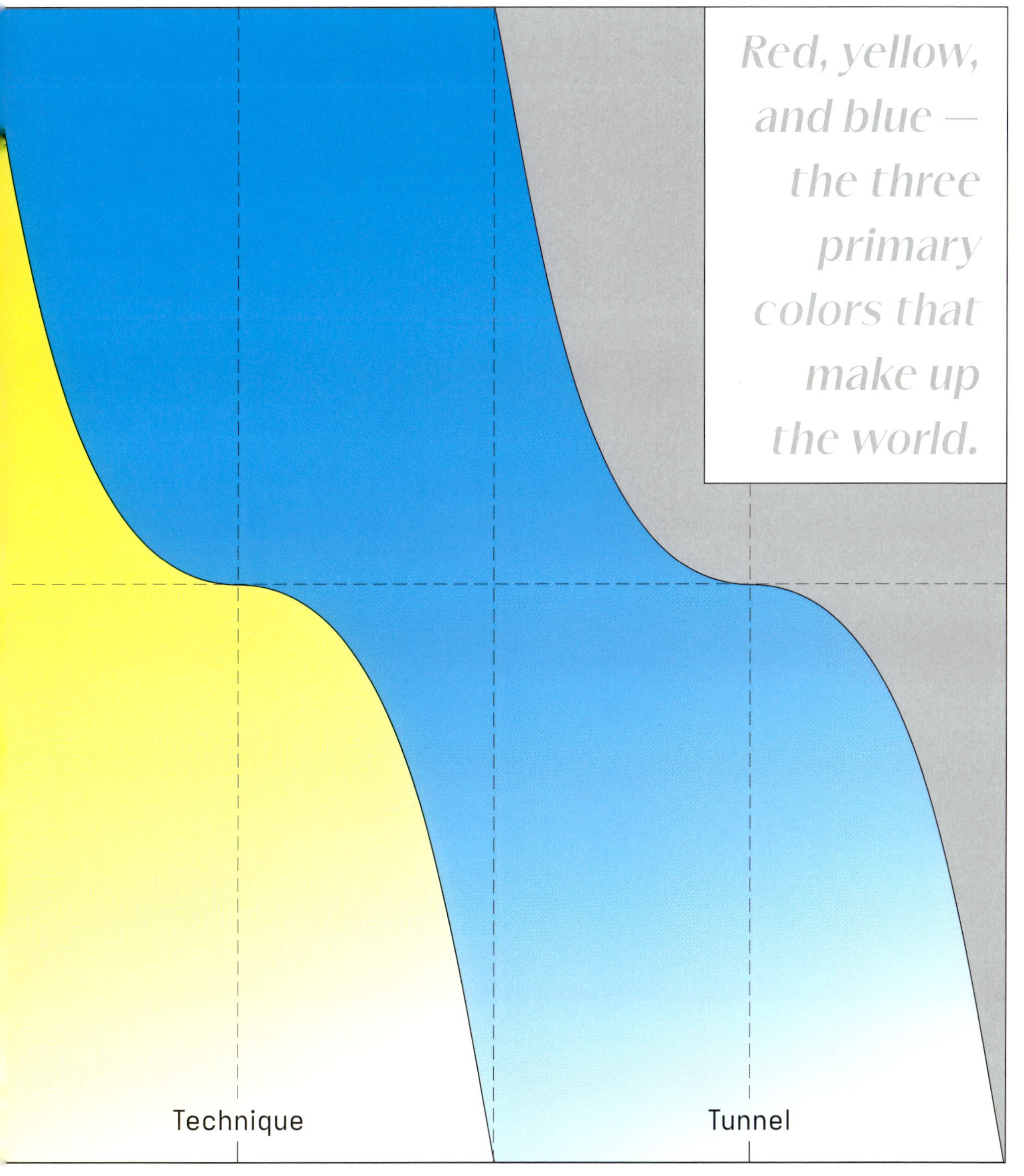
Red, yellow, and blue — the three primary colors that make up the world.
Technique
Tunnel

Theory + Technique + Tunnel = Territory

Color Theory

● Most of us learned in elementary school that we can make almost any color by mixing red, yellow, and blue. However, the emergence of the RYB color model is actually more of a summary of human experience and a historical turning point in color exploration; it is not completely scientifically accurate. ● The earliest works of art we know are cave paintings. The colors used by prehistoric artists were limited to a single ore pigment color, usually black or ochre. Even into the Renaissance, artists had not yet discovered the theory of mixing the three primary colors, while occasional mixing caused disastrous results. Artists had to think in advance about how to paint so that certain pigments would not overlap or be near each other. To obtain usable colors, artists might even have to hunt for rare berries, grind up toxic rocks, or visit local alchemists. ● Classical philosophers in ancient Greece argued that the art world was limited by primitives: colors were different mixtures of black and white. For example, yellow was considered slightly darker than white, while blue was slightly lighter than black. Red and green, in the middle of the light-dark spectrum. But this theory didn't inspire anyone to mix colors but to find unique pigments. Even 150 years ago today, it was still difficult for artists to get colors that didn't interplay. ● It was not until Johannes Itten, a Swiss expressionist painter who taught at the Bauhaus School in Weimar, proposed the concept of the 12-hue color circle in the 1920s that the theory of "red, yellow, and blue as the three primary colors" in the traditional art field began to take root and had a profound influence on the art world and art education for the next century. ● However, the discovery of color theory did not happen overnight. Since childhood, we have learned about the red, yellow, and blue primary color model, knowing it was a habit handed down in the field of painting. However, this does not mean it is completely correct. The term "primary color" actually originated from the biological mechanisms of human beings. In 1802, the British physicist Thomas Young successfully yielded white light by mixing red (R), green (G), and blue (B) three-colored light. This discovery led to the conclusion that the human eye has three types of photoreceptor cells. It turns out that the three kinds of colored light, once mixed in diverse proportions, can yield most of the colors we can see. So for human eyes, the three primaries—red, green, and blue (RGB)—are optimal for

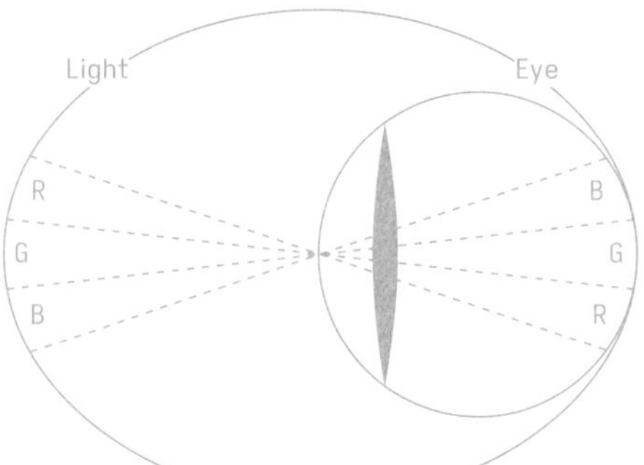

The Three Primary Colors of Light

colored light. The RGB color model is widely used by modern colored televisions, computer monitors, and other devices. By adjusting the brightness of the three colors, red, green, and blue, you can present varying images and colors. For each organism, the number of primaries is different, which depends entirely on the structure of the organism's eyes. For instance, most birds have four color cells, so they have at least four primary colors. ● Therefore, in modern science and technology, the three-primary model of colored light is exclusively applied to any self-luminous display. Computer screens, for example, emit both green (540nm) and red (690nm) light simultaneously to create the perception of a single ray of 580nm yellow light. Although there is no electromagnetic wave in the yellow light range, it elicits the visual effect of a ray of yellow light. ● It's amazing! The "color" you see is not a property of light itself but rather what your brain tells you when this wavelength of electromagnetic waves enters the cone cells of your eye. In everyday life, most of the objects we see do not emit light on their own; they have colors because they can reflect, absorb, and transmit light. We can see color because the light is reflected by the object into our eyes, received by the photoreceptor cells of the eye, and transmitted to the brain, which processes the resultant color of an object that is, in reality, colorless. ● Unlike self-luminous objects, the color of non-self-luminous objects is explained by ""substractive color mixing," which indicates that when light passes through an object, the object absorbs a particular wavelength of light and then reflects other wavelengths of light, forming the color we see. For example, we see a red flower because, when white sunlight reaches it, the flower absorbs green and blue light and only reflects the red light into our eyes, allowing us to perceive it as red. Green leaves, on the other hand, absorb blue and red light, reflecting green light into our eyes. This principle of subtractive color gives rise to the CMY color model. ● In the principle of color mixing, objects that actively emit light are suitable for "additive color mixing," where the three primaries forming colored light are red, green, and blue (the RGB color model). Objects that do not emit light themselves and rely on the reflection of external light for us to see are suitable for substractive color mixing, where the three primaries are cyan, magenta, and yellow (the CMY color model).

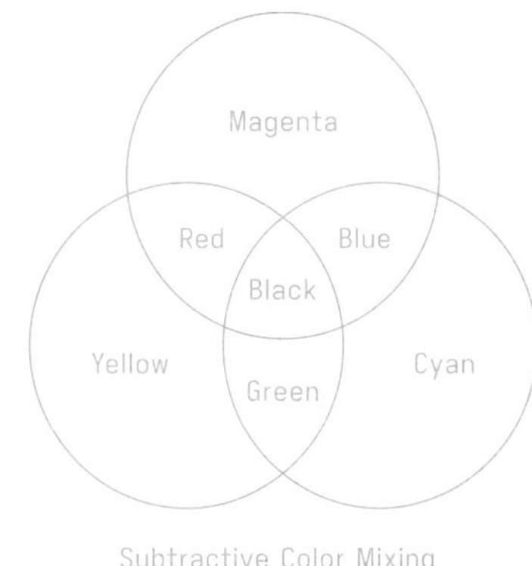

Subtractive Color Mixing

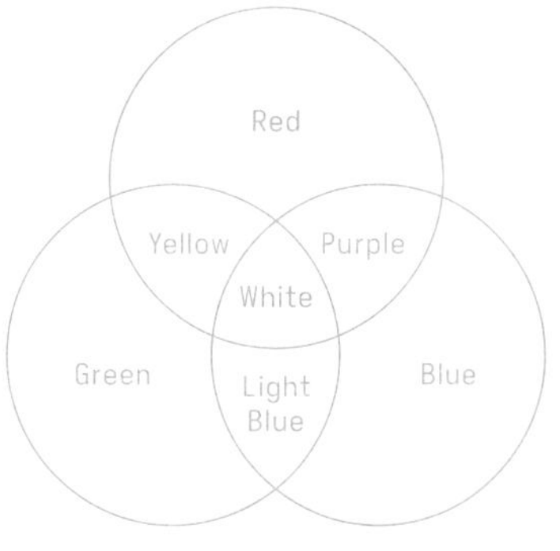

Additive Color Mixing

Technique + Tunnel ● The study of the three primaries aims to understand the principle of color through practical hands-on operations and then build an encompassing pigment mixing model in our minds to meet the ever-changing needs of pigmentary mixtures in the future.

● **The Color Circle** (also known as the 12-hue color wheel) is a ring that combines the colors in a certain order. It serves as a tool in chromatics to help people understand the relationship between colors and facilitate color matching. The basic 12-hue color circle, proposed by the Swiss color master Johannes Itten, has the following structure: the three primaries form an equilateral triangle as the basic hues. Secondary colors are added between the three primary colors, and then the two adjacent colors of these six colors are harmonized to obtain tertiary colors. ● This way, a 12-hue color circle is formed among the six colors. In addition to the basic 12-hue color circle, it can be extended to 24, 48, or even more hues in the color circle.

● **The 12-hue Color Circle** = Primary Colors + Secondary Colors + Tertiary Colors

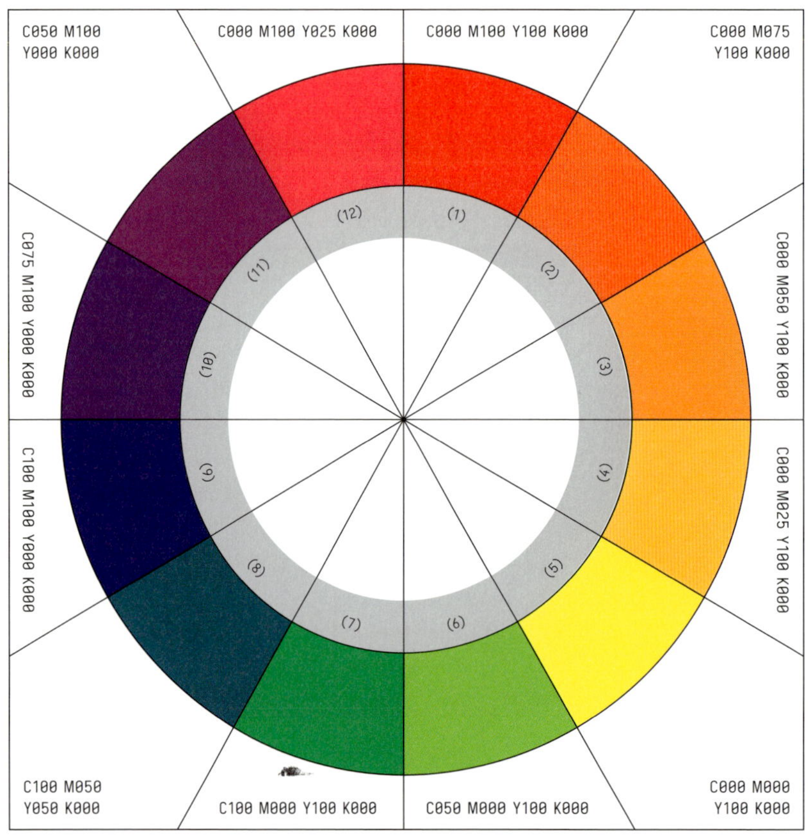

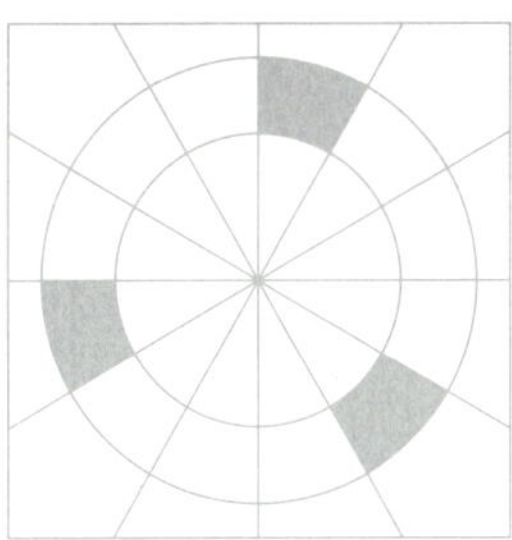

Primary Colors are the most basic colors, not the blended results. In the fields of painting and printing, there are different definitions of the three primaries. The three pigment primaries are red, yellow, and blue (RYB). The three printing primaries are cyan, magenta, and yellow (CMY).

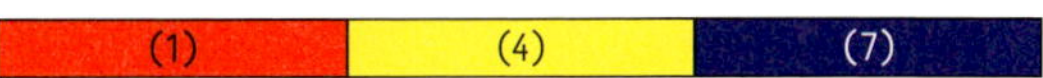

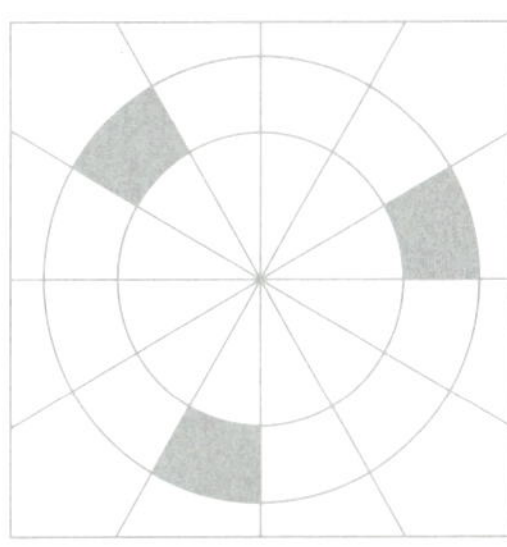

Secondary Colors are mixed by the three primary colors, such as orange, which is made of red and yellow, green, which is made of yellow and blue, and purple, which is made of red and blue.

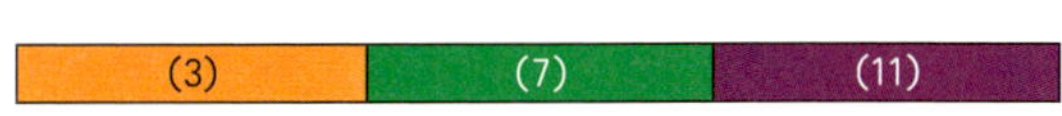

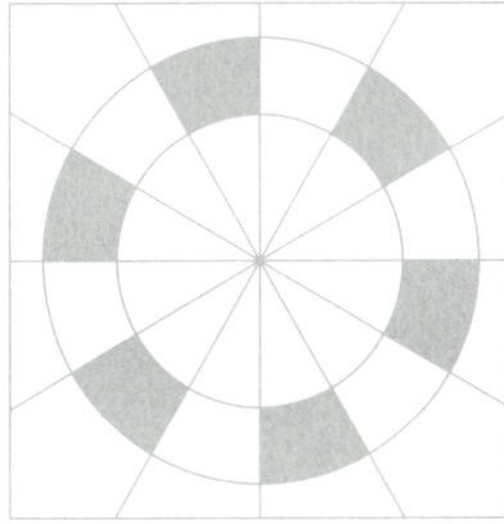

Tertiary Colors are combinations of primary and secondary colors, such as red-purple and blue-purple.

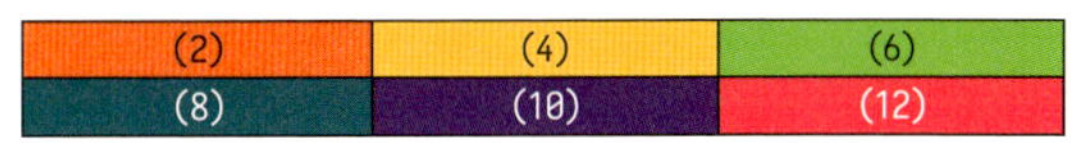

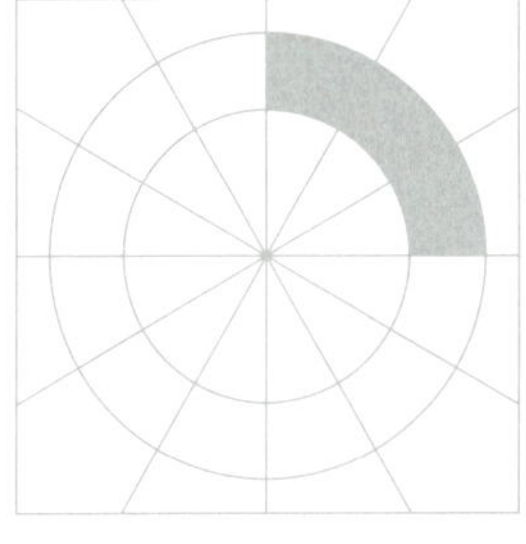

Analogous Colors refer to colors that are adjacent to each other in an analogous color circle. Colors within a 90° angle of the analogous color circle are considered analogous.

(1)	(7)
(2)	(8)
(3)	(9)
(4)	(10)
(5)	(11)
(6)	(12)

- **Complementary Colors** are colors that are opposite each other in the color circle, i.e., two colors that are 180° apart.

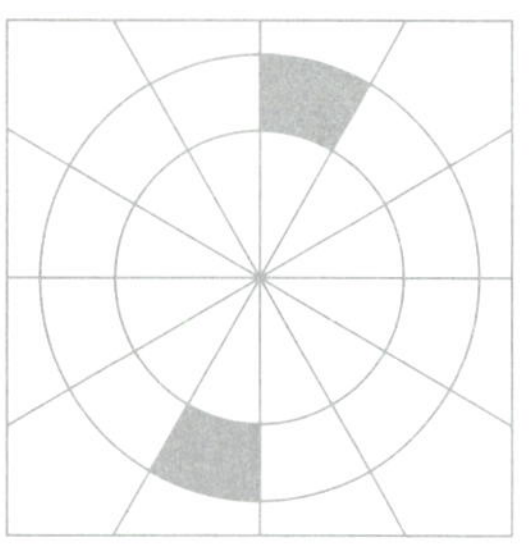

(1) (7)

(2) (8)

(3) (9)

(4) (10)

(5) (11)

(6) (12)

- **Split Complementary Colors** consist of three colors: one color in the color circle and the adjacent colors on either side of the complementary color.

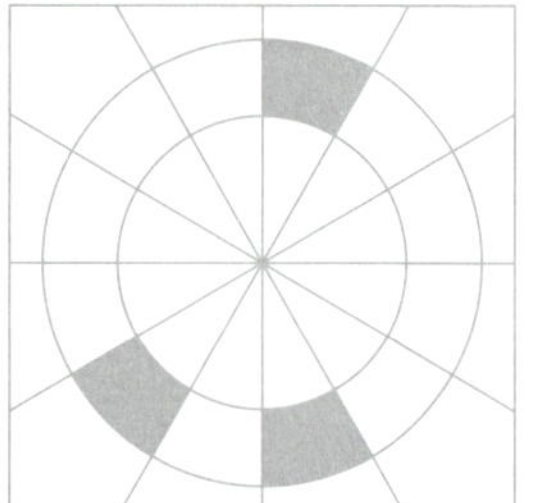

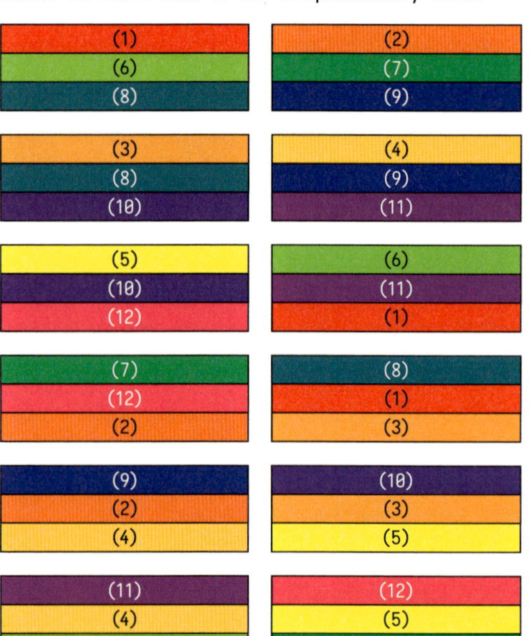

- **Triadic Colors** are the three colors evenly distributed in the color circle, forming an equilateral triangle.

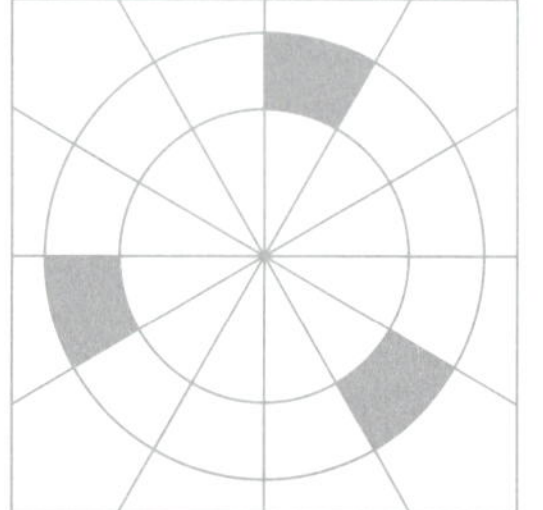

(1) (5) (9)

(3) (7) (11)

(2) (6) (10)

(4) (8) (12)

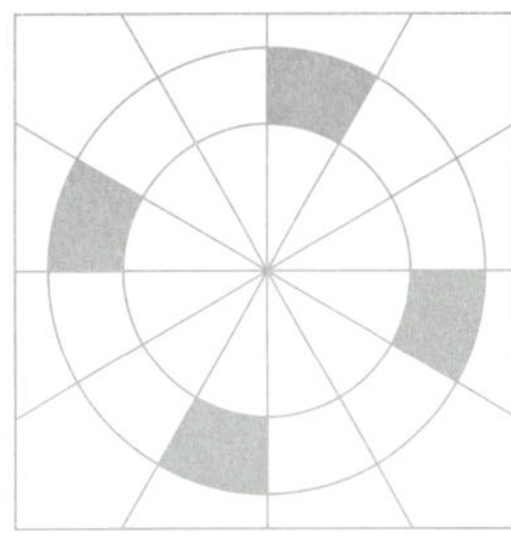

● **Tetradic/Double Complementary Colors** refer to four colors made up of two pairs of complementary colors in a color circle.

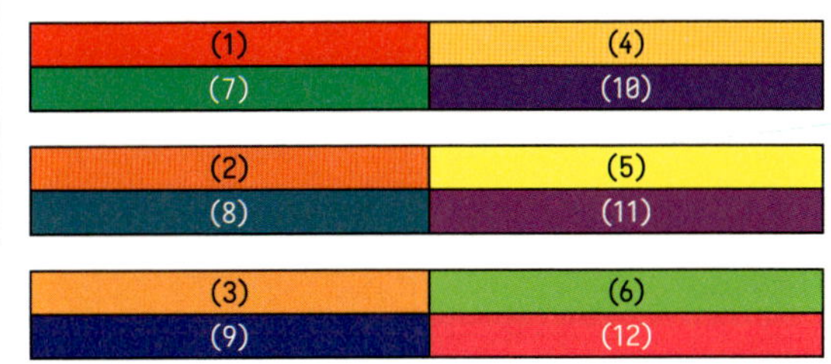

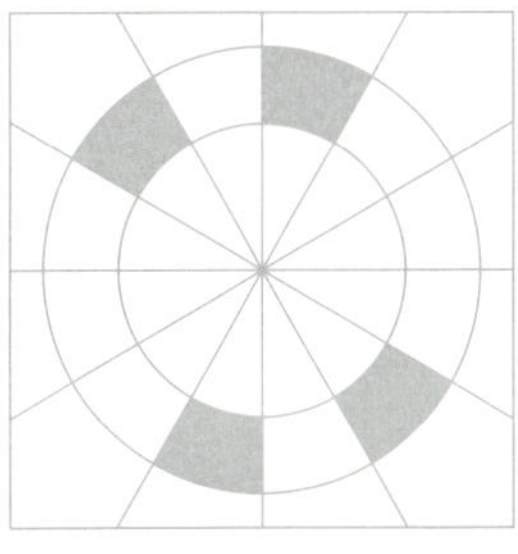

The two pairs of complementary colors can also be in close proximity.

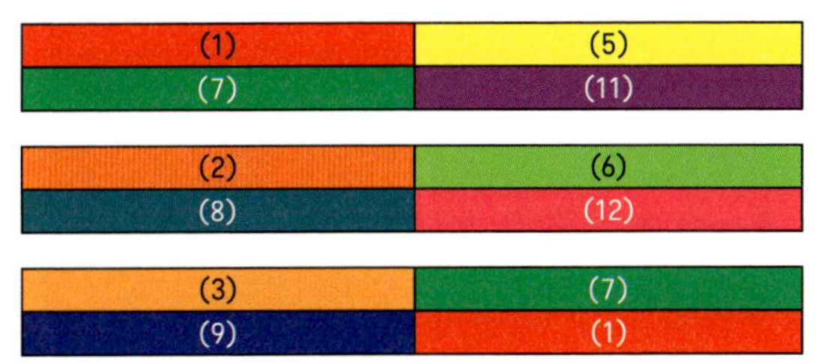

● **Warm and Cool Colors** Warm colors give the impression of warmth. Cool colors give the impression of give the impression of coolness, such as blue, purple, and green.

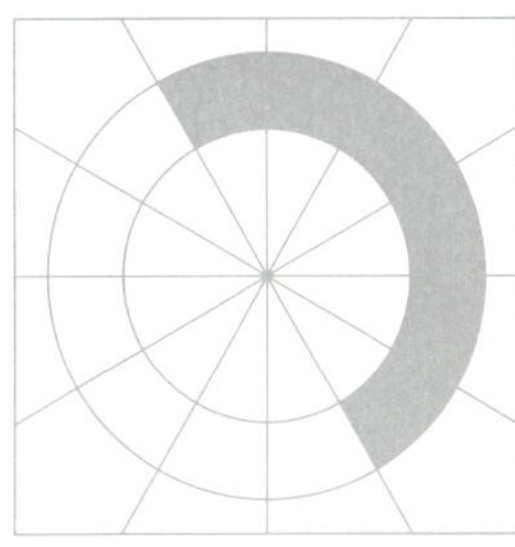

Warm Colors

Warm Colors
(12)
(1)
(2)
(3)
(4)
(5)

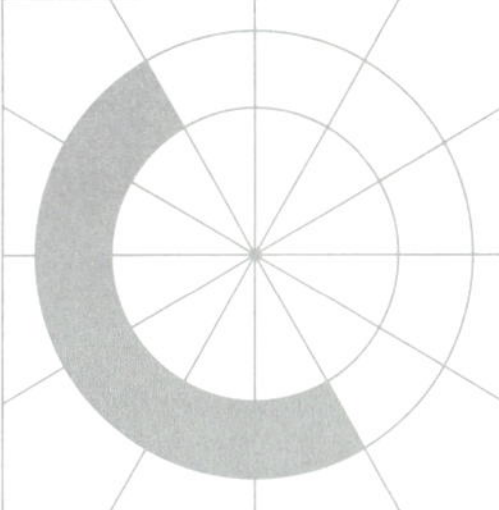

Cool Colors

Cool Colors
(6)
(7)
(8)
(9)
(10)
(11)

To desaturate is to make the original color less vibrant.

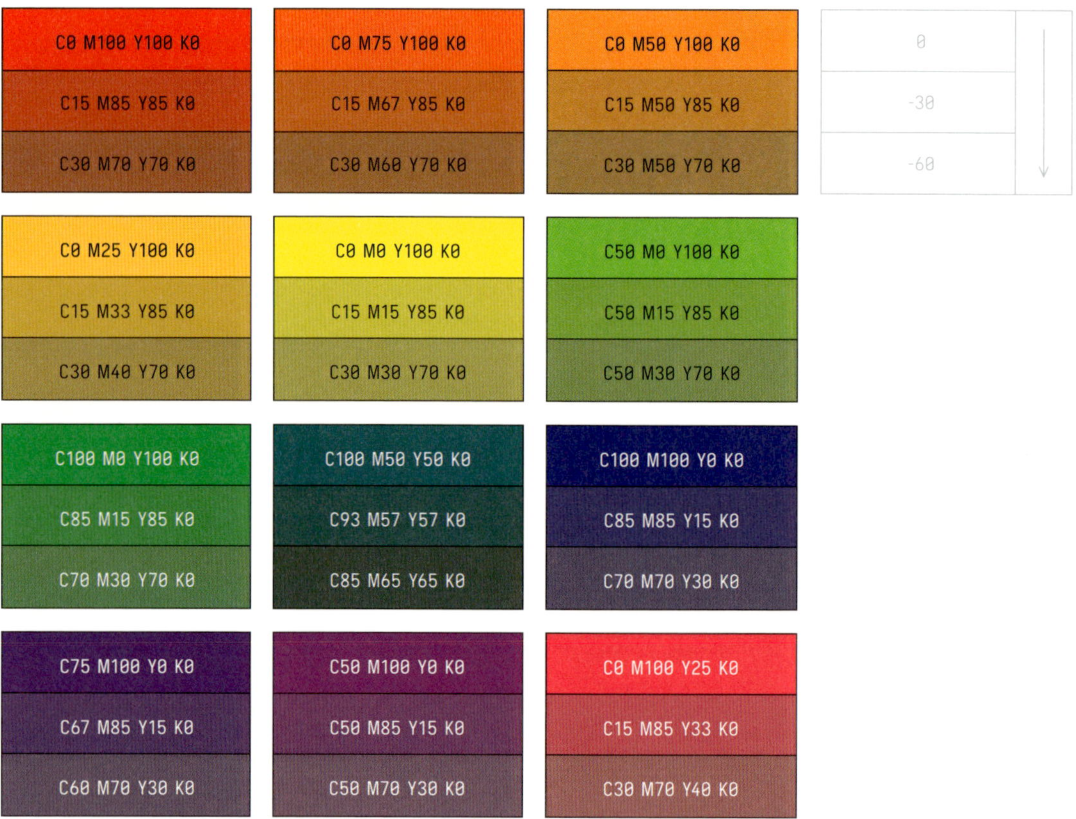

Reducing the brightness involves adding black and gray to the solid color.

C0 M40 Y40 K0	C0 M30 Y40 K0	C0 M20 Y40 K0	60
C0 M70 Y70 K0	C0 M53 Y70 K0	C0 M35 Y70 K0	30
C0 M100 Y100 K0	C0 M75 Y100 K0	C0 M50 Y100 K0	0
C30 M100 Y100 K0	C30 M82 Y100 K0	C30 M65 Y100 K0	-30
C60 M100 Y100 K0	C60 M90 Y100 K0	C60 M80 Y100 K0	-60

C0 M10 Y40 K0	C0 M0 Y40 K0	C20 M0 Y40 K0
C0 M18 Y70 K0	C0 M0 Y70 K0	C35 M0 Y70 K0
C0 M25 Y100 K0	C0 M0 Y100 K0	C50 M0 Y100 K0
C30 M47 Y100 K0	C30 M30 Y100 K0	C65 M30 Y100 K0
C60 M70 Y100 K0	C60 M60 Y100 K0	C80 M60 Y100 K0

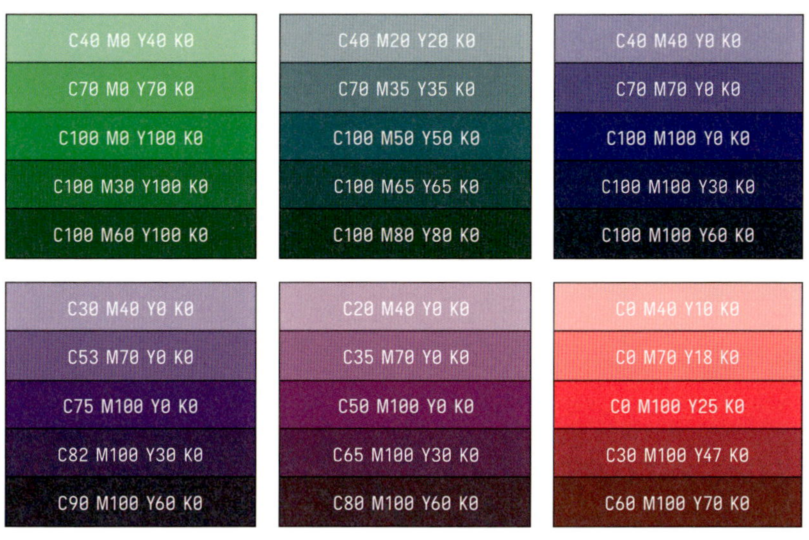

The use of achromatic colors as intermediates provides a visual buffer for color contrast. The "cool + warm + intermediate colors" collide to break the monotony and create a strong sense of layering.

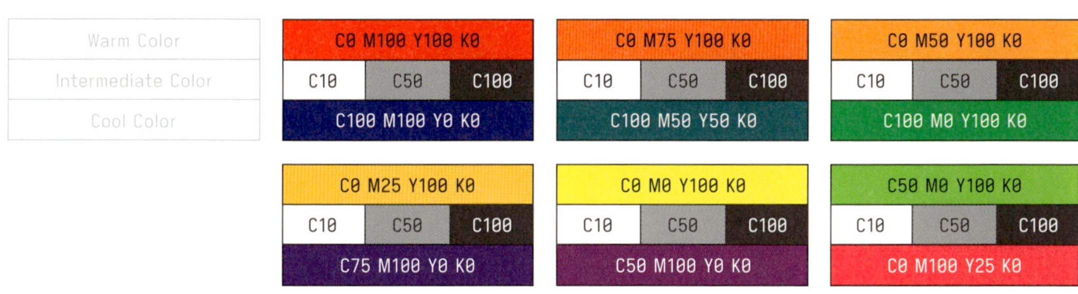

Controlling the color area helps weaken the visual impact. Reducing the color area is particularly effective, as it gives more breathing space and prevents the overall design from being too messy.

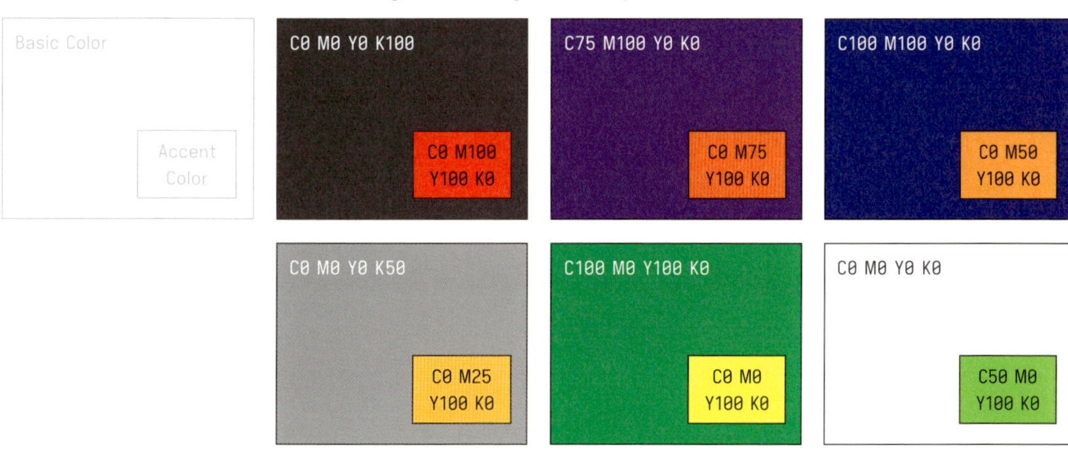

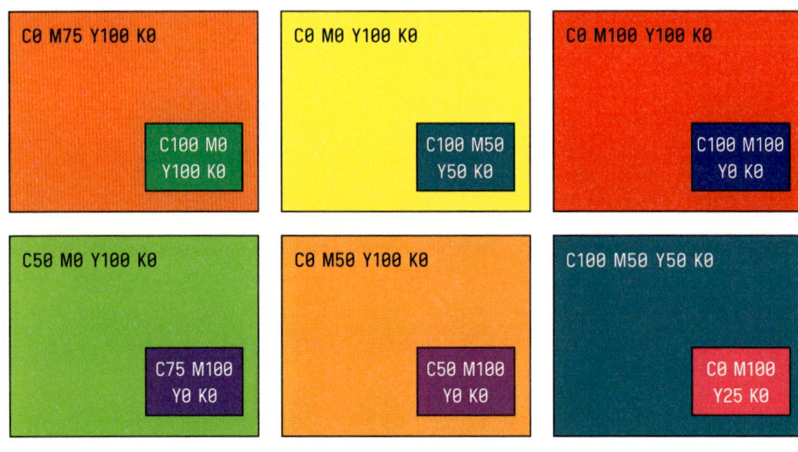

Color contrast is crucial. The "earthy tone" trend in our daily lives is actually composed to strike a contrast. This mild contrast, considered monochrome, results in a composition of natural harmony. For example, a colder tone of blue will make people feel quiet and elegant, while a warmer tone of orange can bring warmth and liveliness. These colors get along well, highlighting a sense of layers and making the visual experience more pleasant. This way of mixing and matching lays a solid foundation for hue contrast.

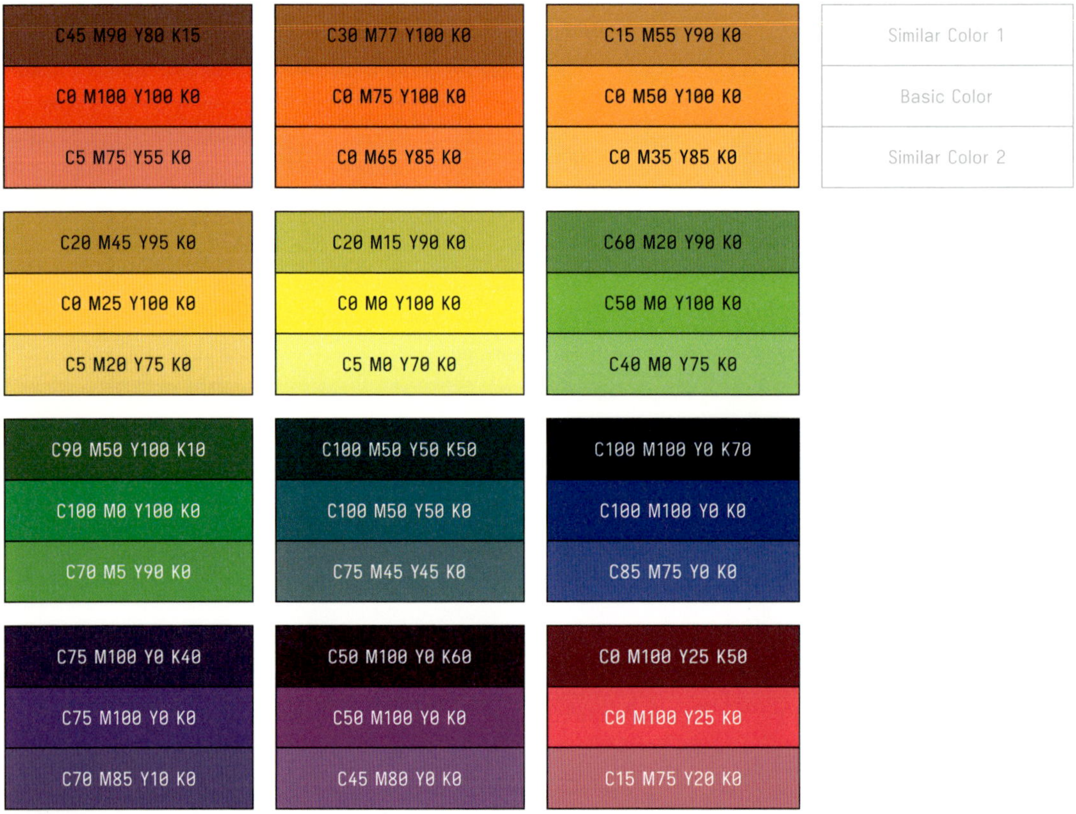

C45 M90 Y80 K15	C30 M77 Y100 K0	C15 M55 Y90 K0	Similar Color 1
C0 M100 Y100 K0	C0 M75 Y100 K0	C0 M50 Y100 K0	Basic Color
C5 M75 Y55 K0	C0 M65 Y85 K0	C0 M35 Y85 K0	Similar Color 2
C20 M45 Y95 K0	C20 M15 Y90 K0	C60 M20 Y90 K0	
C0 M25 Y100 K0	C0 M0 Y100 K0	C50 M0 Y100 K0	
C5 M20 Y75 K0	C5 M0 Y70 K0	C40 M0 Y75 K0	
C90 M50 Y100 K10	C100 M50 Y50 K50	C100 M100 Y0 K70	
C100 M0 Y100 K0	C100 M50 Y50 K0	C100 M100 Y0 K0	
C70 M5 Y90 K0	C75 M45 Y45 K0	C85 M75 Y0 K0	
C75 M100 Y0 K40	C50 M100 Y0 K60	C0 M100 Y25 K50	
C75 M100 Y0 K0	C50 M100 Y0 K0	C0 M100 Y25 K0	
C70 M85 Y10 K0	C45 M80 Y0 K0	C15 M75 Y20 K0	

Practical Color contrast rule: 6(basic color): 3(theme color): 1(accent color)

Basic colors, mainly referring to black, white, beige, and other neutral colors, are easy to match. A theme color is a saturated color that you want to highlight. The accent color is mainly used to create a strong contrast and collision with the theme color. This combination, on the one hand, always considers the big picture or the whole, and on the other hand, the designer can easily base their choice of color on a classic combo that is enduring and versatile.

Basic Color	Theme Color	Accent Color
C0 M0 Y0 K0	C0 M100 Y100 K0	C70 M10 Y0 K0
C5 M10 Y60 K0	C0 M75 Y100 K0	C0 M0 Y100 K0
C0 M10 Y10 K0	C0 M50 Y100 K0	C70 M85 Y0 K0
C10 M10 Y10 K0	C0 M25 Y100 K0	C0 M100 Y100 K0
C20 M0 Y50 K10	C0 M0 Y100 K0	C100 M0 Y100 K0
C15 M5 Y20 K0	C50 M0 Y100 K0	C85 M80 Y0 K0
C35 M0 Y5 K0	C100 M0 Y100 K0	C0 M0 Y80 K0
C45 M0 Y35 K0	C100 M50 Y50 K0	C75 M0 Y55 K0
C20 M15 Y15 K0	C100 M100 Y0 K0	C5 M70 Y25 K0
C50 M0 Y15 K0	C75 M100 Y0 K0	C0 M90 Y45 K0
C70 M0 Y70 K0	C50 M100 Y0 K0	C100 M0 Y0 K0
C0 M25 Y45 K0	C0 M100 Y25 K0	C0 M25 Y100 K0

Territory ● In modern chromatics, do the real three primary colors exist? The examination of this topic reveals that the choice of primary colors is arbitrary and imperfect. Through an in-depth analysis of all the color theories, two main types of primary colors emerge: those explaining how to harmonize colors and those actually used for color harmony—specifically, the RGB and CMY models mentioned earlier. Two paradoxes about primary colors become apparent in practice: First, the primary colors used to explain color mixing are "imaginary primary colors," invisible to the human eye. This means that different people perceive one color differently due to the frequency range of each color, even by using electronic devices that rely on LEDs or cathode-ray tubes to create specific wavelengths of light. In addition, human emotions influence how the brain interprets what the eyes see. ● Secondly, we can blend the primary colors, each corresponding to a specific wavelength of visible light, but it is not possible to adjust all the colors visible to the naked eye (as in the RGB model), making the selection of these primary colors imperfect. For example, you don't need orange paint to create an orange "color." We cannot create three primaries that can be seen simultaneously or blended to cover the entire chromatic range. Thus, whether conceptual or material primaries, they are either nonexistent or imperfect. ● Another factor not considered in the trichromatic model is that color is not always pure; it can be mixed with white. For instance, red mixed with white produces pink. Although red and pink are the same hue, they differ in saturation, influencing their presence under different lighting conditions. ● Modern chromatics has evolved to accept that colors are nothing more than the human eye's perception of light and can produce optical illusions based on how they are refracted. For example, red will appear brighter on a black background than on a white one, and the same applies to shape size, with a red shape appearing larger against a black background. Artists often apply blue backgrounds to emphasize elements or create particular illusions. An interesting and controversial element is the "blue and black (or white and gold) dress" that trended online, with some seeing it as blue and black while others saw white and gold. This phenomenon can be explained by the optical illusion created by colors. ● Specifically, their illusions result from differences

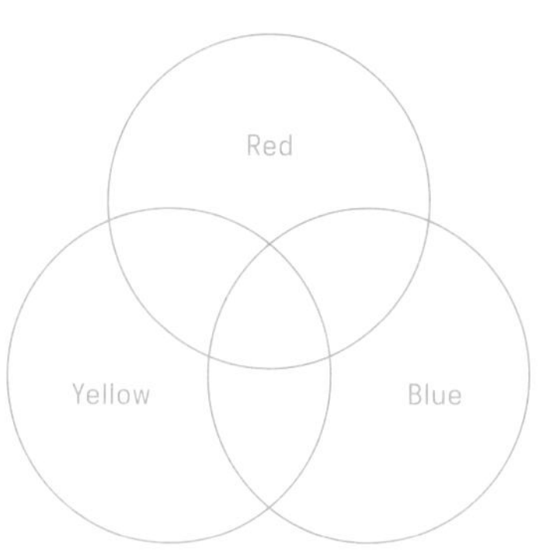

Imaginary Primary Colors

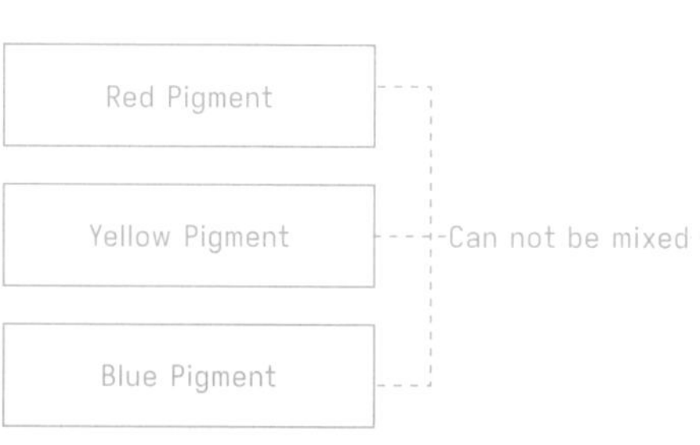

in territory lighting conditions and individual visual systems. In *Concerning the Spiritual in Art*, Kandinsky discusses the effects of color on the eyes and the inner resonance of specific colors. He believes that color can be autonomous, standing alone, independent of visual descriptions of objects. While Kandinsky and his contemporaries focused on the sacred experience of art, today's emphasis on color reflects the consumerist culture we live in. In marketing and brand building, color is used to increase brand awareness, emphasize the visual appeal of goods, and attract attention, even "manipulating" consumers' psychology. ● Modern color theory has not yet developed a clear explanation of how a particular medium affects the appearance of a color. In the digital age we live in, most people experience color on screens. The practices of some artists in virtual reality spaces, such as the Internet, dominate people's sensory and visual perception. Similarly, following the tradition of op art and illusion art, gif creators reduced their color options to 156 colors, introducing an all-new style of minimalist art. Because creators used different resolutions or cameras, our perceptions of color vary. As mentioned earlier, "primary color" is not a physical concept but a biological one. Through different media, people's "virtual" experience of color has formed a huge contrast with the traditional understanding of color in the past. Previously, color was understood to represent changes in light and the mixture of paints, inks, dyes, or pigments. Today's unconventional understanding of design allows for almost any color combination. If the notion that "everyone perceives color differently" is acceptable, so is the proposal to create a new color wheel.

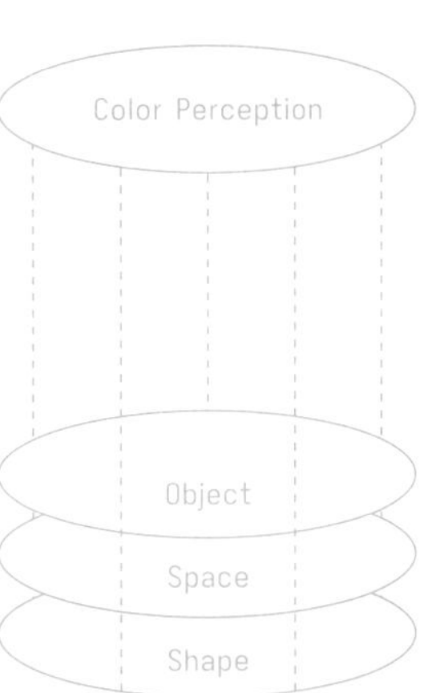

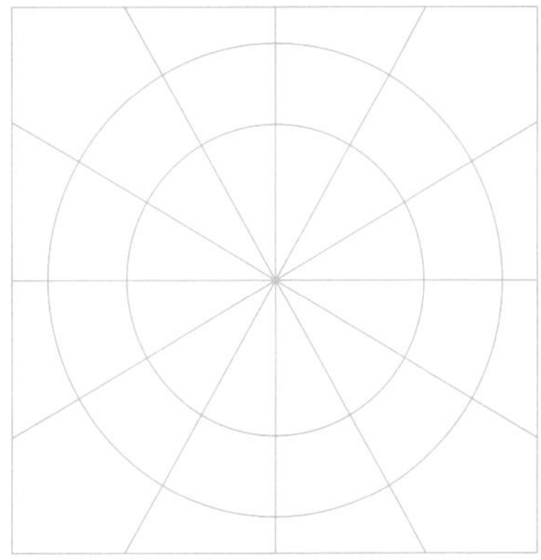

Everyone perceives color differently, and everyone can create a new color wheel.

RYB 3D STORM

1917 THE NEOPLASTICISM MOVEMENT

1918 THE RED AND BLUE CHAIR

1919 THE BAUHAUS WAS FOUNDED

1920 JOHANNES ITTEN AND THE COLOR WHEEL

1922 WASSILY KANDINSKY AND ABSTRACT ART

1923 LÁSZLÓ MOHOLI NAGY AND THE LIGHT-SPACE MODULATOR

2

Red, yellow, and blue, the three primary colors, constitute one of the most influential color combinations in the history of design.

NEOPLASTICISM AND NEOPLASTIC ART
1927

JOSEF ALBERS AND COLOR COMPOSITION
1928

"DYNAMIC MONDRIAN"
1930

THEO VAN DOESBURG DIED
1931

THE BAUHAUS FORCED TO CLOSE
1933

CONTEMPORARY DESIGN
NOW

Figures + Styles = Definite + Dynamic + Desire

- **Definite:** Ever-winning color combo
- **Dynamic:** The retro tone of the Bauhaus
- **Desire:** Beyond time and space

● At the beginning of the 20th century, a group of talented artists and architects launched numerous artistic movements in the name of art, using this interesting approach to heal the postwar wounds of the time and depict avant-garde and fashionable ideals. ● The Dutch De Stijl and the Bauhaus School stand out as among the most representative artistic storms and design movements. ● If Mondrian's use of red, yellow, and blue imparts a calm and restrained sense of order, Kandinsky's interpretation of these same colors is accompanied by music and melody. ● These two masters of abstractism not only profoundly influenced modern design and art but also extended color aesthetics into our daily lives. ● From classical to modern, from figurative to abstract, the enduring trio "red, yellow, and blue" has contributed significantly to artistic design.

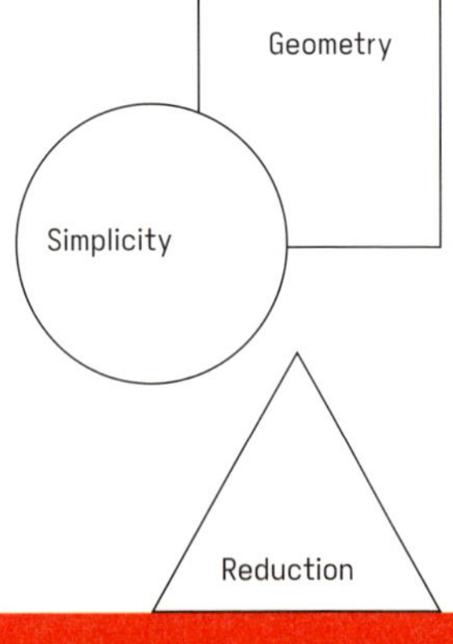

1917: The Neoplasticism Movement ● The Neoplasticism movement was initiated by Dutch artists and architects, including Theo van Doesberg and Piet Mondrian. This school emphasized simplicity, geometry, and the reduction of basic elements in art and design.

1918: The Red and Blue Chair ● "The Red and Blue Chair," an extremely avant-garde creation, announced a determination to break with traditional styles. Crafted by Neoplasticism artist Rietveld, the chair's bare structure is completely undisguised, while the use of the three primaries is subtle. Trained as a craftsman, Rietveld offered a new perspective on architectural design, exploring a new order in an artistic way and highlighting the core tenets of modernism through simple, bright colors.

● ● ● **1919-1924: Neoplasticism and the Abstract Movement** ● Neoplasticism artists, including Mondrian and Van Dusberg, explored abstraction and geometric composition and pursued artistic "abstraction and simplification," reducing color to red, yellow, and blue, as well as black, white, and gray. This new language, based on pure primary colors and flat forms, became a new force against tradition.

● ● ● **1919: The Bauhaus was Founded** ● German architect Walter Gropius founded the Bauhaus School of Design in Weimar, Germany. The Bauhaus focused on the integration of art, craft, and technology, emphasizing functional design. The Bauhaus concept drew inspiration from the pre-war Arts and Crafts Movement, with a close eye on the Progressive Educational Movement and the Total Work of Art, aiming to unite art and art education in every corner of life.

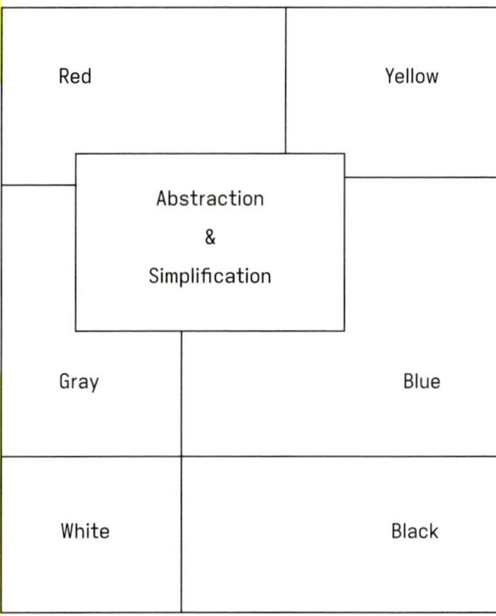

● ● ● **1920: Johannes Itten and the Color Wheel** ● Johannes Itten joined the Bauhaus and developed the influential color theory. His color circle engaged tones and levels, providing the basis for color harmony.

● ● ● **1922: Wassily Kandinsky and Abstract Art** ● Russian artist Wassily Kandinsky joined the Bauhaus as a faculty member, contributing to the exploration of abstract art. Kandinsky's color theory explores the effects of different hues, shapes, and compositions on perception and emotion. In Kandinsky's view, warm and cool colors correspond to different emotions, and the sharper the shape, the warmer, and the blunter the shape, the cooler. So Kandinsky assigned squares red, triangles yellow, and circles blue, until they eventually became black horizontal lines.

● ● ● **1923: László Moholy-Nagy's Light-Space Modulator** ● Hungarian artist László Moholi-Nagy experimented with light and space, creating the lightspace modulator. This dynamic sculpture combines light, movement, and color, marking an unprecedented marriage of technology and art.

● ● ● **1927: Neoplasticism and Neo-plastic Art** ● Piet Mondrain coined the term "neoplasticism" to refer to his unique abstract work. As one of the pioneers of abstract art in the 20th century, Mondrian believed that art should be represented in straight lines and solid colors. Abstract art is sometimes considered challenging to be comprehensible and accessible. Mondrian's works sought a universal unity in art, a pursuit of faith otherwise found in religion. The long-established harmony between art and

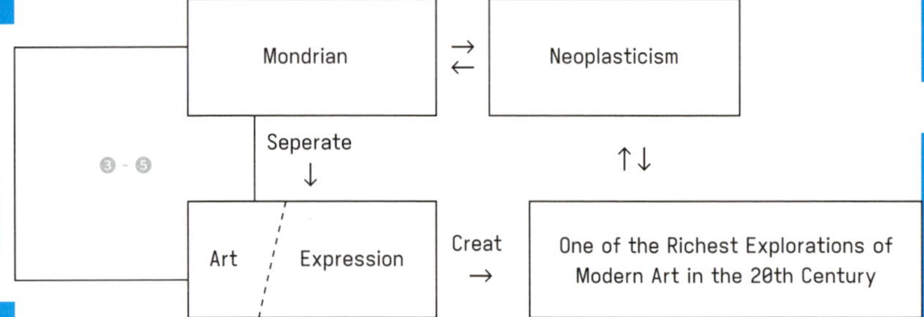

expression was disrupted; however, it led to one of the richest explorations of modern art in the 20th century.

● ● ● **1928: Josef Albers and Color Composition** ● German artist Josef Albers joined the Bauhaus as a master, focusing on color interaction and perception. His research on color relationships and optical illusions formed the basis of his important book, *Interaction of Color*.

● ● ● **1930: "Dynamic Mondrian"** ● The American sculptor Alexander Calder was deeply inspired by his visit to Mondrian's studio, and his style gradually shifted from figurative to abstract, resulting in his first batch of abstract sculptures. With the gradual improvement of the power device, he succeeded in his desire to creat a dynamic Mondrain. Calder explored many ways to change the forms of installations, but the only constant is the motion of red, yellow, and blue, swaying in the air. Calder uses his cosmic intention to give the red, yellow, and blue eternal powers.

● ● ● **1931: Theo Van Doesburg Died** ● The death of Theo van Doesburg, one of the founders of the Neoplasticism movement, marked the end of an active phase of the movement. Afterward, the Neoplastic style continued to influence art, architecture, and design.

● ● ● **1933: The Bauhaus was Forced to Close** ● Due to Nazi political pressure at the time, the Bauhaus was forced to close. Many Bauhaus artists and educators scattered elsewhere, spreading their principles and ideas around the world.

● ● ● **1933–Contemporary: Bauhaus, De Stijl, and Contemporary Color Design** ● The legacy of the Bauhaus and De Stijl continues to inspire contemporary graphic designers, especially concerning color theory and application. The principles of both art movements, namely simplicity, geometric form, and color harmony, remain influential in design education and practice worldwide. ● Amid the torrents of time, the primary colors red, yellow, and blue carry on the spirit of the art movement, never absent from the classic color schemes, sailing boldly beyond time and space into eternity.

⑥

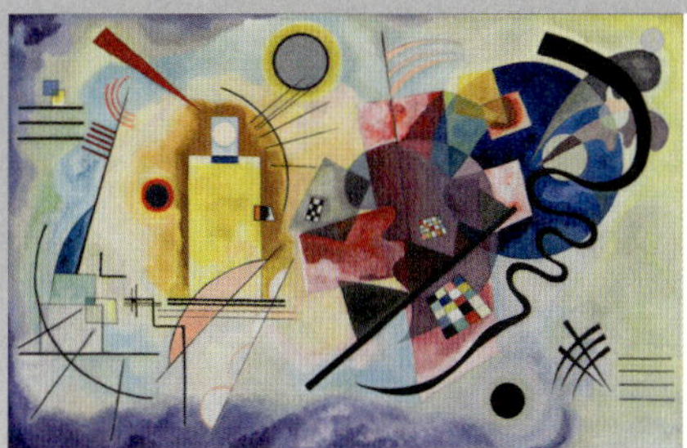

❶ *Yellow, Red, and Blue*, Wassily Kandinsky, 1925, Centre Pompidou, Paris, France.

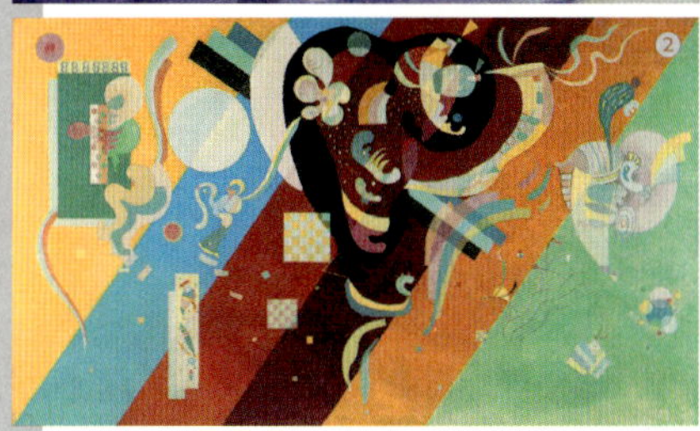

❷ *Composition No.9*, Wassily Kandinsky, 1936, Centre Pompidou, Paris, France.

In Kandinsky's later abstract paintings, he experimented with mixing more colors to evoke emotion. This set of emotion-oriented color rules, recognized and utilized by Bauhaus students, has subtly influenced public aesthetics. When people think of Bauhaus, they often associate the three primary colors of red, yellow, and blue and their basic shapes.

❸ *Red Cloud*, Piet Mondrain, 1907, The Hague Art Museum (Gemeentemuseum Den Haag), Hague, Netherlands.

❹ *View from the Dunes with Beach and Piers, Domburg*, Piet Mondrian, 1909, MoMA, New York, U. S..

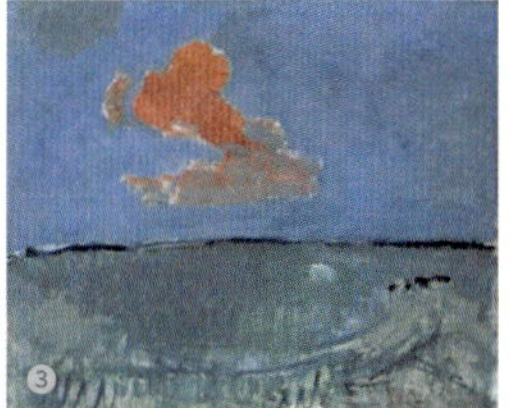

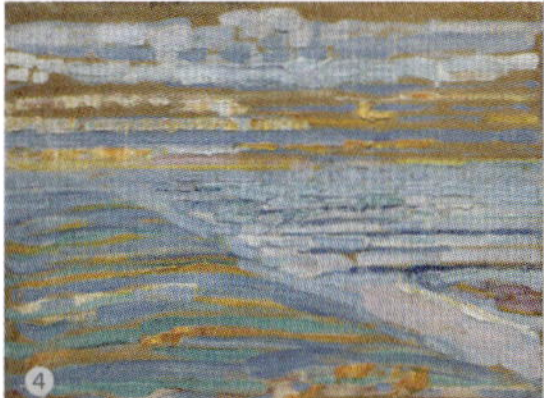

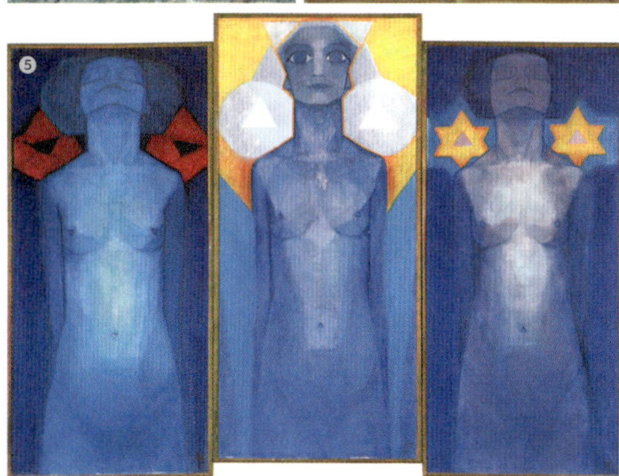

❺ *Evolution*, Piet Mondrian, 1911, The Hague Art Museum, Hague, Netherlands.

Red, blue, and yellow constitute Mondrian's pure and serious art world. In this triptych, three standing human figures look strikingly similar, but the work emphasizes Mondrian's focus on form and visual rhythm rather than visual representation.

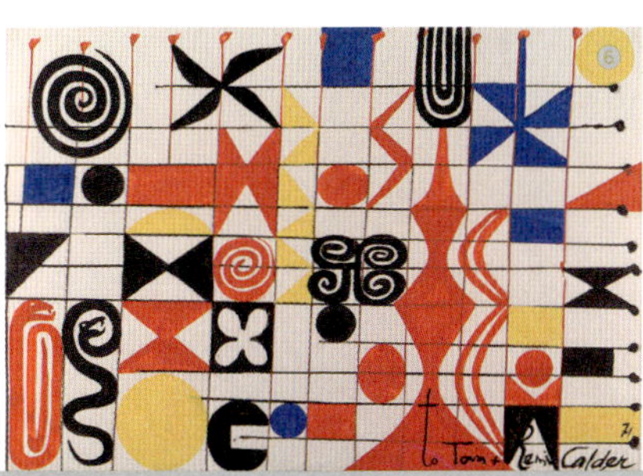

❻ *Untitled*, Alexander Calder, 1971, Solomon R. Guggenheim Museum, New York, U. S..

RYB HARMONY

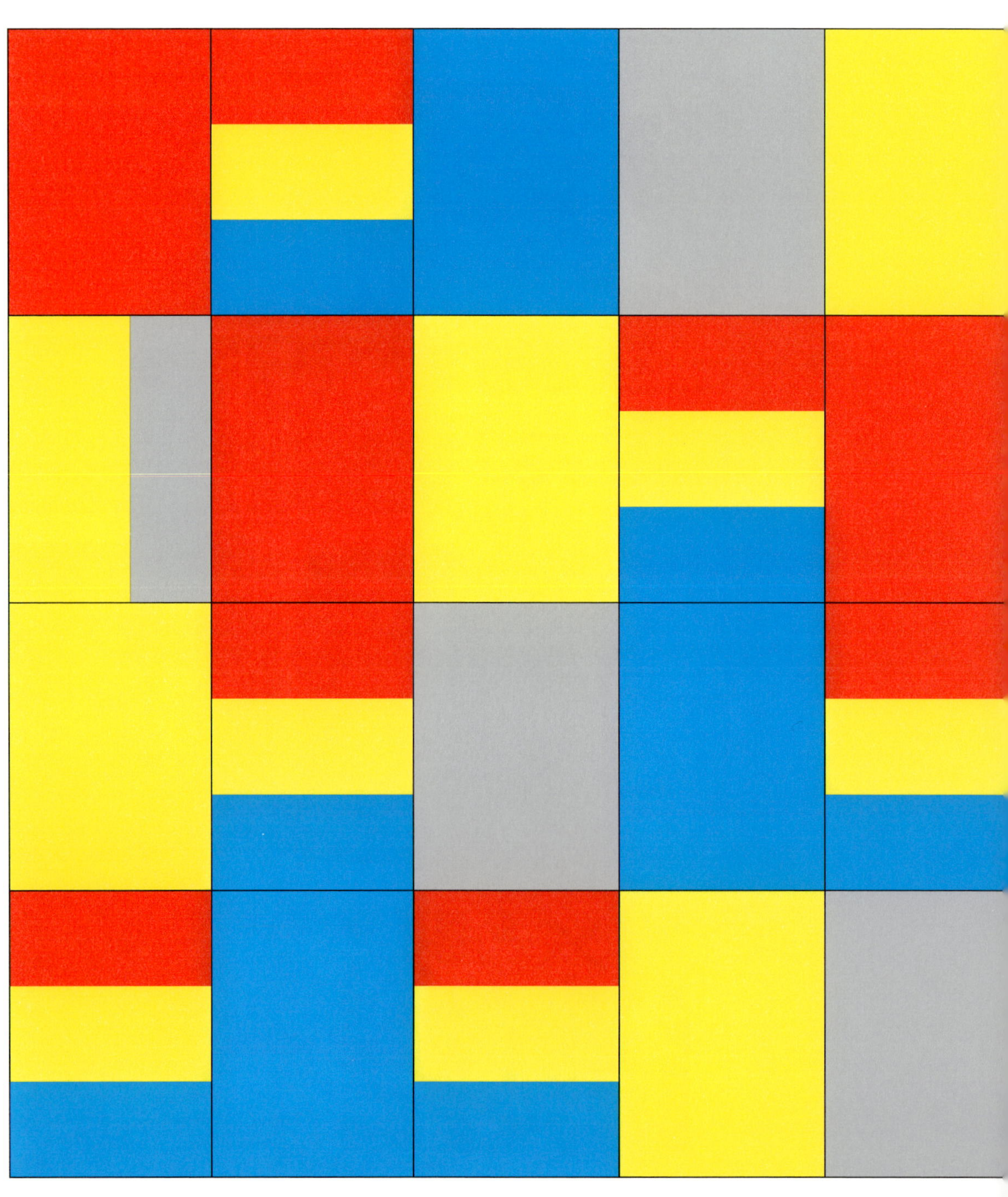

3

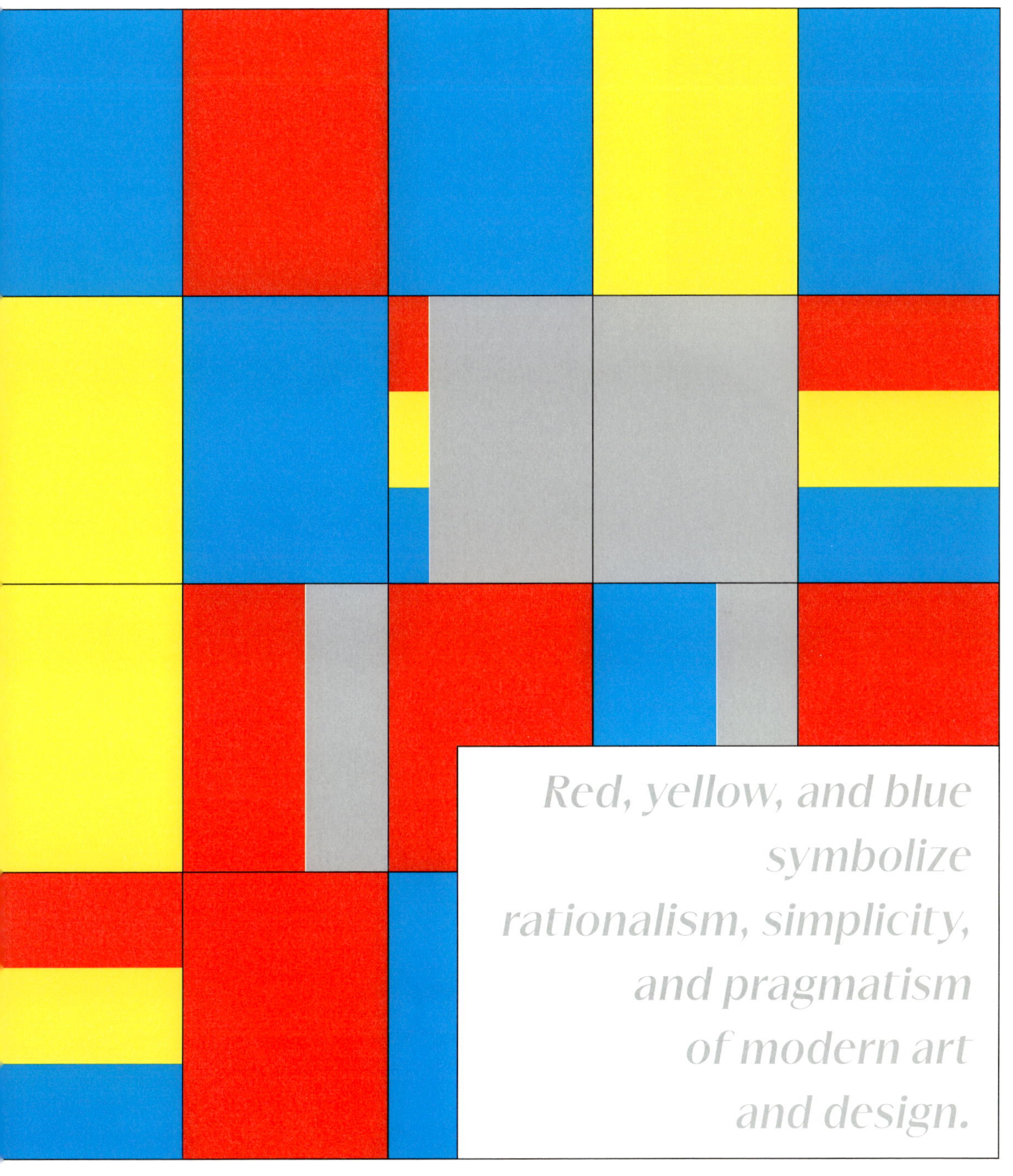
Red, yellow, and blue
symbolize
rationalism, simplicity,
and pragmatism
of modern art
and design.

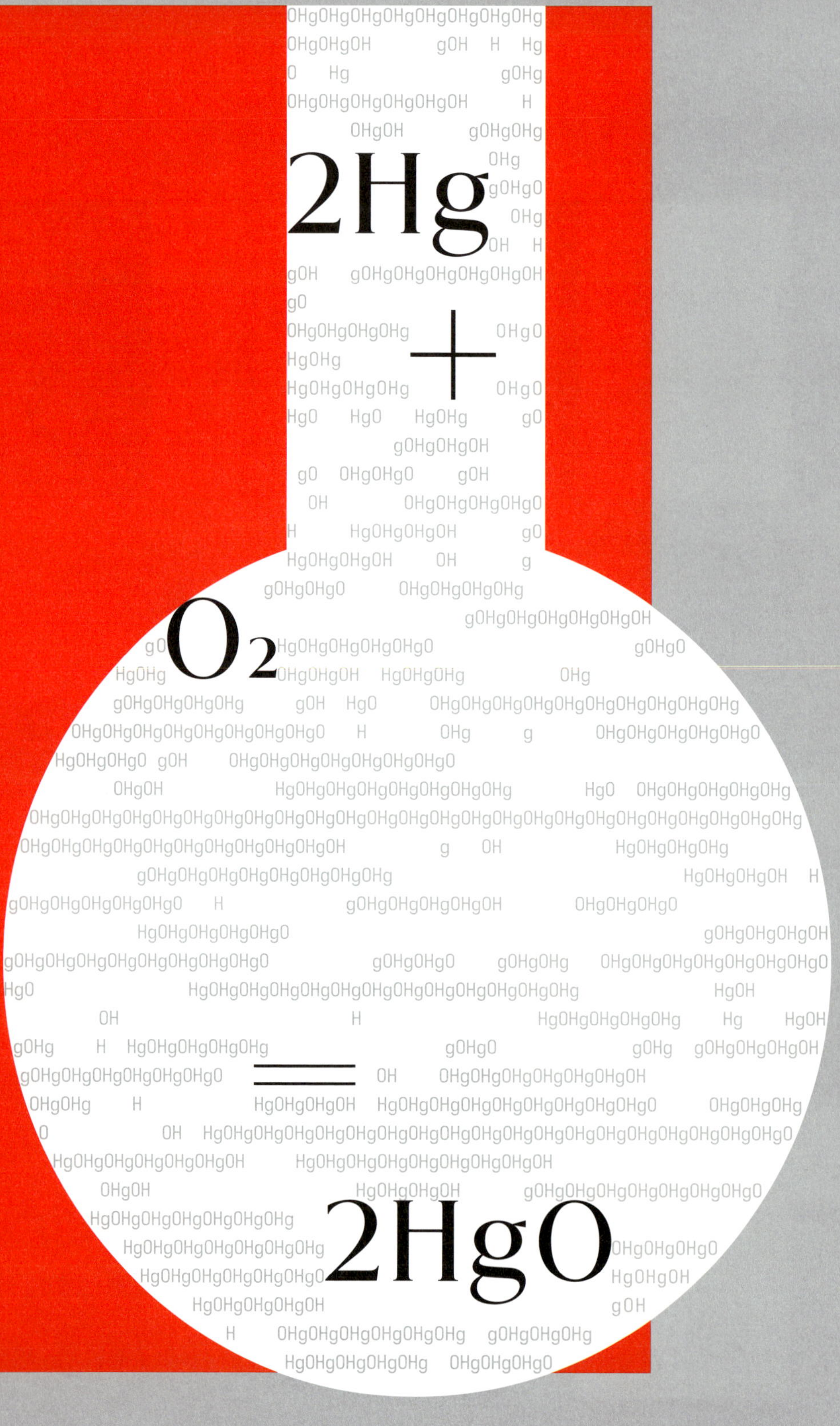
2Hg
+
O_2
=
2HgO

Mercury reacts with oxygen to form red mercury oxide during a high-temperature process.

● The CPK coloring is a representation of atomic or molecular models in chemistry, developed in 1952 by Robert Corey and Linus Pauling. After nearly 70 years of development and improvement, it has become an internationally recognized elemental color scheme. Most of the CPK colors mnemonically refer to colors of pure elements or notable compounds. For example, white represents hydrogen, which is colorless and odorless; black refers to carbon, which is actually black; and yellow is the color associated with sulfur. There are also representative colors that do not come from the actual colors of the elements but from an association of the elements. For example, oxygen has a red CPK color because of its burning color, which is similar to the color of hemoglobin in the blood. Nitrogen, being the most abundant gas in the Earth's atmosphere, and with the sky being blue, has its CPK color set to blue. While oxygen is inactive at normal temperatures, it can directly combine with other elements at high temperatures. For example, silvery-white mercury, when heated with oxygen, can turn into bright red mercury oxide. The redness is the result of a violent chemical reaction, a testament to the power of oxygen. ● Red, with the longest wavelength and the most aggressive penetration, is the most eye-catching color on the spectrum. In Renaissance paintings from the 14th to 16th centuries, red was often used as the cloak color of Christ or the Virgin Mary. Nineteenth-century artists systematically studied color theory, with a particular focus on how complementary colors like red and green accentuate each other. In the 20th century, red represented bloodshed, struggles, and communism, embodying the utopian ideals of the constructivists and supremacists of that time. Avant-garde artists of the same period also preferred to express their pure artistic ideals in red. ● Any incisive designer or artist with a keen eye for color will undoubtedly make the fullest use of red. The great master Titian pioneered the technique of "Titian red," which gives his oil paintings a vaguely ruddy complexion; Henri Matisse, the founder of Fauvism, painted a red background flowing like a flood of beasts; avant-garde artist Yayoi Kusama uses red polka dots to impact vision, obliterating the boundaries of time and space; "Coca-Cola Red" is difficult to find a counterpart in Pantone standards, and this unique red has made the beverage brand enduring for more than a century. They turn red into a catalyst to accelerate aesthetic reactions, transforming the red seen in daily life and the red that has been paid little attention to into experiments in design and art. Designers and artists have various interpretations of "red." They outline red ideas in their minds and display them through their works, so that people can look directly at the red images in their designs.

Hydrogen	White
Carbon	Black
Sulfur	Yellow
Oxygeon	Red
Nitrogen	Blue

CPK Coloring

Story of Red

- SCARLET — R124 G25 B30 — C50 M100 Y100 K25
- COCHINEAL — R168 G0 B18 — C0 M100 Y87 K38
- ROSSO CORSA — R200 G22 B29 — C20 M100 Y100 K0
- VERMILION — R213 G68 B52 — C13 M86 Y80 K0
- PINK — R241 G157 B181 — C0 M50 Y10 K0

Scarlet

• Scarlet is a controversial color with multiple meanings. It has been used to signify fame and power, such as Mary, Queen of Scots, who wore a scarlet robe before her death, symbolizing martyrdom. At first, the word "scarlet" referred to a beloved wool cloth and was later used to describe a bright red color. However, scarlet has also sparked criticism, being seen as a symbol of hypocrisy and sin. This controversy has made scarlet a color of tension and variety. Scarlet historically represented luxury and authority, and was used in the uniforms of the royalty, the church, and the military.

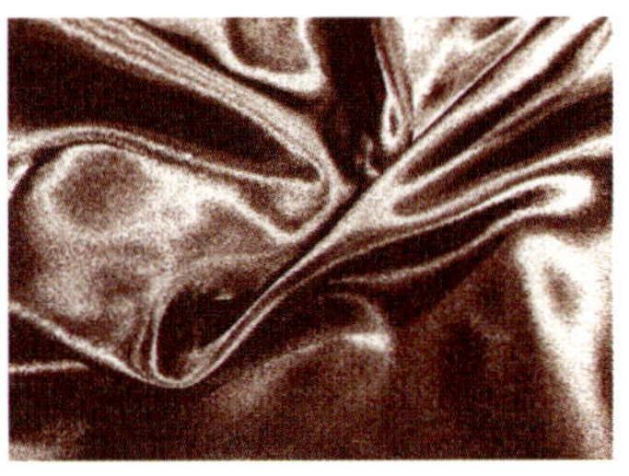

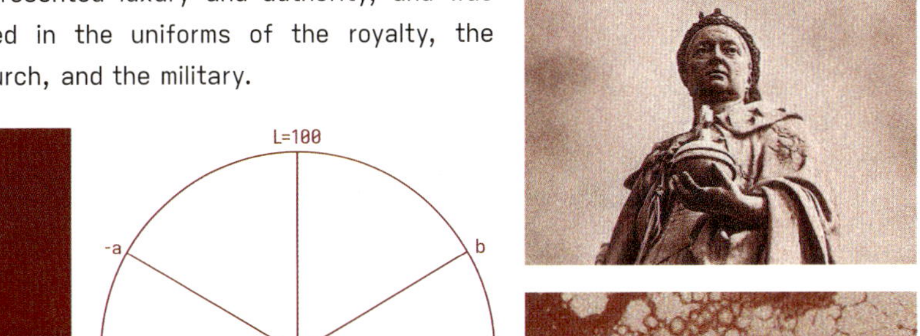

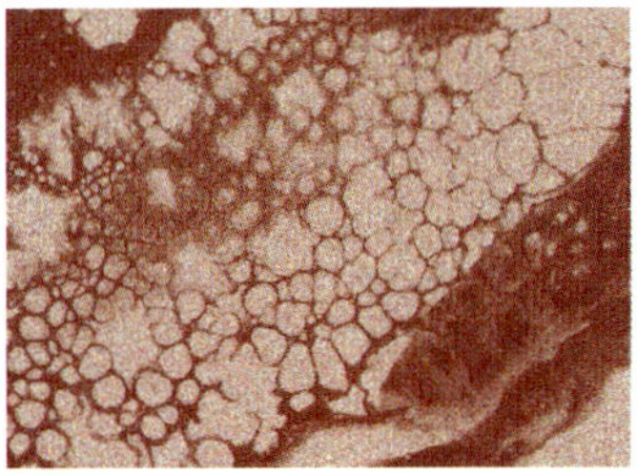

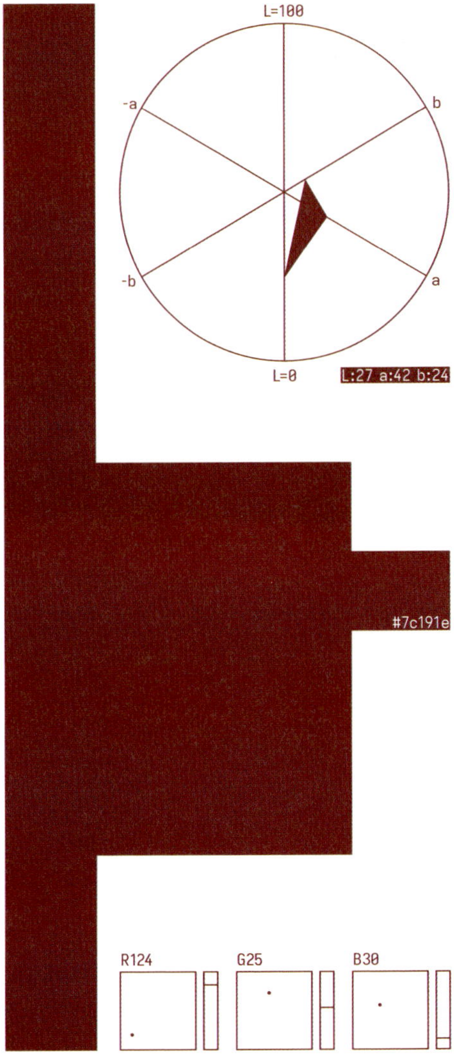

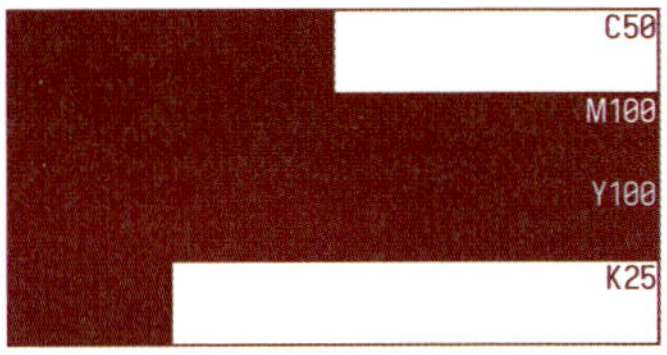

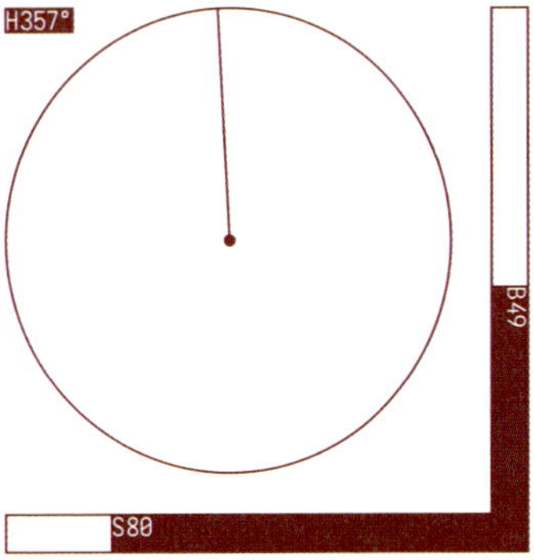

L=100
-a
b
-b
a
L=0
L:27 a:42 b:24

#7c191e

C50
M100
Y100
K25

H357°
B49
S80

R124
G25
B30

Cochineal • Cochineal is a small insect that is often mistaken for a seed Vermilion or gravel. They live in large numbers on cacti in Mexico and South America. These insects can produce a red dye known as cochineal. Cochineal is relatively easy to make. People combine cochineal with a mordant, and then add other chemicals so that they can adjust the hue of the dye. Cochineal is a strong, bright dye used in fabrics and cosmetics. The history of making cochineal dates back to ancient civilizations and is widely used in Central and South American cultures to demonstrate power and status. The Spanish conquistadors brought cochineal back to Europe, promoting the commercialization of red dyes. Artists such as Raphael, Rembrandt, and Rubens used cochineal as a glaze and layered it on top of other red pigments, such as red ochre, to increase its color intensity. Today, cochineal is a popular color in the fashion industry and is also used in medicine and art.

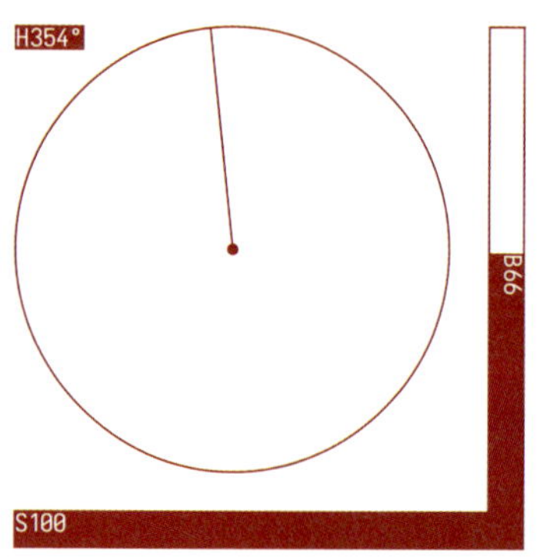

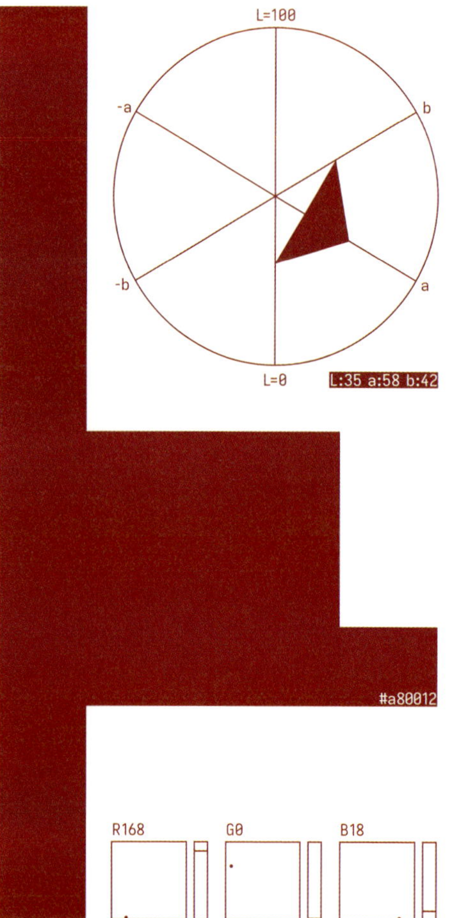

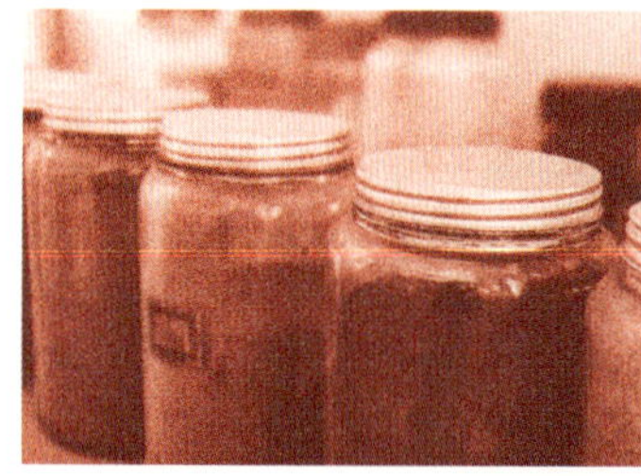

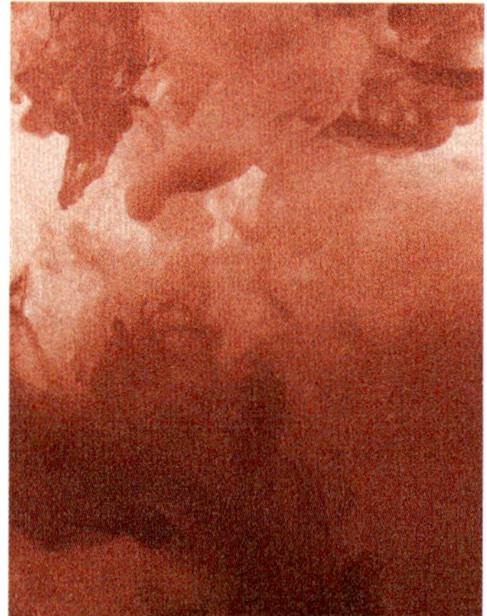

Rosso Corsa • In 1907, Italian Prince Scipione Borghes undertook the challenge of traveling from Beijing to Paris in a poppy-red Itala. This adventurous trip was full of difficulties and challenges, and the car ironed out all the roadblocks. Upon their triumphant return, the red color of the car became the symbol of the Italian national racing team and was named "Rosso Corsa," or racing red. This color has since become the signature hue of Ferrari vehicles, symbolizing speed, passion, and victory. Ferrari Red has, since then, become one of the most iconic colors in the automotive world.

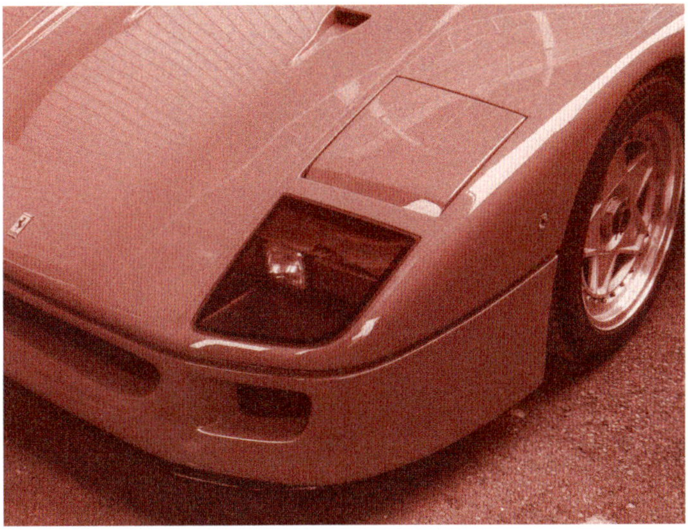

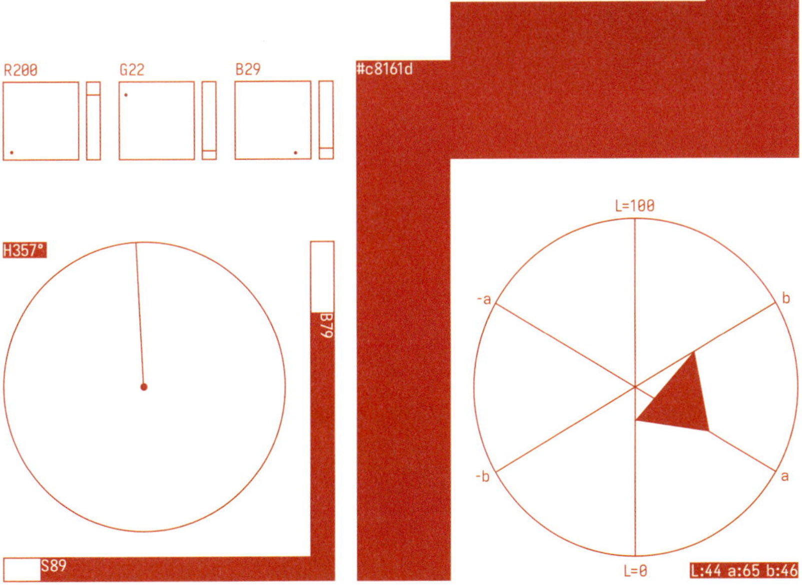

R200 G22 B29

#c8161d

H357°

B79

S89

L=100

-a

b

-b

a

L=0

L:44 a:65 b:46

Vermilion

• Vermilion is a vivid, rich, bright red pigment first seen in the frescoes from Pompeii. The raw material is a mineral called cinnabar, which contains mercury sulfide. The ancient Romans highly valued vermilion and used it in religious festivals and works of art. But natural cinnabar was very rare, and most of the supply came from Spain, which was expensive. Later, alchemists discovered ways to synthesize cinnabar artificially, including dry and wet methods. The dry way requires mixing sulfur powder with mercury and then heating it, while the wet way uses other chemical methods. Vermilion red occupies an important place in medieval art and is widely used in manuscript decoration, tempera paintings, and lacquer works.

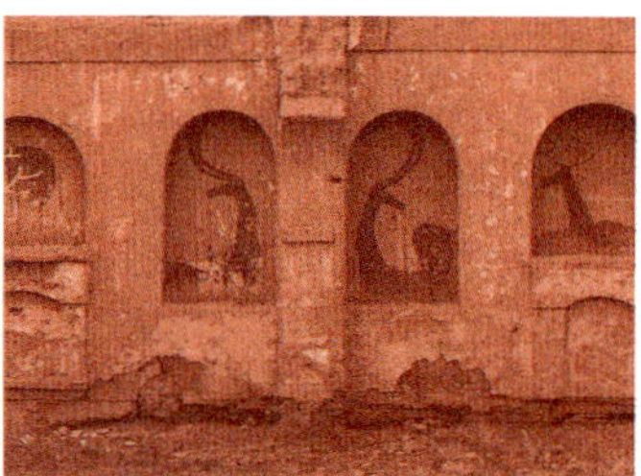

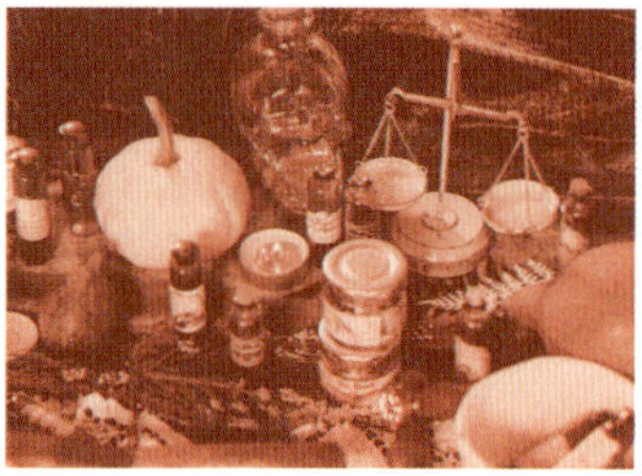

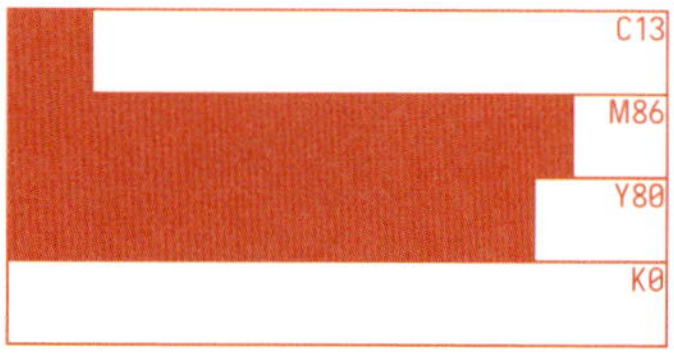

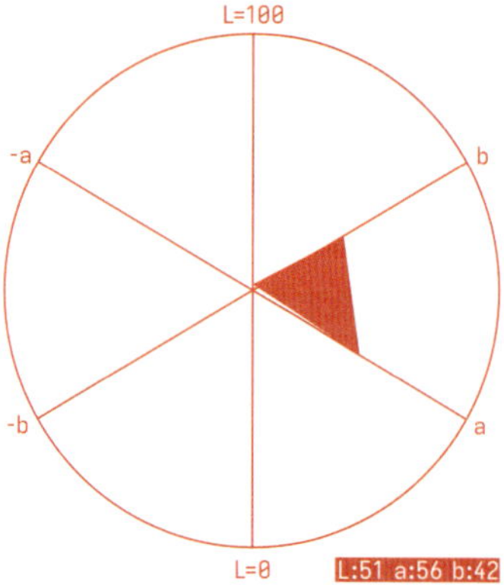

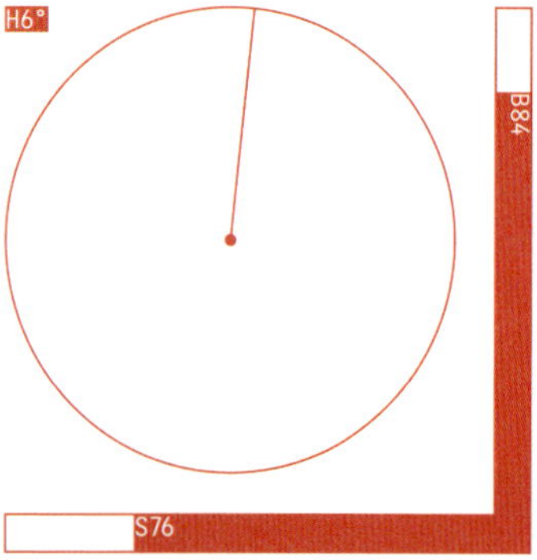

C13
M86
Y80
K0

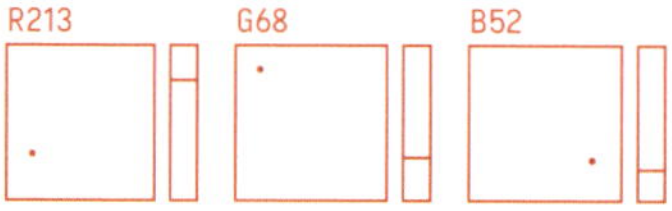

L=100
-a
b
-b
a
L=0
L:51 a:56 b:42

R213
G68
B52

#d54434

H6°
B84
S76

Pink • The word itself is relatively young, too. The first reference in the *Oxford English Dictionary* to describe pale reds dates back to the late 17th century. Before that, "pink" usually referred to a kind of pigment. Pink pigments were made by binding an organic colorant, such as buckthorn berries or an extract of the broom shrub, to an inorganic substance like chalk, which gave it body. They came in several colors—you could have green pinks, rose pinks, or brown pinks—but more often than not, they were yellow. It is an odd quirk that while light reds acquired a name of their own, pale greens and yellows did not, for the most part (although several languages, including Russian, do have different words for pale and deep blues). Most Romance languages make do with a variation of the word "rose," from the flower. English, although uncertain enough, may derive their word for the color from another flower, the Dianthus plumarius, also known as "the pink."

#f19db5

R241 G157 B182

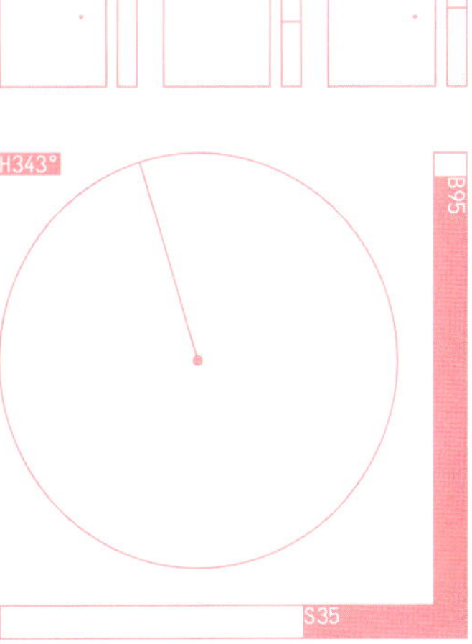

C13
M86
Y80
K0

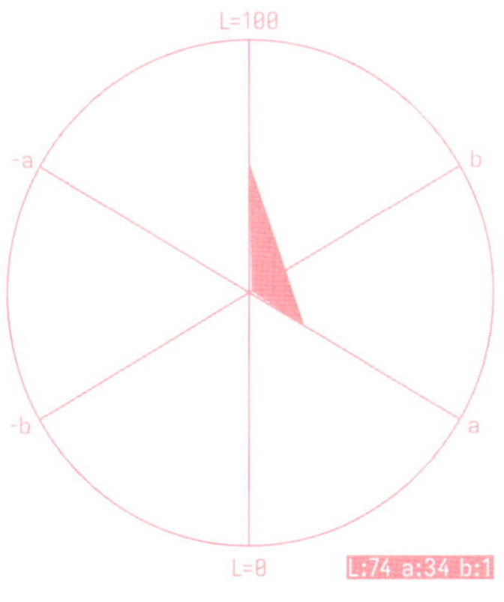

Various Red

C0 M100 Y100 K0	C0 M40 Y30 K0	C10 M90 Y5 K0	C30 M90 Y90 K10	C30 M95 Y100 K0	C0 M60 Y0 K0
C30 M100 Y100 K0	C45 M90 Y80 K15	C10 M85 Y55 K0	C35 M95 Y80 K0	C30 M85 Y75 K0	C15 M60 Y35 K0
C0 M100 Y100 K45	C15 M90 Y50 K0	C50 M100 Y100 K20	C20 M100 Y100 K0	C25 M75 Y50 K0	C0 M60 Y30 K0
C30 M100 Y40 K0	C30 M90 Y80 K15	C15 M60 Y35 K0	C0 M80 Y20 K0	C15 M75 Y55 K0	C25 M90 Y40 K0
C5 M70 Y50 K0	C30 M90 Y90 K0	C0 M100 Y0 K40	C15 M90 Y80 K0	C0 M85 Y40 K0	C30 M80 Y35 K0
C25 M55 Y35 K0	C0 M100 Y20 K50	C20 M100 Y100 K20	C55 M90 Y100 K0	C20 M100 Y0 K0	C40 M100 Y55 K5

…20 …90 …0	C15 M90 Y55 K0	C5 M85 Y30 K0	C0 M100 Y80 K0	C0 M100 Y20 K0	C0 M100 Y60 K0
…0 …100 …30	C50 M100 Y100 K20	C55 M90 Y55 K10	C0 M100 Y0 K50	C10 M90 Y50 K0	C15 M90 Y30 K0
…0 …100 …55	C30 M100 Y75 K0	C0 M30 Y0 K0	C50 M100 Y100 K0	C20 M100 Y85 K0	C35 M100 Y25 K0
…50 …90 …75	C0 M70 Y10 K0	C70 M100 Y90 K60	C0 M70 Y30 K0	C45 M100 Y80 K0	C10 M40 Y0 K0
…35 …100 …0	C0 M100 Y50 K0	C0 M100 Y90 K5	C10 M90 Y60 K0	C0 M100 Y0 K0	C0 M100 Y80 K0
…5 …95 …5	C50 M100 Y100 K50	C45 M100 Y30 K40	C80 M100 Y100 K0	C0 M50 Y10 K0	C0 M20 Y10 K0

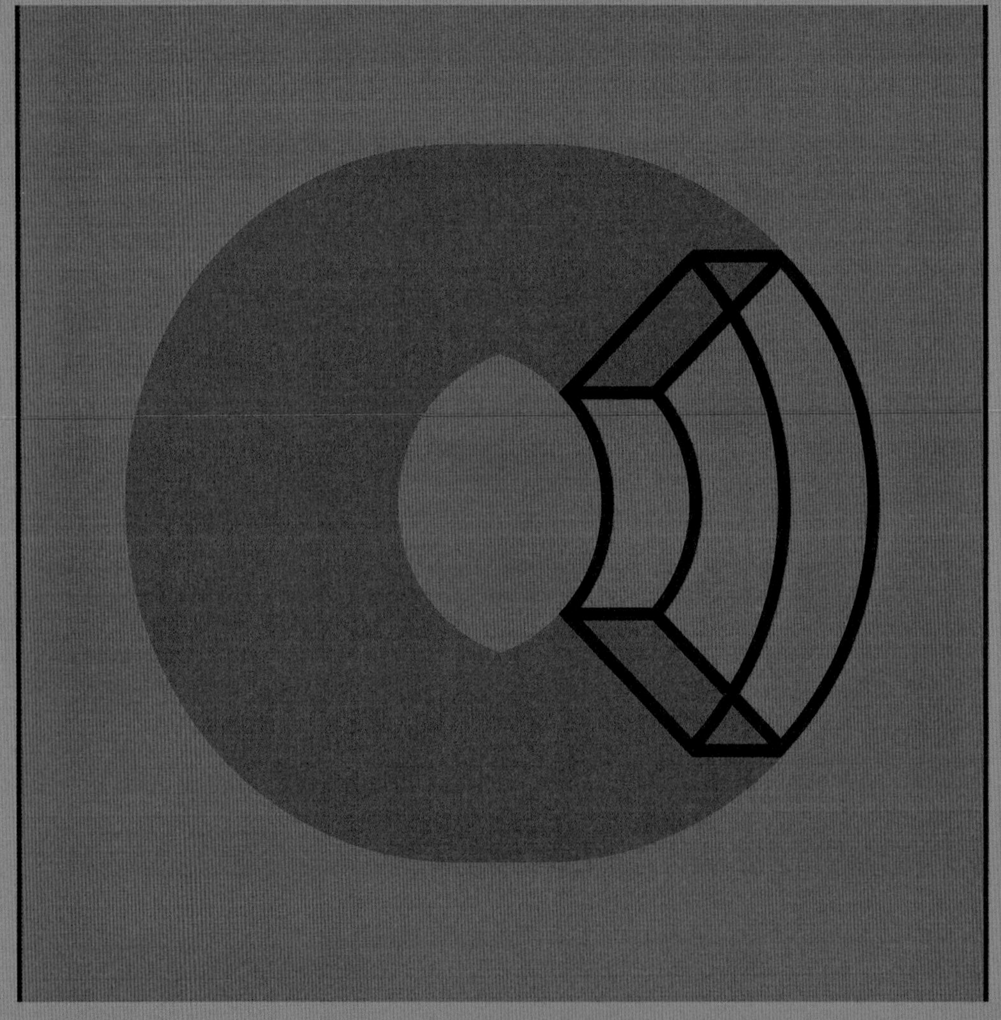

● Design Studio: YOHAK DESIGN STUDIO ● Art Director: Aki Kanai ● Designer: Taku Sasaki

THE CAMPUS ● The CAMPUS is a laboratory by KOKUYO Co., Ltd. centered around the theme of "Work and Live." ● Embracing the concept of "Open Space for Work and Life," KOKUYO transformed a section of its 40-year-old office building into a living area not only for its employees but also for the public. Situated in close proximity to the business hub of Shinagawa Station, it features a lush park, shops, a coffee stand, and other attractions that serve as a communal space, allowing individuals to be their true selves and fostering a diverse and vibrant environment for future generations. ● This concept is visually embodied in a graphic: the letter C, the initial of the facility's name. This design is utilized across various media, including merchandise, videos, the website, and posters and signs within the facility, serving as a representation of the concept and extending a welcoming design to visitors. ● The graphic comprises two primary elements: a solid yet flexible shape and a color that signifies new narratives. ● The three-dimensional form imparts a sense of expansiveness, with the C transformable into various shapes, symbolizing diverse activities that transcend a singular mold.

● Why Red? ● The color, once associated with gender specificity, now symbolizes diversity while emanating a warm and gentle aura that fosters a closer connection between the company and the community. Its unique characteristics, uncommon in both office and town settings, evoke a sense of refreshments.

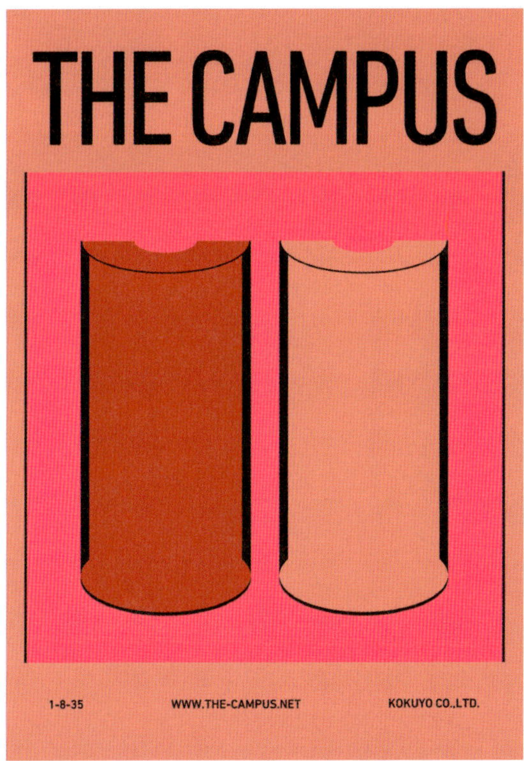

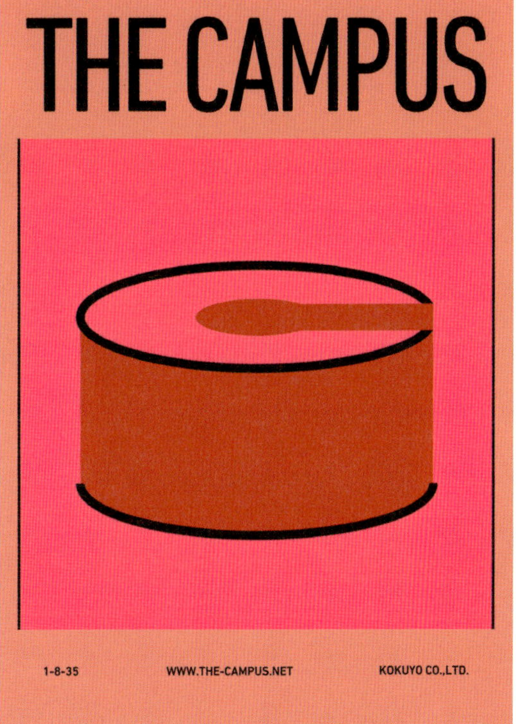

PANTONE 806C PANTONE 197C PANTONE 186C

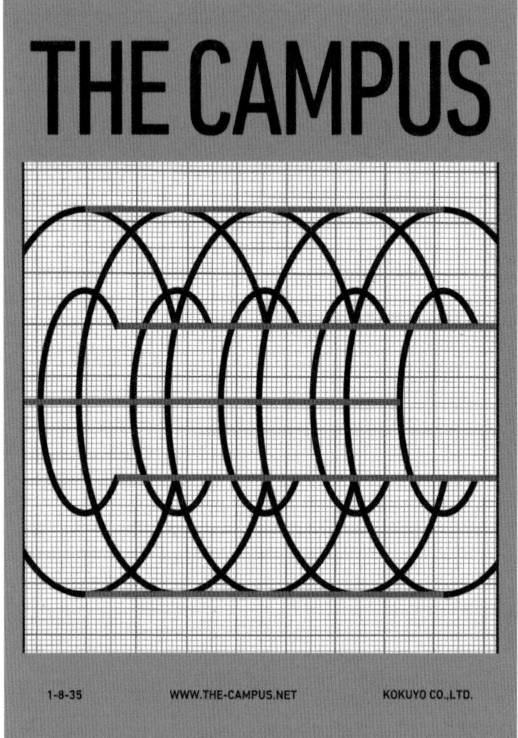

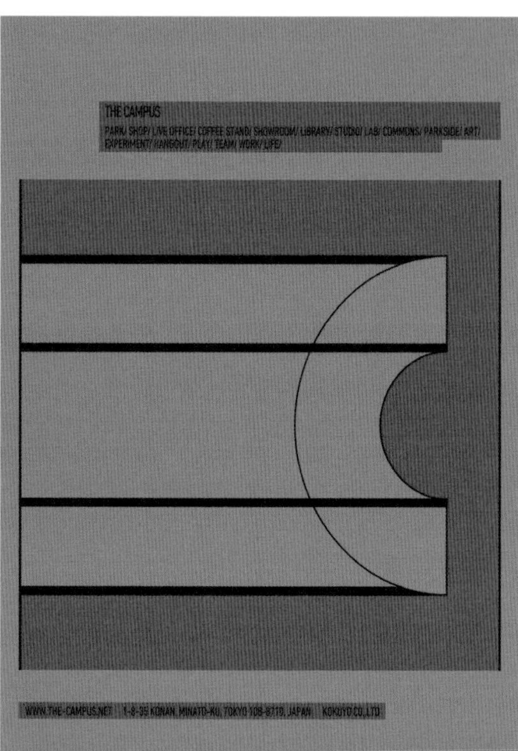

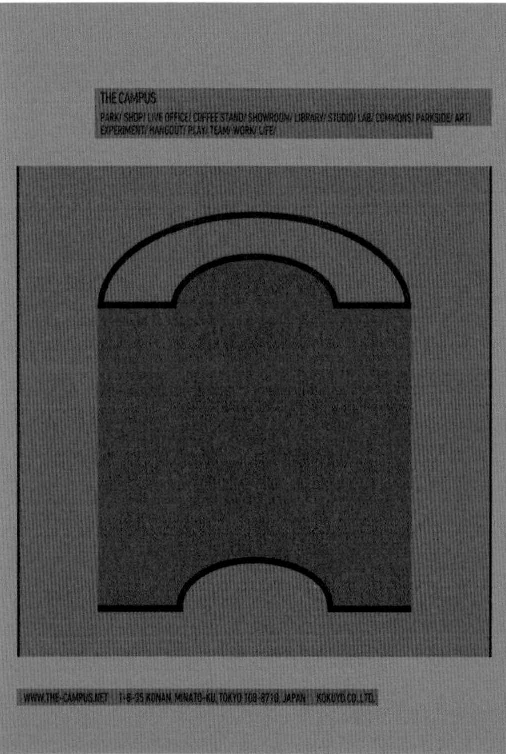

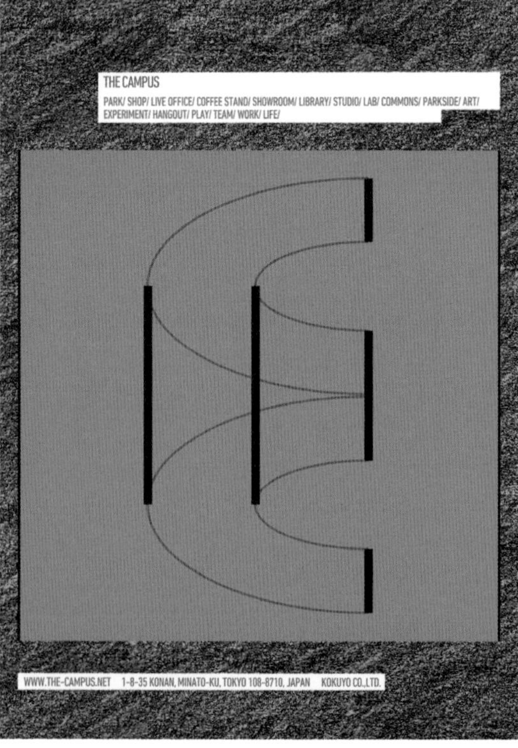

● Client: KOKUYO Co., Ltd.

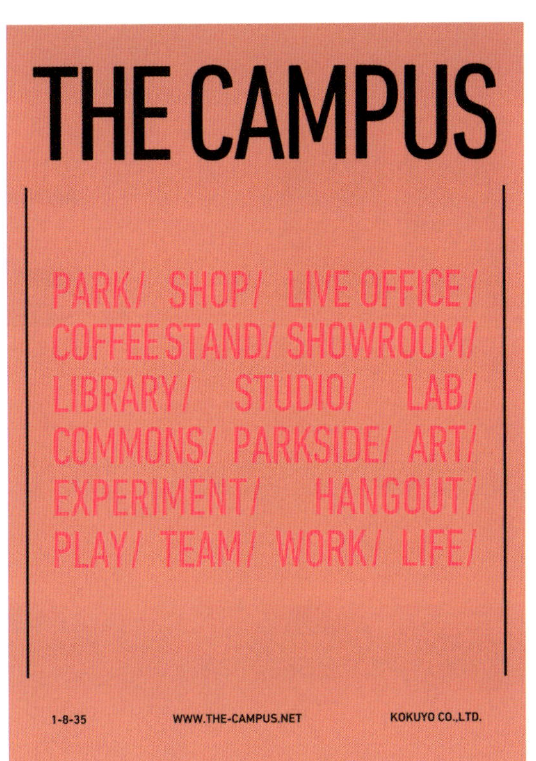
THE CAMPUS
PARK/ SHOP/ LIVE OFFICE/
COFFEE STAND/ SHOWROOM/
LIBRARY/ STUDIO/ LAB/
COMMONS/ PARKSIDE/ ART/
EXPERIMENT/ HANGOUT/
PLAY/ TEAM/ WORK/ LIFE/
1-8-35
WWW.THE-CAMPUS.NET
KOKUYO CO.,LTD.

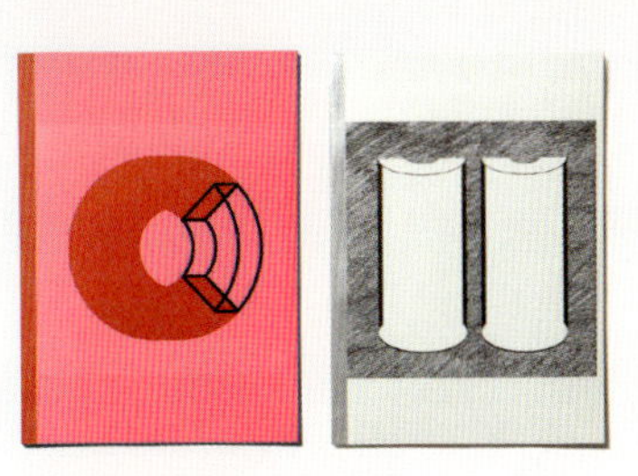

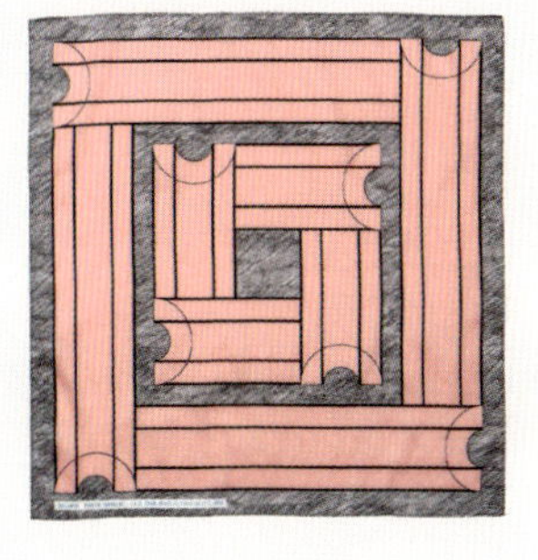

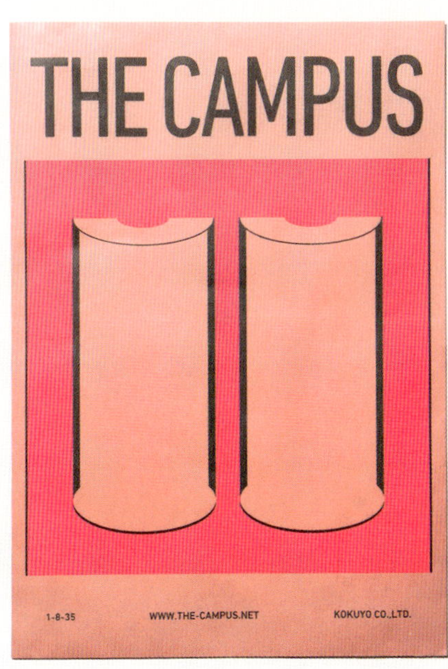
THE CAMPUS
1-8-35
WWW.THE-CAMPUS.NET
KOKUYO CO.,LTD.

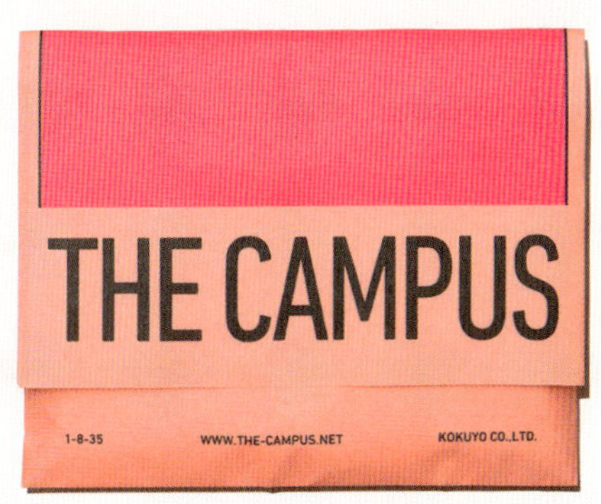
THE CAMPUS
1-8-35
WWW.THE-CAMPUS.NET
KOKUYO CO.,LTD.

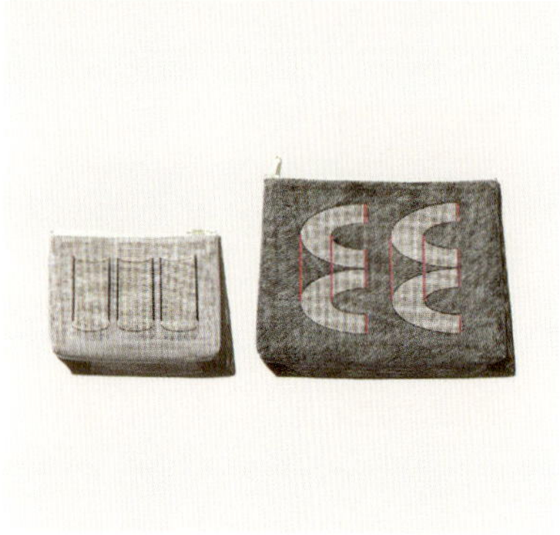

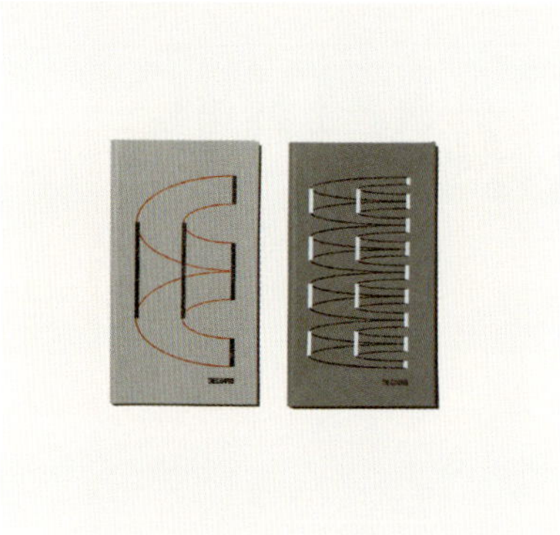

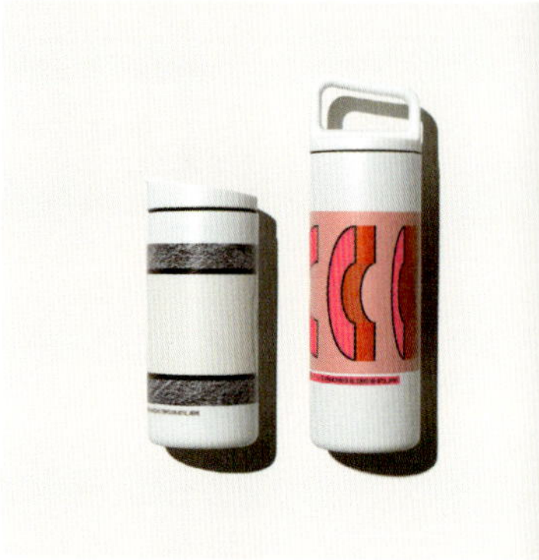

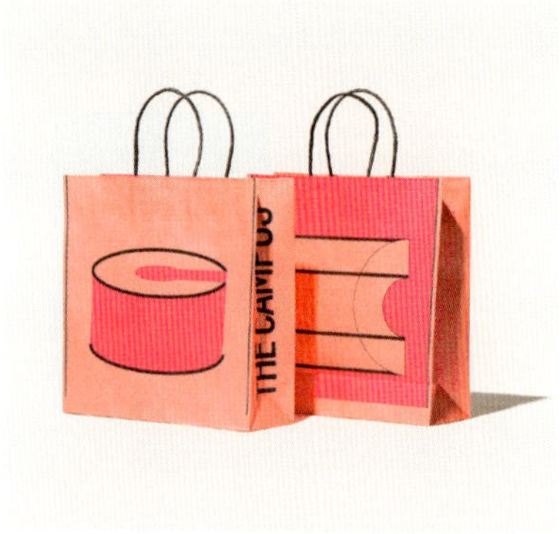
THE CAMPUS

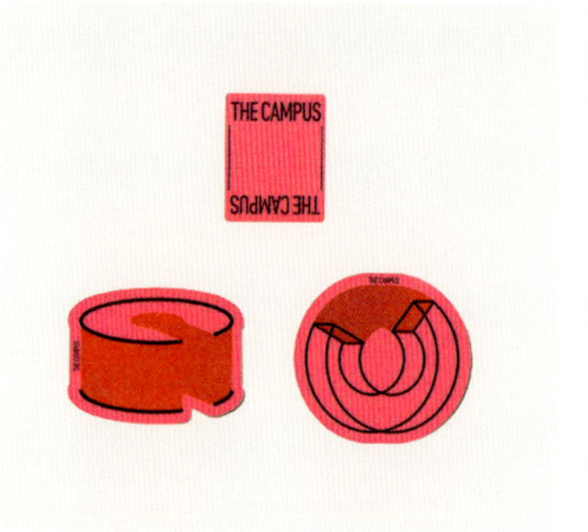
THE CAMPUS
THE CAMPUS

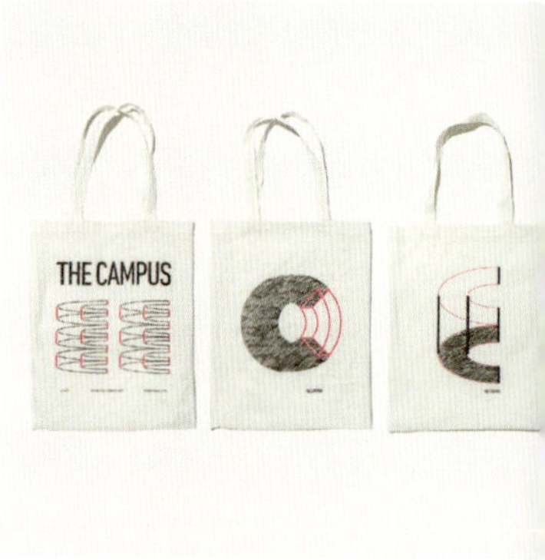
THE CAMPUS

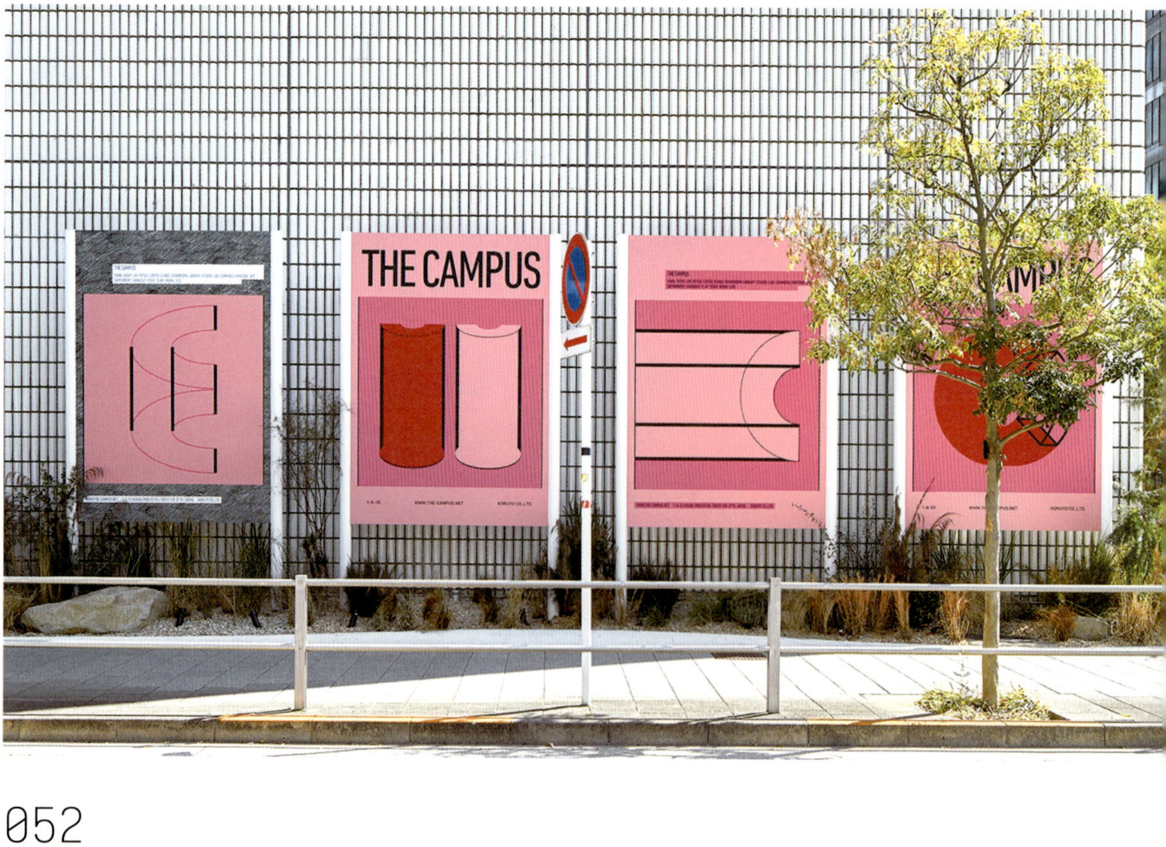
THE CAMPUS

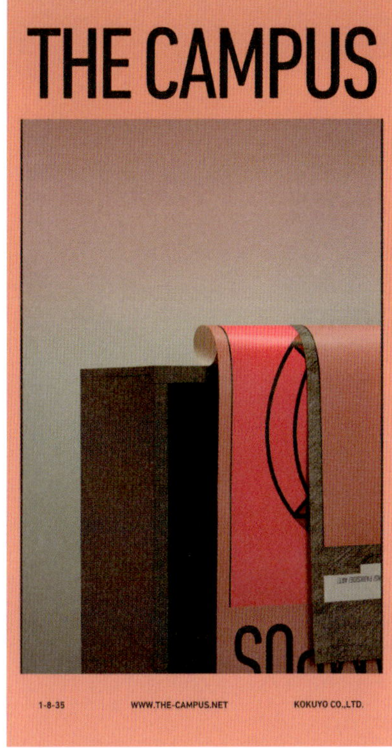
THE CAMPUS
1-8-35
WWW.THE-CAMPUS.NET
KOKUYO CO.,LTD.

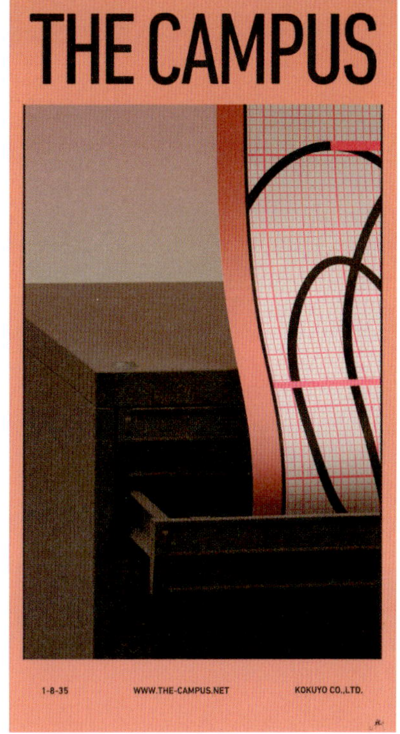
THE CAMPUS
1-8-35
WWW.THE-CAMPUS.NET
KOKUYO CO.,LTD.

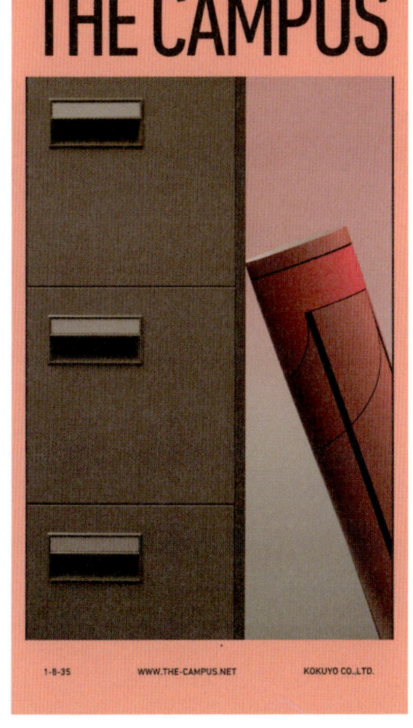
THE CAMPUS
1-8-35
WWW.THE-CAMPUS.NET
KOKUYO CO.,LTD.

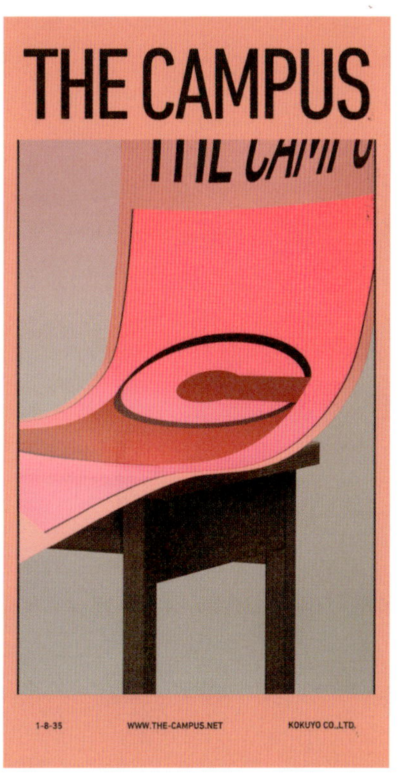
THE CAMPUS
1-8-35
WWW.THE-CAMPUS.NET
KOKUYO CO.,LTD.

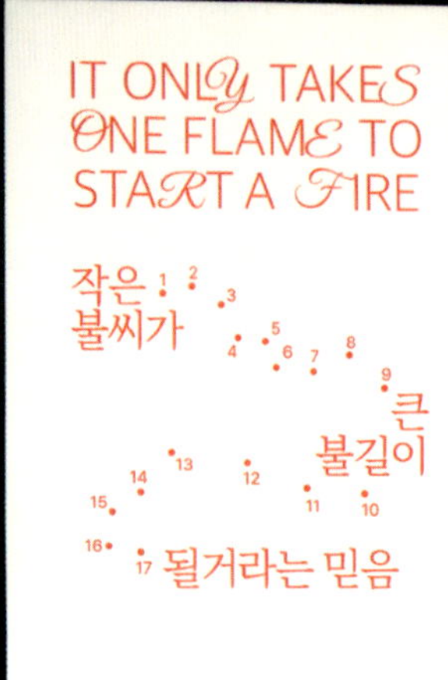

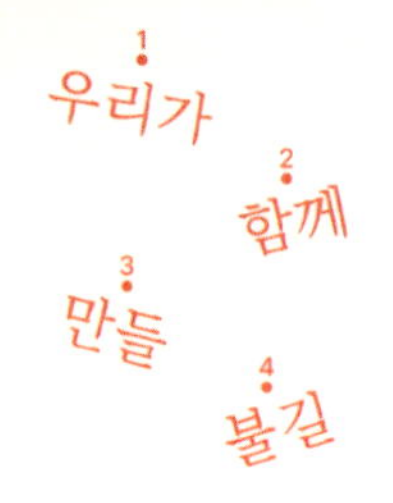

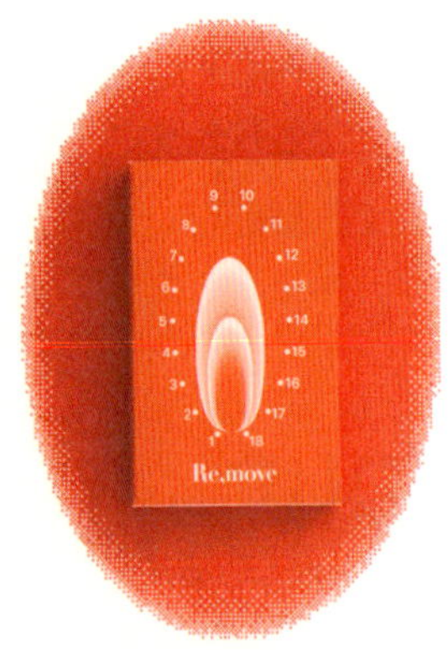

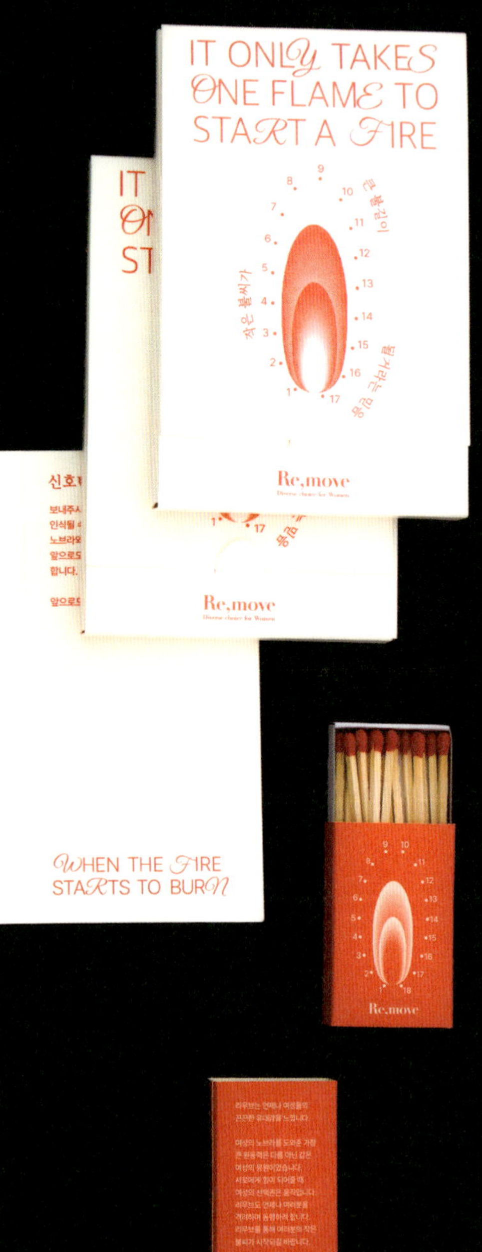

● Design Studio: IN THE GRAPHICS ● Designer: Jungin Lee ● Client: Re,move

It Only Takes One Flame to Start A Fire

● In conveying the theme of this year's Women's Day campaign, "It Only Takes One Flame To Start A Fire," the design team developed an idea rooted in the concept of pointillism and dot pattern. The aim is to illustrate how the unity and resilience of individuals can bring about significant change. ● On the outer cover of the leaflet, a flame is strategically placed alongside a title aligned with numbered dots. These dots are intended to symbolize the "seeds" of the fire, allowing the creation of a larger flame when a line is drawn connecting them. ● Inside the leaflet, an elliptical bitmap element, echoing the primary flame motif, is positioned in the flame attachment area. This creates an extension of the matchbox and leaflet, providing the illusion of a growing fire. The design progression flows seamlessly from the white flame element inside the matchbox to the ember element and culminates in the red oval element on the leaflet. This visually represents individuals who have actively contributed to the advancement of women's human rights.

● Why Red? ● Acknowledging red as the instinctive representation of fire, flames, and "women's solidarity and courage," the designer selected this color. ● The use of red encourages users, upon receiving a skin bra from brand "RE,move" with a matching package of matches, to contemplate the significance of Women's Day and find the courage to explore various choices, including underwear.

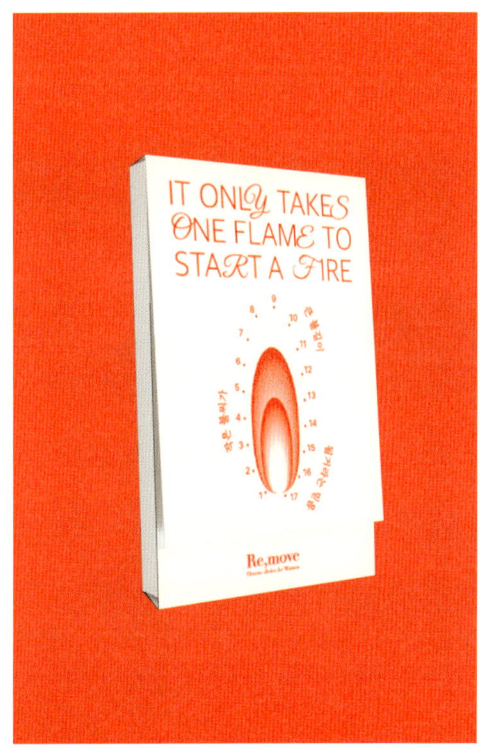

A Pack of 5 Red Packets & 25 Wisdom Sticks

● In a nation without a nationwide New Year celebration, the Lunar New Year has been somewhat overlooked, prompting the designer's response. ● The design is also a friendly invitation to participate in the Lunar New Year tradition of fortune reading through fortune sticks. Instead of traditional wooden sticks, audiences will discover 25 Chinese proverbs on paper sticks, offering inspirational insights for the new year ahead. ● Among five red packets, one provides a glimpse into the Lunar New Year, unveiling its myth and displaying the familiar street sight of the lion dance. The goal was to foster deeper understanding and appreciation for this culturally rich event.

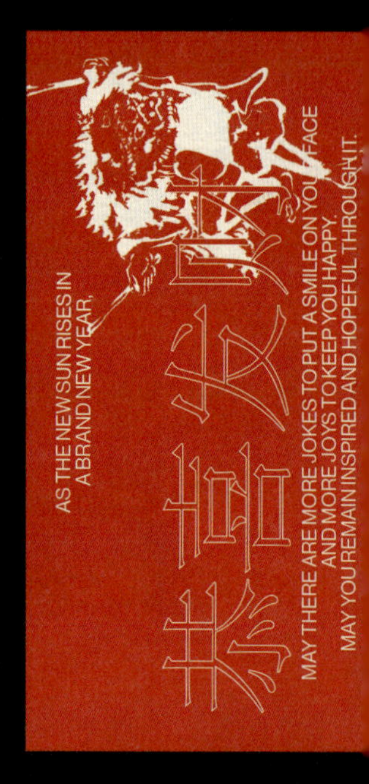

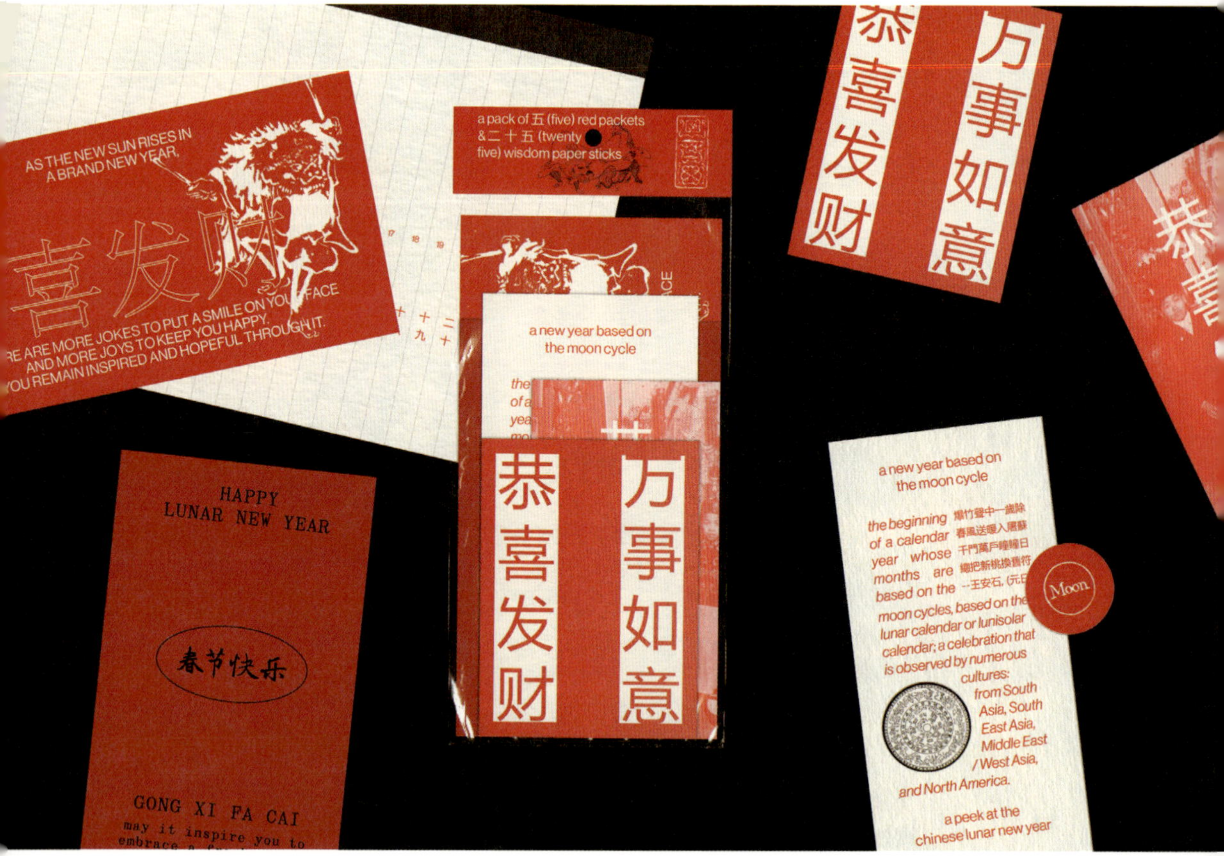

● Designer: Tiffany Wong ● Client: Sore Sore's Shelf

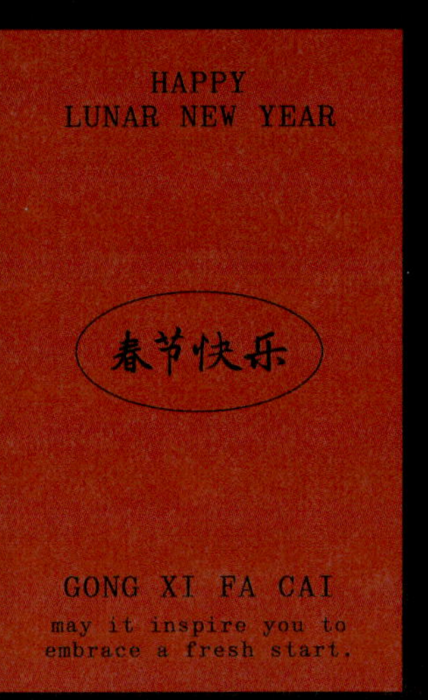

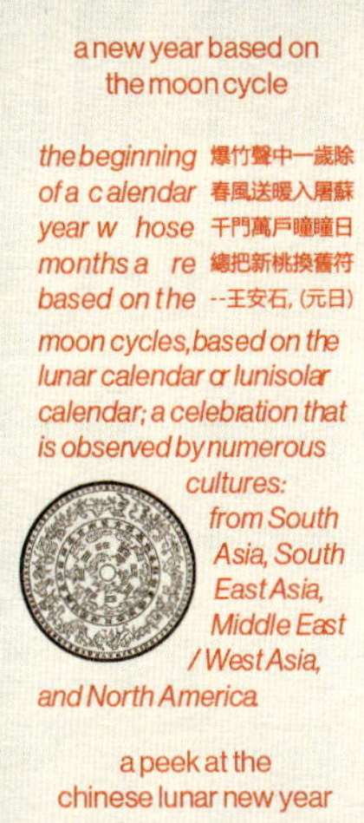

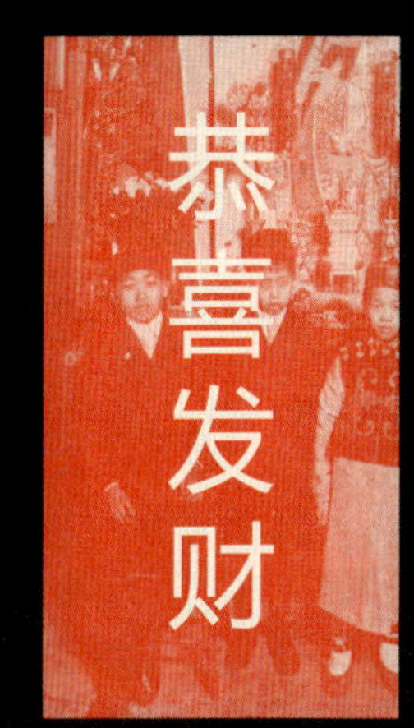

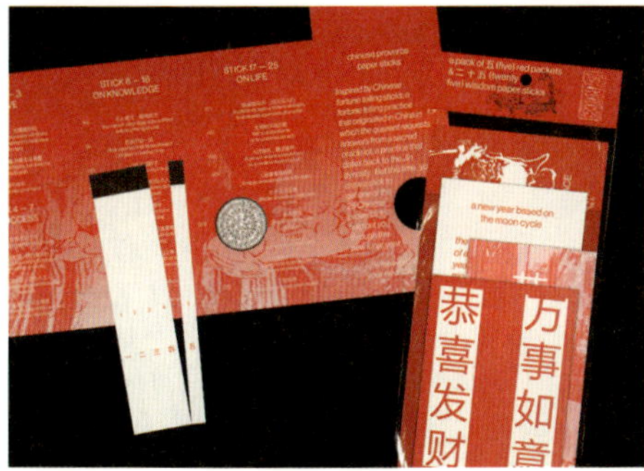

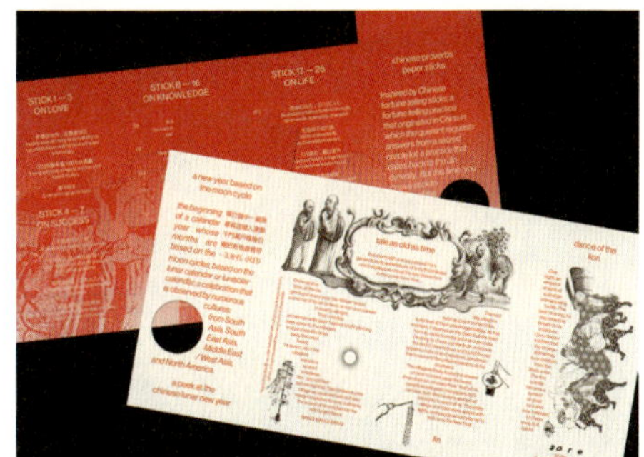

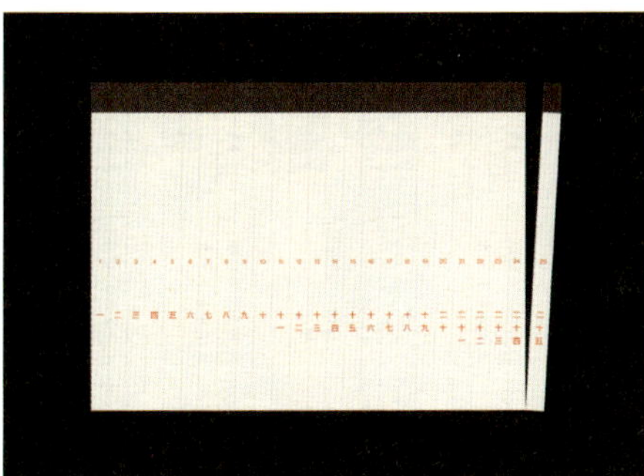

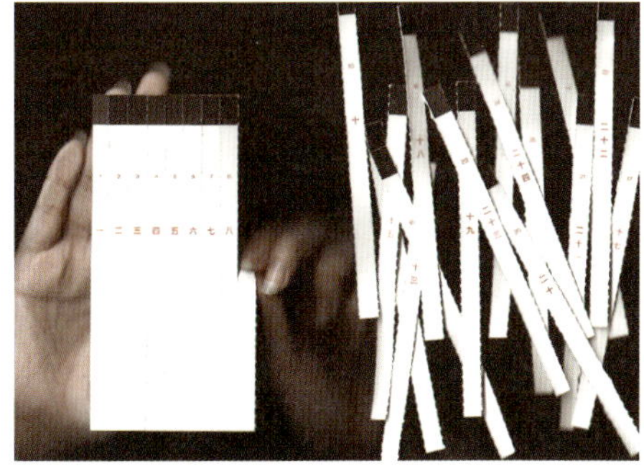

● Why Red? ● Red, a color deeply rooted in Chinese culture for centuries, takes center stage in this contemporary design project, directly associated with the Lunar New Year theme. The vibrant and positive nature of red aims to reflect the cheerfulness and festivity of the celebration, capturing the essence of the Lunar New Year in a more concise and impactful manner.

LOEWE 2022 Chinese New Year Gift

● The team crafted the LOEWE Chinese New Year Gift packaging, ingeniously transforming it into a functional steamer box for customers to use in steaming dumplings. The design is distinctly Chinese, skillfully avoiding clichés while maintaining authenticity.

● Why Red? ● In the context of the Chinese New Year, red serves as the representative color for China. The chosen yellow corresponds to the color of the bamboo cage, a traditional Chinese material. The focal point of the design is the red and yellow gift, embodying a strong sense of Chinese aesthetics.

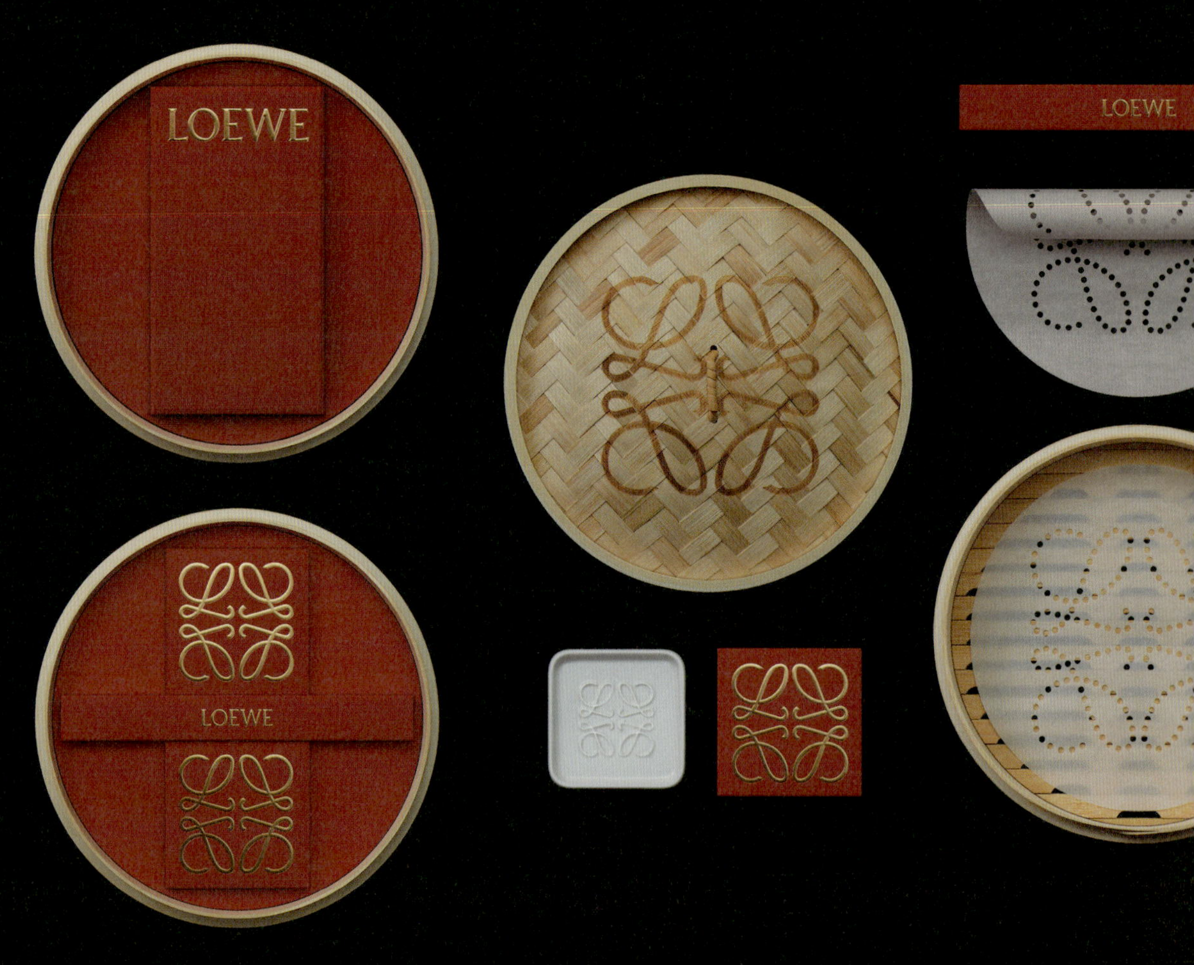

● Design Studio: United Design Lab ● Creative Director: Chen Xing ● Art Director: Xiang Li

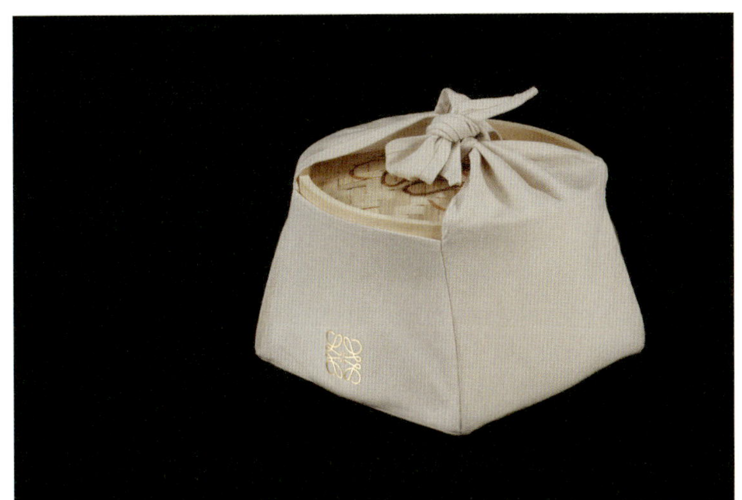

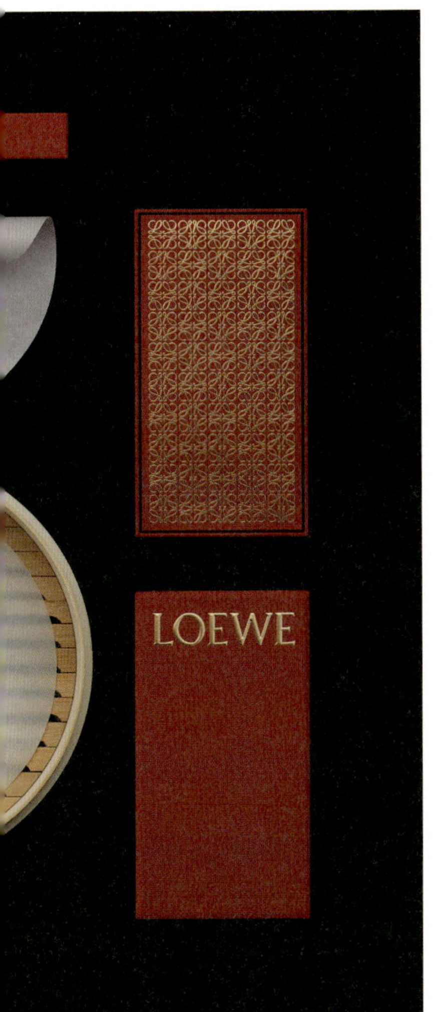

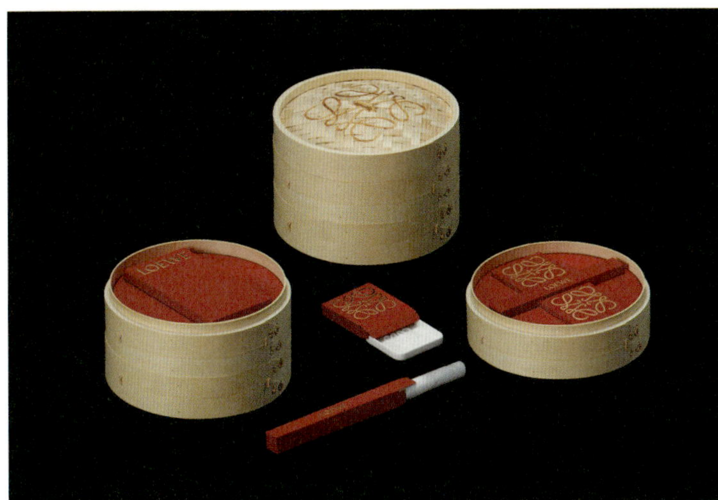

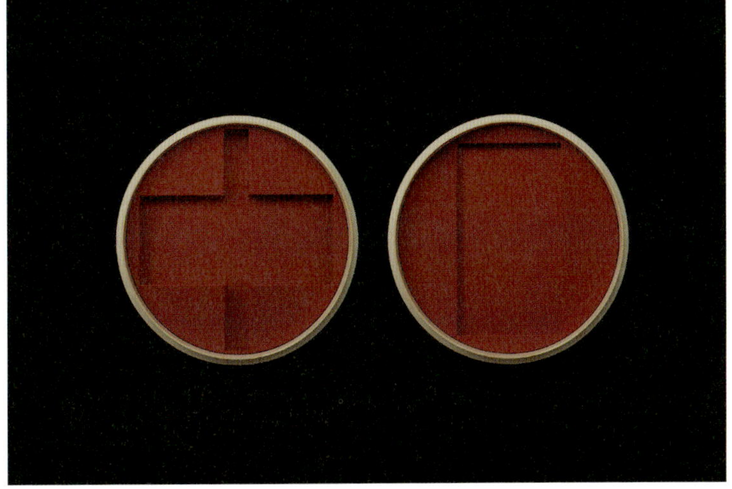

● Graphic Designer: Shuyao Bian ● Client: LOEWE

C0 M100 Y100 K0 | C30 M45 Y55 K0

UUUUU. INFLUENCER KIT

• UUUUU. is a brand that offers accessible and convenient enjoyment of beautiful nails for everyone. The concept of a "nail community" has been reinforced, providing a space where individuals can not only care for their nails but also spend time with friends and forge new connections based on a shared interest in nails. • The design pays tribute to the iconic Macintosh from the 1980s, incorporating retro elements that resonate with the stylistic preferences of Generation Z.

• Design Studio: HEAZ • Graphic Designer: Saerom Lee, Swan Lee, Yeon ho Jeoung • Client: UUUUU.

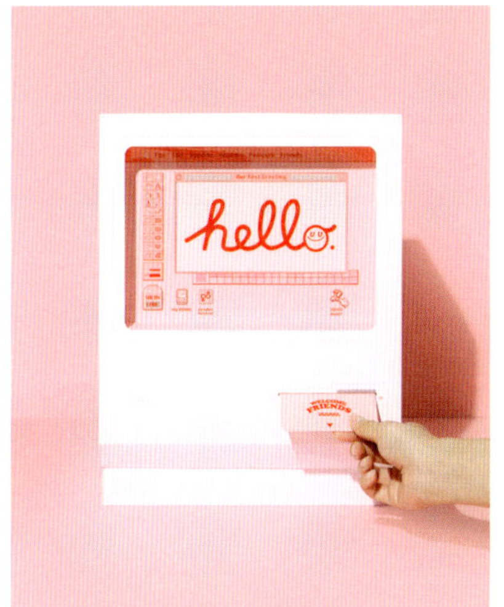

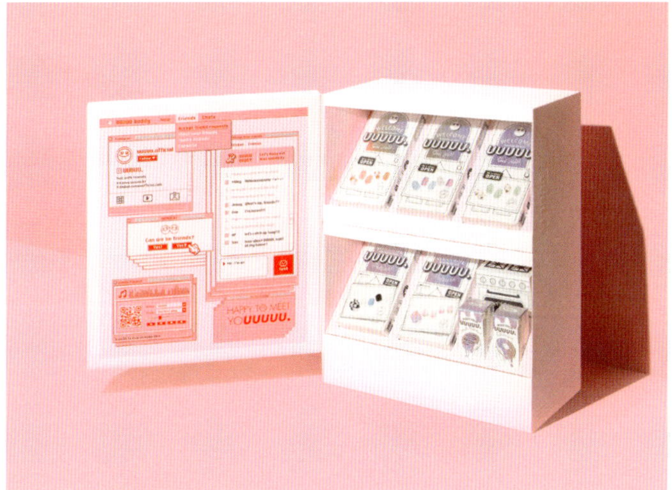

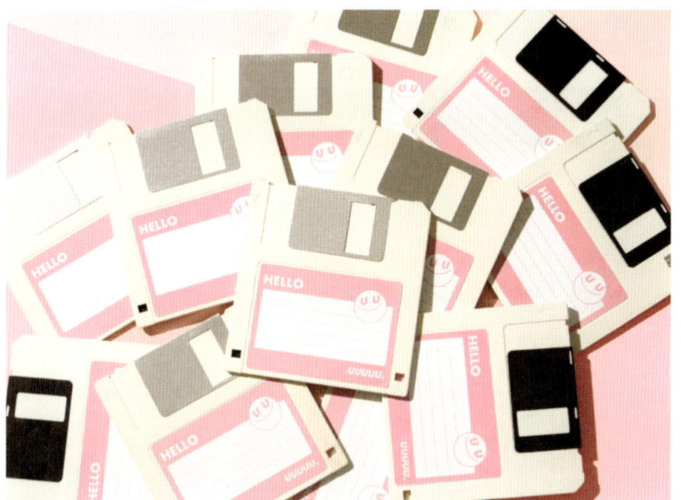

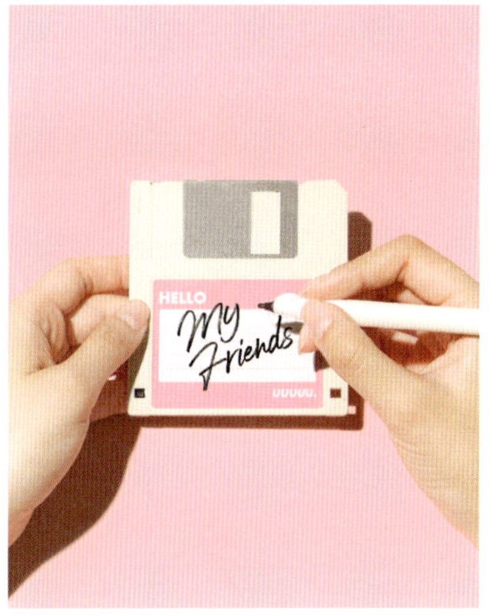

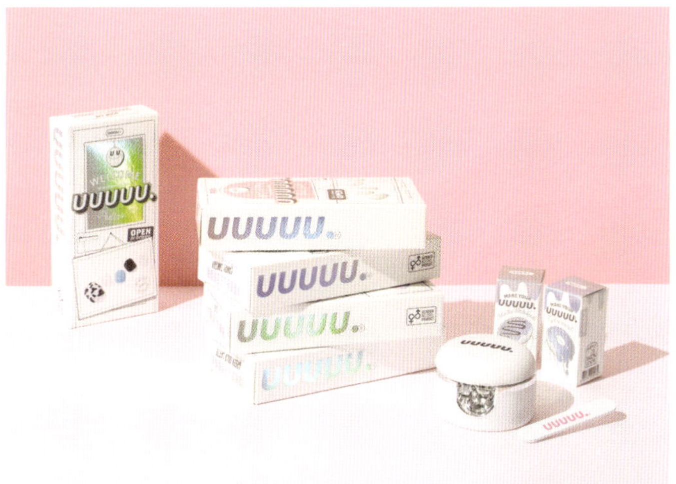

● Why Red? ● The kit employs a palette of pink, red (representing the core brand colors), and white. The meticulously chosen white paper mirrors the tactile feel of the Macintosh computer. The screen showcases the brand's pink and red hues, seamlessly integrating nostalgic graphics to underscore the design's concept. These elements converge to create an engaging and endearing ambiance, capturing the brand's friendly essence.

Cover Design for *Pre-Theoretical Assumptions in Evolutionary Explanations of Female Sexuality*

● Elisabeth A. Lloyd's work, *Pre-Theoretical Assumptions in Evolutionary Explanations of Female Sexuality*, advocates reevaluating traditional discussions on female sexuality within diverse social contexts. ● The designer aimed to offer a unique book-reading experience by altering the conventional role of the book's form, implying the thesis through its elements' structure. ● Utilizing parentheses, braces, and brackets as main graphics, representing the shapes of a woman's genitals, along with a dingbat font, the design aims to structurally reveal the relationship between form and content, emphasizing the study's focal point—feminity.

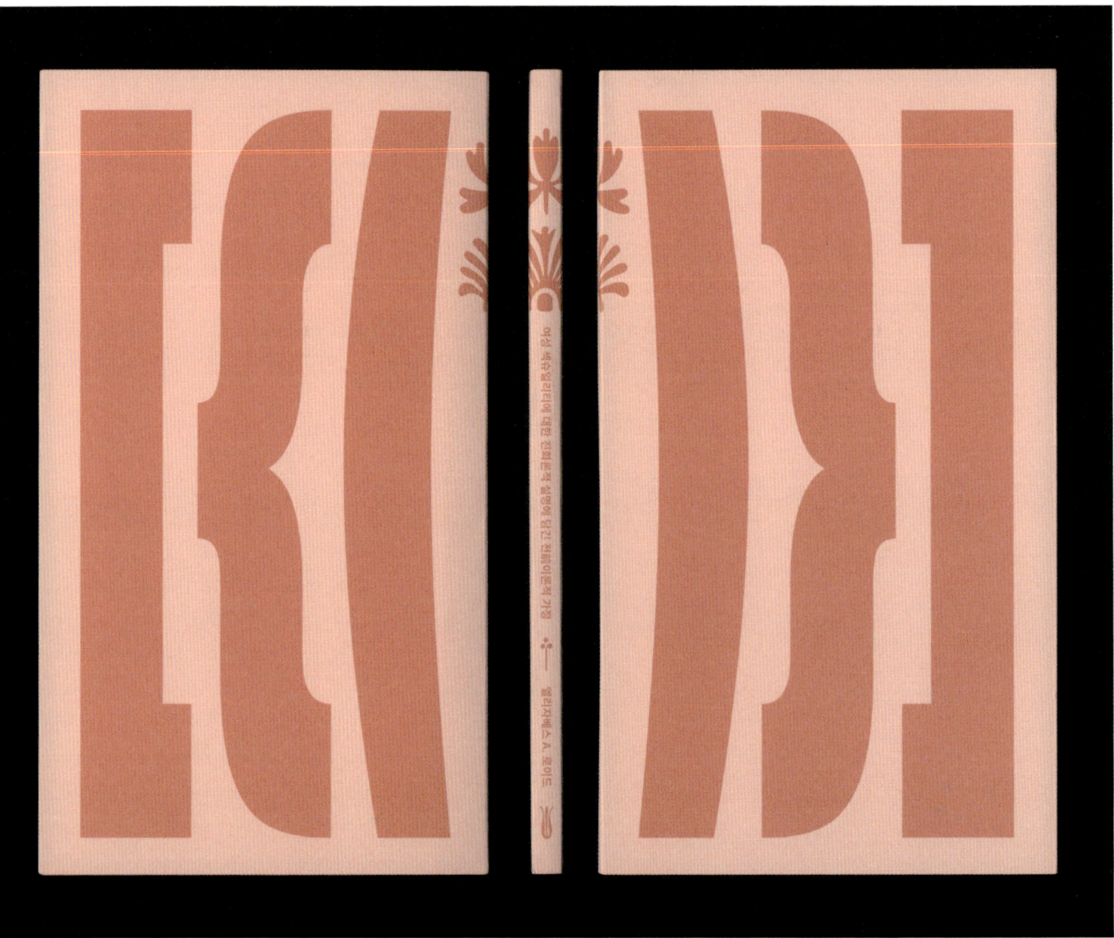

● Designer Studio: PRESS ROOM ● Designer: Jieun Yang ● Publisher: Philo-electro-ray

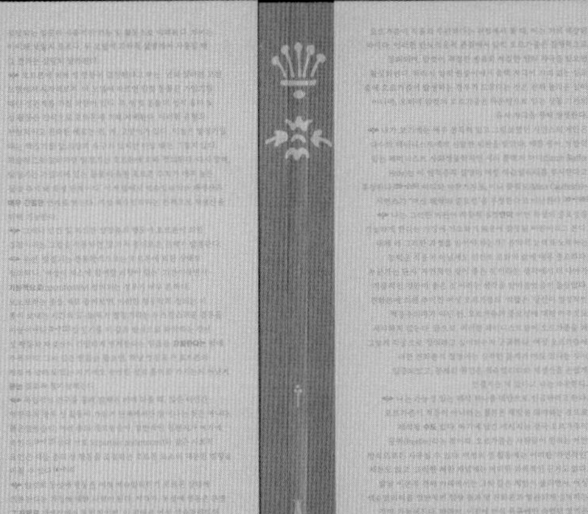

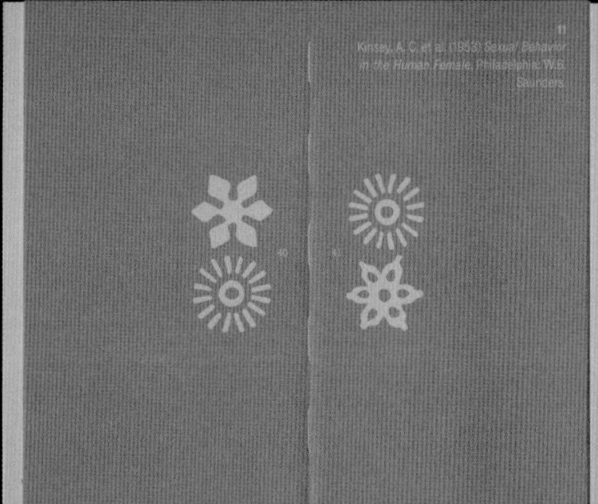

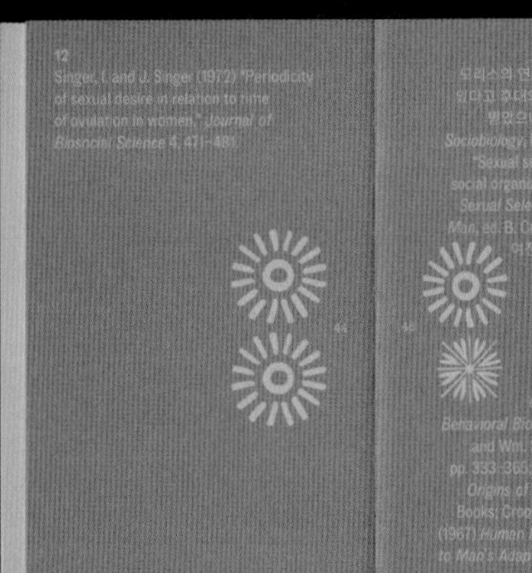

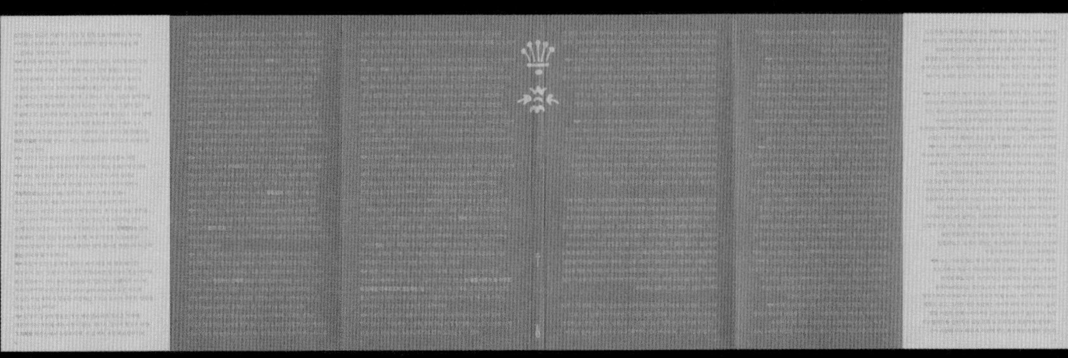

C10 M70 Y60 K0

C5 M40 Y20 K0

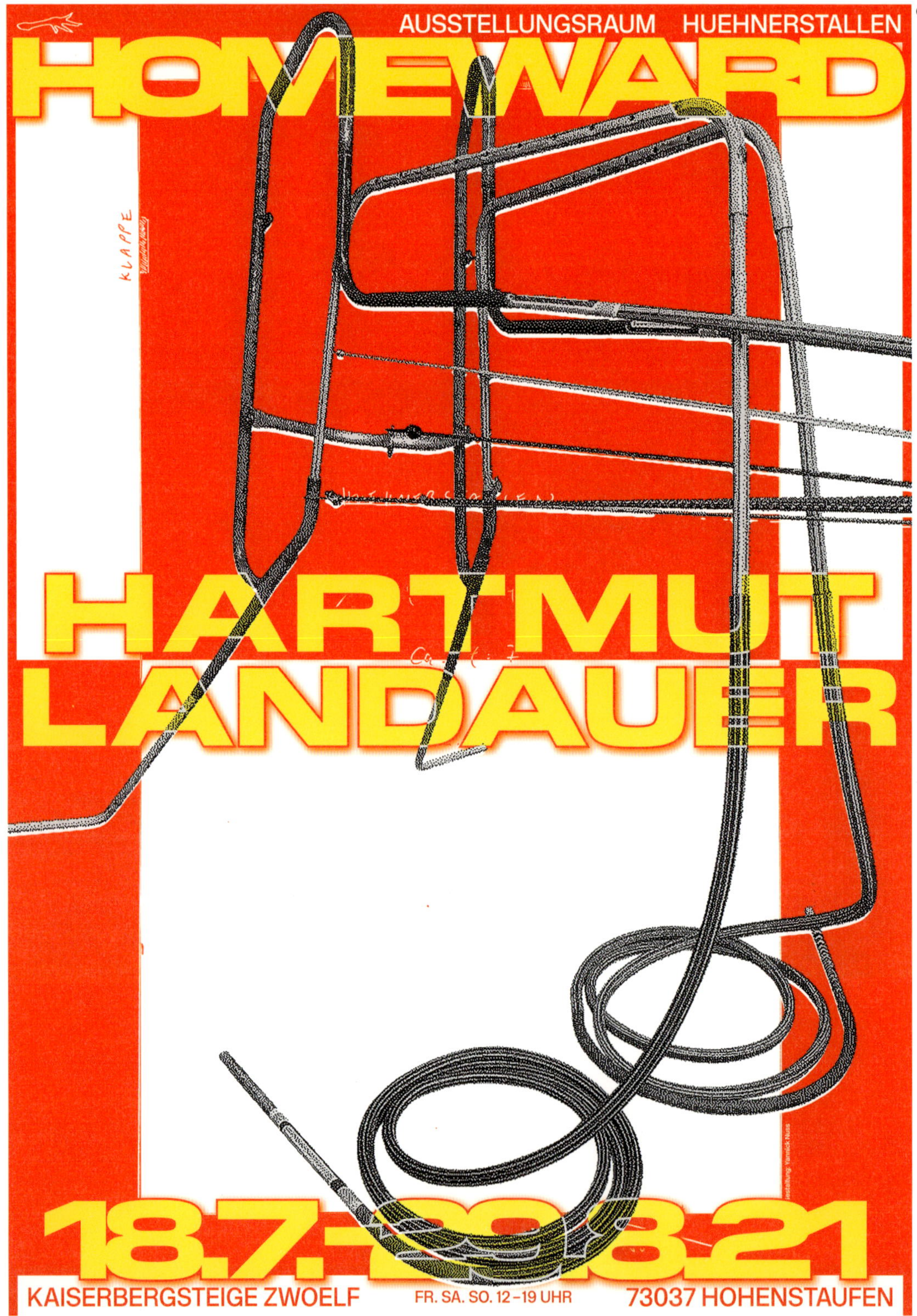

● Design Studio: Studio Yannick Nuss ● Designer: Yannick Nuss

Posters by Yannick Nuss

❶ HOMEWARD—Hartmut Landauer: a poster designed for the exhibition *Huehnerstallen*, a space curated by the artist Bruno Nagel. ❷ HAMMER ANGST: a poster for a lecture performance by the artist Bruno Nagel. ❸ HAUS AU: a poster for an exhibition by the artist Bruno Nagel. ❹ PROTO—Matthew Angelo Harrison: a poster for the exhibition *PROTO* by the artist Matthew Angelo Harrison.

❷

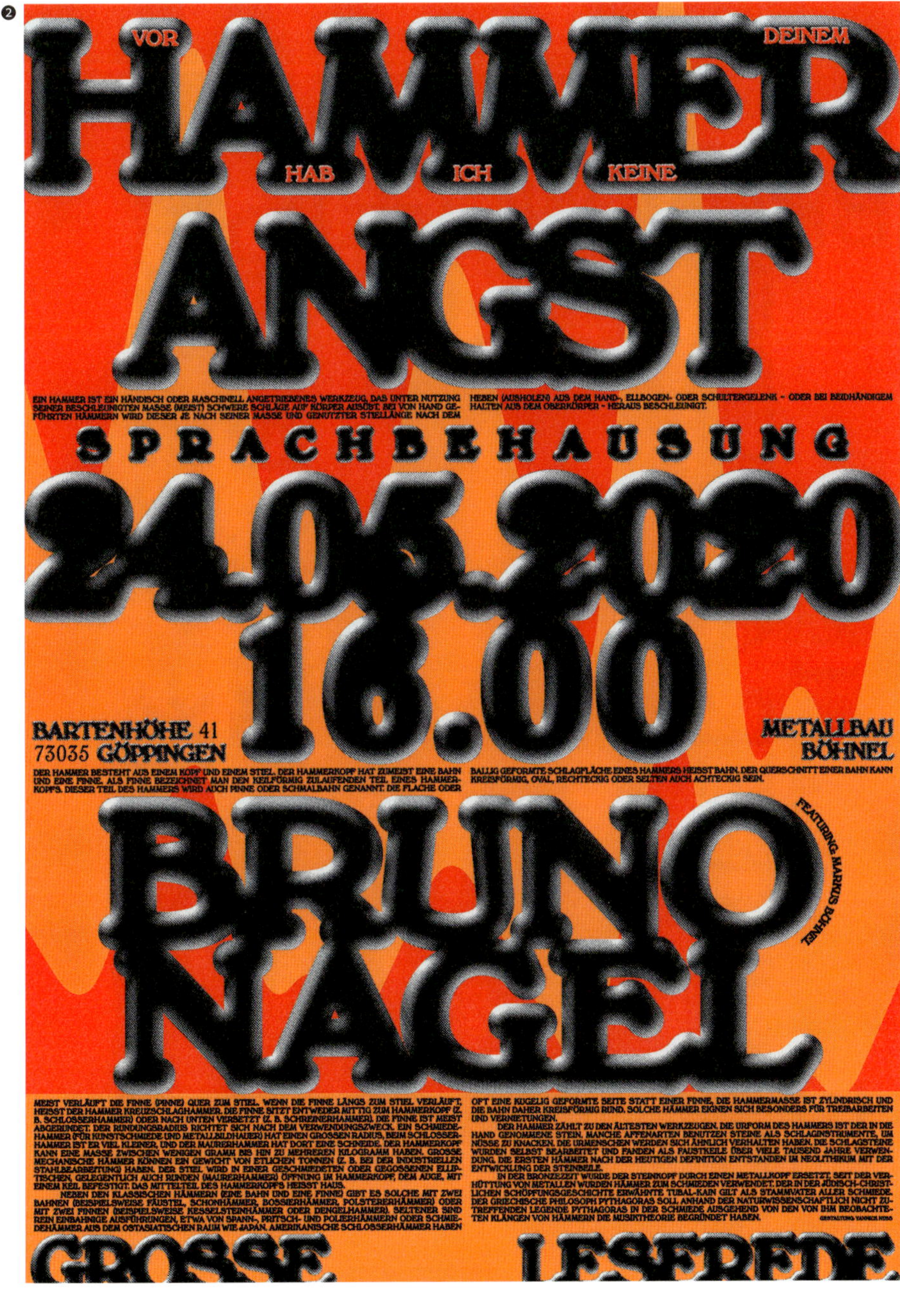

● Why Red? ❶ The poster incorporates red and yellow colors that allude to various artworks created by the artist Hartmut Landauer. Notably, the vibrant hues of the garden hoses featured in his works are highlighted on the poster. ❷ Considering the performance was held in a metal workshop, the poster employs varying shades of red to symbolize the fire and embers utilized in the iron-forging process. ❸ The exhibition venue featured a distinctive exterior facade with yellow and red details, elements that have been incorporated into the poster design. ❹ The poster utilizes a unique color, Pantone Bright Red C, to establish a connection to the artwork of Matthew Angelo Harrison. It serves as a nod to the vibrant hues seen in old UAW protest posters and the personalized jackets worn by employees in the Detroit auto industry.

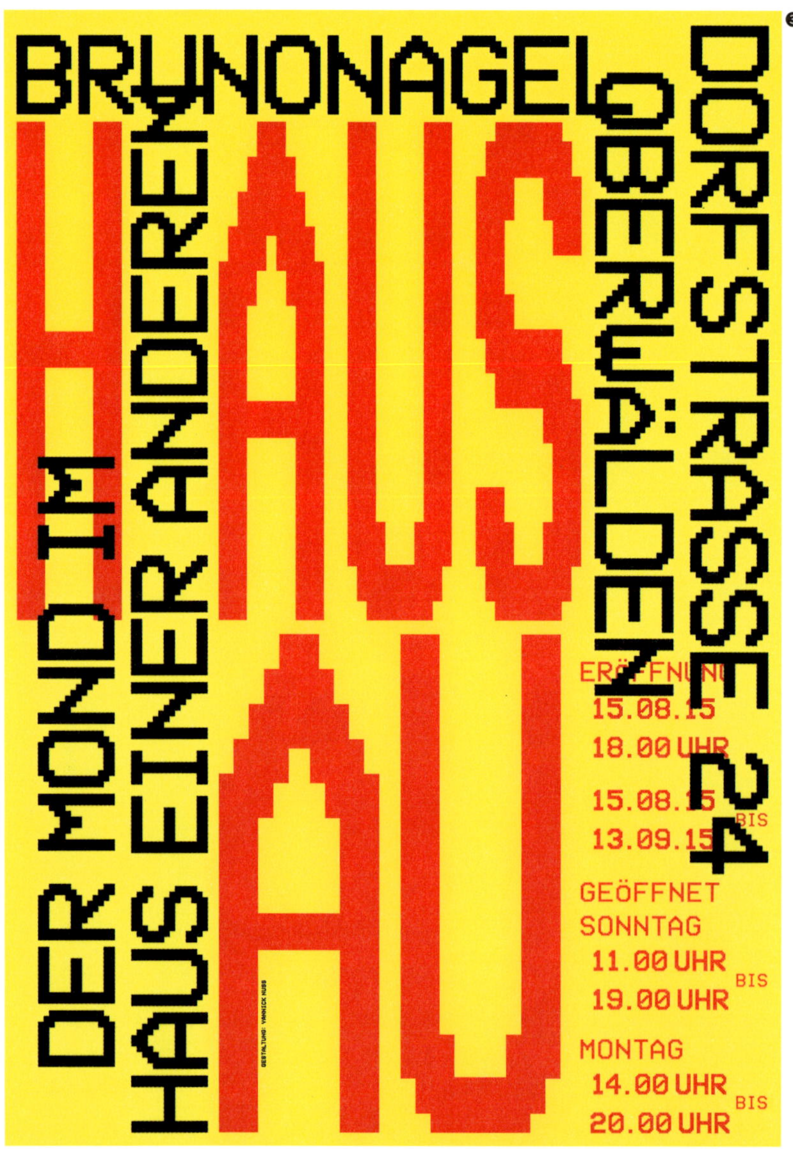

❸

❶–❸ Client: Bruno Nagel ❹ Client: Kunsthalle Basel

4

PROTO
matthew angelo
HARRISON
DARK SILHOUETTE: FORWARD GAZE, 2018 / HOLZSKULPTUR
AUS WESTAFRIKA, GEFÄRBTES KUNSTHARZ,
ELOXIERTES ALUMINIUM, ACRYL / 132,1 × 33 × 33 CM
MK-MIN-ARCHETYPE-002, 2017 / KERAMIK / 12,7 × 12,7 × 22,9 CM
SEER: PEERING THROUGH AURORA, 2020 / SCHEINWERFER, GEFÄRBTES KUNSTHARZ, ELOXIERTES ALUMINIUM, ACRYL / 112 × 20,6 × 21,6 CM
LOCAL 235
UAW
"GODDESS"
4.6.–26.9.
2021
KUNSTHALLE BASEL
Steinenberg 7, CH-4051 Basel
KUNSTHALLEBASEL.CH
Die Ausstellung wird grosszügig unterstützt von Martin Hatebur, Lafayette Anticipations – Fondation d'entreprise Galeries Lafayette, Paris und der Manizeh and Danny Rimer Collection.
DARK SILHOUETTE: ENDURING BOND, 2019 / HOLZSKULPTUR
PEOPLE IN TUNE WITH
TECHNOLOGY
AUS WESTAFRIKA, GEFÄRBTES KUNSTHARZ, ELOXIERTES ALUMINIUM, ACRYL / 160,7 × 29,6 × 23,2 CM

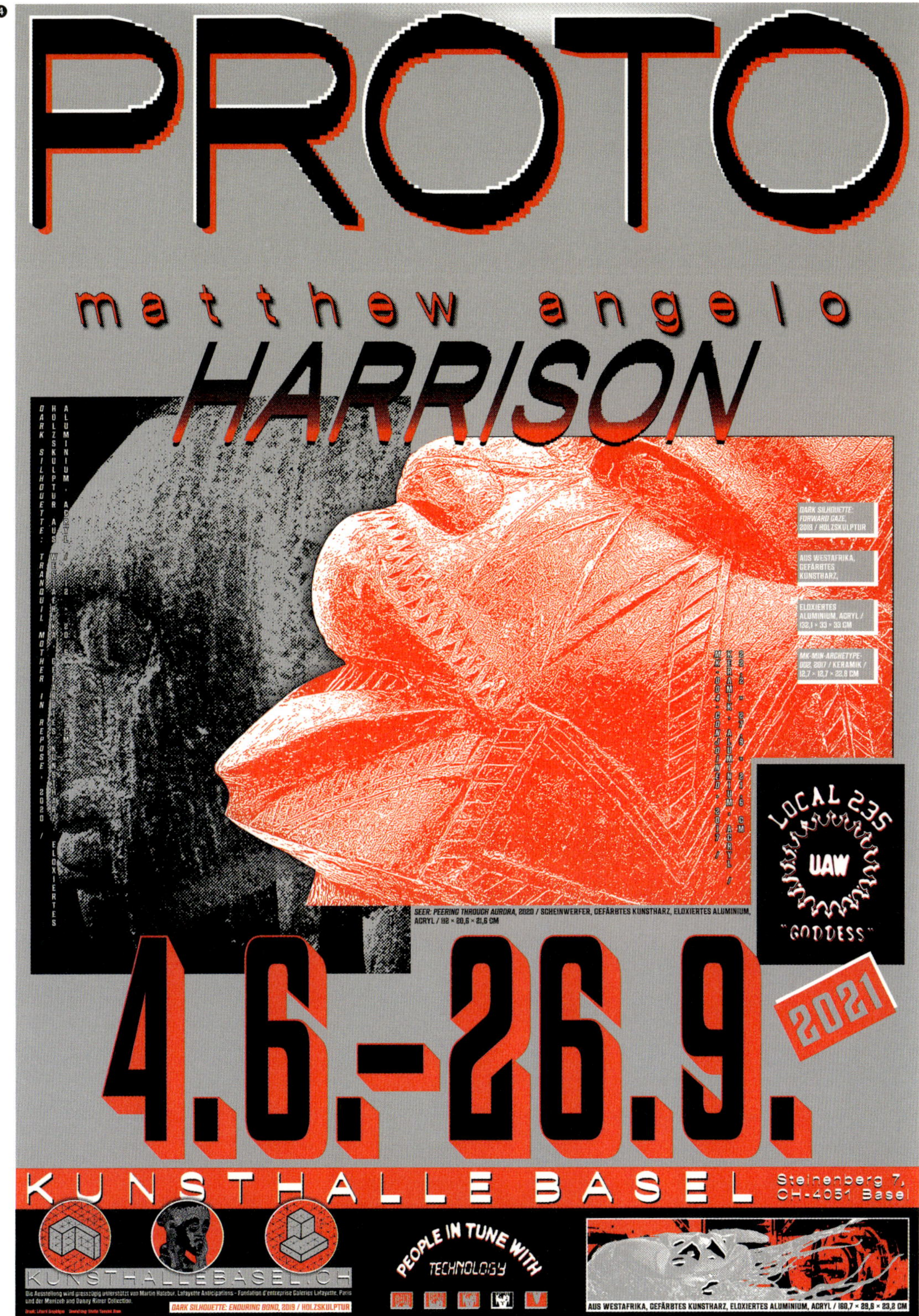

The Heart Director's Cut

● The two-sided poster, later trimmed into a publication, functions as a portable exhibition showcasing the personal items of the artist Bruno Nagel. Comprising objects, poems, and photographs, *The Heart Director's Cut* offers glimpses into the world of Bruno Nagel.

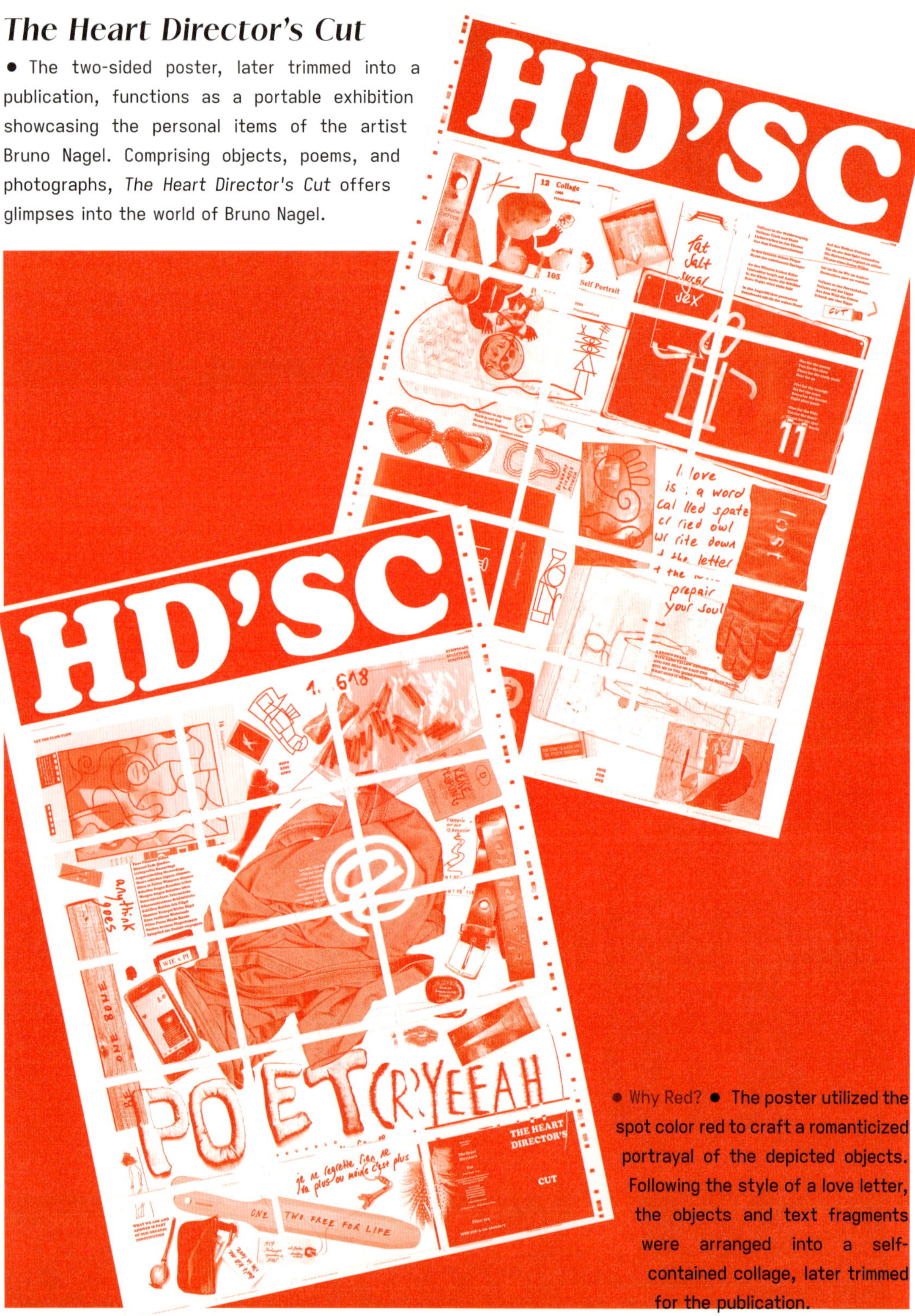

● Why Red? ● The poster utilized the spot color red to craft a romanticized portrayal of the depicted objects. Following the style of a love letter, the objects and text fragments were arranged into a self-contained collage, later trimmed for the publication.

● Design Studio: Studio Yannick Nuss ● Designer: Yannick Nuss ● Client: Bruno Nagel

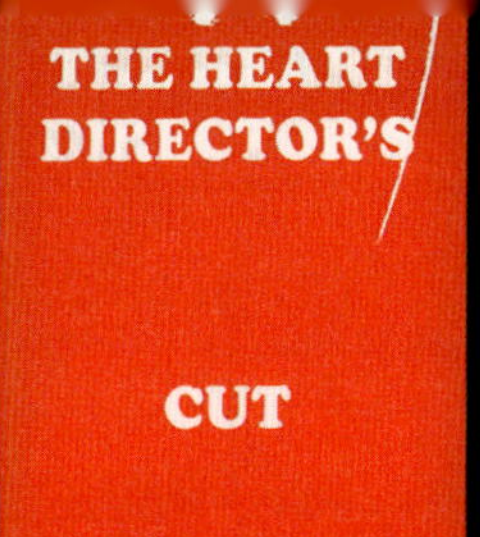

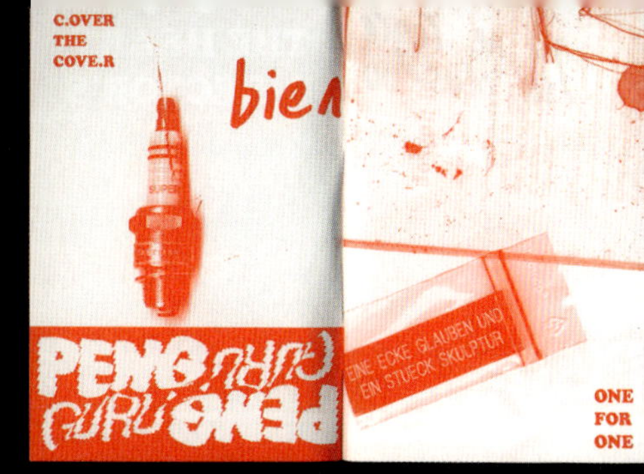

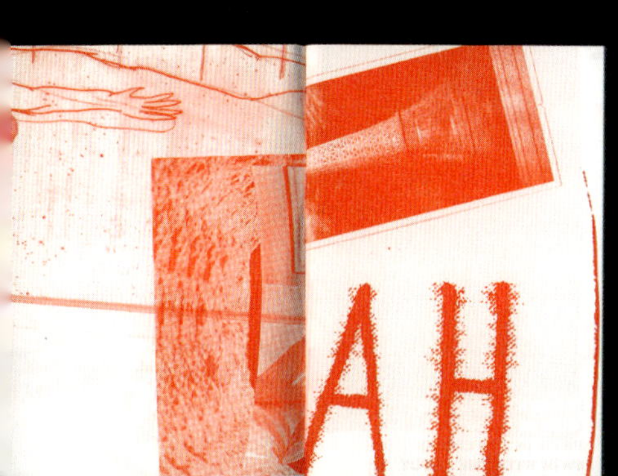

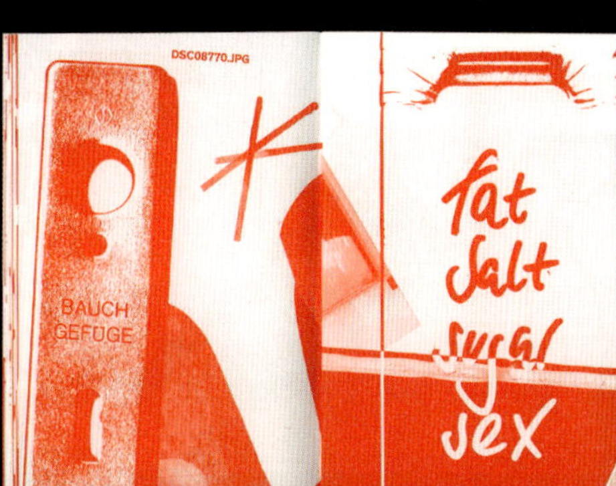

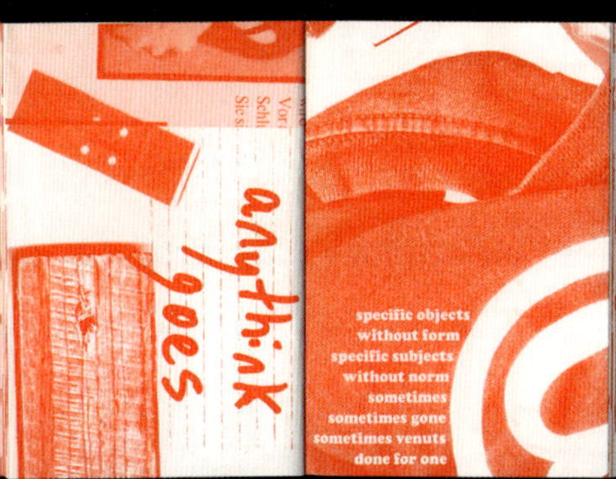

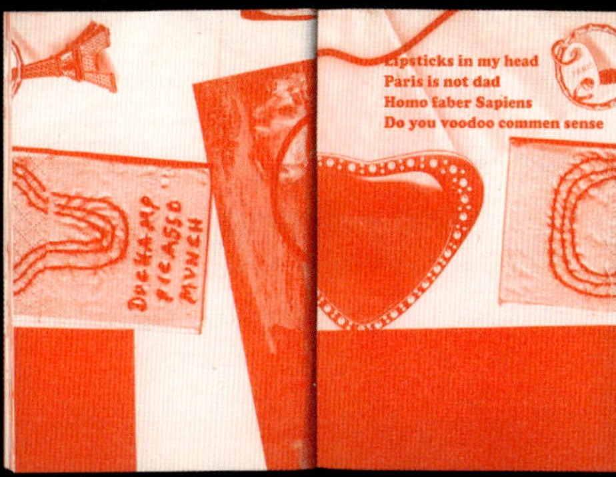

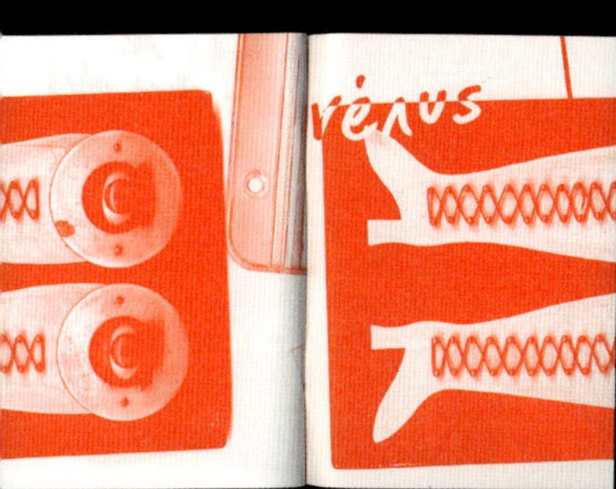

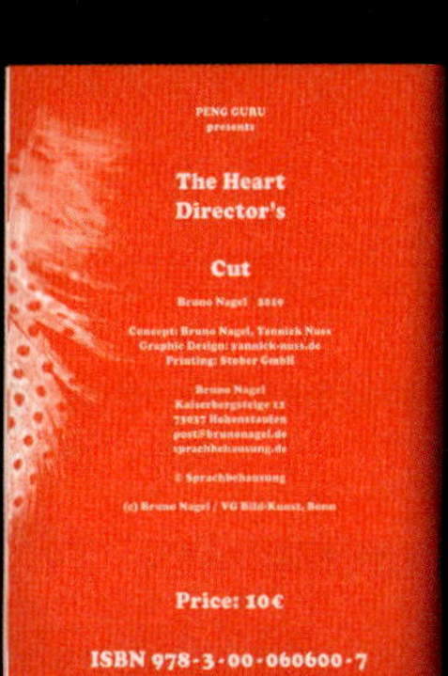

THE HEART DIRECTOR'S
CUT

C.OVER
THE
COVE.R
PENG GURU
EINE ECKE GLAUBEN UND EIN STUECK SKULPTUR
ONE
FOR
ONE

AH

DSC08770.JPG
BAUCH
GEFÜGE
fat
Salt
sugar
sex

anythink
goes
specific objects
without form
specific subjects
without norm
sometimes
sometimes gone
sometimes venuts
done for one

DUCHAMP
PICASSO
MUNCH
Lipsticks in my head
Paris is not dad
Homo faber Sapiens
Do you voodoo commen sense

venus

PENG GURU
presents
The Heart
Director's
Cut
Bruno Nagel 2019
Concept: Bruno Nagel, Yannick Nuss
Graphic Design: yannick-nuss.de
Printing: Stober GmbH
Bruno Nagel
Kaiserbergsteige 12
73037 Hohenstaufen
post@brunonagel.de
sprachbehausung.de
© Sprachbehausung
(c) Bruno Nagel / VG Bild-Kunst, Bonn
Price: 10€
ISBN 978-3-00-060600-7

HKS 13 N (RED)

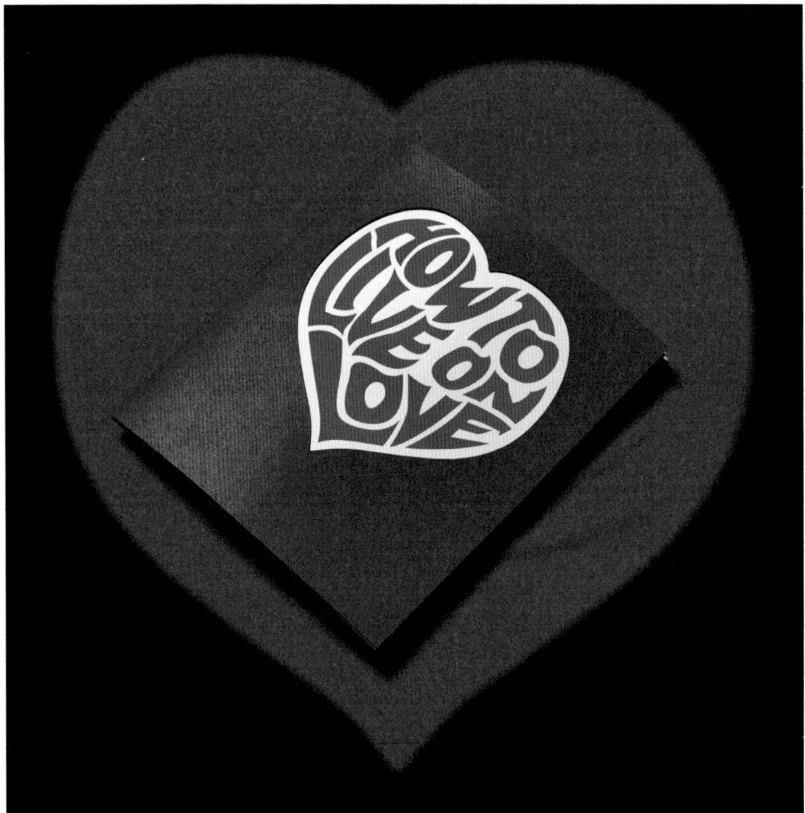

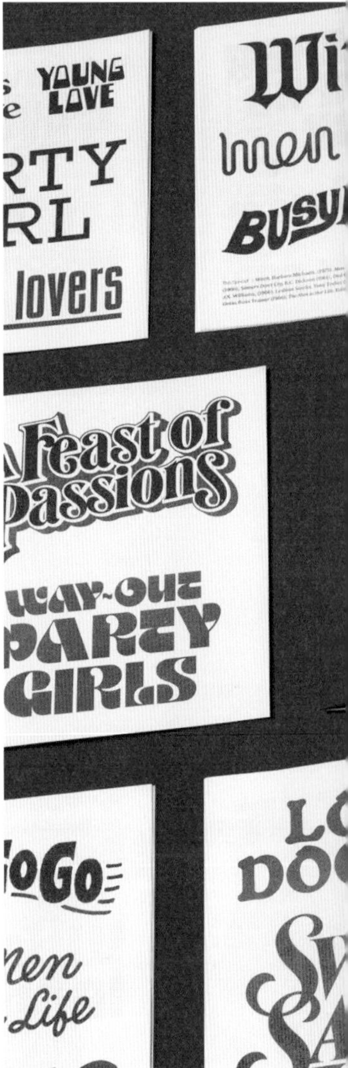

How to Live on Love ● It delves into the distinctive and uncharted typography within the romance and erotic paperback genre. This risoprinted compendium includes an essay detailing the history and design of romance novels, along with a diverse array of lettering samples extracted from erotic pulp covers spanning 1945–1985.

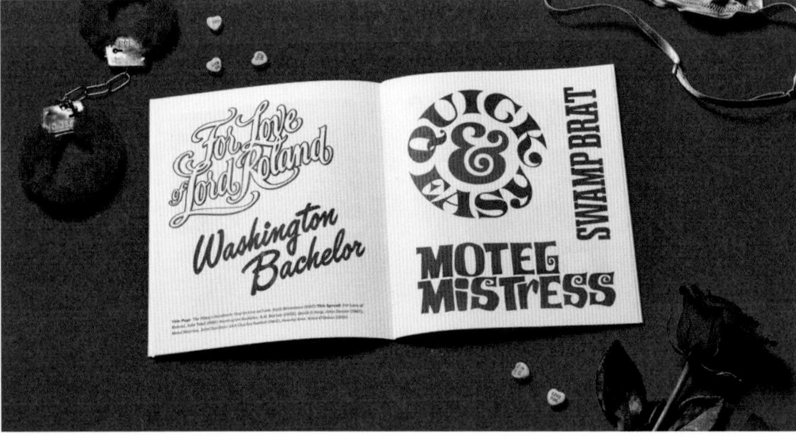

● Designer: Elizabeth Goodspeed ● Photographer: Dylan James Nelson

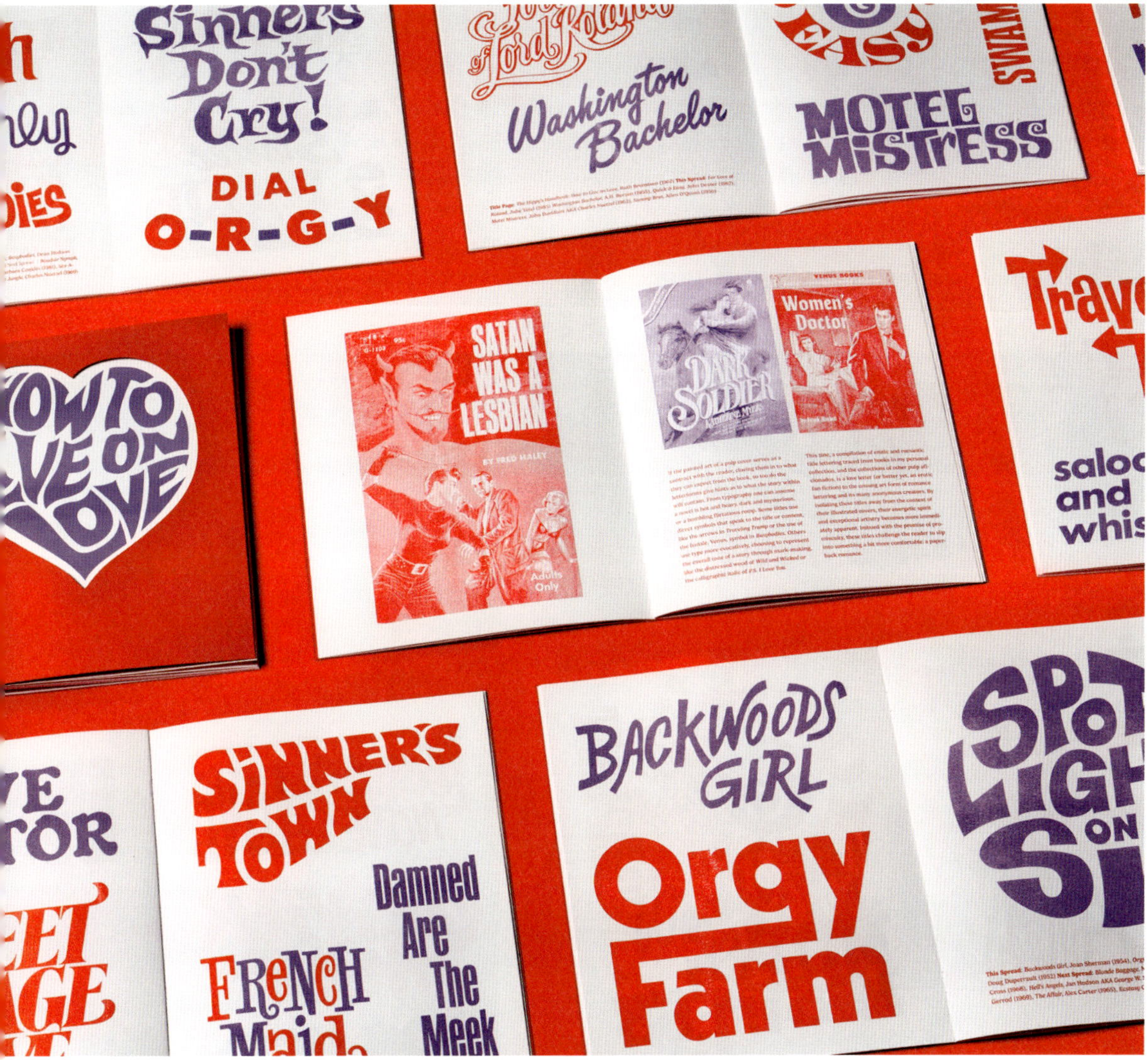

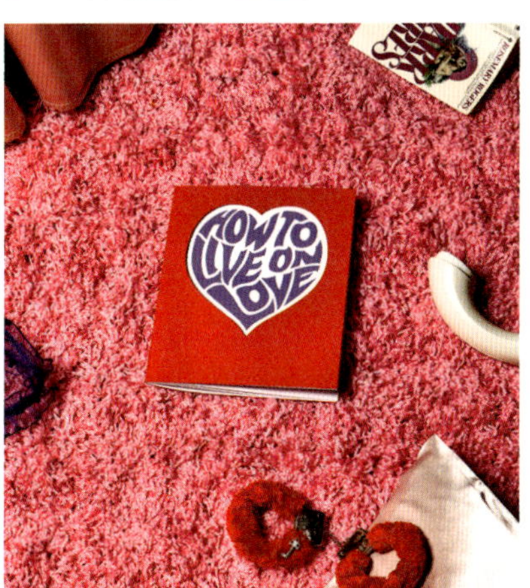

● Why Red? ● In the designer's perspective, red is considered the most sensual color, making it the most fitting choice for a book centered around romance novels and erotica. Given the color limitations of the risograph, purple was selected as a complementary hue to the unexpected but still slightly feminine and bold red, creating a visual effect full of romantic aura.

C3 M99 Y97 K1 | C67 M80 Y0 K0

Poster Design for Hong Kong Visual Arts Center—Art Specialist Course

● Tailored for art enthusiasts, the Art Specialist Course's master class offers a comprehensive learning experience. The symmetric responsive system, driven by a variety of Chinese art courses, showcases every aspect of the program. ● The poster design transforms the mountain image, symbolizing the techniques taught in the courses, with a Pantone silver layer adding texture and creating contrast with the red block representing the mountain. This graphical approach nods to the newly introduced graphical art course.

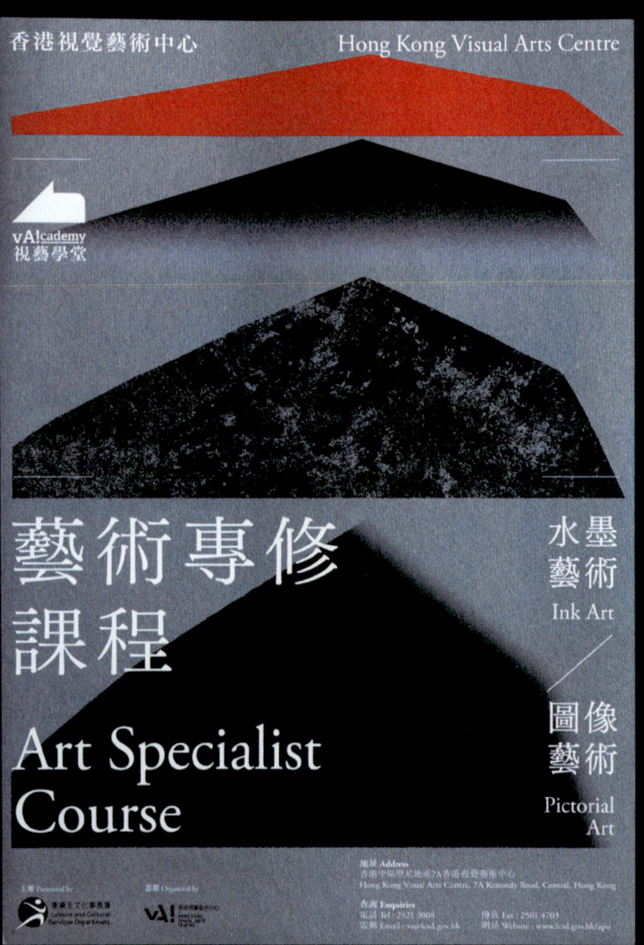

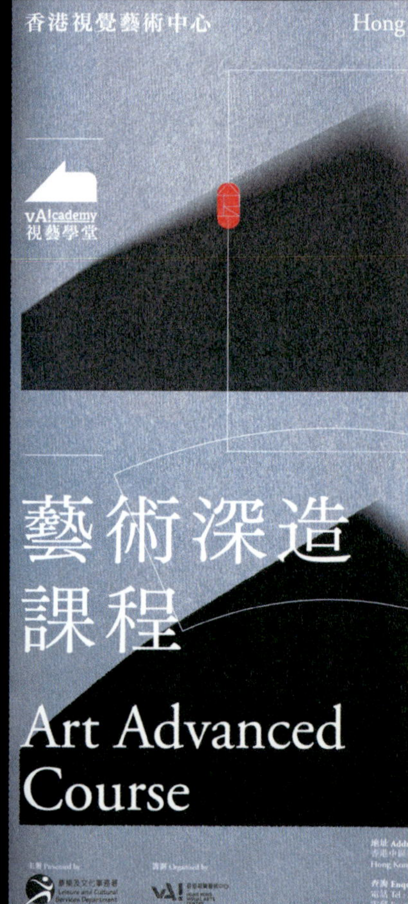

● Design Studio: for&st ● Designer: Ming Cheung ● Client: Hong Kong Visual Arts Center

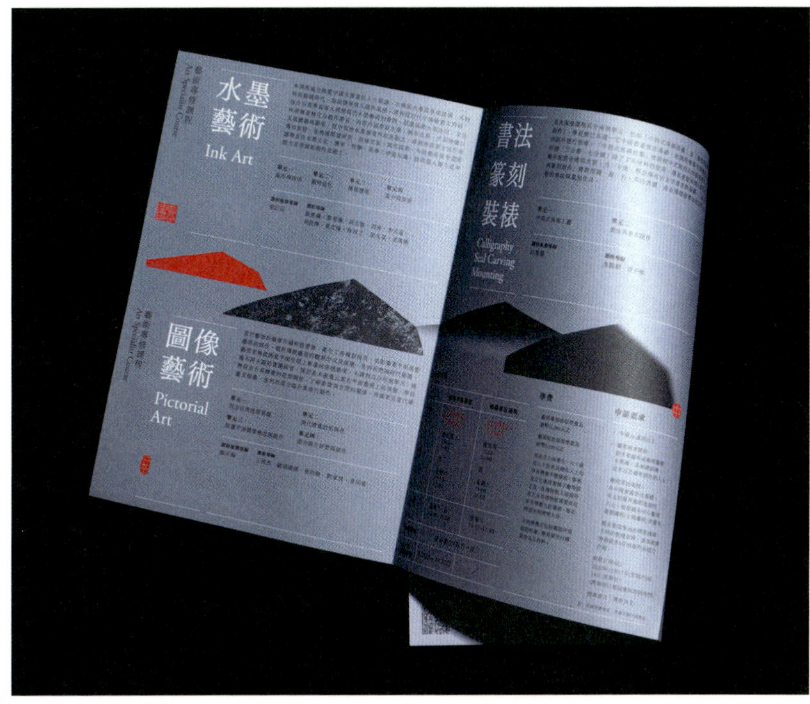

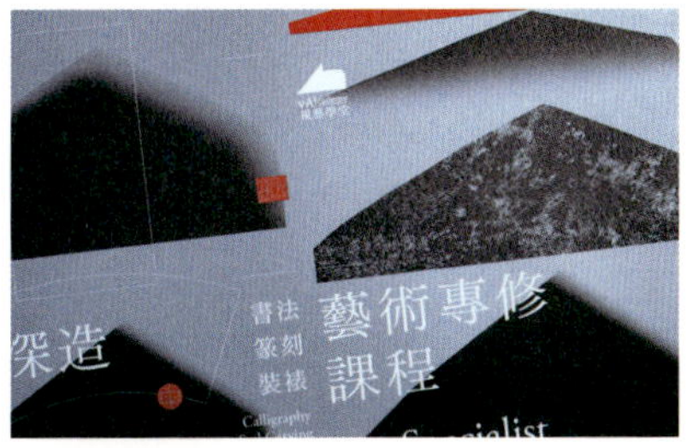

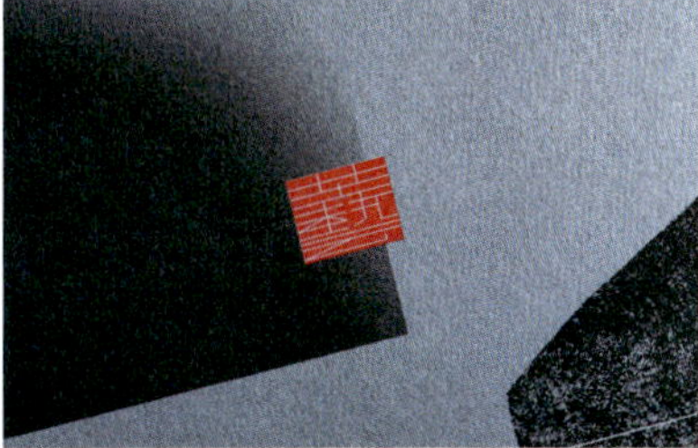

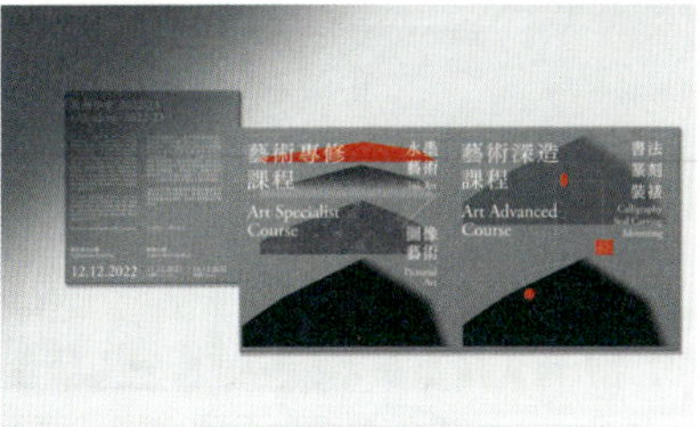

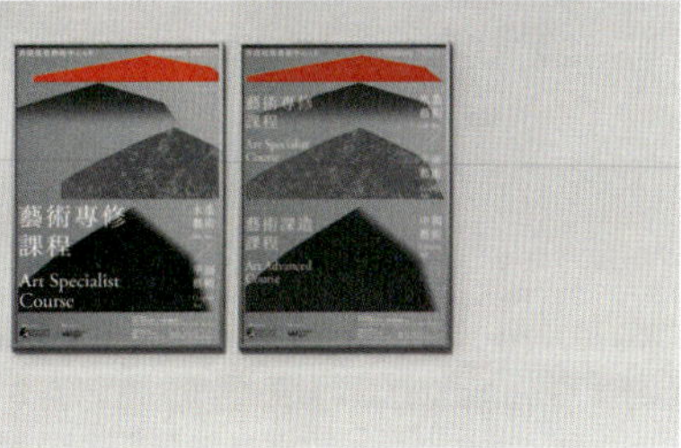

● Why Red? ● The use of red color is intended to resonate with the concept of "progression." The top mountain is depicted in red, symbolizing mastery of all the skills taught in the masterclass. Additionally, as the course focuses on Chinese art, the red color serves as a tribute to the essential element commonly seen in traditional Chinese art.

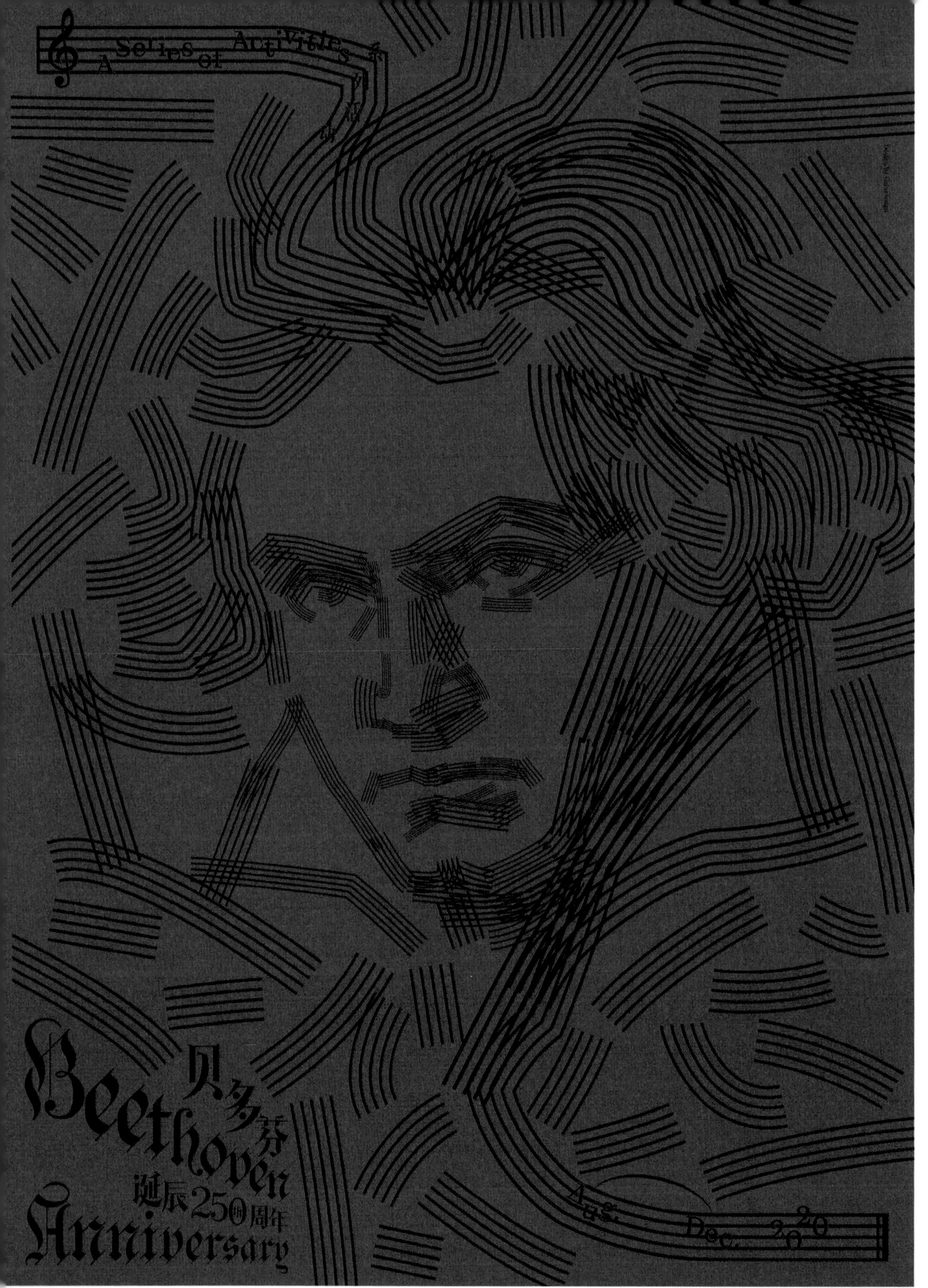

● Designer: Cen Liu ● Client: German Consulate General in Shenyang

Beethoven's 250th Birthday

● A promotional poster designed for the 250th anniversary celebration of Beethoven's birth in Liaoning. Utilizing shredded staff elements, it creatively rearranges and weaves another movement.

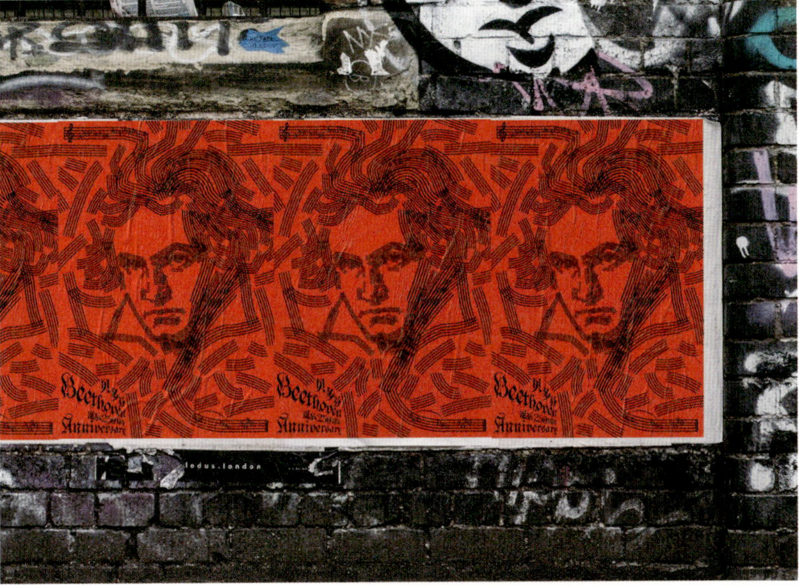

● Why Red? ● The chosen foundational color is a vibrant red, intending on one hand to resonate sensorially with Beethoven's dynamic and emotive musical compositions. On the other hand, it also aims to unveil the rich and fulfilling life of Beethoven.

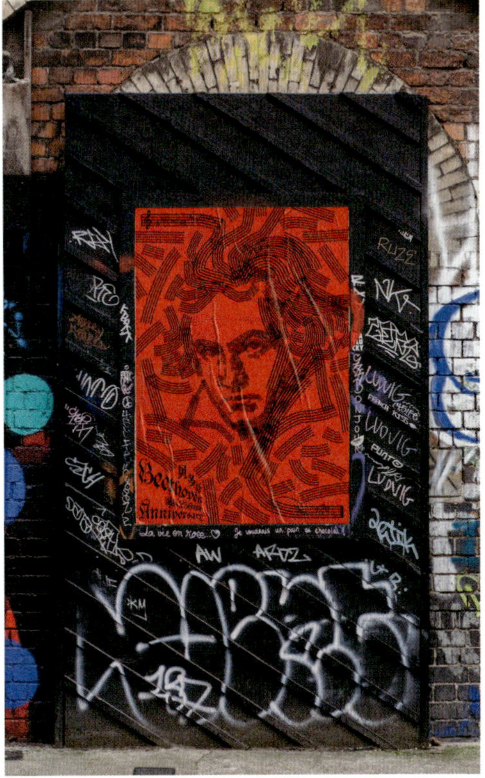

Swish Swoosh

• *Swish Swoosh* archives the code-switching practices of multilingual Asians in the U.S. through interviews. It explores how code-switching extends beyond language to influence personality traits, values, and responsibilities with each spoken language. Interviewees share diverse experiences, from taking on adult roles in immigrant families to adopting Filipino gay lingo, thus fostering closer family bonds.

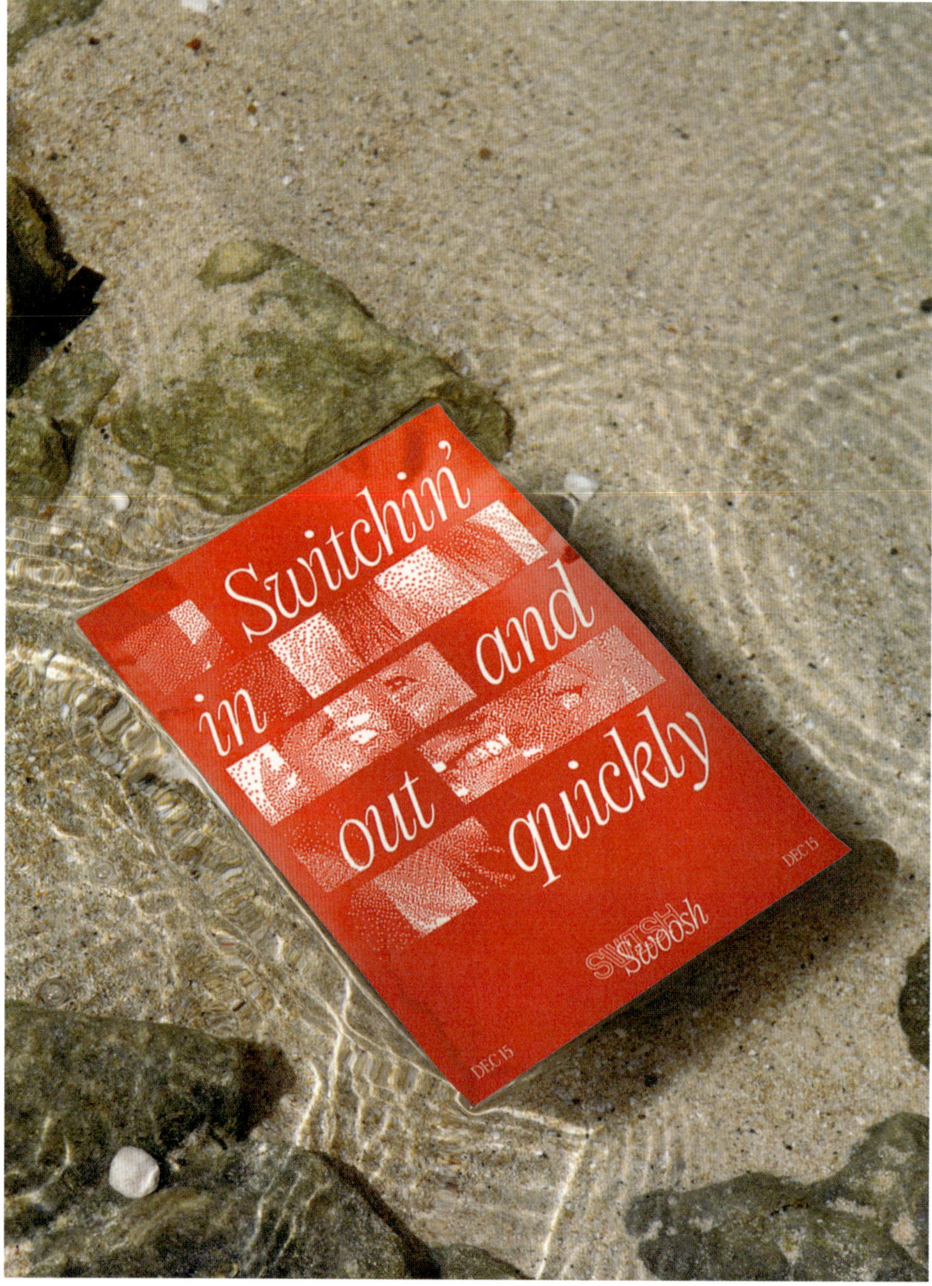

• Designer: Sun Ho Lee

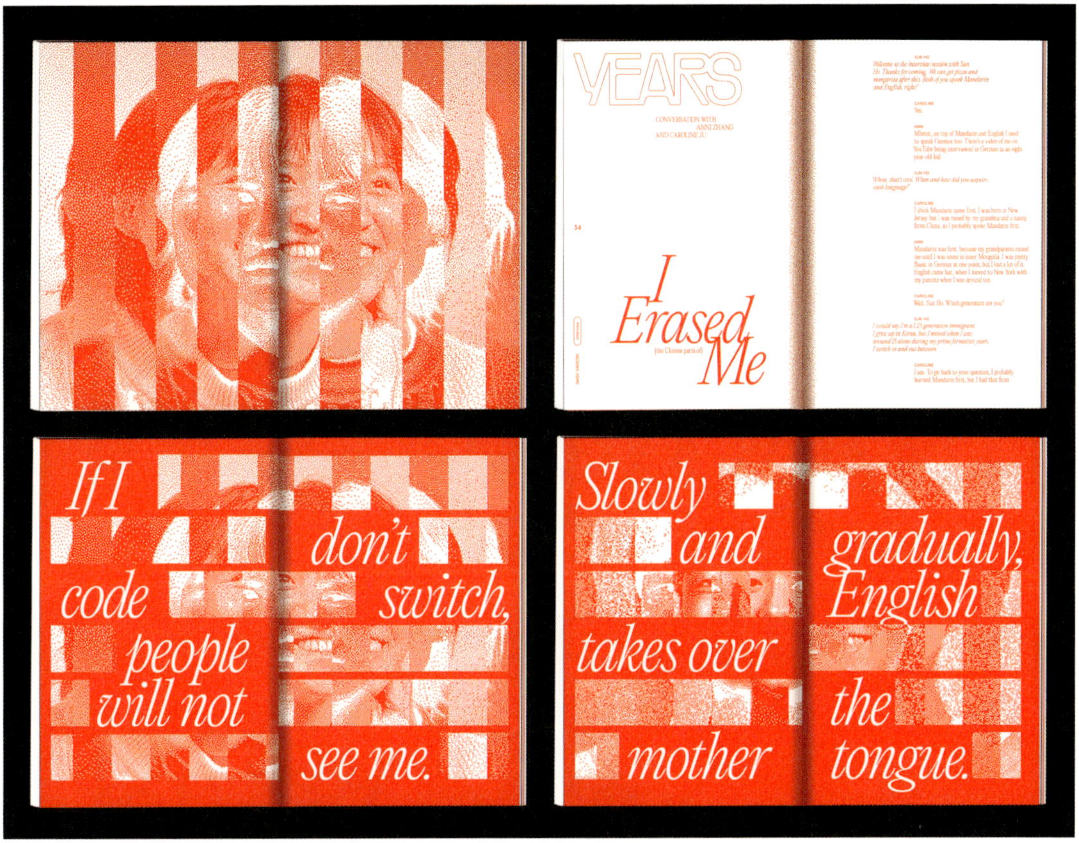

YEARS

CONVERSATION WITH ANNE ZHANG AND CAROLINE JU

I Erased (the Chinese parts of) Me

If I don't code switch, people will not see me.

Slowly and gradually, English takes over the mother tongue.

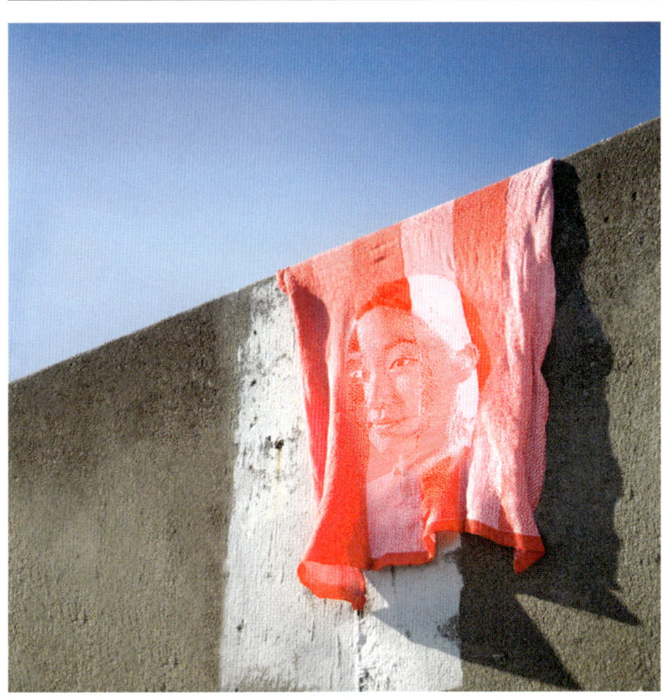

● Why Red? ● Code-switching is a prevalent experience among immigrants in the United States, yet it is often not adequately preserved or documented. The use of a vibrant red shade is to captivate the audience's attention and emphasize the significance of these experiences, prompting meaningful discussions.

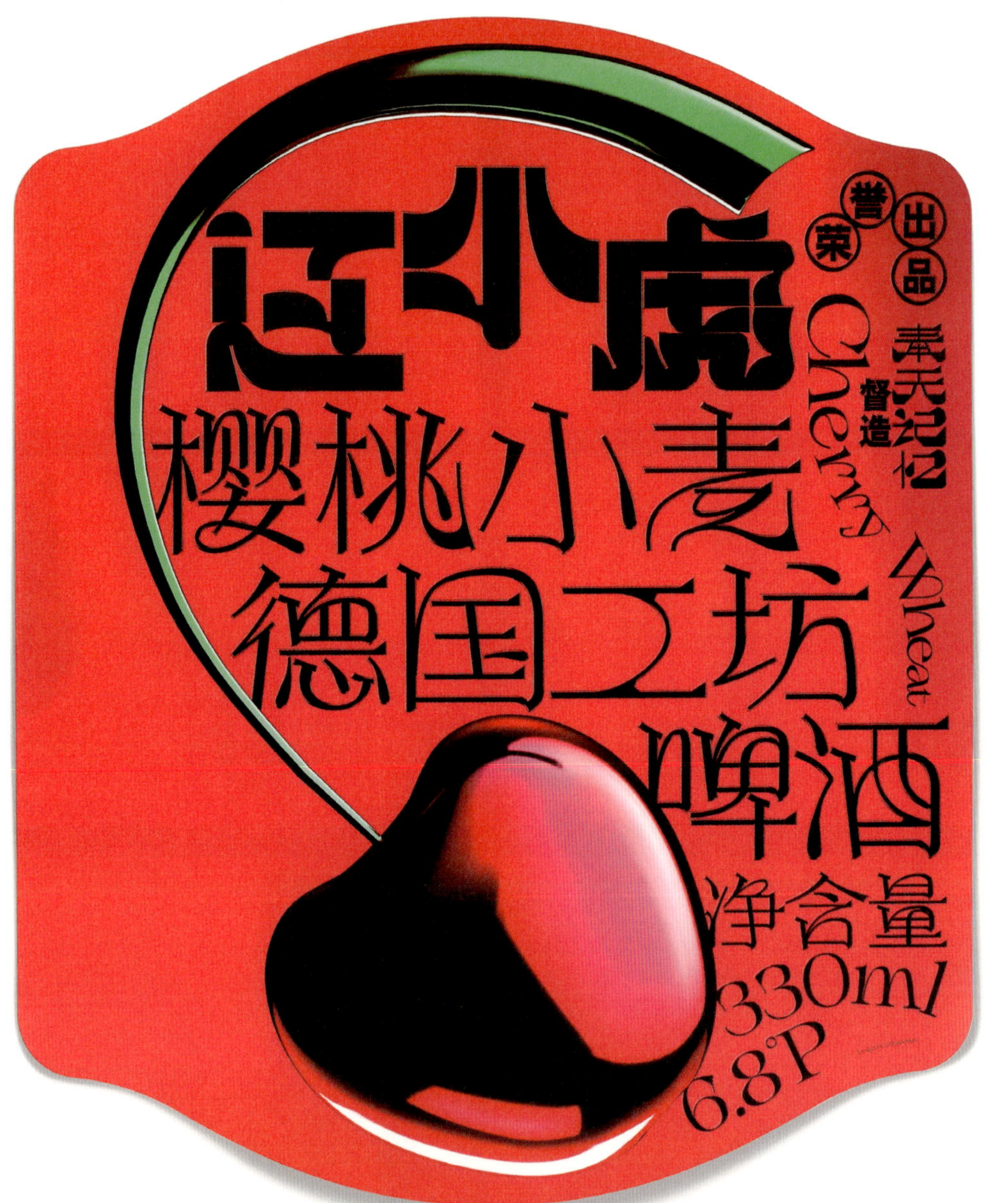

"Liao Xiaohu" Cherry Wheat Beer Packaging Design • "Liao Xiaohu" is a beer brand under the "Memory of Fengtian" craft brewery, specifically designed for nightclubs and bars. The new product launched by the brand, "Cherry Wheat," a fruity beer tailored for women. The packaging design, themed as "Mysterious Cherry," incorporates 3D-rendered metallic cherries, enigmatic and profound lighting effects, and a font design derived from modified Song typefaces to convey the theme. The design aims to express the robust genetic traits unique to the Northeast region while showcasing the mysterious and sensual aspects of women.

• Designer: Cen Liu • Client: Shenyang Jinggongfang Biotechnology Co., LTD

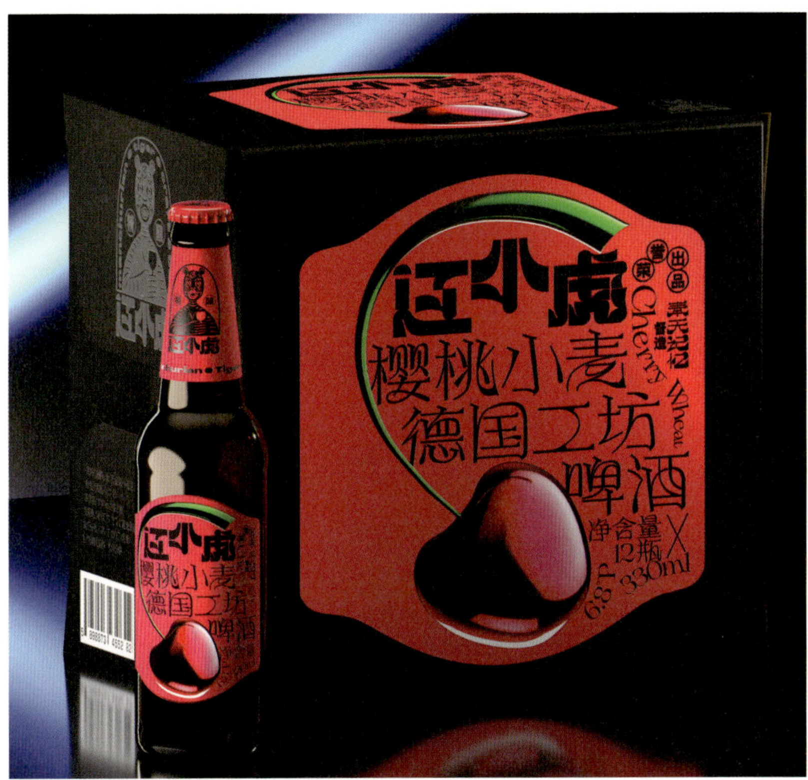

● Why Red? ● The overall design concept aims to create a chemical reaction by skillfully combining the elements of peach red and metallic textures. Similar to the slightly intoxicated women in the dim lights of a nightclub, it exudes a mysterious and sensual atmosphere, unveiling a unique personal charisma.

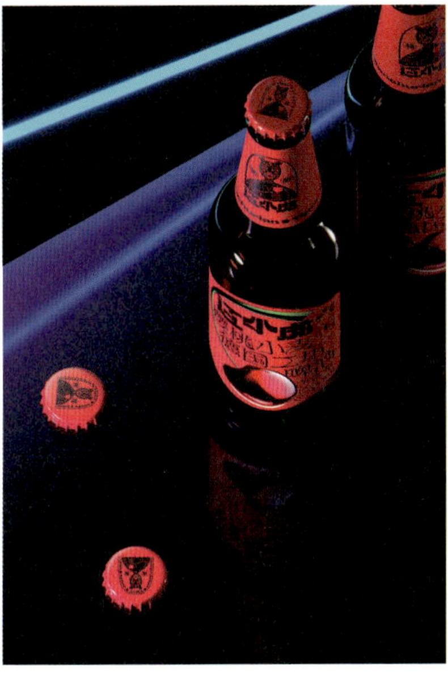

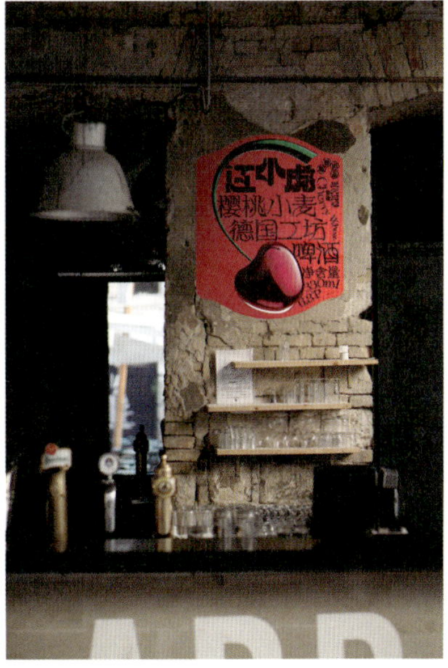

PANTONE 192C PANTONE 225C PANTONE 355C

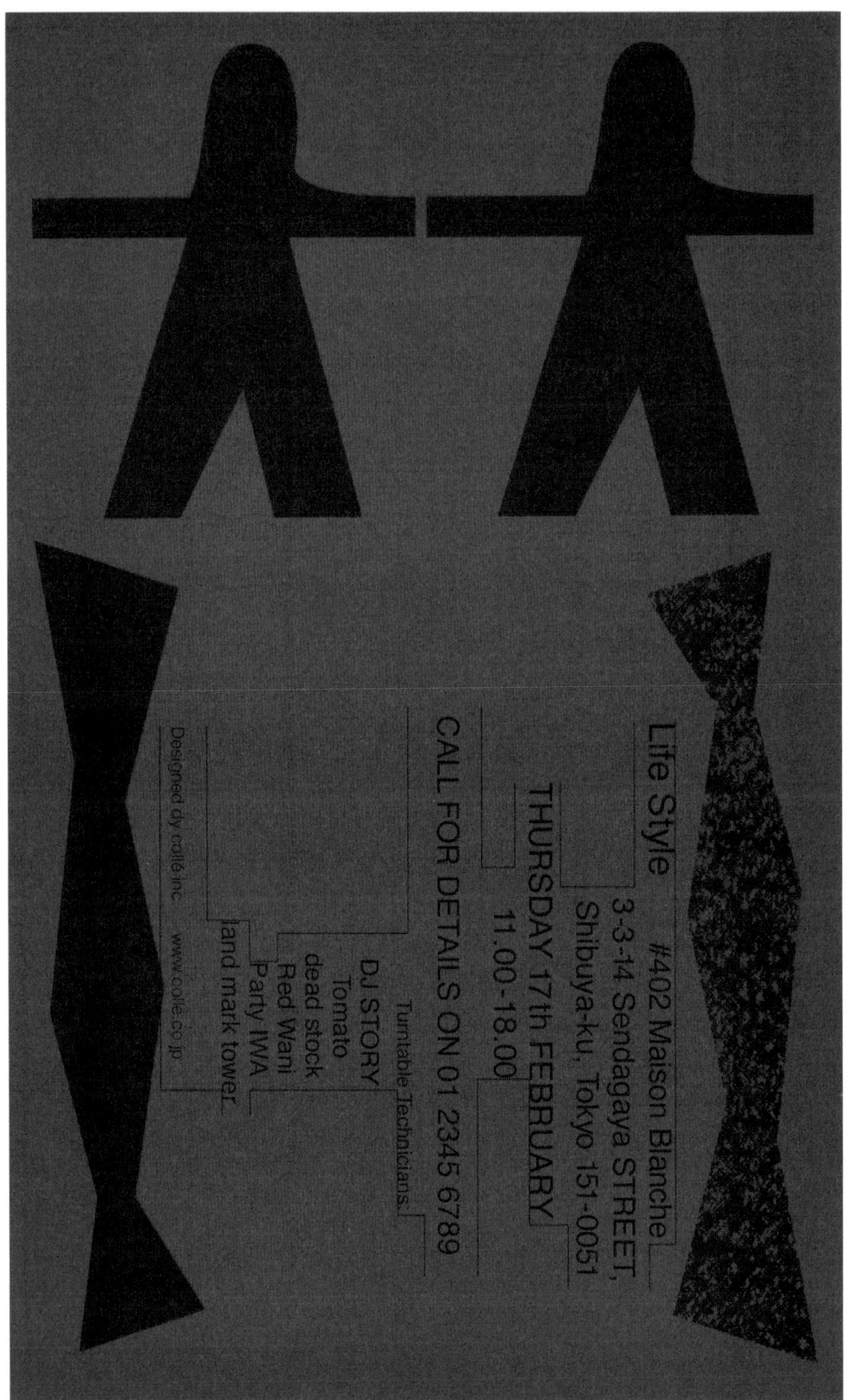

● Design Studio: collé inc. ● Designer: Agata Yamaguchi

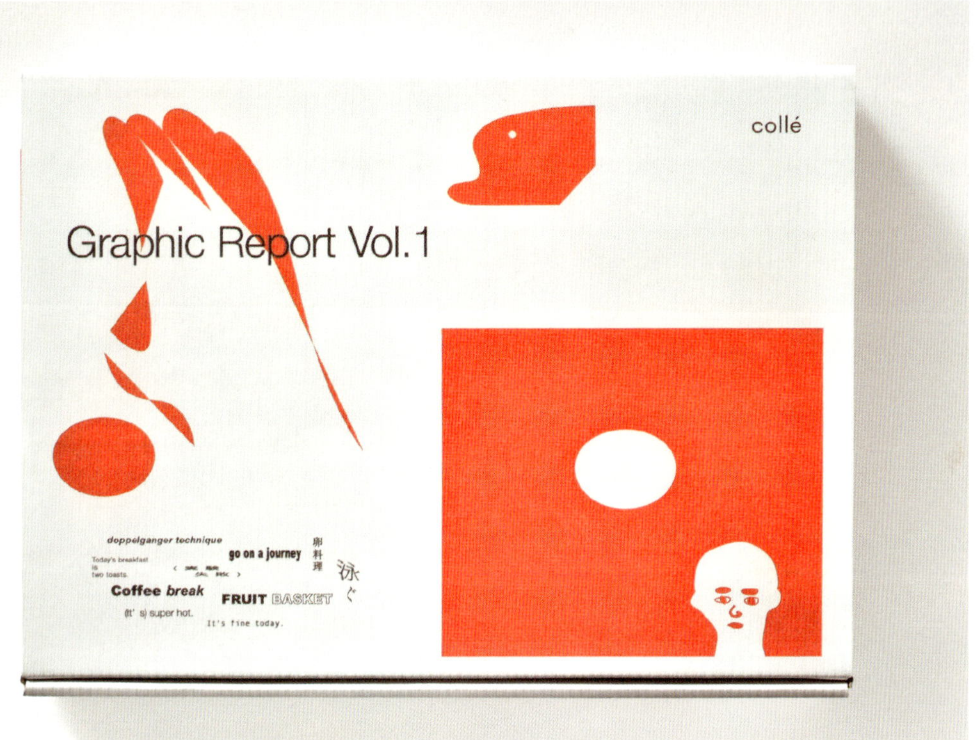

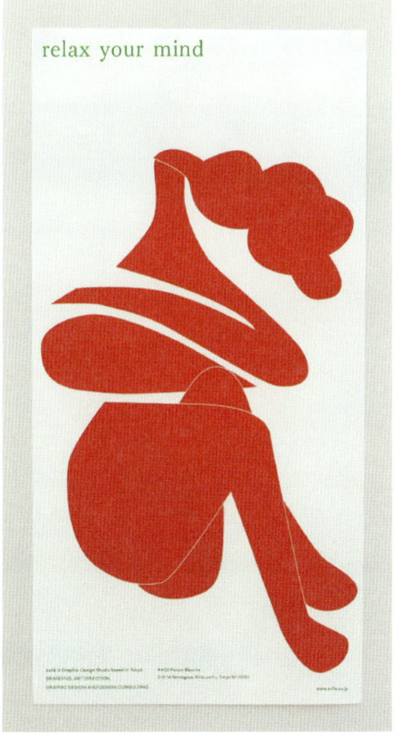

Relax Your Mind ● The designer created a flyer as part of the graphic report production. Crafted with the intention of recommending mental and physical preparation, it consists of two pieces. The central figure practicing yoga symbolizes the balance between stillness and movement. The red flyer specifically emphasizes the concept of stillness. The design utilizes cut and glued colored paper instead of handwritten to make it more clear and dynamic.

● Why Red? ● The designer aimed to create a lasting impression by using colors that evoke contradiction. Blue signifies tranquility, while red represents intensity. This intentional play with emotions, experienced by many, involved using red for static graphics usually associated with blue. The goal was to introduce a subtle sense of incongruity for a deeper viewer experience.

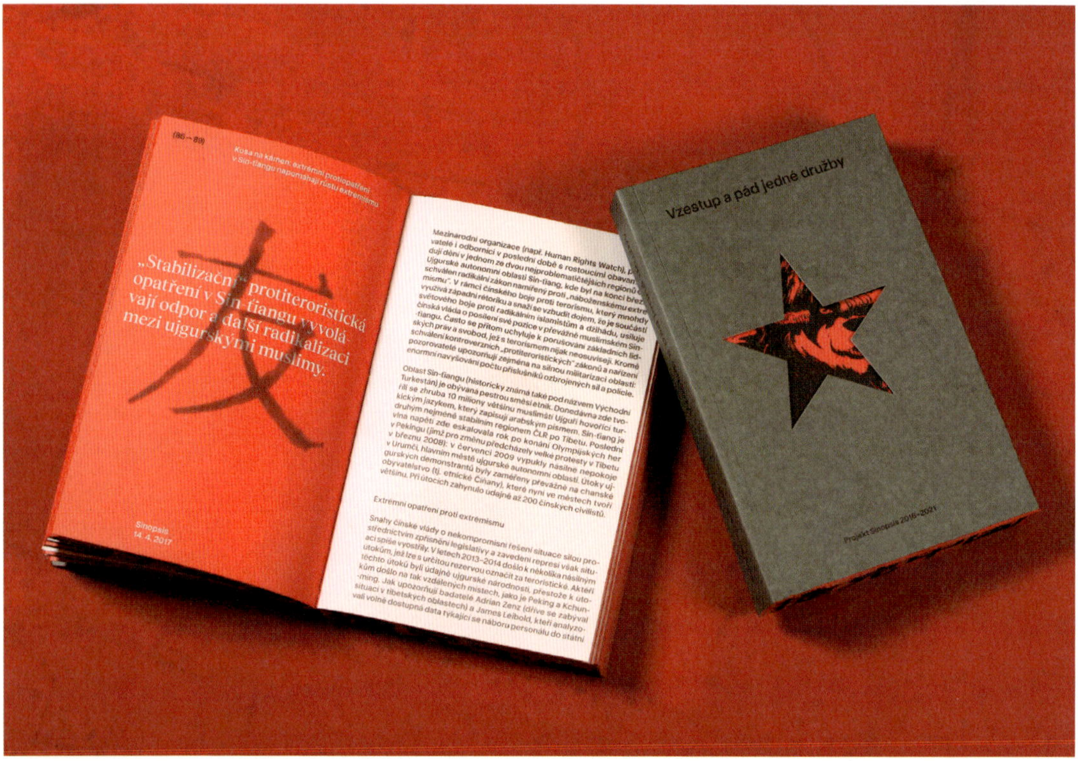

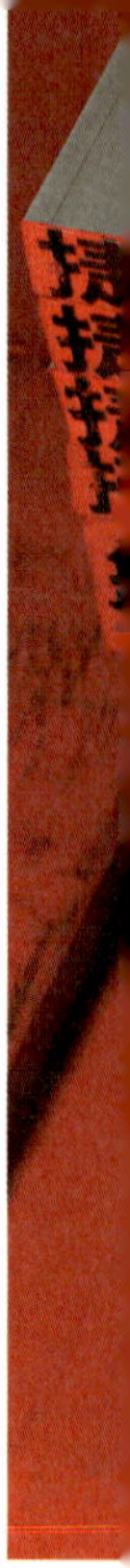

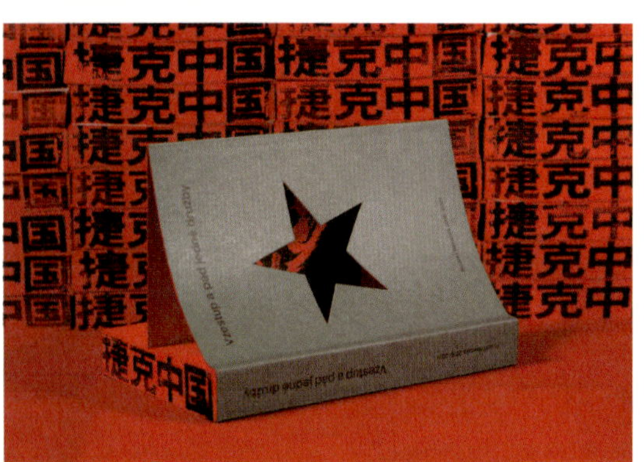

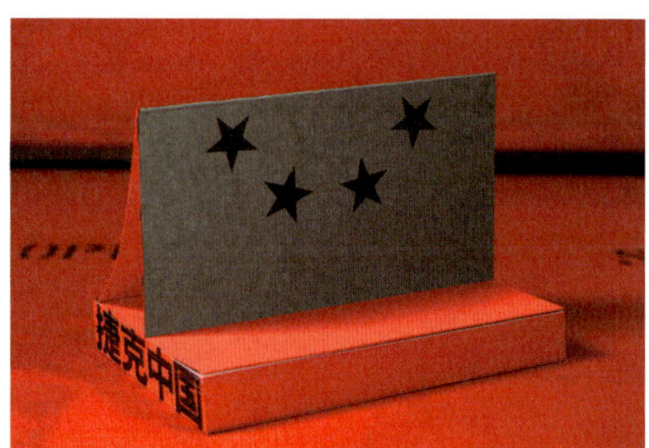

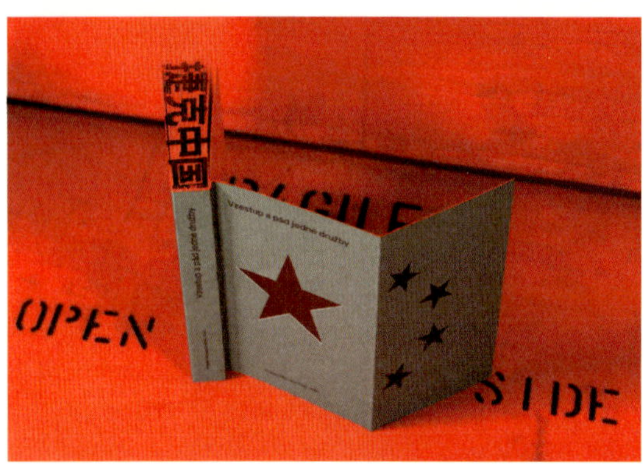

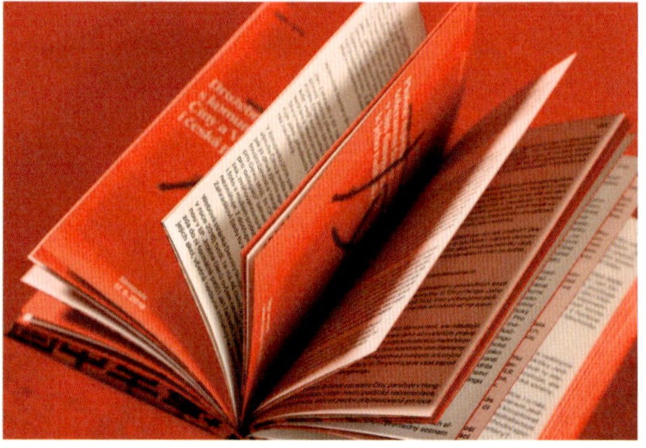

● Design Studio: Lilkudley ● Designer: Petr Kudlacek, Jan Arndt ● Client: Sinopsis

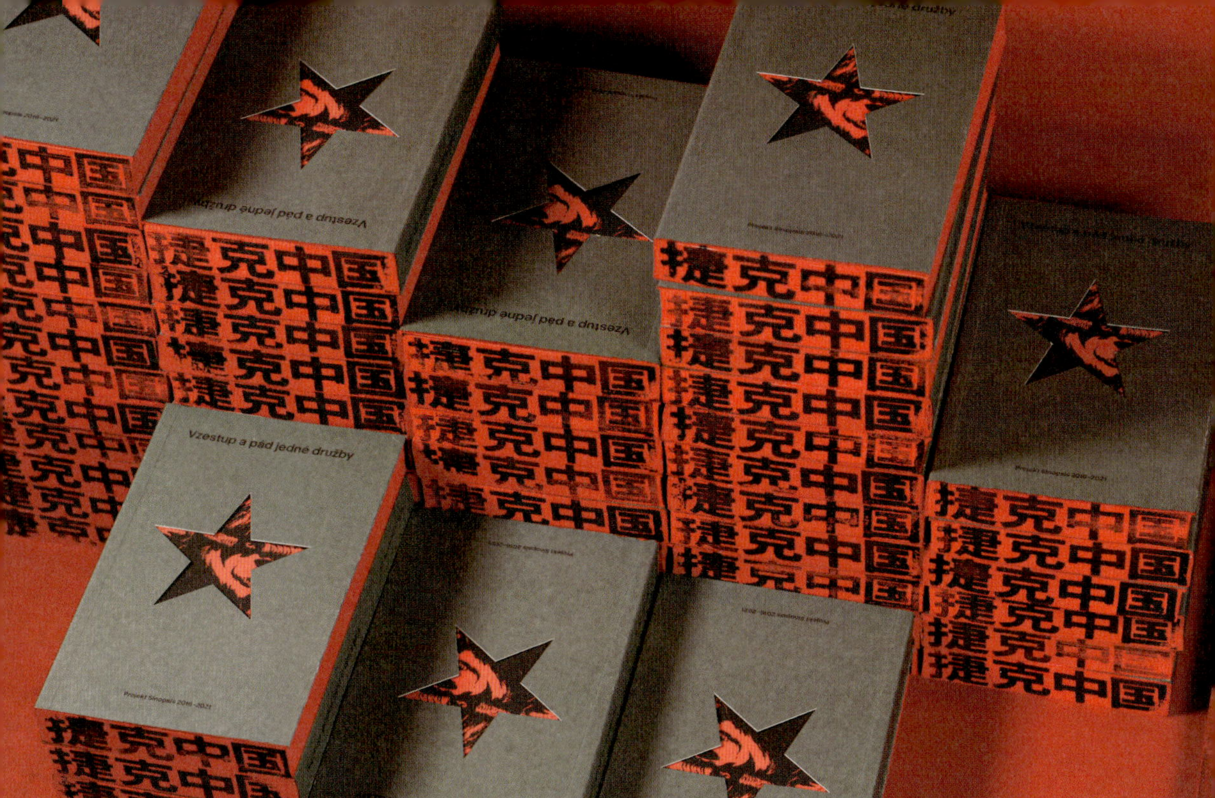

SINOPSIS—China in Context And Perspective

● The task involved compiling internet articles from 2016 to 2021 on the Sinopsis association's platform, exploring the hidden aspects of Czech-China relations. The pocket-sized compilation was designed with engaging visuals. ● Each chapter features the Chinese character for "friendship," gradually unfolding through a timelapse burning effect. By the end, only symbolic ashes remain. Chapter introductions on the left side allow readers to observe this process like flipping through a flip-book. ● The book's crucial color scheme, vivid red against a grayish-green background, is maintained throughout the creative process.

● Why Red? ● The fundamental typographic colors for this project are red and black on white paper. These colors are distinct, uncompromising, and provide clarity. The chosen color scheme is influenced by the given theme.

C0 M95 Y98 K0

"LANGOSBAR"—Together with All Casp

● Langoš stands out as one of Slovakia's cherished streetfood classics. Established by gastronomy legends Lukáš Hesko and Robo Nagy, the LANGOSBAR concept reimagines the traditional dish with unusual options like sourdough lángos topped with pecorino, pastrami, or shrimps. Paired with excellent drinks and regional natural wines, the food shop, nestled in the historic market building, offers a cozy spot for locals and an enticing destination for tourists.

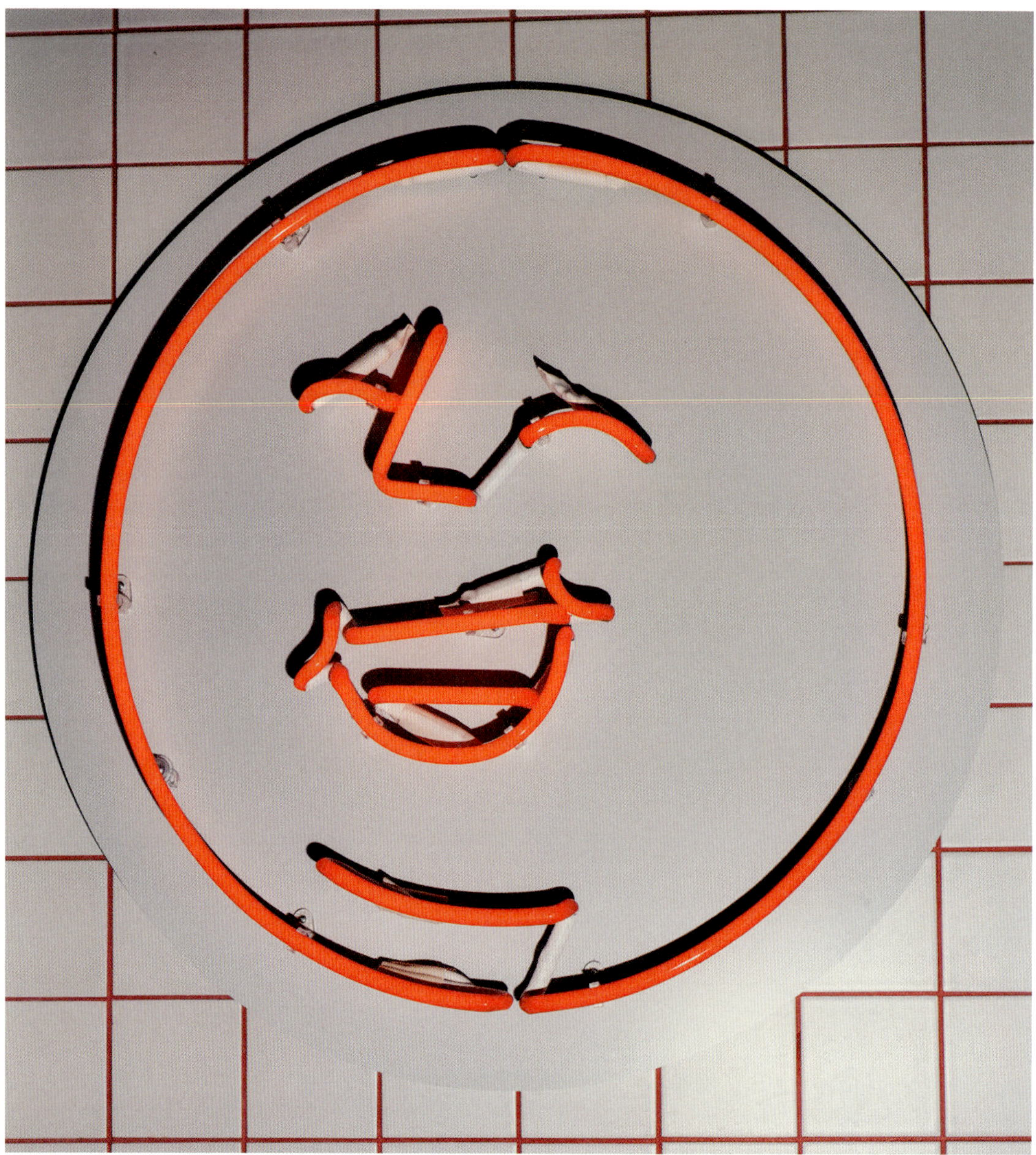

● Design Studio: NICE GUY ● Designer: Matej Špánik, Tomáš Rybár ● Client: LANGOSBAR ● Photography: Miki Čurík

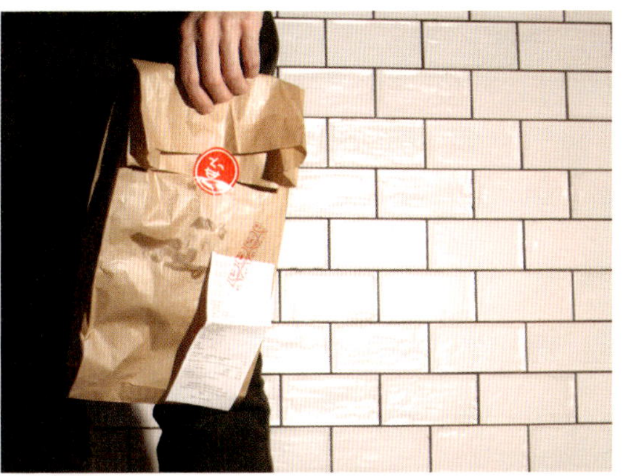

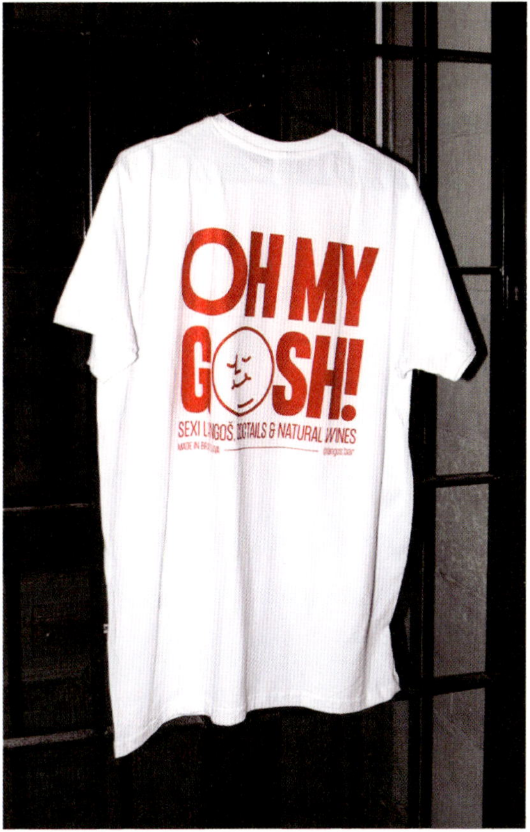

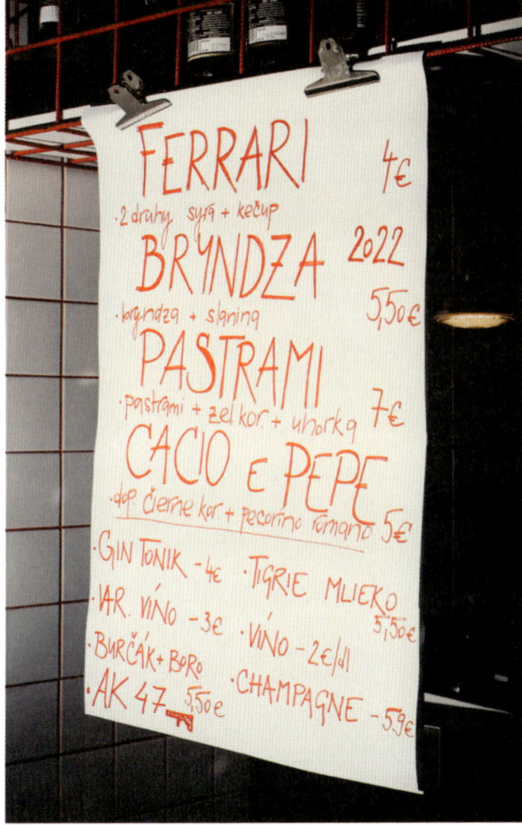

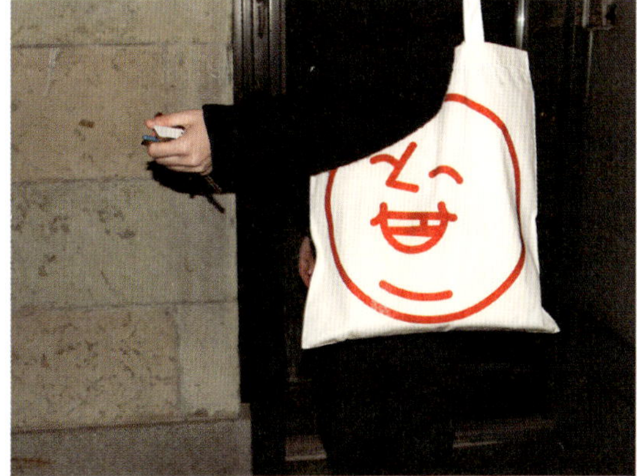

● Why Red? ● The designers' approach aimed at creating a visually bold identity for the modern Lángos concept while maintaining its authenticity. Collaborating with the artists Matej Špánik and Tomáš Rybár, they designed a cheerful, modular face representing the pleasure of enjoying lango. The simple color palette, dominated by red, accentuates the logo's strength. This modularity extends to the typography, using a versatile typeface with different glyph variations for flexibility in text design.

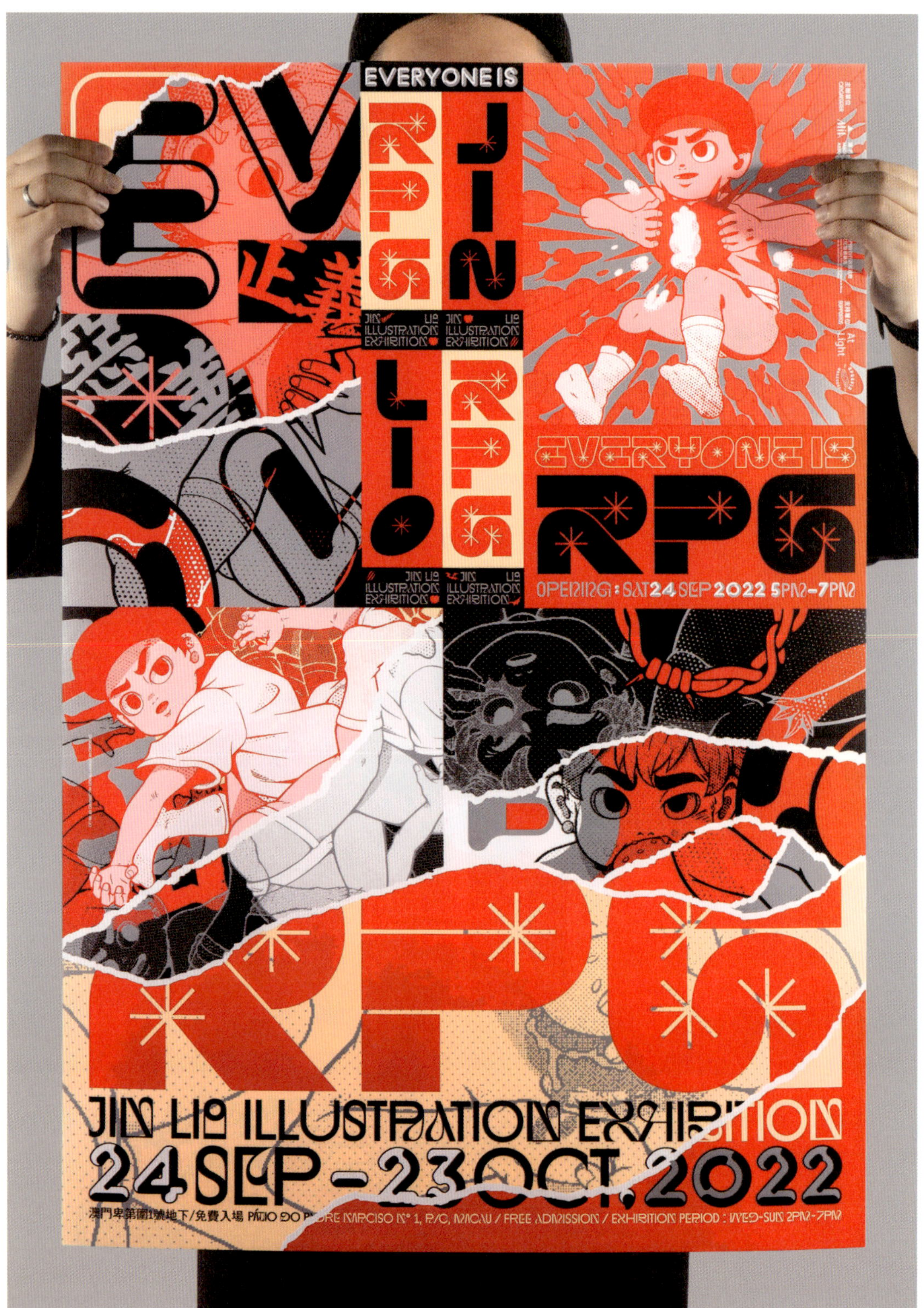

● Design Studio: Indego Design ● Designer: Lam Ieong Kun, Dan Ferreira, Jio Lio

EVERYONE IS RPG ILLUSTRATION EXHIBITION

● The exhibition *EVERYONE IS RPG* by Jin Lio delves into the duality of human nature by using comic book style illustrations. The main design employs paper tearing effects, pixelated visual elements, contrasting colors, and unique printing to emphasize extreme personality traits. Featuring handwritten Chinese calligraphy on emotions and pleasures, the concept explores the mix of positive and negative traits in each person's identity. *EVERYONE IS RPG* invites reflection on the inherent instability and unpredictability of human by creating a tough and tensil visual effect.

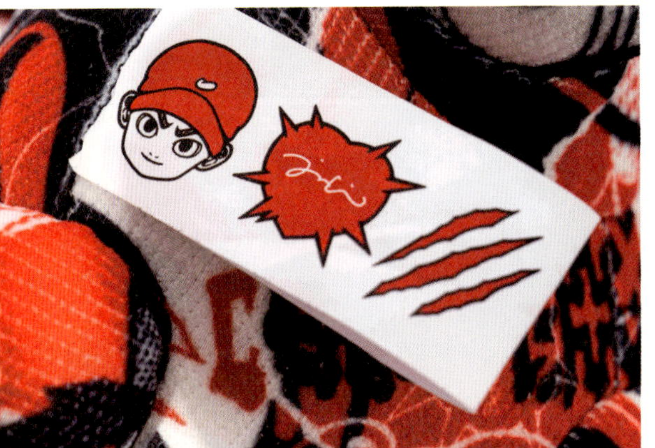

● Why Red? ● The *EVERYONE IS RPG* exhibition employs red and green, contrasting colors representing emotional opposition. These hues emphasize the duality and complexity of human behaviors. Traditional Chinese calligraphy accents the atmosphere, creating a visual narrative of extreme personality tendencies.

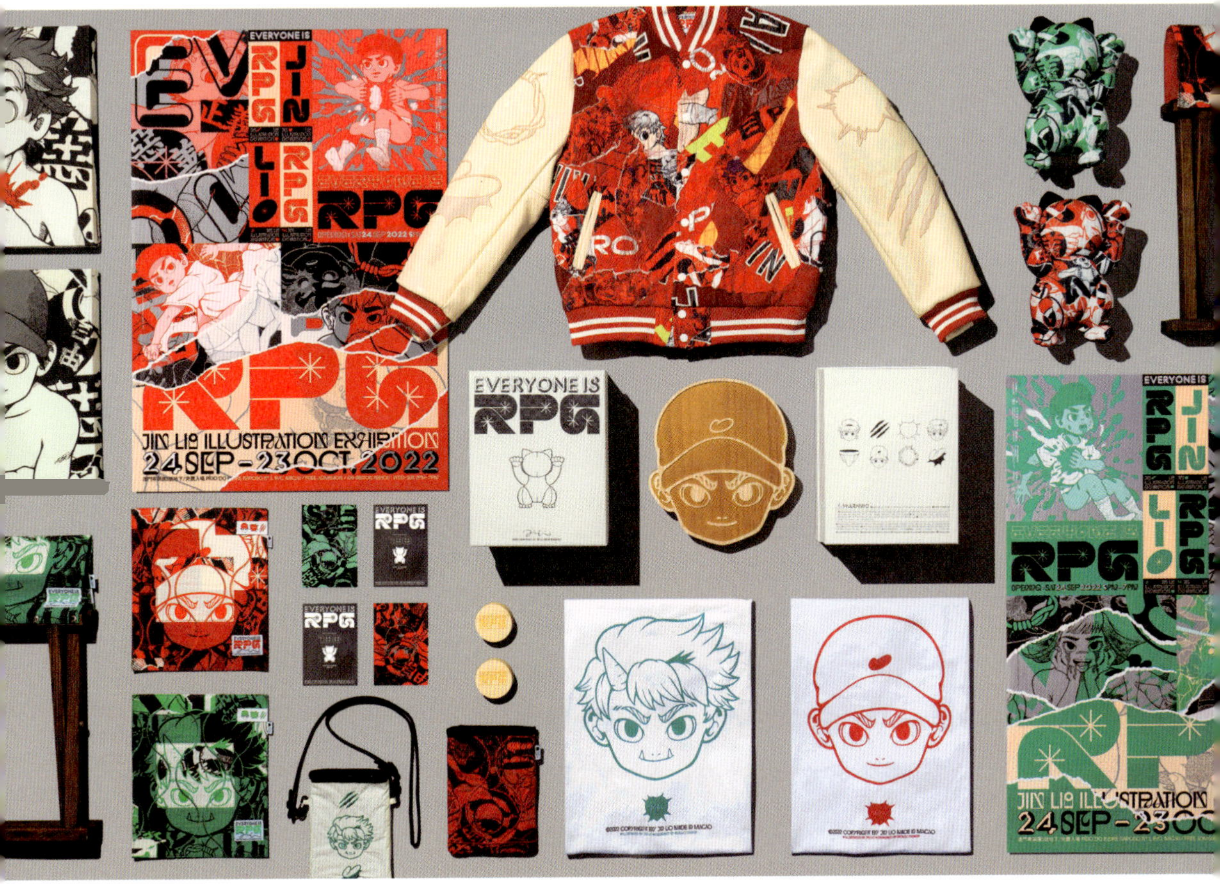

● Client: Macao Illustrators Association

C0 M94 Y89 K0

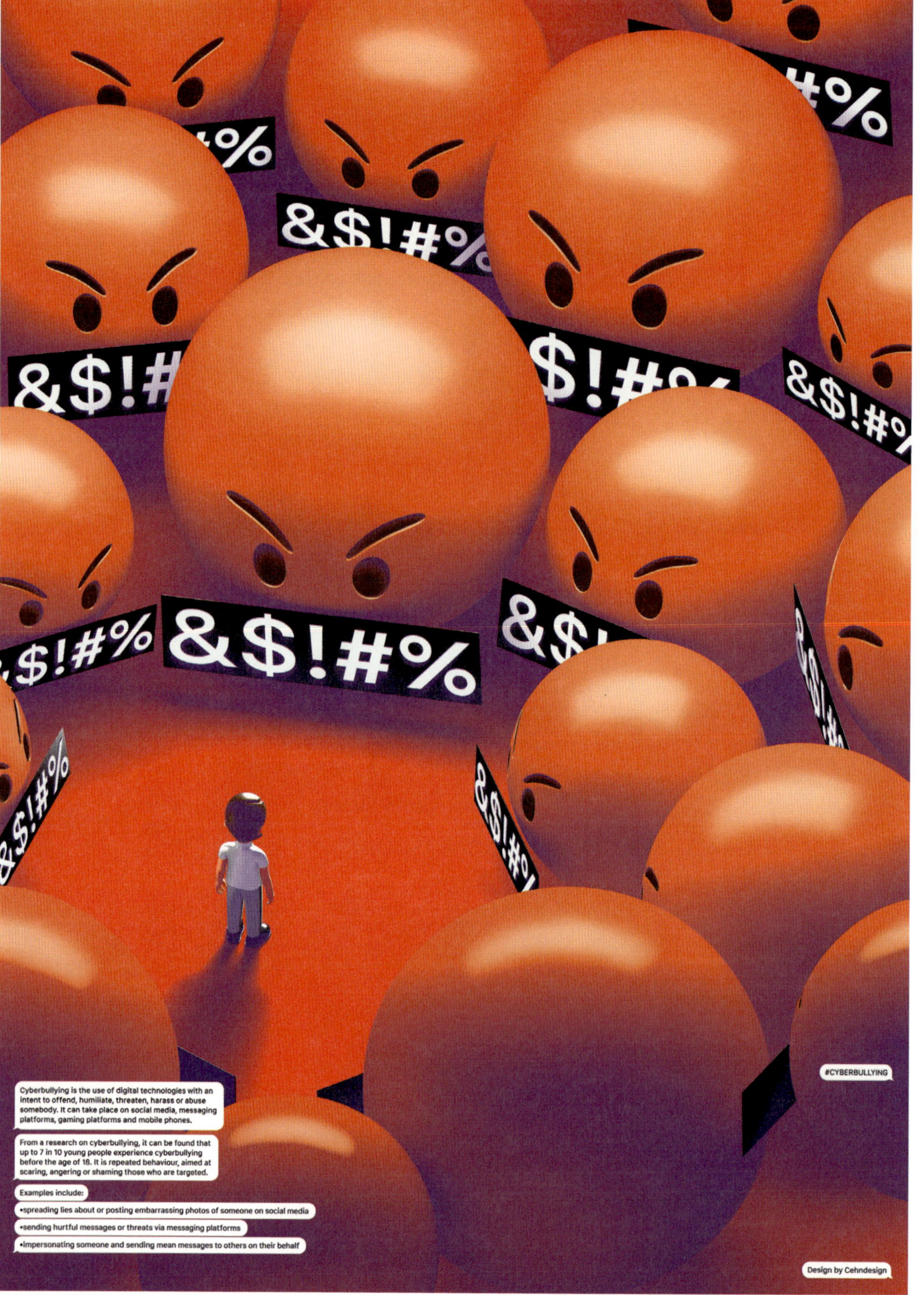

● Designer: Cen Liu ● Client: NoNews Foundation

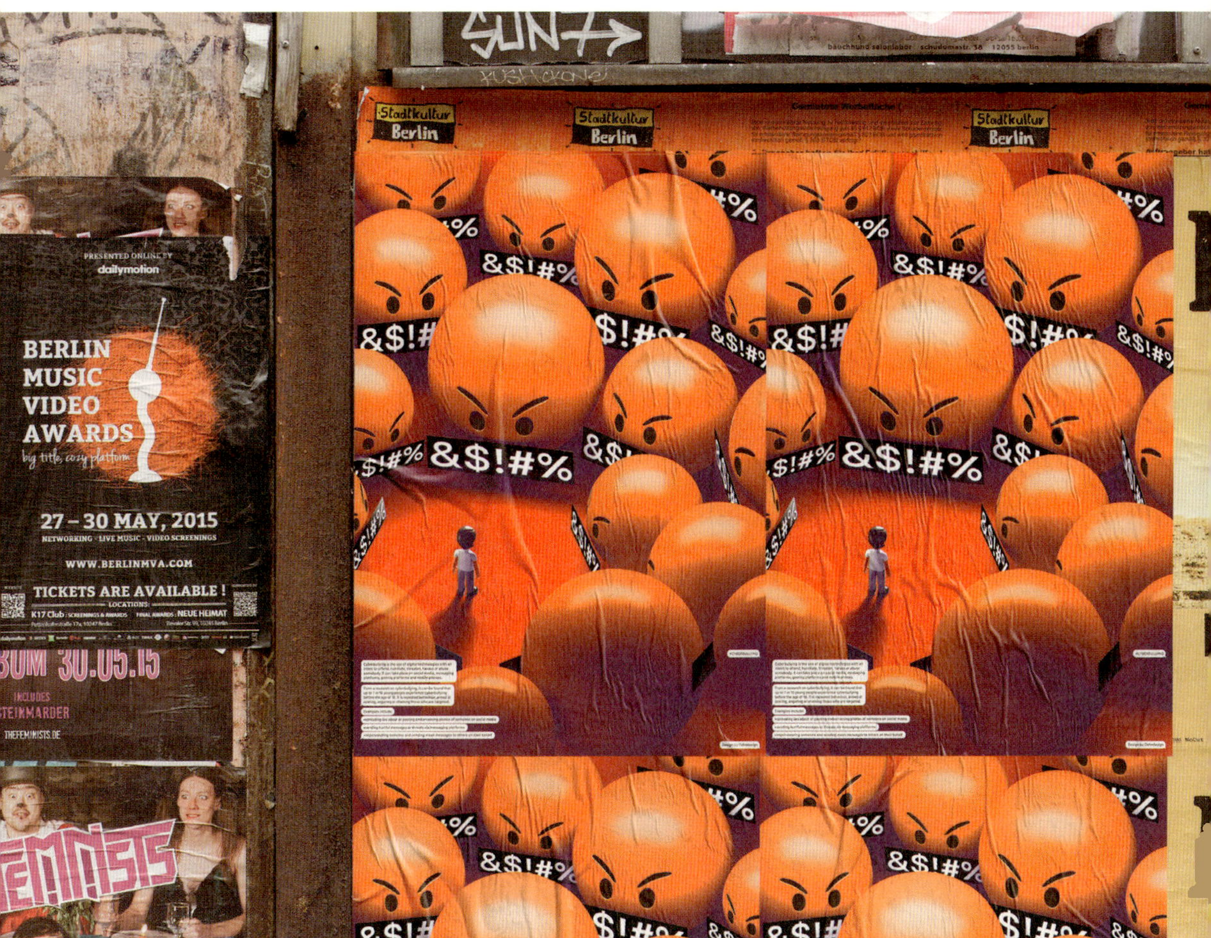

Poster Design for "Cyber Violence" ● The poster addresses the provocation, harassment, abuse, and threats individuals may encounter from unknown sources online. A narrative scene is crafted using Emoji elements, incorporating black humor to convey a sense of oppression.

● Why Red? ● The designers selected the red and orange colors, similar to the "abusive" emoji, as the primary color scheme for the entire design. This choice aims to evoke anger, tension, and opposition, allowing the audience to immersively feel a sense of oppression.

PANTONE ORANGE 021C | PANTONE 811C | PANTONE VIOLETC

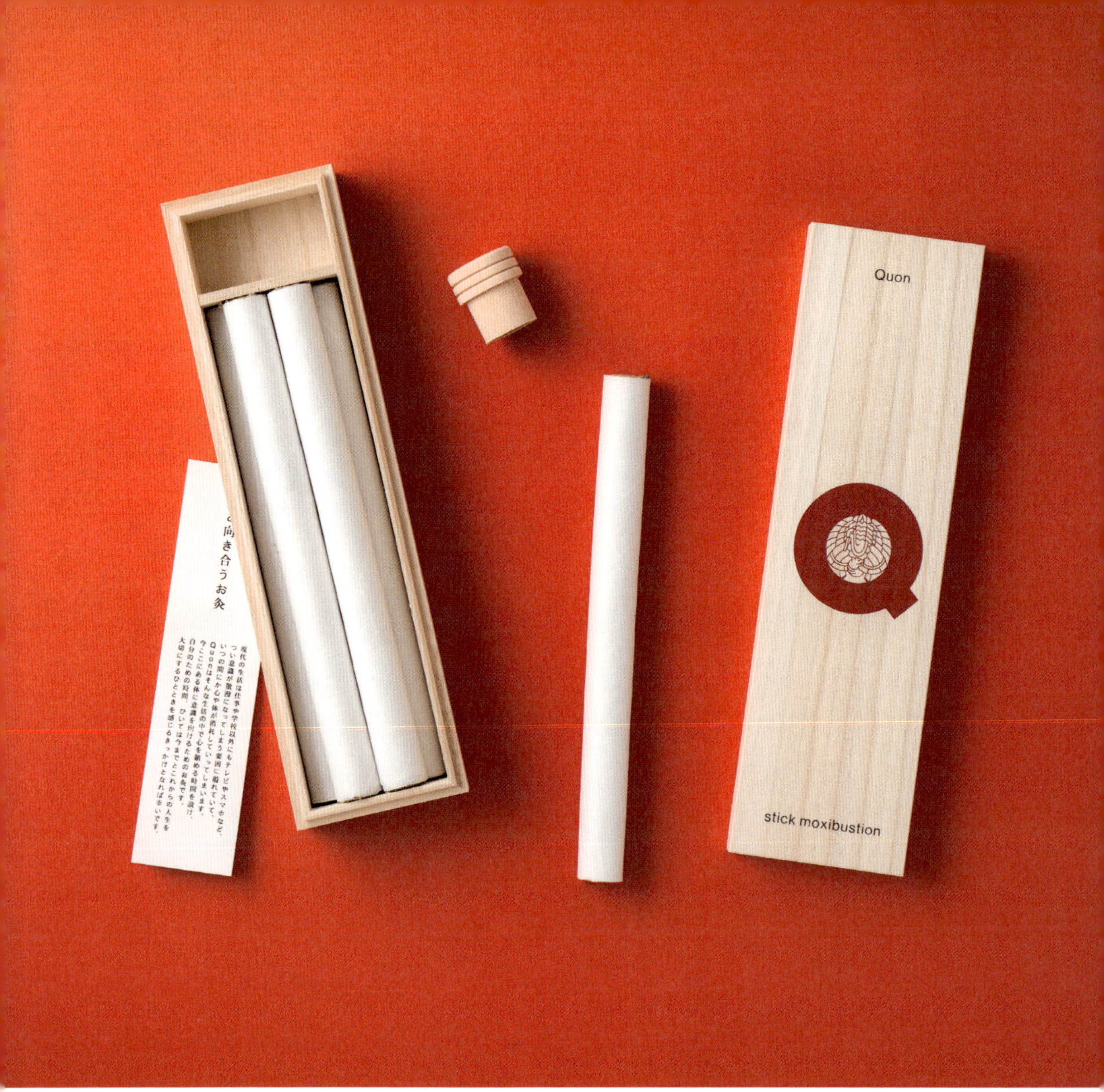

Quon

● Quon, a high-quality mugwort moxibustion (a form of therapy that entails the burning of mugwort leaves) shop, designed its logo and packaging inspired by the "Kameoka Chitose Acupuncture Clinic." The logo incorporates crane and turtle images, symbolizing blessings and longevity. The design combines family crests of cranes and turtles within a thick "Q" circle, implying a long and healthy life through the use of ancient stick moxibustion.

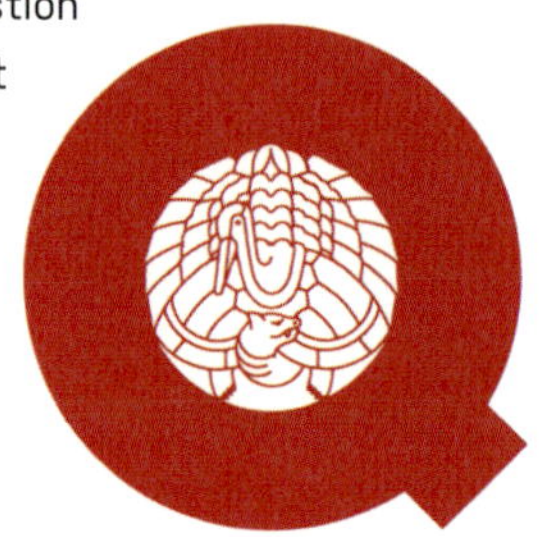

Quon

● Design Studio: Paragram ● Designer: Yusuke Akai

● Why Red? ● The logo, resembling a Japanese seal and inspired by the "Hinomaru" (Flag of Japan), features red for a harmonious feel. The combination of red with geometric shapes creates a sense of stability and security. The modern layout and text, along with the slightly smoky red tone reminiscent of seal ink, convey a solemn and stable atmosphere.

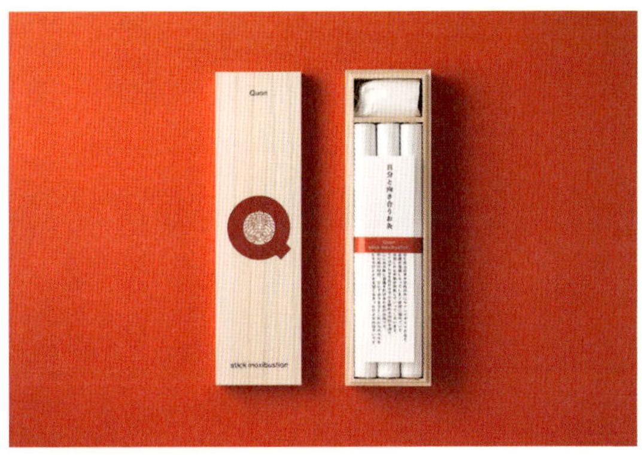

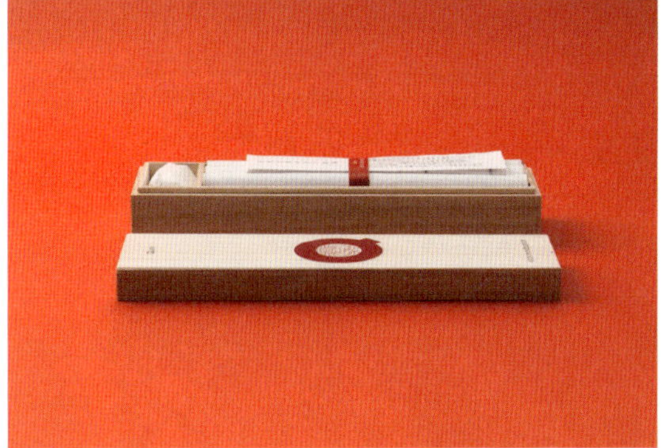

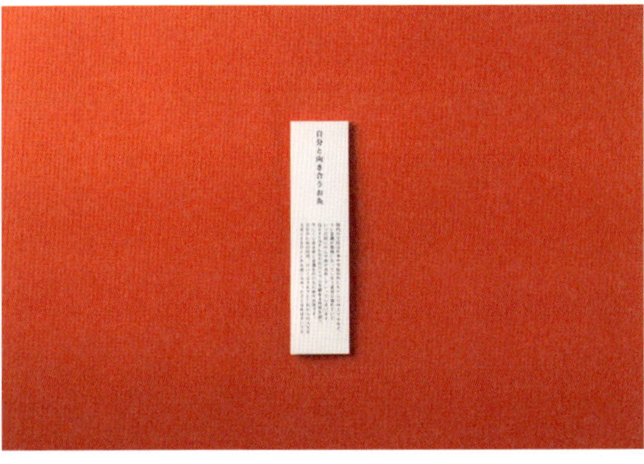

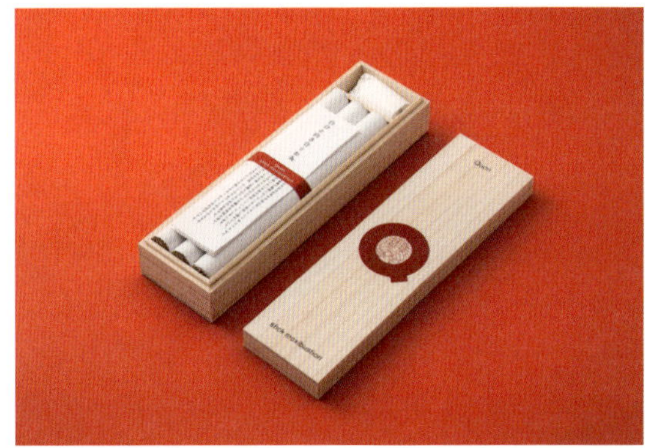

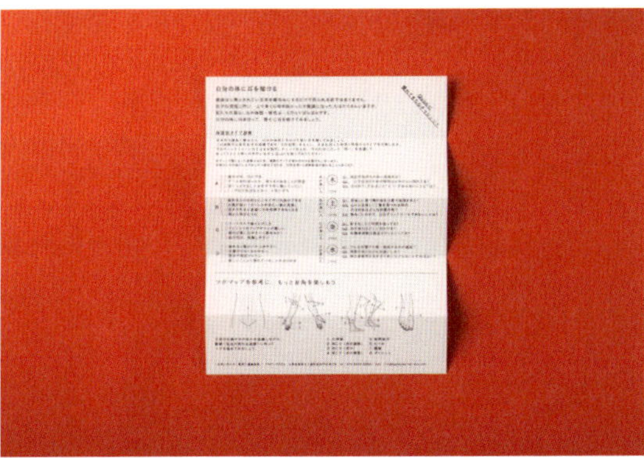

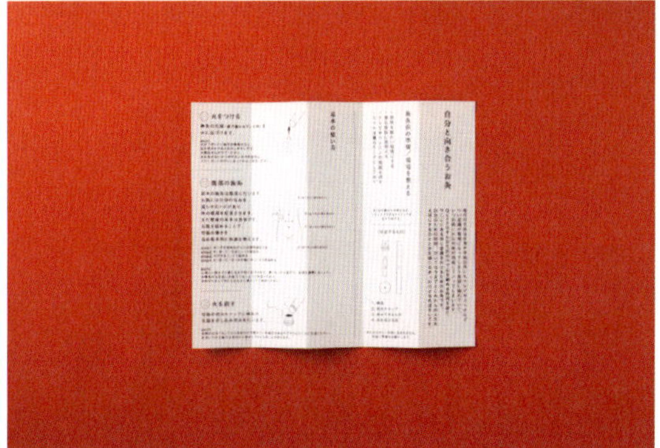

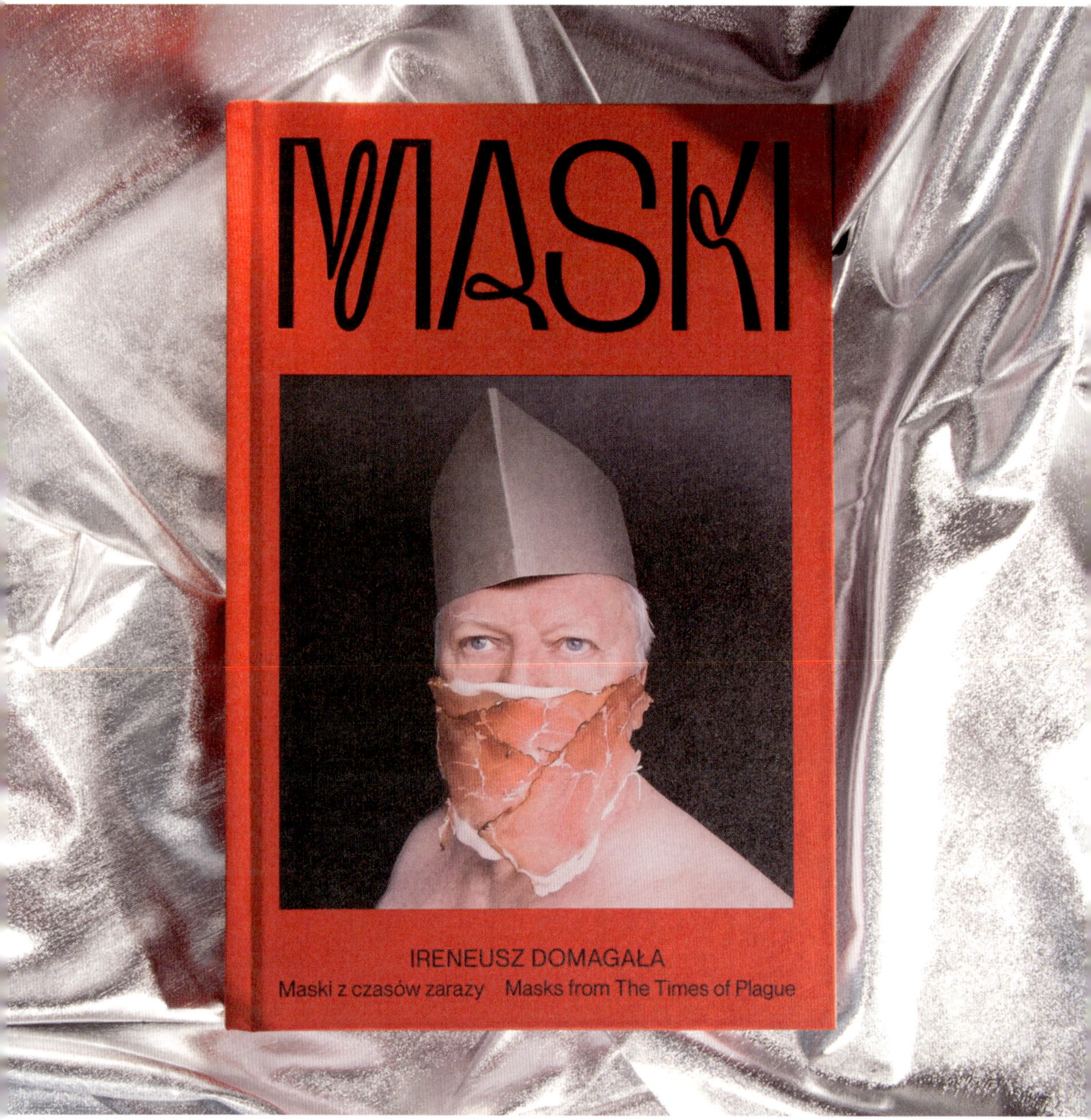

MASKI

IRENEUSZ DOMAGAŁA

Maski z czasów zarazy Masks from The Times of Plague

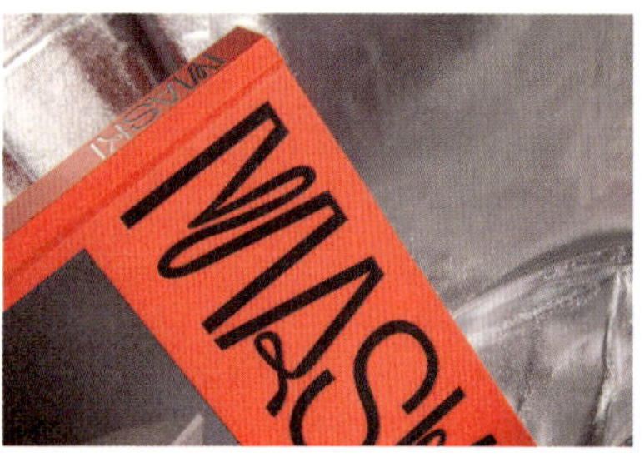

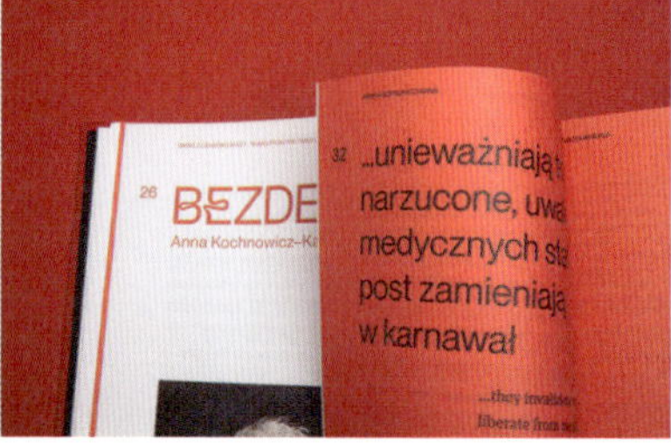

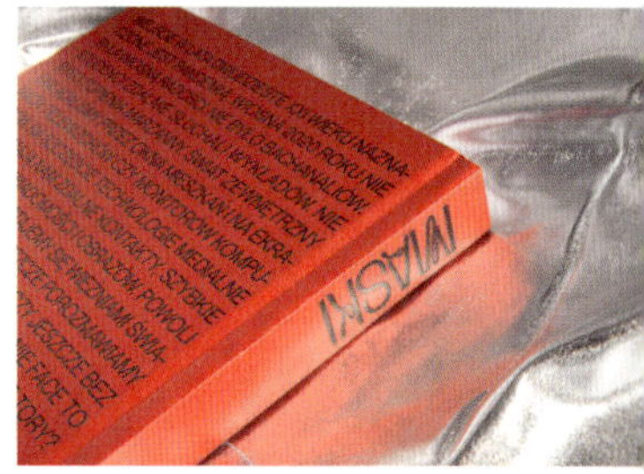

● Designer: Jakub Haremza ● Client: Ireneusz Domagała

Masks from the Times of Plague

● During the COVID-19 pandemic lockdowns and restrictions of 2020–2021, the artist Ireneusz Domagała embarked on an artistic project at the intersection of theater and costume design titled "Masks from The Times of Plague." He created numerous abstract and often fashion/art-inspired versions of face masks, sharing them on his social media. The culmination of this endeavor is a hardcover album that compiles all the projects.

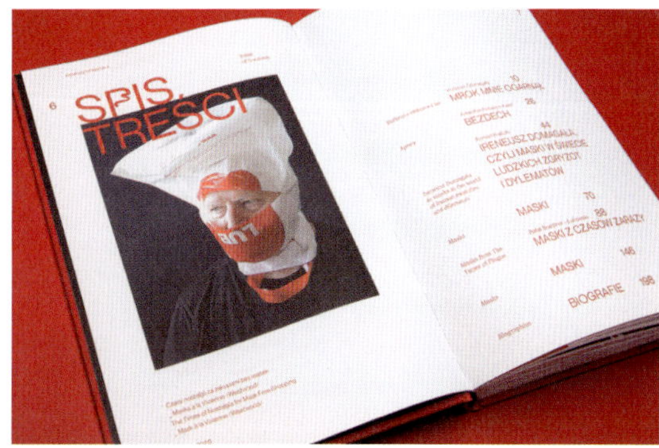

● Why Red? ● A set of intense face masks demands a form reflecting their strength and originality, requiring a strong contrast in the publication to emphasize the project's emotionality. Red, representing strength and devotion, is the natural choice.

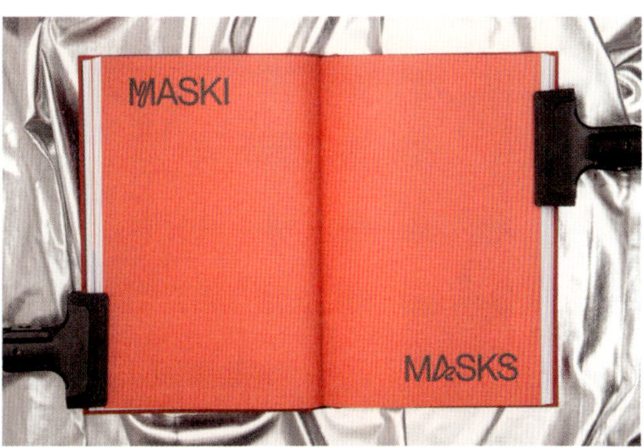

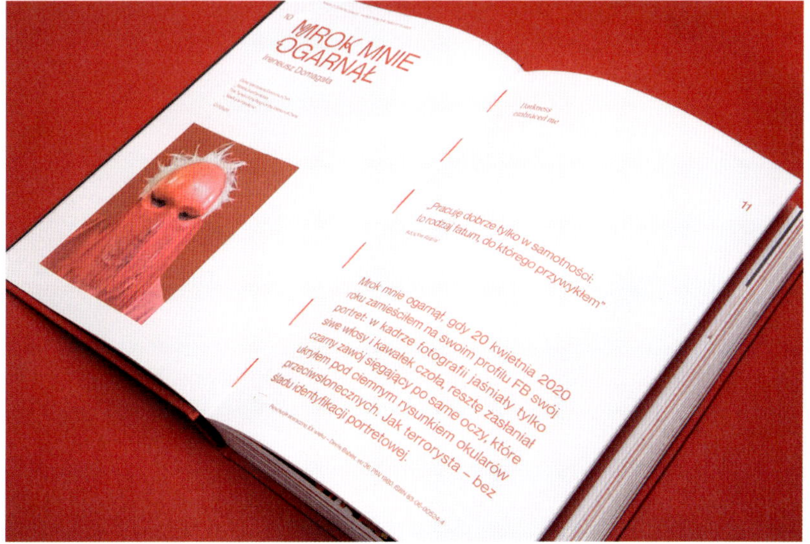

PENNY FOR MY THOUGHTS

● It is a zine comprising a series of diary entries that narrates the story of Anonymous' journey to New Zealand. In contrast to typical travelogues, Anonymous focuses on the anticipation and excitement leading up to the trip rather than the experiences during the journey. The diary entries delve into their emotions, observations of seemingly ordinary things, and overall anticipation, coming to an abrupt end upon reaching the destination.

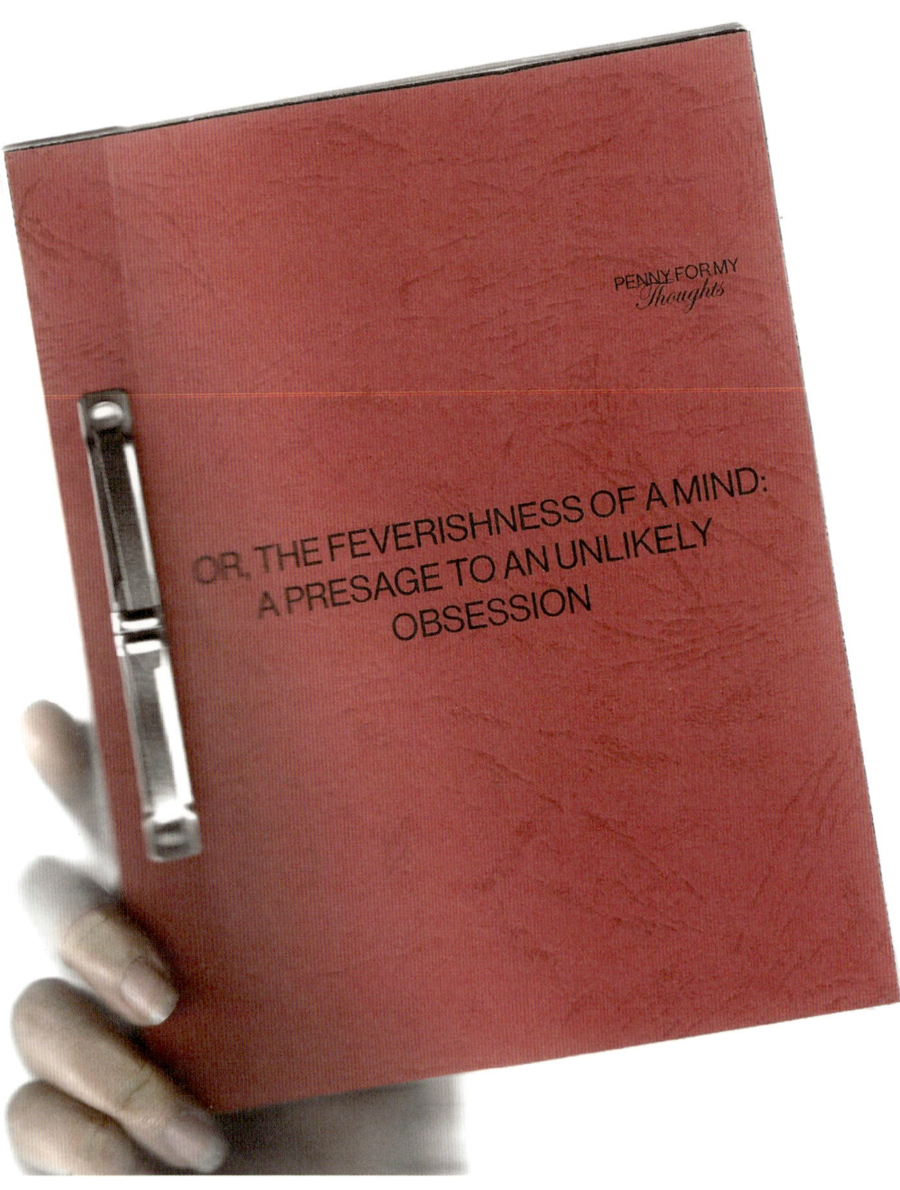

● Designer: Tiffany Wong ● Client: Sore Sore's Shelf

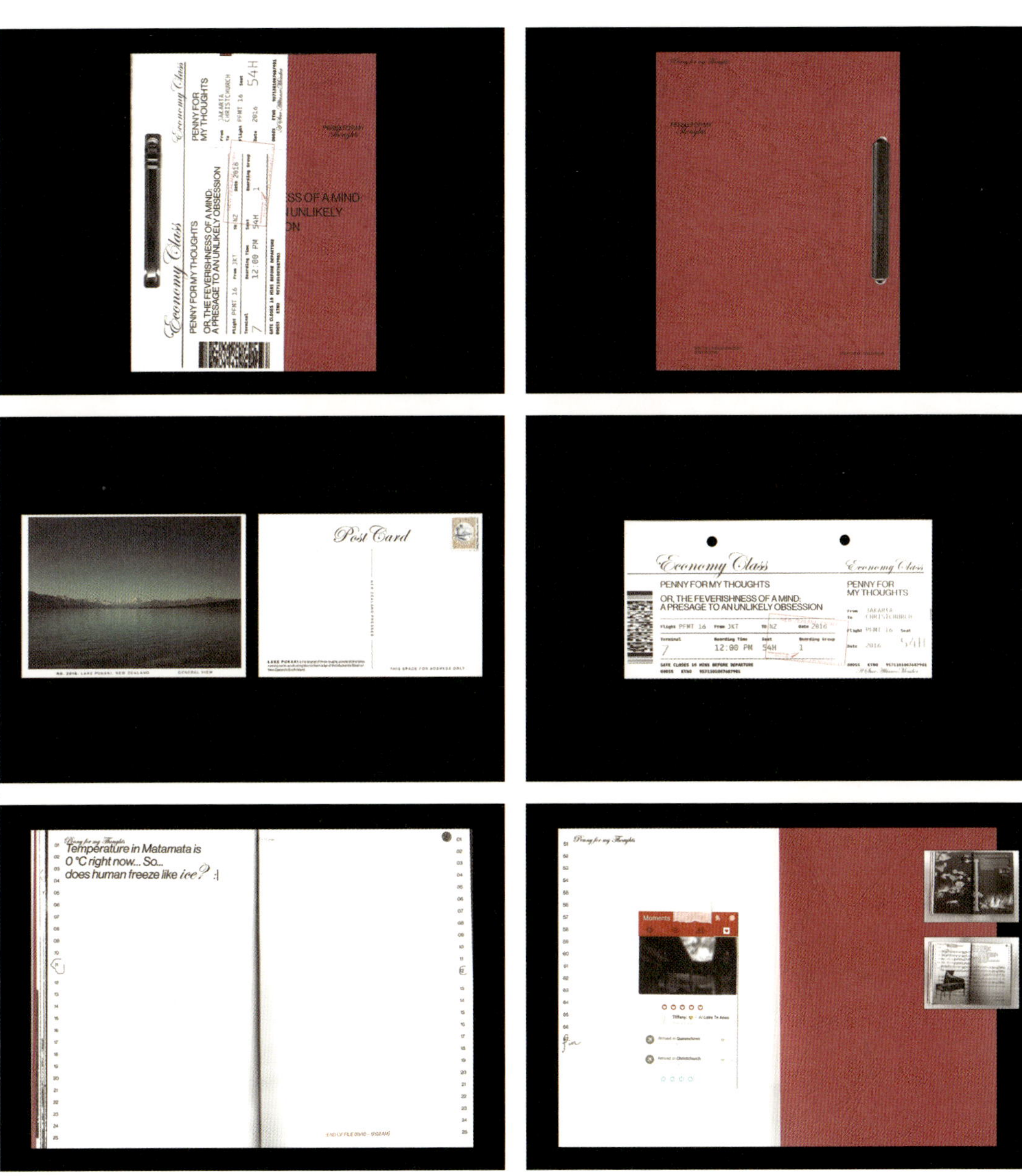

● Why Red? ● The zine tells a cherished memory, emphasized by the touches of red against the black design, highlighting the story's intimacy. The red cover, a crucial element, instantly conveys the zine's amiable and intimate nature.

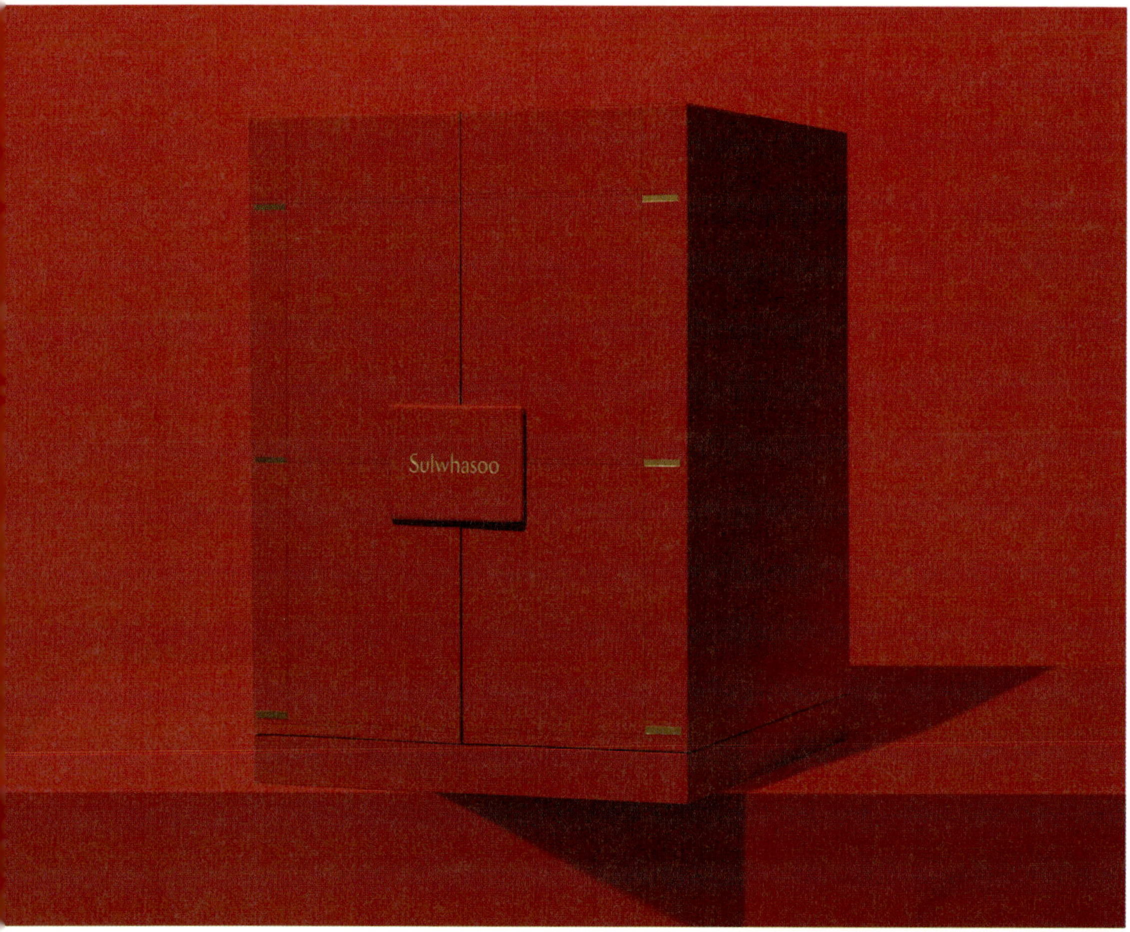

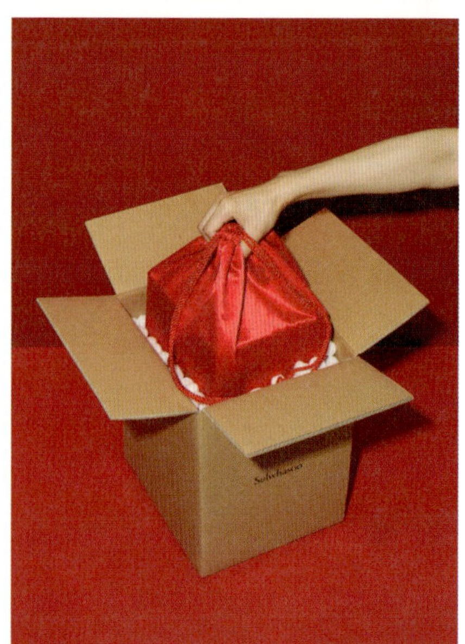

Sulwhasoo Chinese New Year 2021 Press Kit

● Sulwhasoo released a limited collection for the Chinese New Year, featuring intricate graphic motifs with heart and firework elements.
The unique bi-folding door structure wraps up a heart-shaped music box, symbolizing heartfelt wishes for a prosperous New Year.

● Design Studio: HEAZ ● Designer: Saerom Lee, Swan Lee, Yeon ho Jeoung ● Client: Sulwhasoo

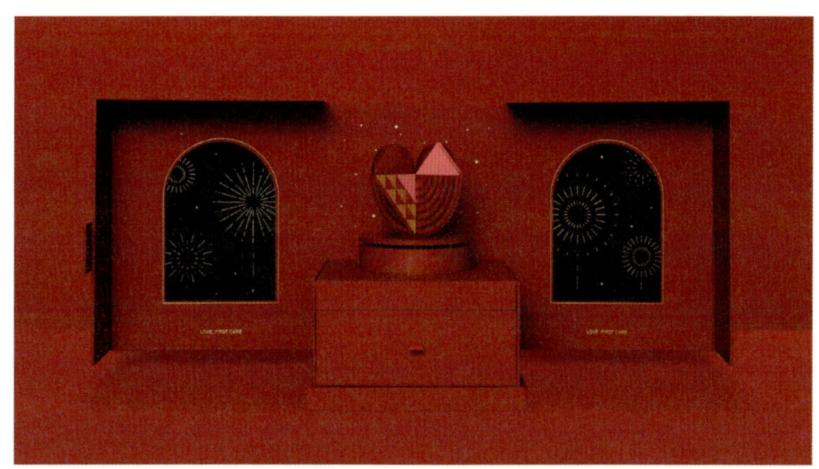

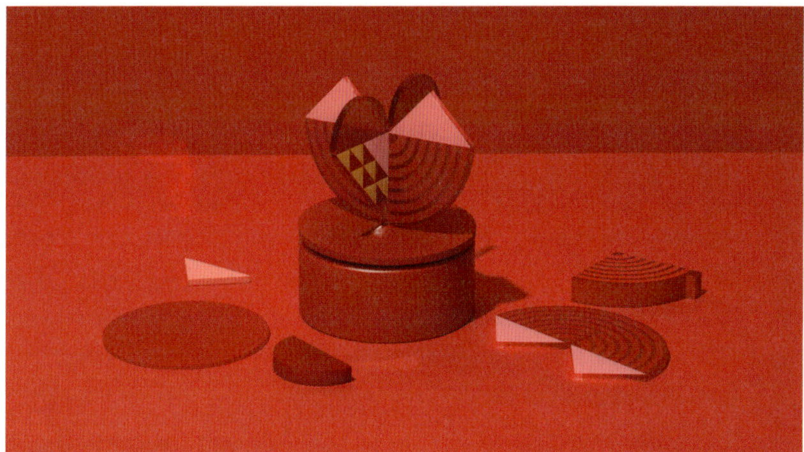

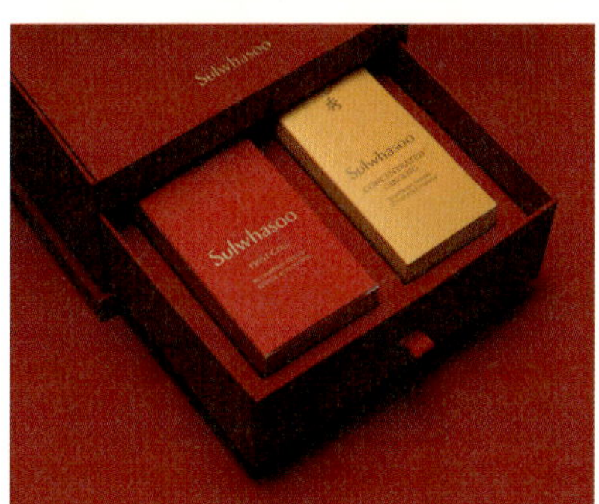

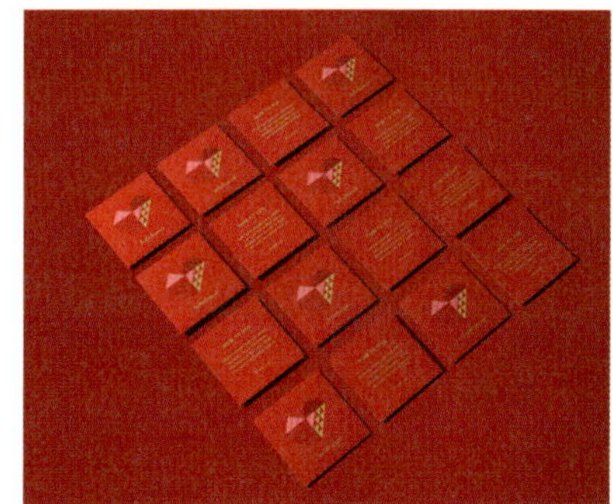

● Why Red? ● Crafted for Chinese VIP customers and influencers, this promotional kit celebrates the Chinese New Year with the symbolic color red, representing blessings and success. The vibrant red hue, teeming with festive air, seamlessly integrated the essence of the season into the kit.

C16 M100 Y77 K7

Fire Sale ● The FIRE SALE event occurred at FISK during the summer of 2017, presenting a variety of T-shirts. The promotional design for this sale drew inspiration from vernacular sale graphics, characterized by a repetitive and stretched typography style. The design prominently features an eye-catching combination of yellow and red colors.

● Why Red? ● The combination of highly saturated red and yellow colors generates a visually energetic effect, making it well-suited for promotional purposes.

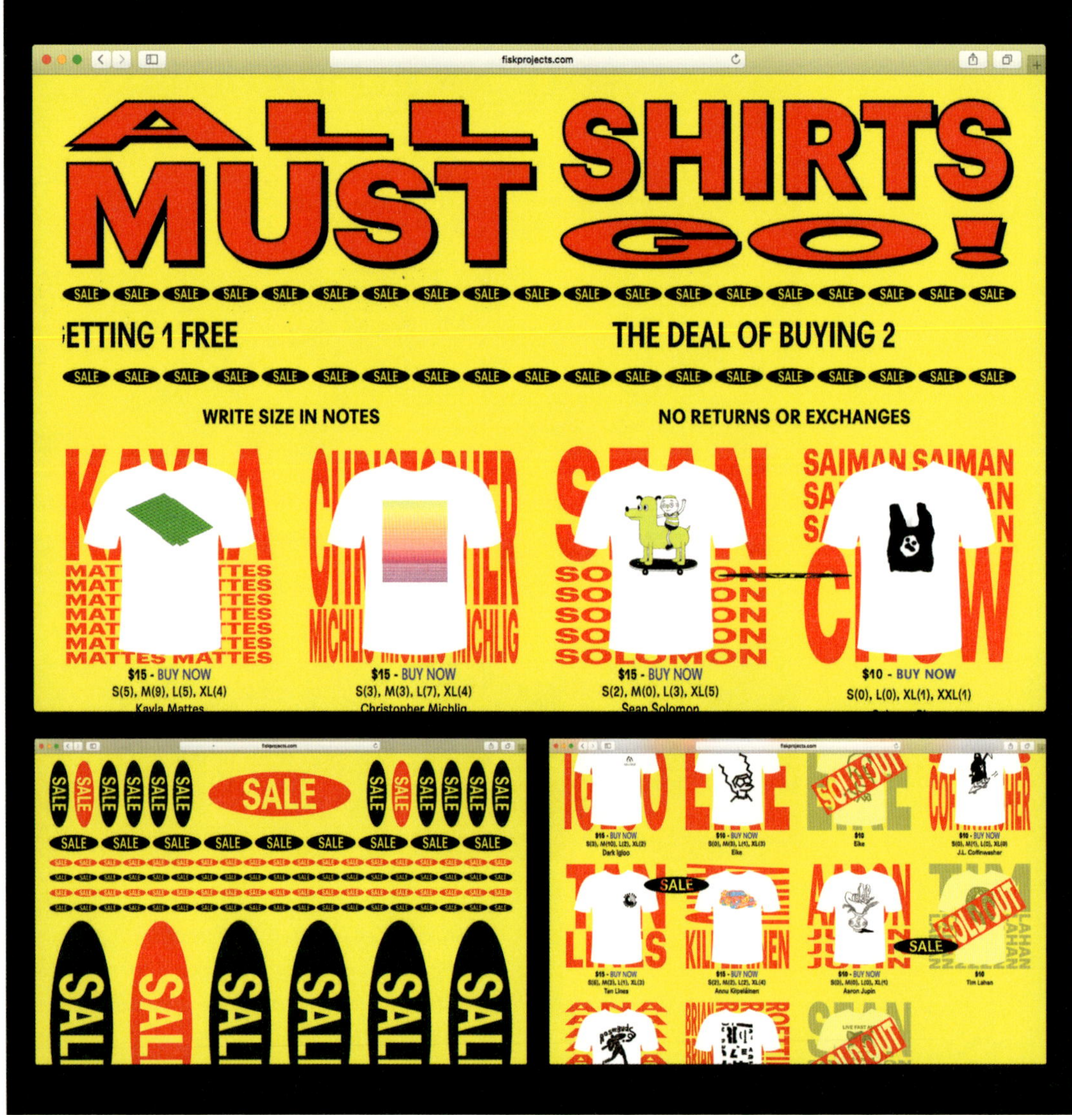

● Design Studio: FISK ● Designer: Jun Ki Hong ● Client: FISK (Internal)

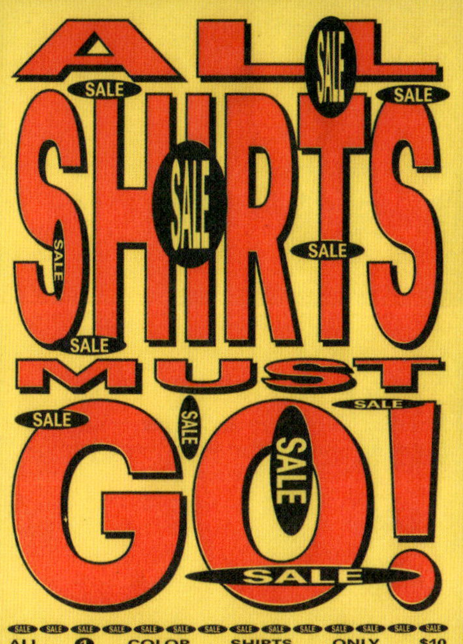

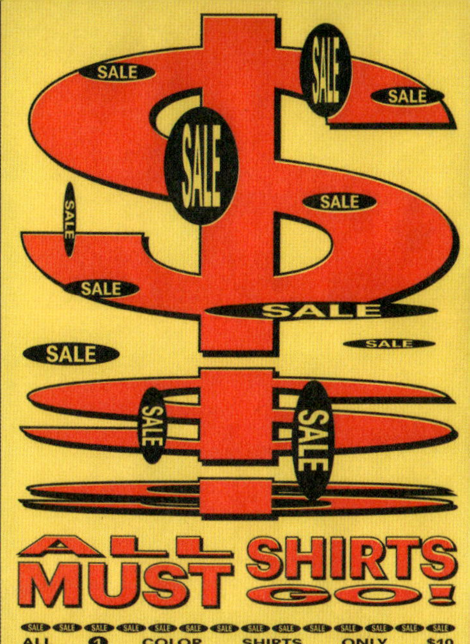

$$$

ALL SHIRTS MUST GO!

ALL 1 COLOR SHIRTS ONLY $10
ALL 2 COLOR SHIRTS ONLY $15
THE DEAL OF BUYING 2 GETTING 1 FREE

FISKPROJECTS.COM/FIRE-SALE

ALL SHIRTS MUST GO!
ALL SHIRTS MUST GO!
SALE

ALL 1 COLOR SHIRTS ONLY $10
ALL 2 COLOR SHIRTS ONLY $15
THE DEAL OF BUYING 2 GETTING 1 FREE

FISKPROJECTS.COM/FIRE-SALE

C0 M96 Y100 K0

C3 M0 Y96 K0

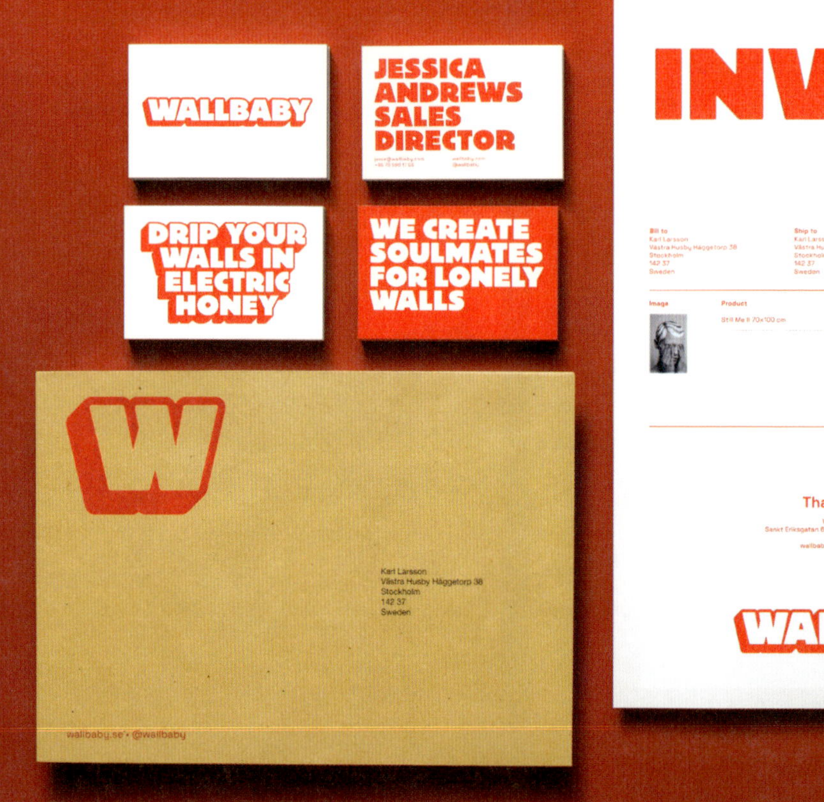

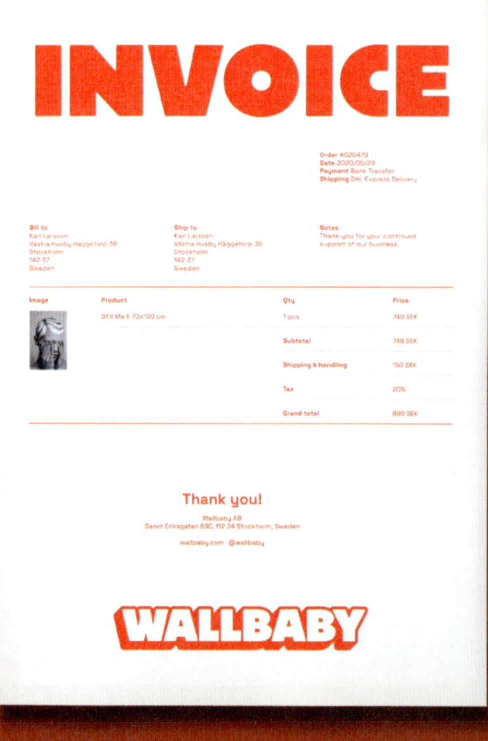

WALLBABY ● WALLBABY, a premium Swedish online poster company, founded by photographers passionate about art and interior design, collaborates with global artists for original expressions. ● Design studio SNASK aimed to create a distinctive brand amidst a saturated market, emphasizing the founders' original motives and quality prints. The name WALLBABY, chosen for its emotional connection, implies bringing better art to homes. The messaging adopts a flirtatious and inspiring tone, prioritizing beauty over functionality.

● Why Red? ● WALLBABY strives to create a deep emotional connection, and the design approach portrays the product as a caring observer, capturing emotions through five sets representing different art collector personas. The bold and soft Graúna typeface, resembling lips, adds a unique touch to the brand's visual identity. The custom-made typographic manner with a frame/shadow dominates the poster, and the bright red color communicates the themes of love and passion.

● Design Studio: SNASK ● Designer: Matej Špánik

WALLBABY

ABCDEFGHIJK
LMNOPQRSTU
VWXYZØÄÖÅ
@1234567890
[&$§?!]#①②③

ABCDEFGHIJK
LMNOPQRSTU
VWXYZØÄÖÅ
@1234567890
[&$§?!]#

FIND THE ONE AT WALLBABY

YOUR HEART'S DESIRE IS WAITING TO MEET YOU AT WALLBABY.

↓↓↓

Find your soulposter at wallbaby.com

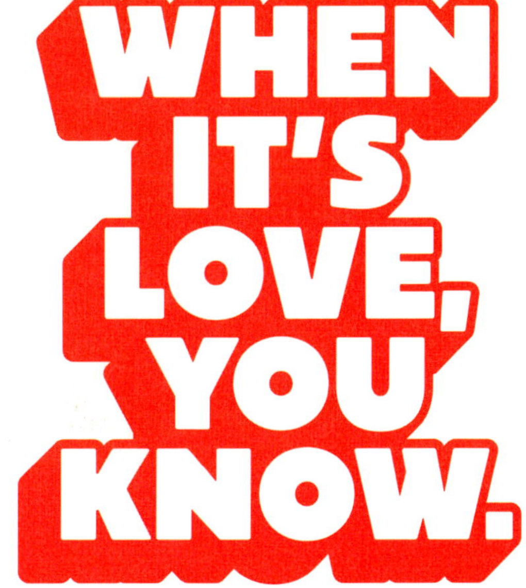

C0 M100 Y95 K0

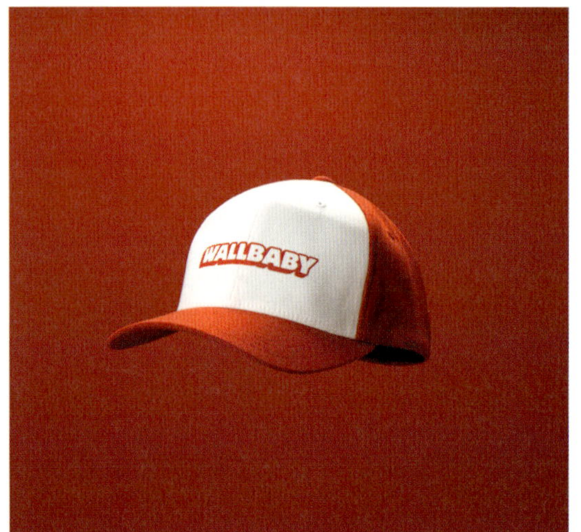

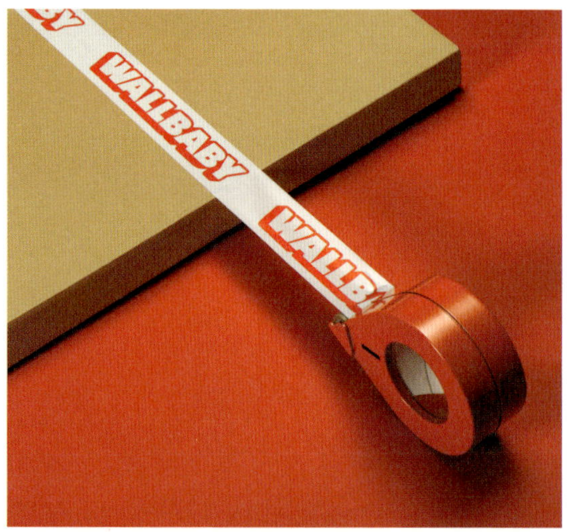

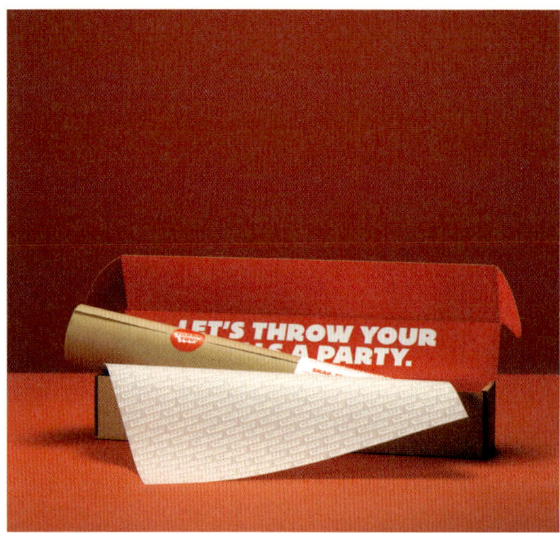

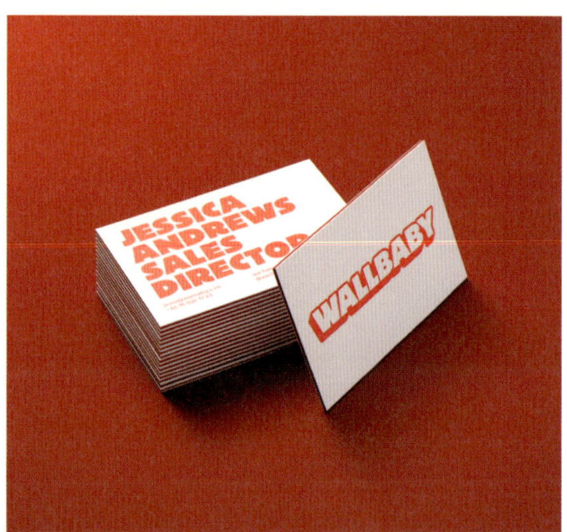

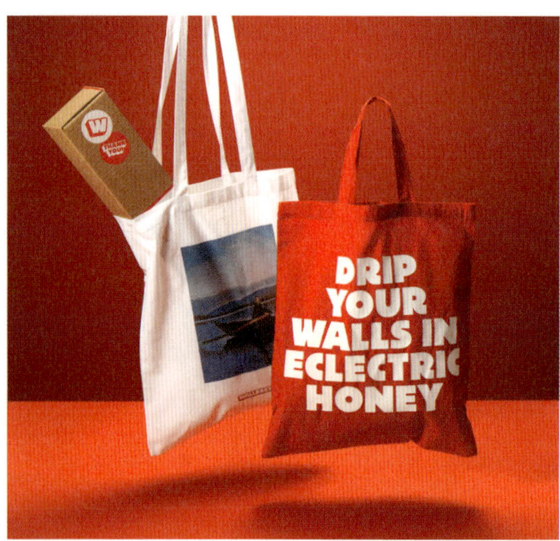

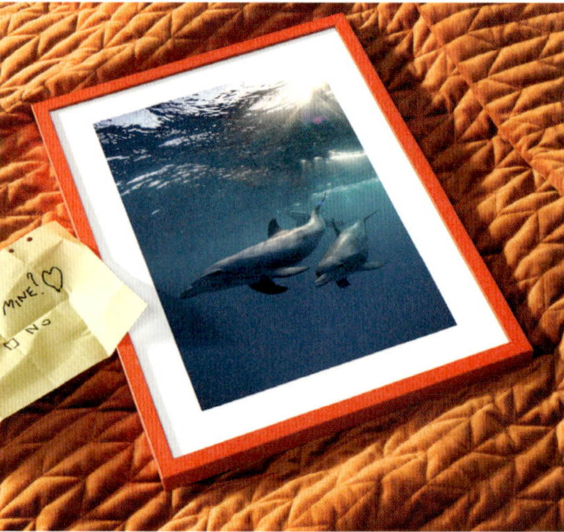

● Client: WALLBABY ● Photography: Golden Retriever

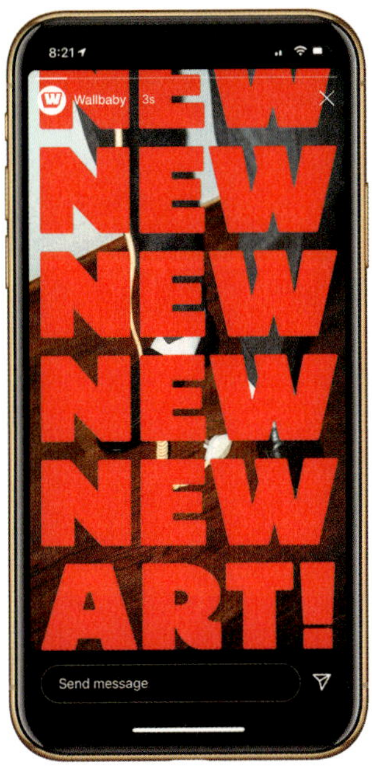
8:21
Wallbaby 3s
NEW
NEW
NEW
NEW
ART!
Send message

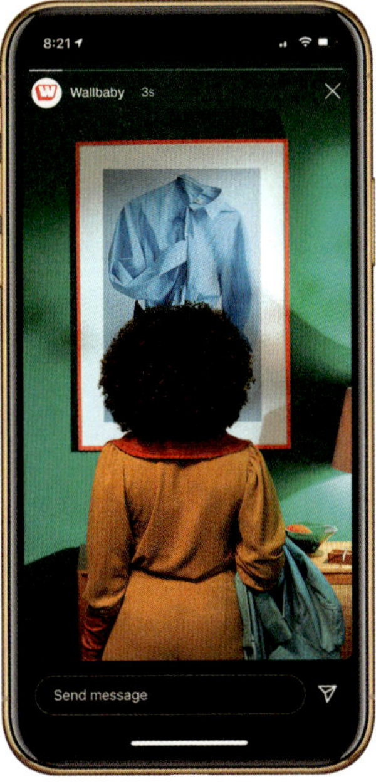
8:21
Wallbaby 3s
Send message

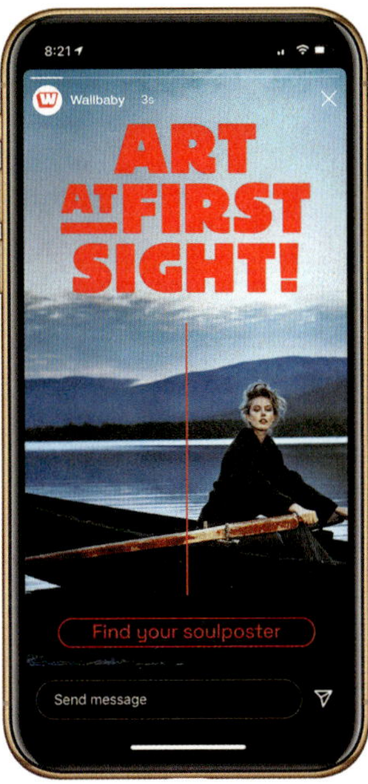
8:21
Wallbaby 3s
ART AT FIRST SIGHT!
Find your soulposter
Send message

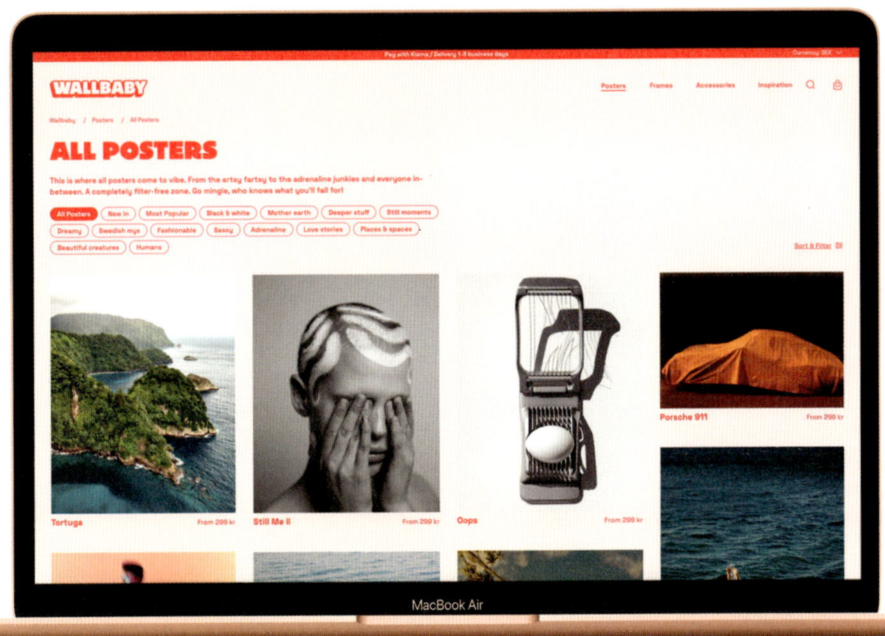
Pay with Klarna / Delivery 1-3 business days
Currency: SEK
WALLBABY
Posters
Frames
Accessories
Inspiration
Wallbaby / Posters / All Posters
ALL POSTERS
This is where all posters come to vibe. From the artsy fartsy to the adrenaline junkies and everyone in-between. A completely filter-free zone. Go mingle, who knows what you'll fall for!
All Posters
New in
Most Popular
Black & white
Mother earth
Deeper stuff
Still moments
Dreamy
Swedish mys
Fashionable
Sassy
Adrenaline
Love stories
Places & spaces
Beautiful creatures
Humans
Sort & Filter
Tortuga
From 299 kr
Still Me II
From 299 kr
Oops
From 299 kr
Porsche 911
From 299 kr
MacBook Air

XU Visual Identity and Package Design

● Xu, an artist brand that uses objects as a narrative medium, focuses on researching the history and cultural phenomena of creation. In the logo design, the four dots of character "煦" (Xu) are evolved into a cluster of flames. The packaging box utilizes a combination of different materials to convey a variety of tactile experiences. The design inspiration for the ribbon handle comes from the rubber bands used to fit molds during pouring.

● Why Red? ● The color scheme is primarily determined by the characteristics of each product and the glaze colors. The designer aimed to convey the warm and gentle qualities of ceramics along with the brand emotion of being "warm and firm."

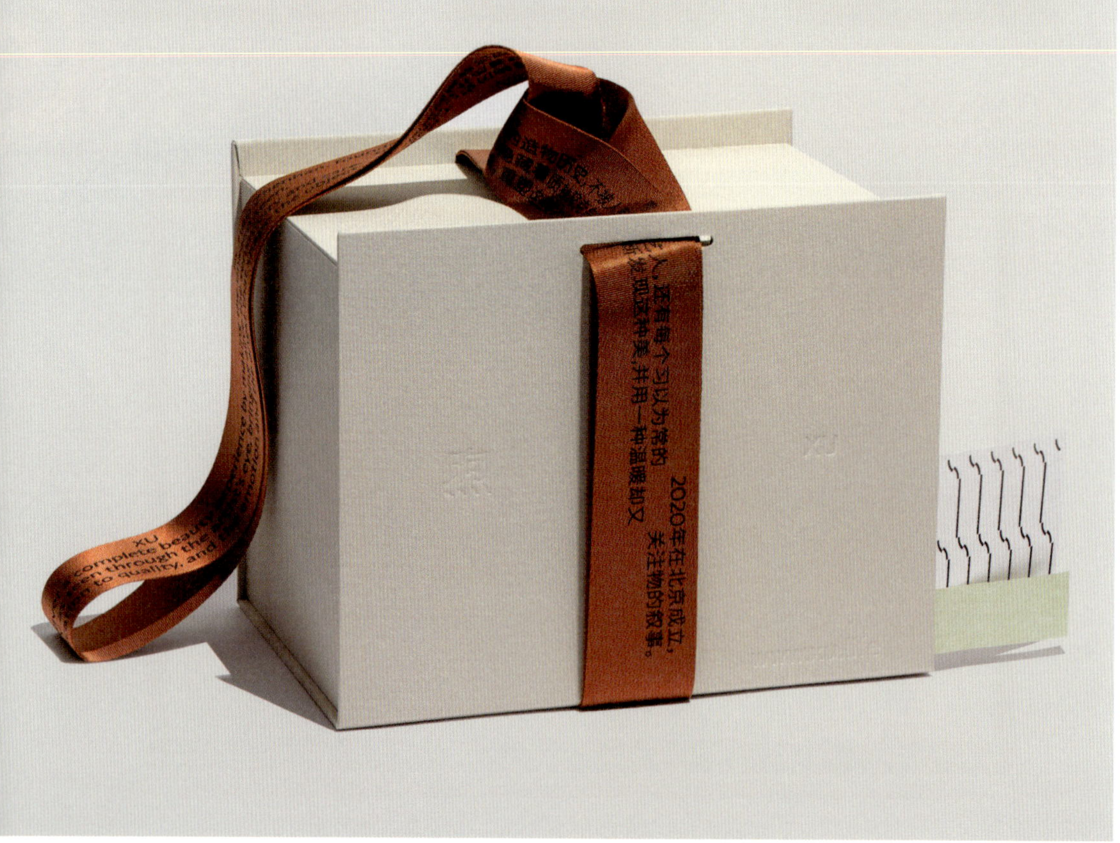

● Design Studio: STUDIO DPi ● Art Director: Ming Ding, Yuanbo Wang ● Designer: Ming Ding,

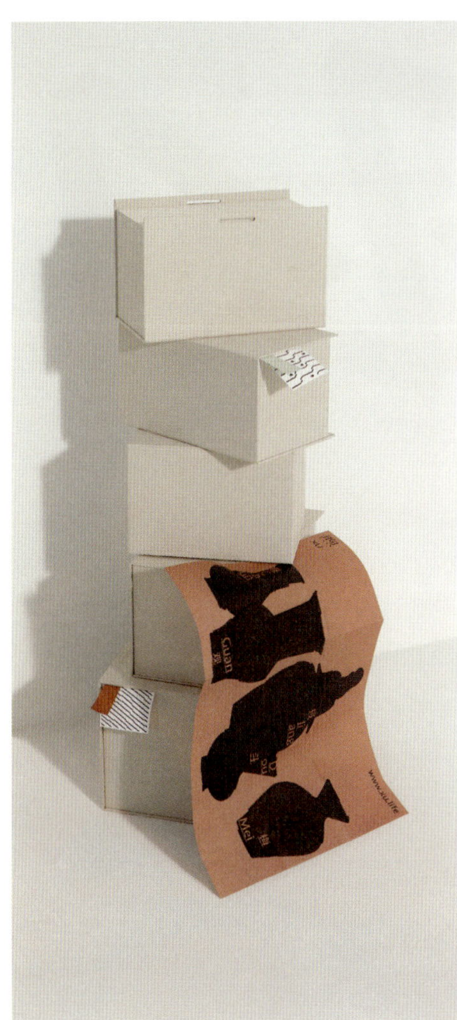

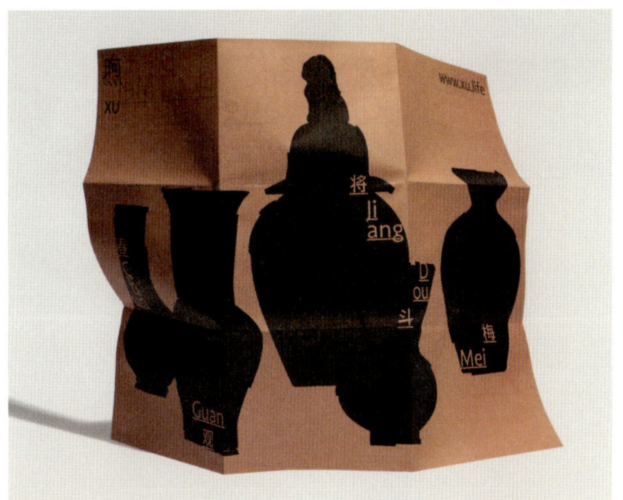

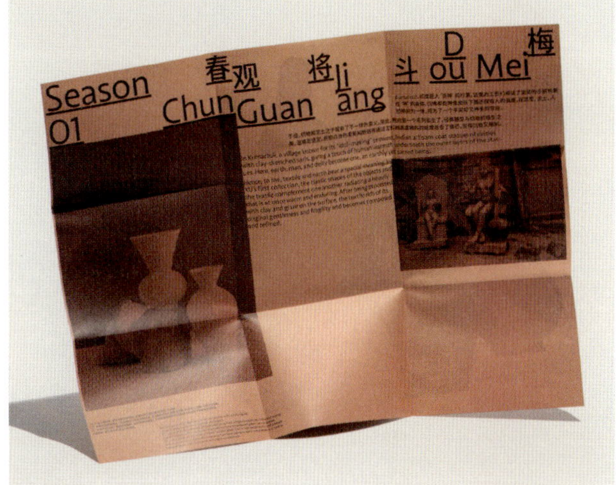

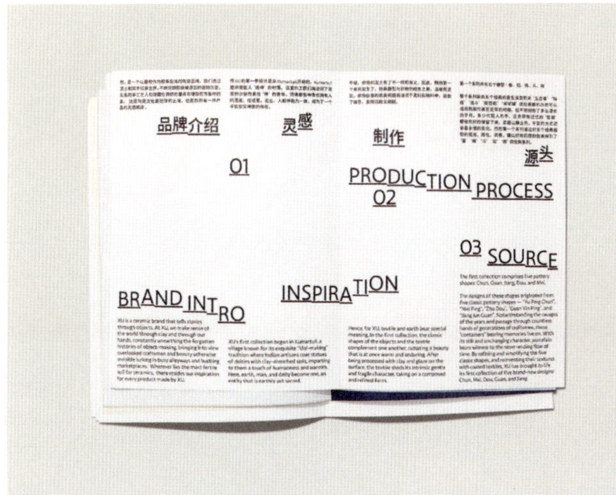

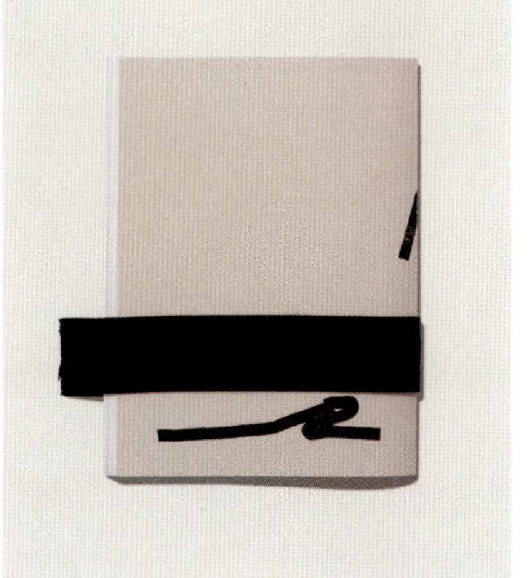

Yuanbo Wang, Chaohao Chen ● Client: XU

C24 M62 Y61 K0

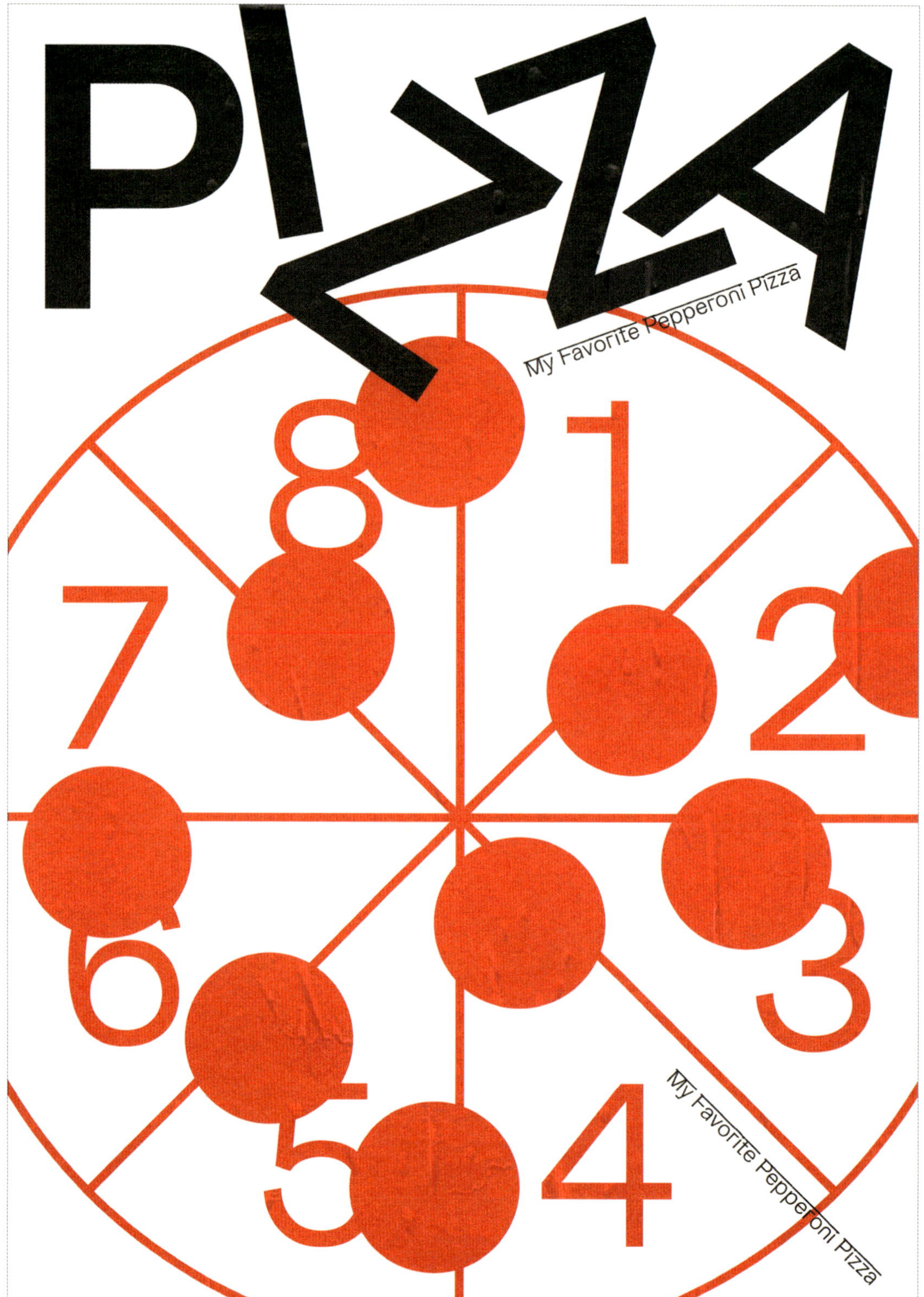

● Design Studio: jun.works ● Designer: Jun Ki Hong ● Client: PizzaTypefaces

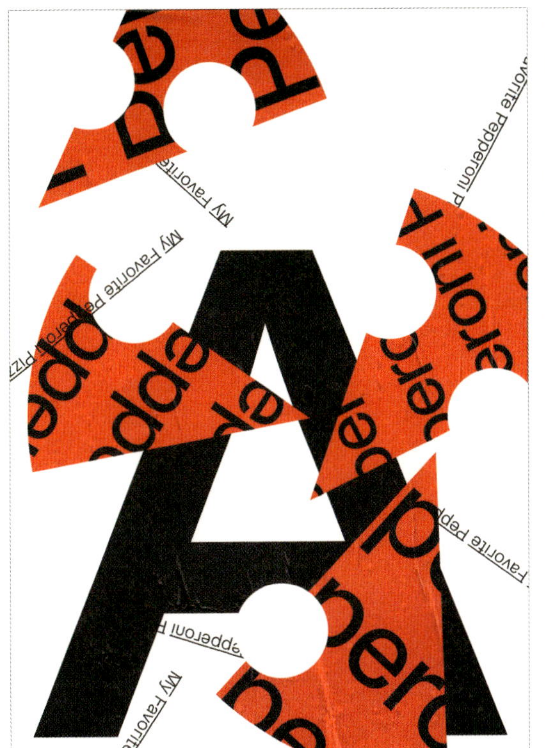

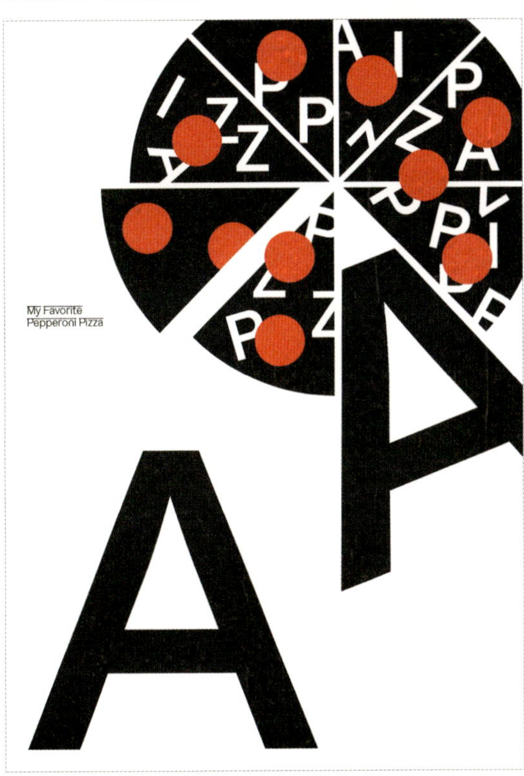

My Favorite Pepperoni Pizza

● The designer crafted eight posters for the Kern font license contest organized by Pizza Typefaces, emphasizing the exclusive Kern typeface with a pizza theme. ● The project showcases diverse iterations of an 8-piece pizza using creative typographic layouts and a pepperoni red color palette to visually express abstract concepts. ● Letter forms, including the "A" representing a pizza slice, were strategically scattered as engaging toppings, adding a dynamic touch to the overall design.

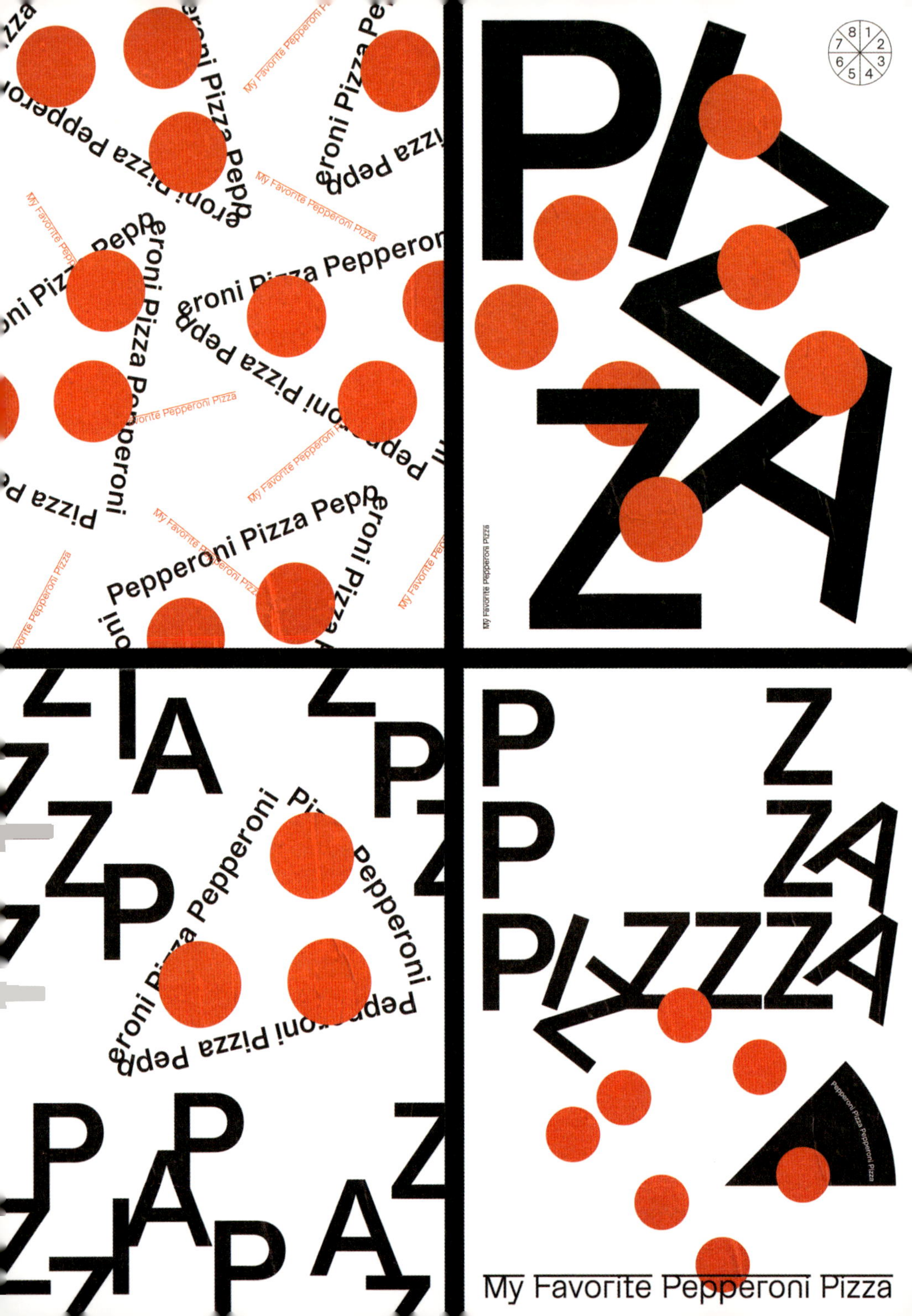
PIZZA
My Favorite Pepperoni Pizza
Pepperoni Pizza Pepperoni Pizza
My Favorite Pepperoni Pizza

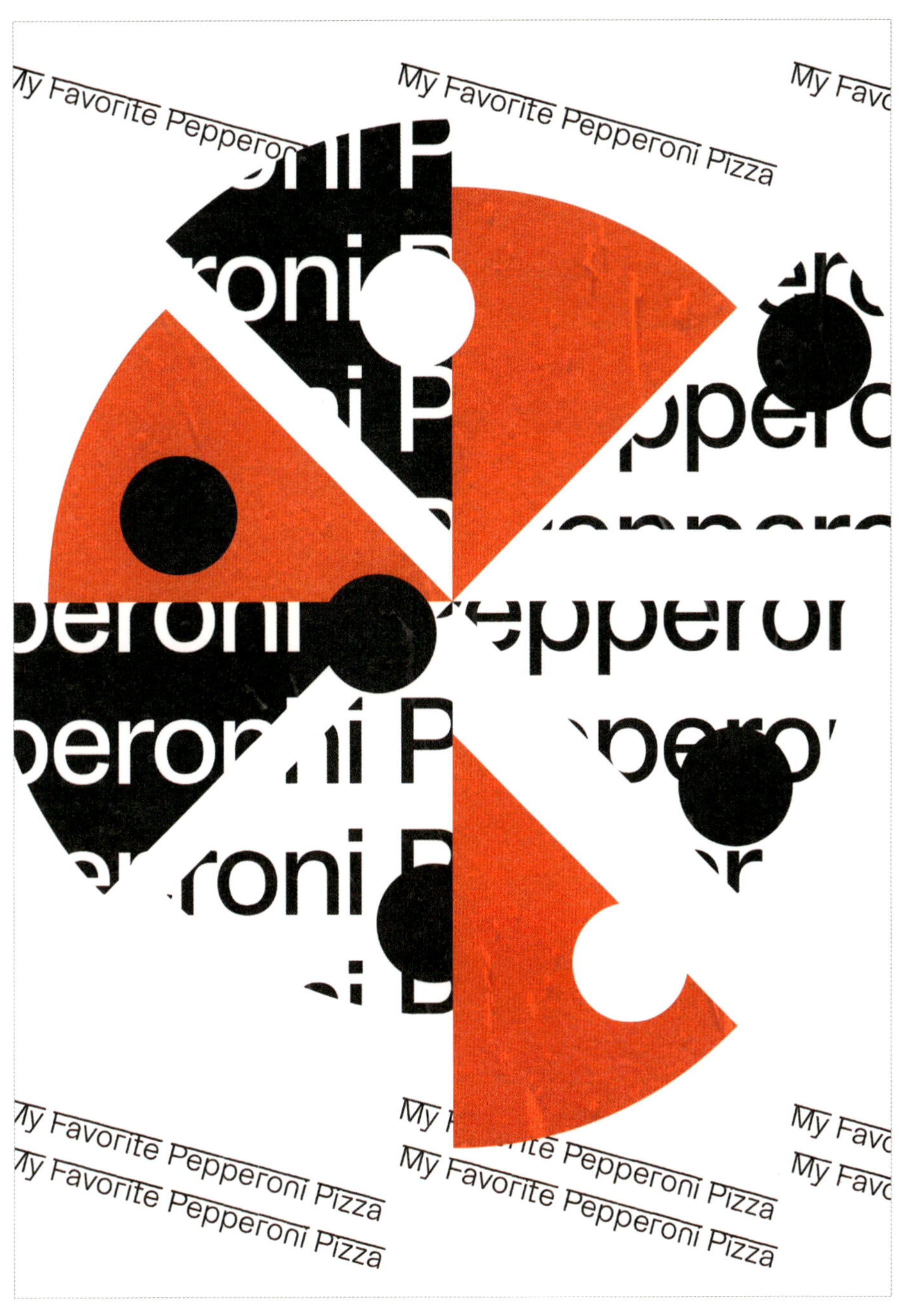

● Why Red? ● The designer intended to evoke an immediate association with pepperoni by using the color red. Without relying on a circular shape, the red color itself is meant to remind people of pepperoni pizza. Using restrained colors, the designer efficiently maximized abstraction.

You and I, tiki-taka • The Korea Disability Art & Culture Center hosted the reporting meeting "I - eum." For this event, graphics and spaces were designed and produced. The primary exhibition graphic, created in 2021, features a graphic display of the young disabled artists' tiki-taka.

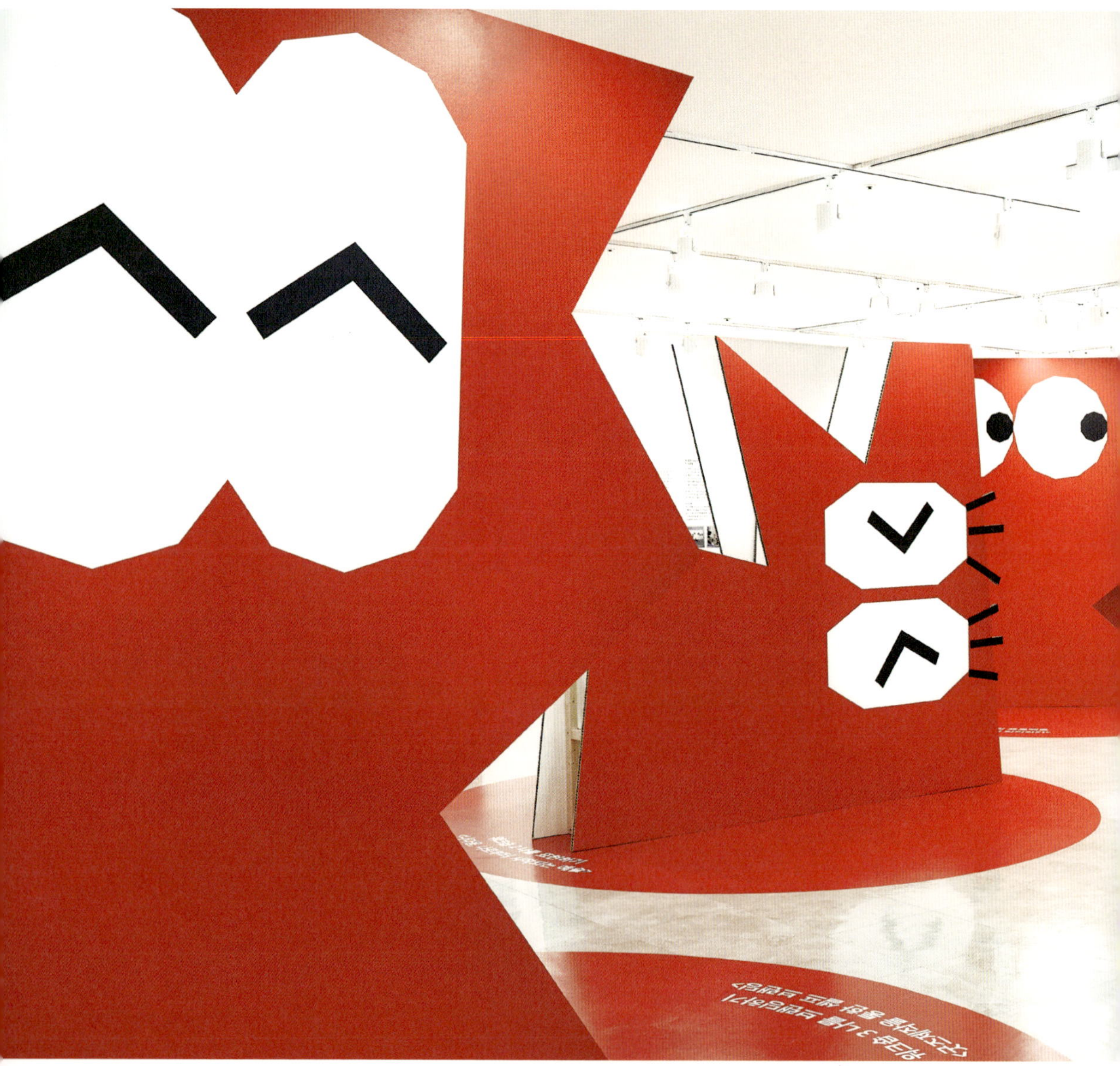

• Design Studio: MAUM STUDIO • Art Direction: Dalwoo Lee • Graphic Design: Yoonji Lee, Jaewon Chung

● Why Red? ● The designer incorporated red into the project with the simple goal of standing out. The intention was to generate increasing interest in showcasing artworks created by disabled individuals, and for that, a bold color choice was deemed necessary.

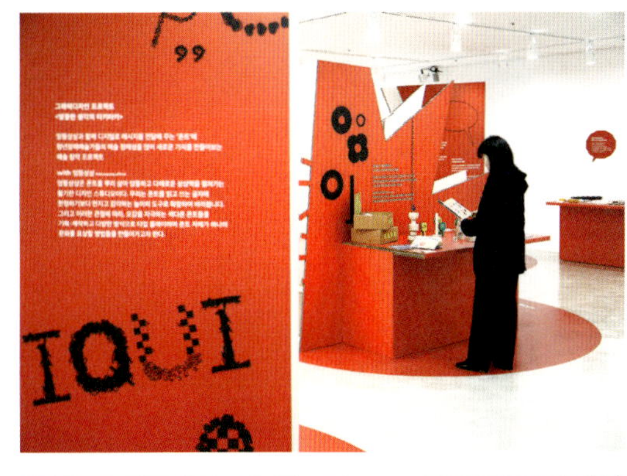

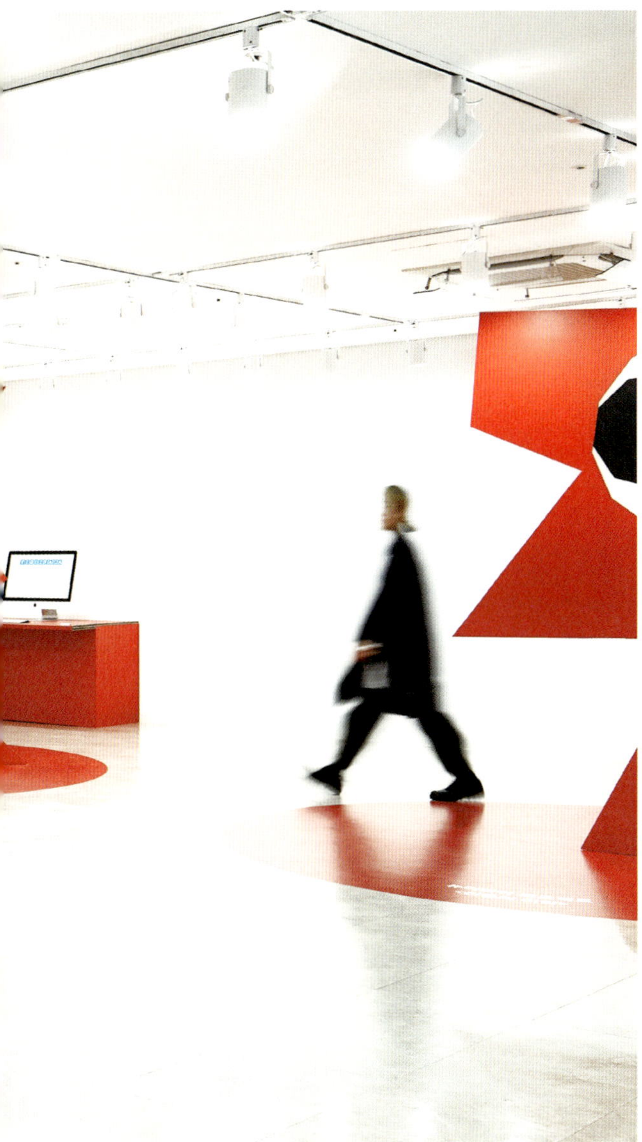

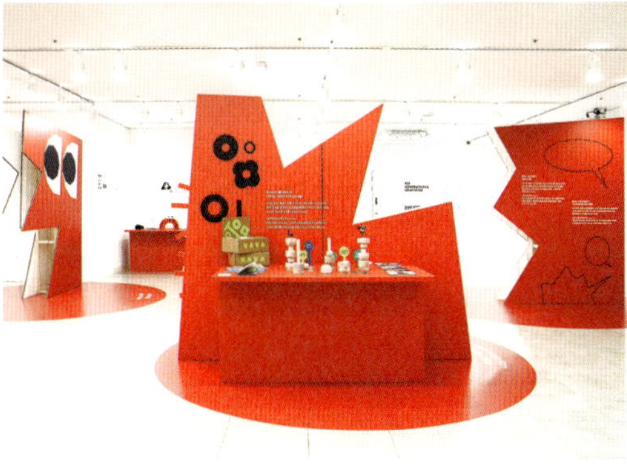

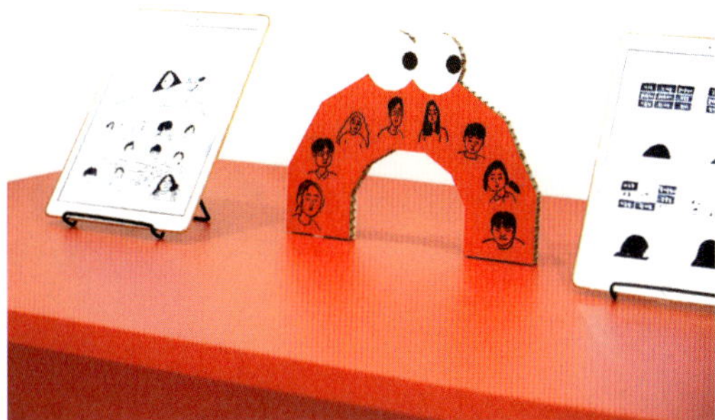

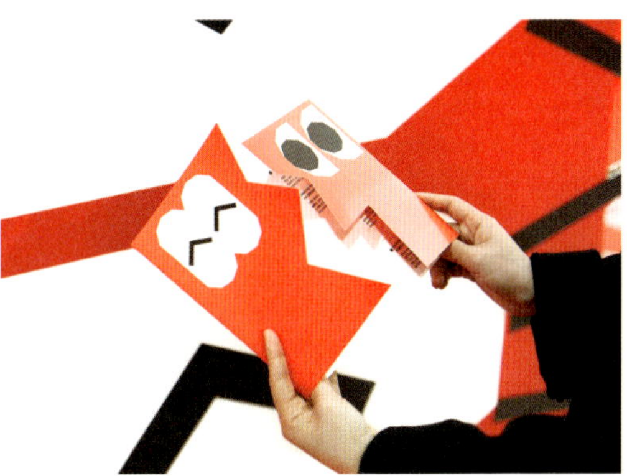

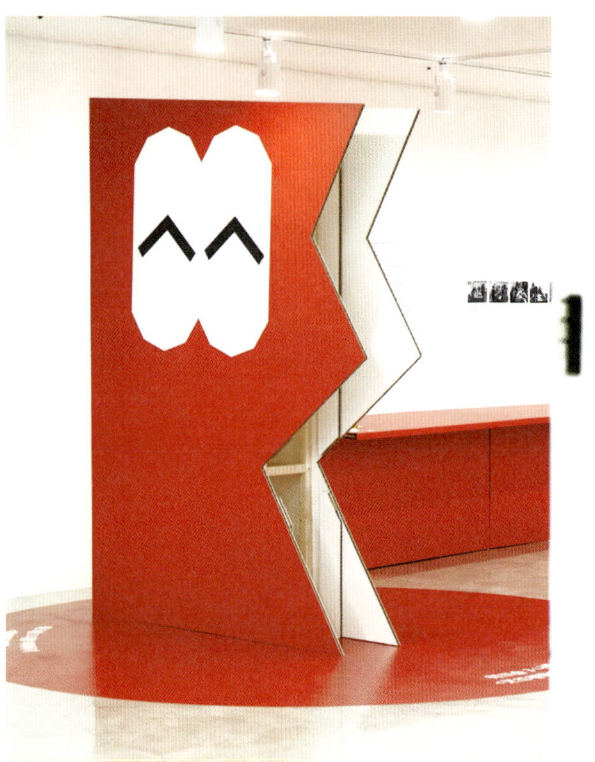

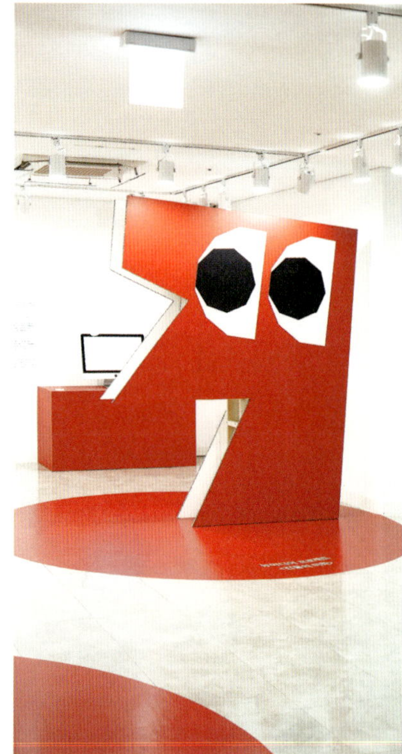

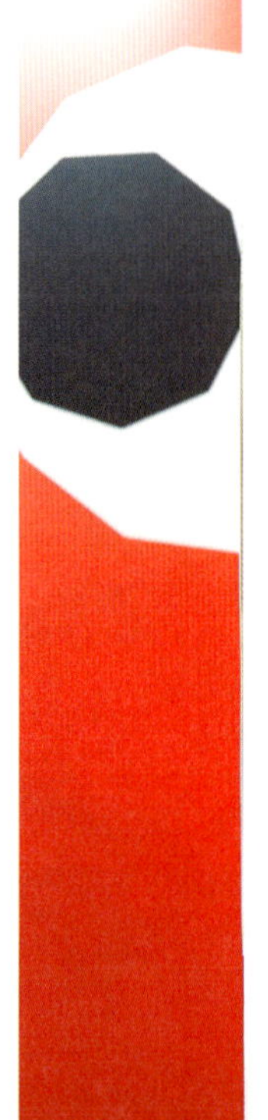

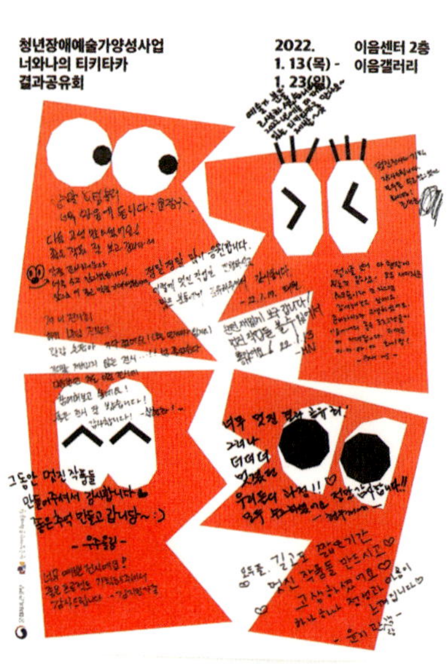

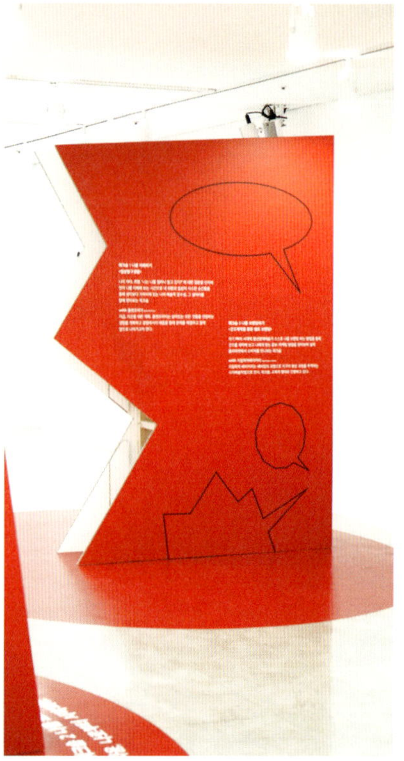

● Space Design: Gyeongjin Kim ● Client: Korea Disability Art & Culture Center

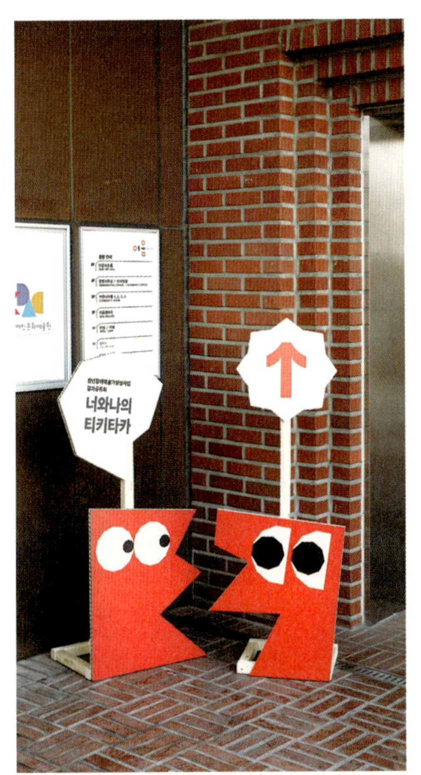
너와나의
티키타카

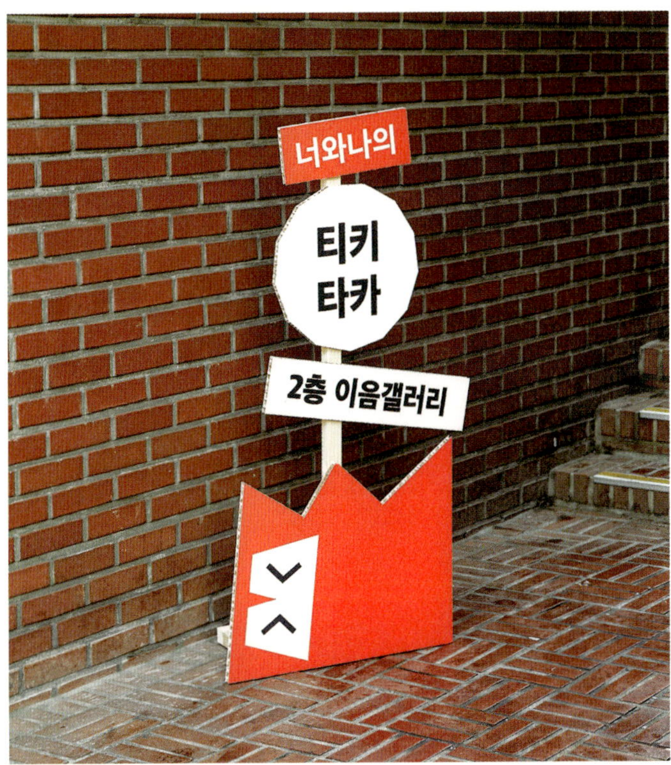
너와나의
티키
타카
2층 이음갤러리

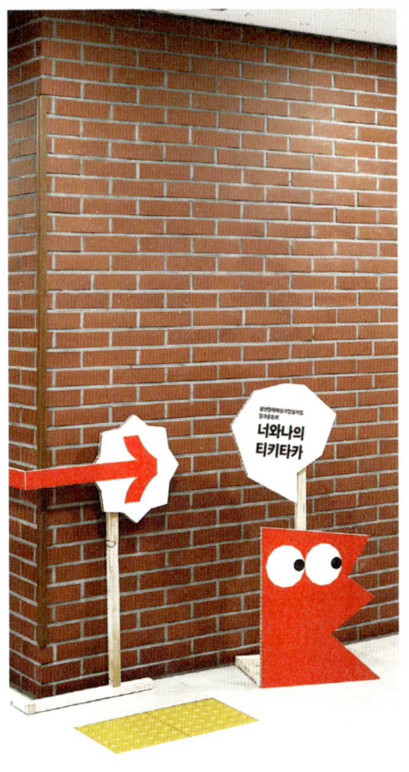
너와나의
티키타카

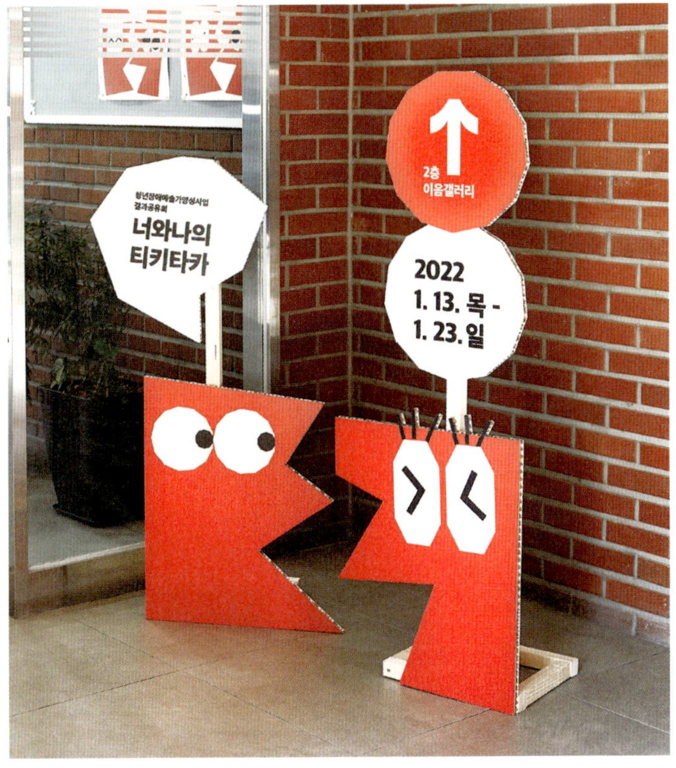
청년장애예술가양성사업
결과공유회
너와나의
티키타카
2층
이음갤러리
2022
1. 13. 목 -
1. 23. 일

Red Matching

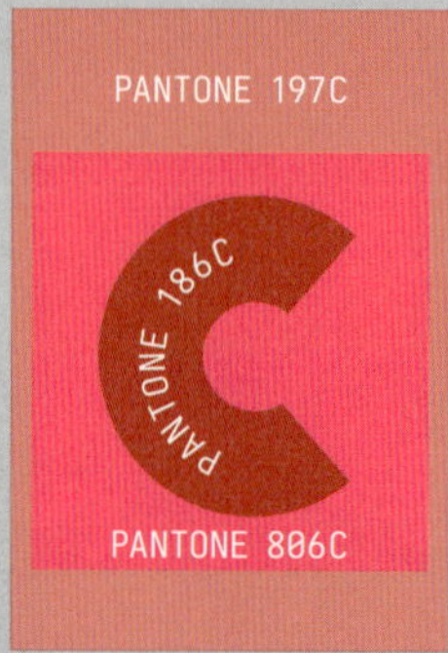

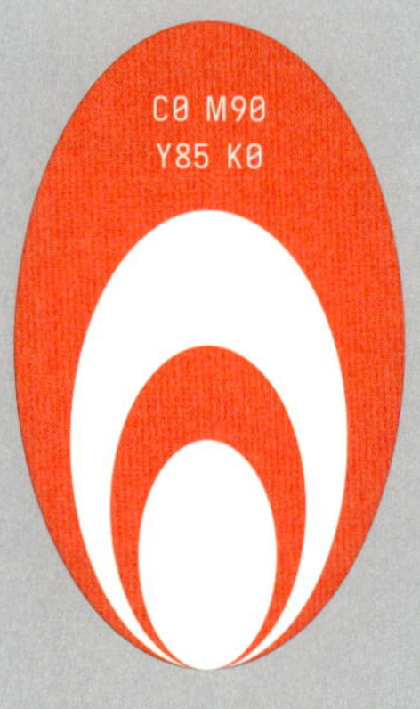

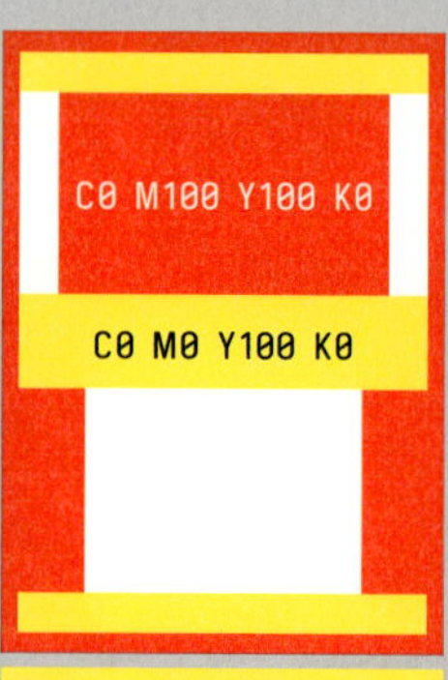

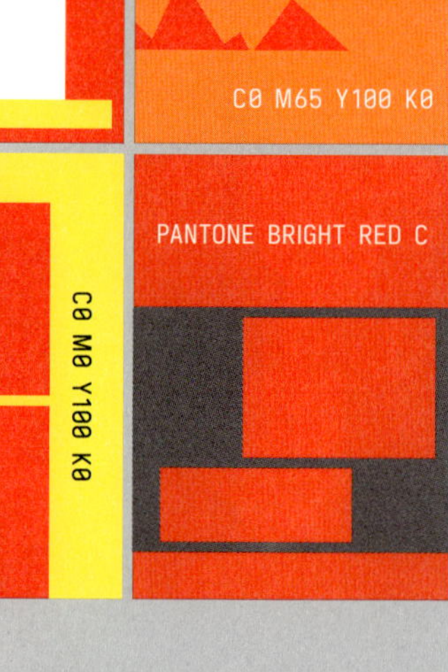

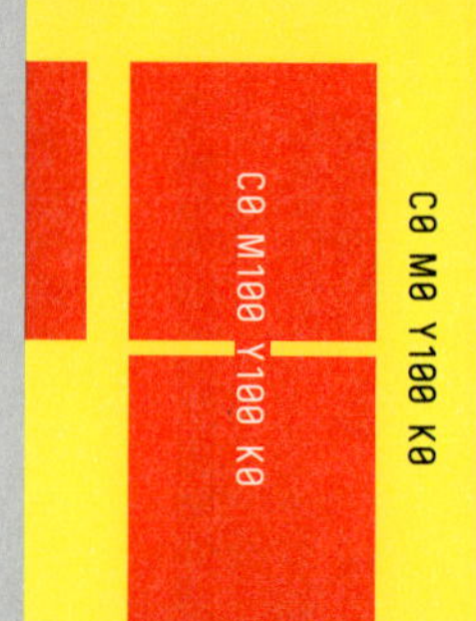

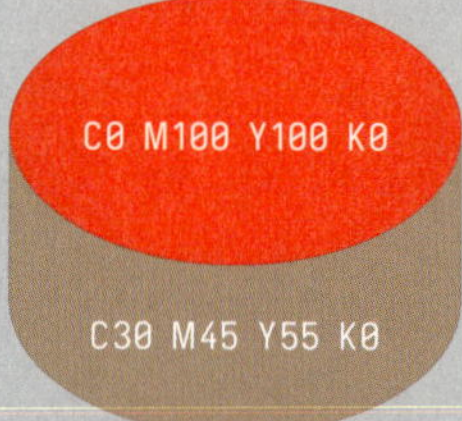

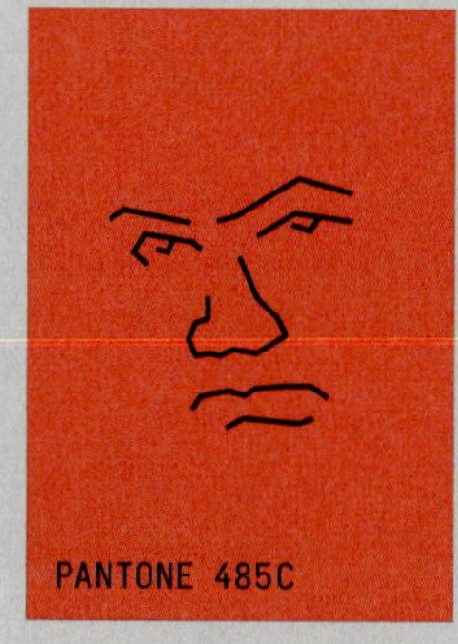

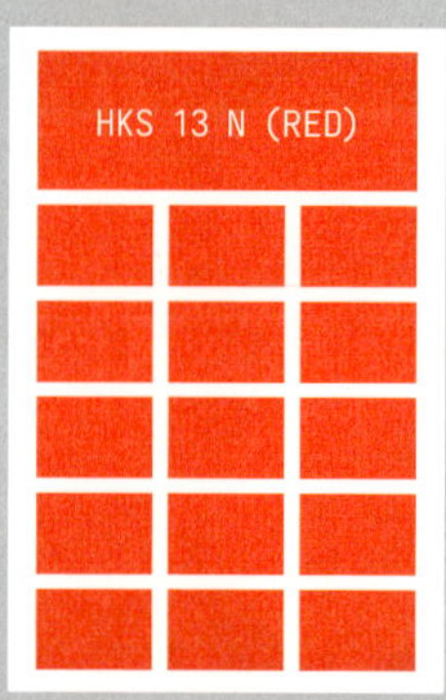

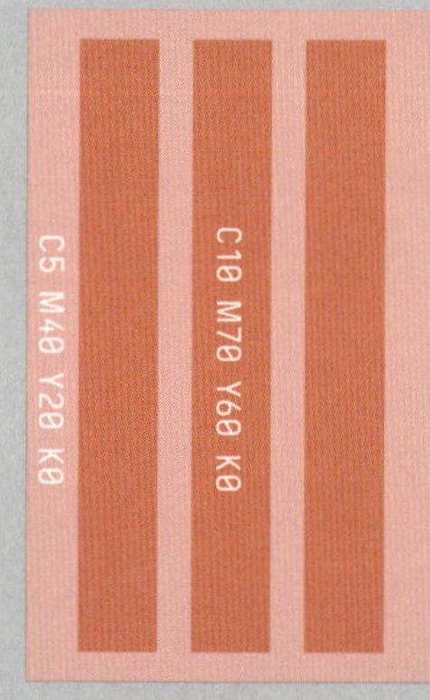

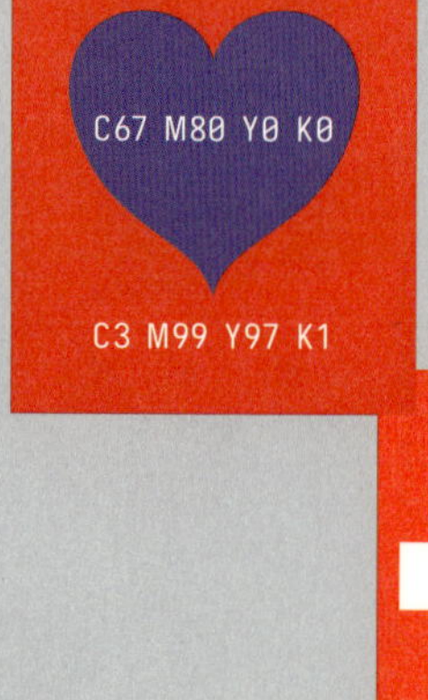

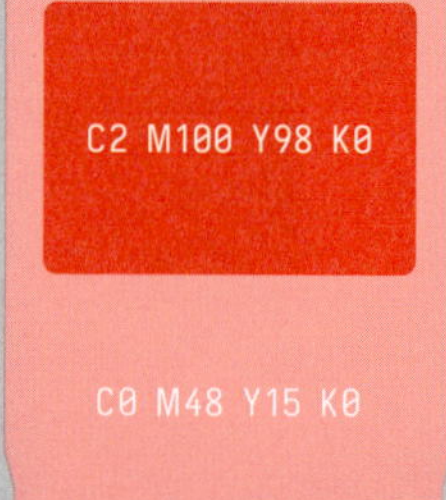

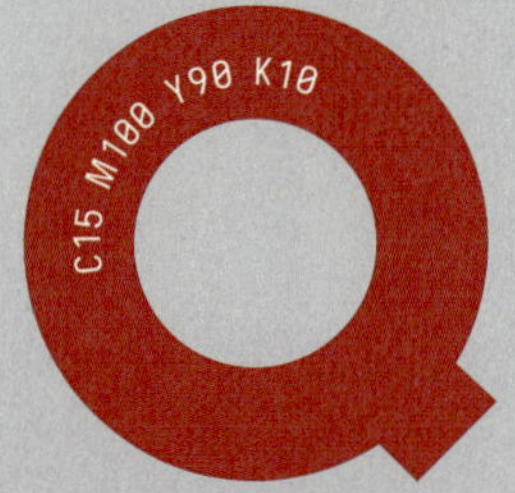

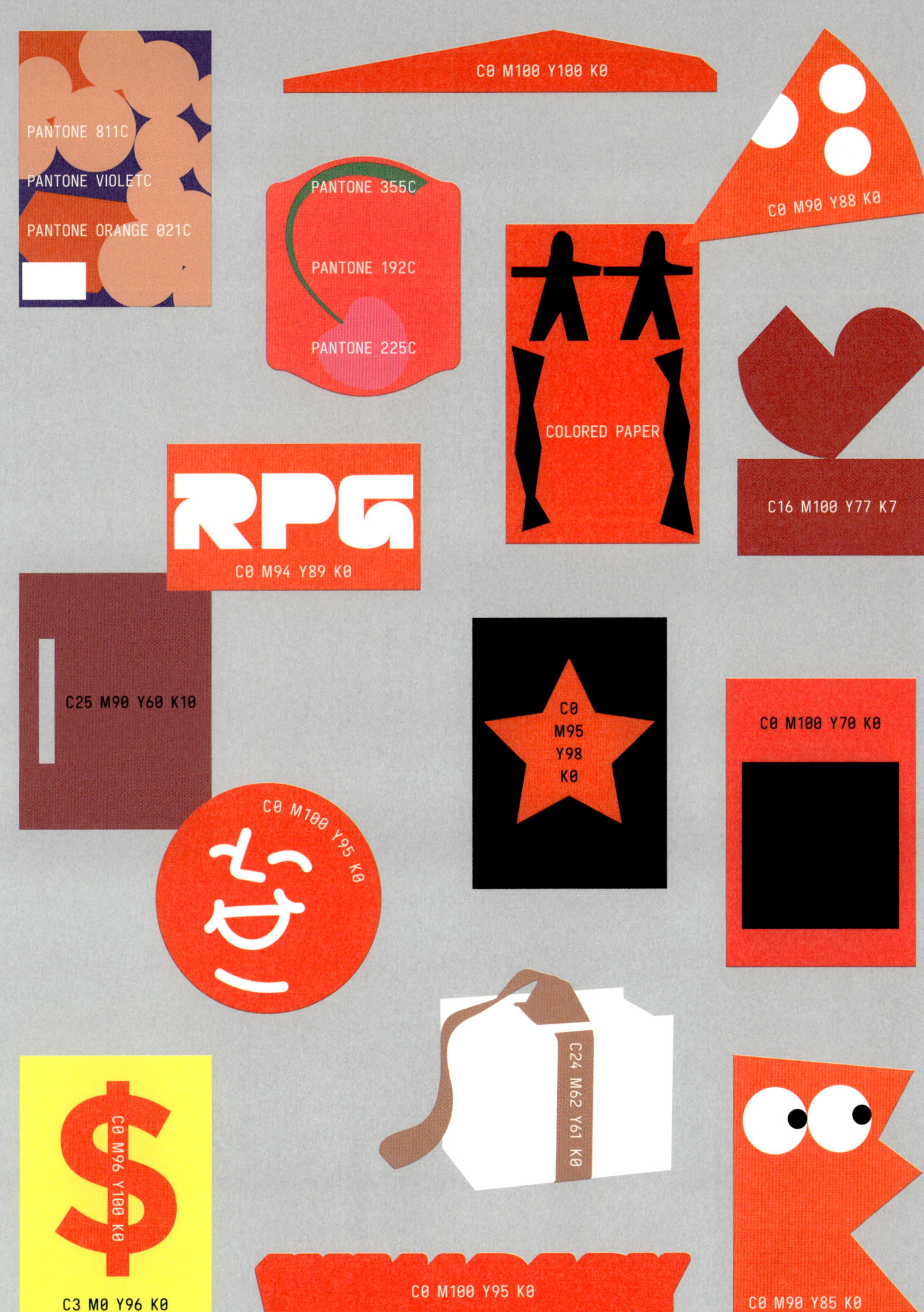
PANTONE 811C
PANTONE VIOLETC
PANTONE ORANGE 021C
C0 M100 Y100 K0
PANTONE 355C
PANTONE 192C
PANTONE 225C
C0 M90 Y88 K0
COLORED PAPER
C16 M100 Y77 K7
RPG
C0 M94 Y89 K0
C25 M90 Y60 K10
C0
M95
Y98
K0
C0 M100 Y70 K0
C0 M100 Y95 K0
C24 M62 Y61 K0
C0 M96 Y100 K0
C3 M0 Y96 K0
C0 M100 Y95 K0
C0 M90 Y85 K0

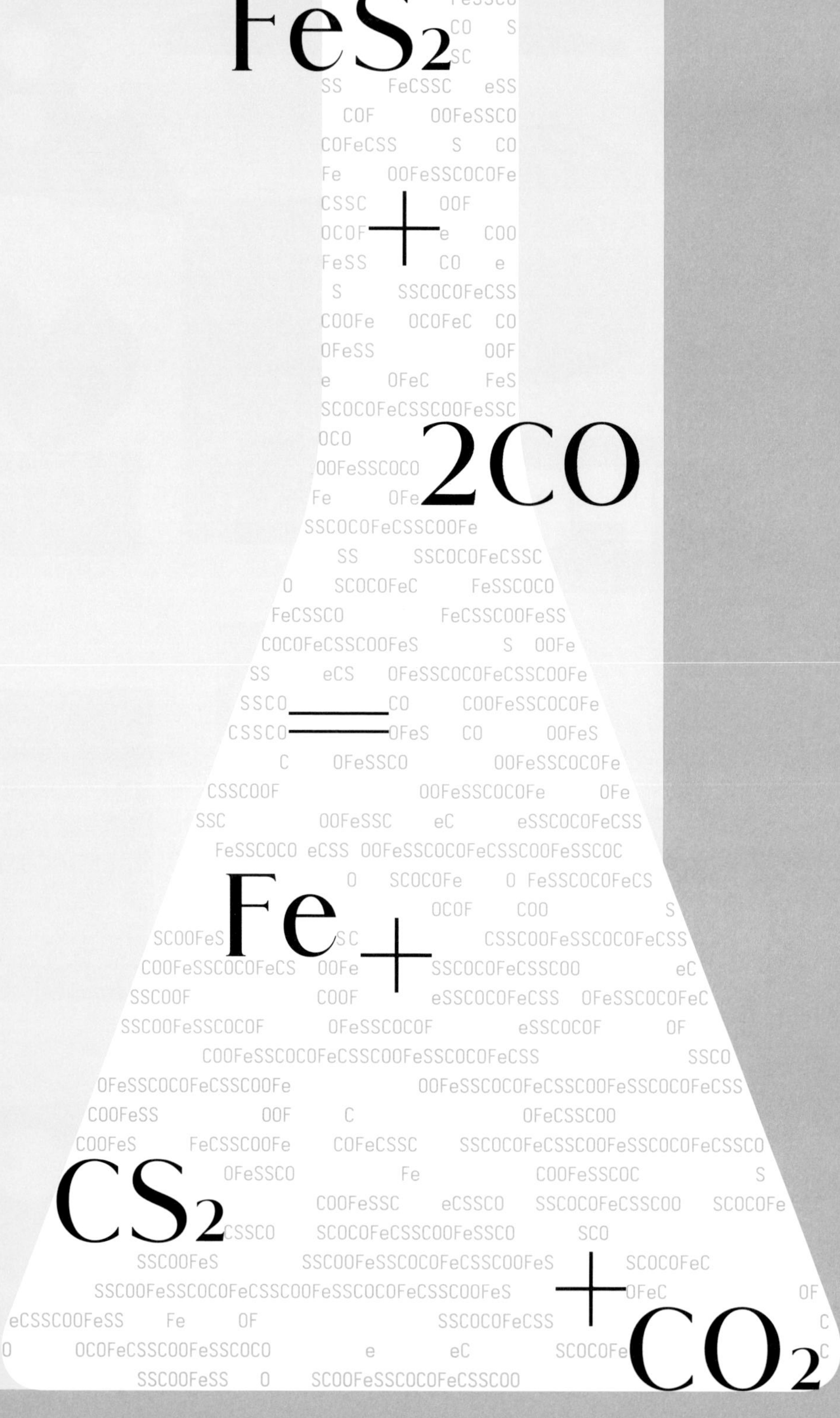
FeS2
+
2CO
=
Fe
+
CS2
+
CO2

Yellow ferrous disulfide reacts with carbon monoxide at high temperatures to form iron, carbon disulfide, and carbon dioxide.

● If you only treat yellow as an ordinary color, you'll miss the opportunity to make this color shine. Designers and artists know its great potential and adopt the eye-catching yellow to embellish ordinary things—similar to iron pyrite. When roasted at a high temperature, pyrite (ferrous disulfide) produces bright and useful iron. Pyrite, bright in color with a light copper yellow hue, is an ancient gem of great ornamental value. It's also the primary raw mineral used for extracting sulfur and manufacturing sulfuric acid. Known as "fool's gold," pyrite was often mistaken for gold due to its metallic luster and gold-like color, making it popular in Victorian England. Besides being polished into ornaments, pyrite serves as a base for jewelry, jade, and other valuable crafts.

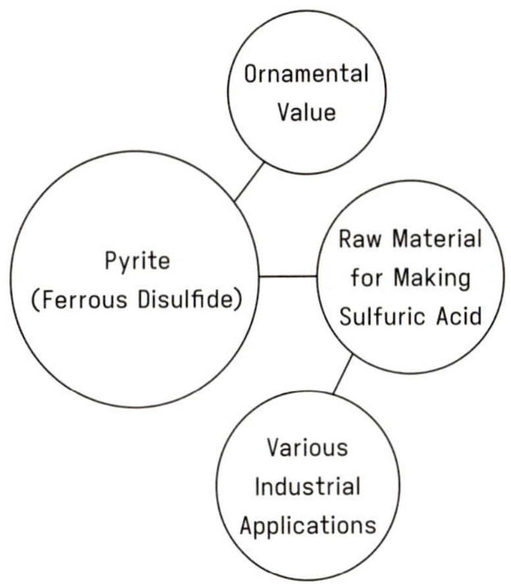

● Pyrite not only holds ornamental value but is also a crucial raw material for extracting sulfur and making sulfuric acid. Through specific processing and reactions, pyrite plays an important role in various industrial applications. Yellow, one of the earliest colors used in human art, appeared in paintings such as the yellow horse in the Caves of Lascaux in France, painted about 17,300 years ago. It was also extensively used in the wall paintings unearthed at Pompeii. In the 18th and 19th centuries, synthetic dyes replaced traditional yellow pigment ores, cow urine, and other materials, becoming the preferred creative pigments for artists. Jean-Honore Fragonard's *A Young Girl Reading* (1776) features a young girl in a bright yellow dress. J. M. W. Turner, recognized as the first to use yellow to render and evoke emotions, prominently used yellow rain clouds as the main background in *Rain, Steam, and Speed—The Great Western Railway*. By the 20th century, yellow was especially valued in the fields of art and design because of its high visibility.

● Yellow arouses different sensory stimuli, making ordinary things stand out. McDonald's famous logo, with its double golden arches on a red background, exemplifies it. Van Gogh, a lifelong lover of yellow, used different shades to portray sunflowers, sun-drenched grapes, and sparkling rivers, expressing both his loneliness and passion with bold yellows.

Story of Yellow

- GOLD — R196 G139 B27 — C27 M50 Y97 K0
- BLONDE — R219 G154 B18 — C15 M45 Y95 K0
- INDIAN YELLOW — R240 G136 B58 — C0 M58 Y79 K0
- ACID YELLOW — R255 G241 B0 — C0 M0 Y100 K0
- CHROME YELLOW — R236 G213 B96 — C10 M15 Y70 K0

Gold

● Gold symbolizes wealth and dignity, arousing the pursuit of desire. As a rare and precious metal, gold has been regarded as a treasure throughout history. Civilizations such as ancient Egypt, Carthage, and the Mali Empire demonstrated their wealth and power through the gold trade. Dazzling gold symbolizes radiance, nobility, glory, luxury, and brilliance—qualities that many aspire to in life. Gold is also used in painting and decoration, such as fabrics woven with gold threads and works of art decorated with gold leaves, which show luxury and divinity.

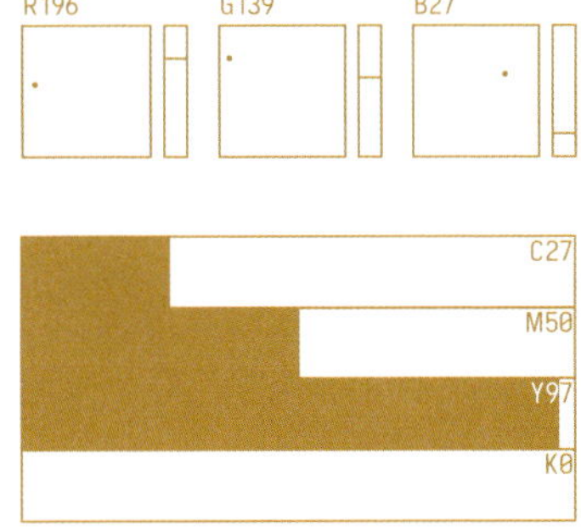

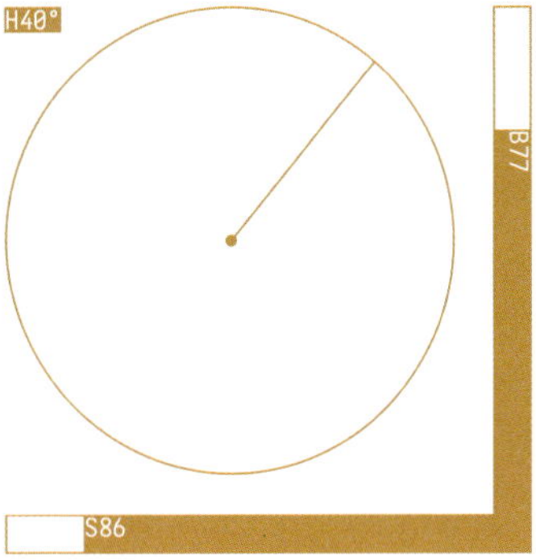

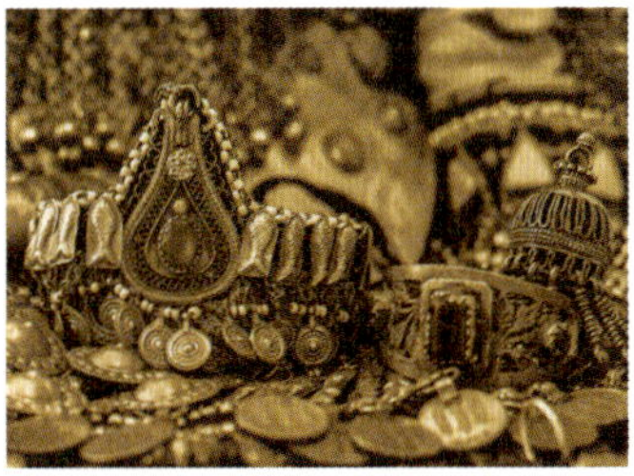

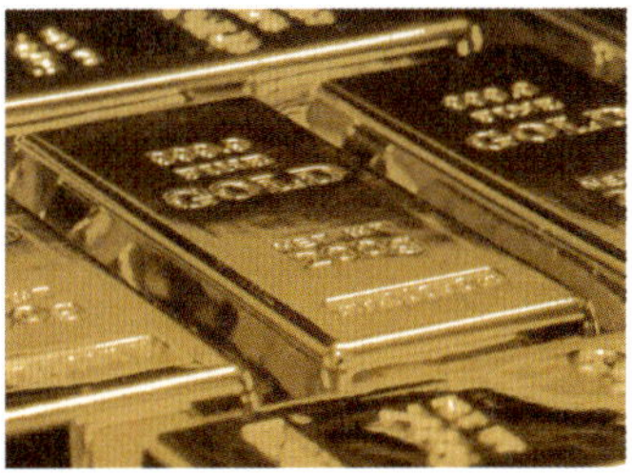

#c48b1b

H40°

B77

S86

L=100

-a

b

-b

a

L=0

L:62 a:16 b:61

Blonde • Blonde has historically been paired with lust and glamour. Blondes are always the focus of attention, and the rarely seen blonde hair makes people envy and resent it more. Blonde hair is often associated with lust. Blonde women often feature prominently in painting, literature, and entertainment, such as Eve in *Paradise Lost* and Lorelei in the play *Gentlemen Prefer Blondes*, or Hollywood star Marilyn Monroe, famous for her blonde hair and charming figure. Gold is the color of chasing, charm, and freedom.

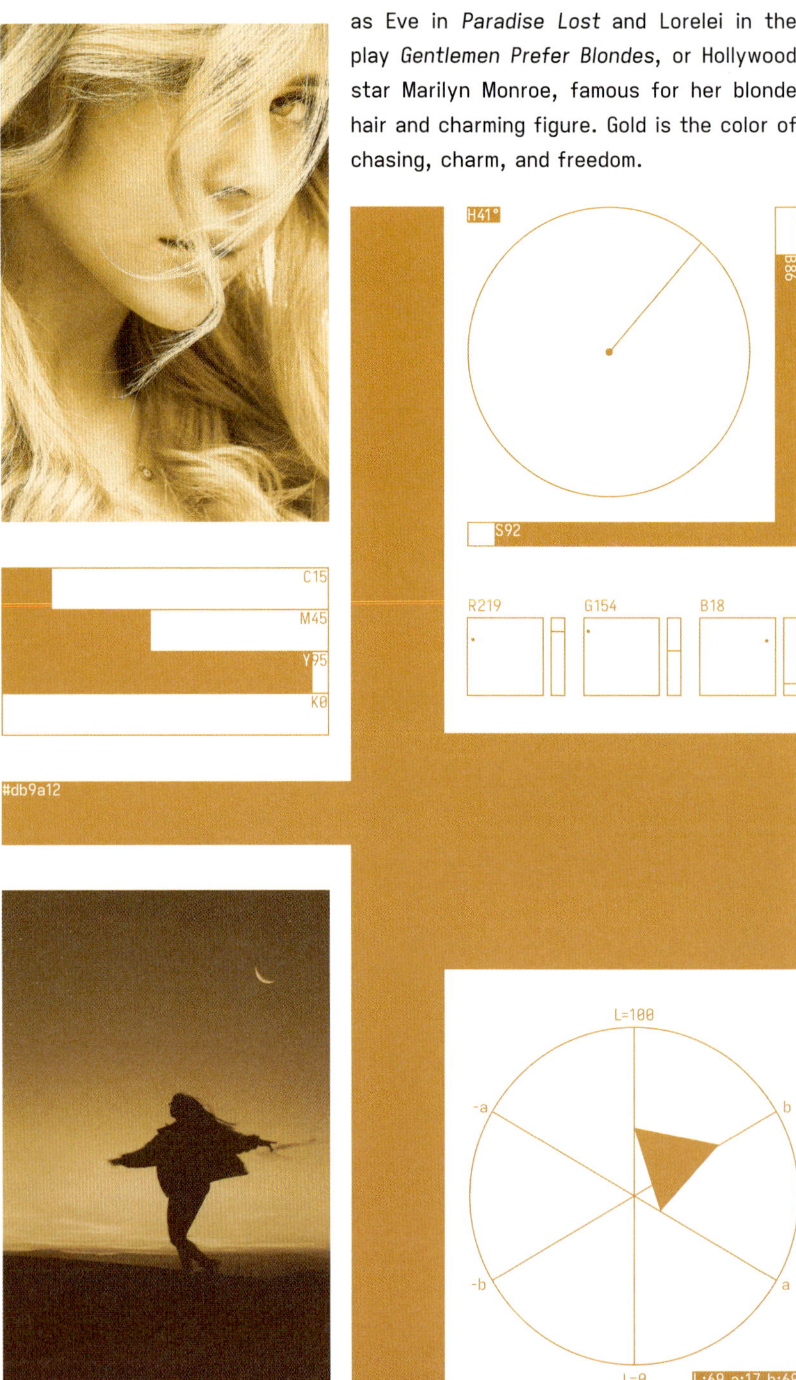

Indian Yellow •

A bright yellow pigment whose history is barely known. In the 17th and 18th centuries, many Indian painters used this pigment, especially those in Rajasthan and Pahari regions. Indian yellow is very similar to garcinia, and for Westerners, this pigment was associated with trade and imperial rule. From the late 18th century, Indian yellow began to flow into Europe from the East. The smell of Indian yellow is unusually pungent and is thought to be similar to animal urine. The truth about Indian yellow is still unknown. Painter Turner once used the experimental watercolor Indian yellow, a fluorescent pigment derived from the urine of cows fed on mangoes.

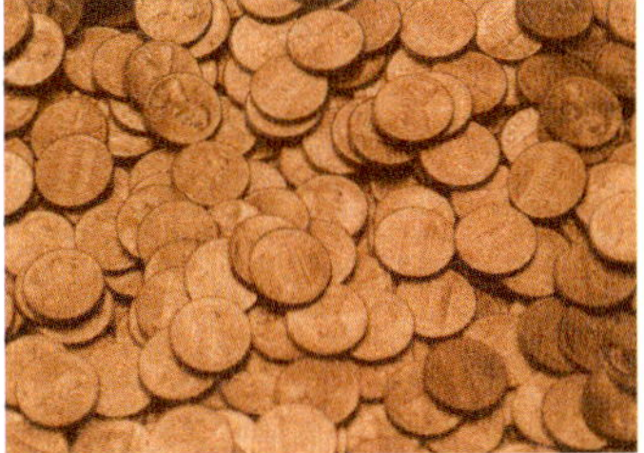

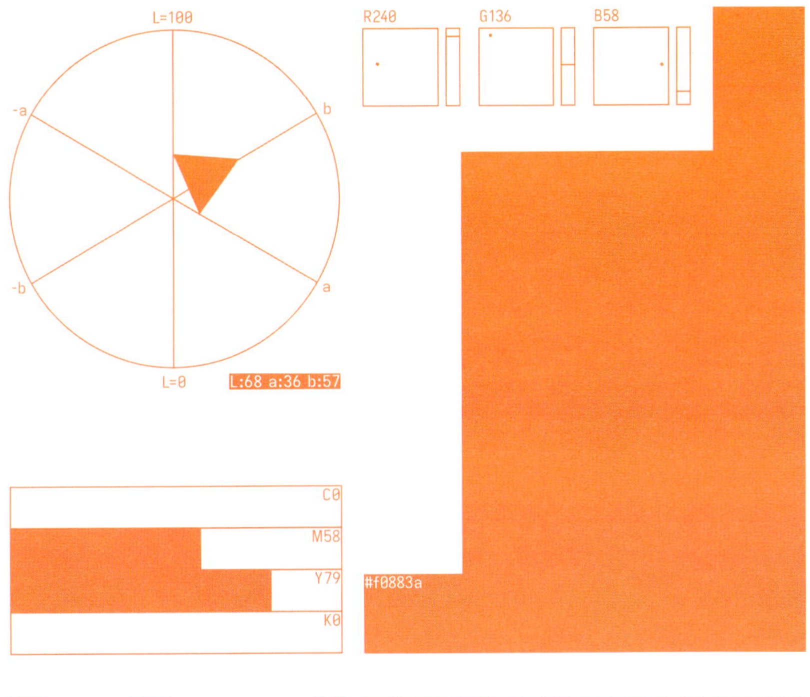

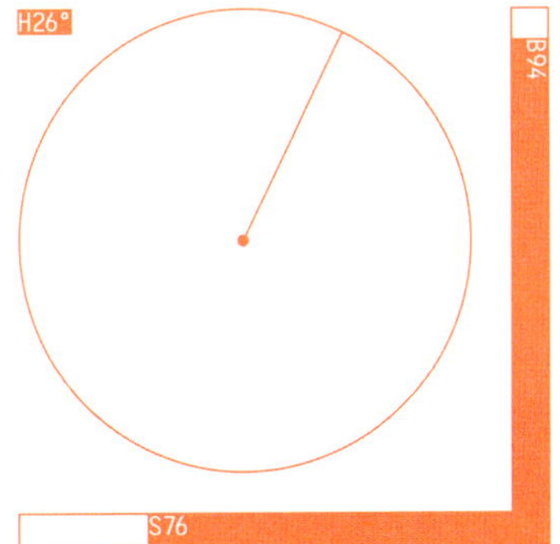

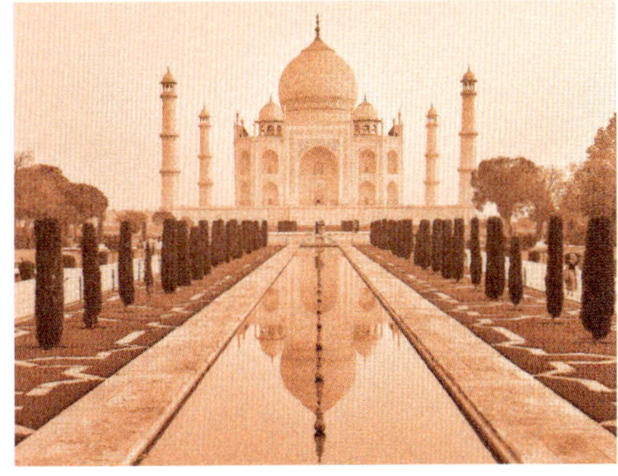

Acid Yellow

• Acid Yellow is a vivid yellow that is closely associated with "Rave Culture" and popular culture. In the 1970s and 1980s, the "yellow smiley face" became a symbol of rebellion and counterculture, appearing on music album covers, nightclub signs, and in pop art. Acid yellow is also associated with acid culture such as "Acid House" music and LSD (a strong artificial hallucinogenic drug), sparking a moral panic. However, smiley emoji has gradually become a part of modern communication, expressing different meanings, and being widely used and internalized as a common means of communication.

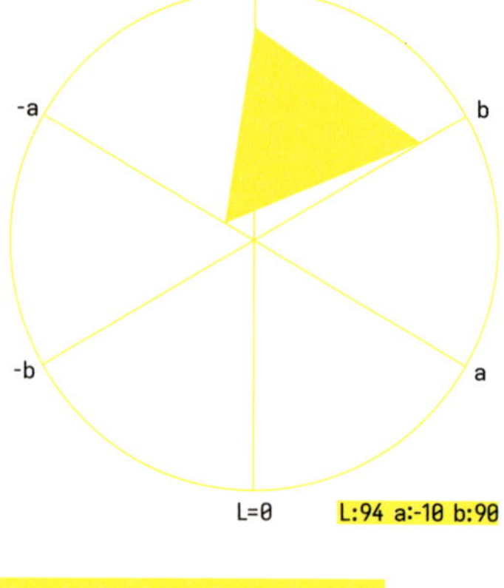

L:94 a:-10 b:90

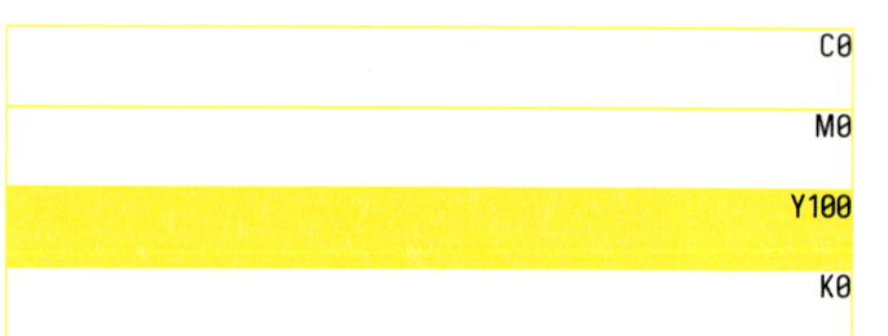

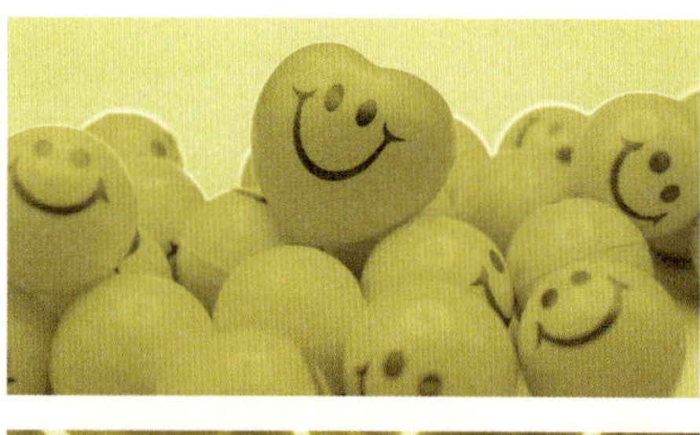

R255 G241 B0

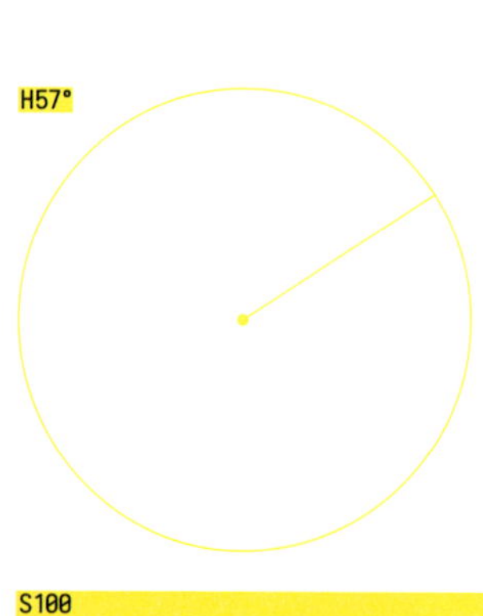

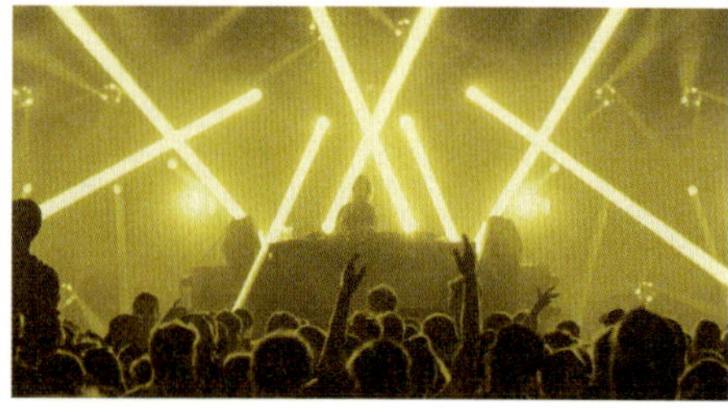

Chrome Yellow

● Chrome Yellow was widely used during the Impressionism period in the late 19th and early 20th centuries. It owed its genesis to the discovery in 1762 of a scarletorange crystal in the Beresof gold mine in the deepest Siberia. The mineral, called crocoite (from the Greek word for saffron, Krokos) by the scientists who discovered it and plomb rouge de Sibérie (Siberian red lead) by the French, wasn't much use as a pigment—the supply was too irregular and the price too high. However, the French chemist Nicolas Louis Vauquelin began working on crocoite and soon discovered that the orange stone contained a new element. It was a metal, which he named chrome or chromium, after another Greek word meaning "color," because chromium salt compounds could come in an extraordinary variety of hues. Chrome yellow became a useful pigment and was widely used by artists in painting. Van Gogh used these bright and cheerful hues of chrome yellow to create images of stars and sunflowers in his eyes.

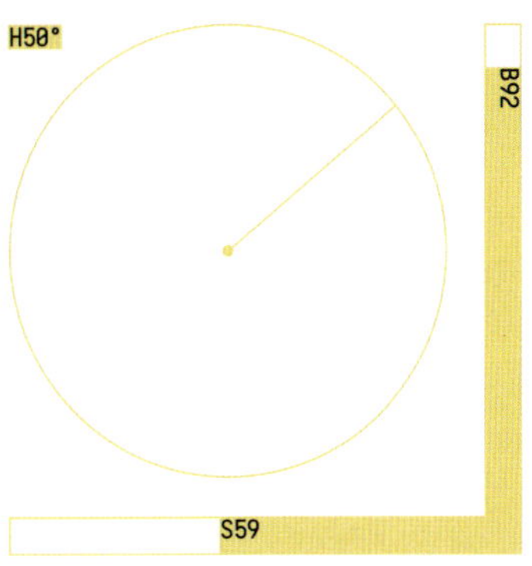

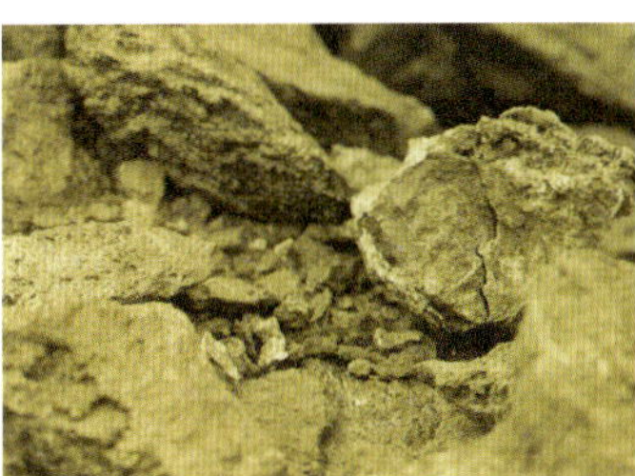

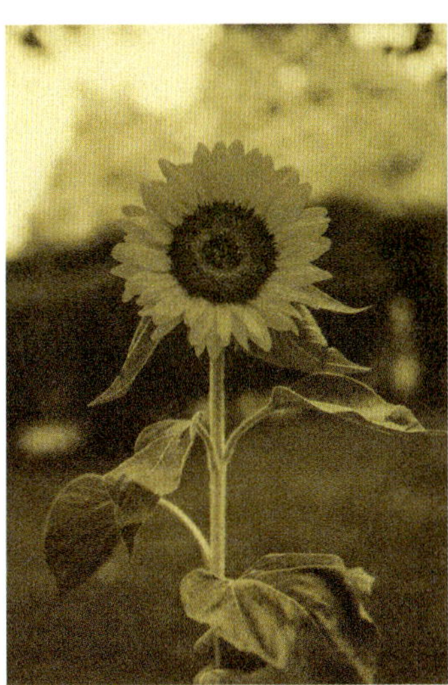

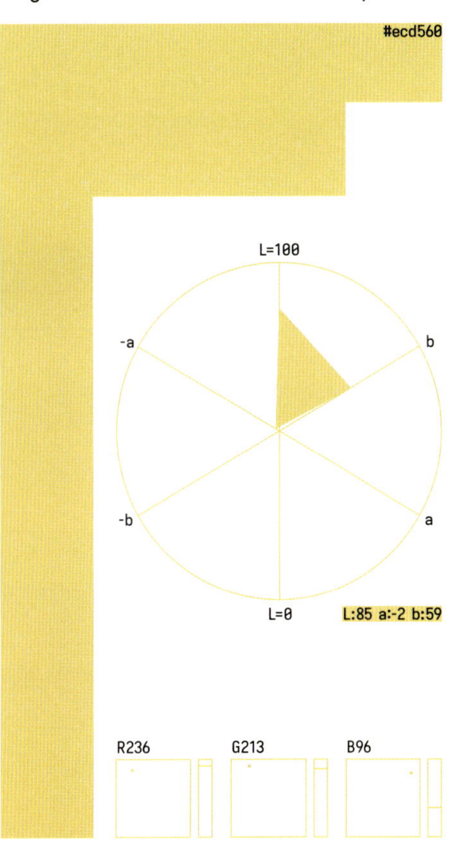

Various Yellow

C0 M0 Y100 K0	C5 M45 Y75 K0	C5 M25 Y55 K0	C20 M45 Y70 K0	C30 M65 Y90 K0	C10 M10 Y70 K0
C20 M25 Y60 K0	C0 M0 Y70 K0	C10 M40 Y100 K0	C20 M20 Y100 K20	C20 M55 Y100 K0	C0 M45 Y80 K0
C0 M60 Y100 K20	C15 M40 Y75 K20	C10 M20 Y80 K0	C20 M45 Y85 K0	C10 M0 Y100 K0	C15 M0 Y60 K0
C30 M35 Y90 K0	C20 M65 Y100 K0	C35 M30 Y70 K0	C0 M20 Y100 K0	C15 M30 Y100 K0	C25 M30 Y70 K0
C40 M50 Y100 K0	C15 M40 Y75 K0	C10 M0 Y55 K0	C10 M15 Y100 K0	C0 M40 Y80 K0	C0 M55 Y85 K0
C0 M40 Y100 K0	C30 M60 Y100 K30	C15 M0 Y100 K10	C0 M0 Y50 K0	C5 M10 Y100 K0	C60 M60 Y100 K10

0 50 100 0	C15 M25 Y75 K0	C10 M45 Y80 K0	C45 M45 Y90 K0	C20 M0 Y100 K0	C30 M40 Y90 K0
0 15 55 0	C0 M50 Y100 K10	C45 M60 Y85 K5	C0 M15 Y40 K0	C0 M25 Y100 K40	C25 M50 Y85 K0
25 25 90 30	C10 M5 Y70 K0	C15 M10 Y80 K0	C50 M50 Y100 K40	C0 M50 Y100 K40	C0 M30 Y100 K5
45 60 100 0	C0 M30 Y100 K25	C30 M60 Y100 K15	C15 M5 Y100 K0	C0 M60 Y100 K50	C0 M15 Y60 K0
25 25 100 0	C60 M60 Y100 K0	C30 M20 Y100 K0	C25 M50 Y90 K0	C15 M15 Y100 K0	C5 M65 Y100 K0
50 45 90 10	C35 M60 Y100 K0	C50 M60 Y100 K10	C15 M10 Y100 K0	C0 M60 Y80 K0	C0 M15 Y80 K0

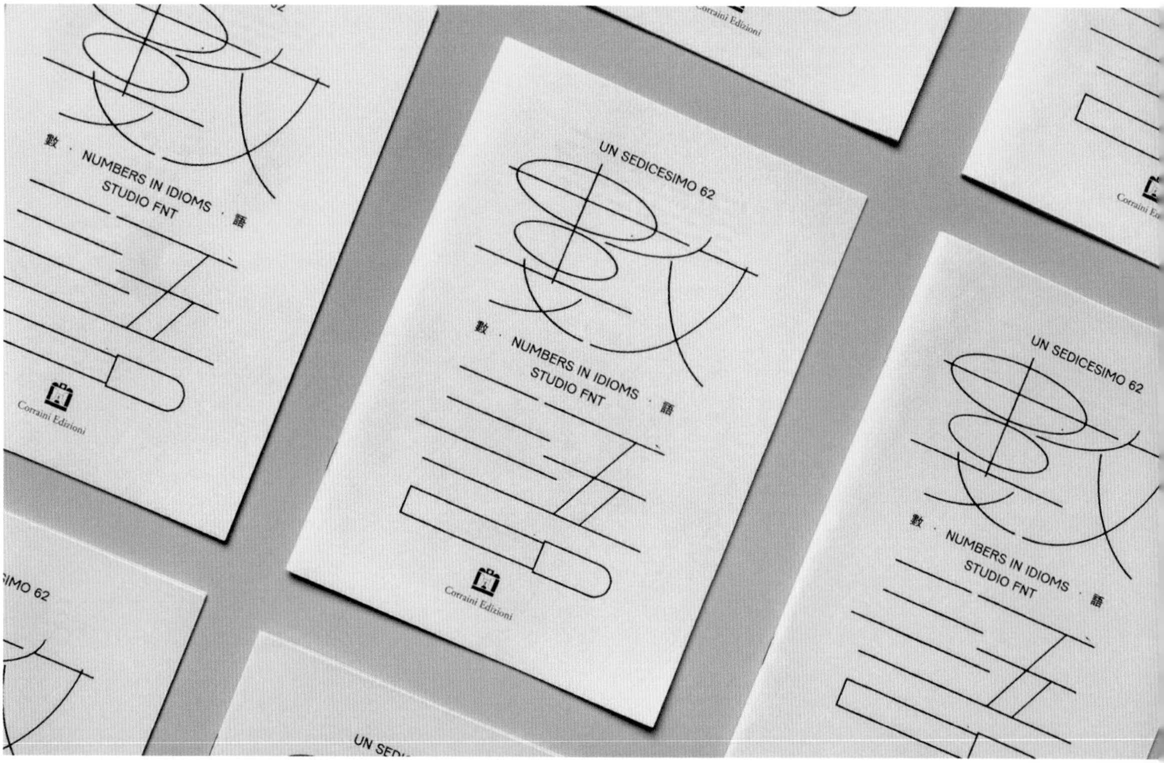

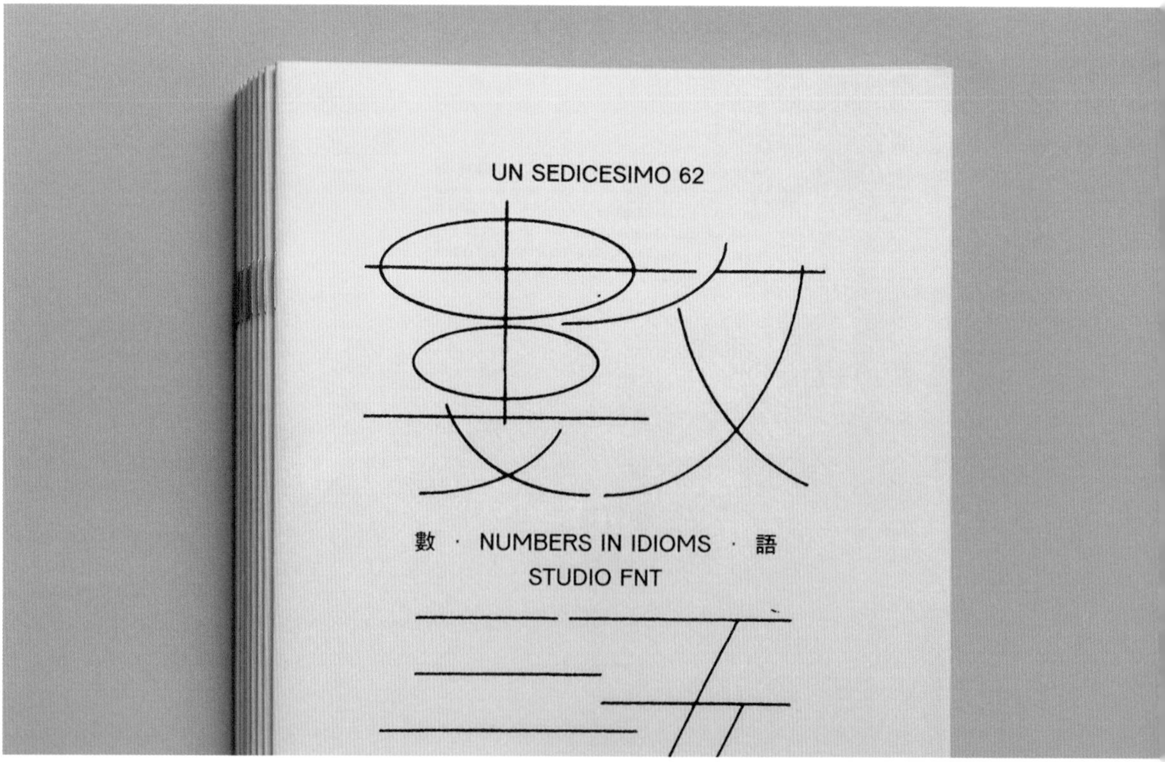

● Design Studio: **Studio fnt** ● Designer: **Jaemin Lee, Heesun Kim** ● Client: **Corraini Edizioni**

Un Sedicesimo 62: Numbers in Idioms

● Corraini Edizioni publishes the zine series *Un Sedicesimo*, named after the standard paper size. Each edition in the series features a different author, including renowned figures like Milton Glaser and Studio fnt, the 62nd author. With freedom in content and design, designers aimed to reflect their perspectives on Asian texts and culture. They explored idioms incorporating numbers one to ten, visualizing them on spreads. The book revisits ancient wisdom, reconsidering its relevance in today's world.

● Why Yellow? ● The designers' aim was to create a simple, distinct color combination for their work through a minimalistic approach with limited colors. The choice of black and yellow, offering a clear and striking contrast, is influenced by the theme centered around Asian thoughts and culture. Among the traditional East Asian colors, yellow, symbolizing balance and resembling Asian skin tones, is chosen as the main color for its comfortable and clear visual representation, aligning with the theme.

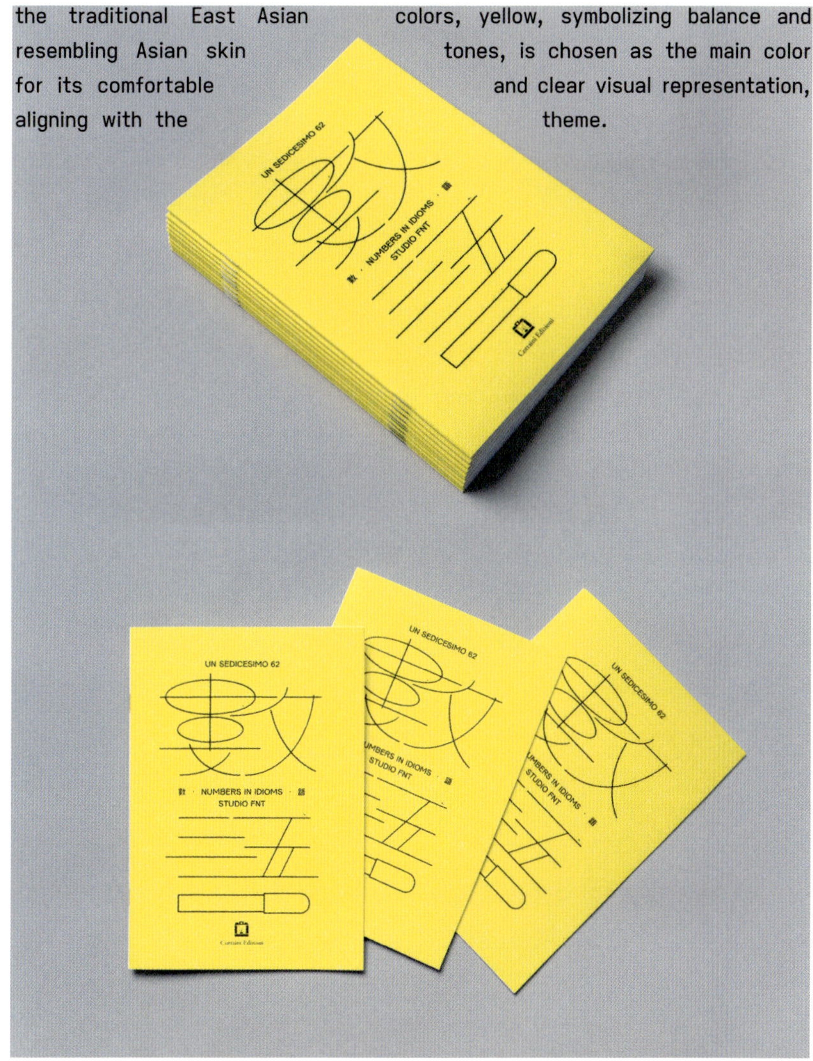

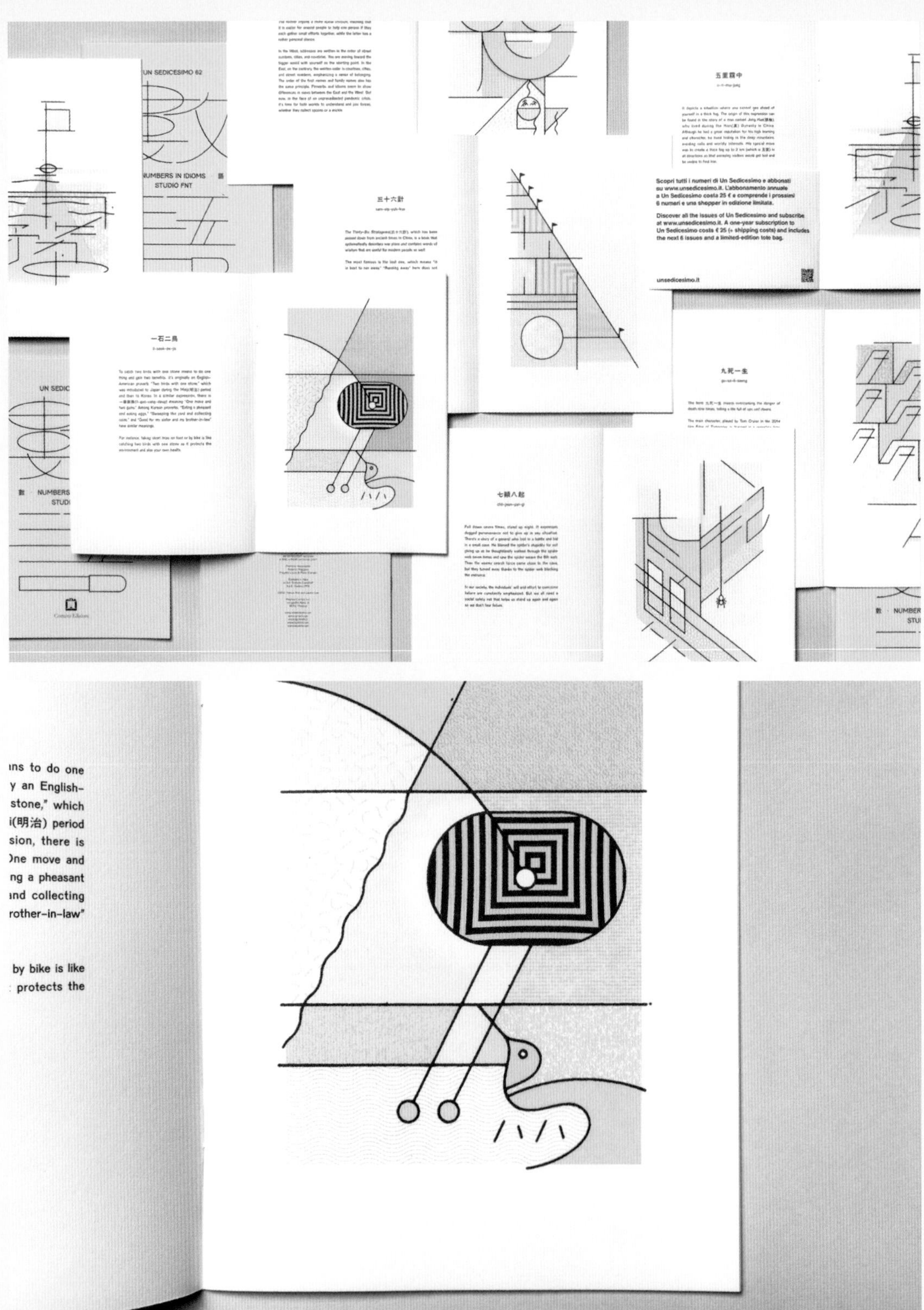
UN SEDICESIMO 62
NUMBERS IN IDIOMS
STUDIO FNT
三十六計
Scopri tutti i numeri di Un Sedicesimo e abbonati su www.unsedicesimo.it. L'abbonamento annuale a Un Sedicesimo costa 25 € e comprende i prossimi 6 numeri e una shopper in edizione limitata.
Discover all the issues of Un Sedicesimo and subscribe at www.unsedicesimo.it. A one-year subscription to Un Sedicesimo costs € 25 (+ shipping costs) and includes the next 6 issues and a limited-edition tote bag.
unsedicesimo.it
五里霧中
一石二鳥
九死一生
七顛八起
ıns to do one
y an English-
stone," which
i(明治) period
sion, there is
)ne move and
ng a pheasant
ınd collecting
rother-in-law"
by bike is like
: protects the

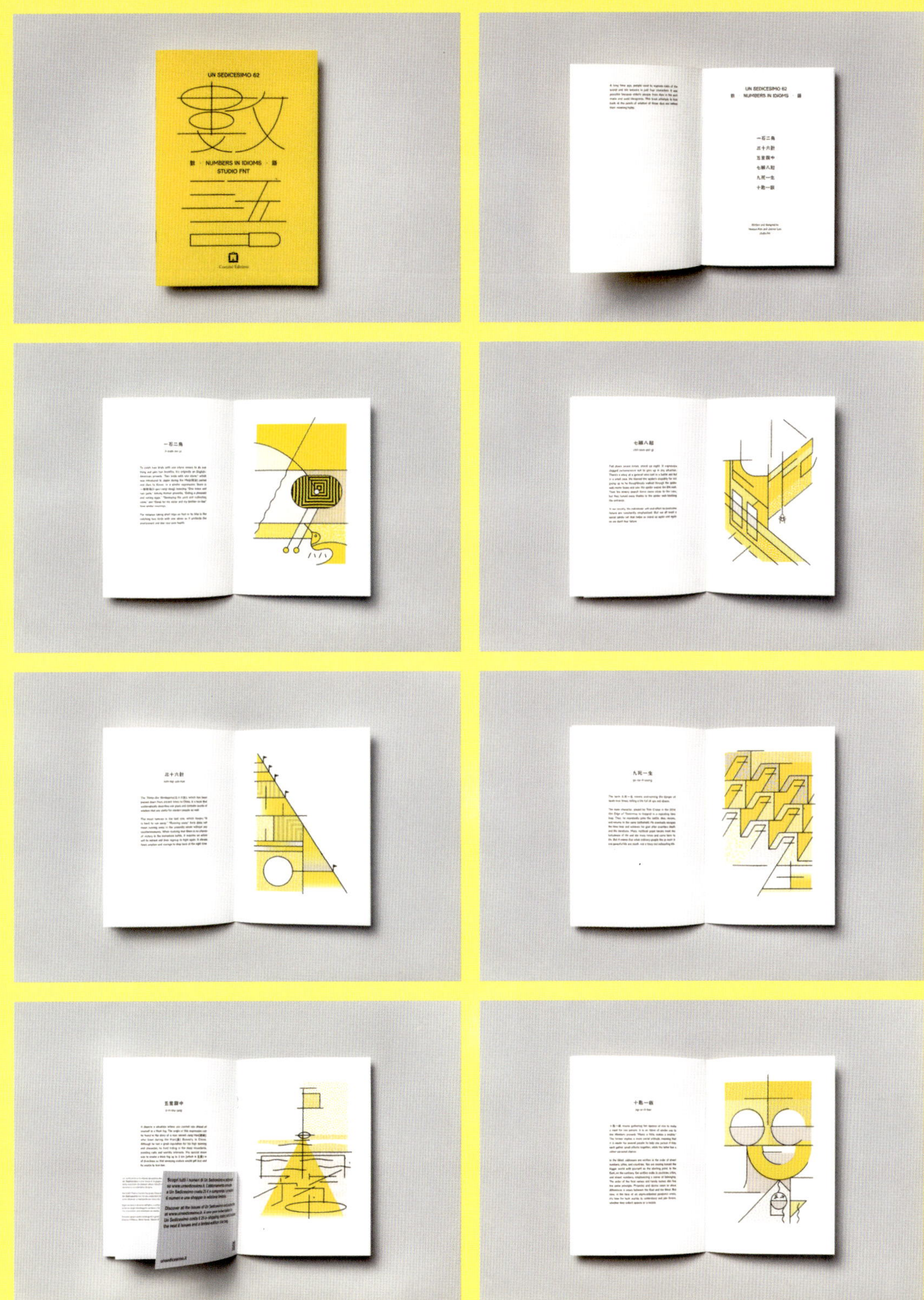
UN SEDICESIMO 62
數
數 · NUMBERS IN IDIOMS · 語
STUDIO FNT
語
UN SEDICESIMO 62
數 · NUMBERS IN IDIOMS · 語

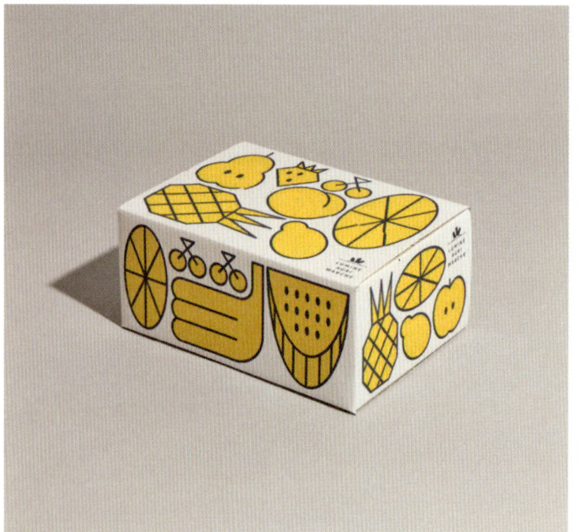

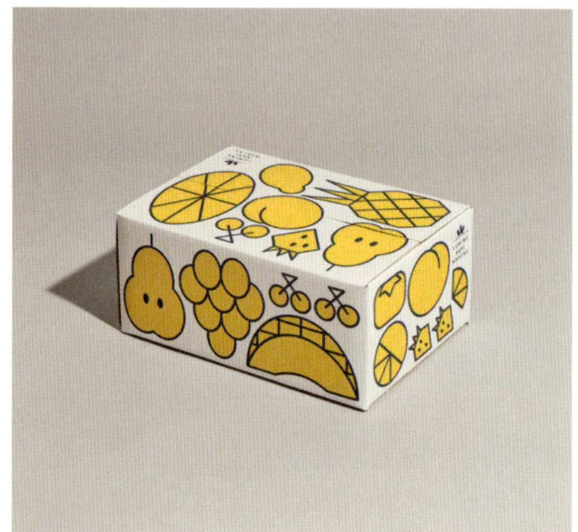

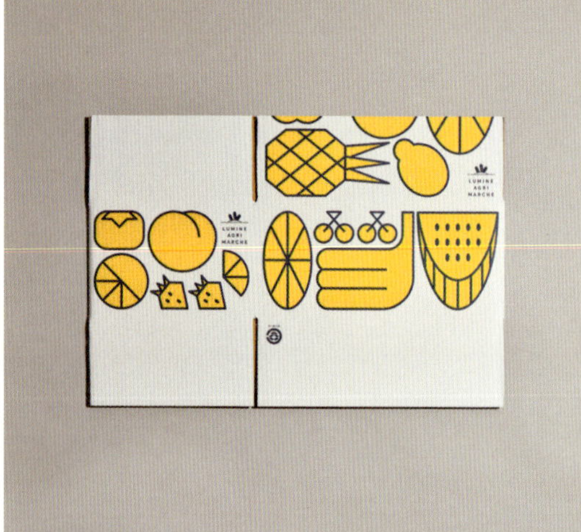

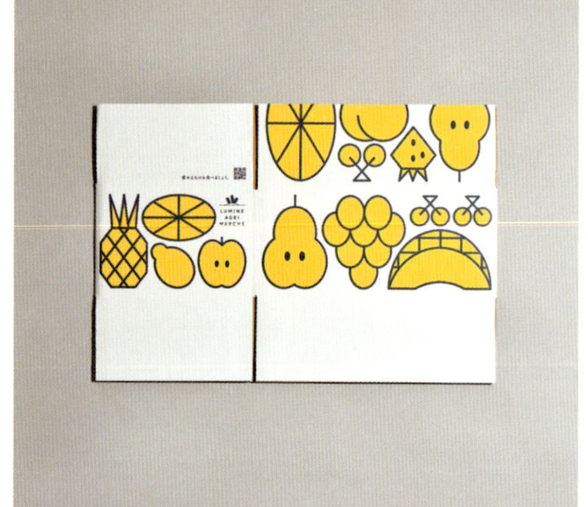

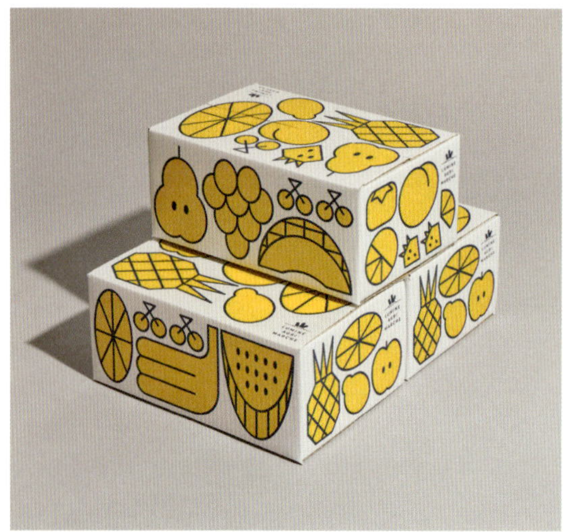

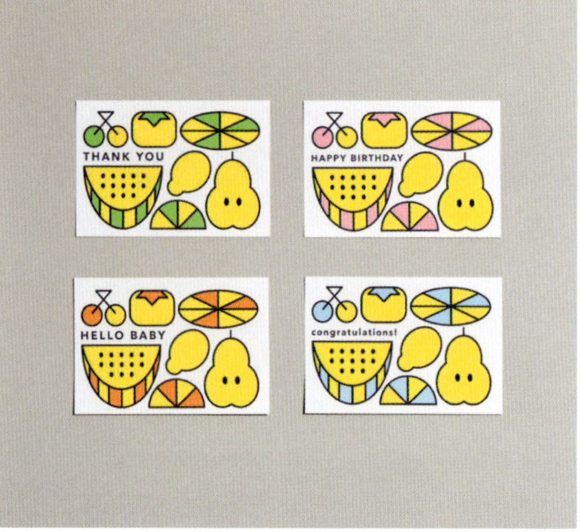

● Design Studio: MOTOMOTO inc. ● Designer: Kenichi Matsumoto ● Client: LUMINE Co., Ltd.

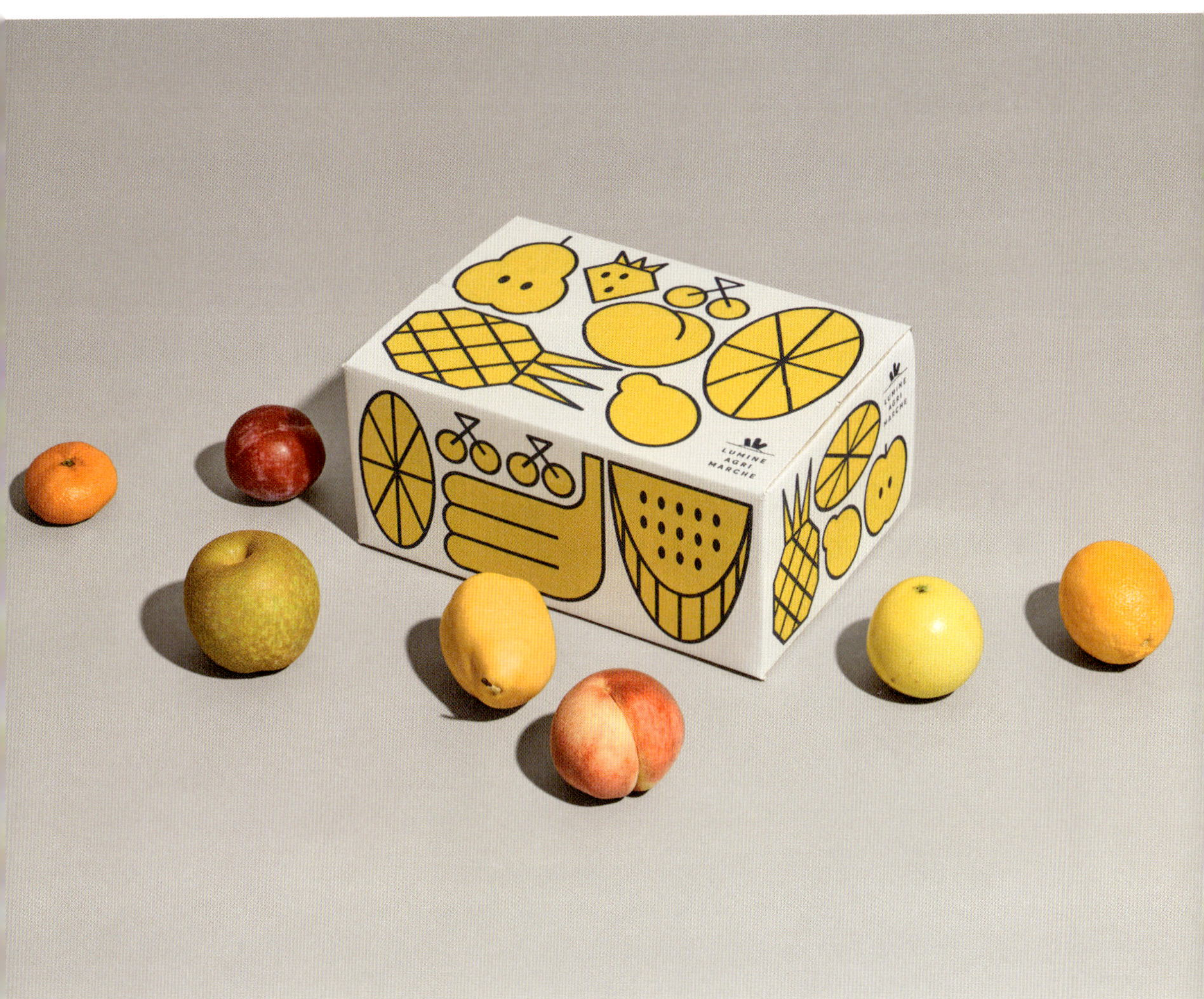

Lumine Agri Marche ● Designed for an agricultural project by Lumine, this cardboard design serves both gifting and transportation purposes, emphasizing environmental friendliness by avoiding over-packaging. Despite its cardboard composition, the graphic representation aims to bring joy to its recipient.

● Why Yellow? ● To maintain the brand image, the design team opted for yellow and navy blue, the logo colors, aiming to convey a fresh impression.

C0 M5 Y100 K0

UFO OUTSIDE

• UFO OUTSIDE is a comprehensive outdoor equipment store. Drawing inspiration from the warning signs on the rear of trucks, this design presents a simple yet impactful visual effect, resonating with clarity and penetration.

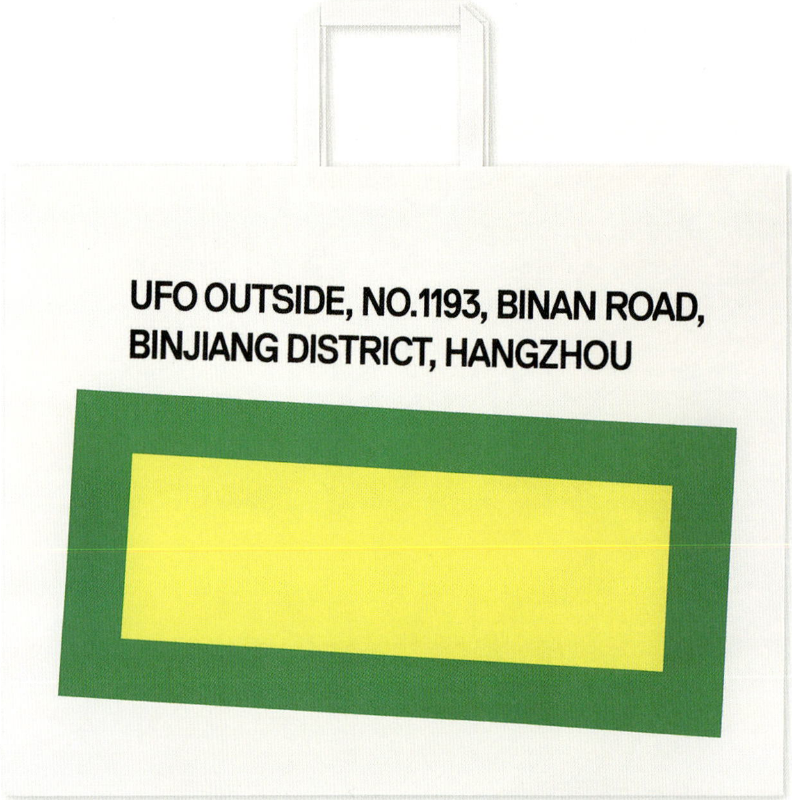

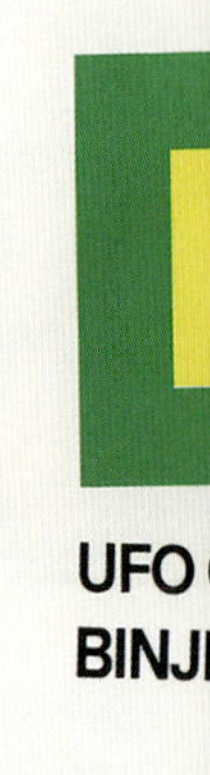

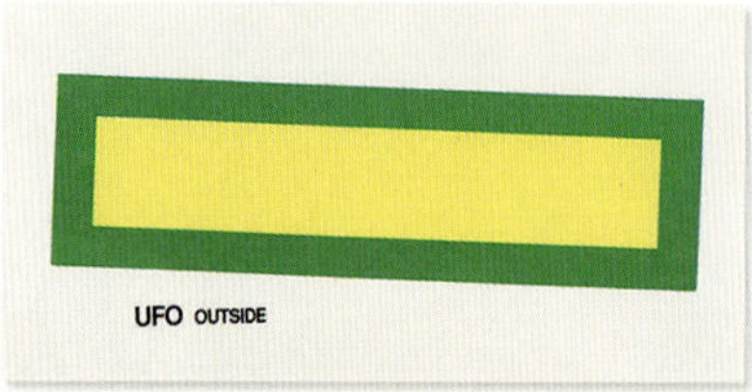

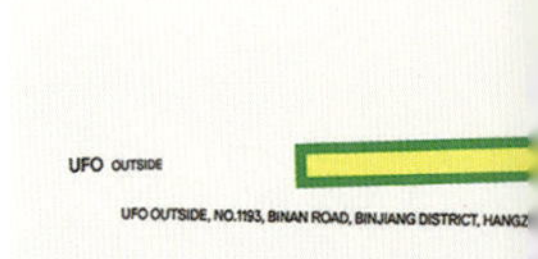

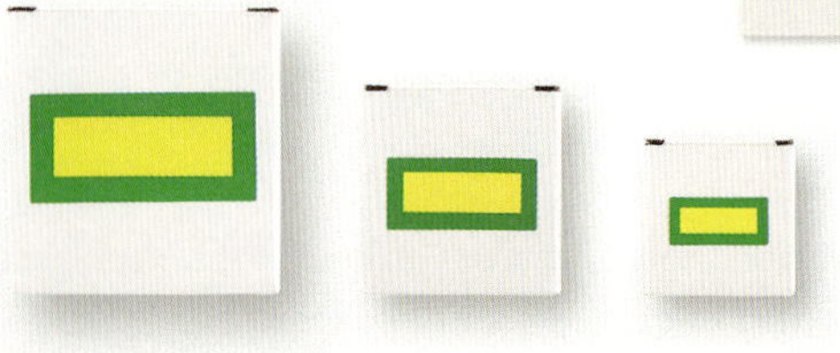

• Design Studio: 702design • Designer: Mei Shuzhi • Client: UFO OUTSIDE

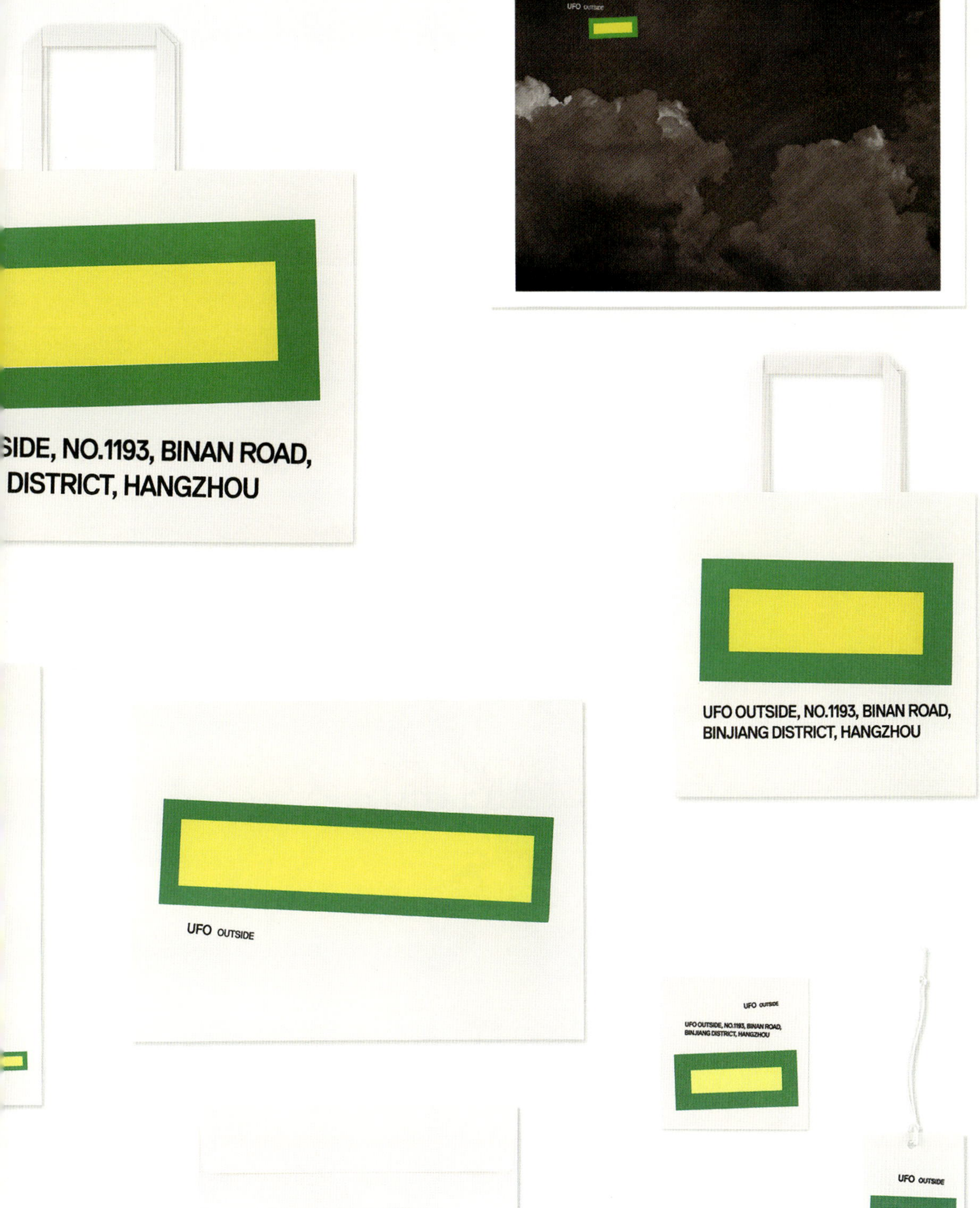

C7 M0 Y100 K0

C100 M0 Y100 K4

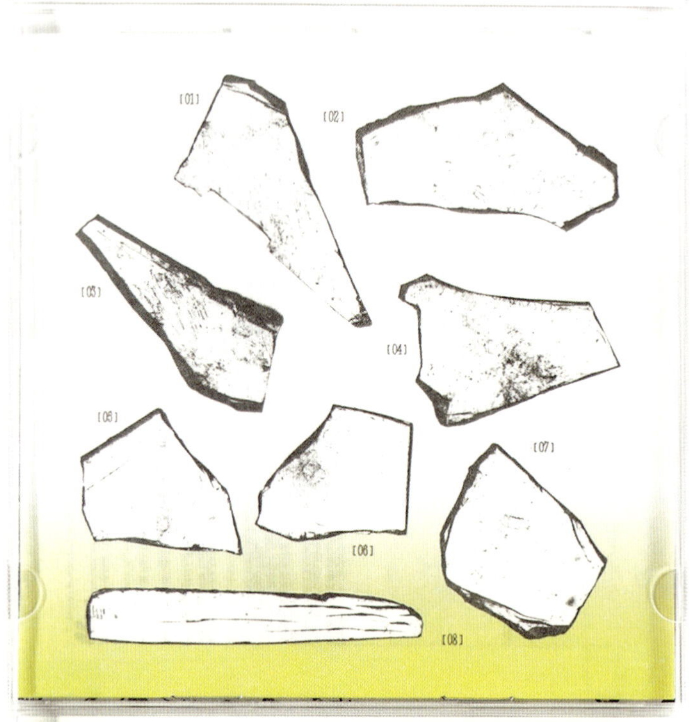

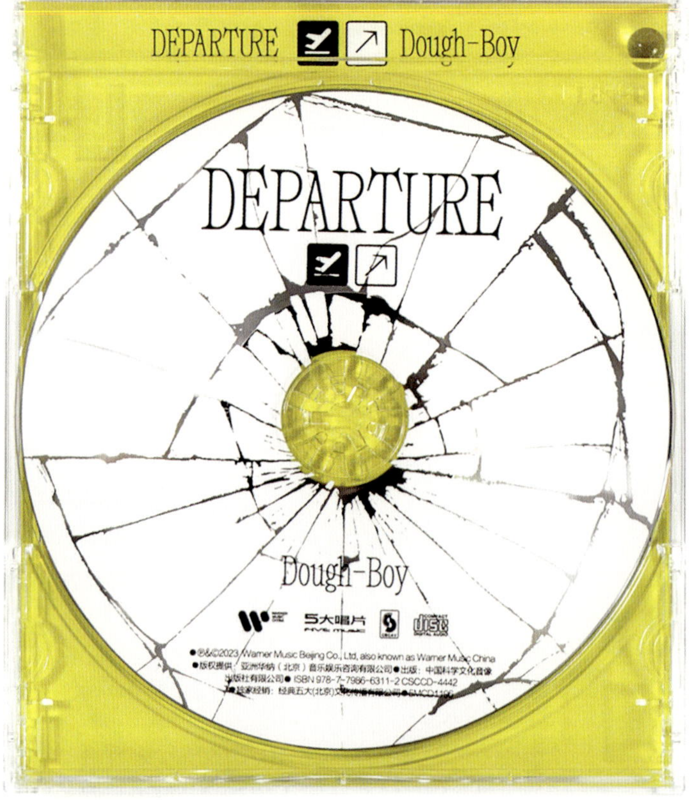

● Design Studio: **Homer & Dreamer Design** ● Designer: **Dreamer** ● Client: **Warner**

Dough-Boy *DEPARTURE* Album Design

● The album is based on the themes of "breaking" and "starting over" with a cover inspired by a mirror. Using three layers of PVC sheets, the design conveys the broken CD shell's aesthetics while ensuring production feasibility. Fragmented material images, representing each song, are integrated into the album. The small embedded ball in the CD symbolizes various elements, from breaking lenses to stubborn stones or simple hearts. Aligning with the album title "Departure," the design incorporates flight information themes, with the tracklist resembling a flight schedule.

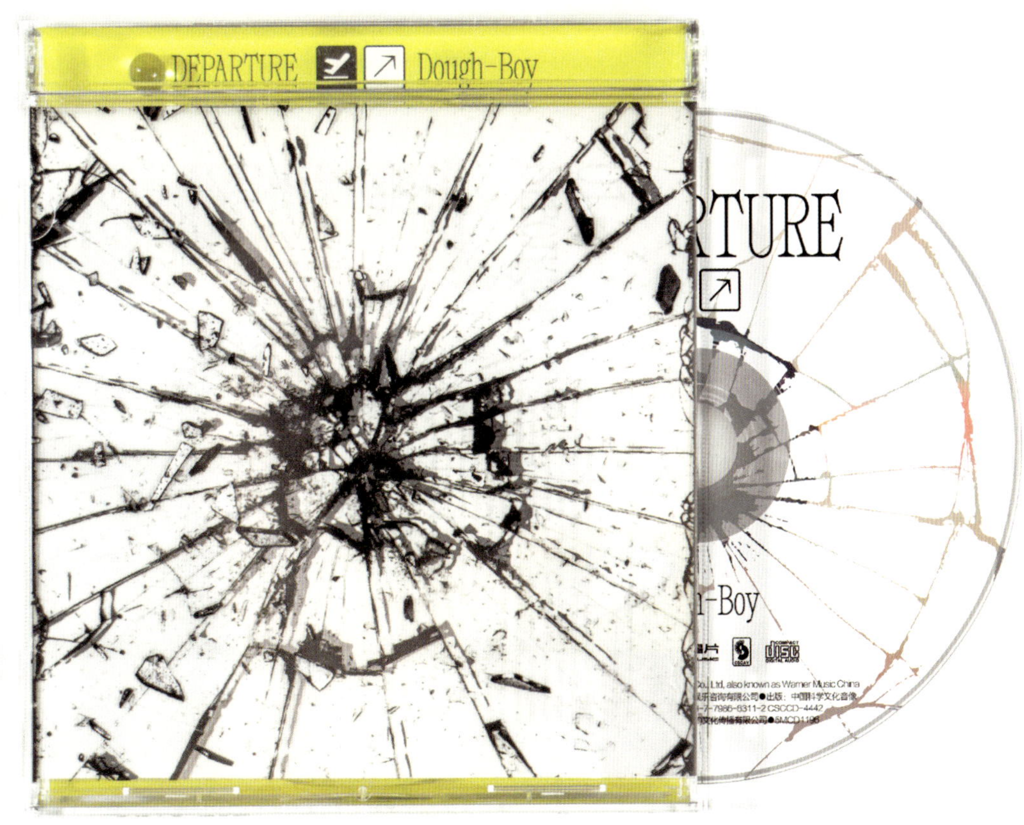

C7 M7 Y86 K0

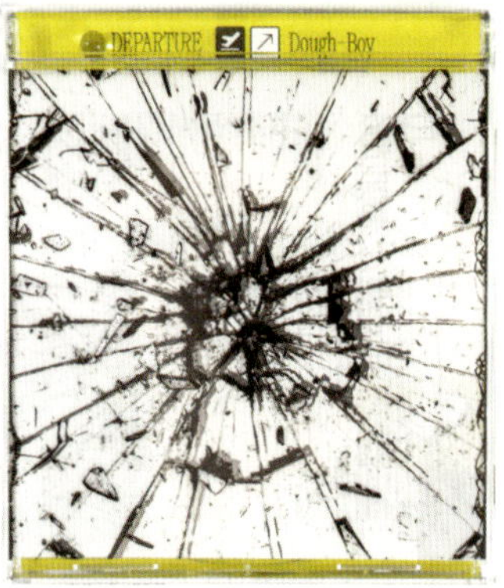

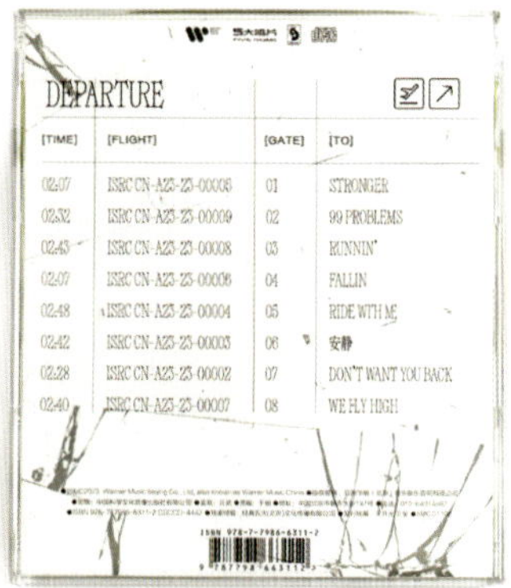

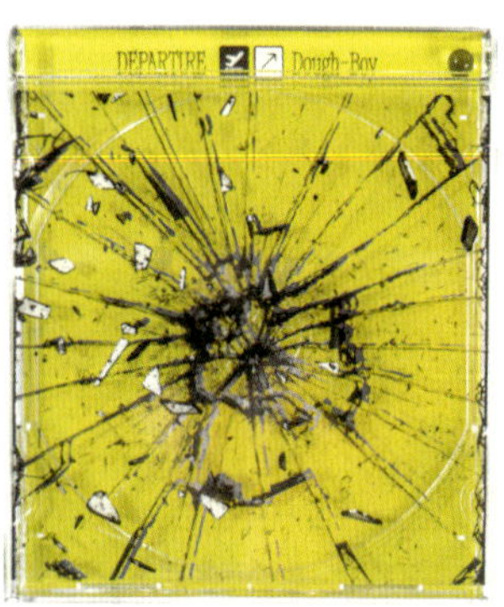

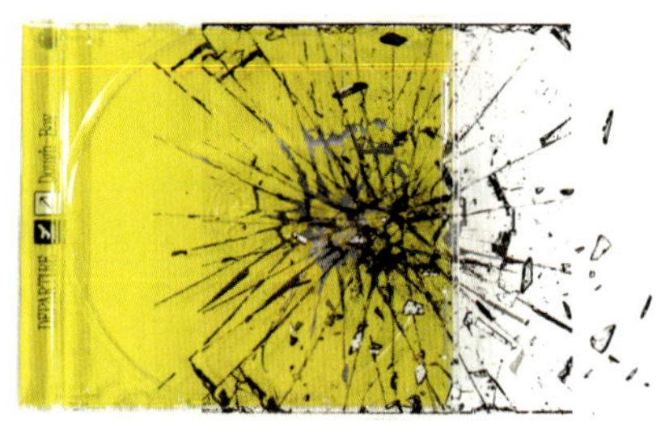

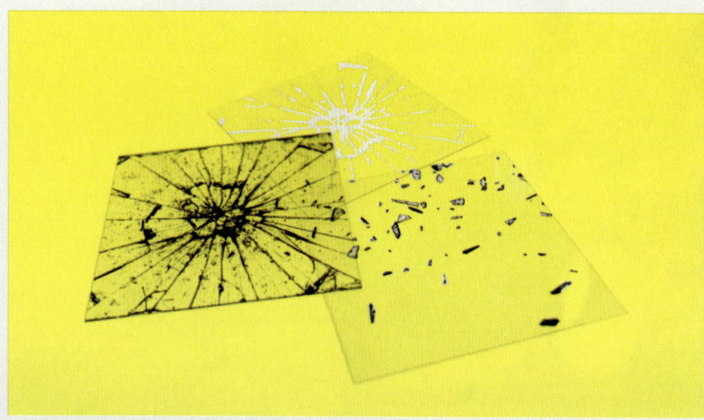

● Why Yellow? ● The entire album adopts a vibrant yellow, which is not only very fresh but also carries a sense of aggressiveness. This choice aligns with the album's concepts of "breaking" and "starting over."

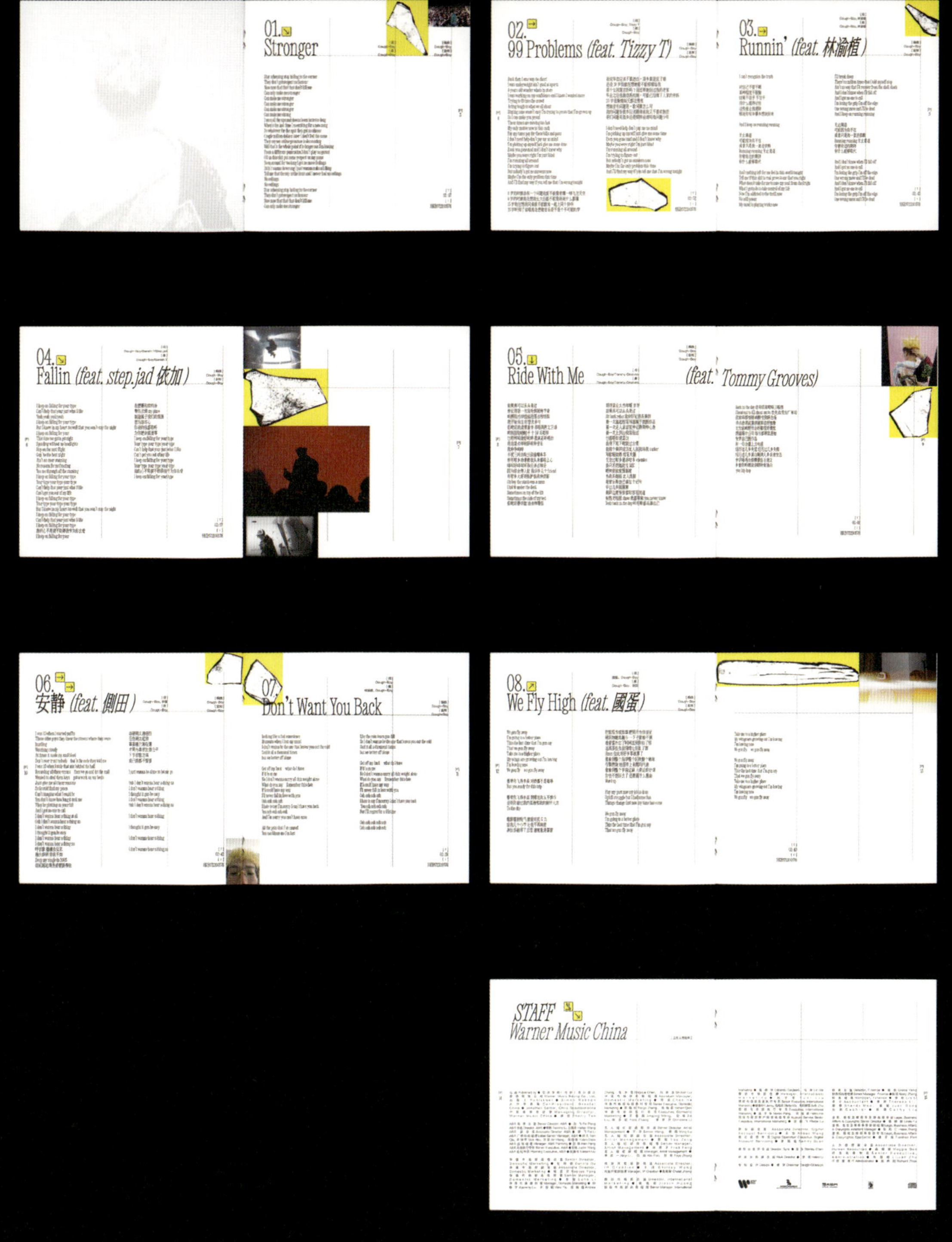
01. Stronger
02. 99 Problems (feat. Tizzy T)
03. Runnin' (feat. 林渝植)
04. Fallin (feat. step.jad 依加)
05. Ride With Me (feat. Tommy Grooves)
06. 安静 (feat. 側田)
07. Don't Want You Back
08. We Fly High (feat. 國蛋)
STAFF
Warner Music China

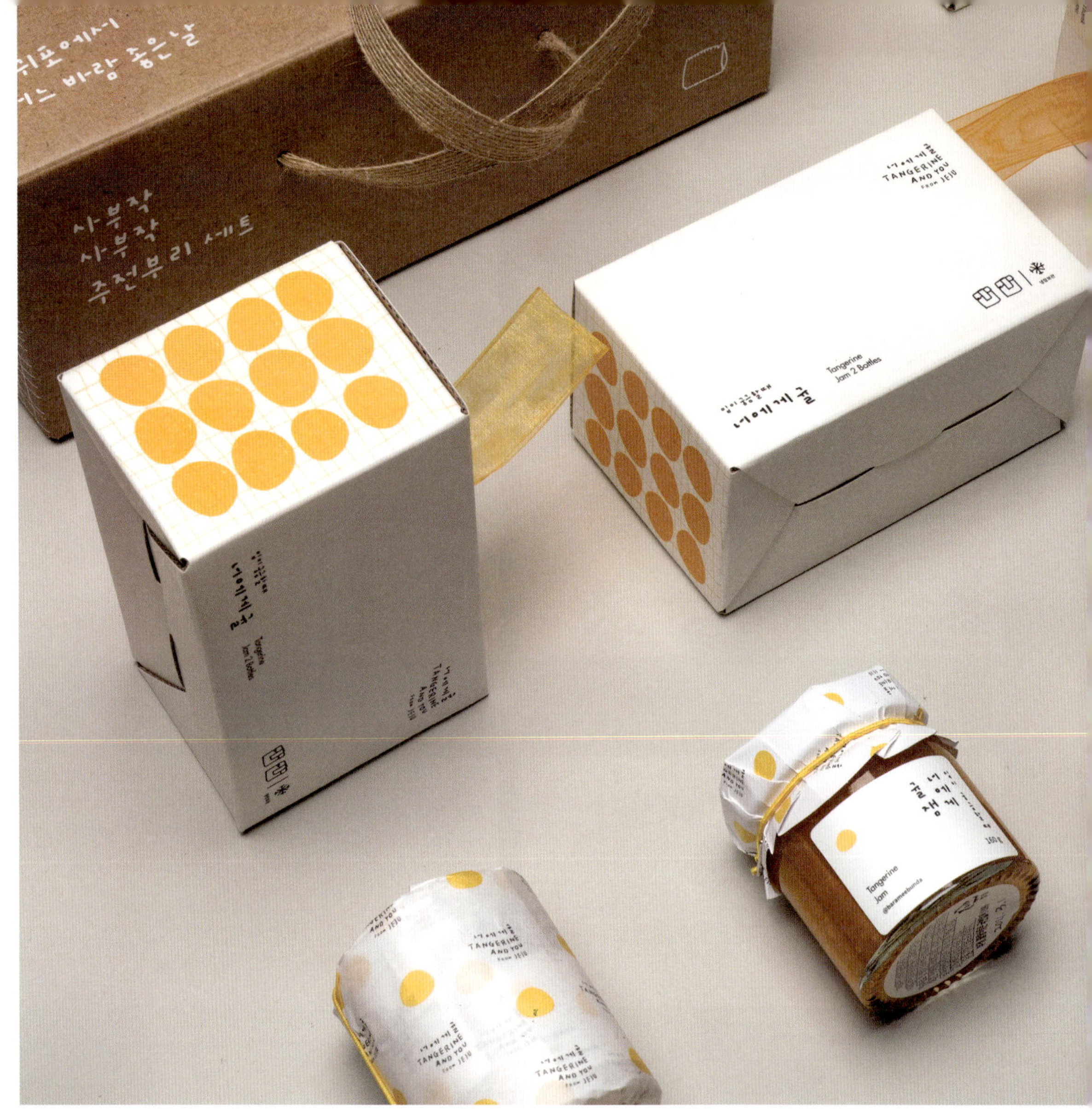

Tangerine and You • "Tangerine and You" is a Jeju Island tangerine farm. The designer conveyed warmth and innocence through abstract depictions of natural elements like tangerines, flowers, stone walls, and the island's wind. These elements tactfully form patterns for a consistent visual identity across multiple products.

• Design Studio: AURG Design • Designer: Songyee Paek • Client: Tangerine and You

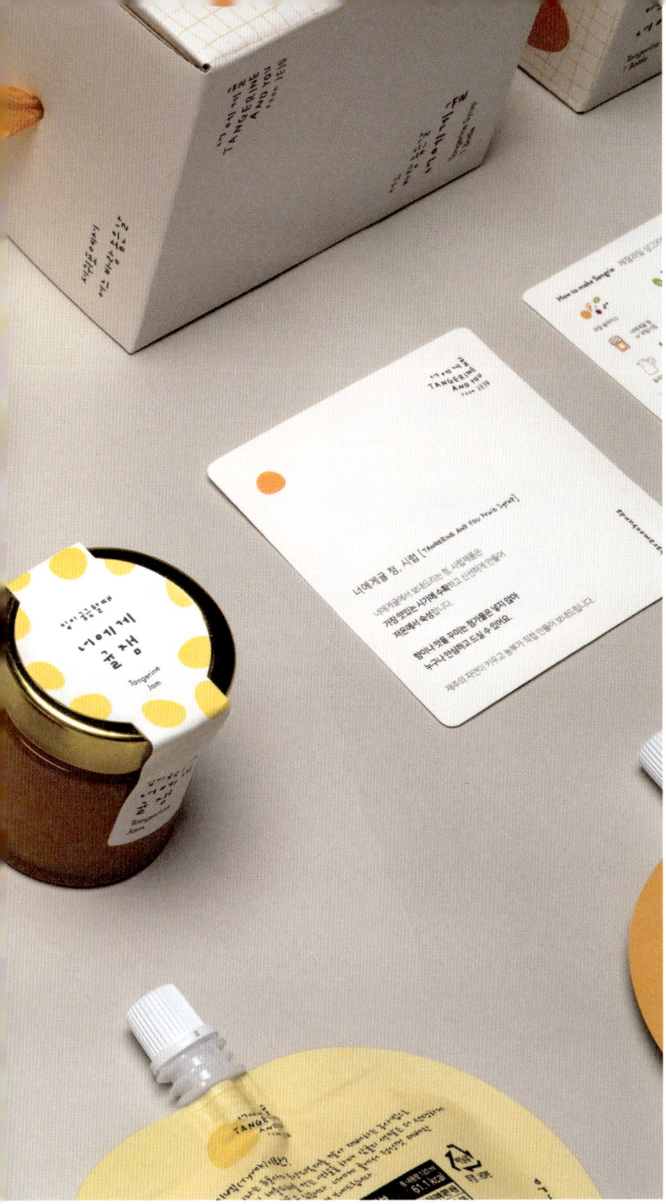

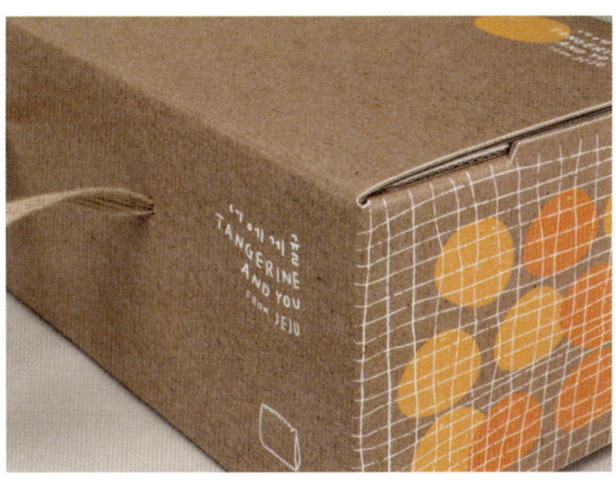

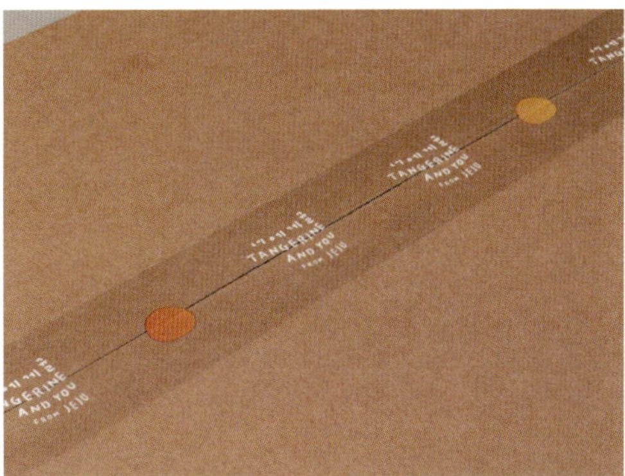

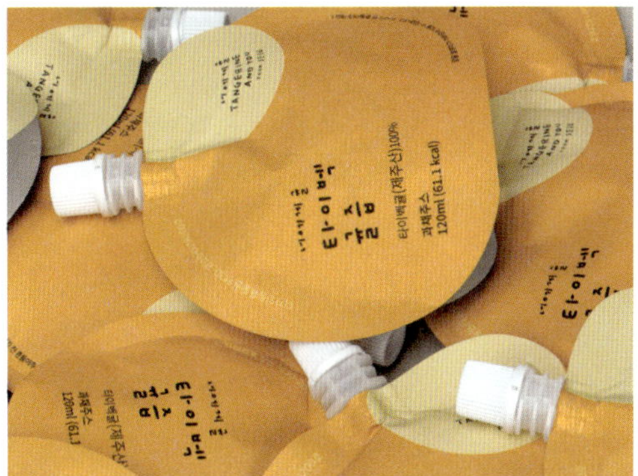

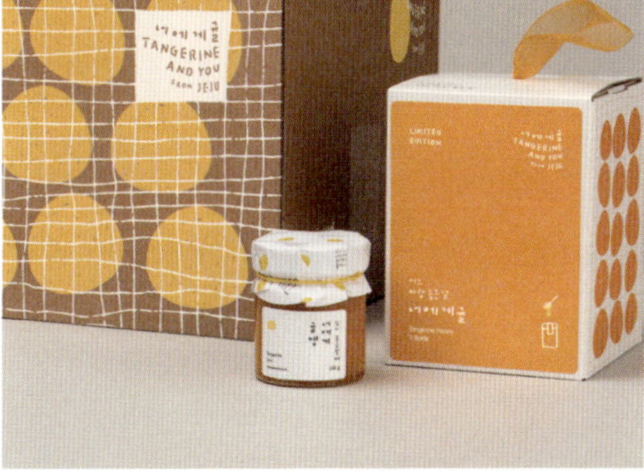

● Why Yellow? ● The essence of this design is to convey warmth with bold simplification. Yellow is deemed most fitting for intuitively delivering both tangerines and warmth. The guiding principle here is that simple is the best.

C0 M56 Y97 K0

C0 M29 Y89 K0

C0 M2 Y8 K0

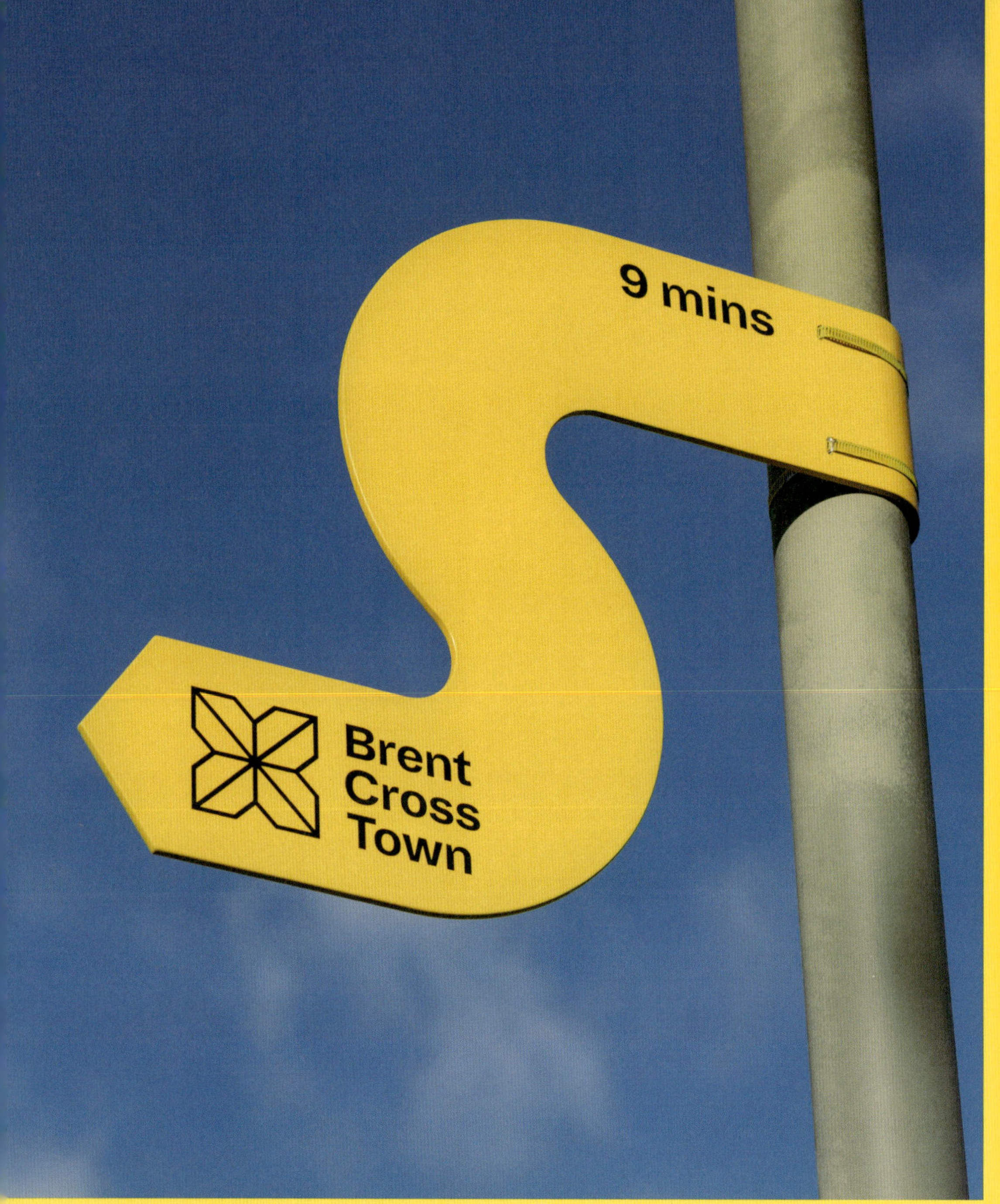

Brent Cross Town Way Finding • Pedestrian wayfindng system for Brent Cross Town in London, to guide people to participate in sport and play.

• Design Studio: Fieldwork Facility

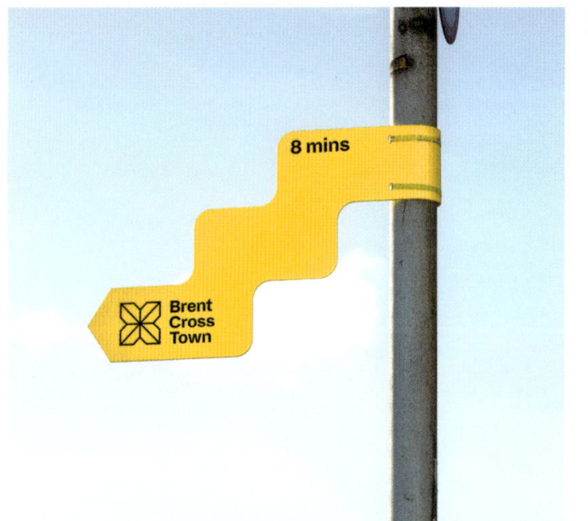
8 mins
Brent
Cross
Town

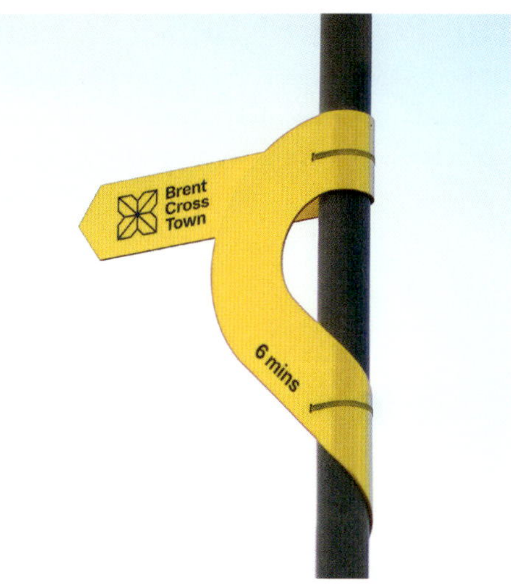
Brent
Cross
Town
6 mins

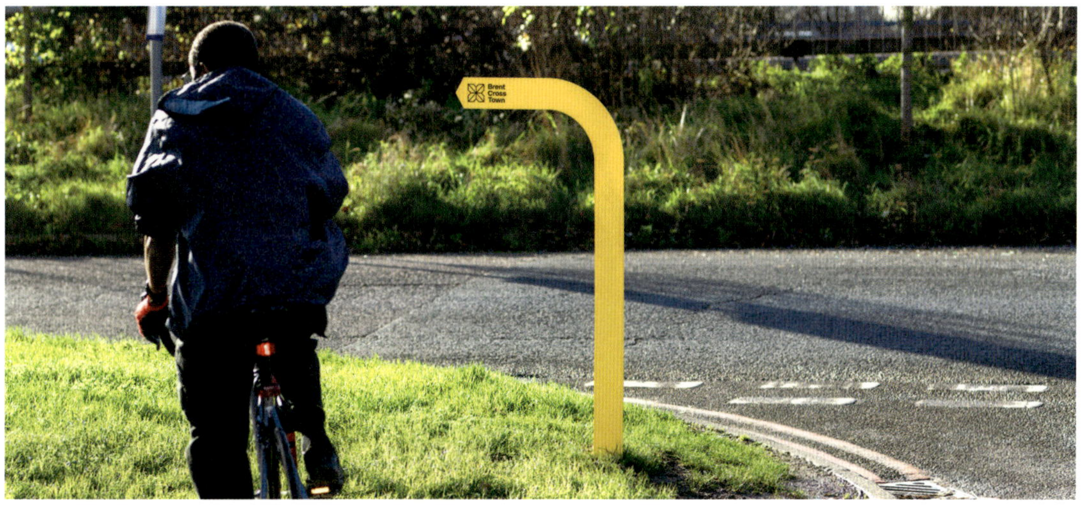

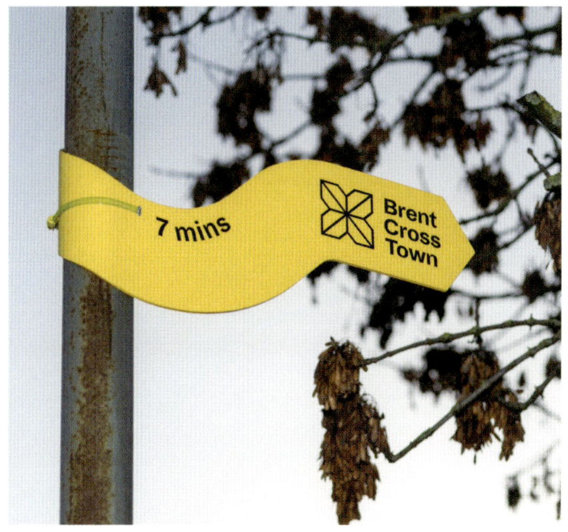
7 mins
Brent
Cross
Town

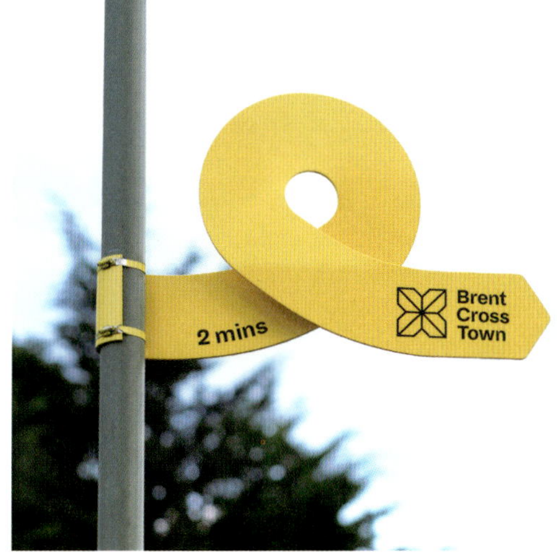
2 mins
Brent
Cross
Town

The Power of Belief is Endless

● The design of the record revolves around the album title, focusing on the concept of "endless." By repeatedly displaying this phrase, the Chinese characters undergo variations in size, spacing, and density, creating a visually rich effect that conveys a sense of oppression. The primary color is a bright yellow, aiming to attract attention and make the album title more prominent. The cover features an image of a canine tooth, serving as the artist's metaphor.

● Why Yellow? ● It expresses a penetrating and relaxed feel, dissolving, to an extent, the serious connotation of the music.

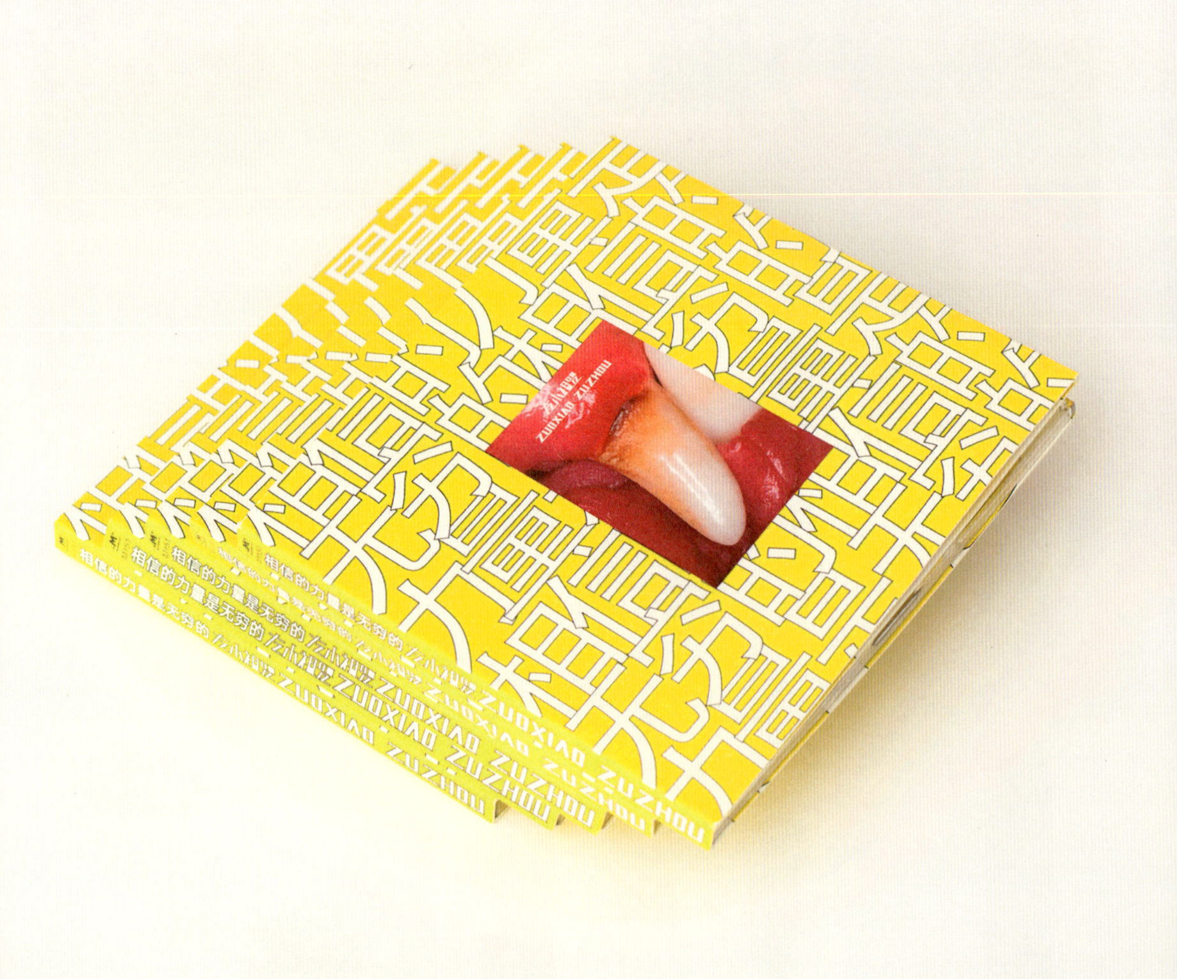

● Design Studio: PAY2PLAY ● Designer: Xiaoxi Sun ● Client: Zuoxiao Zuzhou Studio, Modern Sky

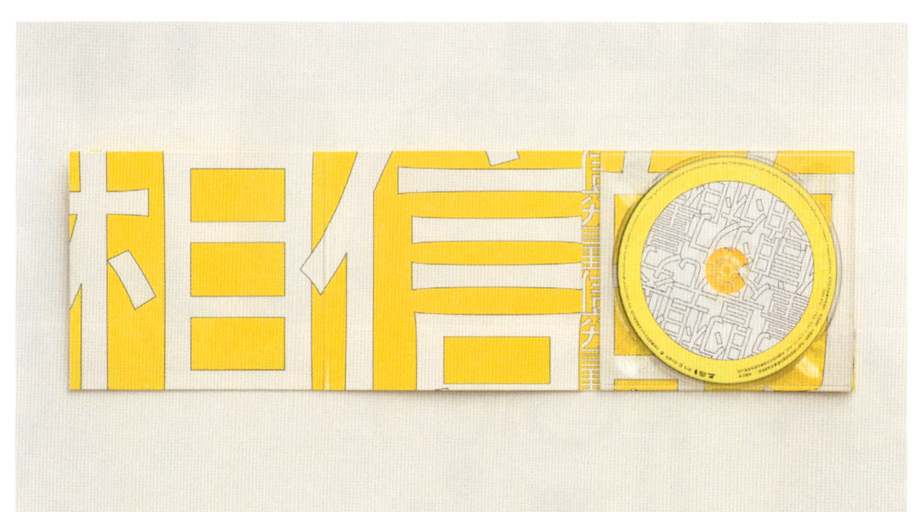

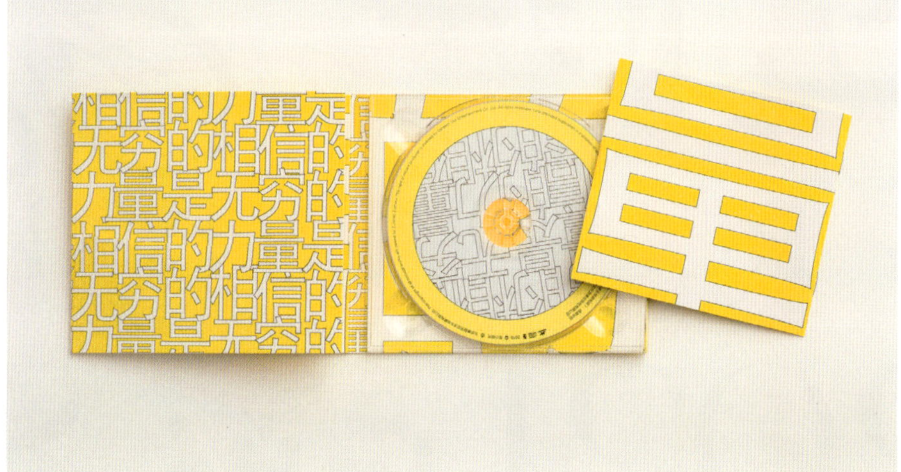

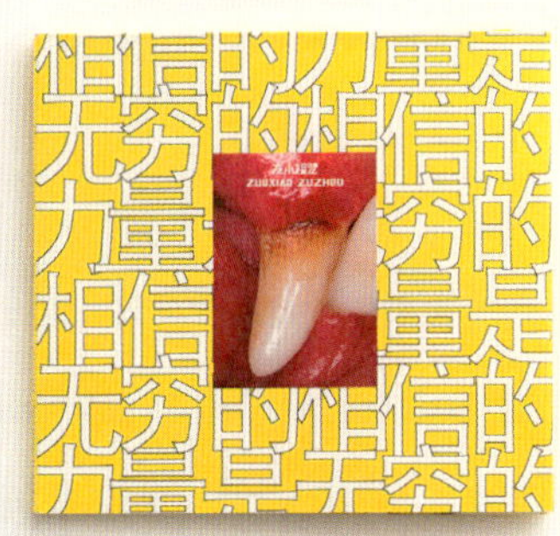

01 百年之后 04:59
02 卖花的小姑娘 05:32
03 她的男朋友 03:53
04 哲学 04:25
05 建筑师 13:02
06 罗马湖 09:09
07 在苏州卖花的小姑娘去哪里了 05:31

The copyright of all musical works are owned by Zuoxiao Zuzhou.
The right of record producer is owened by Modern Sky Entertainment Co.,Ltd.
All rights reserved. Unauthorized duplication is a violation of applicable laws.

ISBN 978-7-7986-5561-2

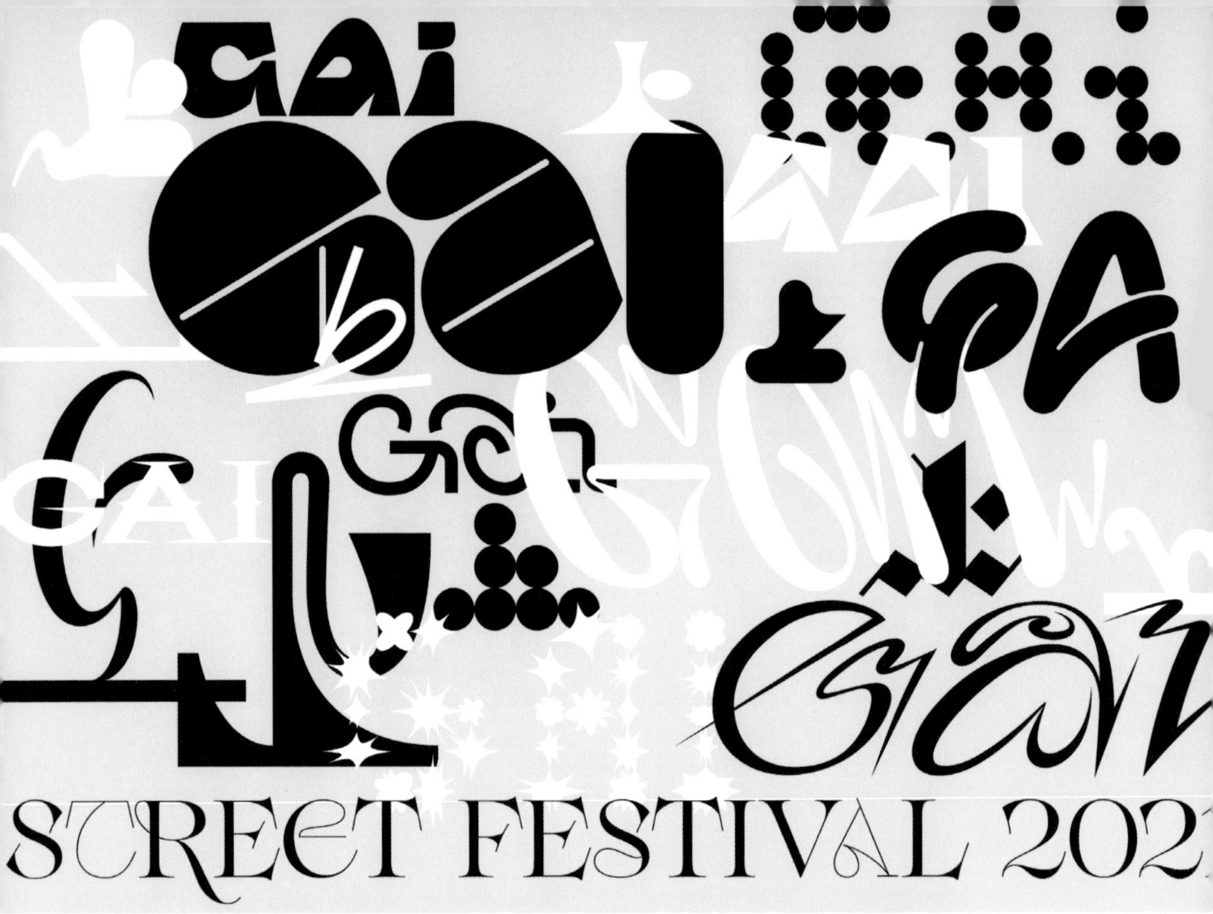

2021 GAI S

TIVAL 2021 GAi ST

2021 GAi STREET F

ET FESTIVAL 2021 GAI STREE

STIVAL 2021 GAI STREET FES

L 2021 GAI STREET FESTIVAL

• Designer: Cen Liu • Client: Deep Promotion Culture Communication Co., Ltd

"Shang Gai" Street Culture Festival

● "Shang Gai" Street Culture Festival is an annual celebration spotlighting design excellence and fostering cultural dissemination. "上(Shang) Gai" originates from Northeastern Chinese slang "上街" (Shang Jie), conveying the leisurely joy of strolling. This project seamlessly blends local attributes with diverse expressions of street culture. By employing typographic designs and vibrant colors for a captivating fusion, the design team promised a visually immersive and culturally rich experience for the festival.

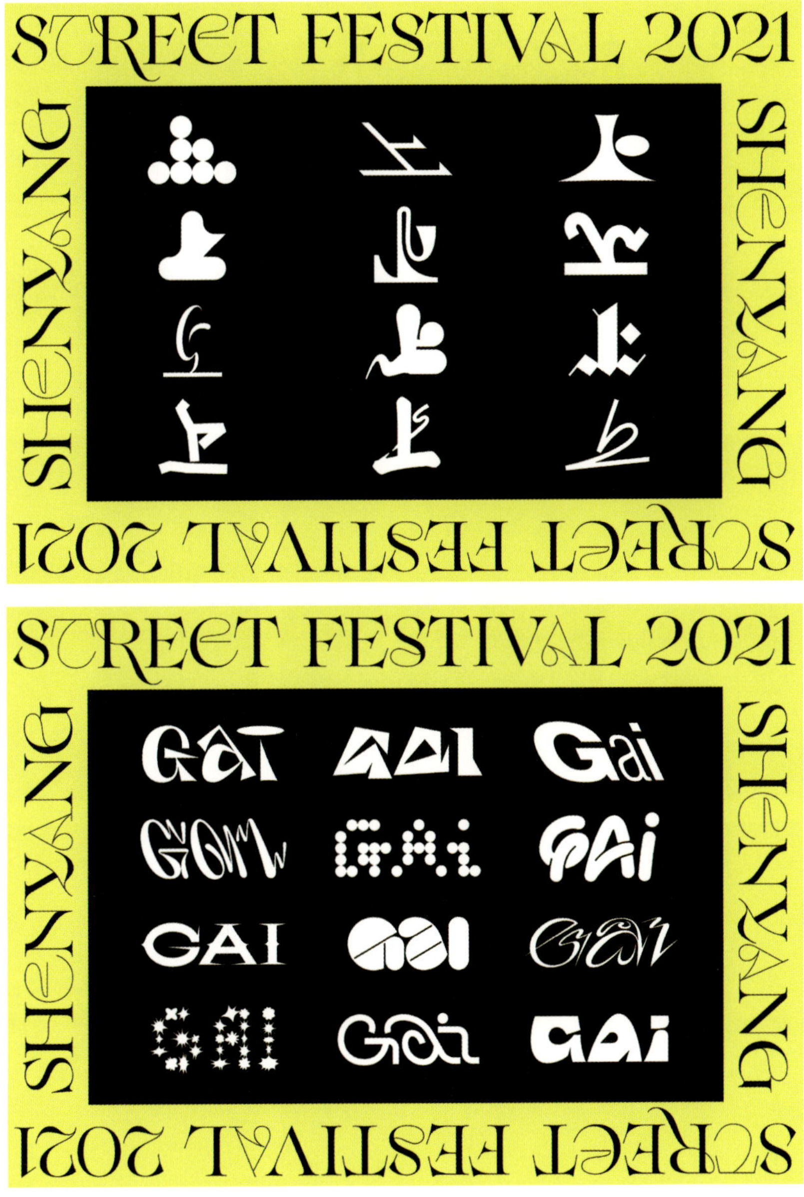

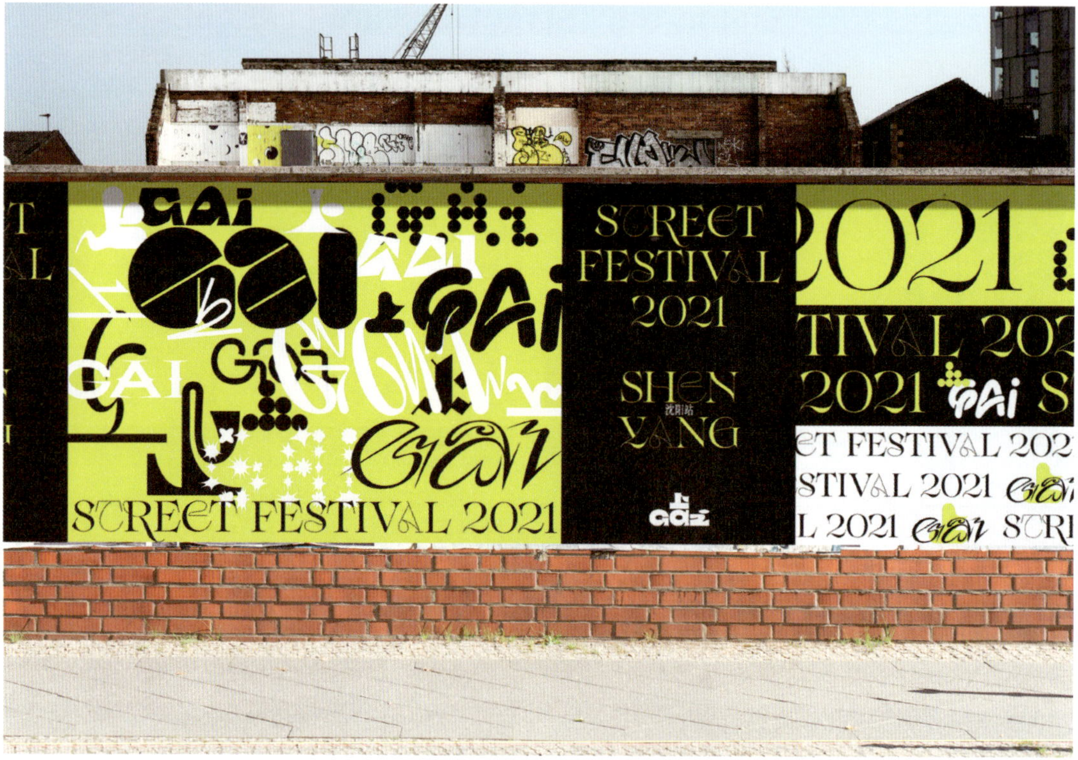

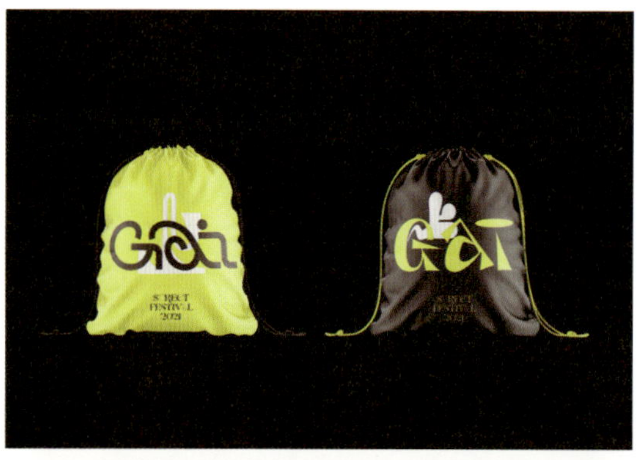

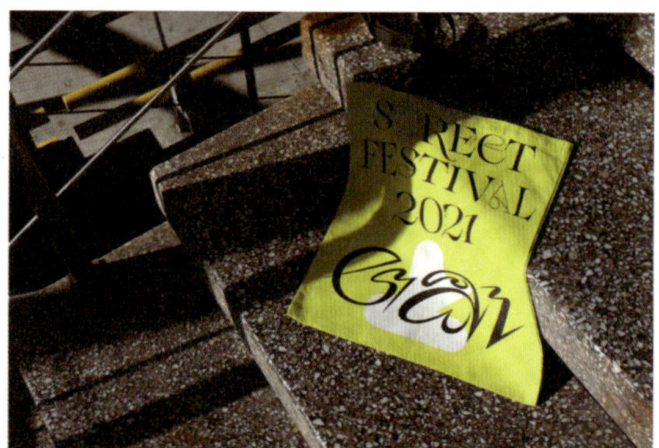
STREET
FESTIVAL
2021

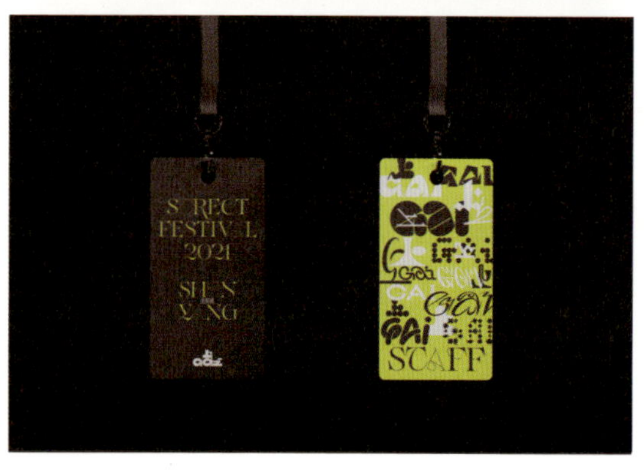
STREET
FESTIVAL
2021
SHEN
YANG
STAFF

STREET FESTIVAL 2021

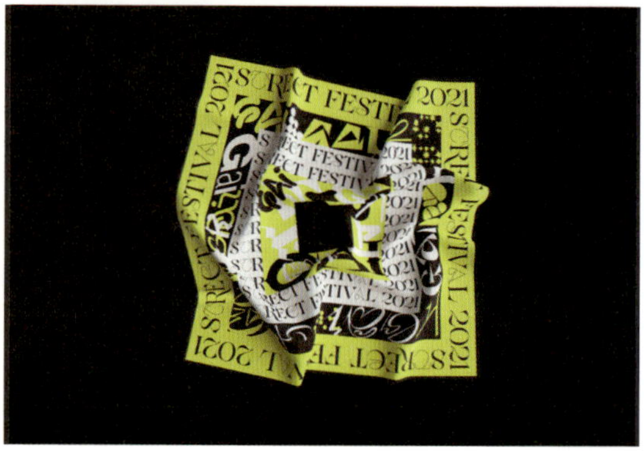

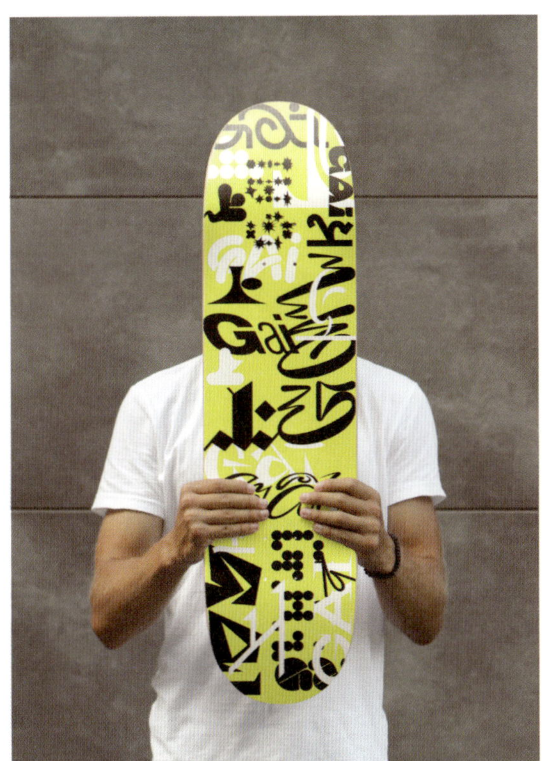

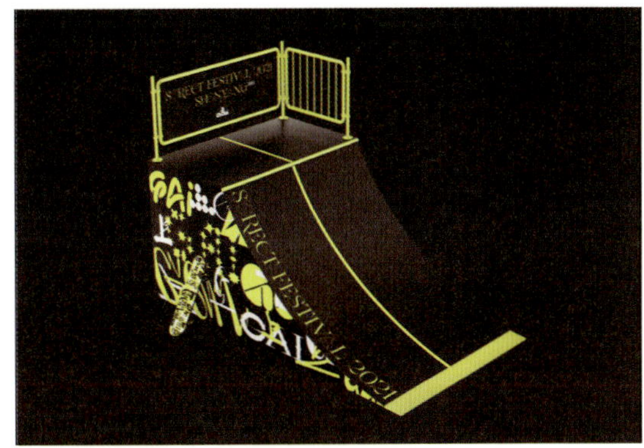

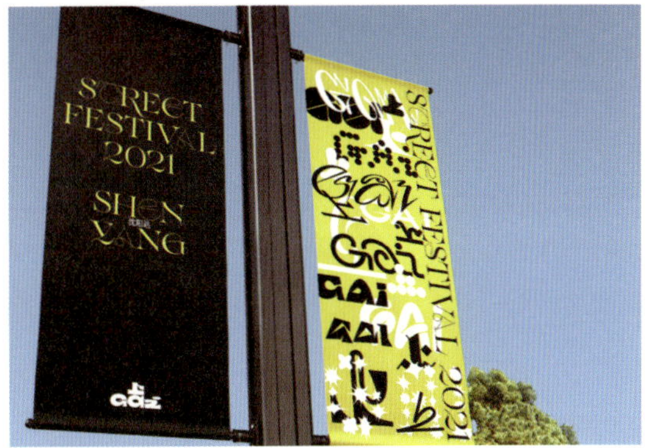

● Why Yellow? ● The visual identity combines bright yellow with black/white, blending high brightness and high-purity yellow for ornamental value. Diverse font designs for characters "上" and "Gai" reflect street culture's tolerance and showcase youth's self-esteem, forming a visually dynamic identity system that adapts while staying visually appealing.

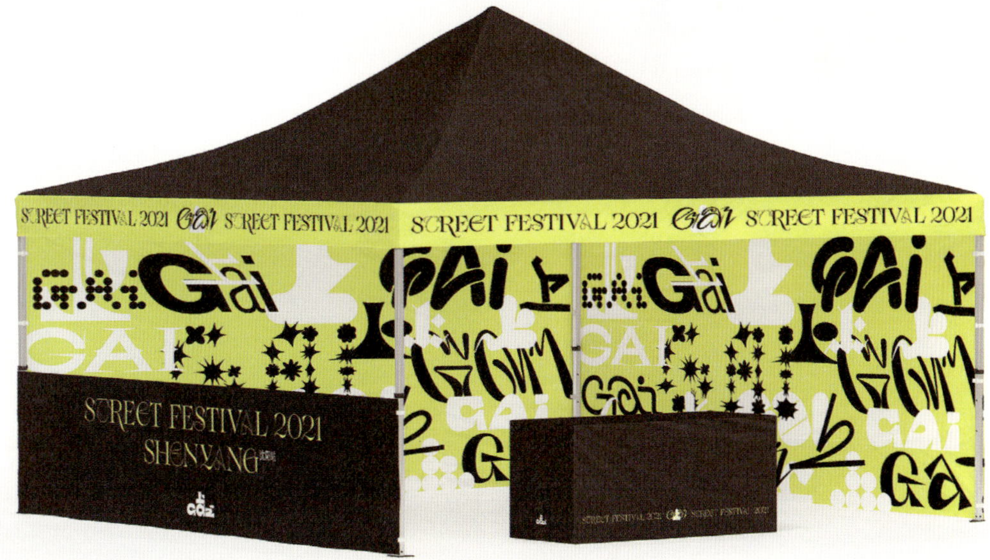

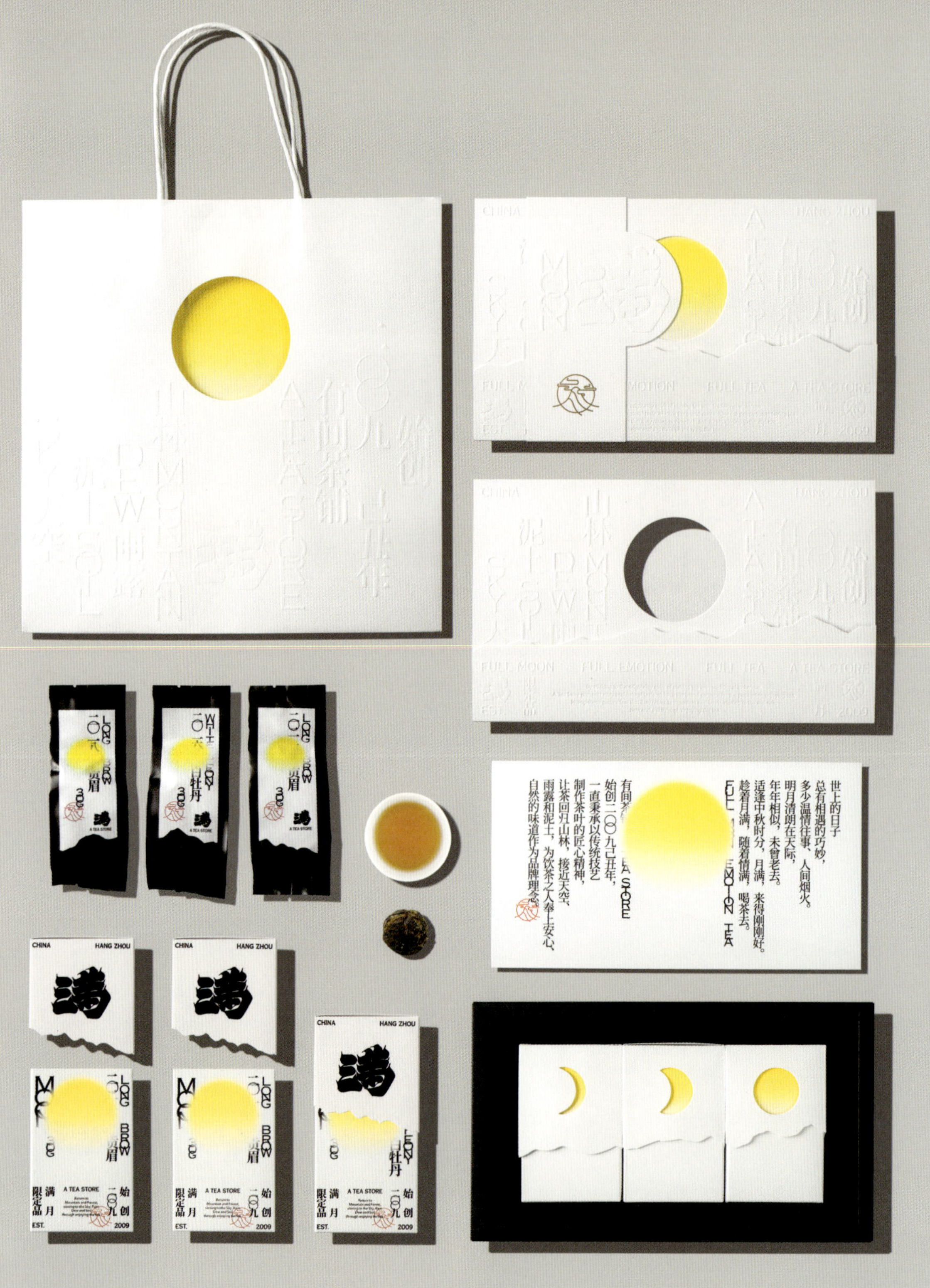

● Design Studio: **Design by AO** ● Designer: **Young Ho** ● Client: **A Tea Store**

Full Moon Tea Gift

● "Full Moon Tea Gift" seamlessly integrates the symbolism of full moon with the brand's philosophy, featuring a combination of three distinct vintages of white tea. ● The design team skillfully employed paper cutting and embossing technique to depict the refreshing and delicate mountainous landscape under the full moon. Every vintage of white tea is housed in its own independent paper box, arranged within the outer set box to create a cohesive depiction of a moonlit mountain forest. This seemingly simple design offers an intricate, refined visual experience.

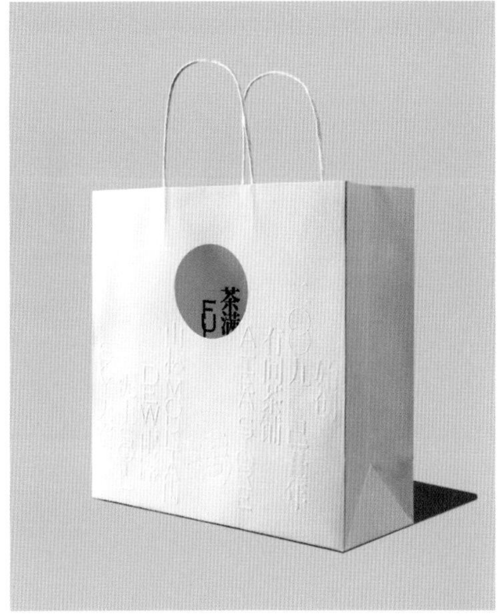

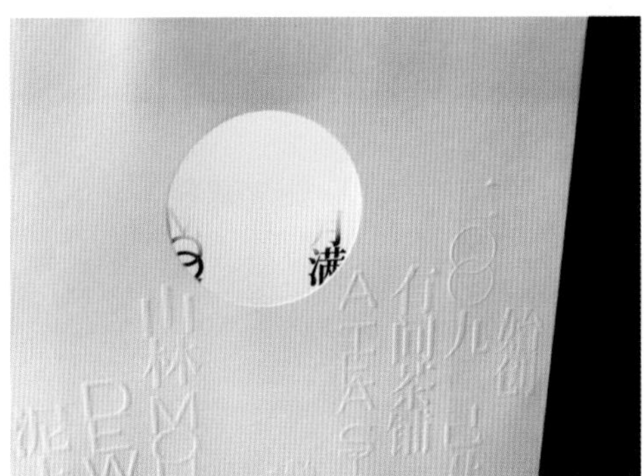

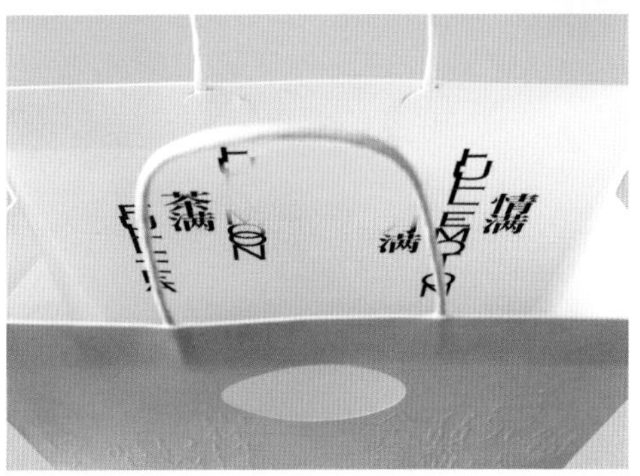

● Why Yellow? ● The choice of bright yellow allows viewers to have a more visual connection to the artistic conception of the full moon.

Mighty Oaks—*All Things Go*

● *All Things Go* marks Mighty Oaks' third studio album, infusing elements of folk and indie music with a fresh layer of singer-songwriting visualized through double-exposed images in the artwork. The band's dedication to handmade music is reflected in their new logo, coherently integrating strings and drums. The setup comes to an end with carefully designed packaging and merchandise.

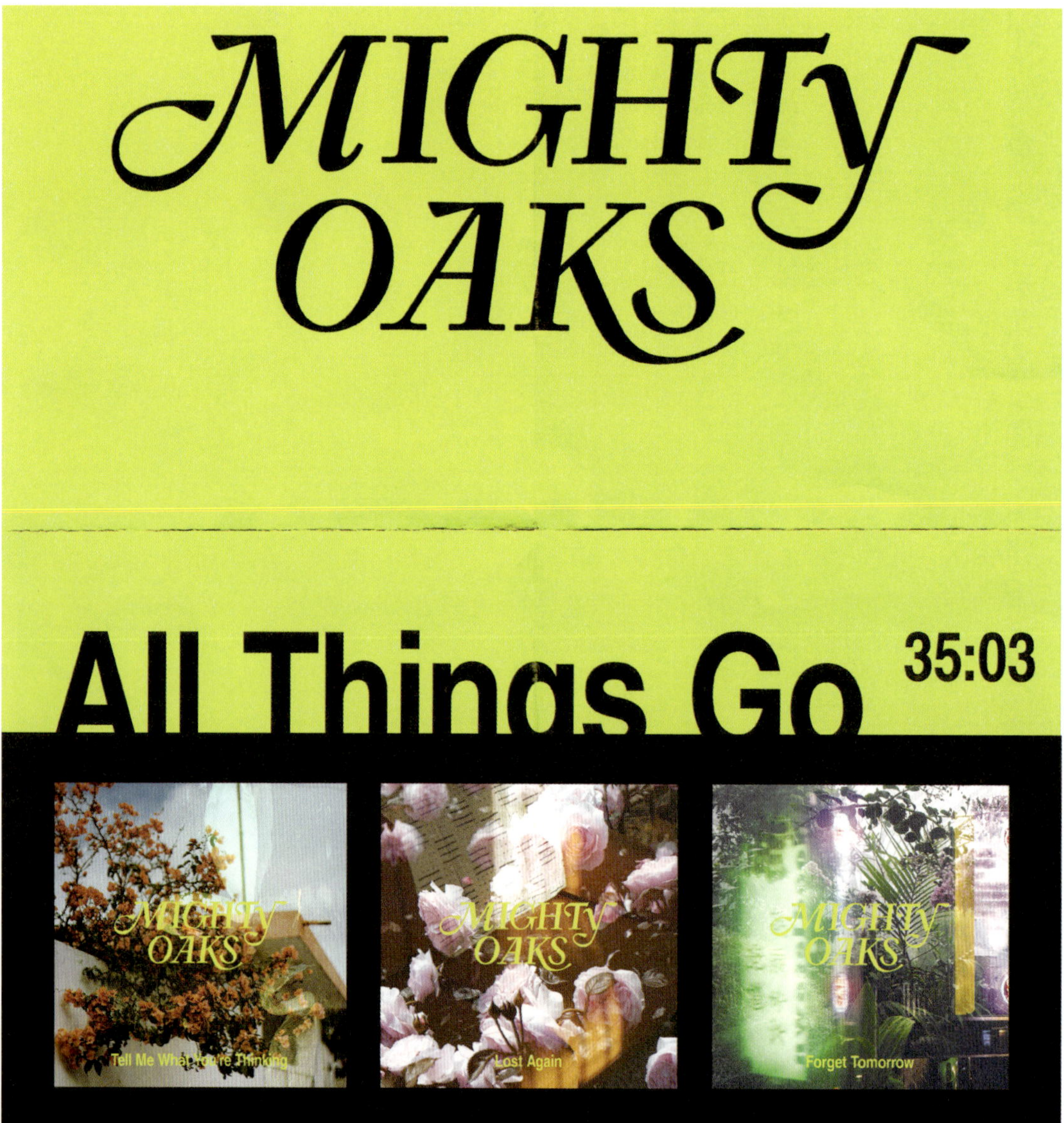

● Why Yellow? ● The band's third album shifts from classic folk to embrace singer-songwriter elements, signaling a new beginning. Neon yellow, as a bright signal color, stands contrast to the earthy tone of folk music, injecting fresh vitality into the music.

 ● Design Studio: Deutsche & Japaner ● Designer: David Wolpert, Julian Zimmermann, Ina Yamaguchi, Moritz Firchow

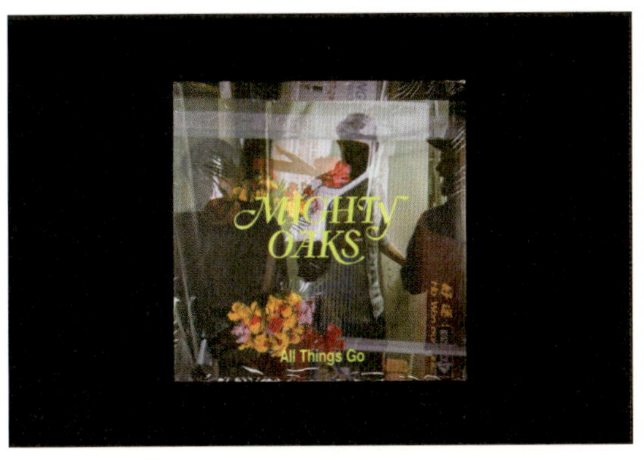
MIGHTY OAKS
All Things Go

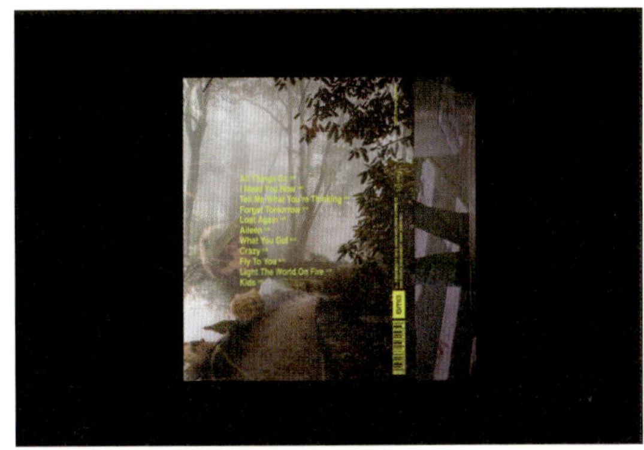
All Things Go
I Need You Now
Tell Me What You're Thinking
Forget Tomorrow
Lost Again
Aileen
What You Got
Crazy
Fly To You
Light The World On Fire
Kids

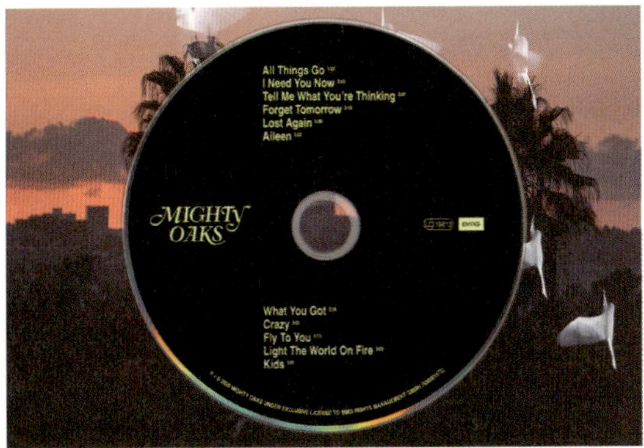
All Things Go
I Need You Now
Tell Me What You're Thinking
Forget Tomorrow
Lost Again
Aileen
MIGHTY OAKS
What You Got
Crazy
Fly To You
Light The World On Fire
Kids

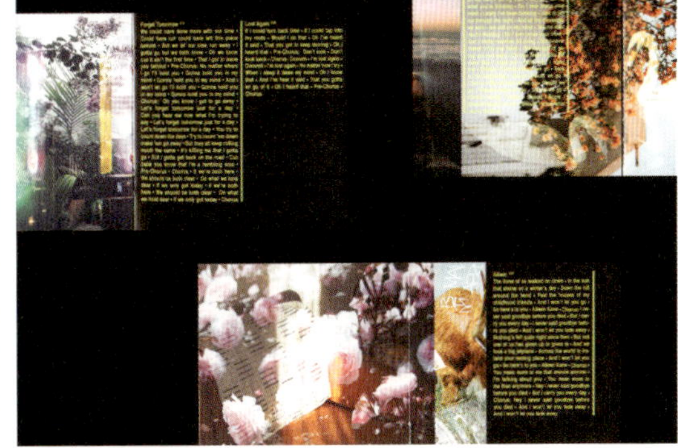

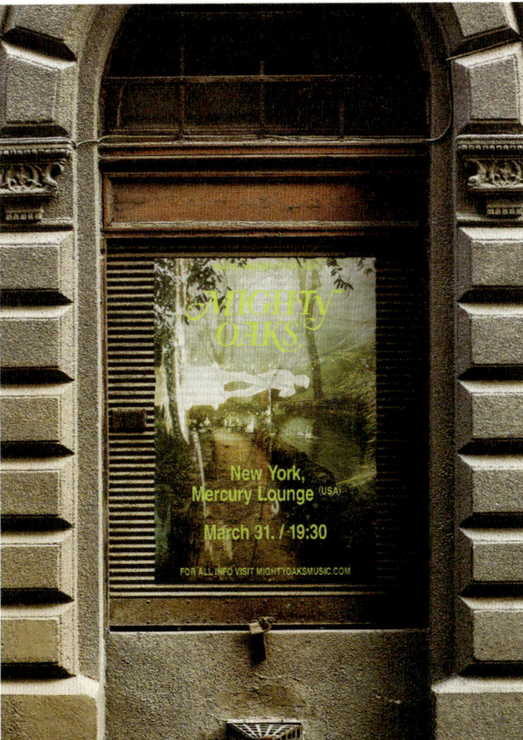
MIGHTY OAKS
New York,
Mercury Lounge (USA)
March 31. / 19:30
FOR ALL INFO VISIT MIGHTYOAKSMUSIC.COM

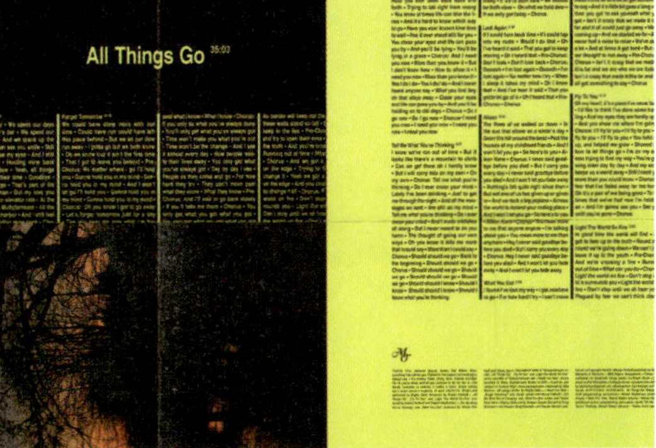
All Things Go 35:03

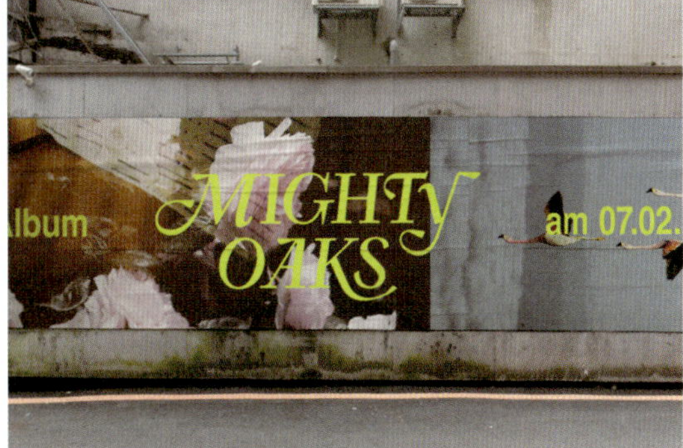
Album
MIGHTY OAKS
am 07.02.

2022년 예술창작활동지원사업 선정 프로젝트

오버더떼창 : 문전본풀이

2022.8.6 ~2022. 8.20 화,수,금 20:00 | 토,일 15:00

두산아트센터 Space111

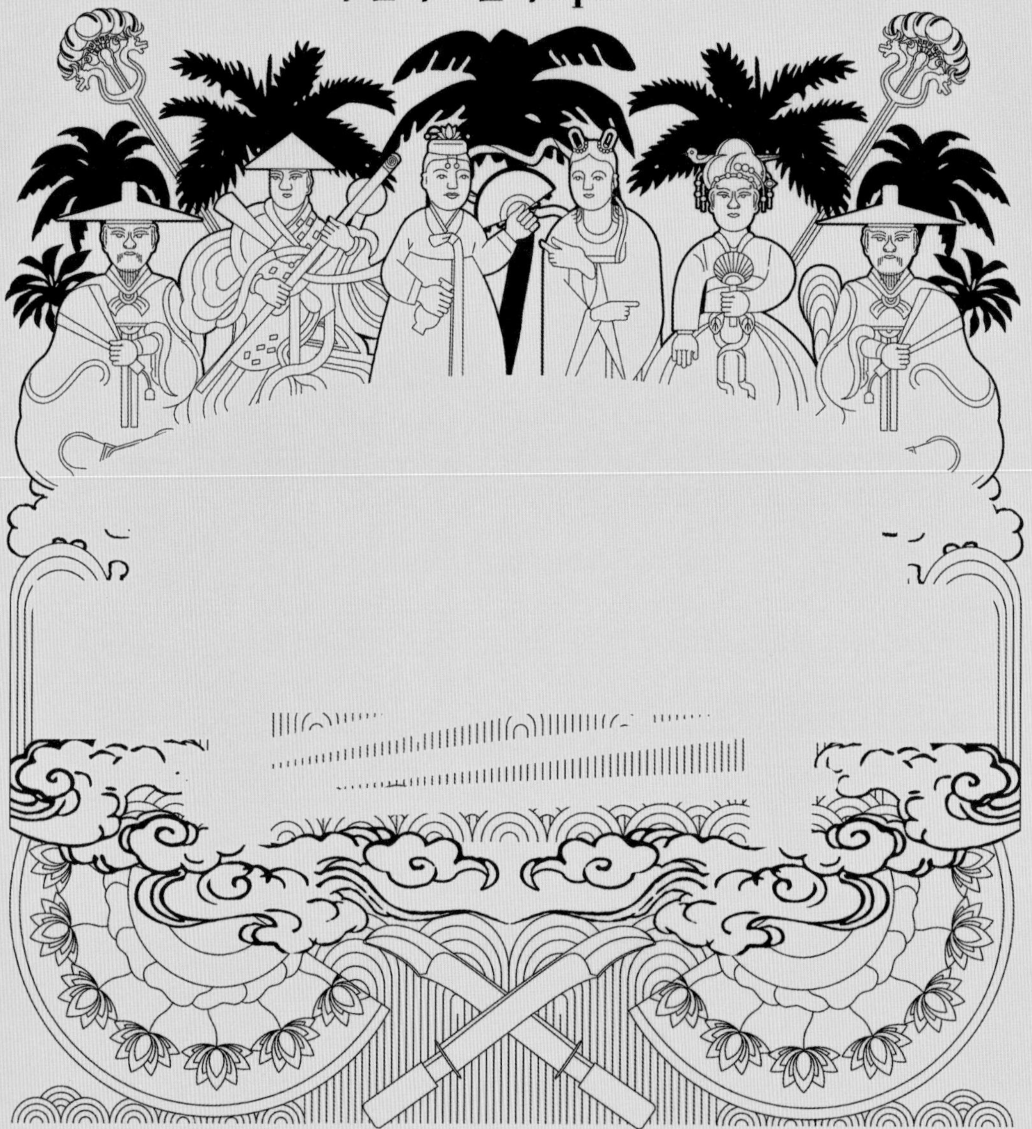

원작 [문전본풀이] **각색·작사·연출** 박인혜 **작창·음악감독** 박인혜 **드라마터그** 이경화 **무대디자인** 박동우 **조명디자인** 김건영 **음향디자인** 권태훈 **의상디자인** 김영진(차이킴)
무대감독 박종훈 **영상** 우인제 **음원** 서순실 심방 **홍보물 디자인** 스튜디오 다솔 **출연** 박인혜, 양승은, 이예린, 한아윤, 황지영, 이해원 **음악** 심미령, 조봉국 **PD** 안지은, 신아름 **조연출** 이은채
주최·주관 판소리아지트 놀애박스 **기획** 두산아트센터, 판소리아지트 놀애박스 **제작** 의정부문화재단, 판소리아지트 놀애박스 **후원** 서울특별시, 서울문화재단
판소리 <오버더떼창 : 문전본풀이>는 2021년 3월 두산아트센터 두산아트랩(DOOSAN ART LAB)을 통해 쇼케이스로 선보인 후 발전시킨 작품입니다

● Design Studio: Studio Dasol ● Designer: Dasol Lee ● Client: Pansori Azit Nohlaebox

Over the Crowd—singing of Pansori: Munjeonbonpuri

● *Over the groupcrowd singing: Moonjeonbonpuri* is a modern "Pansori[1] choir play" inspired by Jeju Island's shamanistic mythology, rooted in the belief of gods protecting households. The design draws inspiration from Jeju's traditional "Painting of Shamanistic Spirits." Featuring shamanistic bells, folding fans, knives, palm trees, and a silhouette of a Jeju house, the contemporary illustration encapsulates key narrative elements. The designer skillfully reimagined this enthralling tale with intricate details.

1.Pansori: a genre of narrative song of Korea, typically performed dramatically by a vocalist, accompanied by a puk (double-headed barrel drum). Built from the word "pan," meaning "open space," and "sori," meaning "singing" or "sound," the term pansori itself is a reference to the markets, public squares, and other such open venues where performances originally took place. (Britannica)

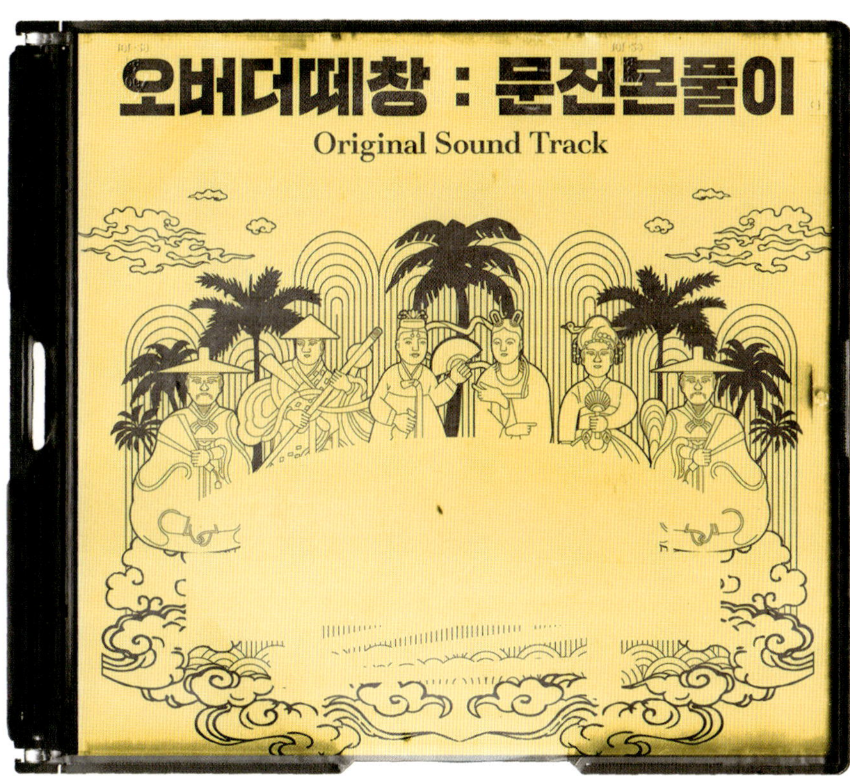

● Why Yellow? ● The client requested an implicit story expression, avoiding fairytale or cute elements while maintaining a light touch. The designer chose a bright yet simple yellow and black color scheme, symbolizing vitality and calmness, respectively. The strong contrast aligns with the client's vision. ● Using black lines on a yellow background aims for restrained beauty, allowing focus on the poster's story. ● The color scheme and design are deemed suitable for a poster as they naturally can attract attention.

C0 M15 Y70 K0

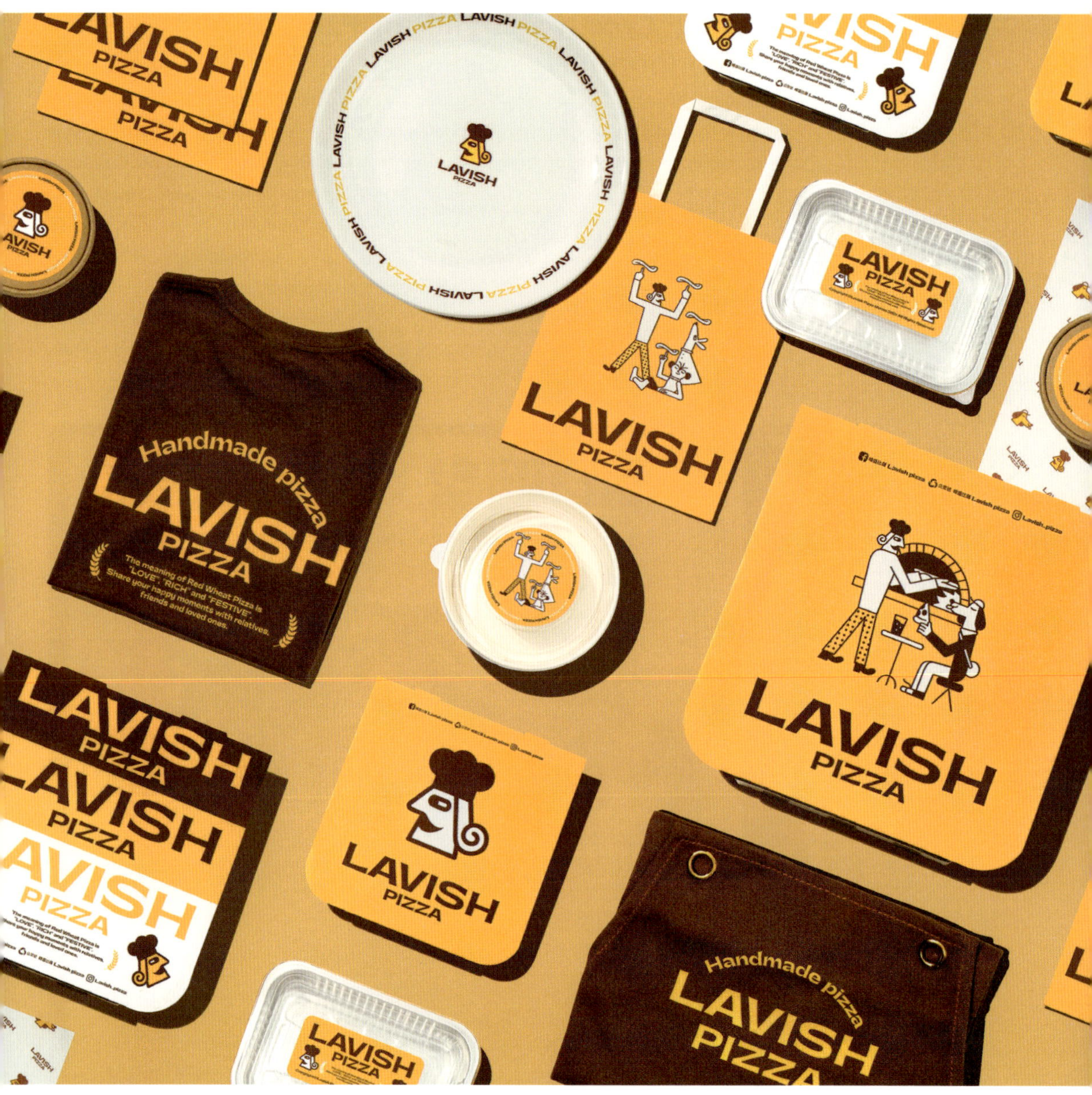

LAVISH PIZZA • "Lavish Pizza," a prominent Macau chain, is famed for its innovative "Red Dough Pizza." In a rebranding effort, characters take center stage, led by Lavish, the pizza chef with a passion for creating new flavors. Alongside Lavish is a loyal dog, a discount-loving office lady, and an alien KOL sharing culinary delights. The brand's story revolves around these characters, fostering a stronger customer connection. The new visual identity, encompassing logos, fonts, colors, and characters, inherits Lavish's innovative spirit, injecting vitality into the design and making the brand irresistibly contagious.

• Design Studio: Indego design • Designer: Lam Ieong Kun, Dan Ferreira • Client: LAVISH PIZZA

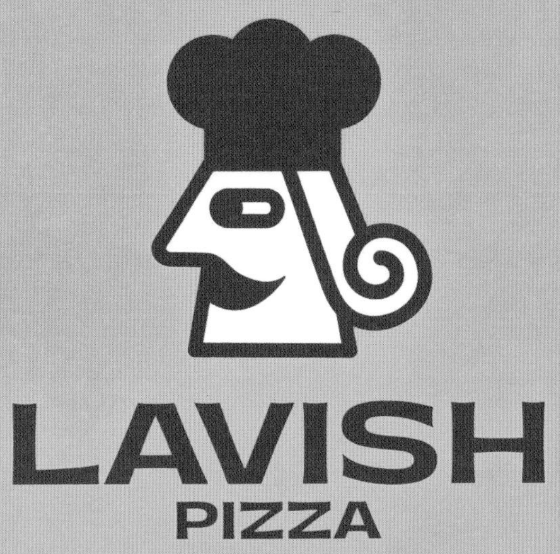

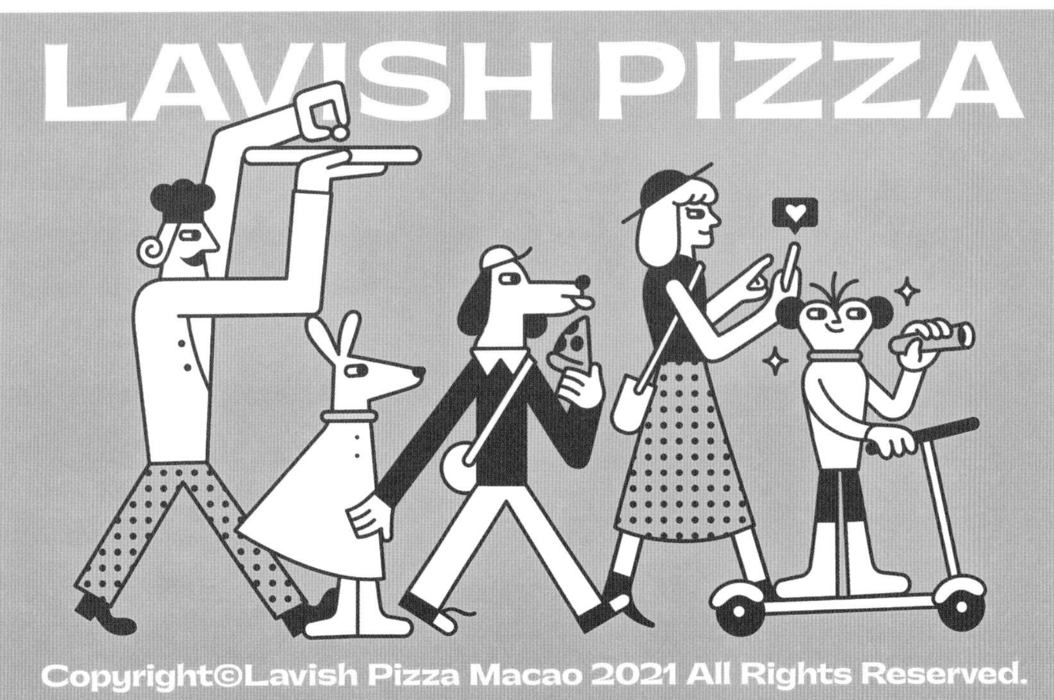

C0 M30 Y97 K0 C53 M80 Y100 K26

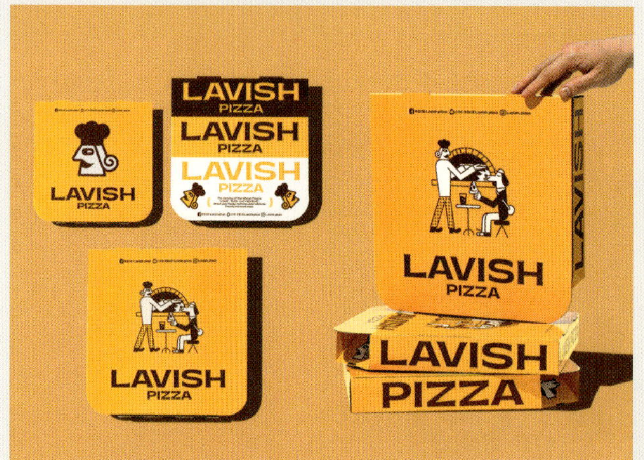

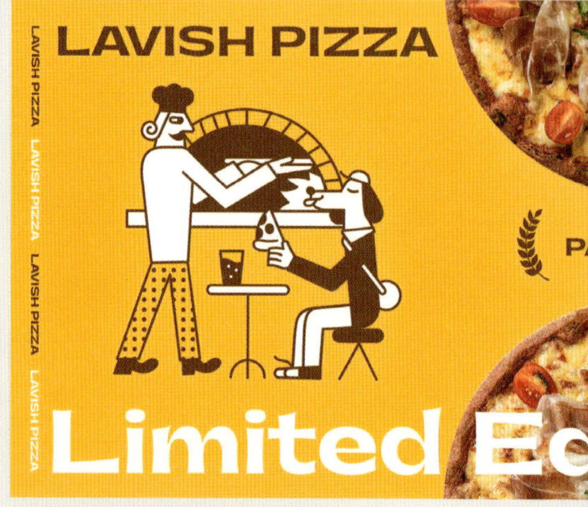

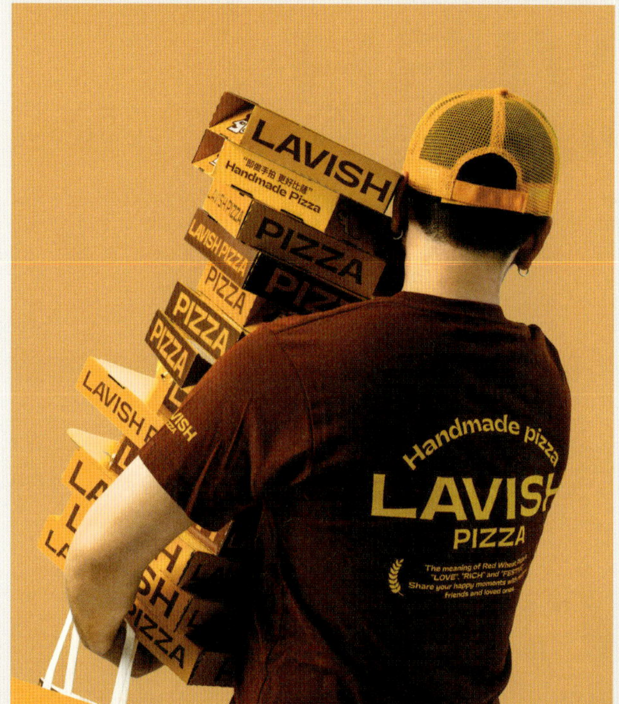

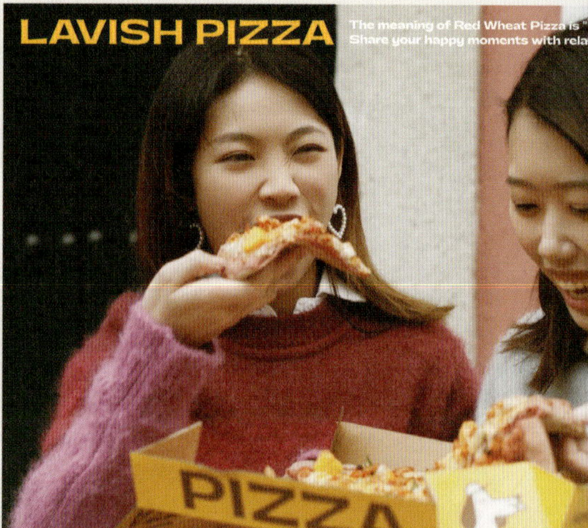

LAVISH
PIZZA

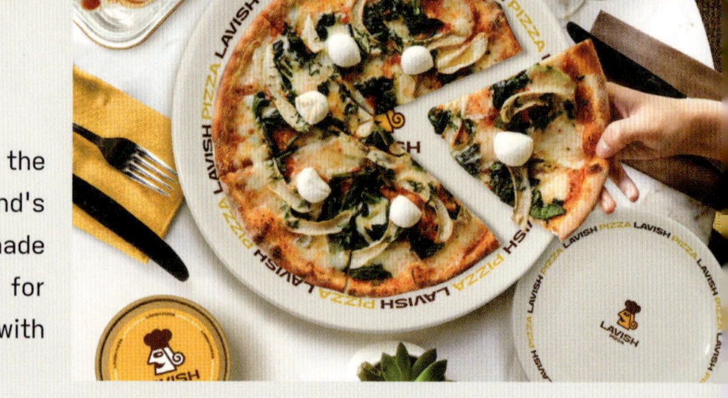

● Why Yellow? ● Choosing yellow as the main color in the rebranding stems from its previous role in the brand's identity. The decision was made to refine the yellow shade to better cater to market preferences. ● Yellow, known for representing happiness, vitality, and creativity, aligns with the brand's energetic and innovative spirit.

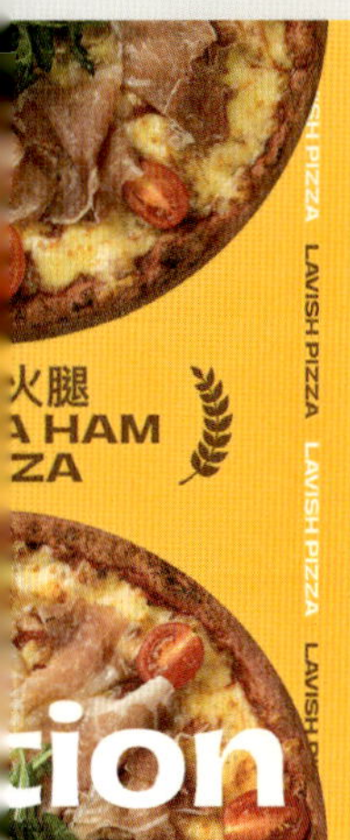
LAVISH PIZZA

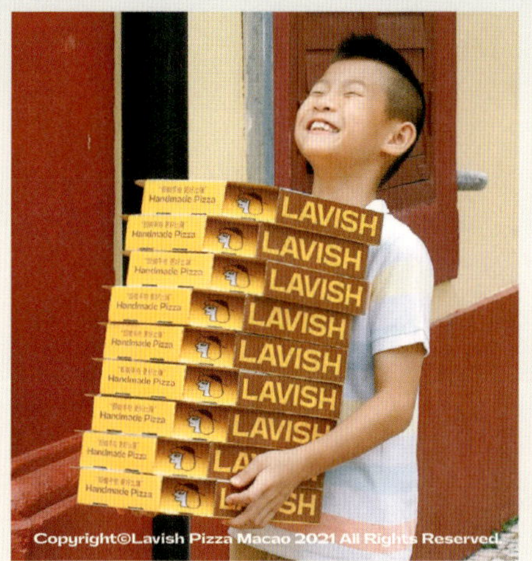
LAVISH
Handmade Pizza
Copyright©Lavish Pizza Macao 2021 All Rights Reserved.

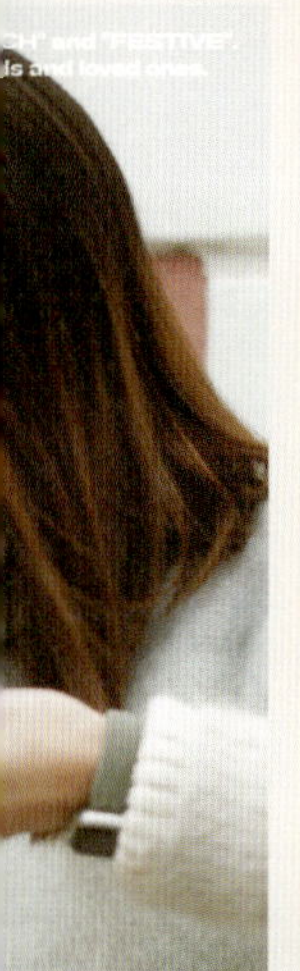

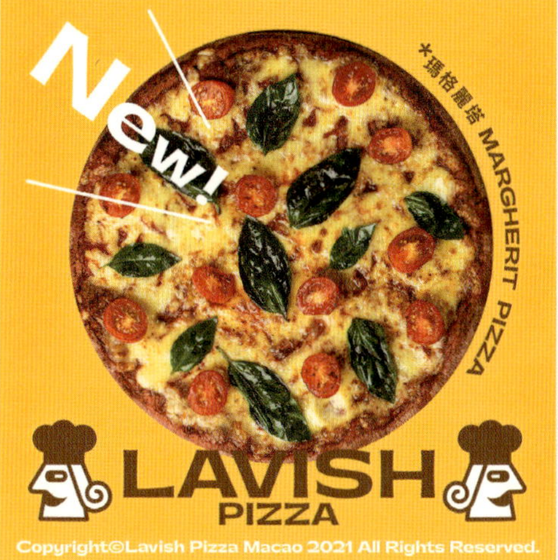
New!
*瑪格麗塔 MARGHERIT PIZZA
LAVISH
PIZZA
Copyright©Lavish Pizza Macao 2021 All Rights Reserved.

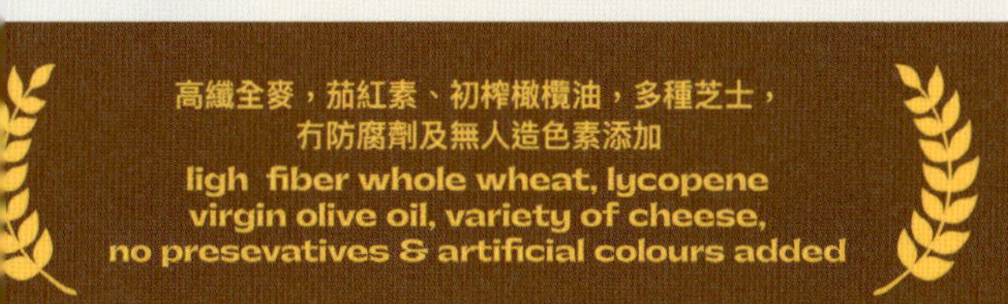
高纖全麥，茄紅素、初榨橄欖油，多種芝士，
冇防腐劑及無人造色素添加
ligh fiber whole wheat, lycopene
virgin olive oil, variety of cheese,
no presevatives & artificial colours added

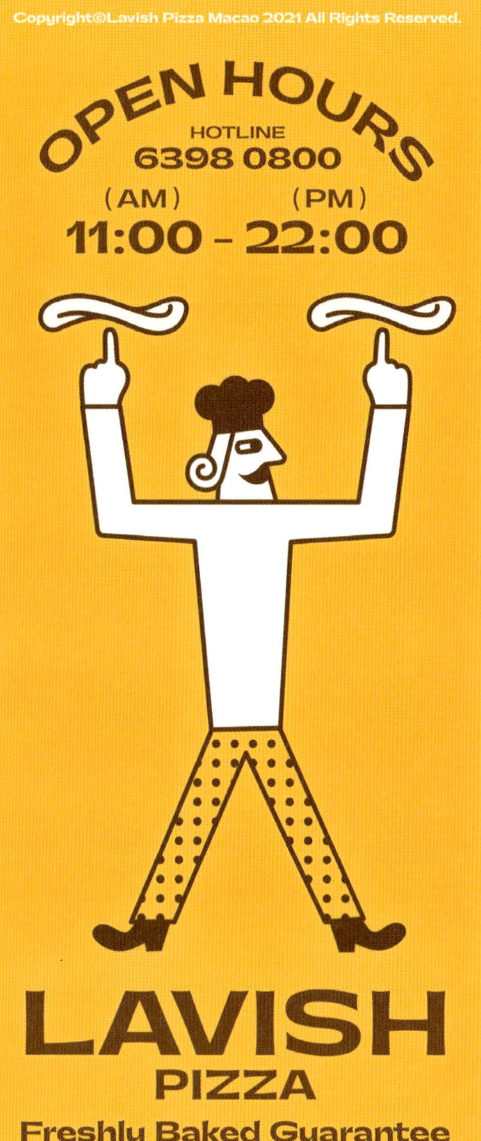
Copyright©Lavish Pizza Macao 2021 All Rights Reserved.
OPEN HOURS
HOTLINE
6398 0800
(AM) (PM)
11:00 - 22:00
LAVISH
PIZZA
Freshly Baked Guarantee

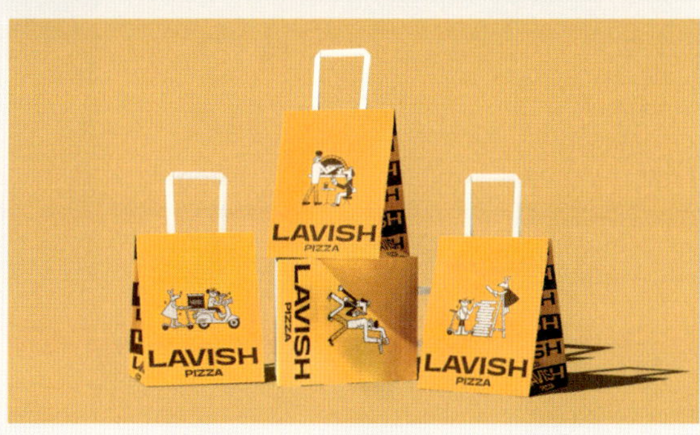
LAVISH
PIZZA

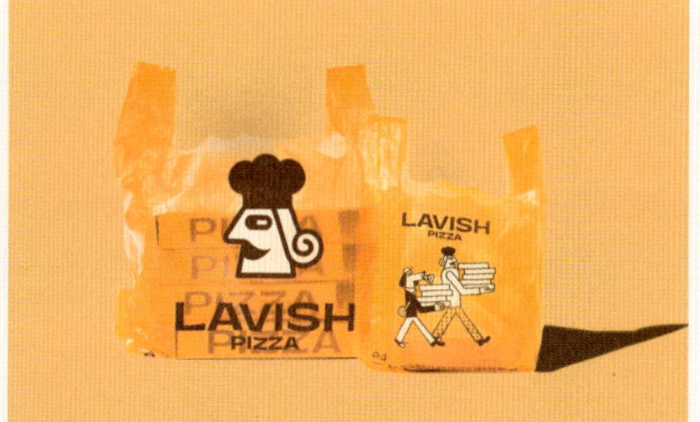
LAVISH
PIZZA

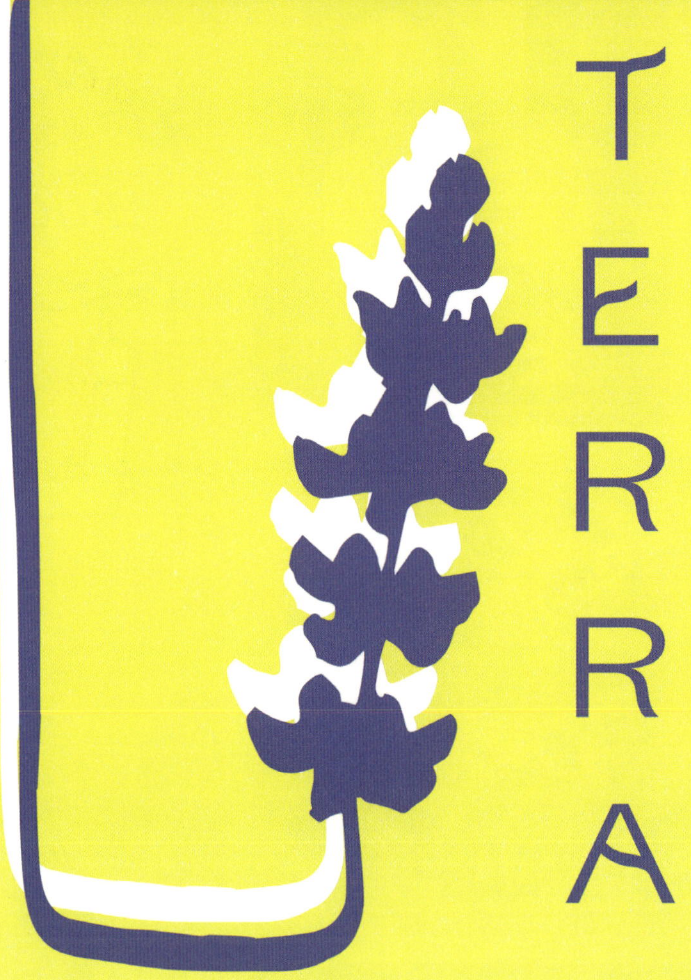

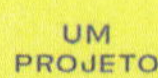
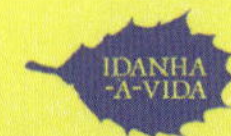

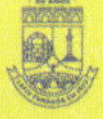

• Design Studio: ilhas studio • Client: Pela Terra

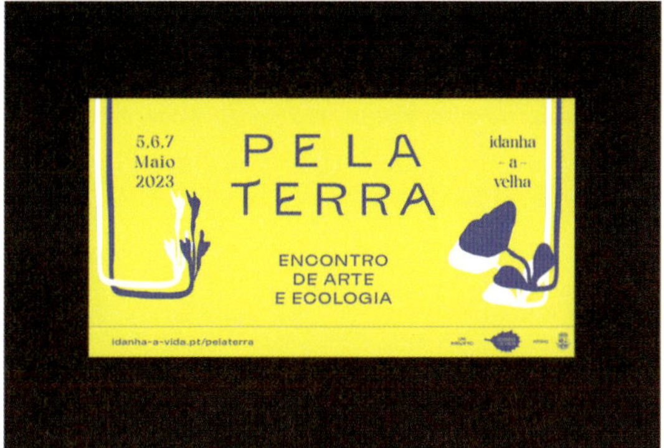

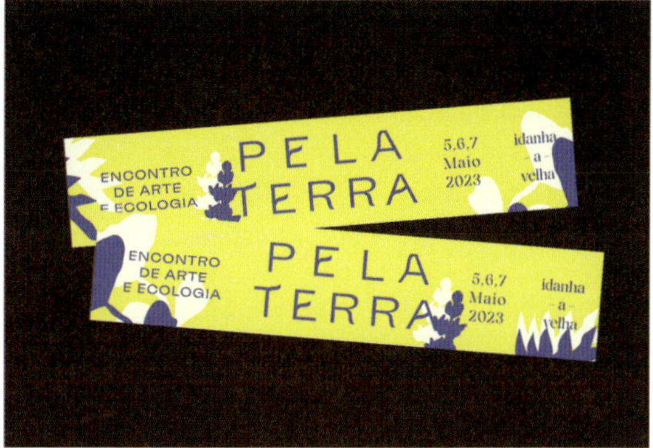

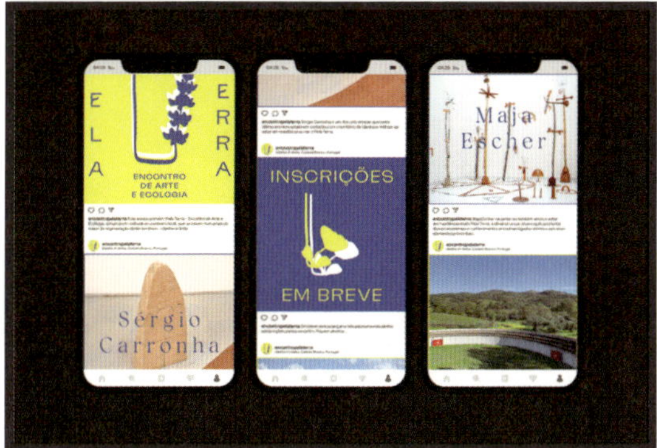

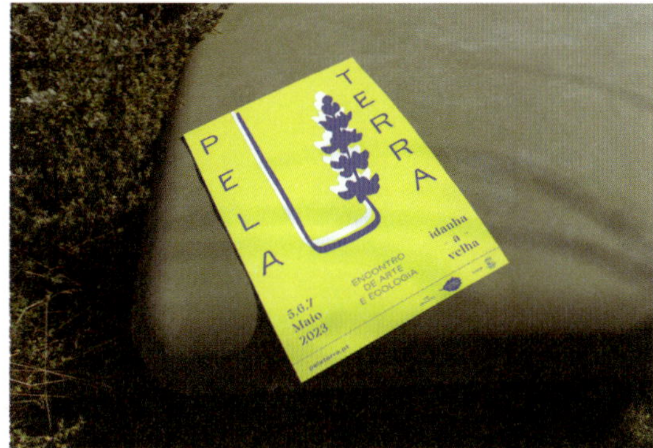

Pela Terra ● The graphic identity for the annual "Pela Terra" (For the Earth) festival in Idanha-a-Velha represents the convergence of art and ecology. Over three days, the festival serves as a platform for a profound connection with the earth, showcasing artistic interventions along a circular trail in Idanha's landscape. Eight resident artists, inspired by the village spirit, community, and surroundings, create these installations throughout the year.

● Why Yellow? ● "Pela Terra" celebrates the connection between art, ecology, and land during spring. The festival's identity prominently features the vital posture of the land's awakening, captured through yellow and blue, symbolizing the meeting of land and sky in nature.

C8 M0 Y87 K0 | C89 M74 Y0 K0

G120 Package Design

● Brand Holistic Bio aims to transform its image, moving away from traditional ginseng associations. The designer targeted a younger audience with a contemporary, trend-focused approach, without relying on traditional ginseng imagery. The structure, typography, and color palette were carefully crafted to convey a modern and future-oriented vibe.

● Why Yellow? ● The design team chose "yellow" as the main color for the project, considering it the most suitable to convey the desired energy and vitality of the product. In alignment with the future-oriented design concept, there is also a deliberate effort to evoke the sensation of light emerging from an achromatic space.

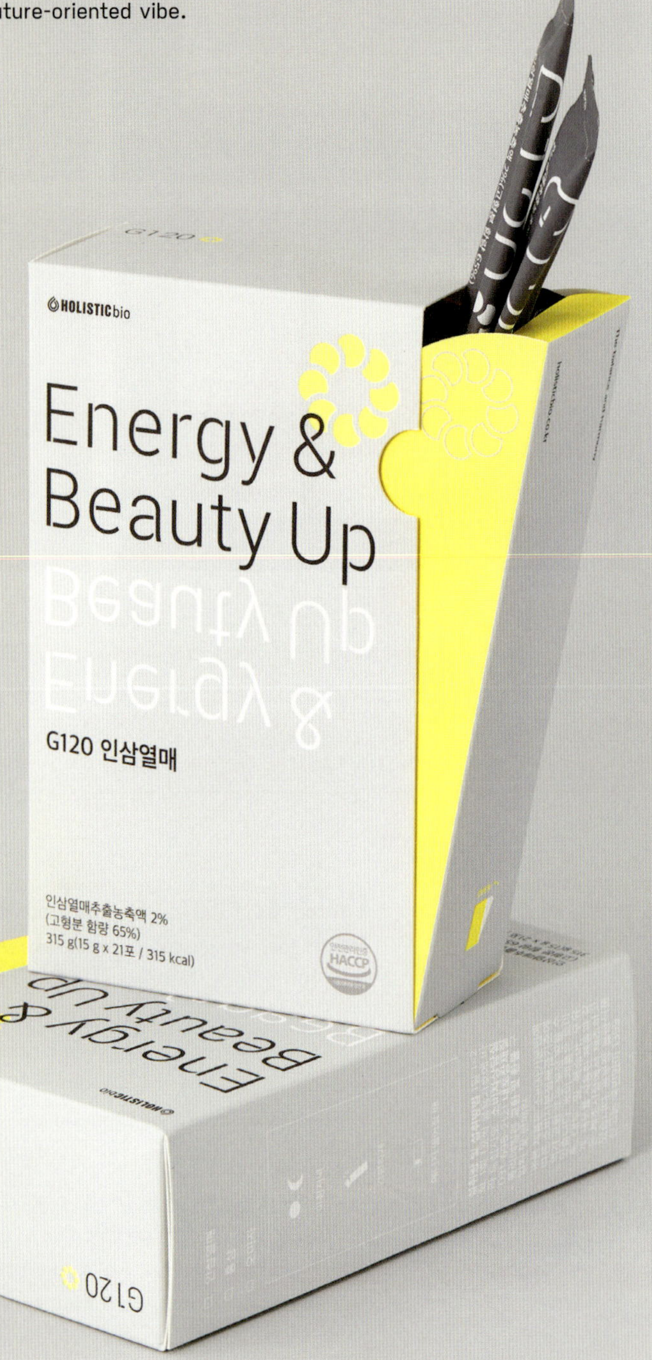

● Design Studio: LONG&SHORT ● Designer: Joohyung Yun ● Client: Holistic Bio

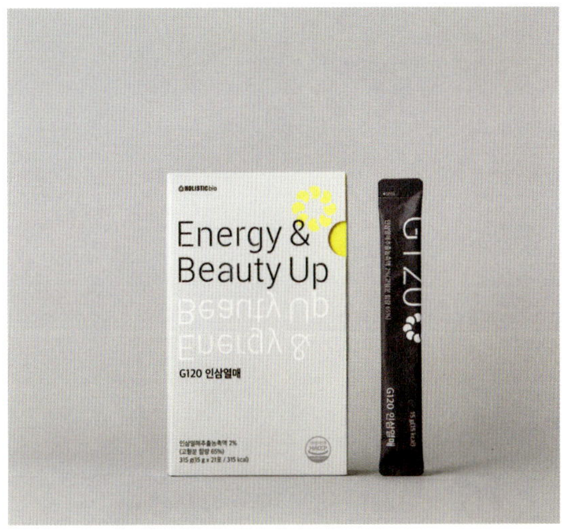
HOLISTICbio
Energy &
Beauty Up
G120 인삼열매
G120
G120 인삼열매

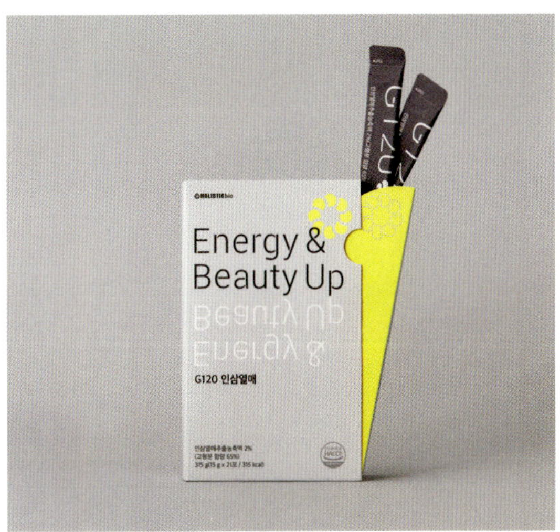
HOLISTICbio
Energy &
Beauty Up
G120 인삼열매

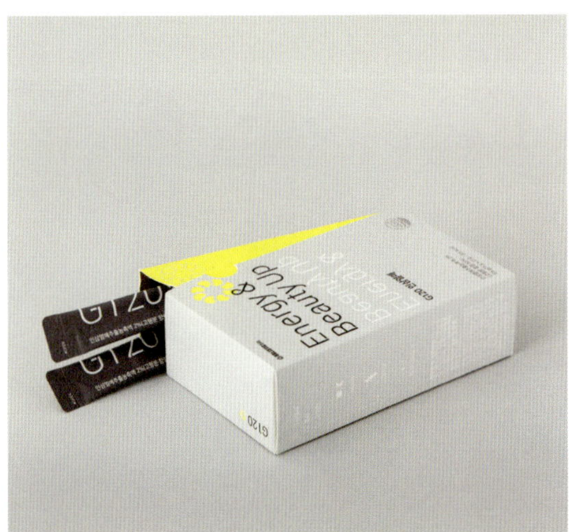
Energy &
Beauty Up
G120 인삼열매
G120

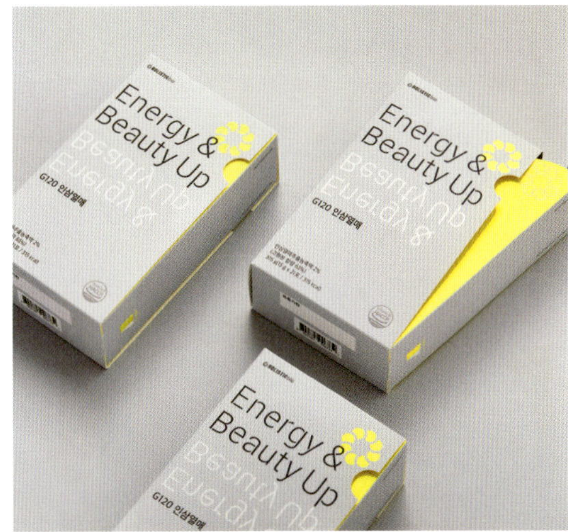
Energy &
Beauty Up
G120 인삼열매
Energy &
Beauty Up
G120 인삼열매
Energy &
Beauty Up
G120 인삼열매

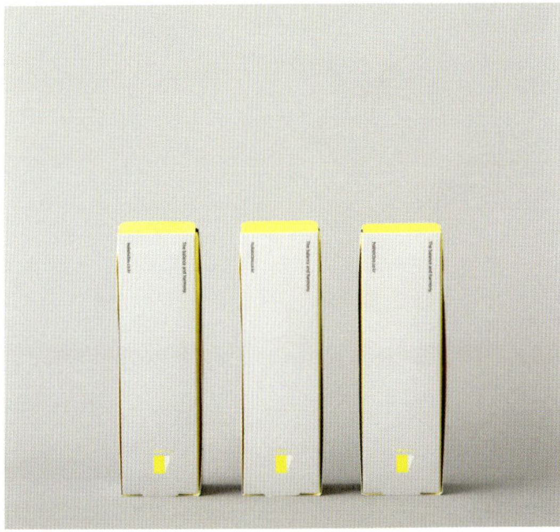

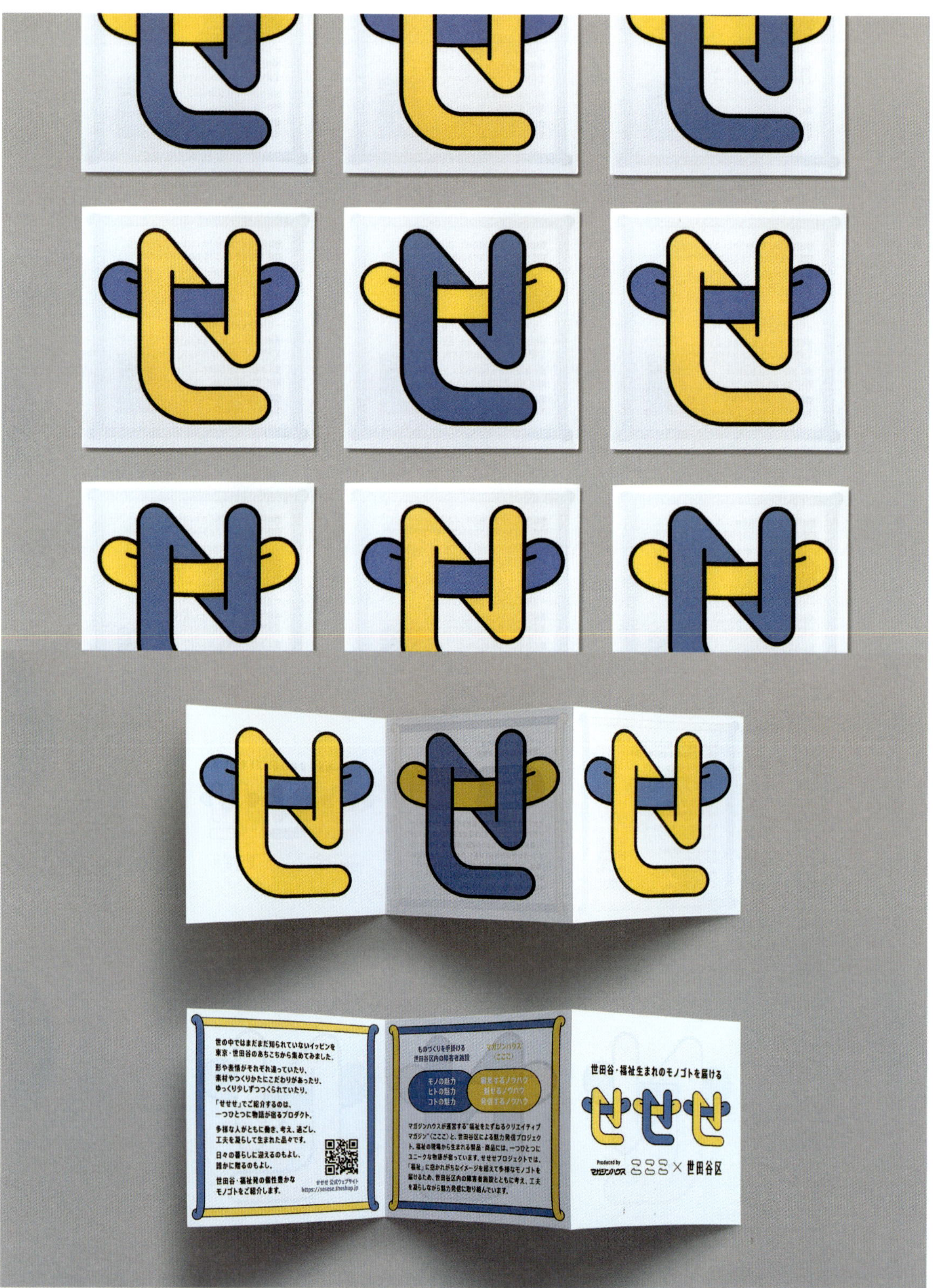

 • Design Studio: MOTOMOTO inc. • Designer: Kenichi Matsumoto • Client: SETAGAYA CITY & MAGAZINE HOUSE CO., LTD.

SESESE ● The design team created the logo for "Sesese," a project by "Kokoko," a creative magazine about welfare operated by Magazine House and Setagaya city. The goal was to promote the attractiveness of products and goods born in the field of welfare, making the serious theme more fun and appealing.

● Why Yellow? ● The two colors used in the logo contrast different hues, emphasizing the theme of connection and gentleness based on the image of people interacting with each other. ● Rather than the strength of the primary colors as they are, the mixed colors are meant to create an image of softness and brightness.

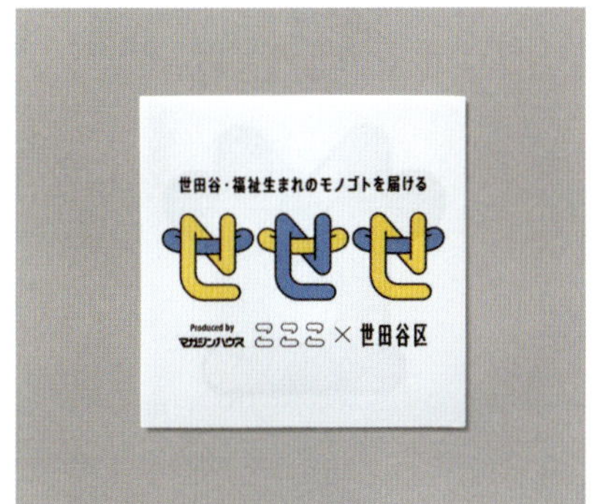

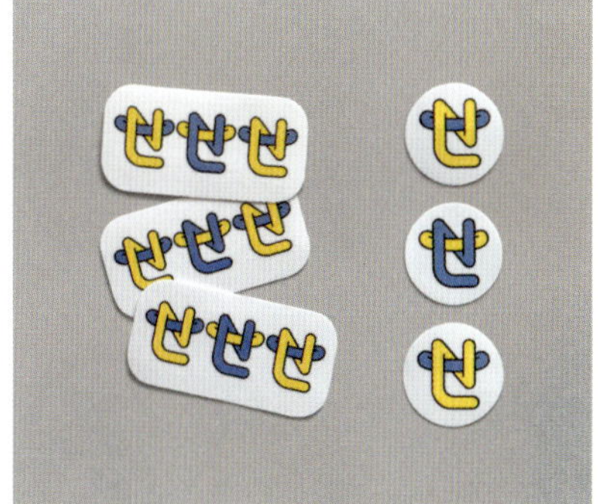

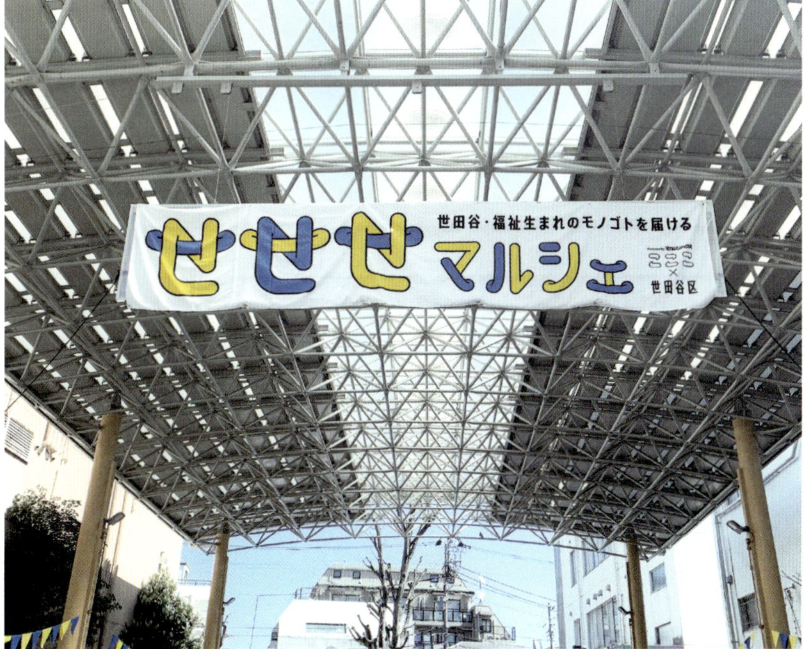

C0 M15 Y100 K0 | C70 M30 Y0 K0

SITO NATA • Sito Nata, a popular bakery in Macau, known for its Portuguese tarts, incorporates doodles drawn by global food enthusiasts on its wall. The logo highlights a Portuguese tart and a headcloth, a nod to the shop owner Sito. Inspired by tart spots and wall doodles, the packaging uses vibrant yellow and blue, featuring Portuguese style, with a tart color enhancing the design's distinctiveness and vitality.

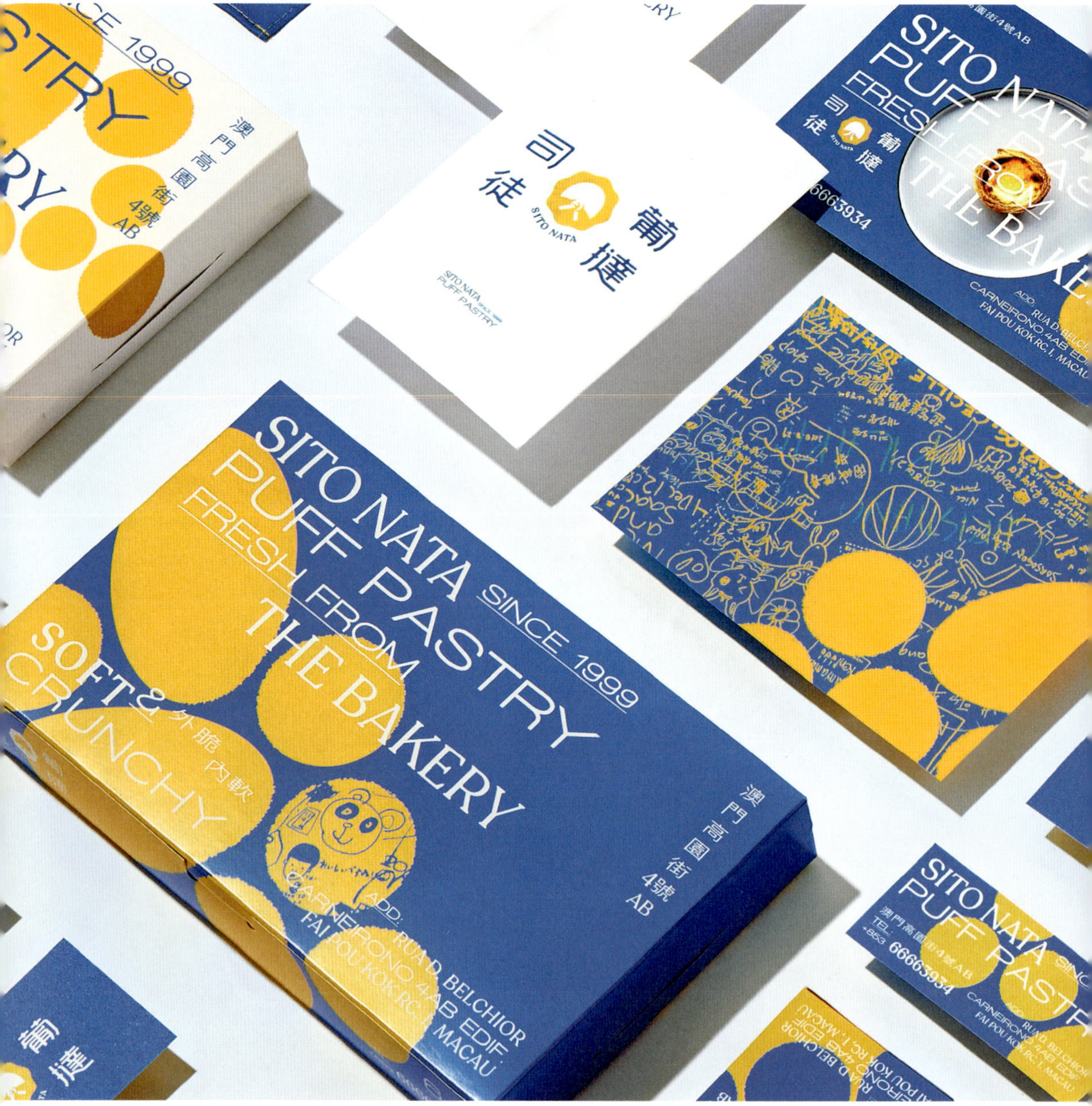

• Design Studio: Indego design • Designer: Lam Ieong Kun, Dan Ferreira • Client: SITO NATA

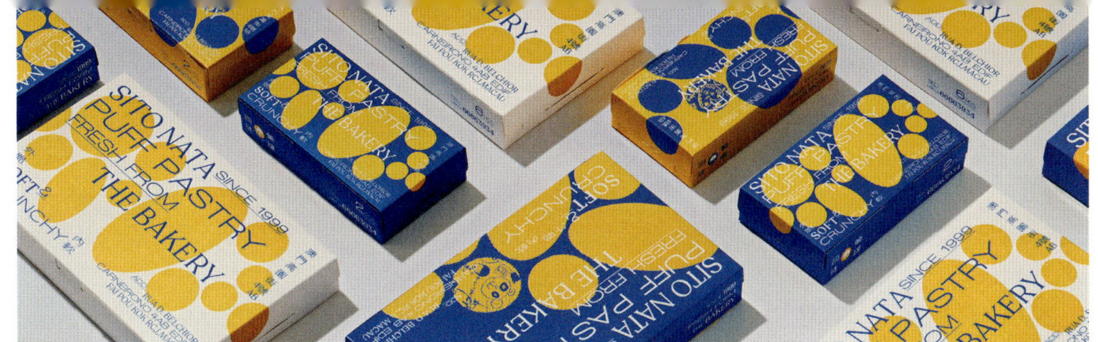

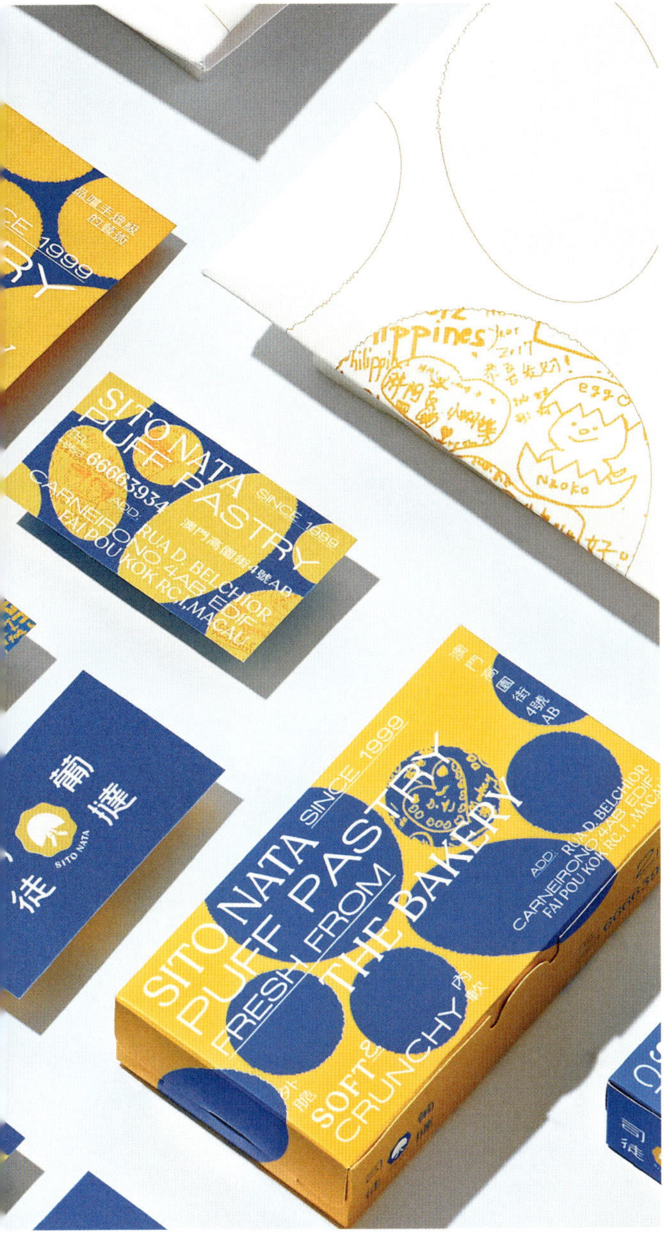

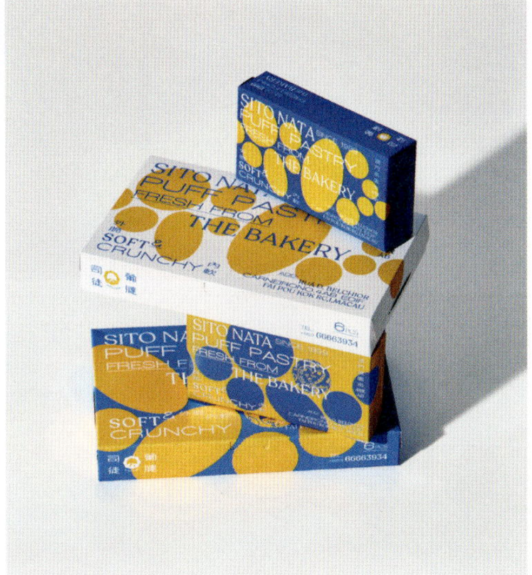

● Why Yellow? ● The design team opted for yellow and blue as the main colors, with yellow representing the color of Portuguese tarts and blue embodying a Portuguese style. This color choice aims to elevate the overall design, making it more distinctive and vibrant.

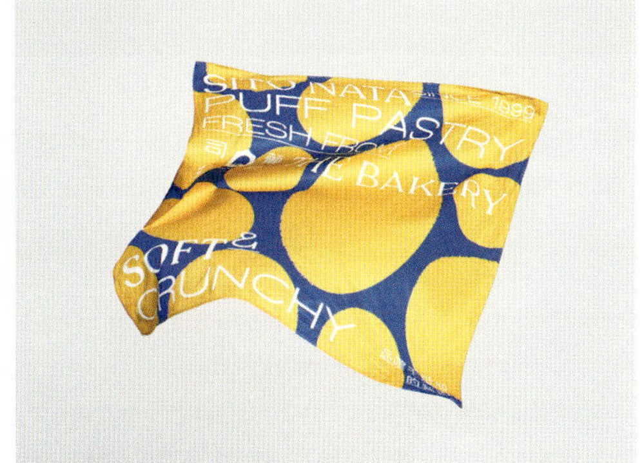

C5 M21 Y86 K0 | C87 M65 Y0 K0

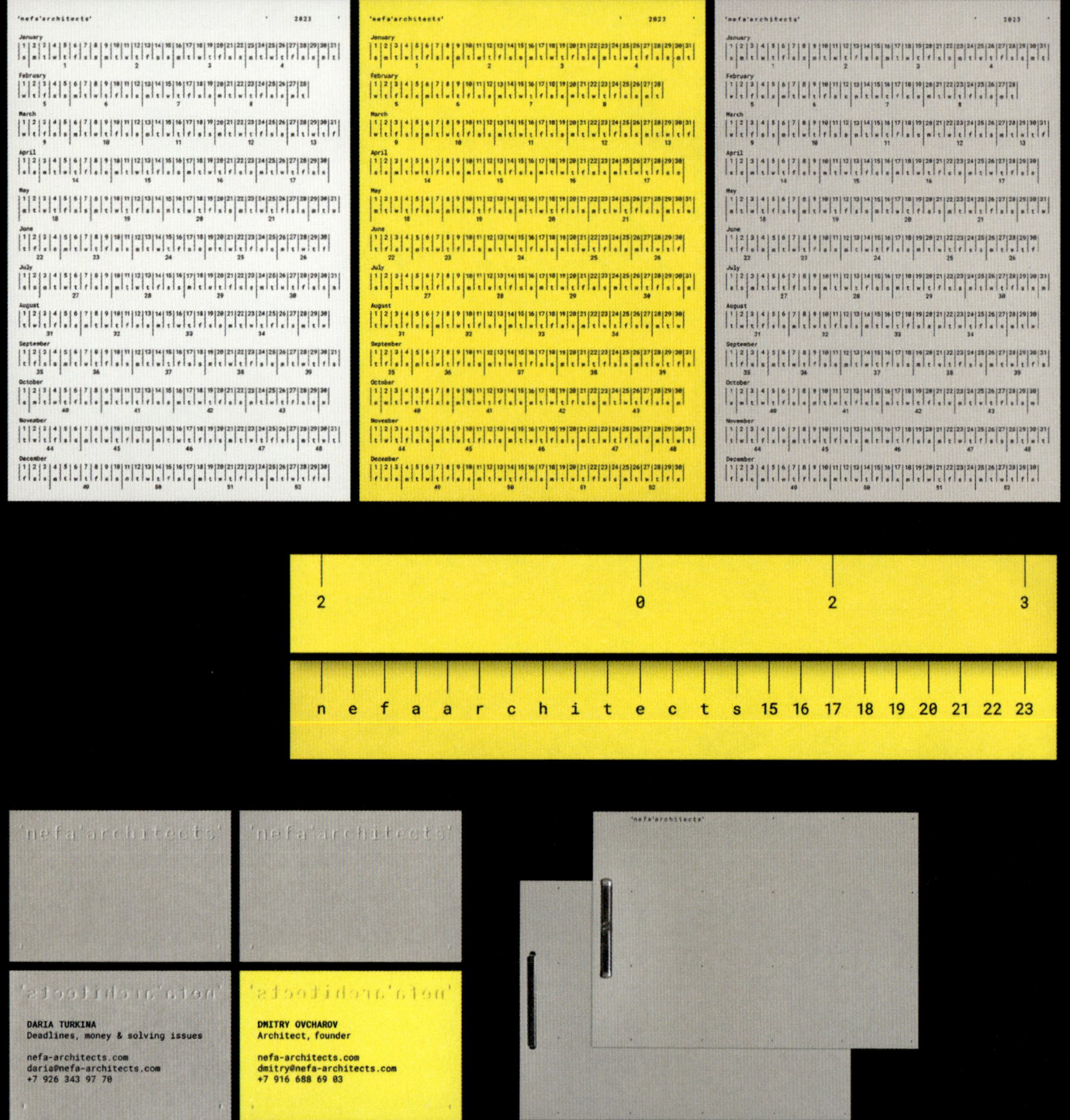

Nefa Architects Visual identity

• With a 25-year history, Nefa Architects specializes in custom projects. The design team revamped the logo and brand identity to embody an engineering approach to space design. Inspired by architectural drawings, the visual language features measuring ruler markings, while the corporate font, Roboto Mono, adds a modern touch. The lowercase logo emphasizes an open and friendly bureau, integrated into a modular grid with serifs. The color palette draws from project images, including monochrome tones representing architects' favorite materials—metal and concrete. Yellow symbolizes the bureau's love for experimentation and self-expression.

• Design Studio: Leit Design • Designer: Ekaterina Nikolaeva, Daria Kazakova

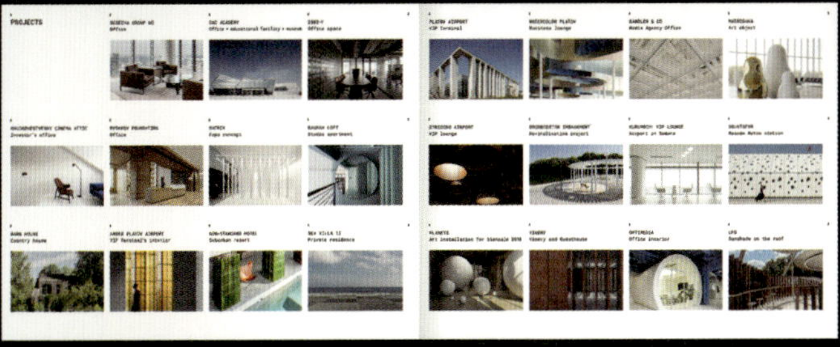

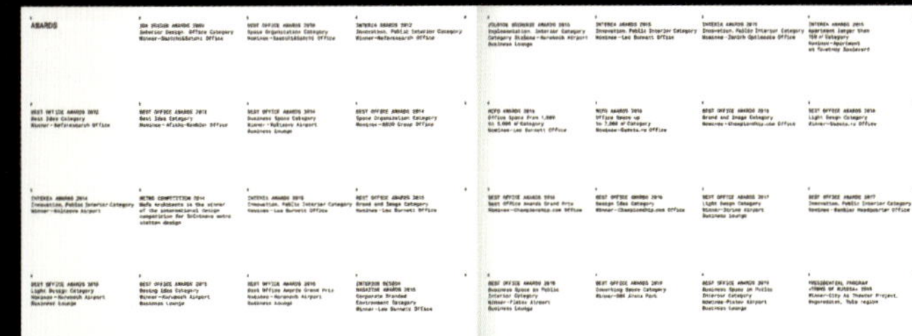

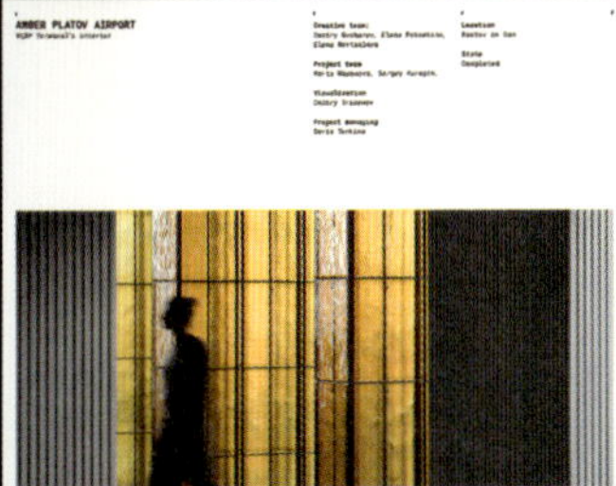

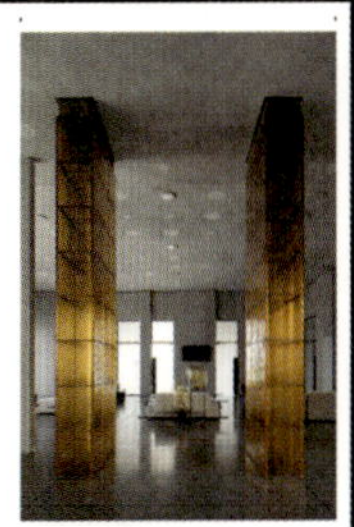

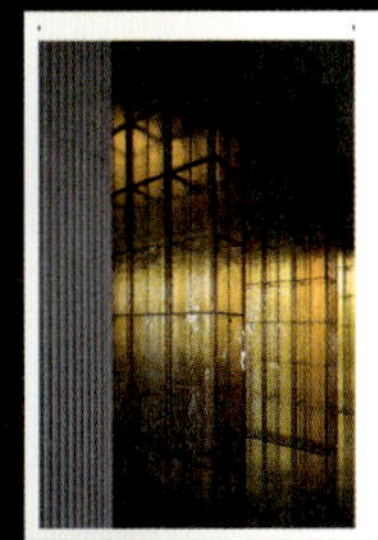

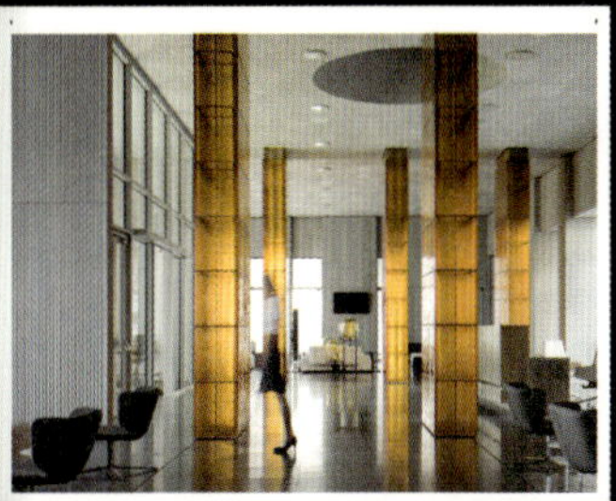

● Why Yellow? ● In this project, the yellow color signifies the bureau's passion for experimentation and self-expression. The chief architect, associating yellow with architecture, integrates it as the featured color into the monochrome palette.

● Client: Nefa Architects

C0 M0 Y100 K0

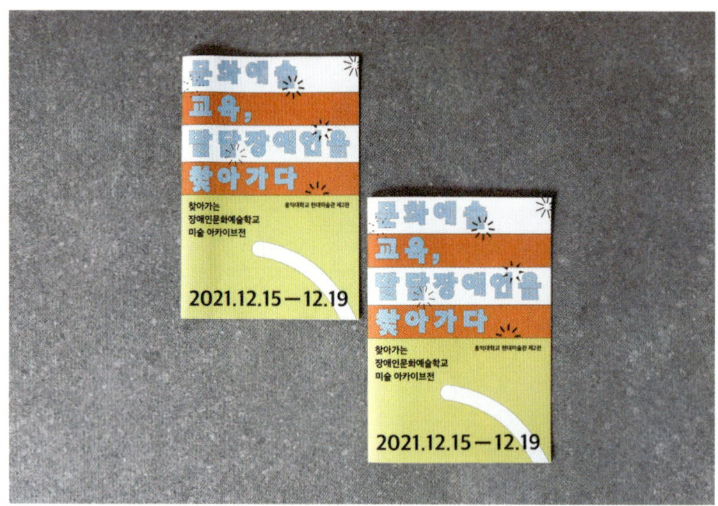
문화예술
교육,
발달장애인을
찾아가다
찾아가는
장애인문화예술학교
미술 아카이브전
2021.12.15—12.19

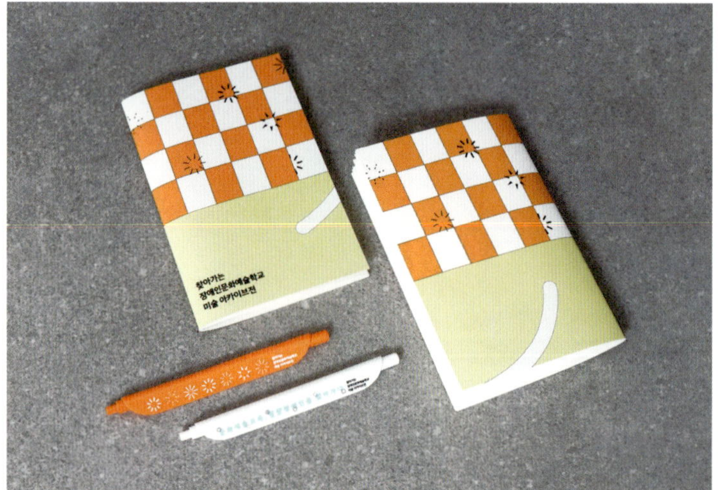
찾아가는
장애인문화예술학교
미술 아카이브전

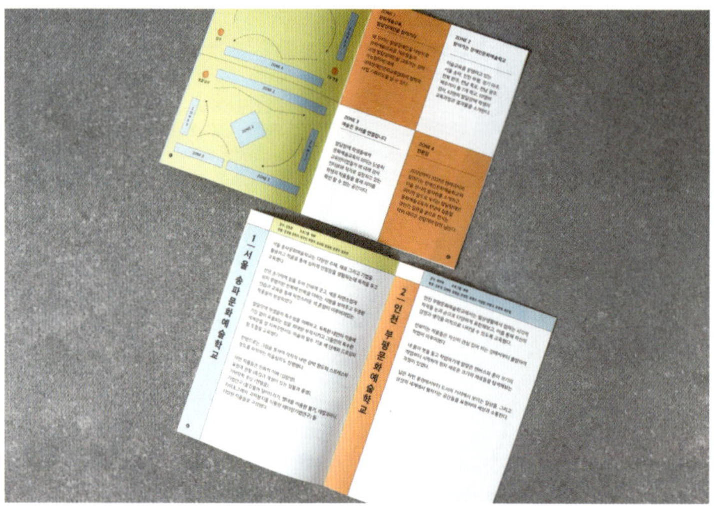
1 서울 송파문화예술학교
2 인천 부평문화예술학교

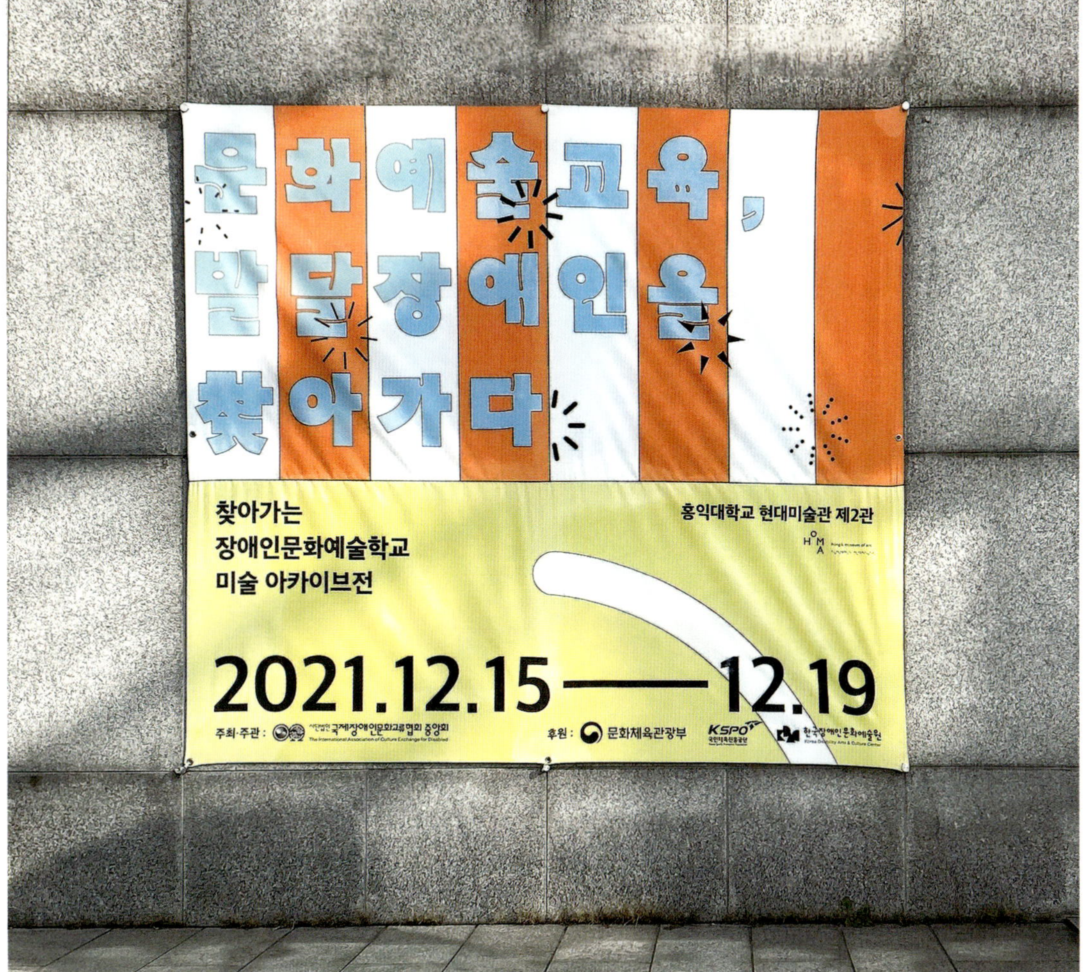

Exhibition Design of Arts School for the Disabled

● The Art Archive Exhibition of the Culture and Arts School for Disabled showcases the philosophy and history of culture and arts education for the developmentally disabled and announces the results in 2021. The exhibition encourages reflection on the arts education philosophy for the disabled and future focuses by using a positive and flexible visual centered around the keyword "possibility," while expressing hope with the keyword "light."

● Why Yellow? ● The project primarily utilizes orange, light blue, and yellow as its main colors, to convey the possibilities and diversity of the exhibition's subjects, with a central focus on creating an overall "positive" mood.

C0 M53 Y74 K0 | C5 M2 Y57 K0 | C31 M0 Y13 K0

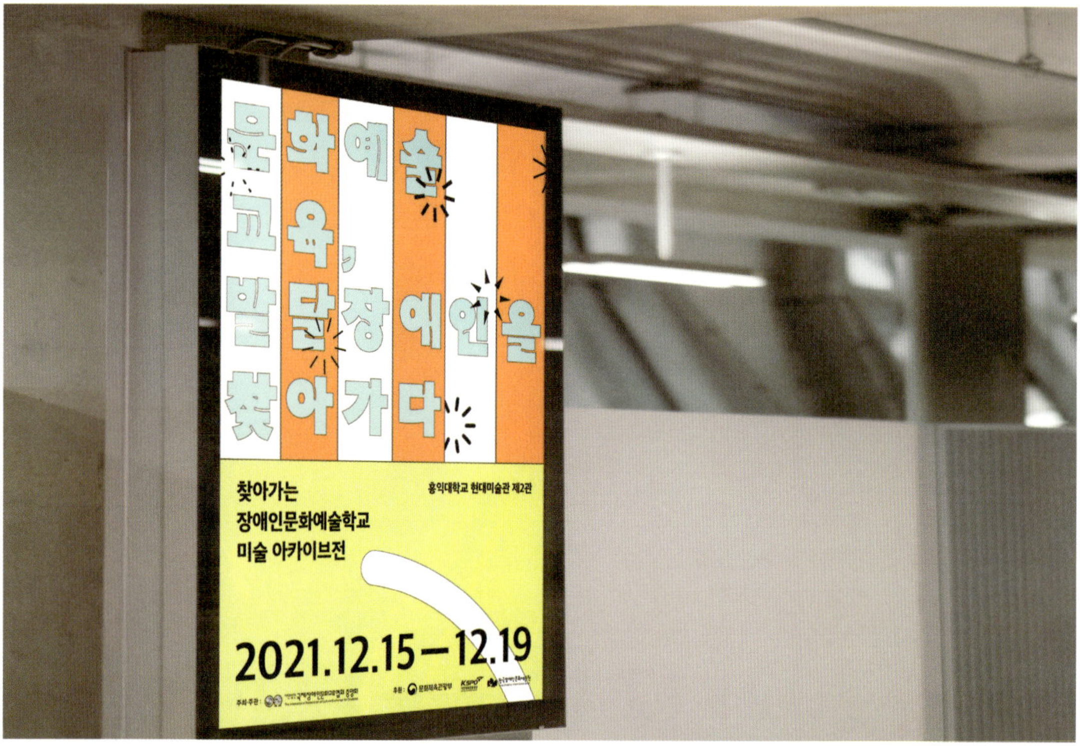
문화예술
교육,
발달장애인을
찾아가다
찾아가는
장애인문화예술학교
미술 아카이브전
홍익대학교 현대미술관 제2관
2021.12.15—12.19

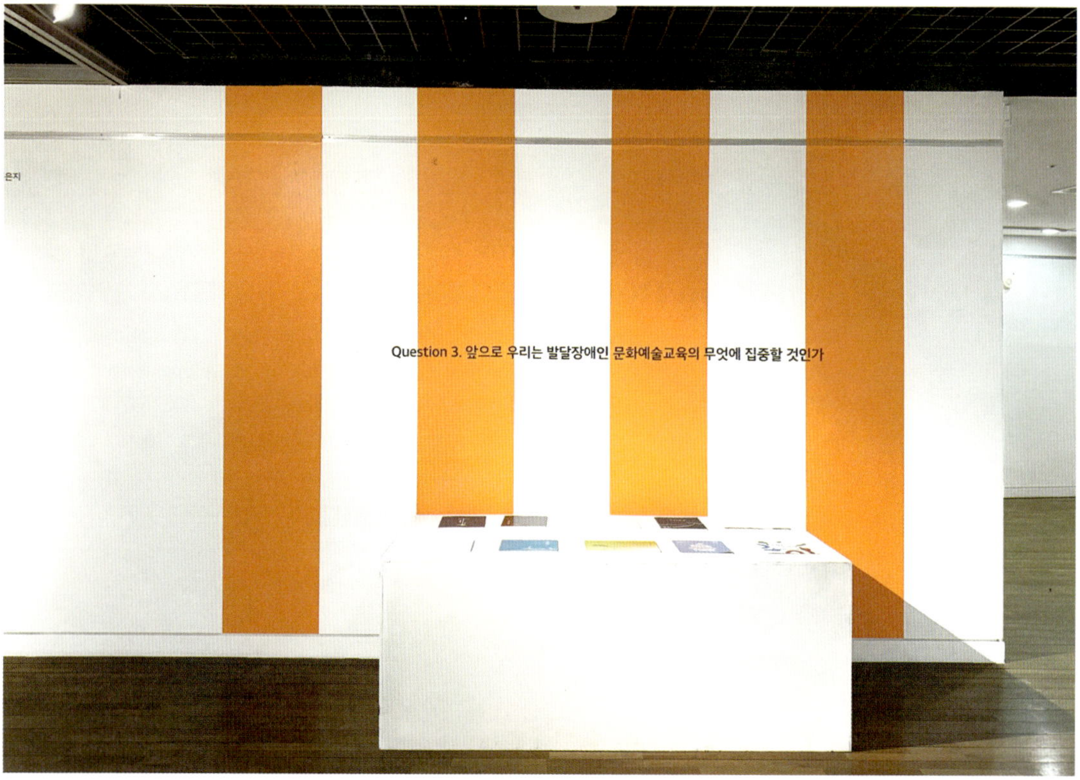
Question 3. 앞으로 우리는 발달장애인 문화예술교육의 무엇에 집중할 것인가

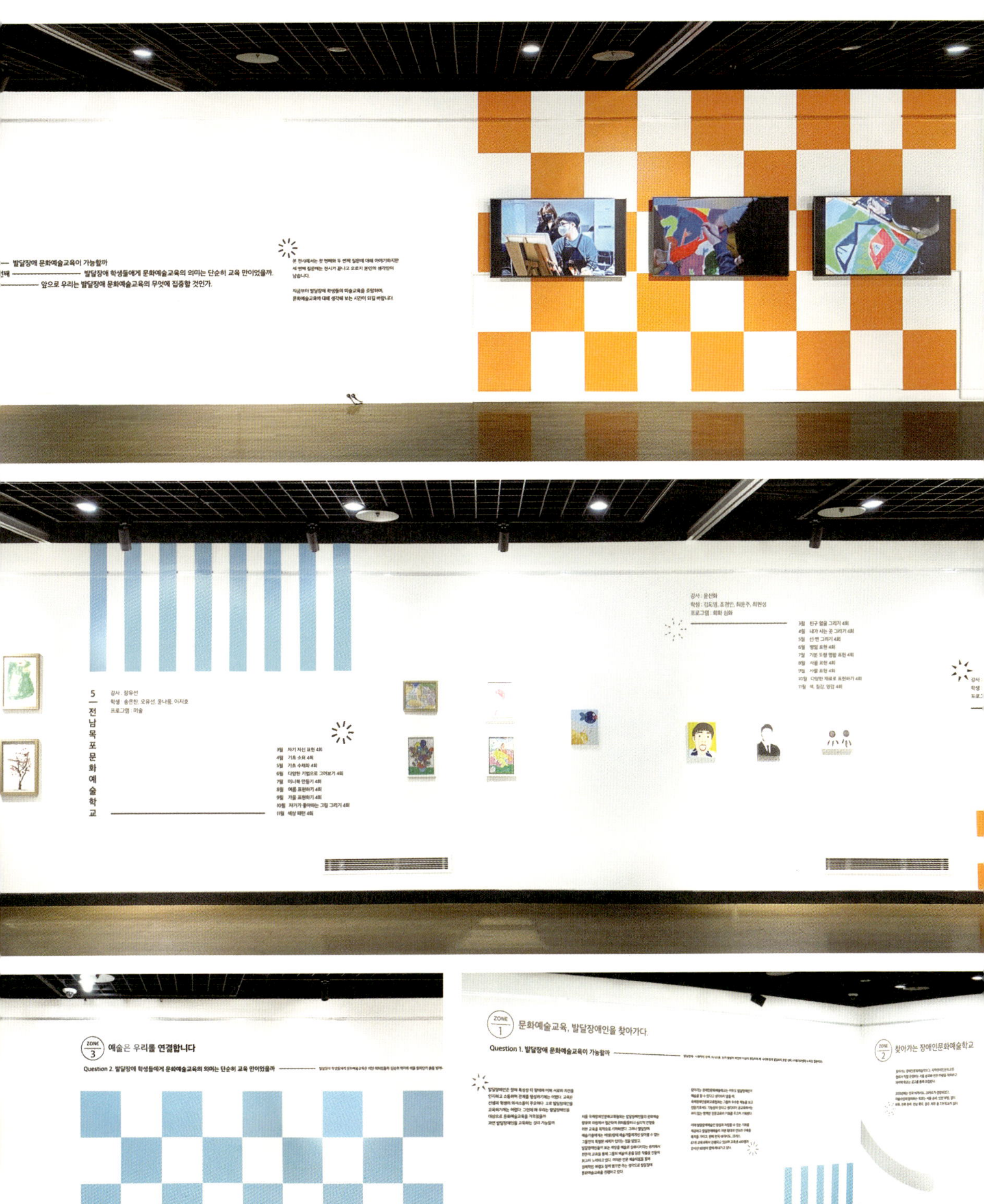

Breadwinner • Joined by a team of engineers in the early stage, the designer played a key role in shaping Breadwinner, a tech company for detail-oriented bakers. From guiding the company to establishing its brand identity, the designer fused European bread-making history with a DIY punk ethos. The blackletter-inspired logo and typography, along with anthropomorphized loaf-and-starter characters, aim to simplify the bread-making process.

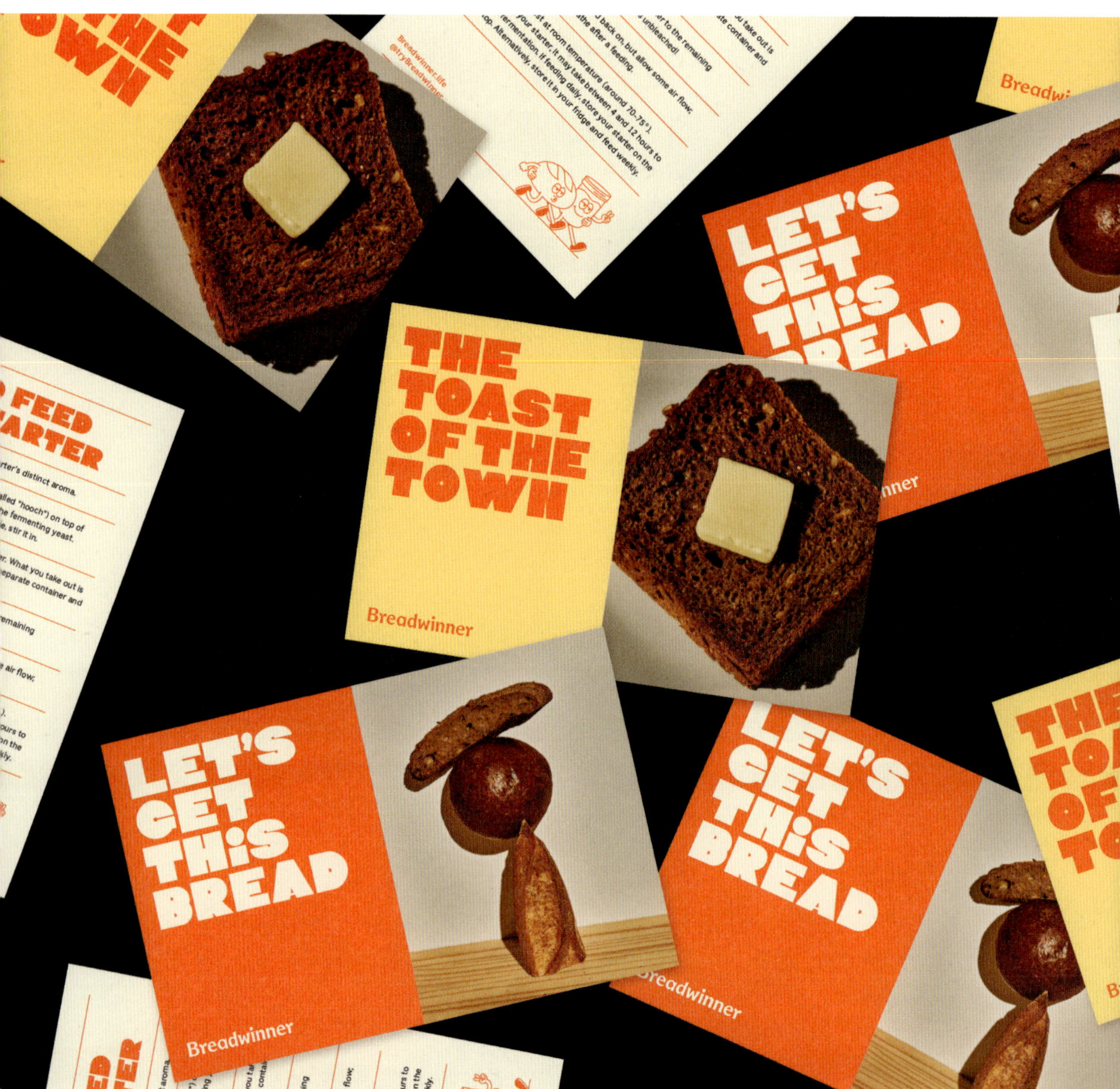

 • Design and Creative Director: Elizabeth Goodspeed • Illustrator: Steve Gavan • Photographer: Cody Guilfoyle

● Why Yellow? ● The yellow and orange-red tones in this project exude warmth, evoking a sense of hominess reminiscent of a kitchen. Besides, they infuse a bold and contemporary flare into a brand deeply entrenched in history.

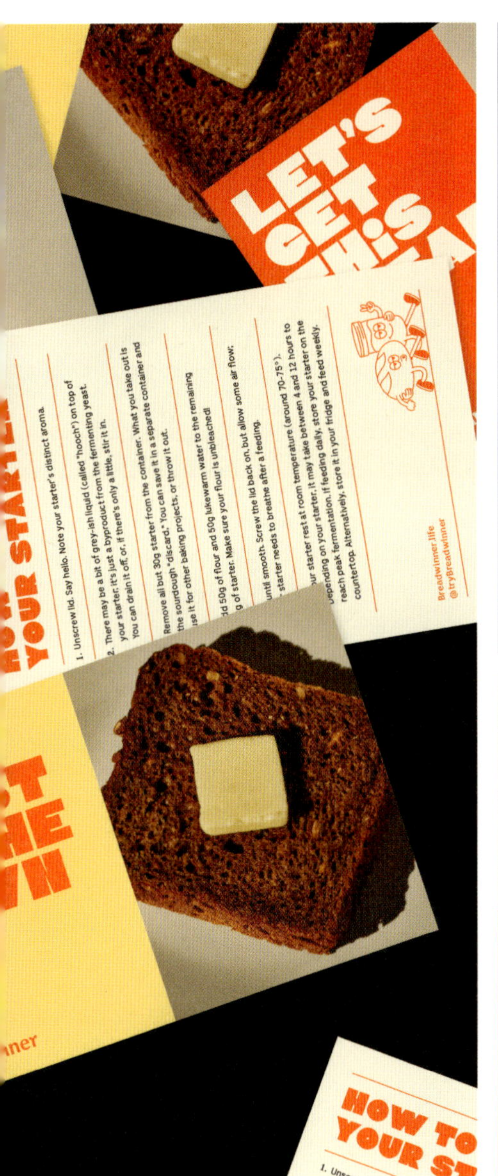

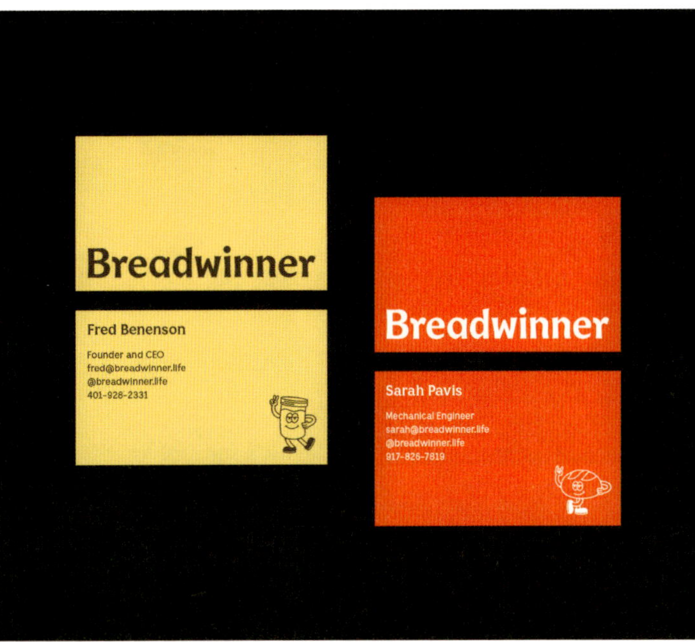

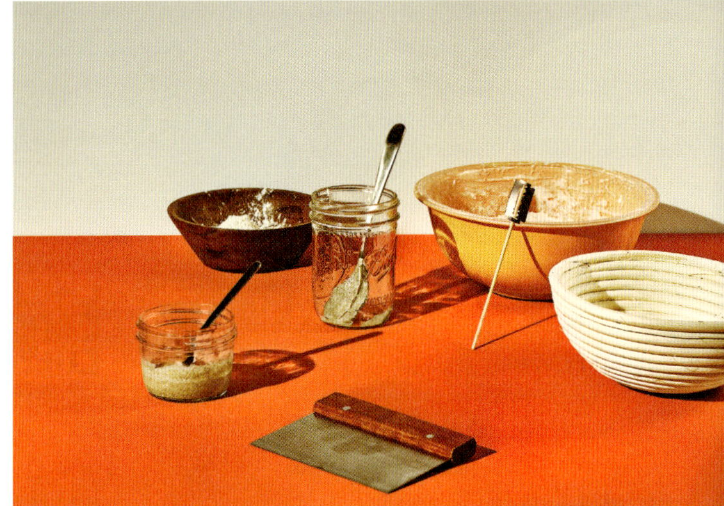

● Client: Fred Benenson

C0 M76 Y100 K0 | C3 M14 Y64 K0

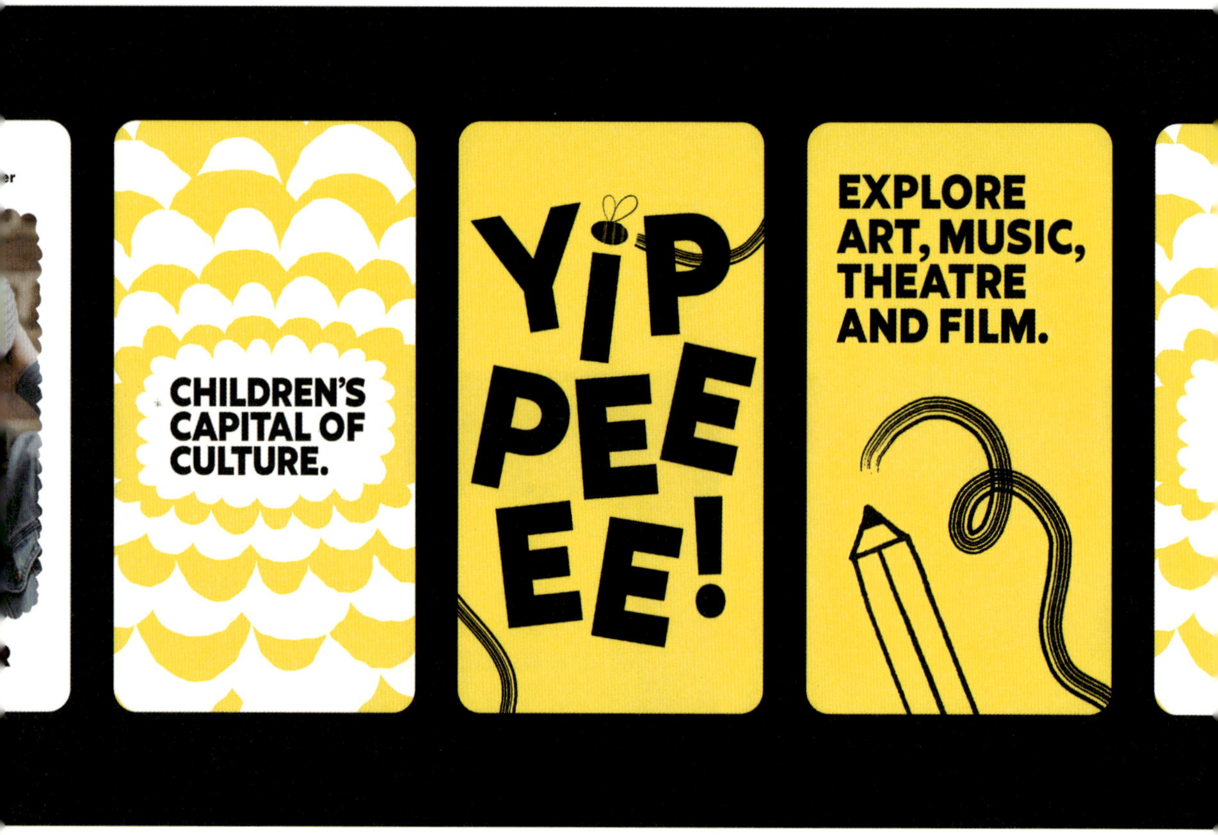

Children's Capital of Culture

● The town of Rotherham will be awarded the world's first Children's Capital of Culture in 2025. The design team crafted a dynamic brand identity, including illustrations, an advertising campaign, and merchandise, to celebrate this huge achievement. ● With a playful aesthetic, the identity engages the young audience, fostering positivity and encouraging active community involvement.

Inspired by traits of imagination and ambition, the brand promotes the idea that "anything is possible," motivating young people to pursue ambitious paths in their early careers. The illustrative elements cover diverse subjects, symbolizing the spirit of limitless possibilities.

● Why Yellow? ● The design team chose yellow for its impactful vibrancy, especially when paired with black, aiming to captivate attention, ensure brand recognition, and convey positive, encouraging messages through entertaining illustrations.

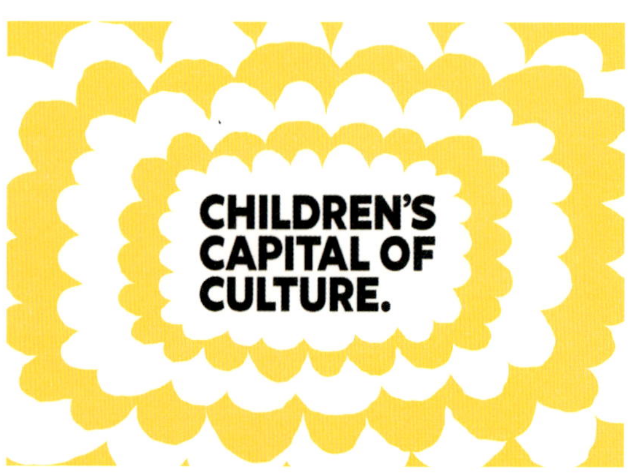

● Design Studio: Foundry ● Client: Rotherham Metropolitan Borough Council

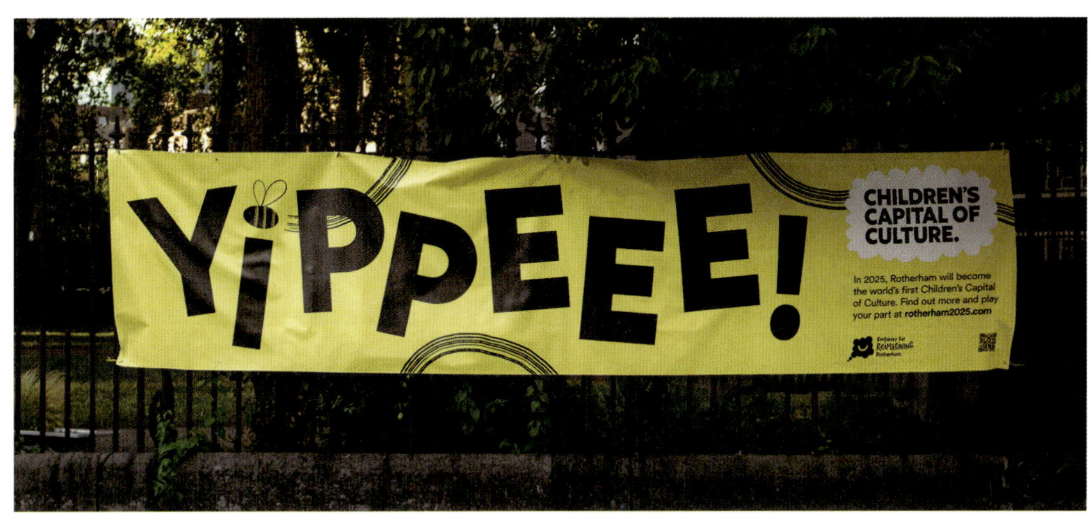
YIPPEEE!
CHILDREN'S CAPITAL OF CULTURE.
In 2025, Rotherham will become the world's first Children's Capital of Culture. Find out more and play your part at rotherham2025.com

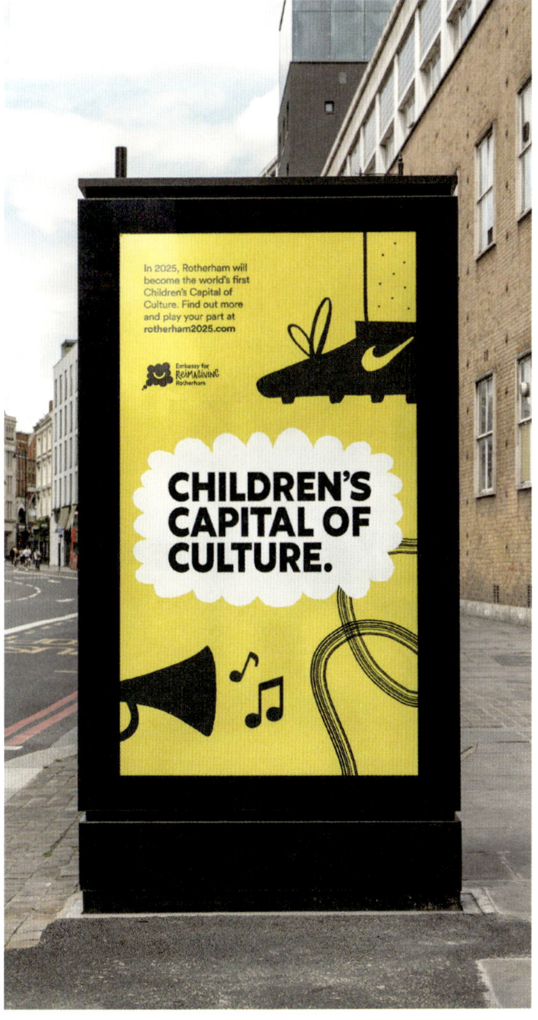
In 2025, Rotherham will become the world's first Children's Capital of Culture. Find out more and play your part at rotherham2025.com
CHILDREN'S CAPITAL OF CULTURE.

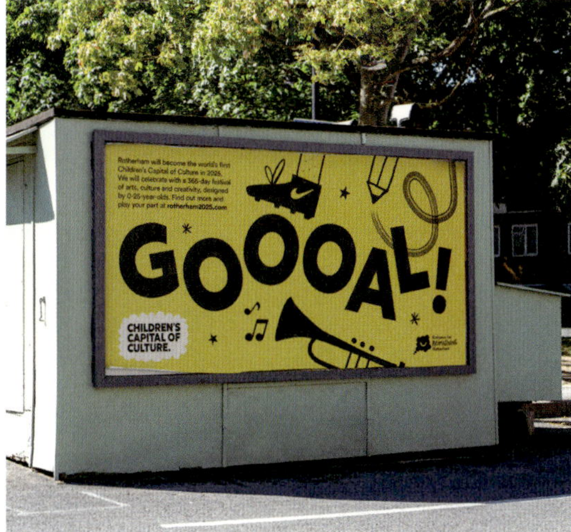
Rotherham will become the world's first Children's Capital of Culture in 2025. We will celebrate with a 365-day festival of arts, culture and creativity, designed by 0-25-year-olds. Find out more and play your part at rotherham2025.com
GOOOAL!
CHILDREN'S CAPITAL OF CULTURE.

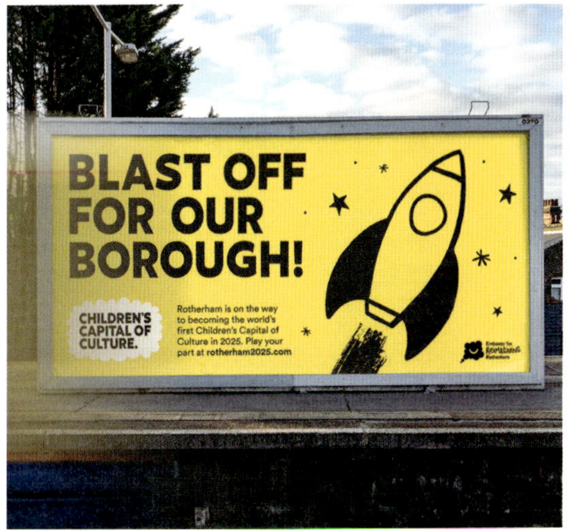
BLAST OFF FOR OUR BOROUGH!
CHILDREN'S CAPITAL OF CULTURE.
Rotherham is on the way to becoming the world's first Children's Capital of Culture in 2025. Play your part at rotherham2025.com

C2 M7 Y91 K0

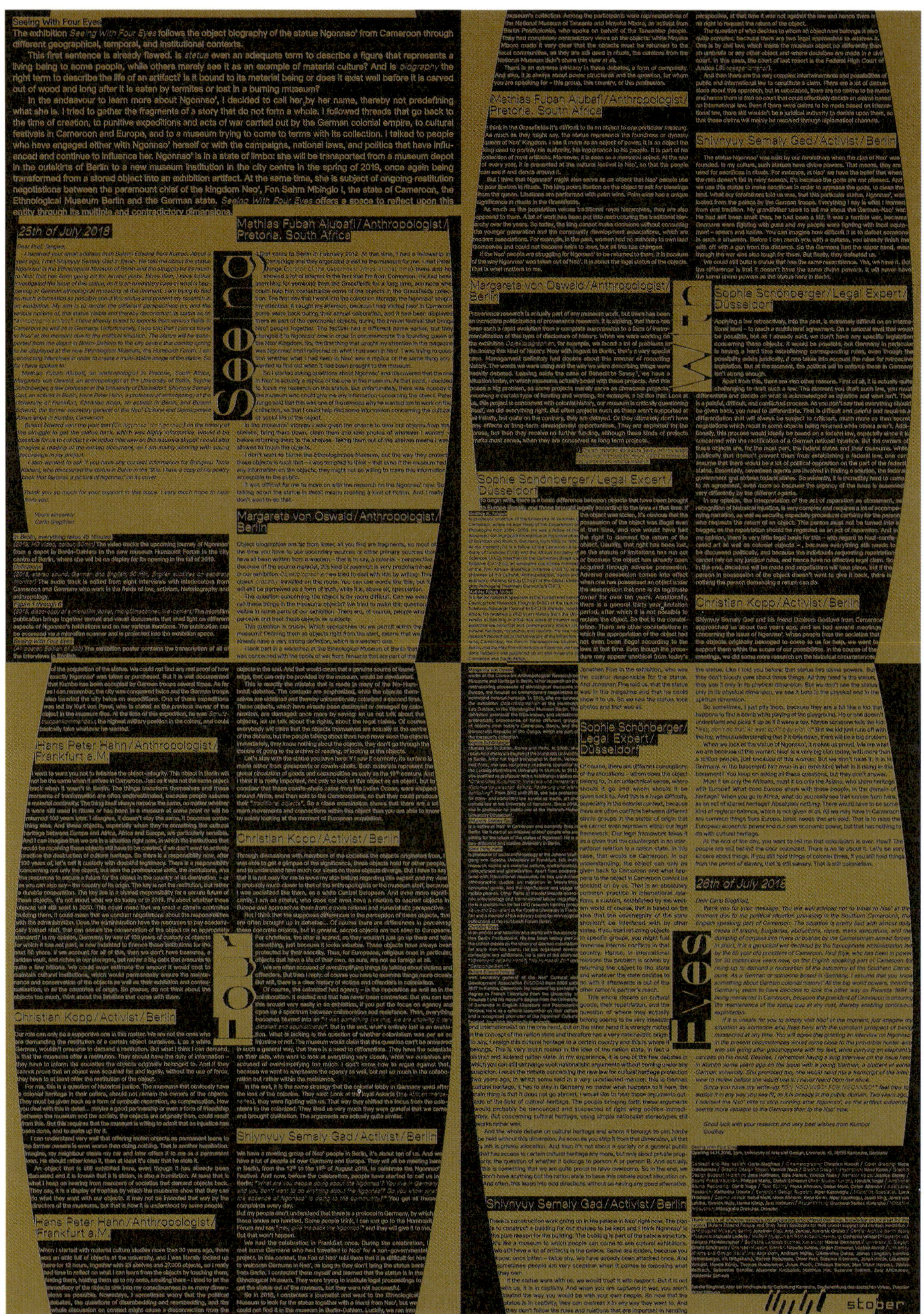

● Design Studio: Studio Yannick Nuss ● Designer: Yannick Nuss ● Client: Carlo Siegfried

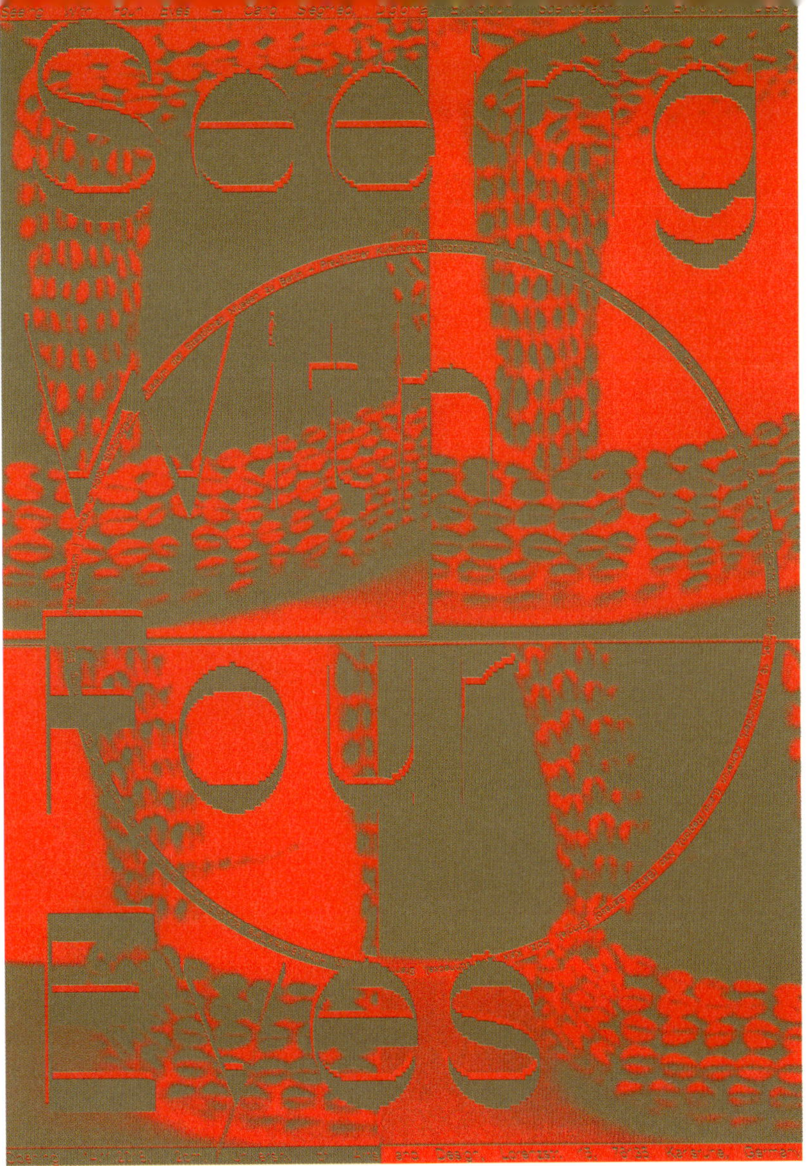

Seeing With Four Eyes • Posters for the exhibition *Seeing With Four Eyes* by the artist Carlo Siegfried at the University for Arts and Design in Karlsruhe. The exhibition explored the biography of the Ngonnso[1] statue and its travels through different German ethnological institutes.

• Why Yellow? • The designer created a double-sided poster utilizing spot colors, specifically Pantone 485 C for red and Pantone 871 C for gold. These colors, along with black, subtly alluded to the German flag and evoked associations with blood and gold.

1.Ngonnso: refers to a traditional African statue with cultural and artistic significance, often associated with specific rituals or traditions.

PANTONE 871C PANTONE 485C

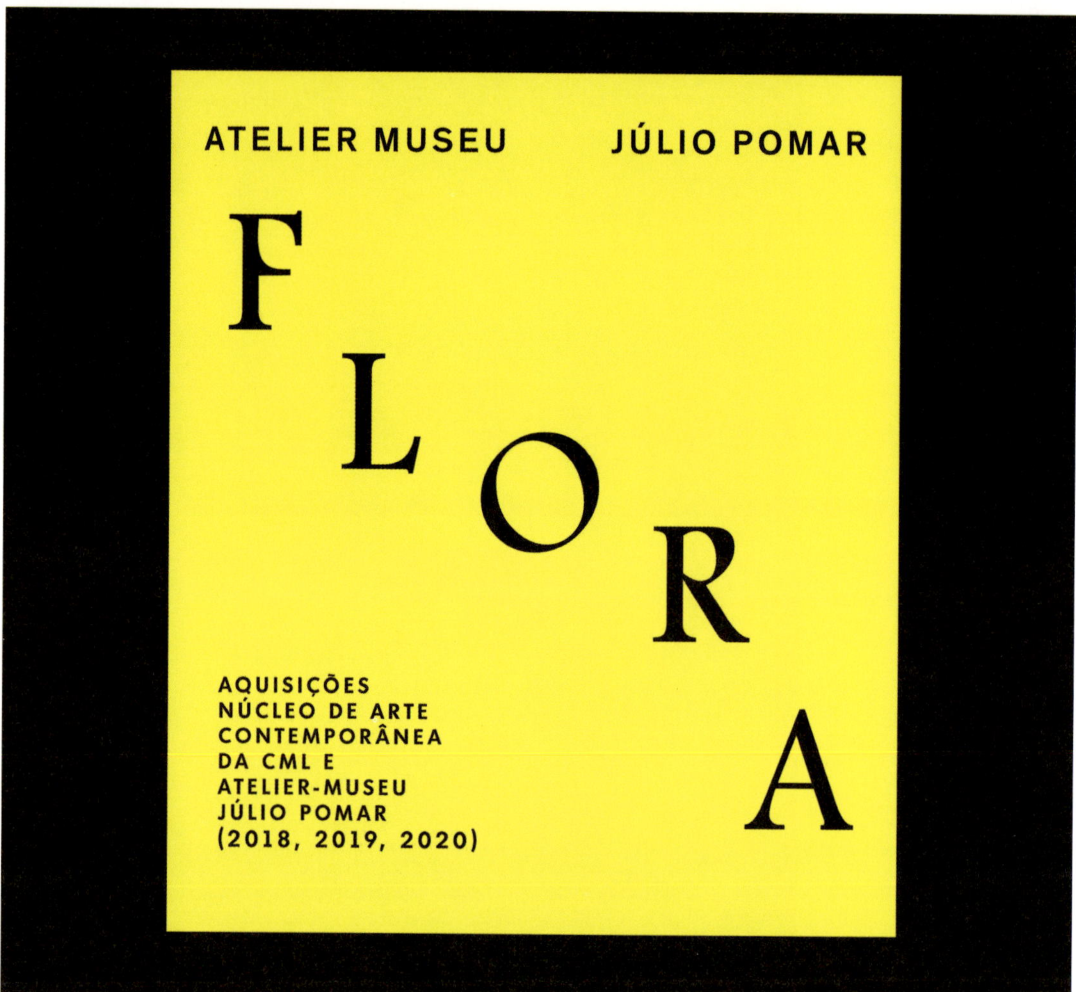

Flora • The graphic image for the *FLORA* exhibition, curated by Sara Antonia Matos and Pedro Faro, explores the diversity of themes in Portuguese contemporary art. Named after a reception of Andre Romao's works, the exhibition aims to engage visitors directly with the pieces and respond to questions raised by them. The extensive body of works led to the use of typographic language for the exhibition's poster and graphic identity.

• Why Yellow? • During the COVID-19 pandemic, the team worked on projecting and designing the visual identity for the exhibition. Despite the challenges, they felt a sense of hope and brightness in the idea of bringing people together through the exhibition. This led to the choice of such a vibrant and warm color for the visual identity.

• Design Studio: ilhas studio • Client: Atelier-Museu Júlio Pomar

ATELIER MUSEU
JÚLIO POMAR

F L O R A

AQUISIÇÕES
NÚCLEO DE ARTE
CONTEMPORÂNEA
DA CML E
ATELIER-MUSEU
JÚLIO POMAR
(2018, 2019, 2020)

5 de Abril
a 13 de Junho

Inauguração
5 de Abril
11h às 17h

EGEAC ATELIER MUSEU JULIO POMAR
Pomar

ATELIER MUSEU
JÚLIO POMAR

F L O R A

Ana Santos
André Cepeda
André Romão
Augusto Alves da Silva
Bruno Cidra
Bruno Pacheco
Carla Filipe
Catarina Dias
Cecília Costa
Dalila Gonçalves
Dealmeida Esilva
Francisco Tropa
Henrique Pavão
Hugo Canoilas
Igor Jesus
Isabel Madureira Andrade
Isabel Simões
João Onofre
Joana Escoval
João Maria Gusmão
& Pedro Paiva
João Pedro Vale
& Nuno Alexandre Ferreira
Jorge Queiroz
Júlio Pomar
Kiluanji Kia Henda
Mafalda Santos
Maria Capelo
Maria José Cavaco
Mariana Silva
Marta Soares
Mattia Denisse
Miguel Branco
Miguel Palma
Noé Sendas
Nuno Henrique
Nuno Nunes-Ferreira
Patrícia Garrido
Pedro Casqueiro
Pedro Tropa
Ricardo Jacinto
Rita Ferreira
Rui Calçada Bastos
Sara Bichão
Tatiana Macedo
Teresa Carepo
Tiago Alexandre
Tiago Baptista

curadoria:
Sara Antónia Matos
e Pedro Faro

AQUISIÇÕES
NÚCLEO DE ARTE
CONTEMPORÂNEA
DA CML
E ATELIER-MUSEU
JÚLIO POMAR
(2018, 2019, 2020)

5 de Abril
a 13 de Junho

Inauguração
5 de Abril
11h às 17h

EGEAC ATELIER MUSEU JULIO POMAR
Pomar

ATELIER MUSEU JÚLIO POMAR

F L O R A

AQUISIÇÕES
NÚCLEO DE ARTE
CONTEMPORÂNEA
DA CML E
ATELIER-MUSEU
JÚLIO POMAR
(2018, 2019, 2020)

5 de Abril
a 13 de Junho

EGEAC ATELIER MUSEU JULIO POMAR
Pomar

ATELIER MUSEU JÚLIO POMAR

F L O R A

AQUISIÇÕES
NÚCLEO DE ARTE
CONTEMPORÂNEA
DA CML E
ATELIER-MUSEU
JÚLIO POMAR
(2018, 2019, 2020)

curadoria:
Sara Antónia Matos
e Pedro Faro

5 de Abril
a 13 de Junho

EGEAC ATELIER MUSEU JULIO POMAR
Pomar

Inauguração:
5 de Abril das 11h às 17h

C3 M0 Y100 K0

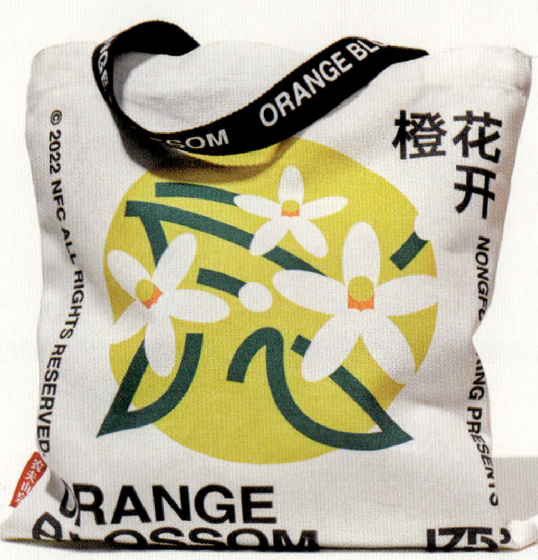

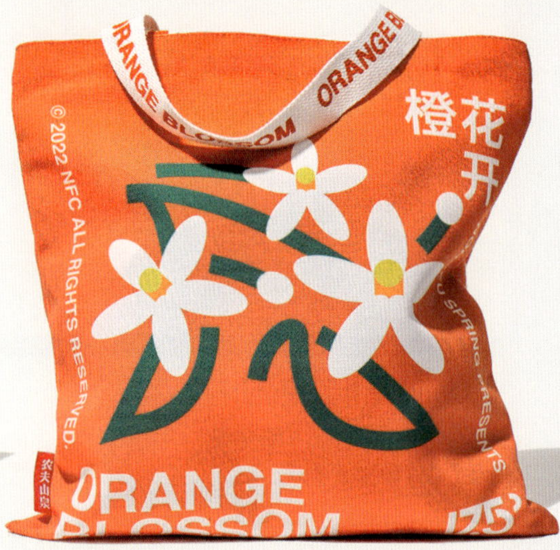

Nongfu Spring 17.5° Orange Blossoms Bloom

● Orange Blossom is a marketing IP created by Nongfu Spring for its 17.5° Orange brand. The design team employed strong color contrast, concise orange blossom shapes, and a fashionable information layout to successfully craft a youthful, stylish, and vigorous brand image for 17.5° Orange.

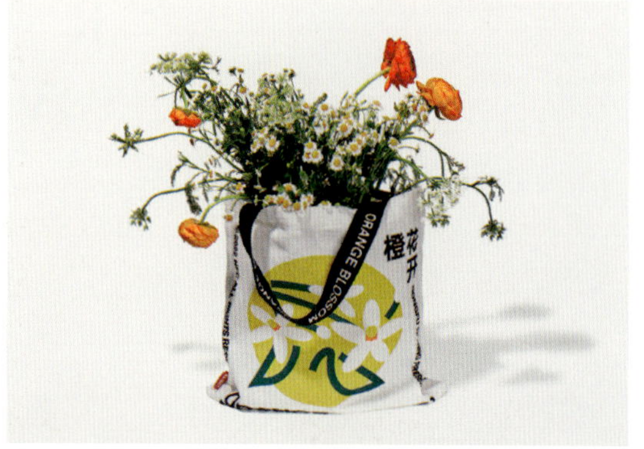

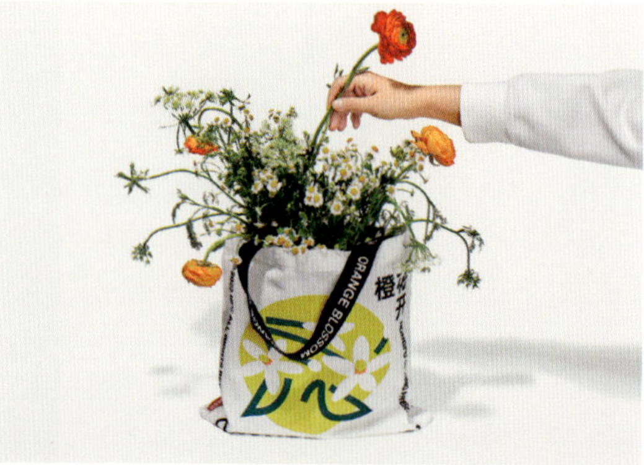

● Design Studio: Would Design ● Designer: Yunlong Li, Ying Zhang ● Client: Nongfu Spring

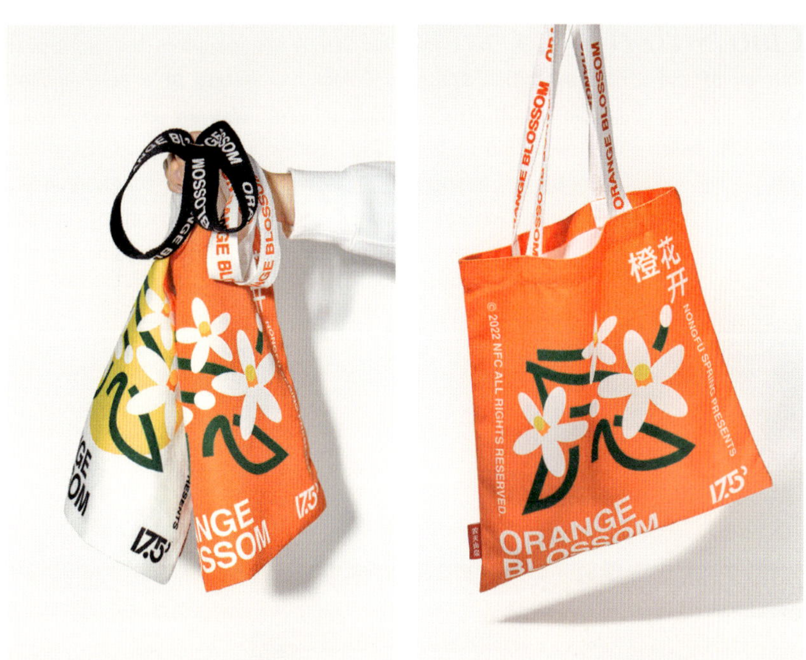

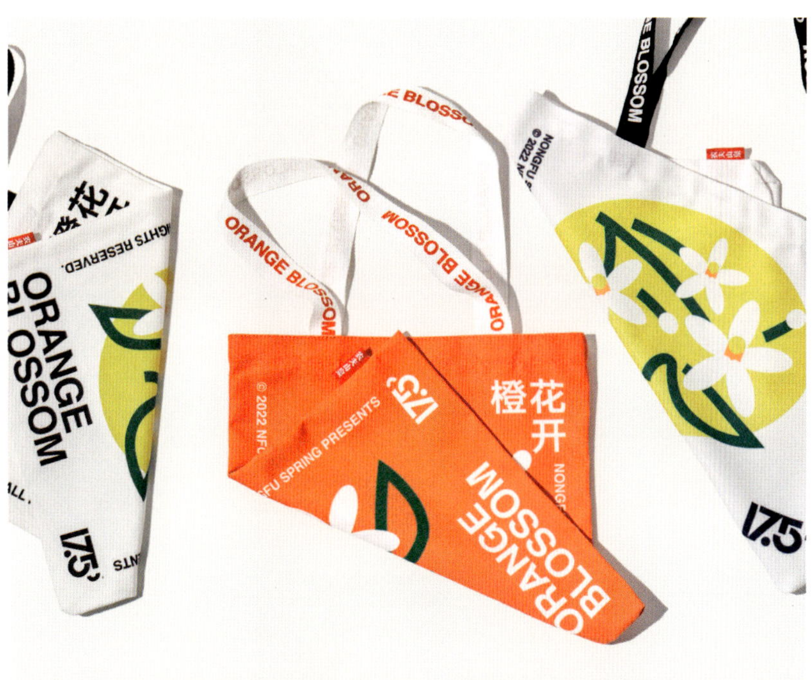

● Why Yellow? ● The choice of high-saturation orange and yellow, extracted from orange fruit and orange blossom respectively, conveys an atmosphere of youth, enthusiasm, and fashion.

C0 M71 Y87 K0 | C0 M11 Y87 K0 | C90 M46 Y91 K8

Ciao Strizzi

• The book *Ciao Strizzi* encapsulates the eight-year journey of the Strizzi exhibition space in Cologne, adhering to a self-imposed strict principle that plays with the tension between anarchy and commerce. The color palette was simplified to black and neon-yellow, visually unifying the content of 8 years of art exhibitions into a cohesive work. This publication uniquely combines exaggerated content complexity with a clear reduction in bright color, emphasized by small, intricate, and meticulous typography.

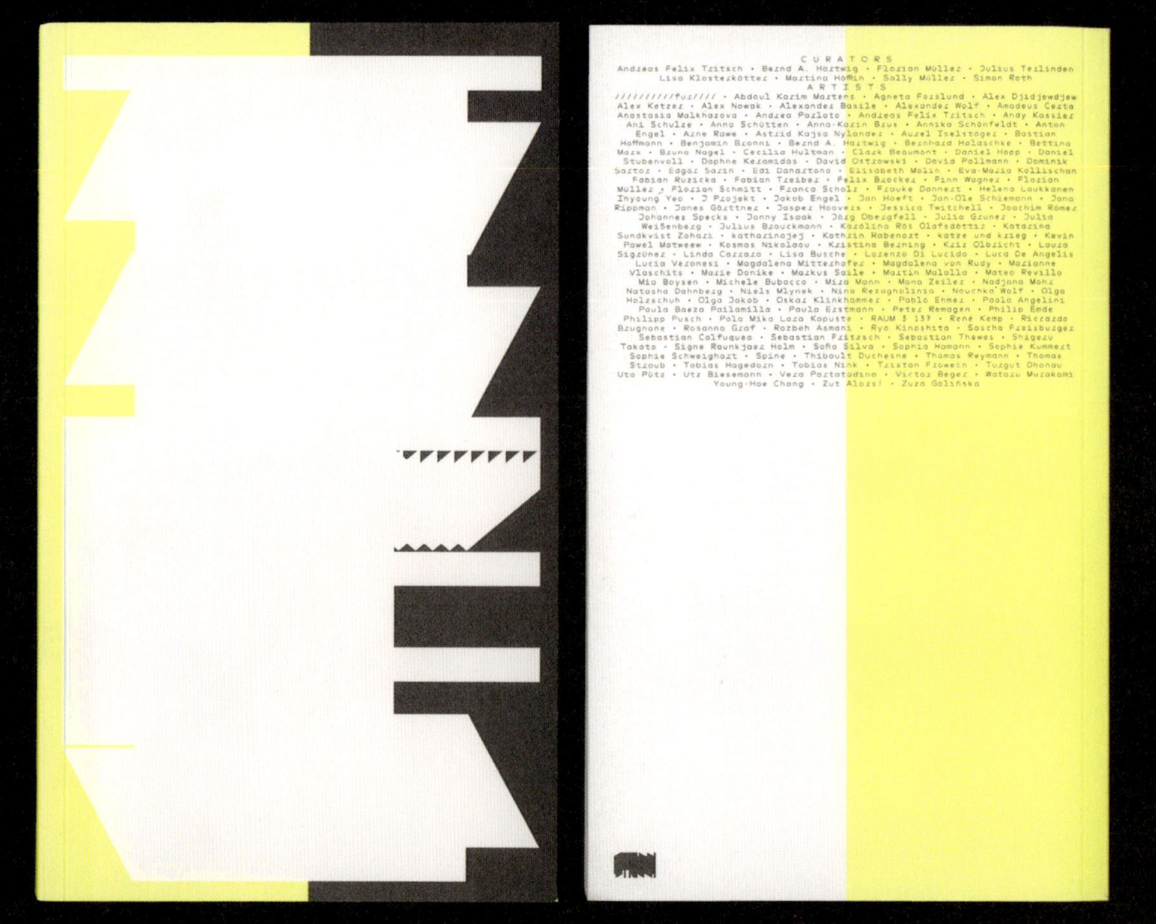

• Design Studio: Serve and Volley • Designer: Simon Roth, Klaus Neuburg

● Why Yellow? ● The design team chose yellow and black for their strong contrast. Yellow, appearing calm alongside black, is more neutral in conveying emotion and information compared to other colors. The paper color, white, contrasts with black and aligns with yellow.

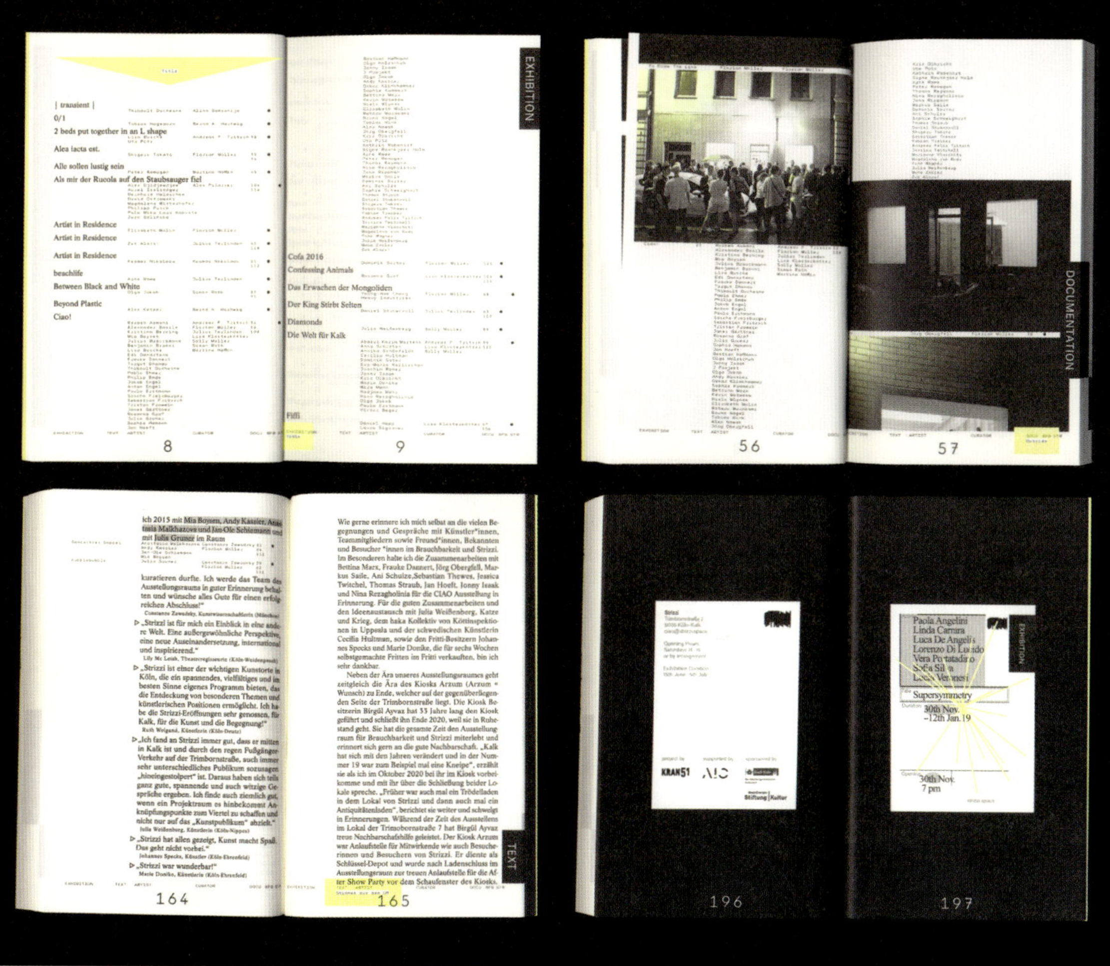

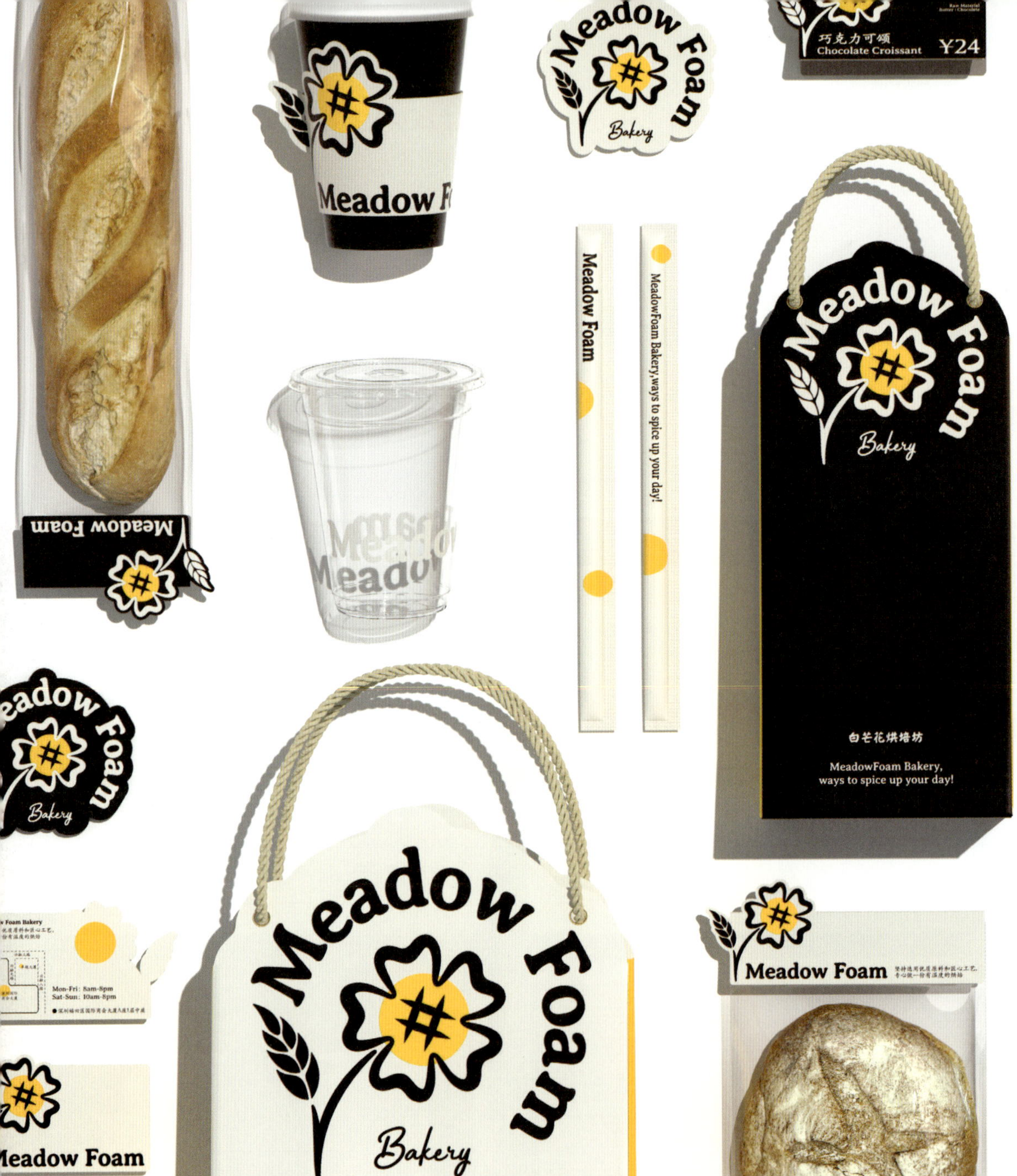

Meadow Foam

● Meadow Foam, a coffee brand in Shenzhen CBD, China, creatively uses the white grass flower as its iconic symbol for brand recognition. Dynamic lines with varying thickness capture the flower's vitality and the essence of baking, with a touch of retro quality in the circular English typesetting.

● Design Studio: XXD DESIGN ● Designer: Yuqing Xu, Qiyuan Xiao, Jia Tan

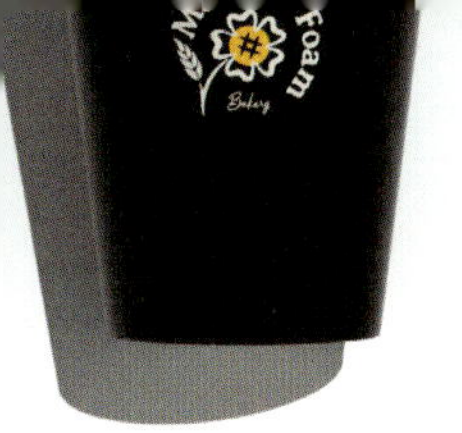

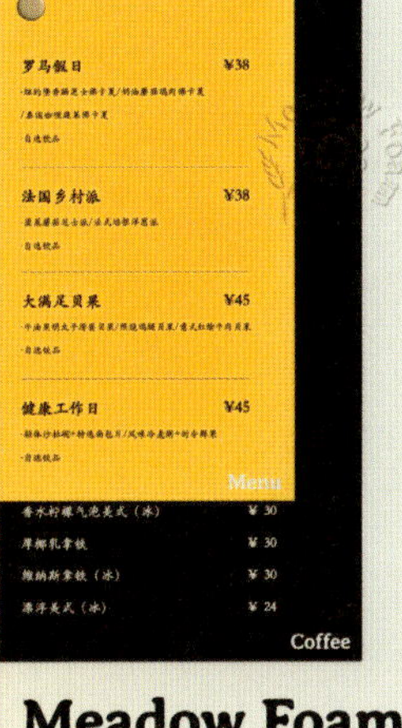

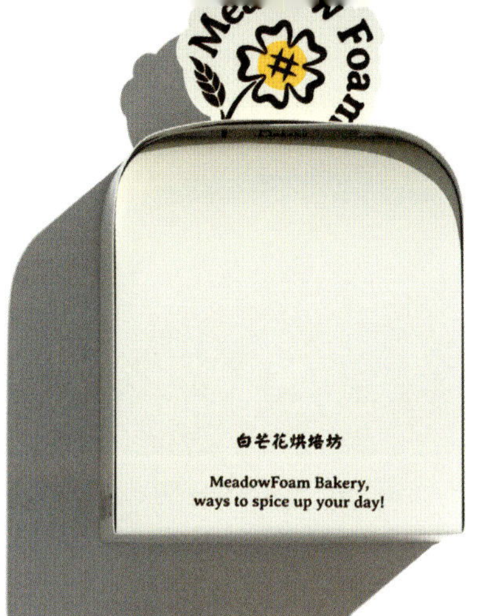

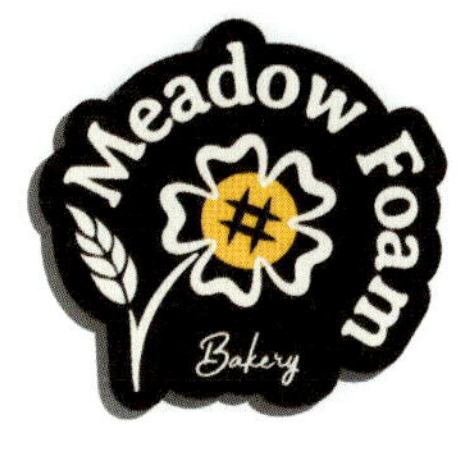

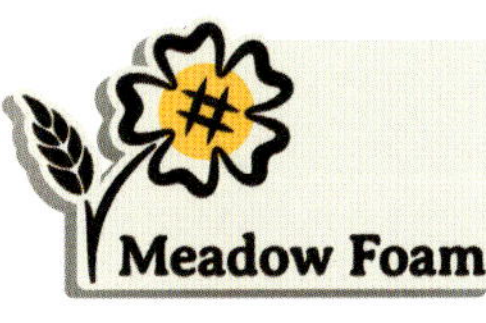

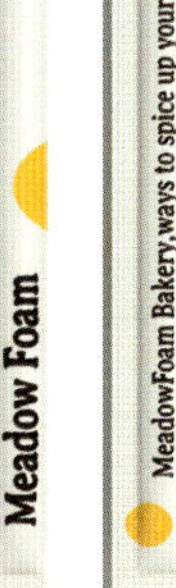

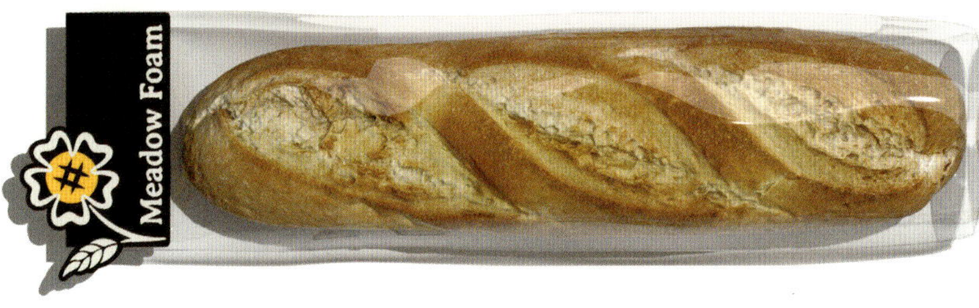

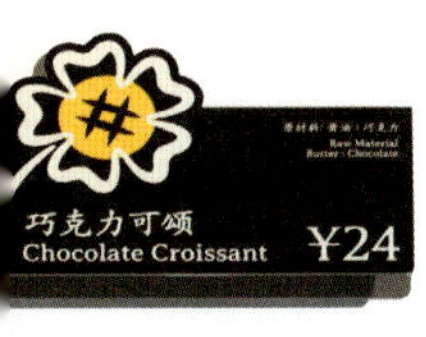

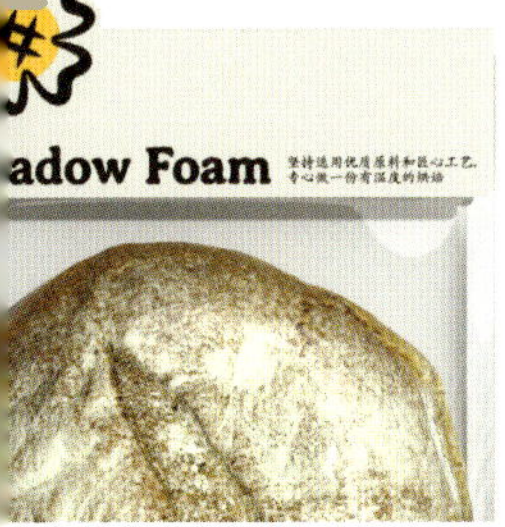

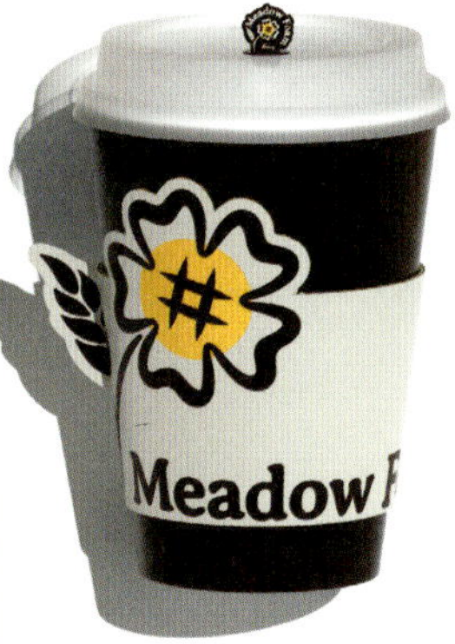

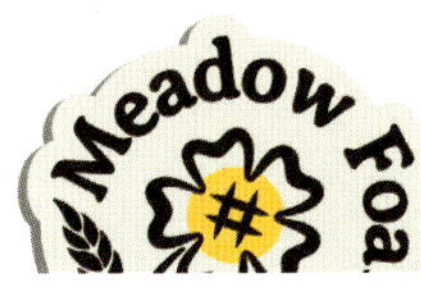

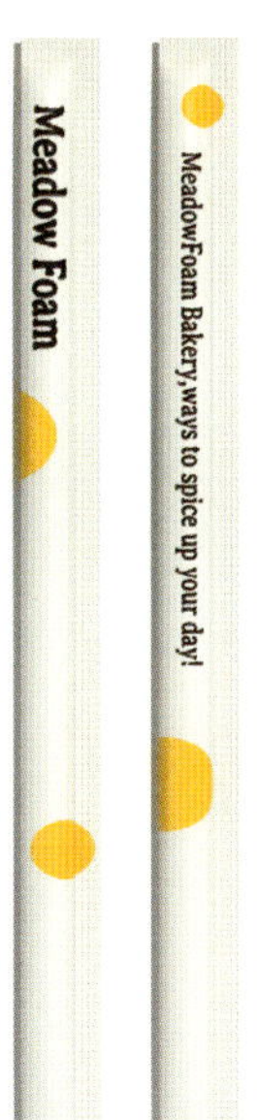

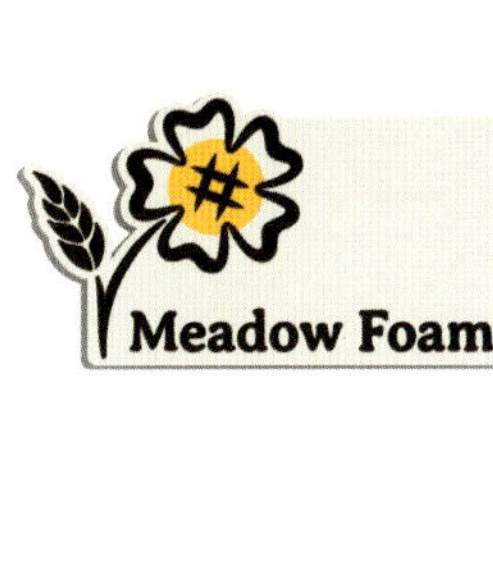

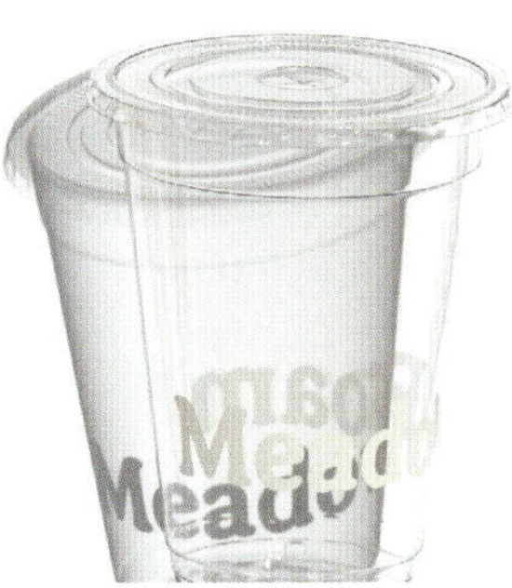

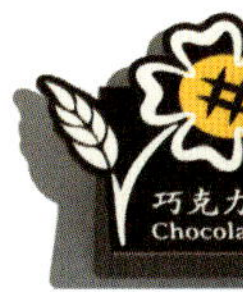

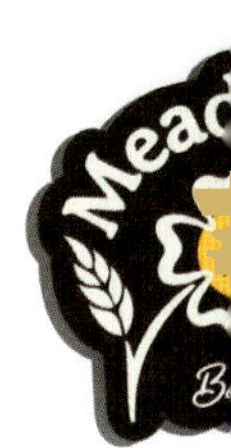

C6 M32 Y100 K0 | C71 M88 Y96 K67 | C11 M12 Y17 K0

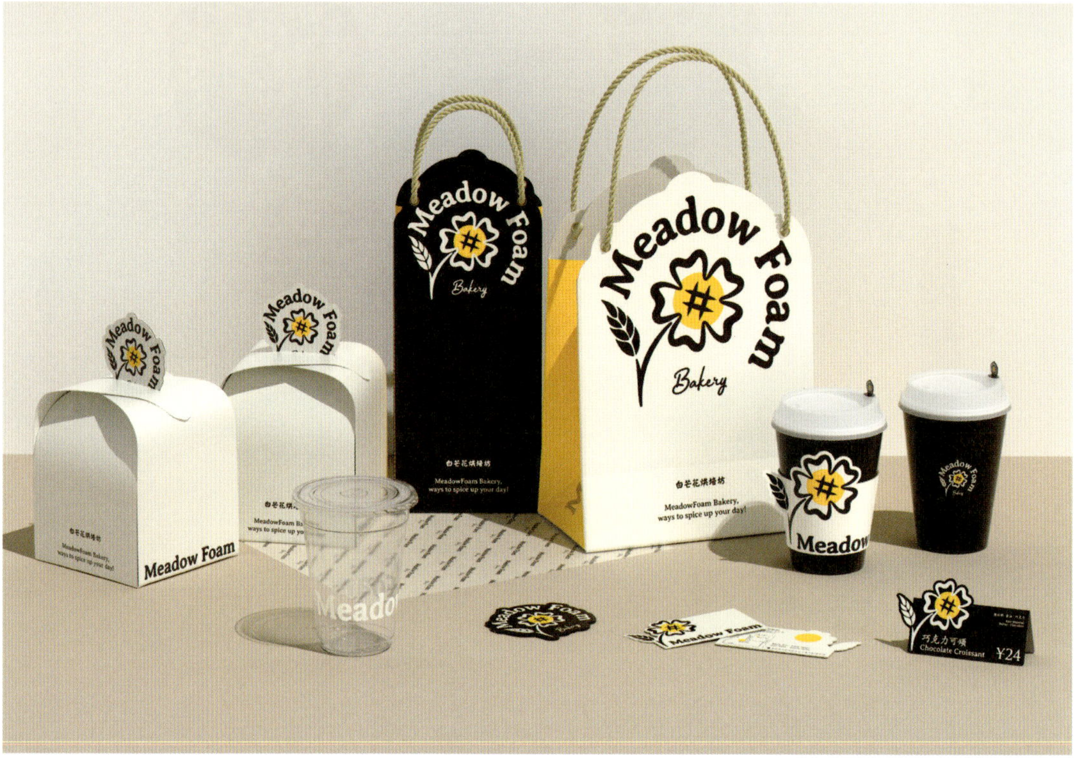

● Why Yellow? ● The design team opted for warm yellow as the brand color, enhancing the appetizing appeal of this bakery brand. Additionally, yellow, commonly associated with happiness, aims to create a warm and comfortable experience for customers.

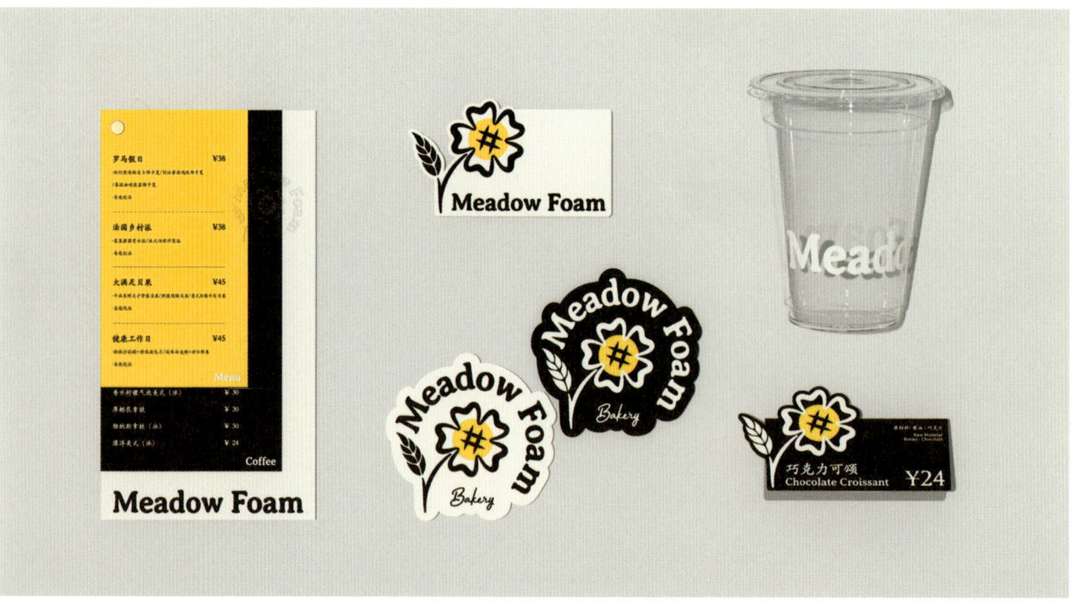

● Client: Shenzhen Yongyun Brand Investment Co., Ltd.

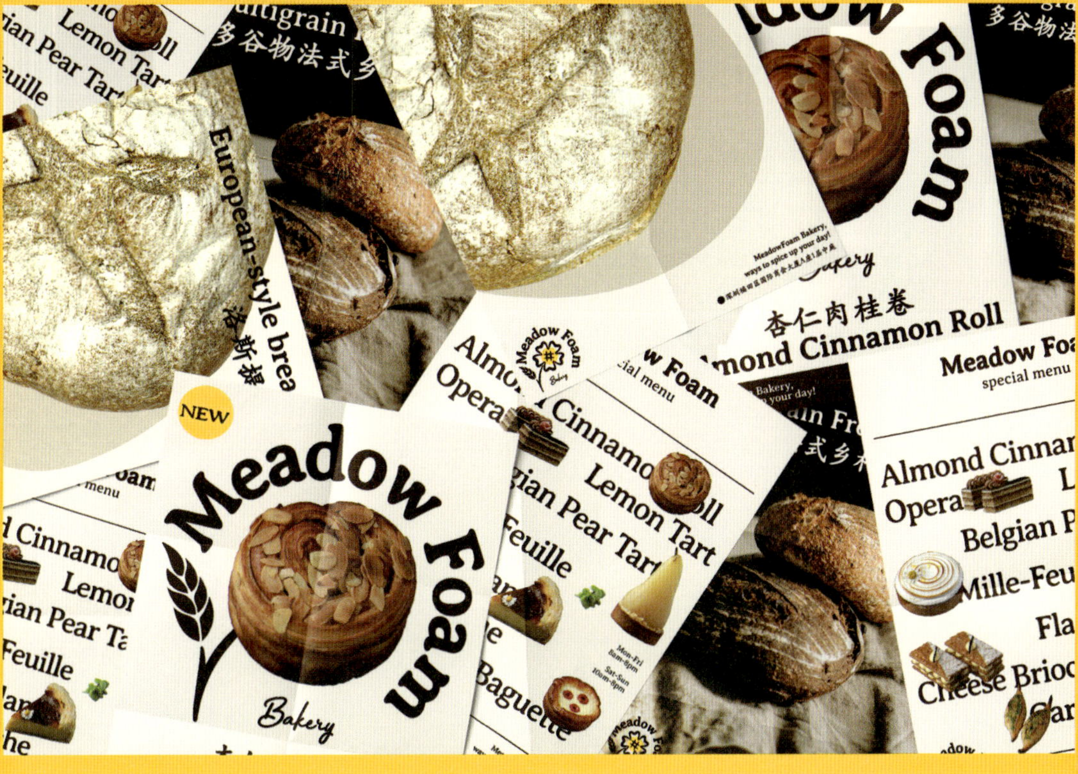

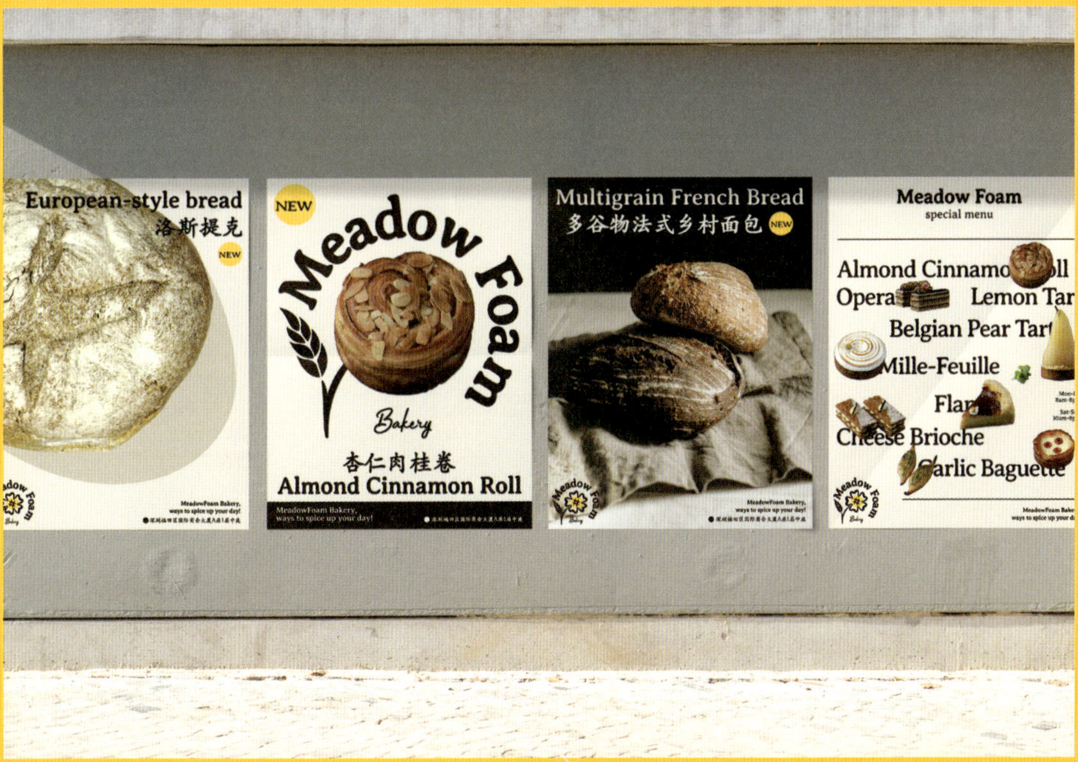

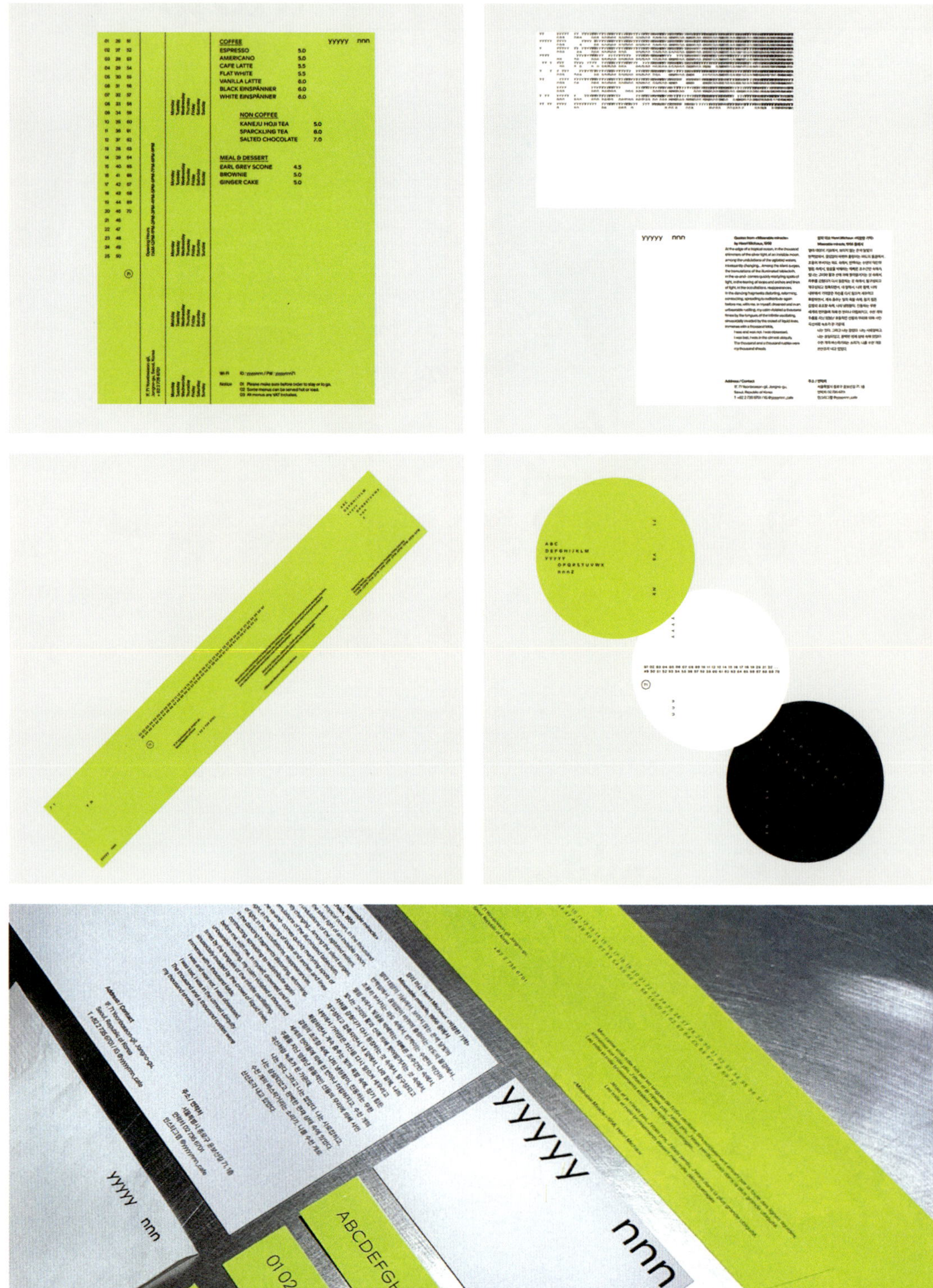

yyyyy nnn
COFFEE
ESPRESSO 5.0
AMERICANO 5.0
CAFE LATTE 5.5
FLAT WHITE 5.5
VANILLA LATTE 6.0
BLACK EINSPÄNNER 6.0
WHITE EINSPÄNNER 6.0
NON COFFEE
KANEJU HOJI TEA 5.0
SPARCKLING TEA 6.0
SALTED CHOCOLATE 7.0
MEAL & DESSERT
EARL GREY SCONE 4.5
BROWNIE 5.0
GINGER CAKE 5.0
yyyyy nnn
yyyy
nnn
ABCDEFGHIJKLM

yyyyynnn ● The branding for the cafe "yyyyynnn," situated in Jongnogu, Seoul, is an in-house project of Creative Studio Unravel, where the graphic design was led by a team member. The design features a structured layout and typographic style tailored to match the repetitive alphabet name and the brutalist interior design.

● Why Yellow? ● Considering colors that provide a bold accent within the gray, neutral-colored cafe interior, the designer aimed to extend their use of bright yellow to cup sleeves, stickers, and other elements, ensuring easy and consistent identification throughout the space.

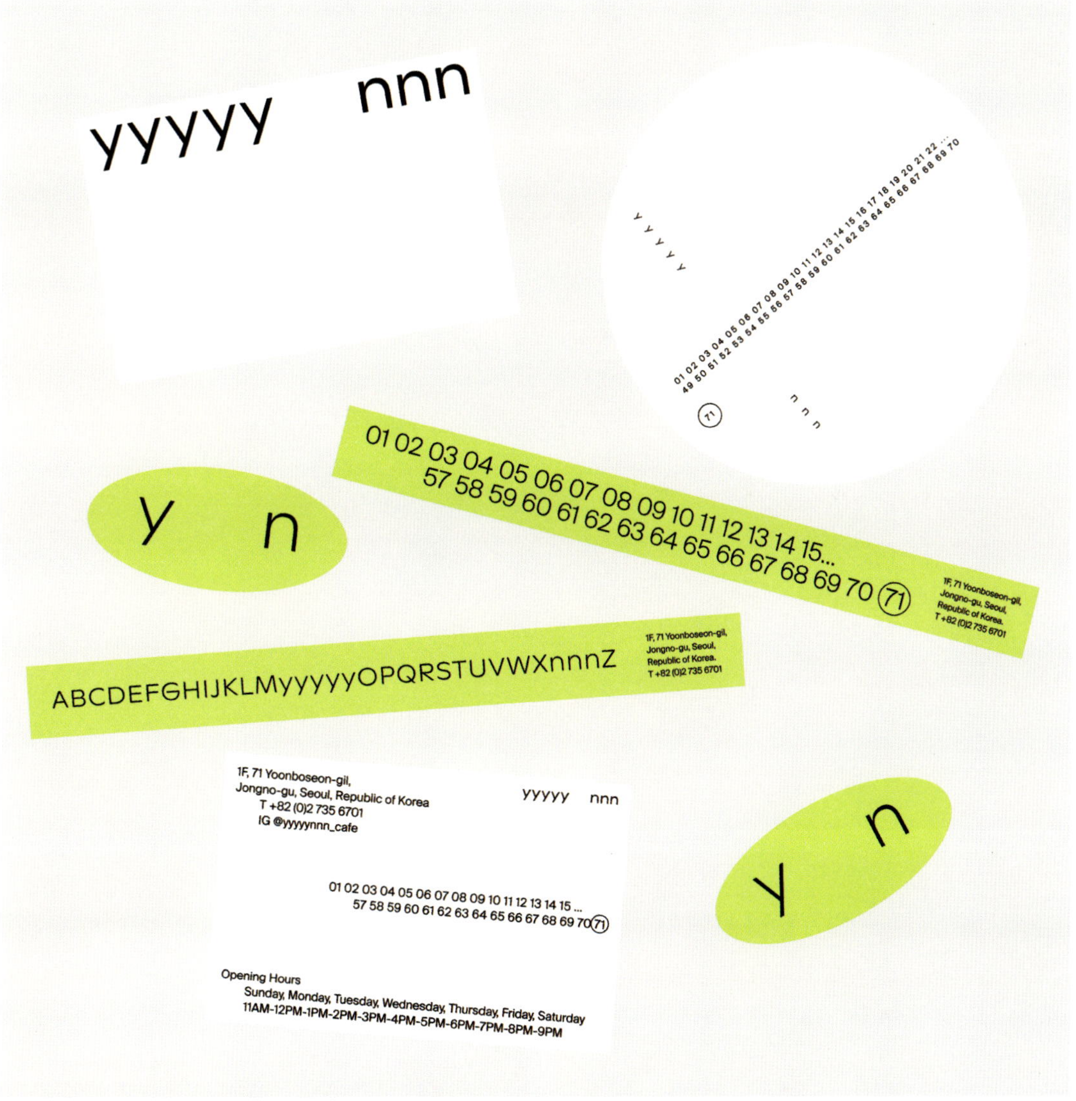

Do it—China 2021

● *Do it—China 2021* is a collaborative publication project curated by Hans Ulrich Obrist and Cao Dan, featuring proposals from 108 contemporary Chinese diaspora artists. Inspired by the 108 heroes in the classic Chinese novel *Water Margin*, it symbolizes the diversity of contemporary Chinese art. ● The book adopts traditional Chinese stitched binding, using rice paper for the inner pages. The artists' names are imprinted on the book edges in alphabetical order, creating a visual index. The inner layout varies according to each artist's proposal, maintaining overall coherence. The cover is crafted from fabric with the title embossed in black. The unique rectangular format, spanning 400 pages and with a thickness of 6 centimeters, adds a ceremonial aspect to the reading experience. ● Fonts include both serif and sans-serif, using orange and black to differentiate between Chinese and English. Continuing the iconic orange theme from *Do it*, the entire book exudes a sculptural strength, vividly showcasing the influence of contemporary Chinese art. The book itself is akin to a piece of contemporary art.

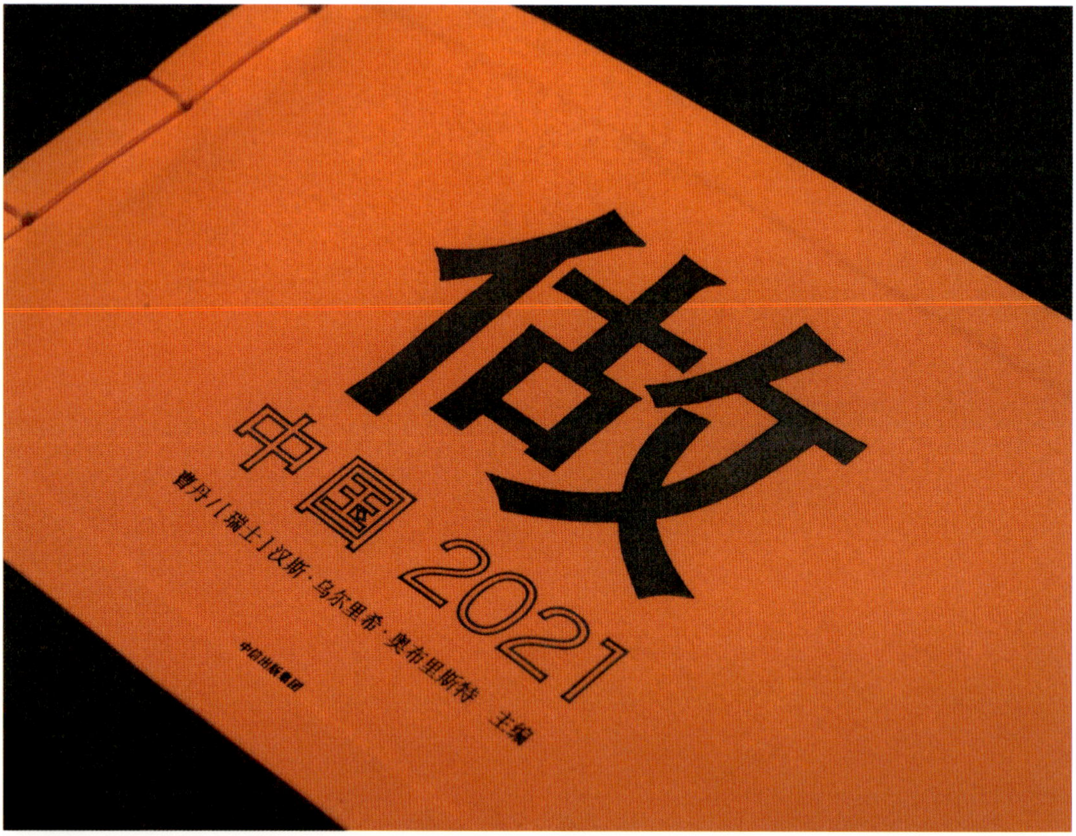

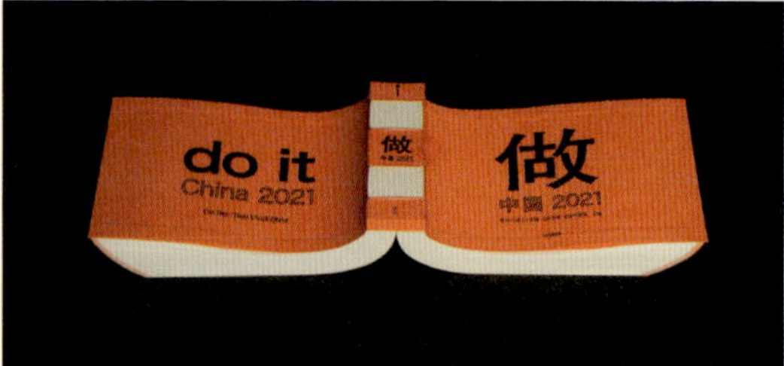

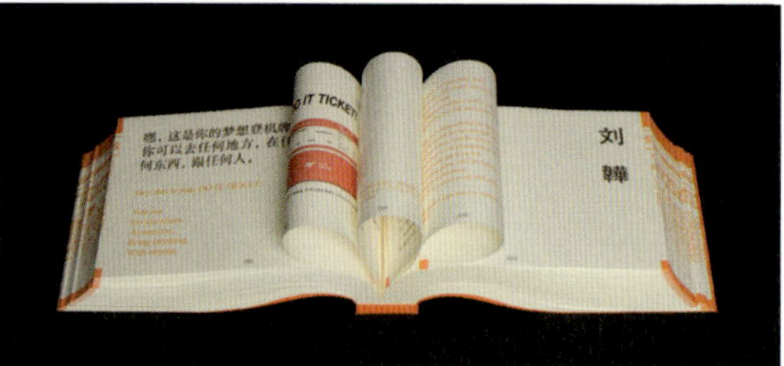

● Design Studio: PAY2PLAY ● Designer: Xiaoxi Sun ● Client: CITIC Press Group

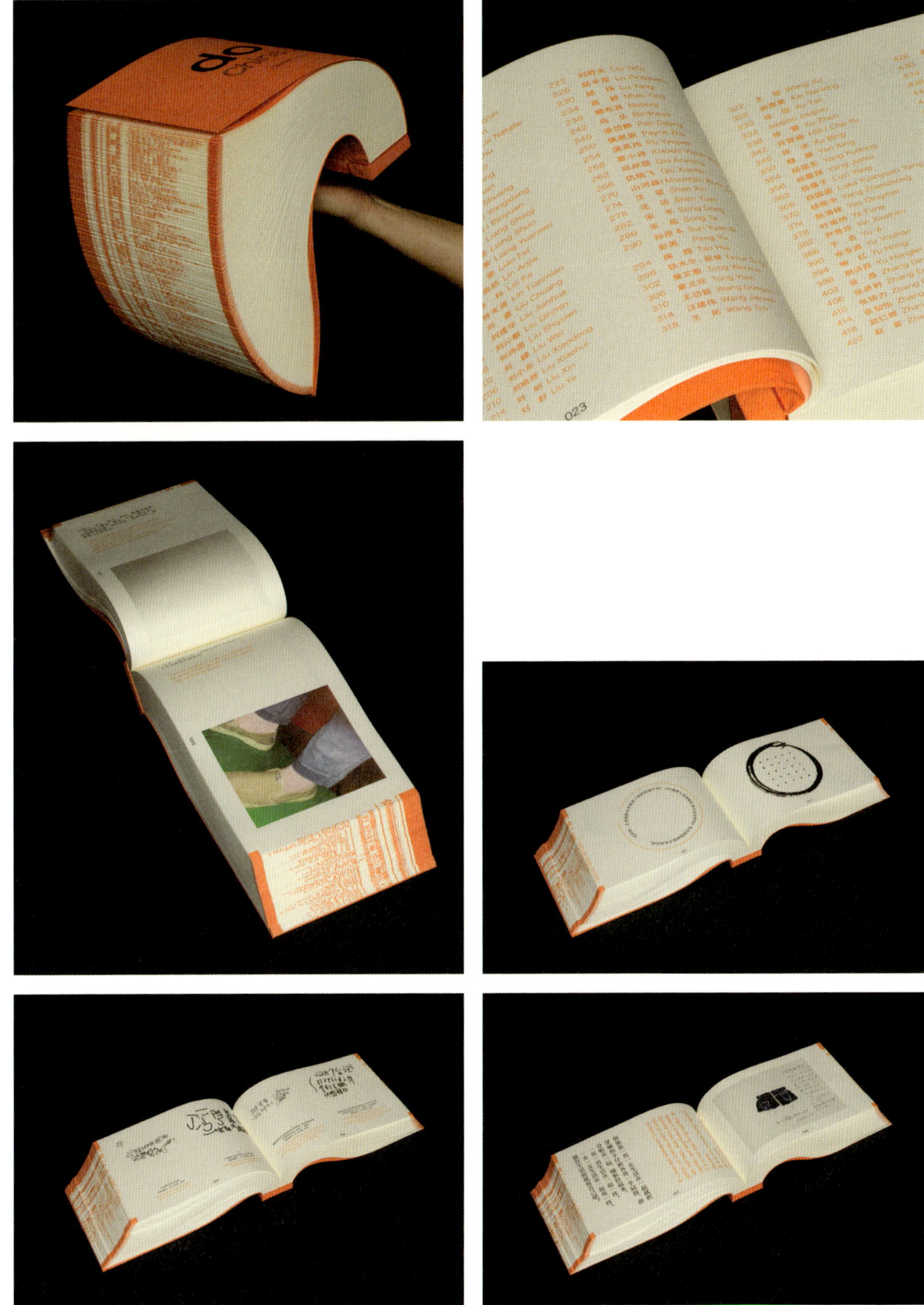

Yellow Matching

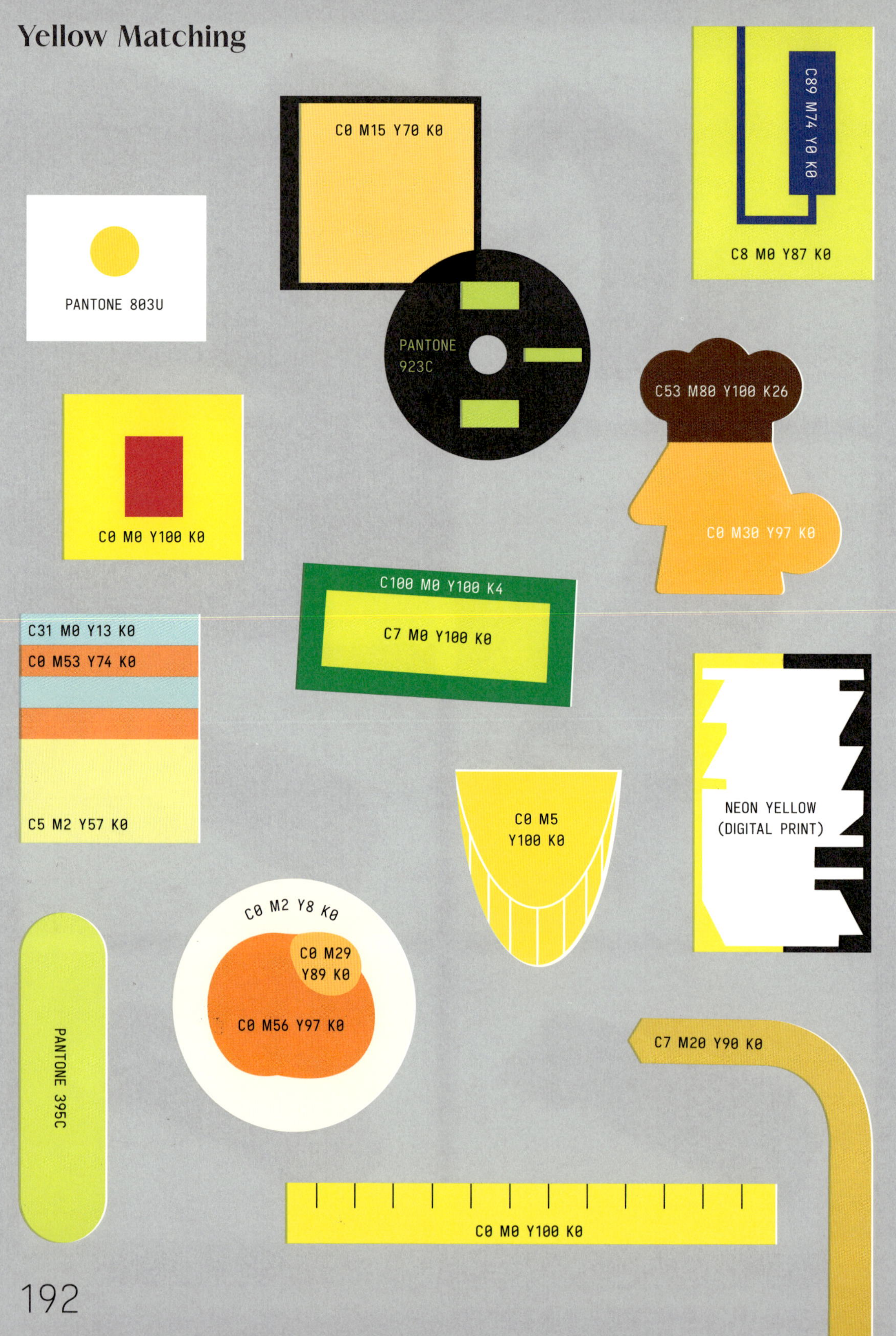

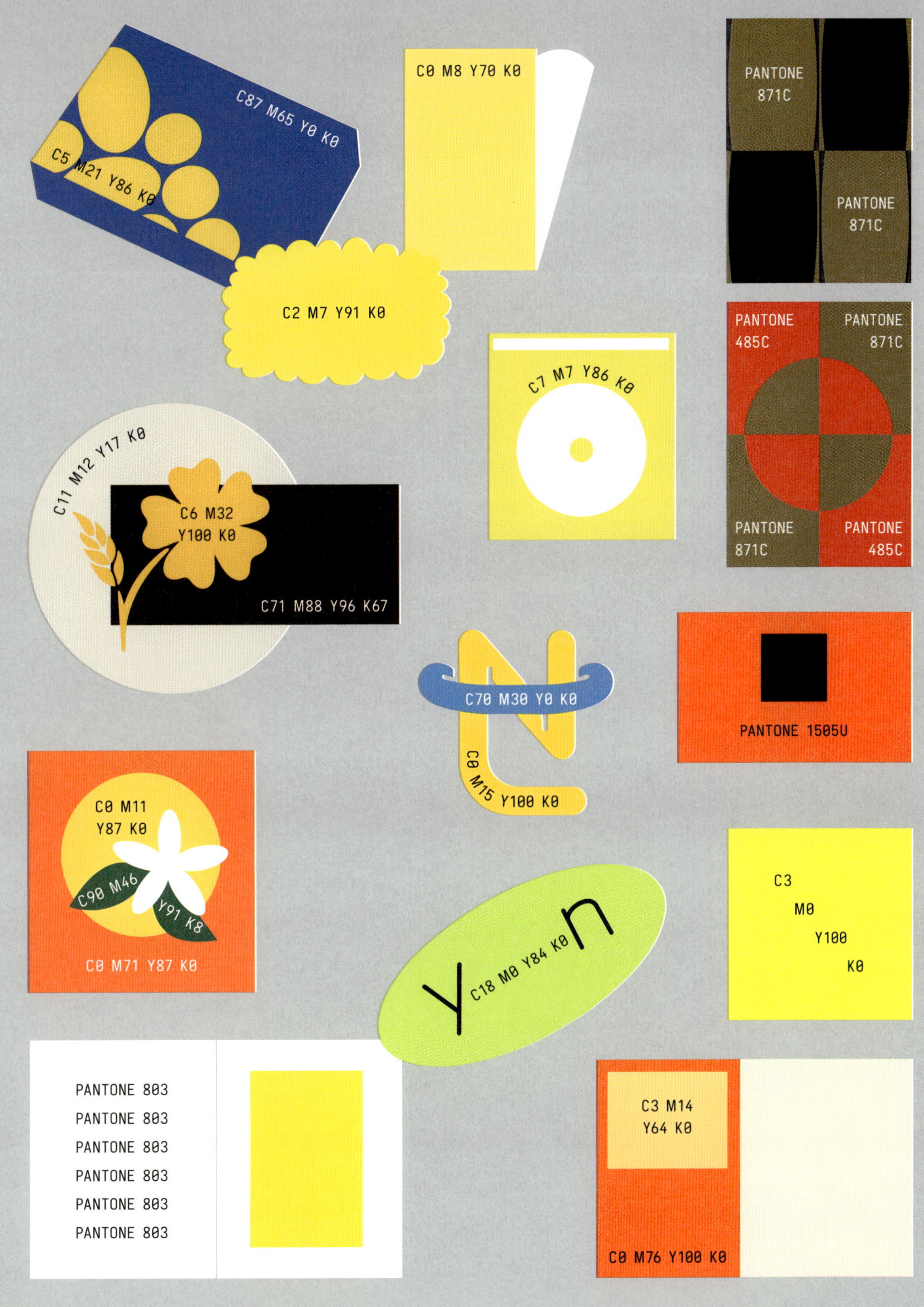
C87 M65 Y0 K0
C5 M21 Y86 K0
C0 M8 Y70 K0
PANTONE 871C
PANTONE 871C
C2 M7 Y91 K0
C7 M7 Y86 K0
PANTONE 485C
PANTONE 871C
PANTONE 871C
PANTONE 485C
C11 M12 Y17 K0
C6 M32 Y100 K0
C71 M88 Y96 K67
C70 M30 Y0 K0
C0 M15 Y100 K0
PANTONE 1505U
C0 M11 Y87 K0
C90 M46 Y91 K8
C0 M71 Y87 K0
C18 M0 Y84 K0
C3 M0 Y100 K0
PANTONE 803
PANTONE 803
PANTONE 803
PANTONE 803
PANTONE 803
PANTONE 803
C3 M14 Y64 K0
C0 M76 Y100 K0

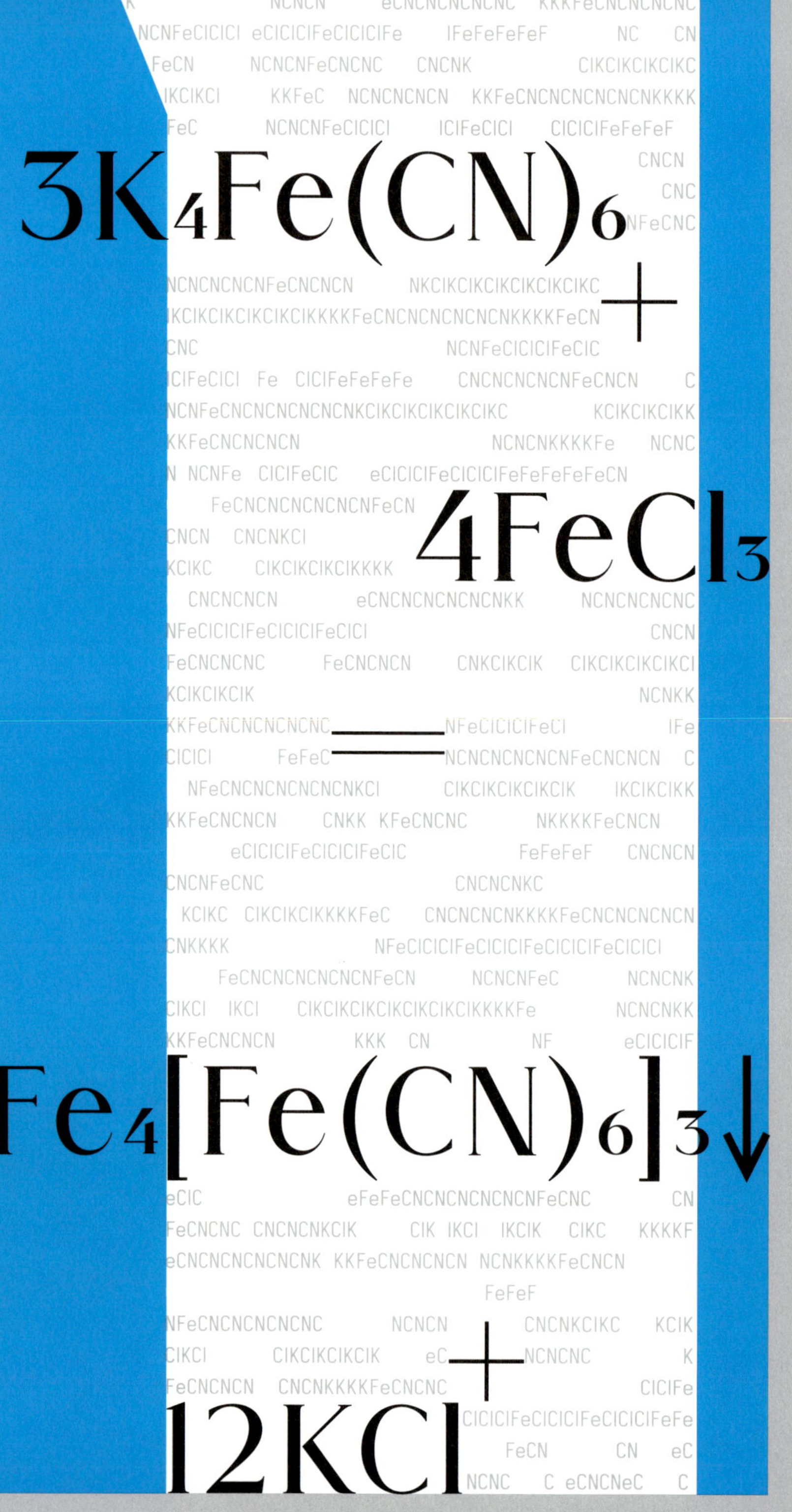
3K4Fe(CN)6
+
4FeCl3
=
Fe4[Fe(CN)6]3↓
+
12KCl

The Prussian blue (iron ferrocyanide) is produced by the reaction of potassium ferrocyanide with ferric chloride. ● The birth of Prussian blue was almost a stroke of fate, a serendipitous discovery. At the beginning of the 18th century, due to the mistake of Johann Diesbach, a worker who made and used paint, he originally intended to make a batch of cochineal red lake. But Diesbach inadvertently added potassium carbonate mixed with bone oil to the mixture of potassium sulfate and accidentally invented the blue pigment with an excellent advantage—Prussian blue. This pigment has a strong coloring ability and stability, making it beloved by painters. Its application is not limited to the field of painting but also in wallpaper, wall paint, and textile dyes. Later, Prussian blue was also evolved for carbon paper and the treatment of thallium poisoning. Although the process of making Prussian blue is complex, it becomes a precious and unique pigment. ● On the visible spectrum, blue is between purple and green, but in fact blue does not come from the natural world. We have hardly ever seen blue animals or plants. The naked eye can see the "sea and sky" only because of the scattering principle that plays visual tricks in the human eyes. Blue, together with red and yellow, constitutes the most basic primary colors in color theory and dominates the art world. The wavelength of blue is 440nm–470nm, and its color is pure and subtle, eliciting boundless associations and various symbolic meanings. ● As the "classic blue" of Pantone in 2020, it once again rode the crest of the trend and retro waves. During the Renaissance, the introduction of oil painting changed the way colors were perceived and utilized. Artists carefully struck a balance between blue and other colors. Lapis lazuli, used to extract the blue, is mined from Afghanistan, so the price of the ultramarine dye was once even higher than that of gold. ● In the 18th and 19th centuries, the invention of Prussian blue, as a synthetic pigment, allowed painters to expand their use of colors. The impressionists emerged, making good use of blue to depict nature and evoke emotions. In the early 20th century, many artists recognized the emotional power of blue and made it a core element of their paintings. In the mid to late 20th century, abstract expressionists used blue in an unaffected and neat fashion, in order to stimulate emotion and thought. Perhaps blue was too precious in the past, or has long been etched into people's DNA as the color of the sky and the sea, blue is always the favorite of designers and artists, so building up a character with complex connotations and rich expressiveness. They use Prussian blue to express elegance and melancholy, sky blue to depict innocence and dream, and azure blue to symbolize peace and relaxation. They bring different connotations to blue in design and art, and also the audience can feel the nuances brought about by color construction.

Prussian Blue	Elegance and Melancholy
Sky Blue	Innocence and Dream
Azure Blue	Peace and Relaxation

- ULTRAMARINE — R38 G15 B98 — C89 M94 Y0 K44
- EGYPTIAN BLUE — R0 G58 B125 — C94 M69 Y0 K35
- INDIGO — R43 G87 B166 — C86 M66 Y0 K0
- WOAD — R0 G64 B113 — C100 M39 Y0 K58
- COBALT — R96 G142 B169 — C66 M36 Y25 K0

Ultramarine

● The word comes from the Italian word "Oltramarino," meaning "beyond the sea." Since the Middle Ages, painters have depicted the Virgin Mary in bright blue robes, a color chosen not for its religious symbolism but for its expensive price tag. Ultramarine, the iconic hue of the Virgin Mary, is the most precious and famous pigment of the late Middle Ages and Renaissance. The natural ultramarine comes from the rare lapis lazis, and can only be found on a remote mountain in Afghanistan. This precious material became popular around the world and was used to decorate funeral portraits in Egypt, the Quran in Iran, and later the headdress in Johannes Vermeer's *Girl with a Pearl Earring* (1665). For hundreds of years, the price of lapis lazuli even rivaled the price of gold.

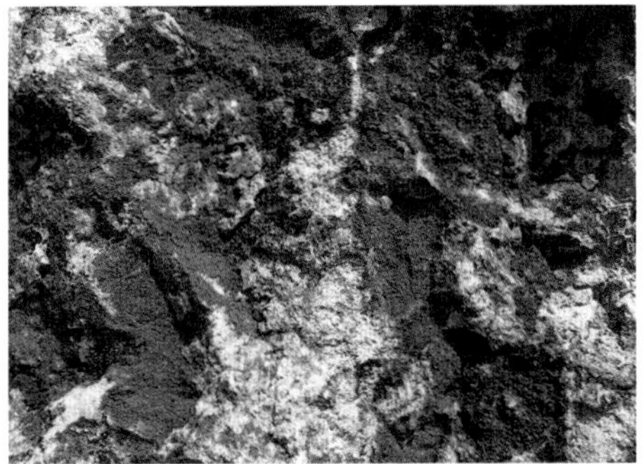

In the 1950s, Yves Klein, working with a Parisian paint supplier, invented a synthetic version of ultramarine blue, a color that became the French artist's hallmark. Explaining the appeal of this historic hue, Klein once said, "Blue has no dimensions, it is beyond dimensions."

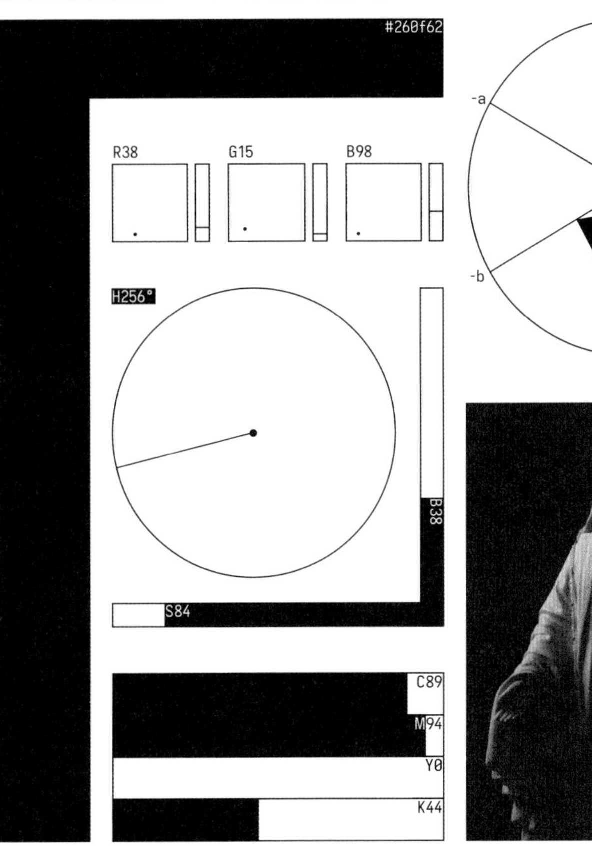

Egyptian Blue

• Egyptian Blue is an ancient pigment. The ancient Egyptians admired blue as a sacred color, representing the sky and the gods. Egyptian blue is complex to make, but brightly colored and stable. It is widely used in writing, wall and coffins decoration. The ancient Romans called it "Egyptian blue," but the craft was gradually lost. The raw material of Egyptian blue is composed of ground limestone and sand mixed with copper-containing minerals such as azurite or malachite, which can at high temperatures produce blue opaque glass crystals. Although Egyptian blue was gradually replaced by ultramarine after the 13th century, its unique value is widely recognized.

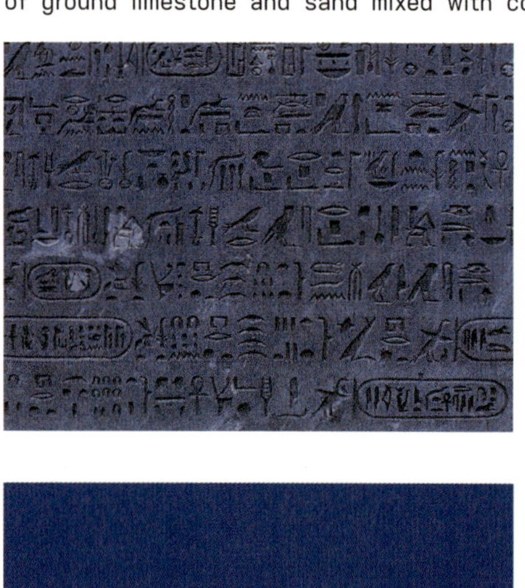

C94
M69
Y0
K35

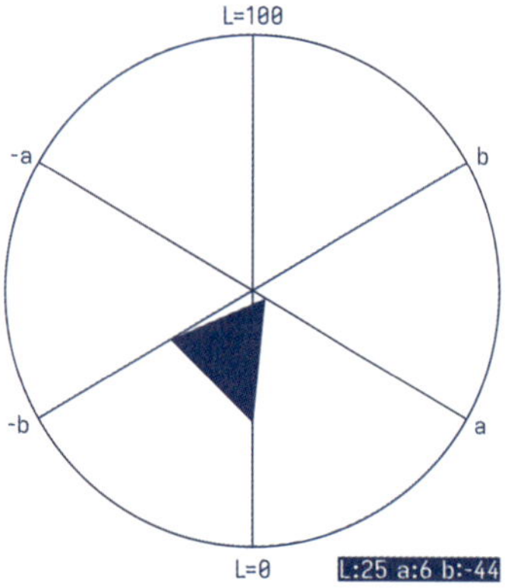

L=100
-a
b
-b
a
L=0
L:25 a:6 b:-44

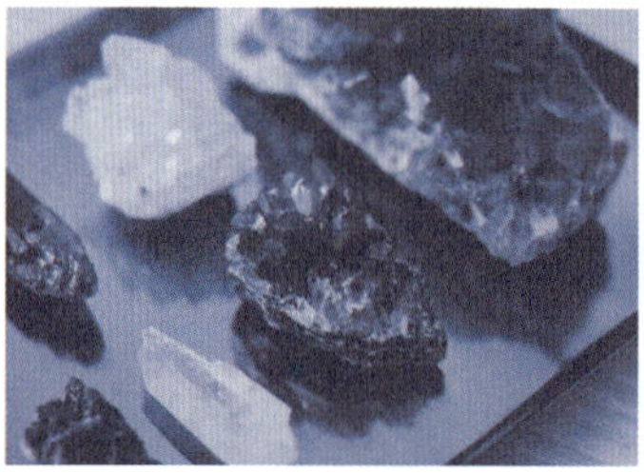

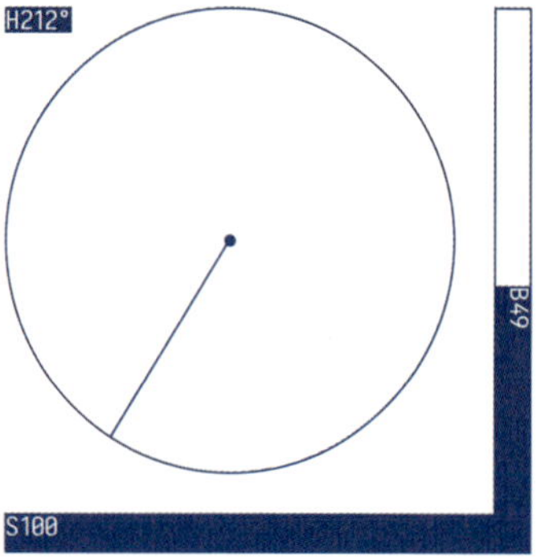

H212°
B49
S100

#003a7d

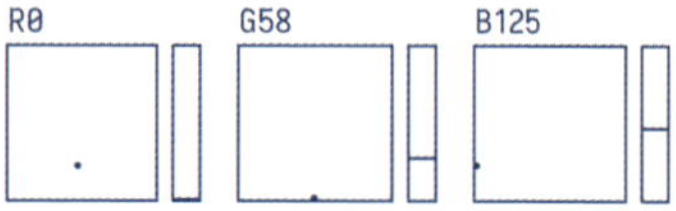

R0
G58
B125

Indigo ● Indigo is a precious color. Between 600 and 500 BC, Babylonian inscriptions on a pottery tablet revealed the technique of dyeing wool with indigo. Indigo, a plant from which the dye is extracted, is difficult to grow and susceptible to disasters. The production process of indigo dye is complex and needs to be extracted and made by hand. Indigo has a strong color-fixing power and is widely used in funeral ceremonies and artistic creation. Trade in indigo was restricted, but with the rise of colonialism and changes in trade routes, the price of indigo dropped. Today, indigo is the color of blue-collar workers, especially in the denim industry. Indigo blue jeans have become a symbol of democracy in fashion.

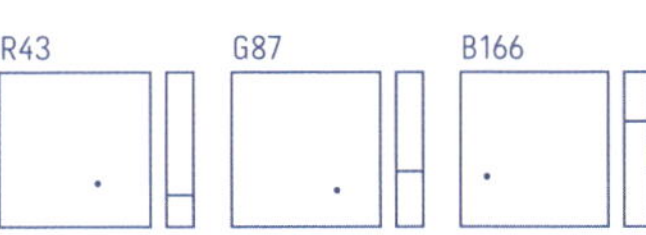

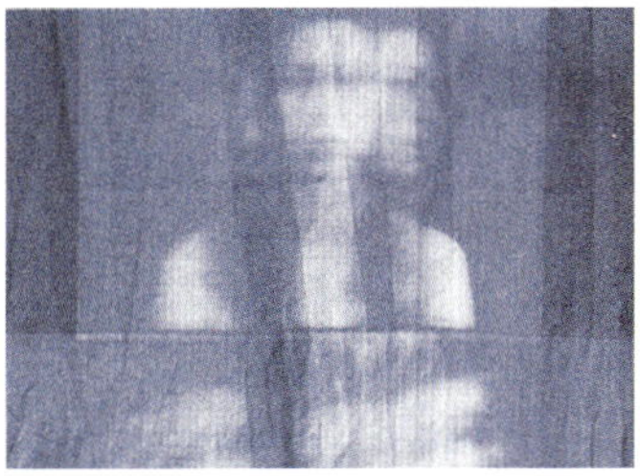

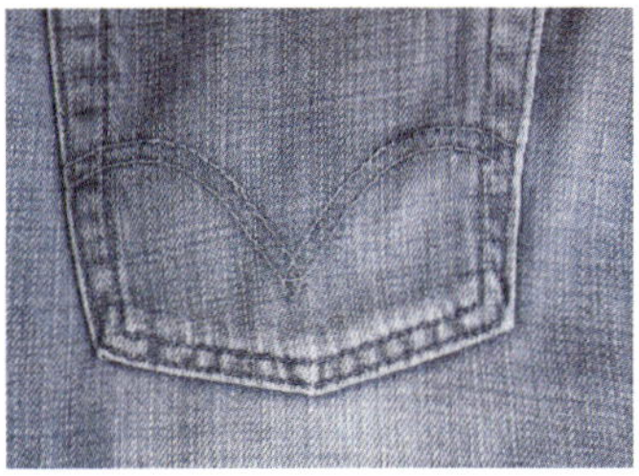

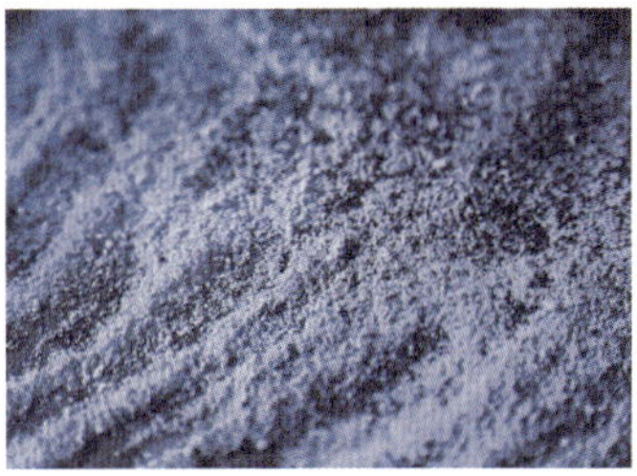

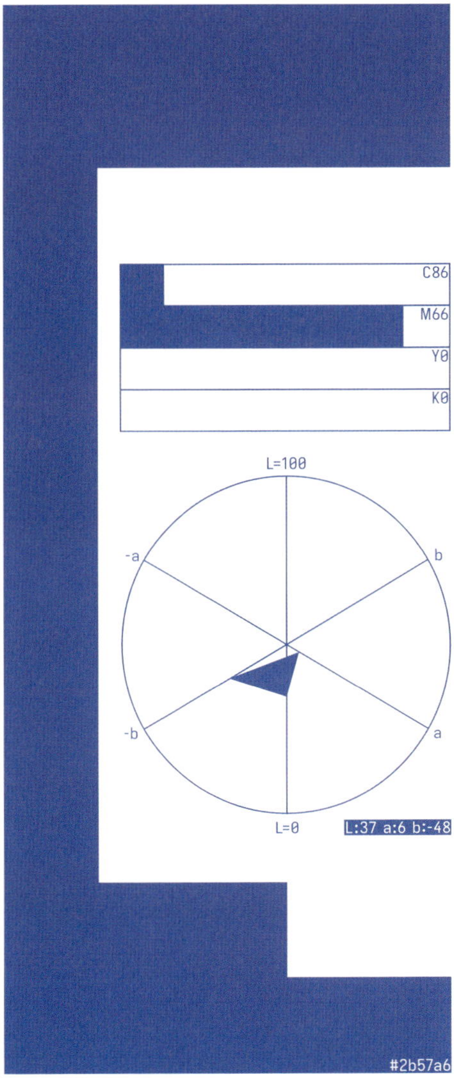

C86
M66
Y0
K0

L=100
-a
b
-b
a
L=0
L:37 a:6 b:-48

#2b57a6

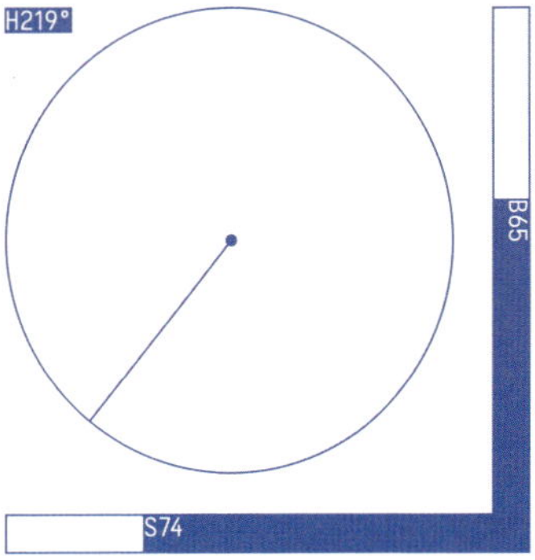

H219°
B65
S74

Woad

• Woad was an ancient blue gold. William Morris loved using isatis indigotica for Cobalt vintage fabrics and wallpaper. Isatis dye is derived from plants and is complicated and expensive to make. To this day, the French "Pays de Cocagne" is still a metaphor for "land of plenty." The unique charm of woad is displayed before visitors, and the change from grass green to deep sea green to bright blue is amazing. Woad was widely used in the textile industry and even became a body pigment for the Celts. However, the production of isatis has a negative impact on the environment, with its wastewater polluting rivers and resulting in barren land. Over time, as other indigo plants appeared, the isatis trade declined and was replaced by the cheaper and more potent indigo. Eventually, the isatis trade collapsed, leaving only abandoned farmland and lost merchants.

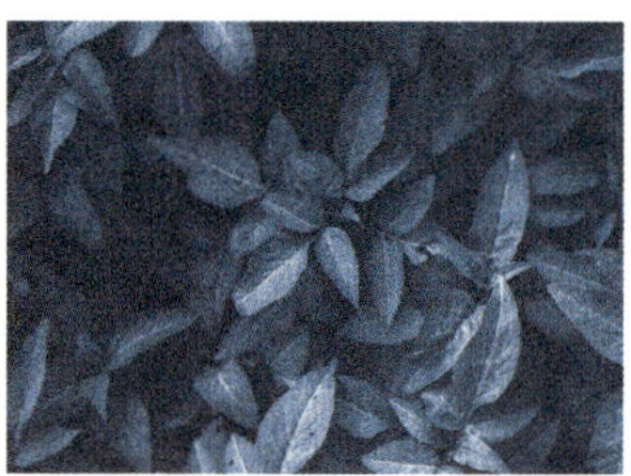

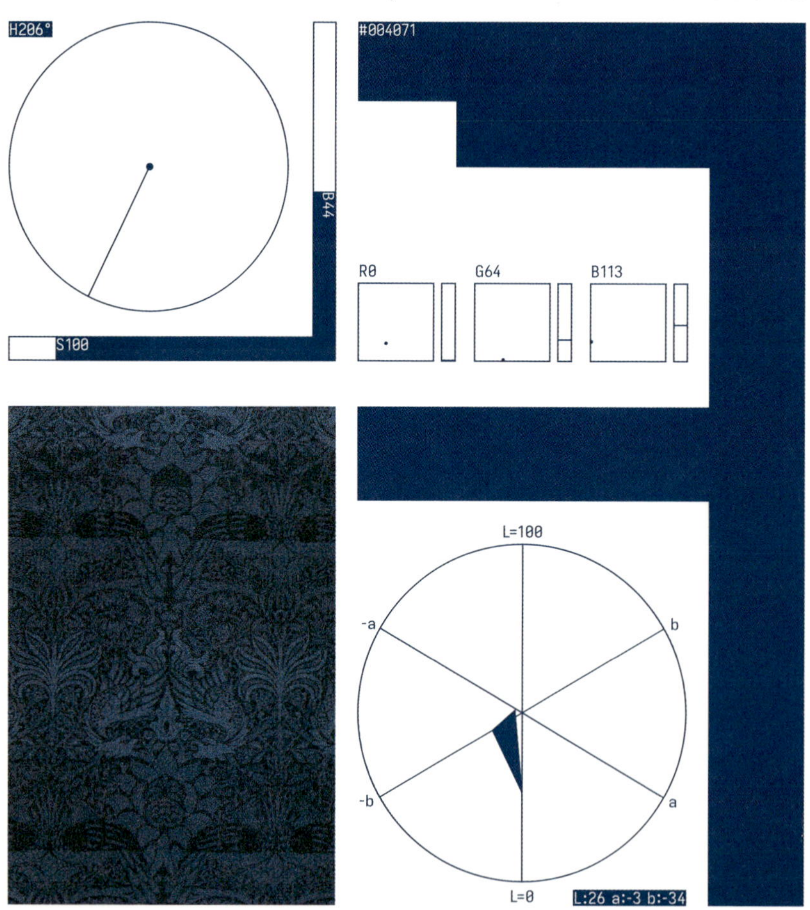

Cobalt • Cobalt blue was discovered in 1802 and was used as a substitute for the expensive lapis lazuli; Van Gogh used it extensively in his paintings. Cobalt blue is a strong color that displays excellent light resistance, high saturation, a slight matte texture, and coverage, along with weak precipitation. In 1945, the artist Han Van Meegeren was accused of collaborating with the enemy and trading Vermeer's work. He defended the painting traded as his own and claimed to have exchanged them for the lost masterpieces of Vermeer seize by the enemy. One of the key pieces of evidence that proved his defense correct was that he used cobalt blue, a pigment that only appeared after Vermeer's death. Van Meegeren was eventually convicted of forgery, not collaboration. This story reveals the importance of cobalt as a special pigment and a shift in attainability.

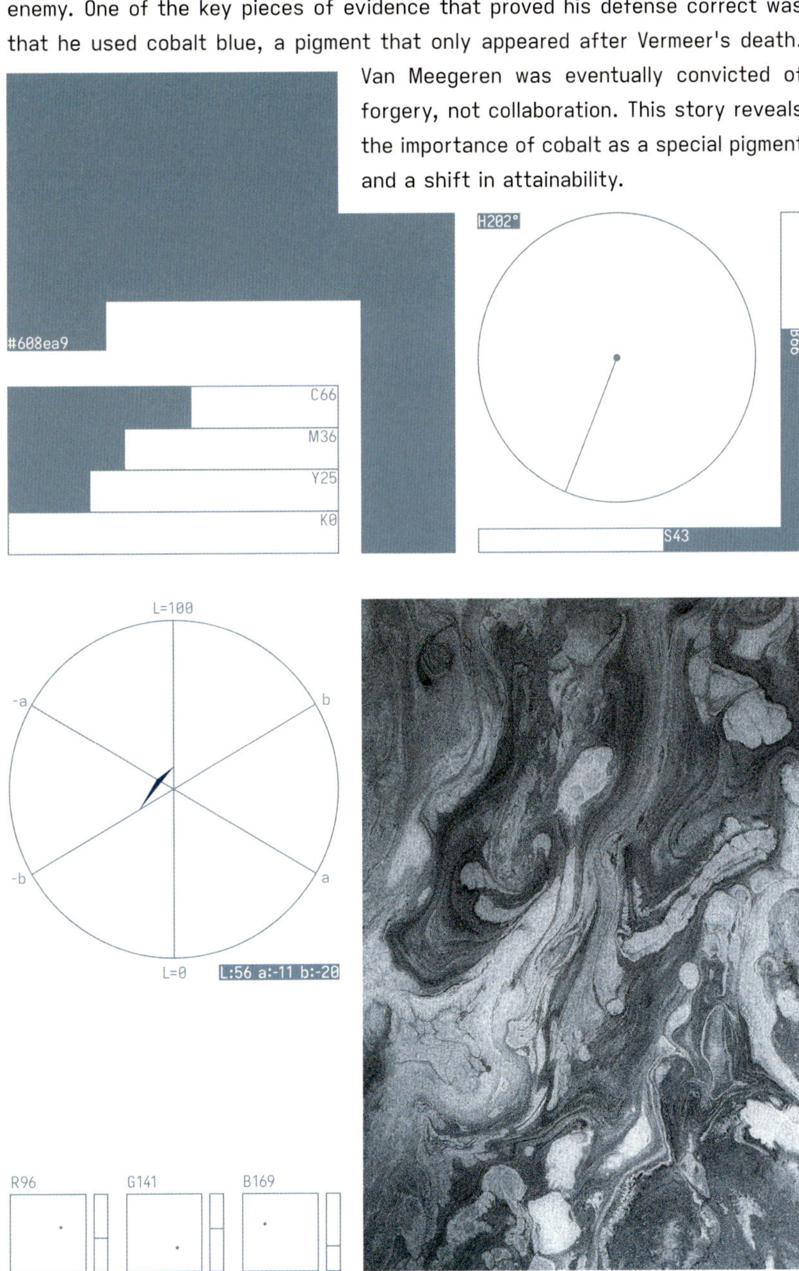

Various Blue

C100 M0 Y0 K0	C60 M25 Y40 K0	C60 M35 Y30 K0	C20 M10 Y10 K0	C55 M5 Y5 K0	C80 M50 Y20 K0
C50 M0 Y20 K0	C80 M70 Y0 K0	C65 M30 Y0 K0	C80 M45 Y10 K0	C80 M80 Y50 K10	C40 M5 Y15 K0
C45 M15 Y10 K0	C30 M5 Y5 K0	C90 M70 Y40 K5	C100 M90 Y50 K20	C65 M40 Y5 K0	C50 M25 Y5 K0
C65 M20 Y5 K0	C90 M70 Y0 K0	C40 M20 Y0 K0	C95 M90 Y0 K0	C40 M5 Y20 K0	C40 M30 Y15 K0
C50 M25 Y5 K0	C90 M40 Y0 K10	C80 M55 Y0 K0	C65 M50 Y5 K0	C30 M20 Y0 K0	C70 M50 Y0 K0
C100 M90 Y30 K0	C25 M10 Y10 K0	C45 M25 Y0 K0	C100 M80 Y55 K10	C70 M60 Y40 K20	C80 M70 Y20 K10

0 5 5	C75 M30 Y20 K0	C80 M60 Y65 K20	C55 M15 Y20 K0	C70 M20 Y20 K0	C25 M5 Y10 K0
0 0 5	C90 M55 Y65 K15	C80 M50 Y60 K5	C70 M20 Y25 K0	C90 M30 Y30 K0	C50 M10 Y20 K0
5 5 0	C95 M0 Y50 K15	C100 M90 Y40 K5	C65 M55 Y50 K5	C50 M35 Y0 K0	C80 M60 Y0 K0
5 70	C80 M55 Y60 K10	C90 M70 Y70 K40	C75 M55 Y40 K0	C100 M100 Y60 K50	C75 M60 Y40 K0
0 70 5 5	C100 M75 Y0 K0	C100 M100 Y40 K0	C85 M55 Y60 K10	C90 M45 Y60 K0	C80 M40 Y25 K0
5 30	C100 M100 Y60 K0	C30 M20 Y0 K0	C55 M0 Y15 K0	C50 M0 Y35 K0	C20 M5 Y5 K0

KORE A PILOT OFFICE

• KOREA PILOT's inaugural pop-up store is a project designed to share the joy of writing, embodying the philosophy of supporting the value of writing over time. Titled "Precious Words Collection Office," it offers an emotional experience of PILOT Pen's excellent technology. Visitors can record the joy of using a pen, appreciate the impact of a single stroke, and cherish the precious words that add color to their daily lives.

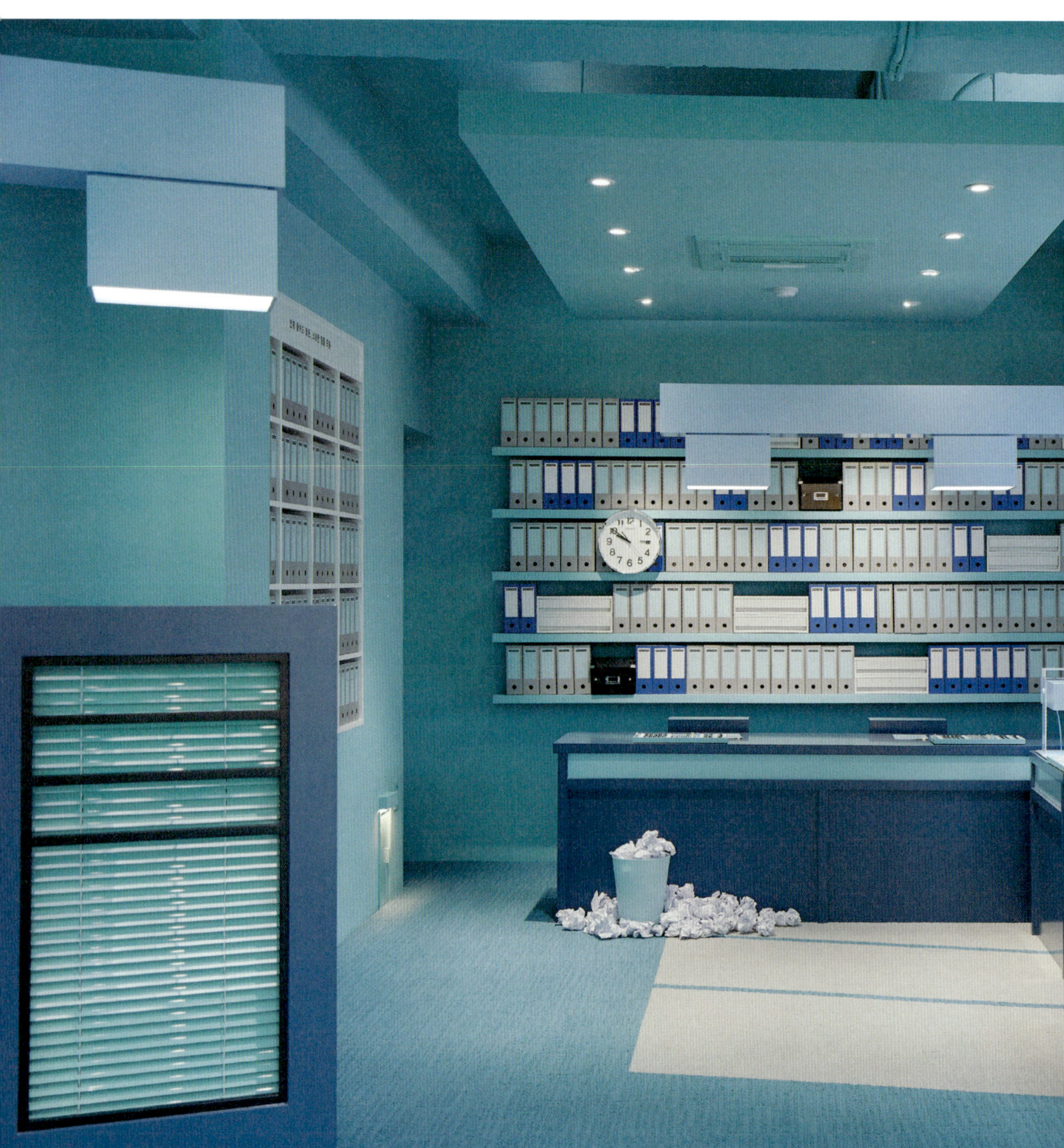

• Design Studio: MAUM STUDIO • Creative Direction: Dalwoo Lee

● Why Blue? ● The design studio adjusted the saturation of the existing color of the Pilot to align with the pop-up store's theme. This blue color was chosen as the primary hue to convey a tranquil and impactful visual impression.

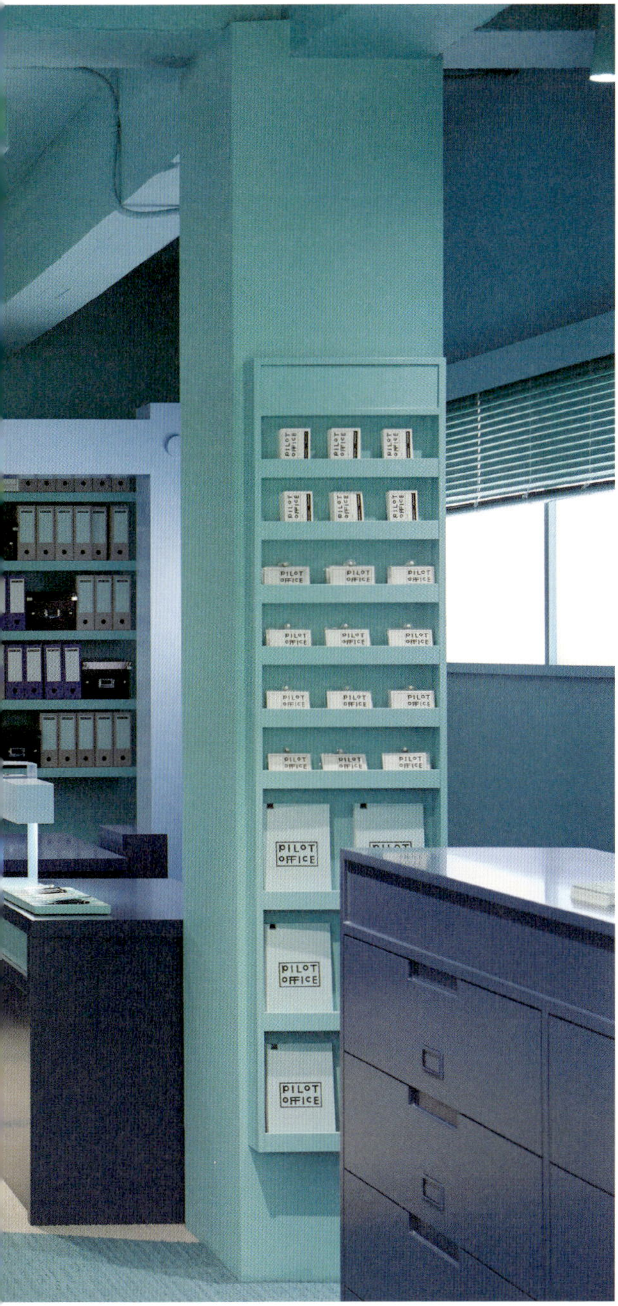

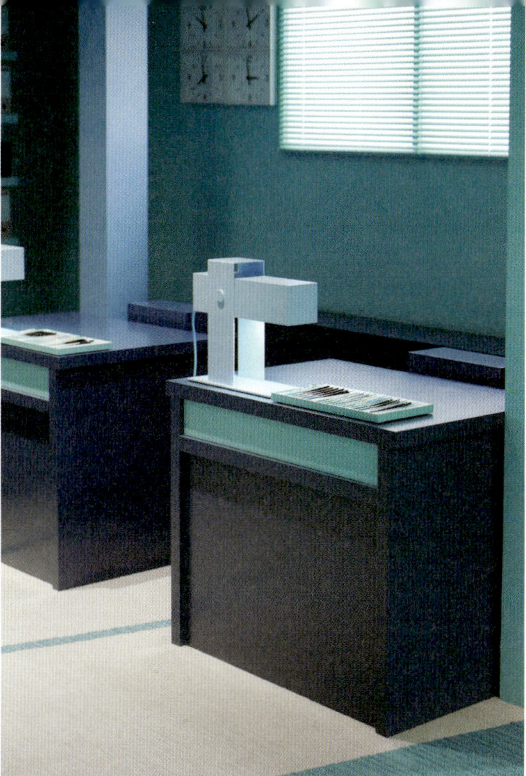

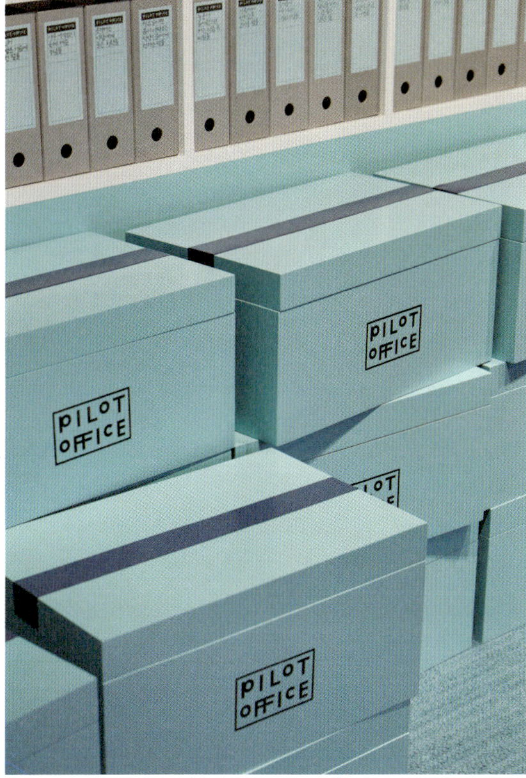

C39 M0 Y10 K0

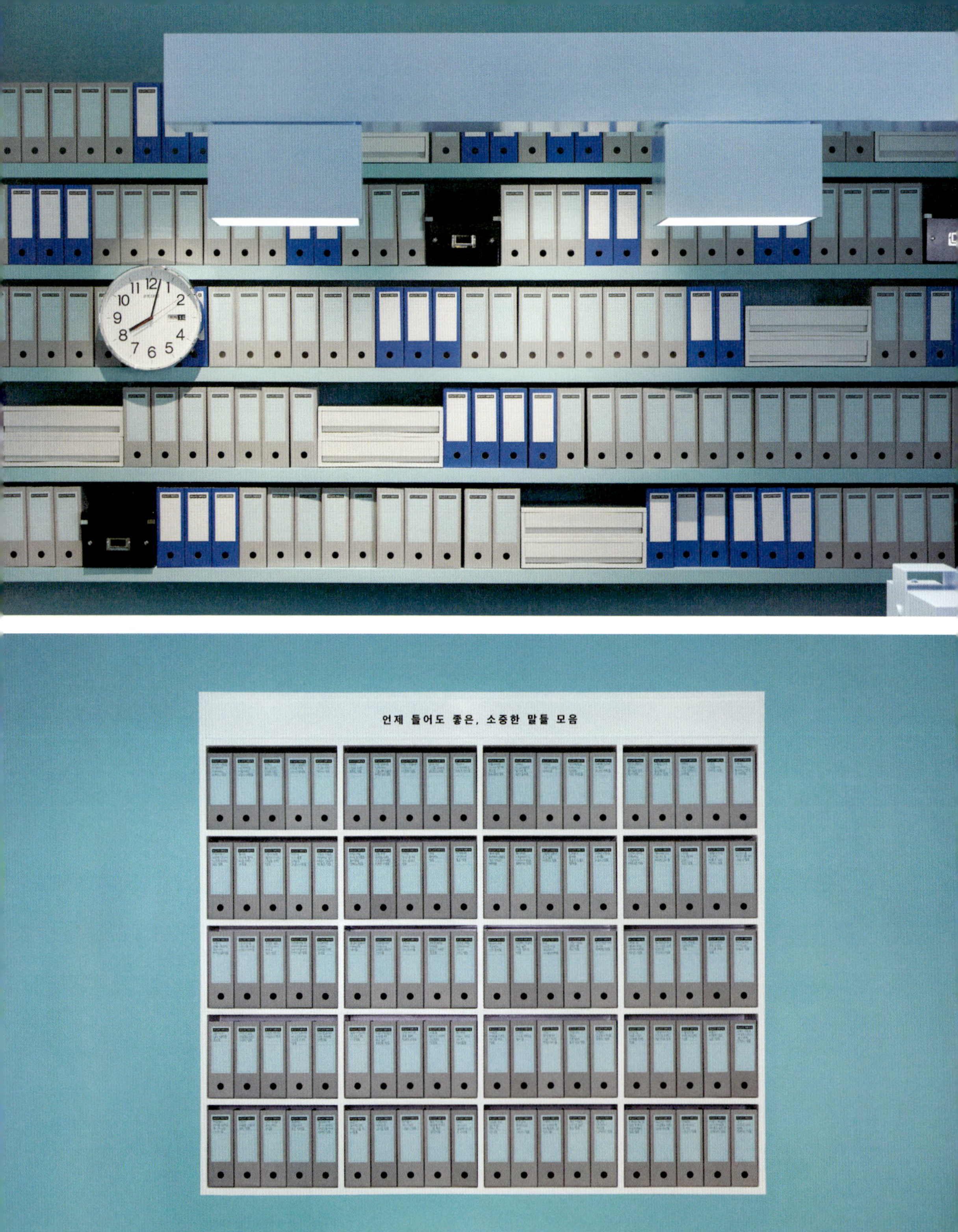

● Space Design: Eunhye Oh, Youngbak Jeong, Hanwool Kim, Kyoungjin Kim

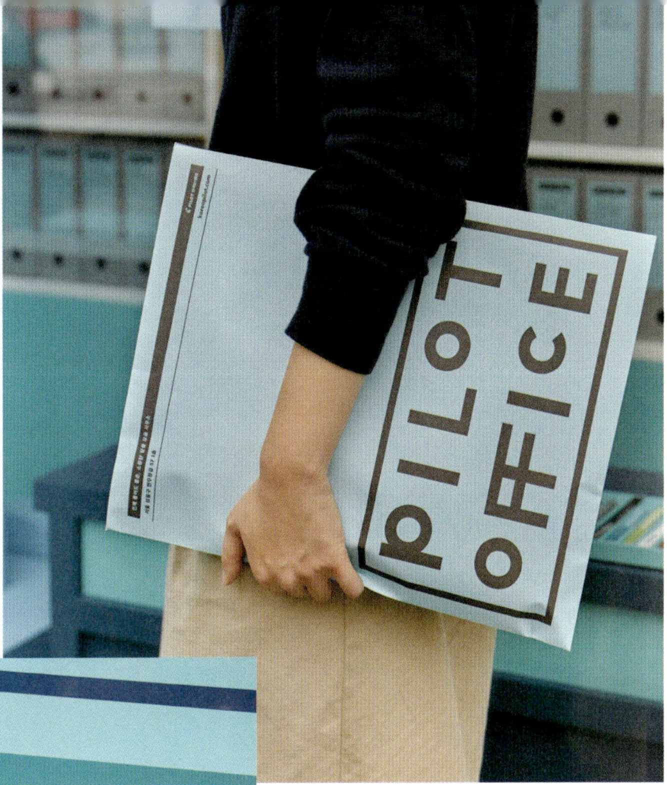

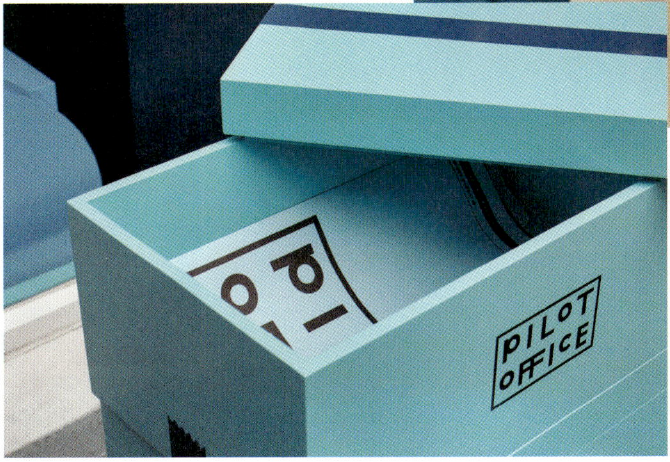

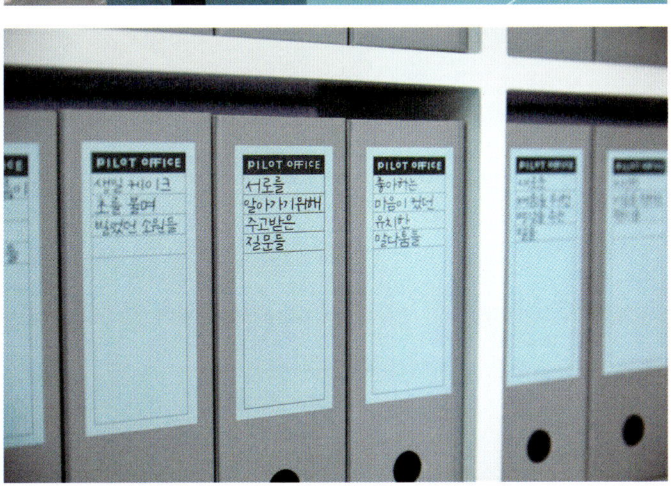

● Graphic, Product Design: Yoonji Lee, Jeawon Chung, Hyunjin Lee ● Photography: Juyeon Lee ● Client: KOREA PILOT

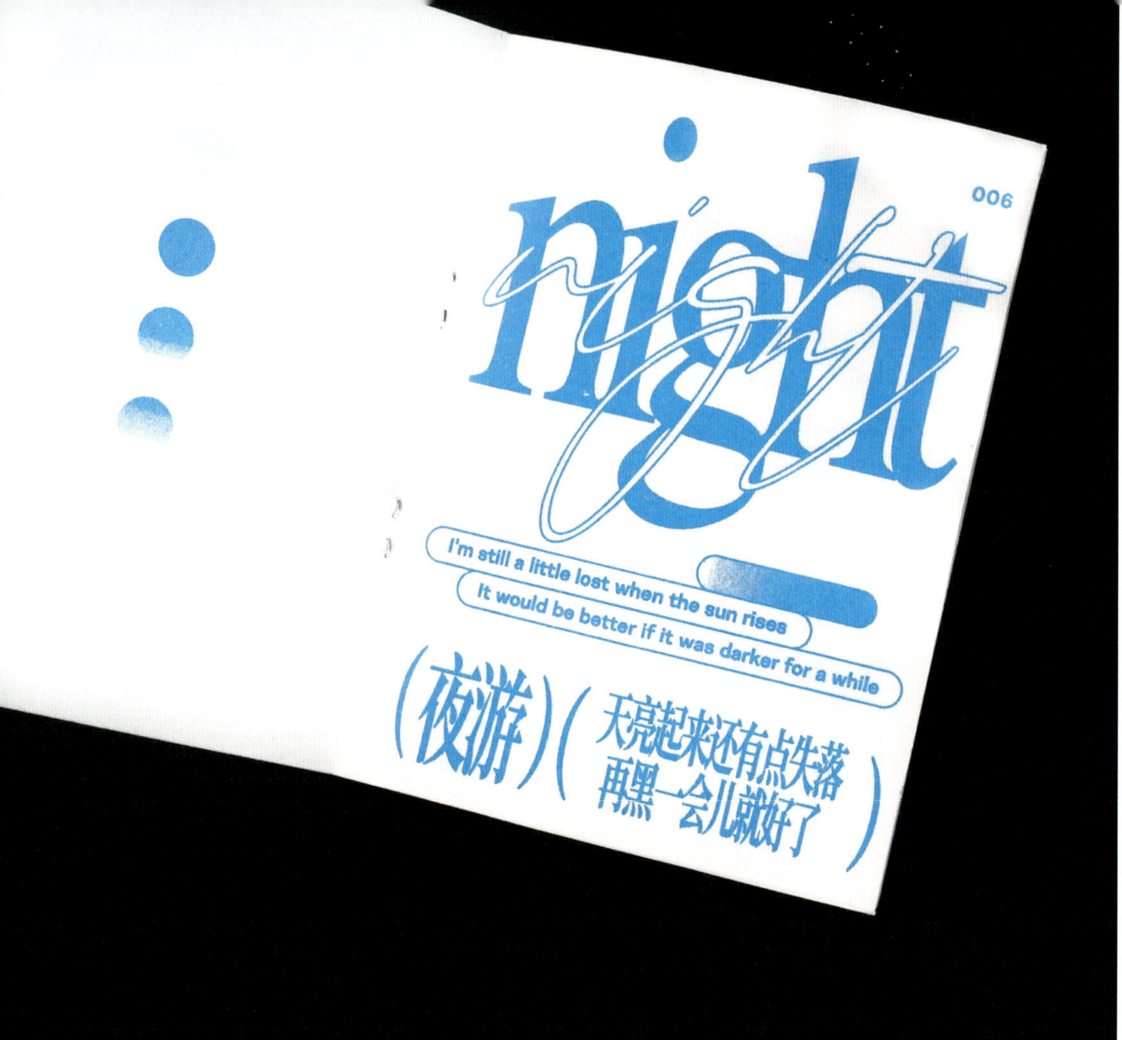

I Can't Swim ● In the designer's philosophy, the metaphor serves as a key, to create an infinite closeness between two individuals—a sensation that approaches genuine understanding. The designer once openly shared her emotions on social media, stating, "The printer and I are both malfunctioning, stuck in the same chapter." A friend responded, understanding the underlying sense of sadness. ● The designer hesitates in expressing emotions because "clear expression often means being misunderstood." However, she is also aware that the world shouldn't always be perfect and immune to scrutiny. In her view, expressing vulnerability is, in fact, an act of courage.

● Why Blue? ● The first piece of the Zine *I Can't Swim* consists of just two sentences, succinctly explaining: "Depression is like drowning, but I can't swim."
Colors have the power to evoke a range of emotions, and blue, in particular, conveys a sense of calm and melancholy, much like the vast and sometimes brutal sea. The dialogues captured in this Zine unfold a state of continuously sinking.

● Designer: WANG SHUO

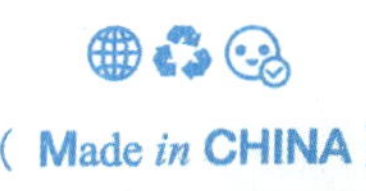

(Made *in* CHINA)

EMOTION
SERIES
01

I CAN'T SWIM

（我不会游泳）

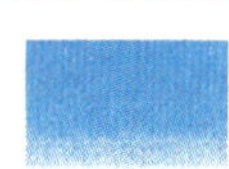

WRITTEN & DESIGNED
BY
WANG SHUO

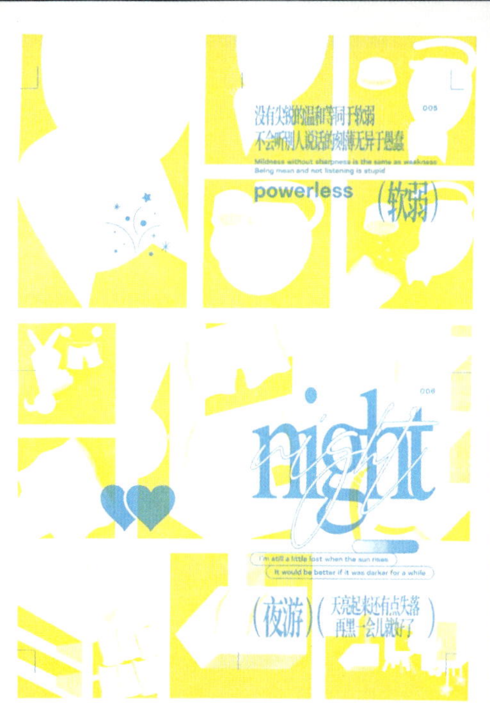

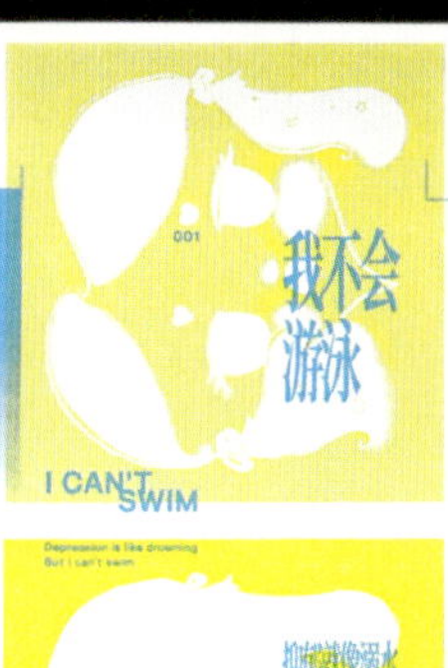

Depression is like drowning
But I can't swim

抑郁就像溺水
但我不会游泳

002

容器

RECEPTACLE

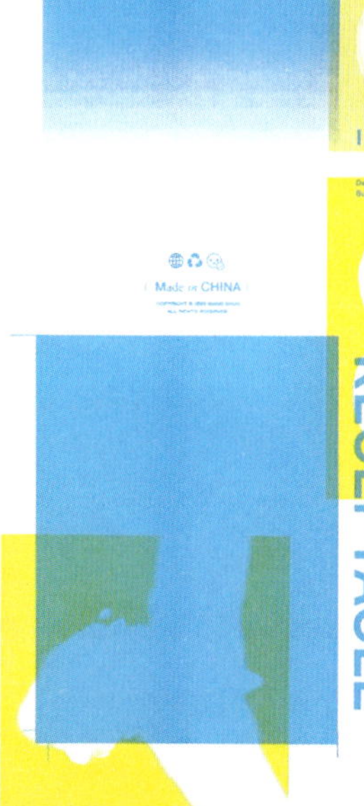

When I fell asleep
Body full of tears
Close your eyes and it will overflow
The bed became the ocean
I became a receptacle

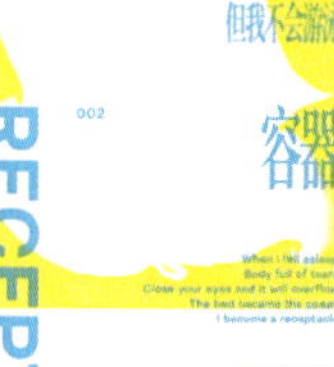

睡觉的时候
身体蓄满眼泪
闭上眼睛溢了出来
床变成了海洋
我变成了容器

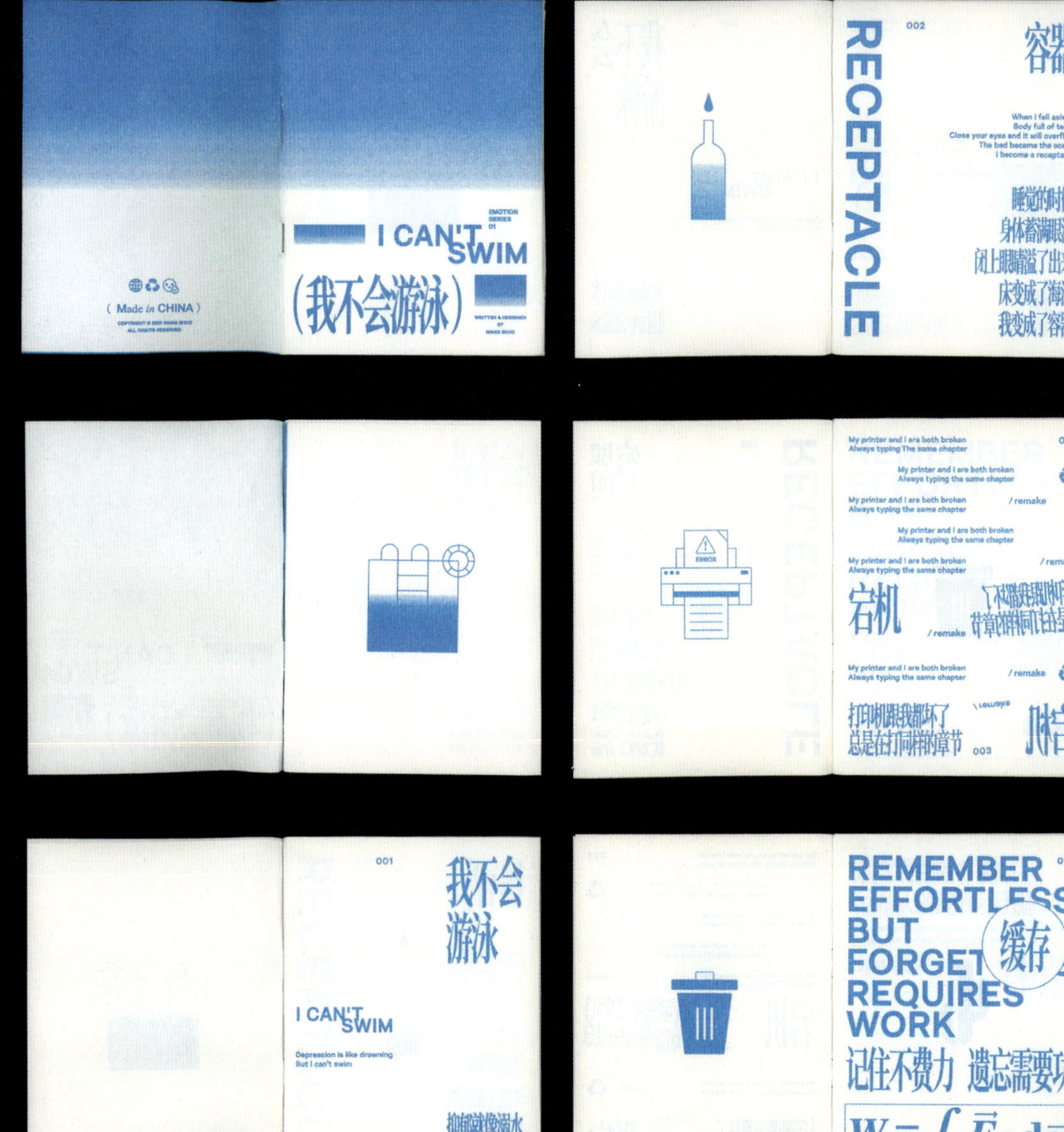
(Made in CHINA)
EMOTION SERIES 01
I CAN'T SWIM
(我不会游泳)
002
容器
RECEPTACLE
When I fell asleep
Body full of tears
Close your eyes and it will overflow
The bed became the ocean
I become a receptacle
睡觉的时候
身体蓄满眼泪
闭上眼睛溢了出来
床变成了海洋
我变成了容器
ERROR
003
My printer and I are both broken
Always typing The same chapter
/remake
宕机
打印机跟我都坏了
总是在打同样的章节
001
我不会游泳
I CAN'T SWIM
Depression is like drowning
But I can't swim
抑郁就像溺水
但我不会游泳
004
REMEMBER EFFORTLESS BUT FORGETTING REQUIRES WORK
缓存
记住不费力 遗忘需要功
$W = \int_c \vec{F} \cdot d\vec{x}$

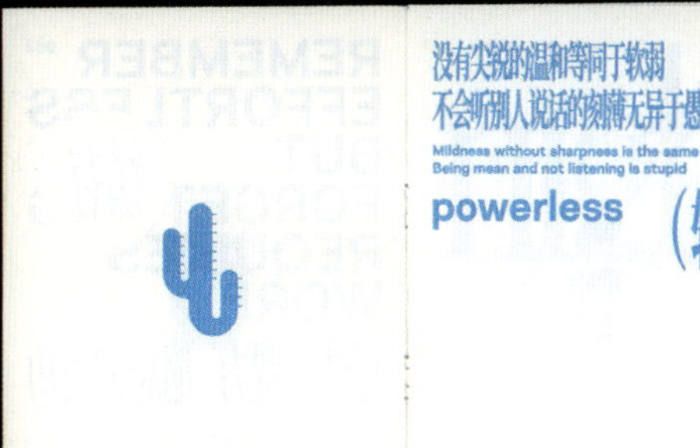

005
没有尖锐的温和等同于软弱
不会听别人说话的刻薄无异于愚蠢
Mildness without sharpness is the same as weakness
Being mean and not listening is stupid
powerless
(软弱)

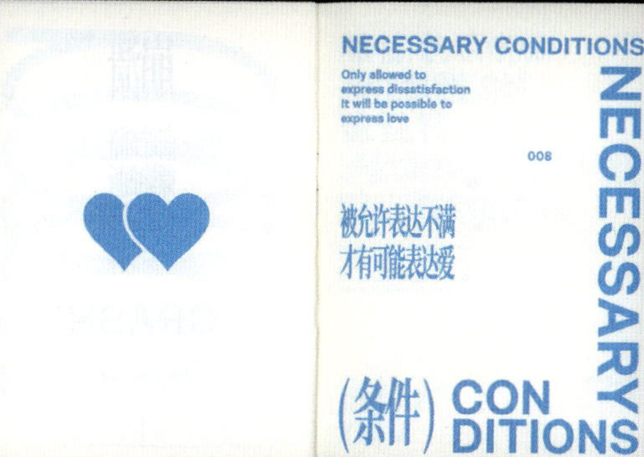

NECESSARY CONDITIONS
Only allowed to
express dissatisfaction
It will be possible to
express love
008
被允许表达不满
才有可能表达爱
(条件) CON
DITIONS
NECESSARY

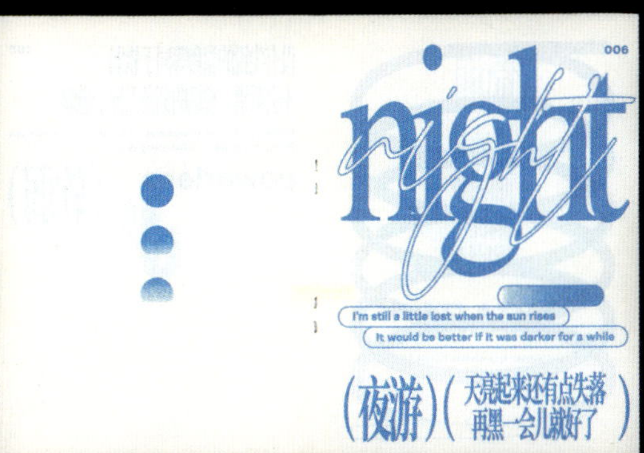

006
night
I'm still a little lost when the sun rises
It would be better if it was darker for a while
(夜游)(天亮起来还有点失落
再黑一会儿就好了)

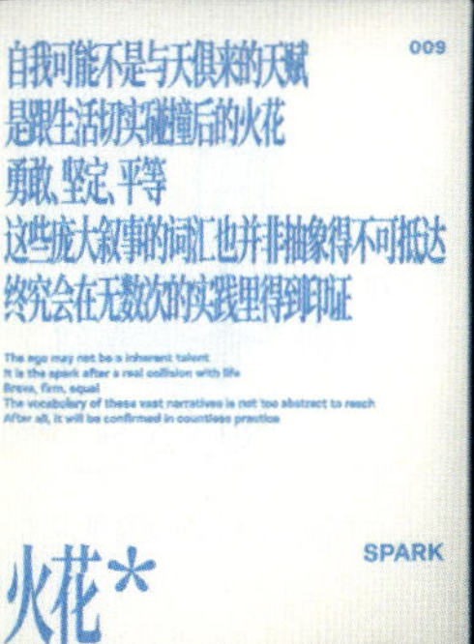

009
自我可能不是与天俱来的天赋
是跟生活切实碰撞后的火花
勇敢、坚定、平等
这些庞大叙事的词汇也并非抽象得不可抵达
终究会在无数次的实践里得到印证
The ego may not be a inherent talent
It is the spark after a real collision with life
Brave, firm, equal
The vocabulary of these vast narratives is not too abstract to reach
After all, it will be confirmed in countless practice
火花*
SPARK

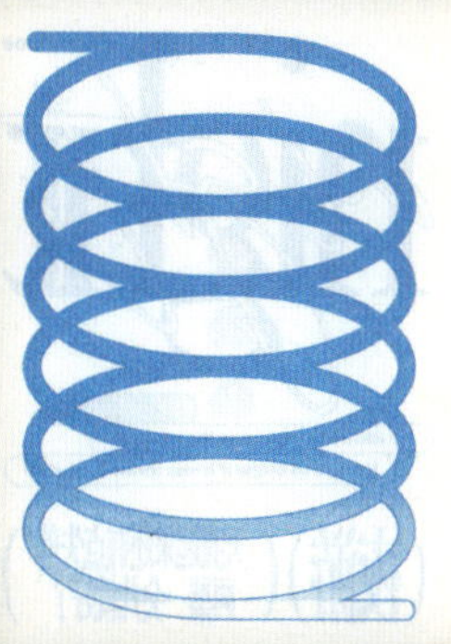

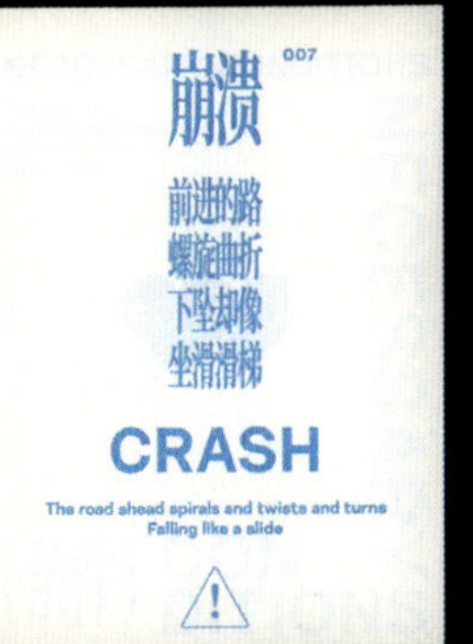

007
崩溃
前进的路
螺旋曲折
下坠却像
坐滑滑梯
CRASH
The road ahead spirals and twists and turns
Falling like a slide

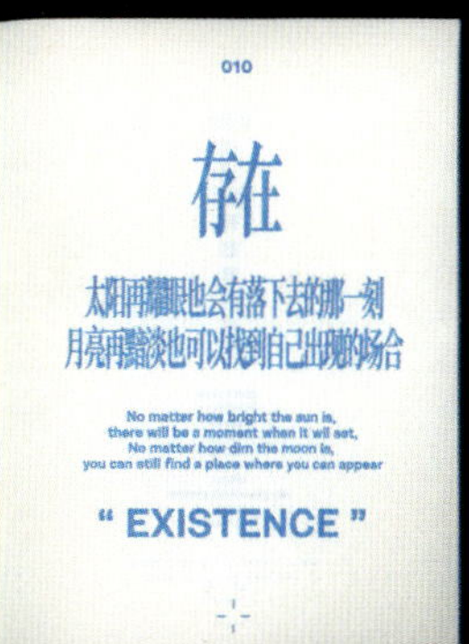

010
存在
太阳再耀眼也会有落下去的那一刻
月亮再黯淡也可以找到自己出现的场合
No matter how bright the sun is,
there will be a moment when it will set,
No matter how dim the moon is,
you can still find a place where you can appear
" EXISTENCE "

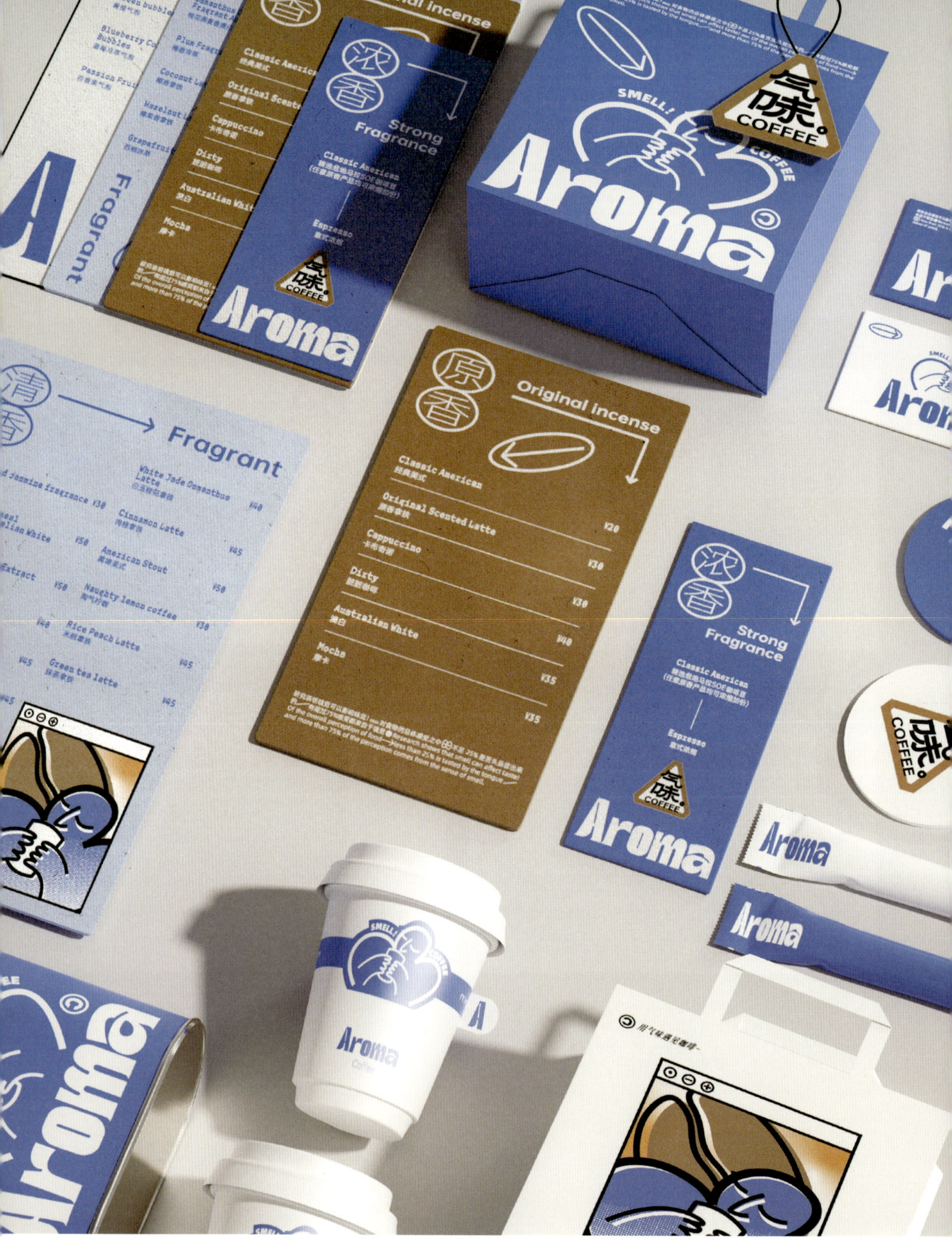

● Design Studio: SURPRISE ● Designer: Thirteen ● Client: Aroma Coffee

Aroma Coffee ● In the realm of packaging and brand design, a deep dive into research highlights the crucial impact of smell on taste. Less than 25% of the taste experience in food and beverages comes from the tongue, while over 75% is influenced by olfaction. Guided by the principle of "olfaction first," the design team is inspired to reconnect with the essence of coffee. Carefully curated for each coffee cup, the packaging aims to create unique olfactory symbols, emphasizing the diversity of coffee culture and the brand's commitment to varied coffee experiences. Aroma Coffee's brand design centers around "Meeting Coffee with Aroma," categorizing aromas into four levels (light, fresh, original, and intense) for a convenient and swift consumer selection experience.

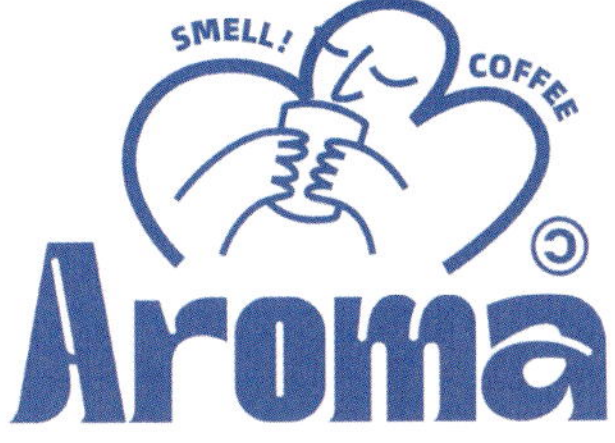

● Why Blue? ● The brand aims to convey a professional visual experience to consumers.

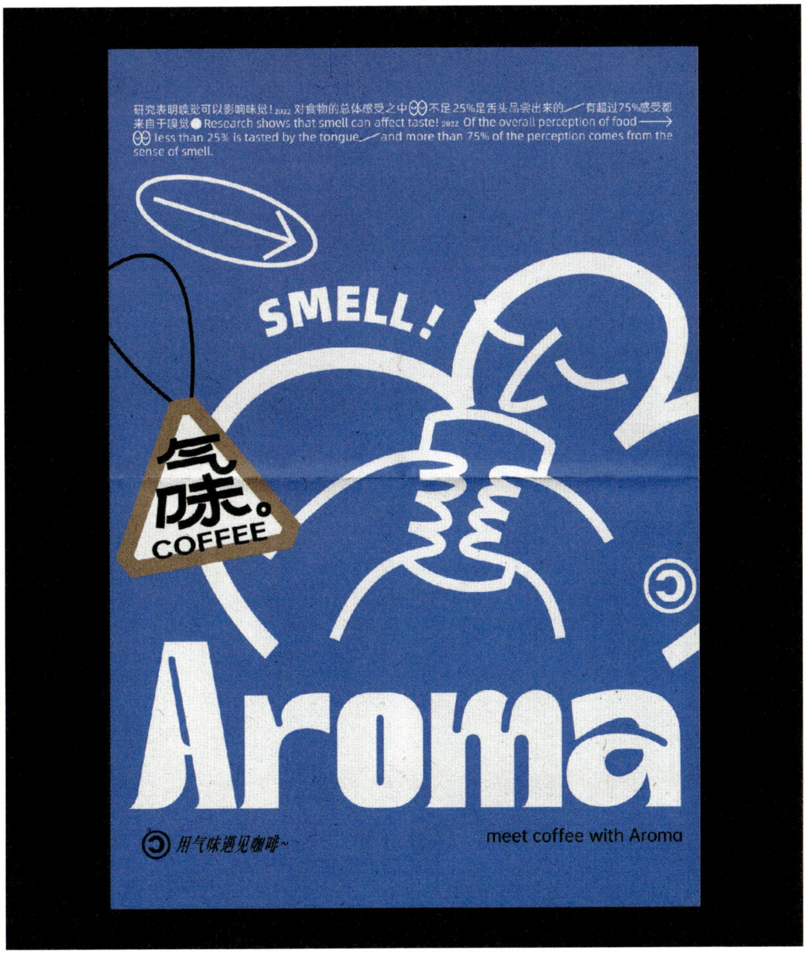

C70 M47 Y0 K0　C7 M45 Y66 K18

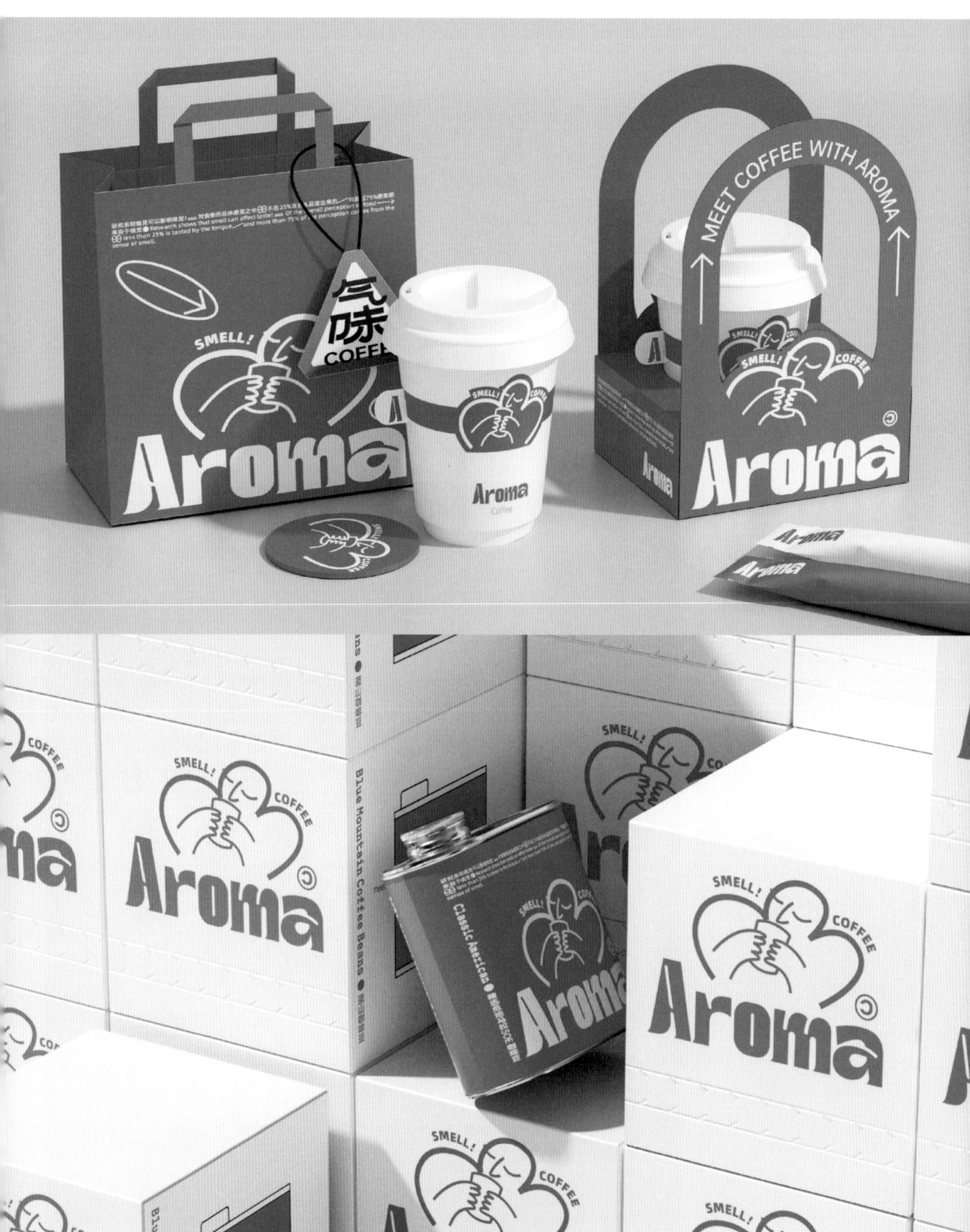
SMELL!
COFFEE
Aroma
MEET COFFEE WITH AROMA
Aroma
Coffee
Blue Mountain Coffee Beans
Classic Americano

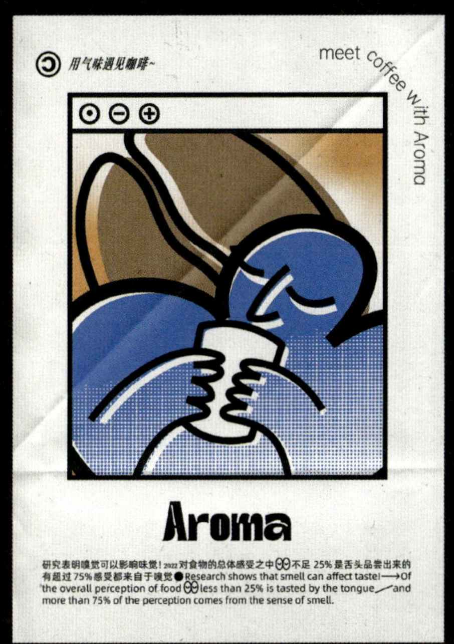
用气味遇见咖啡~
meet coffee with Aroma
Aroma
研究表明嗅觉可以影响味觉！2022 对食物的总体感受之中 不足 25% 是舌头品尝出来的
有超过 75% 感受都来自于嗅觉 Research shows that smell can affect taste! Of
the overall perception of food less than 25% is tasted by the tongue and
more than 75% of the perception comes from the sense of smell.

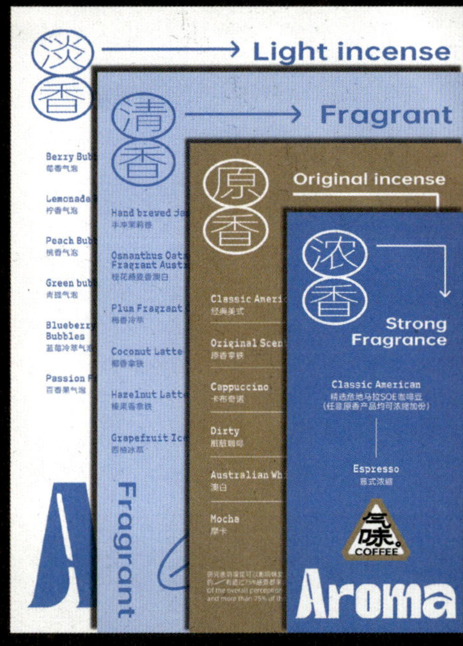
淡香
Light incense
清香
Fragrant
原香
Original incense
浓香
Strong Fragrance
Berry Bub
莓香气泡
Lemonade
柠香气泡
Peach Bub
桃香气泡
Green bub
青提气泡
Blueberry Bubbles
蓝莓冷萃气泡
Passion F
百香果气泡
Hand brewed
手冲果莉拾
Osmanthus Oat
Fragrant Austr
桂花燕麦澳白
Plum Fragrant
梅香冷萃
Coconut Latte
椰香拿铁
Hazelnut Latte
榛果香拿铁
Grapefruit Ice
西柚冰萃
Fragrant
Classic Ameri
经典美式
Original Scen
原香拿铁
Cappuccino
卡布奇诺
Dirty
脏脏咖啡
Australian Wh
澳白
Mocha
摩卡
Classic American
Espresso
意式浓缩
气味
COFFEE
Aroma

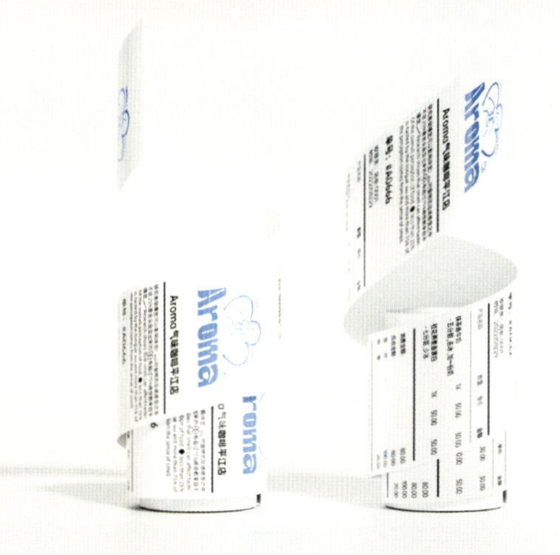

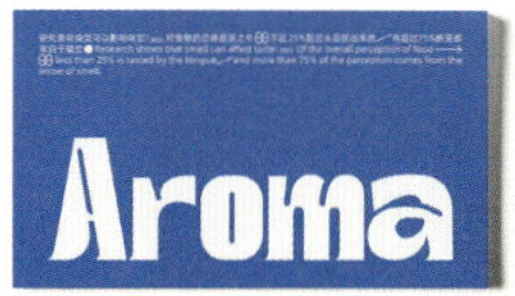
Aroma

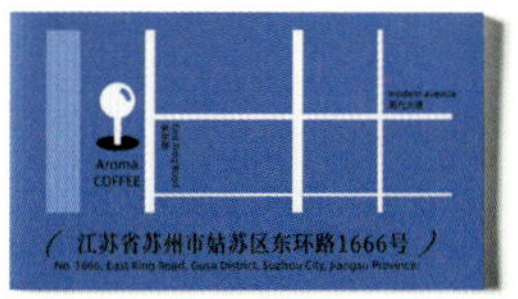
江苏省苏州市姑苏区东环路1666号

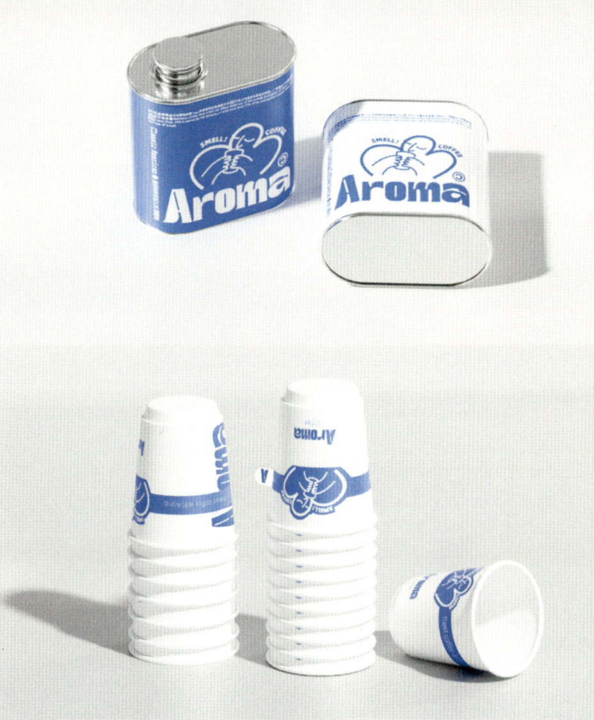
Aroma
Aroma

Diverseddie's *Emotional Harbor* Album Design

● This CD marks the musician's debut album, capturing his journey of growth and insights. Music, akin to a safe harbor, holds a special place for him. The album, with its refined design featuring clouds, sea, and a bear emblem, aims to convey the musician's emotional experience. The inner pages unfold to reveal a navigational route symbolizing the river of time and the path back home. The CD design exposes a mirrored sea beneath the clouds.

● Why Blue? ● The deep blue hue, mirroring the album's songs and the musician's ambiance, resembles an overcast sea filled with unease and untold stories. The album predominantly features a palette of deep gray and blue, with light gray as the background. Gray draws the outlines, while the blue elements stand out with clarity and composure.

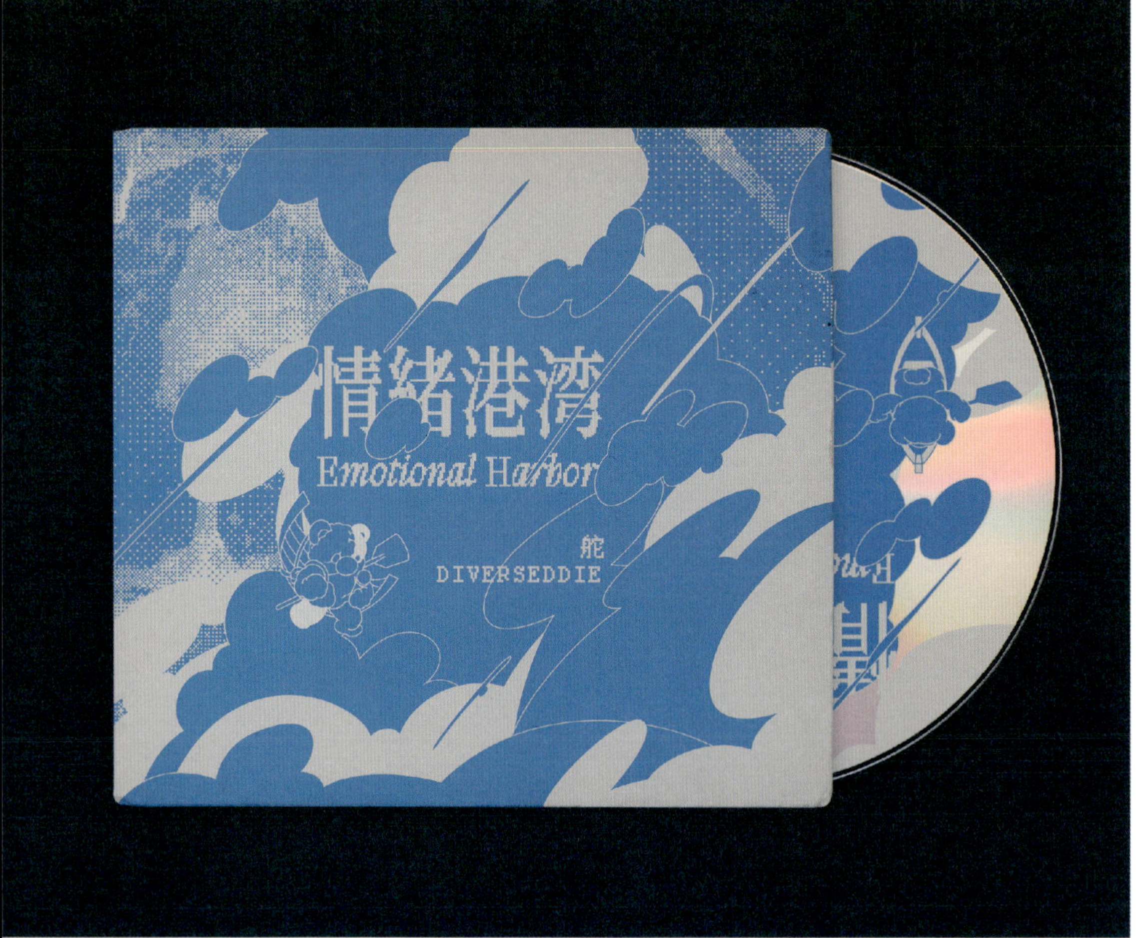

● Design Studio: Homer & Dreamer Design ● Design: Homer ● Client: SHOOC Studio

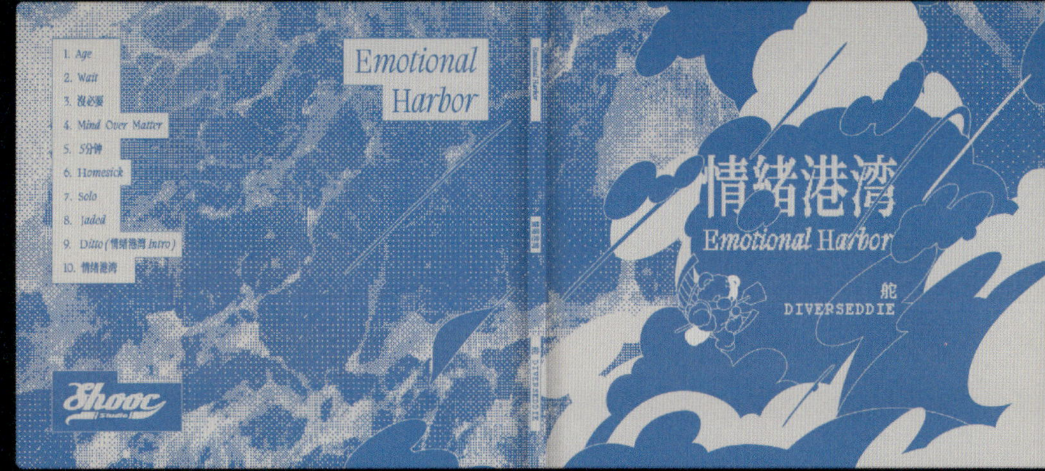

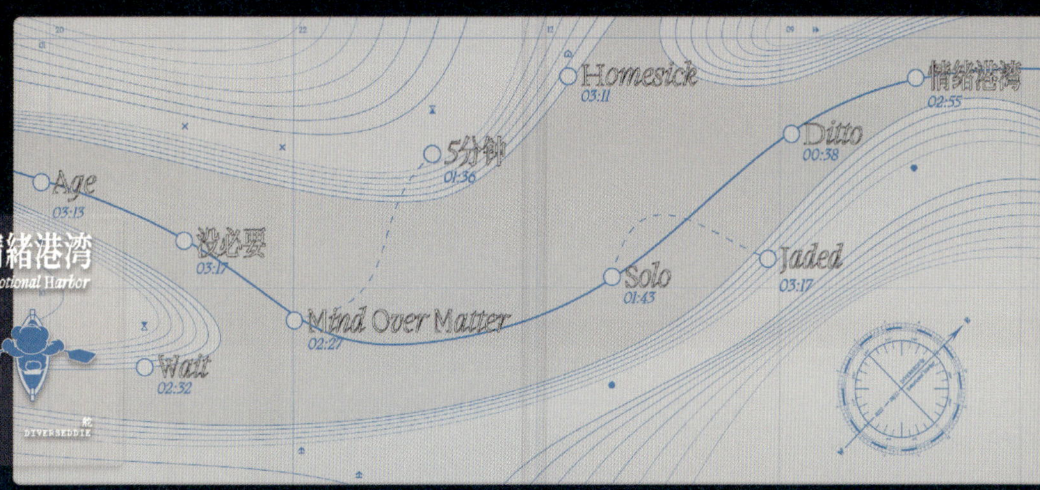

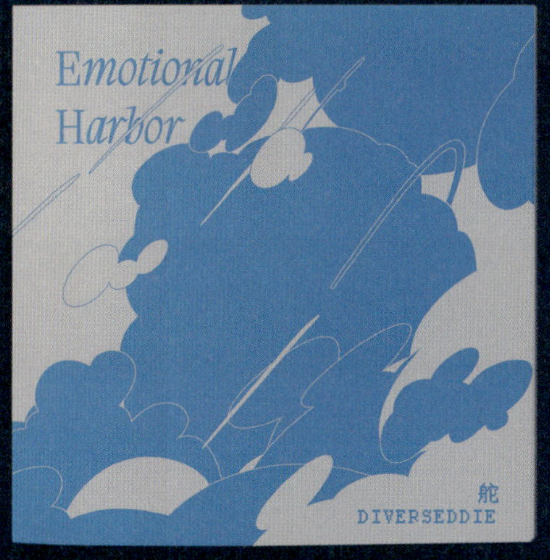

C94 M36 Y13 K3

C0 M0 Y0 K35

"Am I doing fine for my age?"
Spinning on their minds questioning
You see the dollar signs on their pay
But I got a peace of mind
So I'mma wait
Ride my wave
With my WAV
In my way

Started writing rhymes around when I was 15
I gave it all my time, but only I was listening
I wasn't in it for attention
Just the instinct to go on a venture to reinvention, self sustained
In the midst of the abyss, singing through the storm
Solving puzzles in myself, playing nimble chords
It was all a dream, till I pushed it into orbit
Catch me recording in my university dormitory
Not a perfect story

03

01.Age

作曲：FYKSEN

We always complicate
Made things exaggerated
Never stop to think
Messages automated
Maybe we're stuck too long, inside this conversation
Maybe we need escape, maybe a long vacation
Either way, yeah we're back to basics
Walking out the maze

A moment later we
are putting on a smiling face
We don't even know why
It was raining in the first place
Cause we care enough, per se

08

09

Jetlagged but Im only sitting at my desk,
Segue,
and I keep on moving either way
Caught up on my favorite animes,
I dont got the time to hibernate no way,
Write it down,
Then I start it from the ground,
Journey look like a mountain,
But Im walking what is in front of me,
Focus on my endeavors,
Instead of fold under weather,
Be ready where or whenever go,
Sitting waiting wishing nah that I cant afford,
Pen and paper are my dawgs and were never bored,
Mind over matter always no matter what,

I've been working lowkey, now I'm back
AFK now Im resonating on high pass,
Like day and night feels like on time lapse,
Jetlagged but Im only sitting at my desk,
Segue,
and I keep on moving either way,
Caught up on my favorite animes,
I dont got the time to hibernate no way,
Sitting waiting wishing nah that I cant afford,
Pen and paper are my dawgs and were never bored,
Opportunities are knocking at the door,
Mind over matter always no matter what,
Sitting waiting wishing nah that I cant afford,
Pen and paper are my dawgs and were never bored,
Mind over matter always no matter what,
Among the brightest of stars,
Shine in the dark uh,
Maybe the journeys a blessing in disguise uh,
Life is ready or not well here it comes.

and a sharpenedup mindset,
is the only shining armor,
4AM in the morning,
Manifesting not yawning
and Im learning how to dream while staying awake
Even though it is alluring to sleep,
I got that micro speed and that macro patience.
Moving steadily
Slowly finding my haven
Putting mind over matter
and the win is adjacent
You know
Ive been working lowkey now Im back,
AFK now Im resonating on high pass,
like day and night feels like on time lapse,

04.Mind Over Matter

编曲：ZUUSEK
混音／母带：Nani Beats

that I could really be their
Stomping on my stage
yeah I wished that they could see that someday
and I'm proud to say we came a long way
Yeah I'm reppin' for my folks
Also rep a few dumbbells
You don't see me though
I'd be working, I don't come out
On my tunnel vision
writing lyrics to the moon
and record them when the sun's out
on a mission in a booth
I'm just sticking to my purpose
and staying as a wordsmith
I'mma save a few purchases
and write a lot more verses
Got me working through the day
Retrospective in the nighttime
Working through the day
Reminiscing in the night
When I'm hungry, I lift weights, yeah

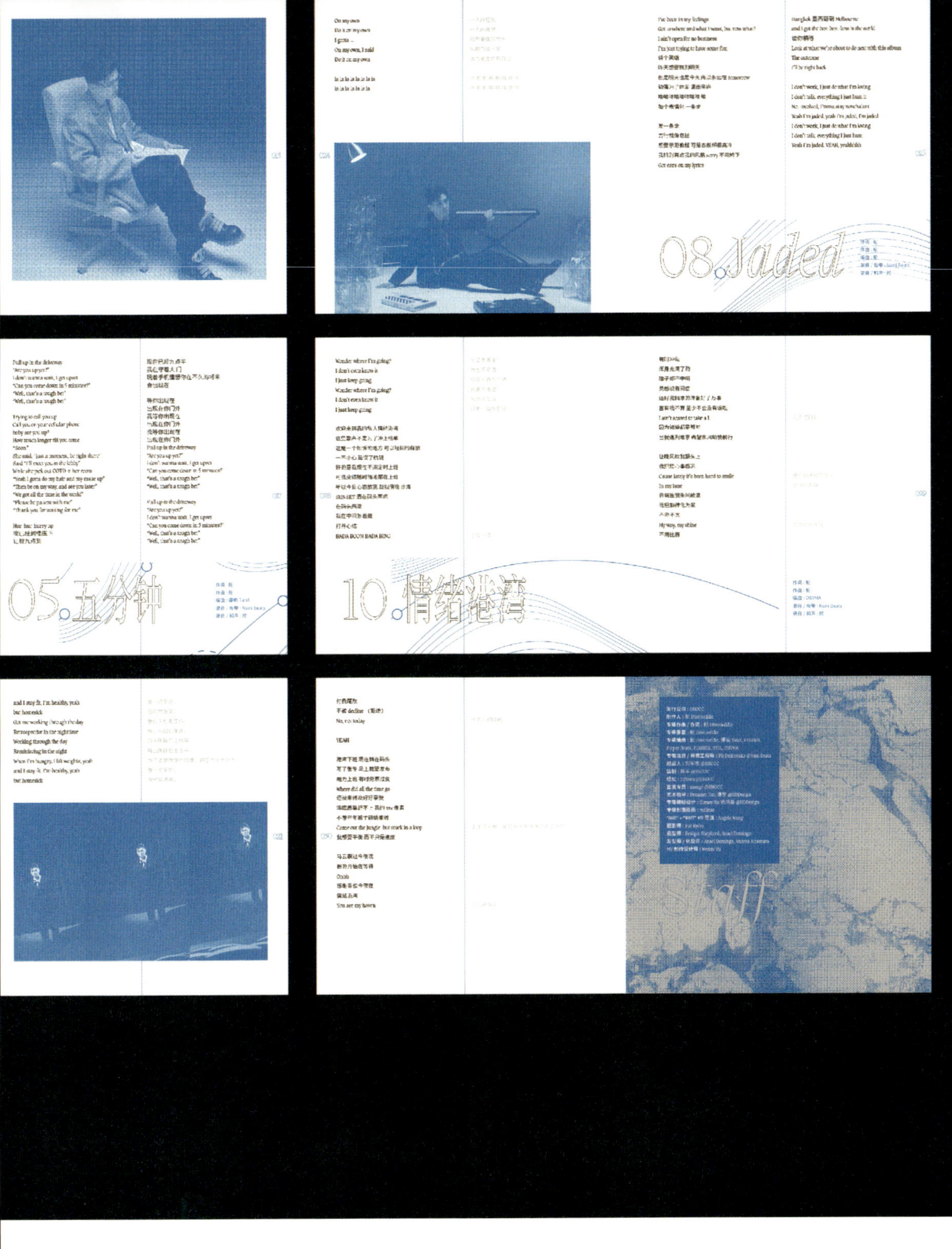

BETHANY KIM—YIN

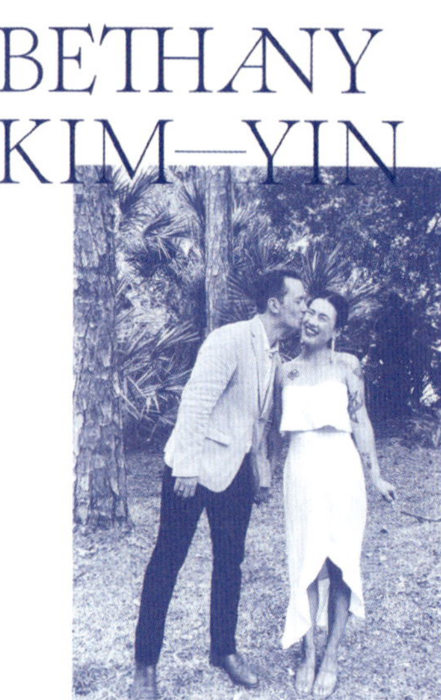

Bethany with her husband.

As I reclaim my racial identity
I try on what I never thought fit me

My birth name is Yin
My mother's is Kim

Upon adoption, she was Brown
And I was Brown until Goodson

But I wonder how it might have felt
To have identified with my Asian self

So as I imagine what might have been
I play around with Kim-Yin

Learning the cost of tradition
If I want to say no, then saying so

I was told to take my husband's name
I was always told I couldn't wear yellow

But I try it on, and realize
Yellow is my perfect size ☼

*BORN IN UNKNOWN

*CURRENTLY IN USA

15

SADIA SOHANI QUDDUS

سادية

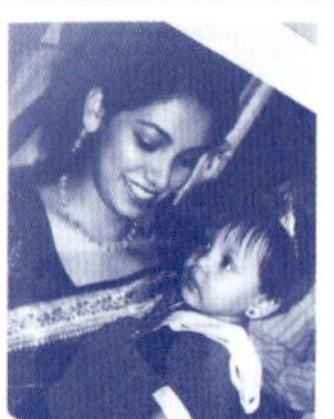

Sadia comes from Arabic word for joy. Sohani is a Bangla word for beauty.

17

I'VE IMAGINED BEING CALLED A DIFFERENT NAME COUNTLESS TIMES.

22

BUT NOTHING FELT FULLY MYSELF.

☼

23

Is This a Typo? ● In the American context, many Asians adopt an English name alongside their given name to streamline communication. The publication *Is This a Typo?* challenges this norm, featuring stories from thirty-nine contributors about their names—often mispronounced or treated as typos in English. The publication highlights the thoughtful process behind choosing these names, ultimately paying tribute to their significance and the individuals who bear them.

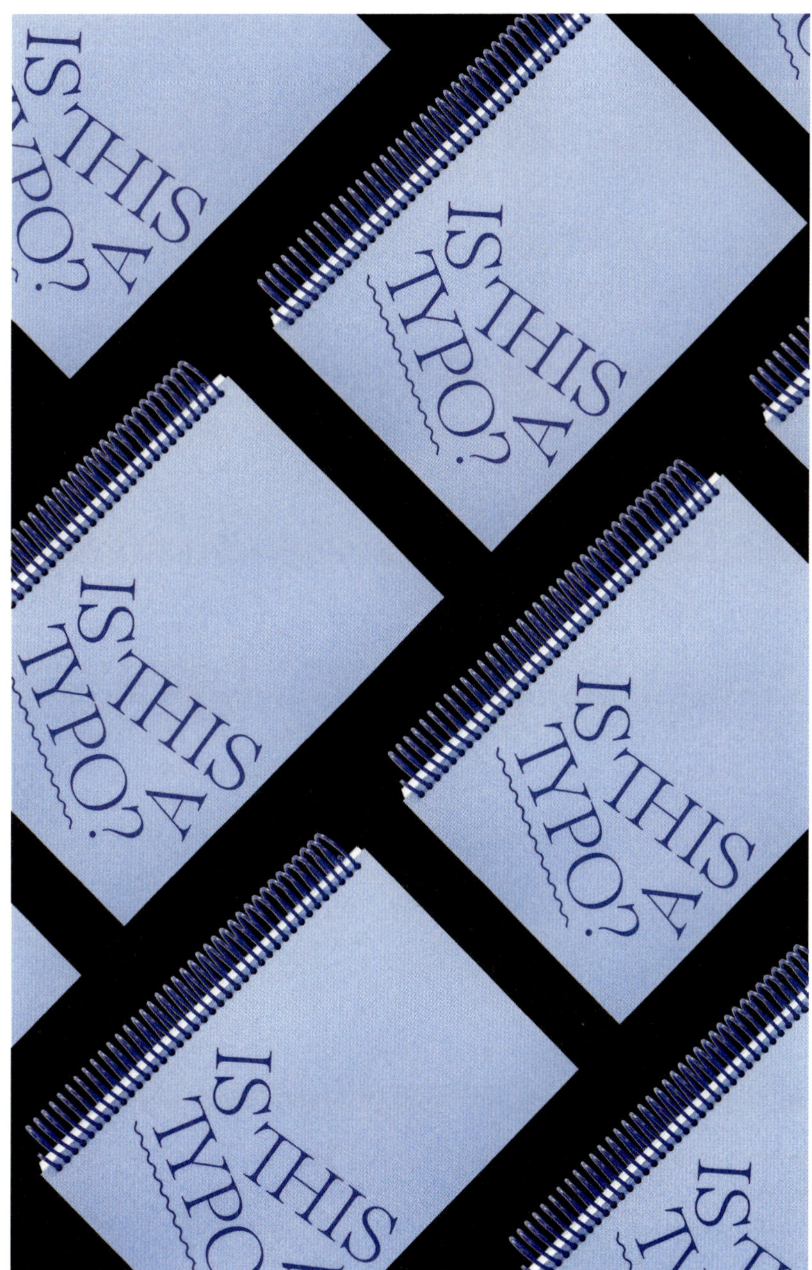

● Why Blue? ● The designer aimed to elevate and show respect for names that are frequently mispronounced and casually disregarded. A profound shade of royal blue was chosen to accentuate the significance of honoring these names.

C98 M90 Y0 K0

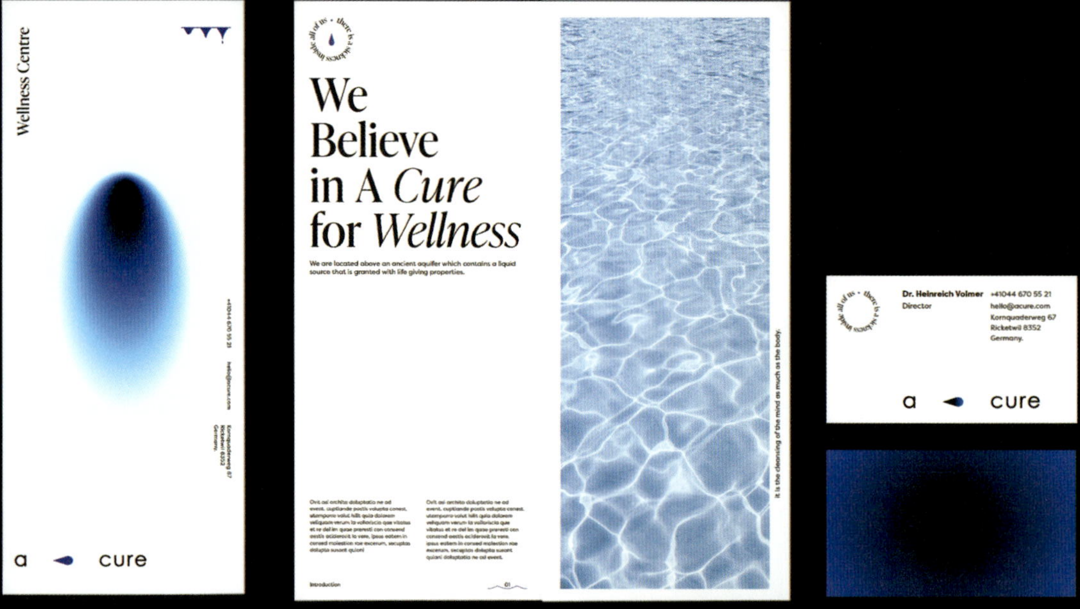

A Cure • A premier hydrotherapy company, A Cure specializes in providing luxurious wellness experiences with water's transformative power. Meticulously designed facilities feature stunning water elements, pleasant landscapes, and private areas fostering peace. A Cure is dedicated to delivering an unparalleled hydrotherapy experience with design elements inspired by water's qualities. It positions itself as the ultimate natural solution for health concerns, visually reinforced through a gradational iconic droplet logo. The elegant typefaces and minimal layout create a visual ambiance of luxury and tranquility.

• Why Blue? • The project, being centered around the element of water, naturally gravitates towards the color blue. By incorporating gentle blue gradients, the designer aimed to evoke a sense of tranquility and calmness throughout the visuals. The choice of blue gradients, transitioning gradually from a darker to a lighter hue, mirrors the concept of "the cure" slowly dissipating and being absorbed by the bodies.

• Design Studio: Jien Li Design • Designer: Chua Jien Li

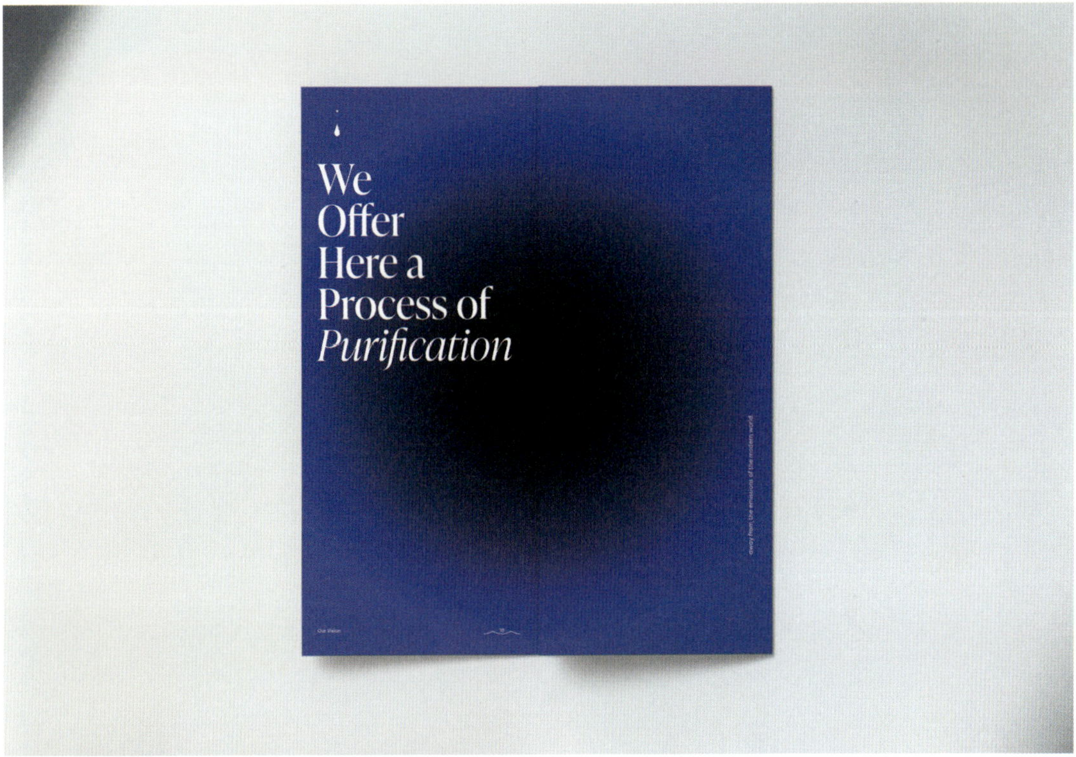

We
Offer
Here a
Process of
Purification

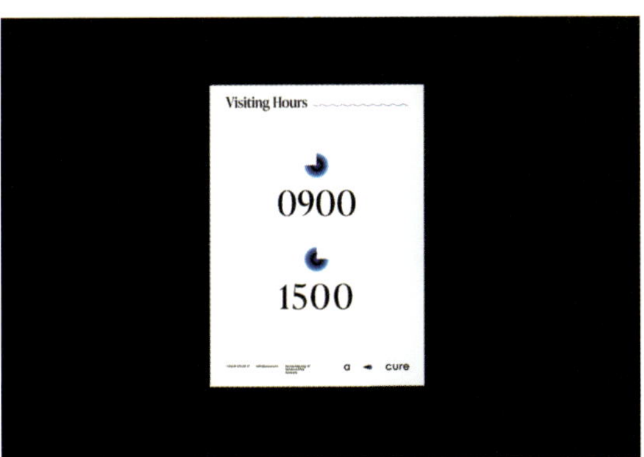

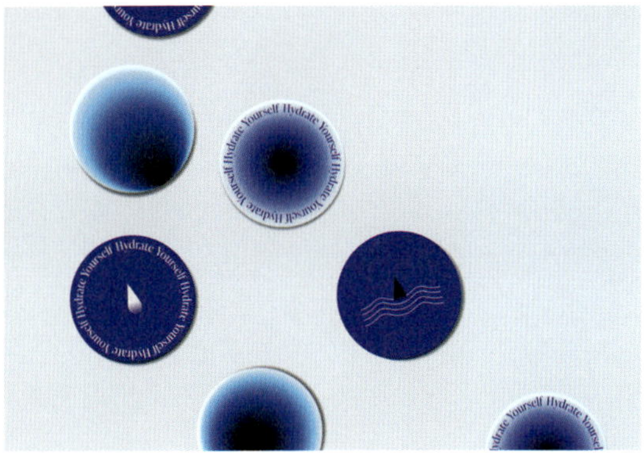

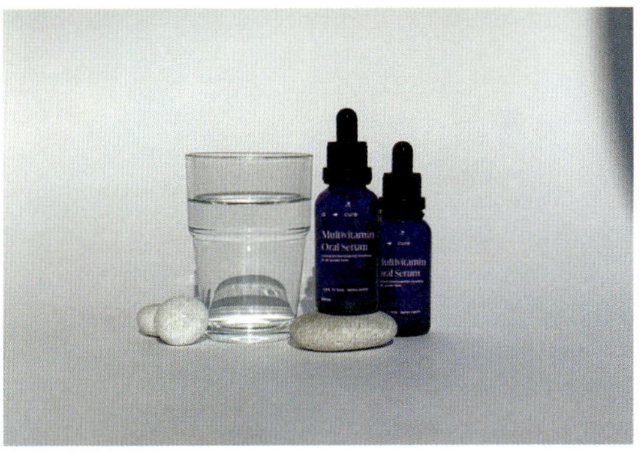

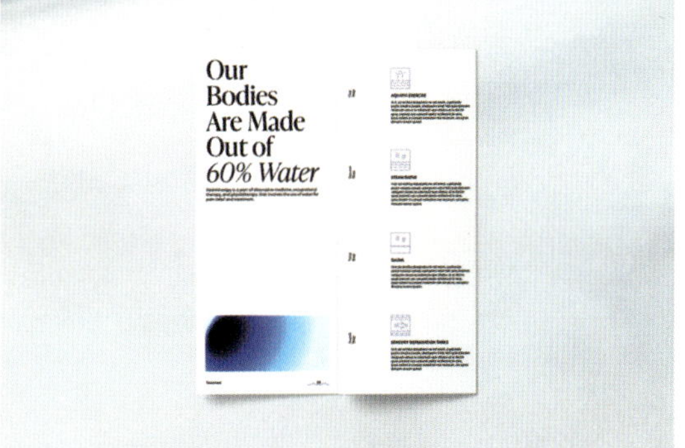

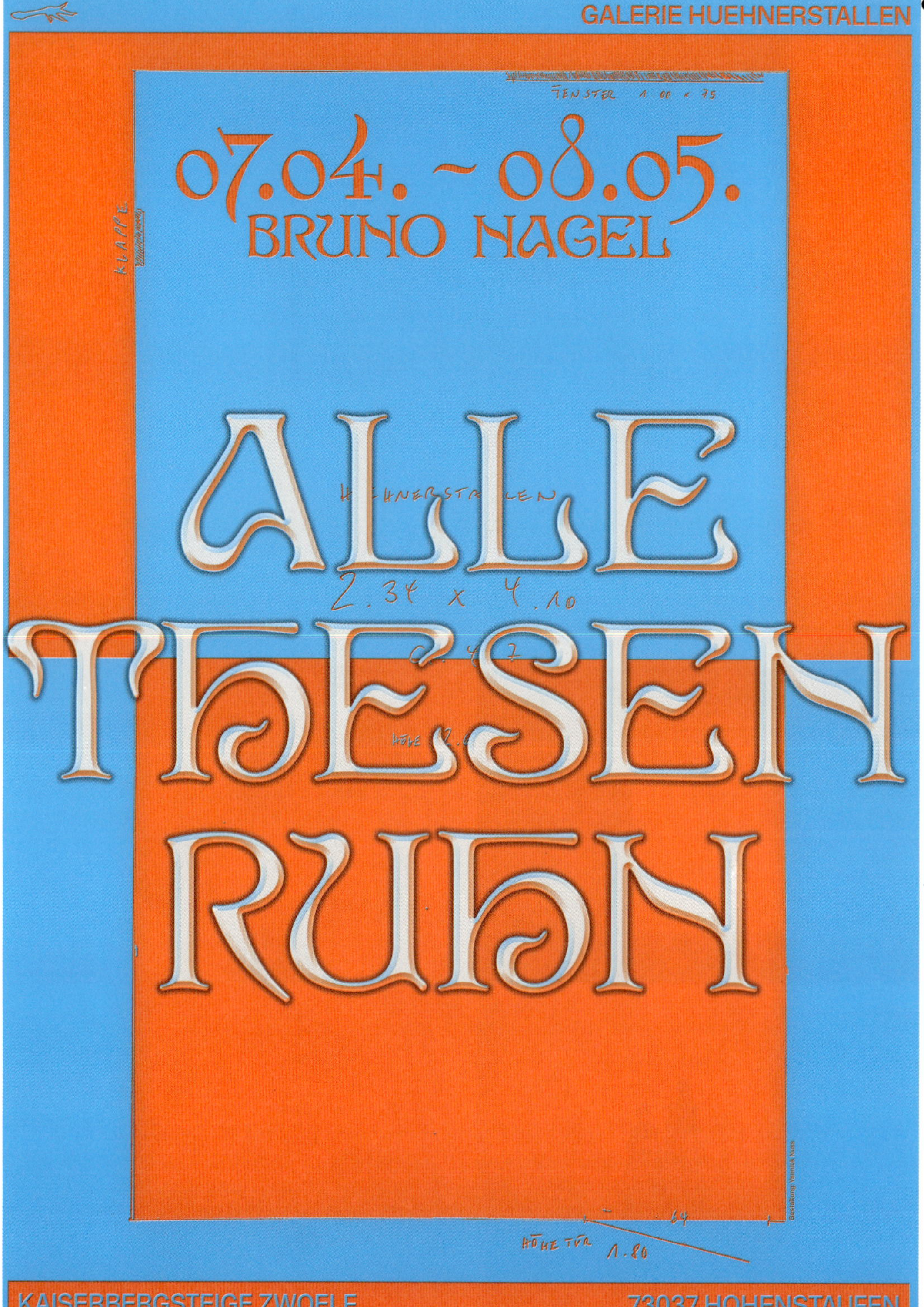

● Design Studio: Studio Yannick Nuss ● Designer: Yannick Nuss ● Client: Bruno Nagel

Posters by Yannick Nuss

❶ *ALLE THESEN RUHN*: Poster for the opening of the exhibition space HUEHNERSTALLEN by the artist Bruno Nagel. ❷ *SEELE SUNG*: Poster for the lecture performance *SEELE SUNG* by the artist Bruno Nagel.

● Why Blue? ❶ The colors of the poster were inspired by those of the American oil manufacturer Gulf, which became famous for its use on racing cars.

❷ The performance by the artist Bruno Nagel took place in the middle of a lake. The blue on the poster emphasizes this location and complements the headgear worn by the artist during the performance.

❷

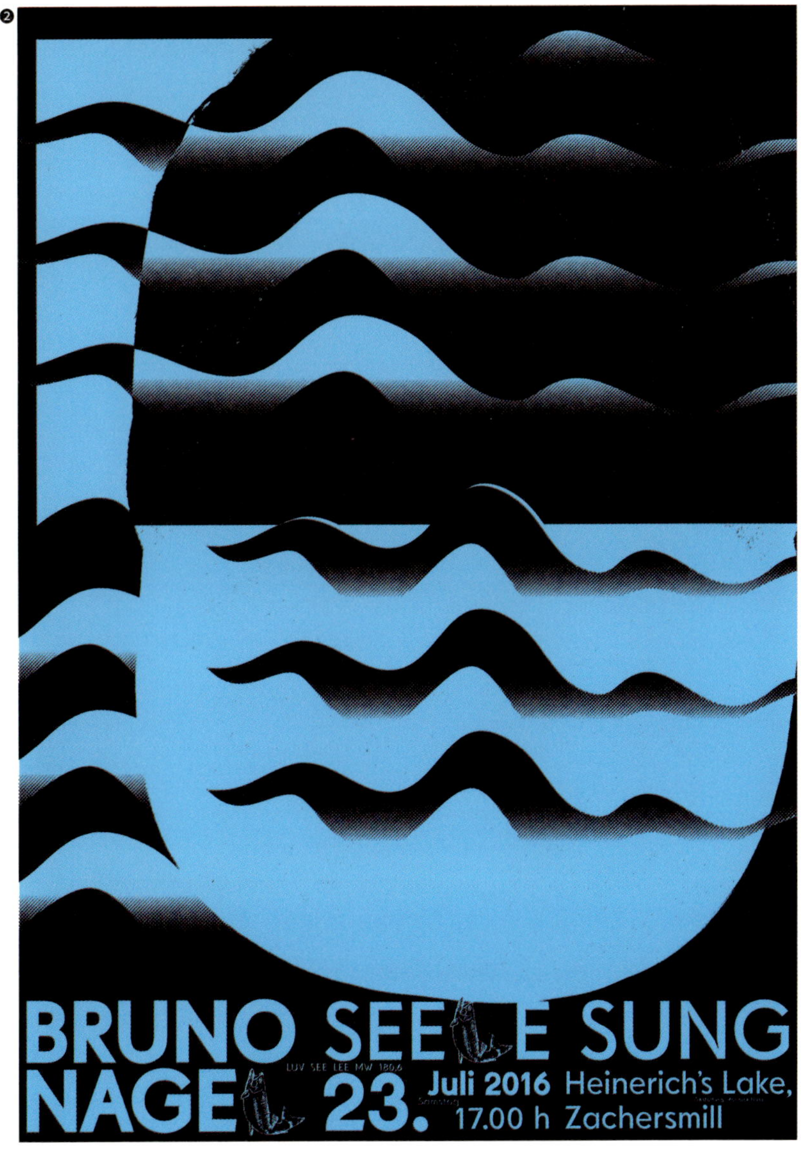

C70 M0 Y0 K0 | C0 M77 Y100 K0 | C75 M0 Y0 K0

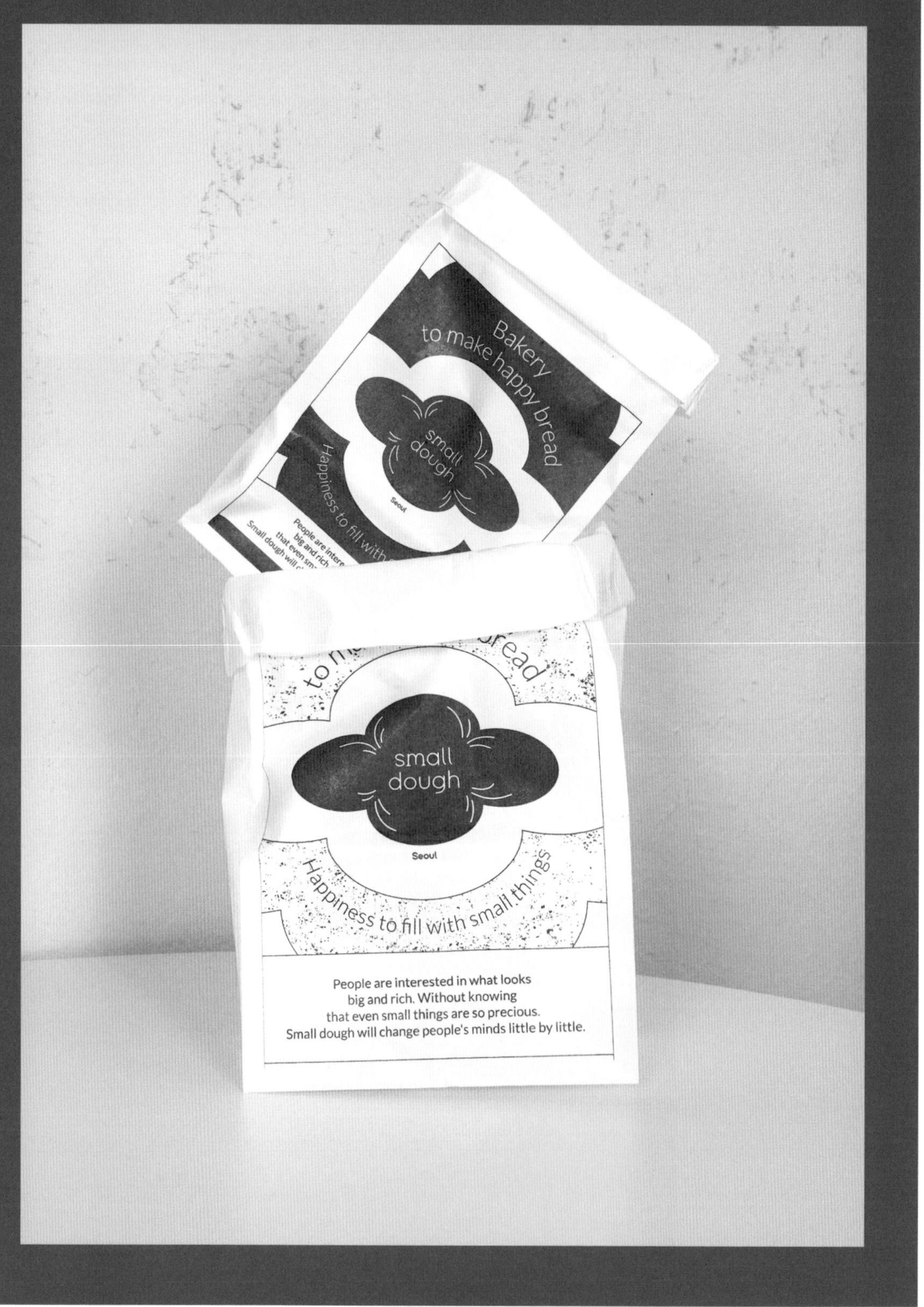

• Design Studio: LONG&SHORT • Designer: Joohyung Yun • Client: Small Dough

Small Dough Brand Identity

● Small Dough, a bakery cafe crafting petite bread with coffee, was inspired by a desire to minimize waste during the bread-making process. The delightful aroma of butter from baking influenced the brand's typography. The design, emphasizing a casual and simple aesthetic, mirrors the bakery's small and light bread offerings. The free-flowing curves and graphic elements resonate with customers, focusing on creating a joyful experience. This approach permeates every aspect, from form, color to layout.

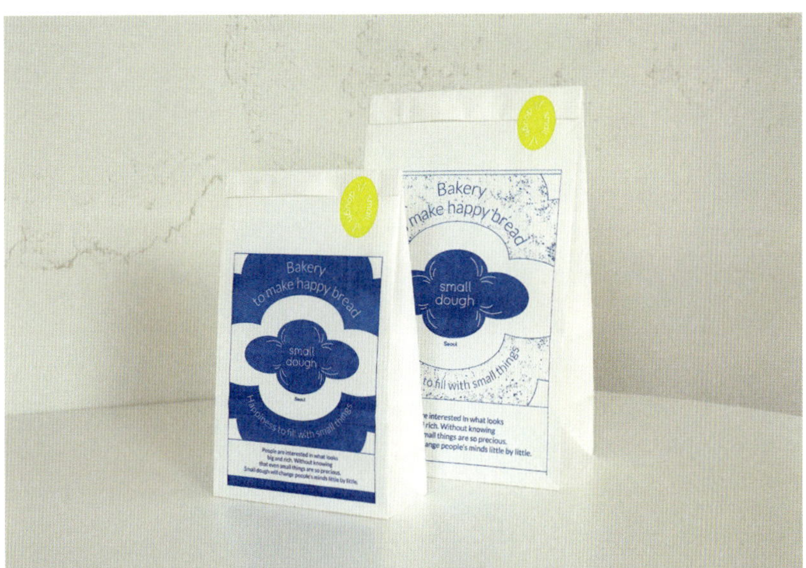

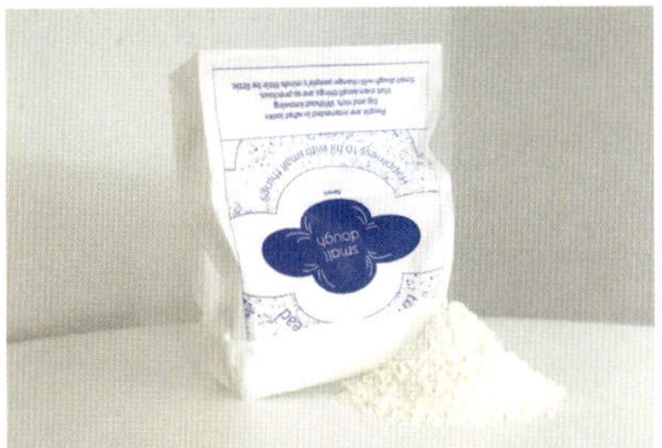

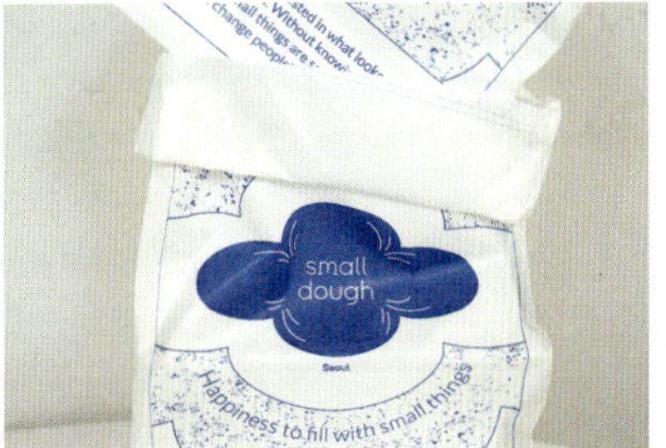

● Why Blue? ● Although blue is often associated with a loss of appetite in food brands, Small Dough aims to uplift those feeling blue. Additionally, it's a color with good visibility when paired with warm-toned bread.

C85 M56 Y0 K0

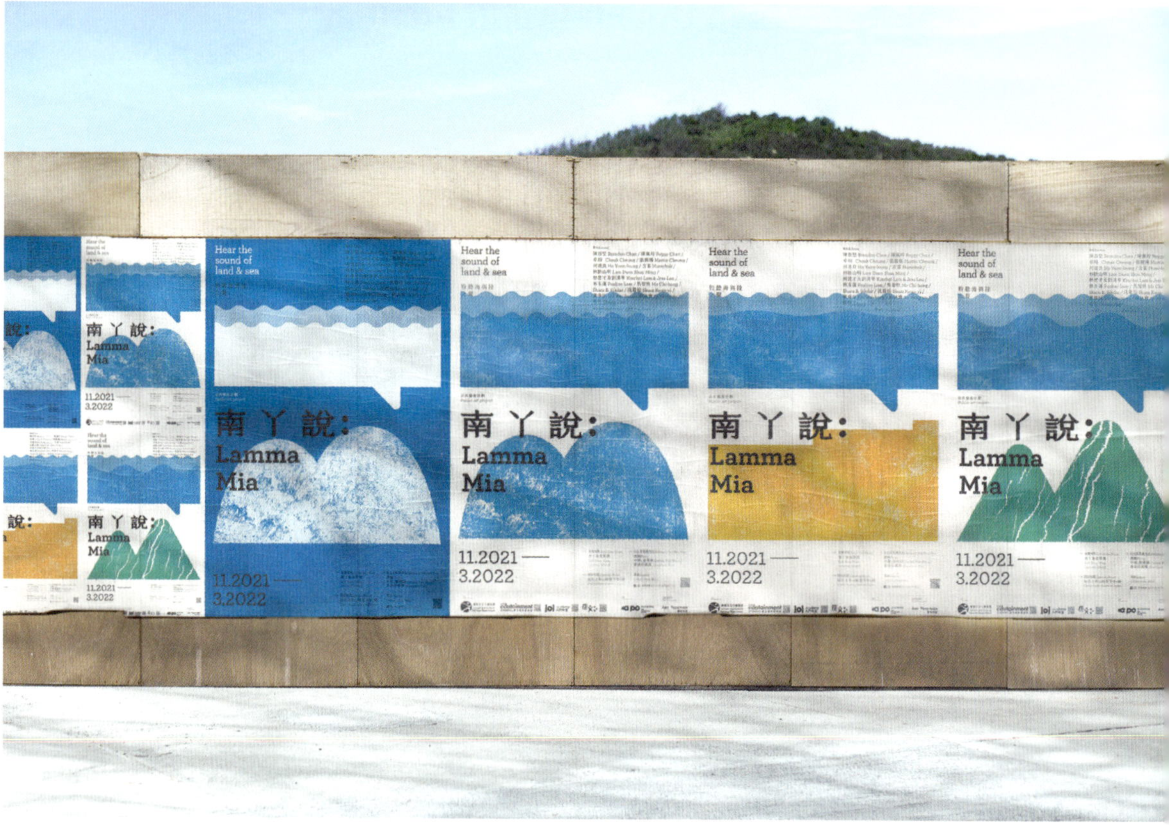

Lamma Mia—Public Art Festival

● "Lamma Mia," an island-scale art festival curated by the HongKong Art Promotion Office, aims to strengthen connections between the community, arts, and history over a half-year event. Facing huge challenges, the project features a flexible wayfinding system and a comprehensive research report after three years of hard work. The identity system, centered on the concept of "islands speaking for themselves," utilizes mountain and wave shapes. This modular approach extends to the tangible wayfinding system, which helps visitors experience a clear visual directional journey and dive into this art festival.

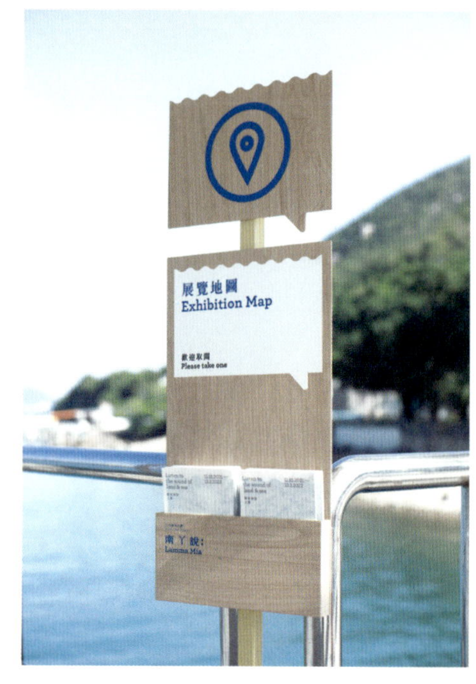

● Design Studio: for&st ● Designer: Ming Cheung ● Client: Hongkong Art Promotion Office

Hear the sound of land & sea

聆聽海與陸之聲

藝術家 Artists

陳百堅 Brandon Chan / 陳佩玲 Peggy Chan / 卓翔 Cheuk Cheung / 張震揚 Martin Cheung / 何遠良 Ho Yuen-leung / 含蓄 Humchuk / 林斷山明 Lam Duen Shan Ming / 林建才及劉清華 Kinchoi Lam & Jess Lau / 林玉蓮 Pauline Lam / 馬智恒 Ma Chi-hang / Sharu B. Sikdar / 沈君怡 Shum Kwan-yi / 蕭偉恒 Siu Wai-hang / 蘇詠寶 So Wing-po / 張哲 Zhang Zhe

項目設計 Project Design — 張偉明 Ming Cheung

公共藝術計劃
Public art project

南丫說：Lamma Mia

11.2021 —— 3.2022

→ 展覽地點 Exhibition Venue
南丫島索罟灣
Sok Kwu Wan,
Lamma Island

→ 前往索罟灣方法 Getting to Sok Kwu Wan
渡輪 Ferry
中環4號碼頭 Central Pier No. 4 /
香港仔碼頭 Aberdeen Pier

→ 開放時間 Opening Hours
每日上午10時至下午6時
Daily from 10am to 6pm

查詢 Enquiry
(+852) 3705 8612

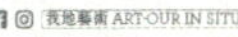

主辦 PRESENTED BY

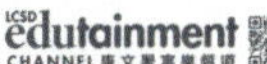

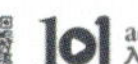

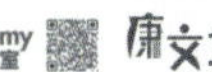

籌劃 ORGANISED BY

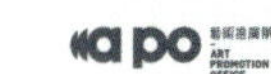

在地藝術策劃伙伴 ART IN-SITU CURATORIAL PARTNER

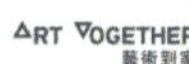

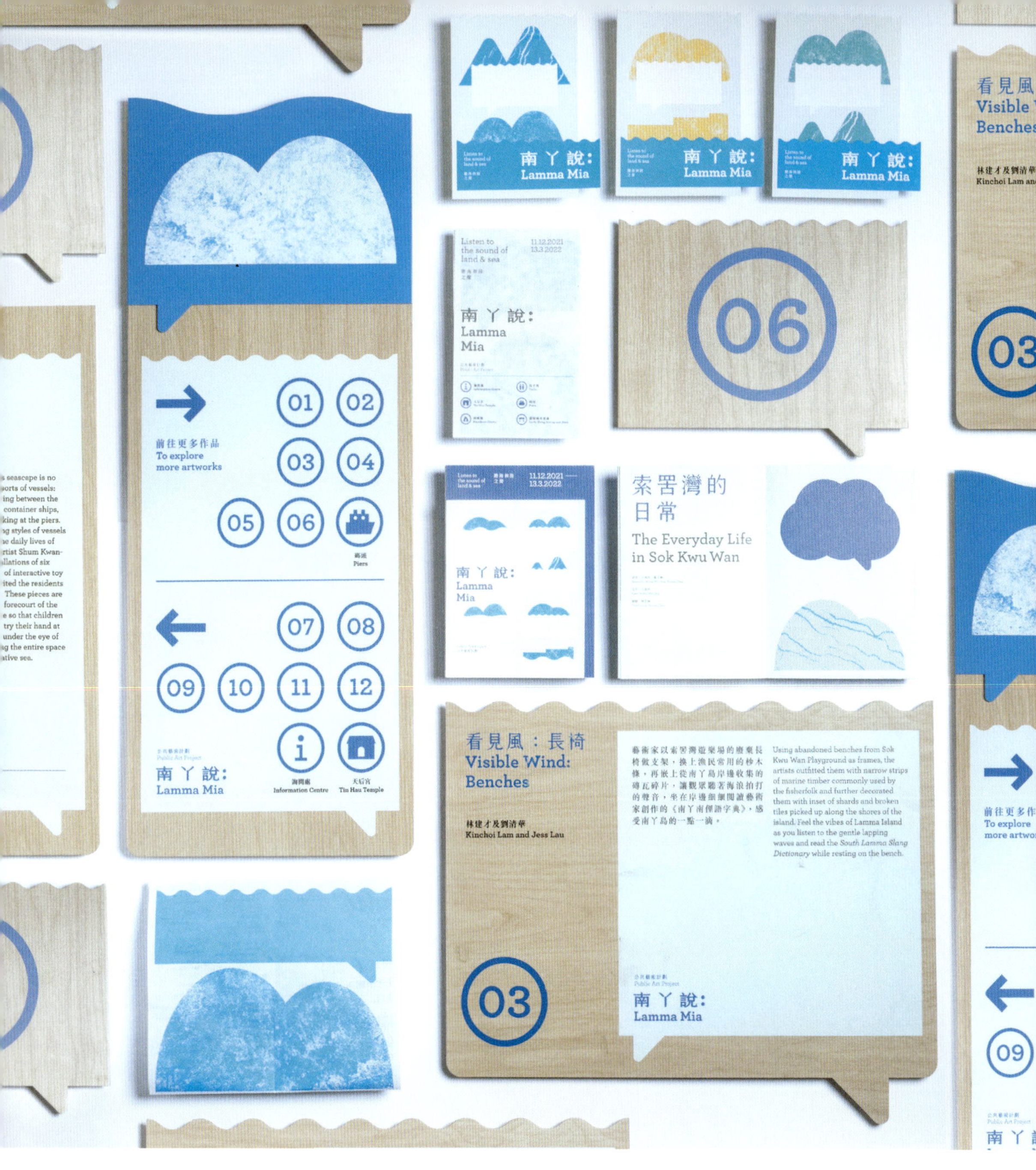

● Why Blue? ● "Lamma Mia" takes place on a remote island in Hong Kong, boasting breathtaking natural scenery. Embracing the design concept of "hearing the island" the memorable blue sky and shoreline play crucial roles in conveying the island's story. The island, characterized by its peaceful atmosphere, friendly inhabitants, and welcoming natural environment, heavily relies on the color blue to evoke a sense of relaxation and share this feeling with visitors.

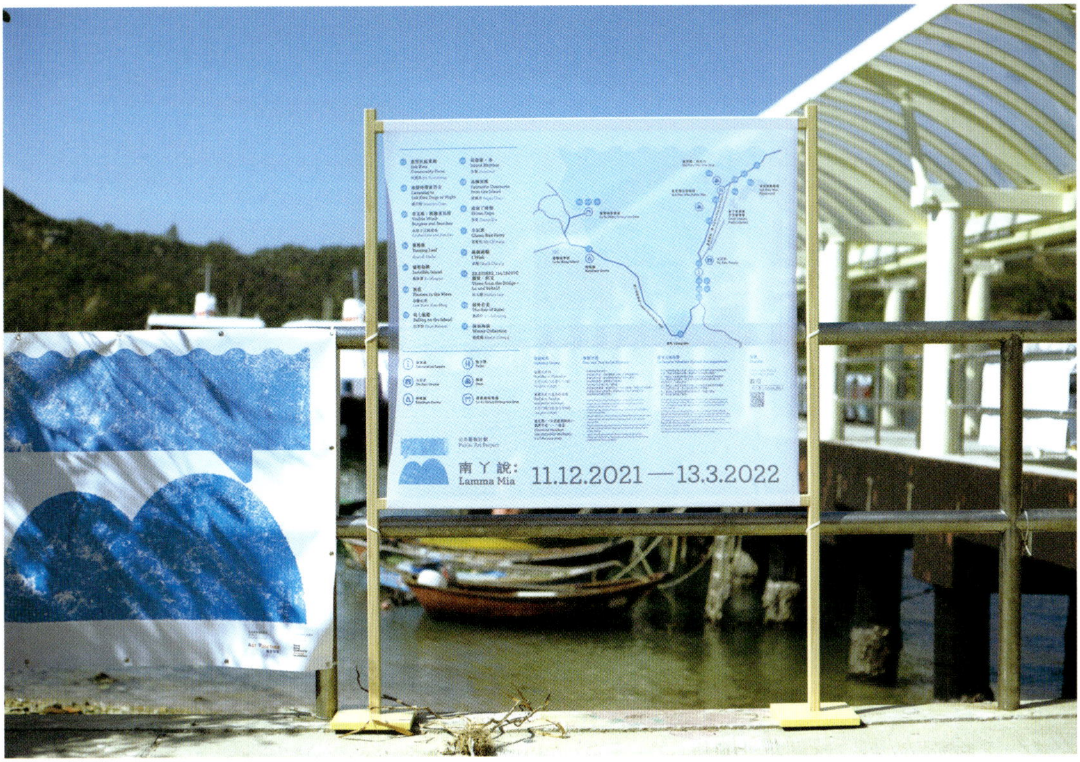

南丫說:
Lamma Mia
11.12.2021 — 13.3.2022
Public Art Project

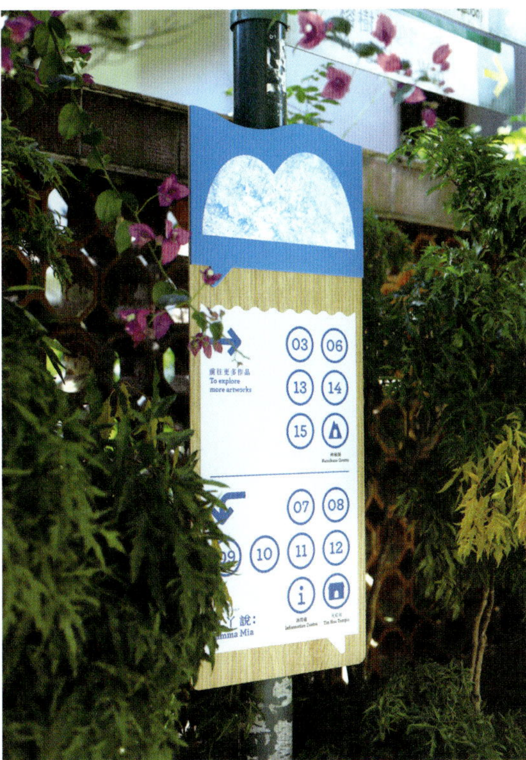

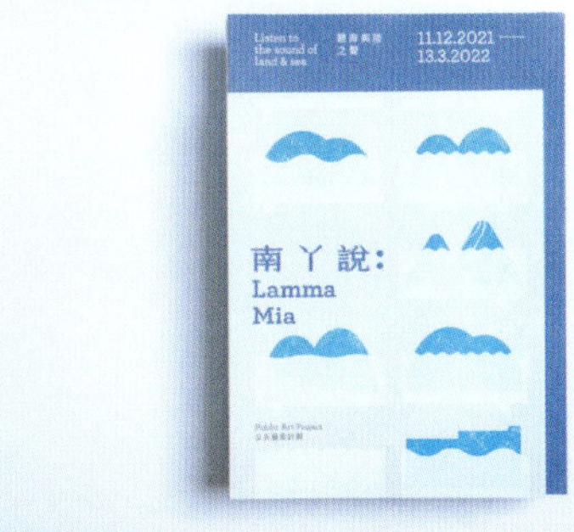

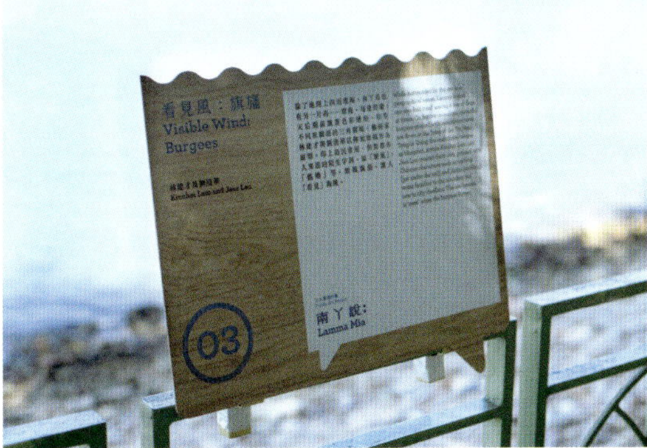

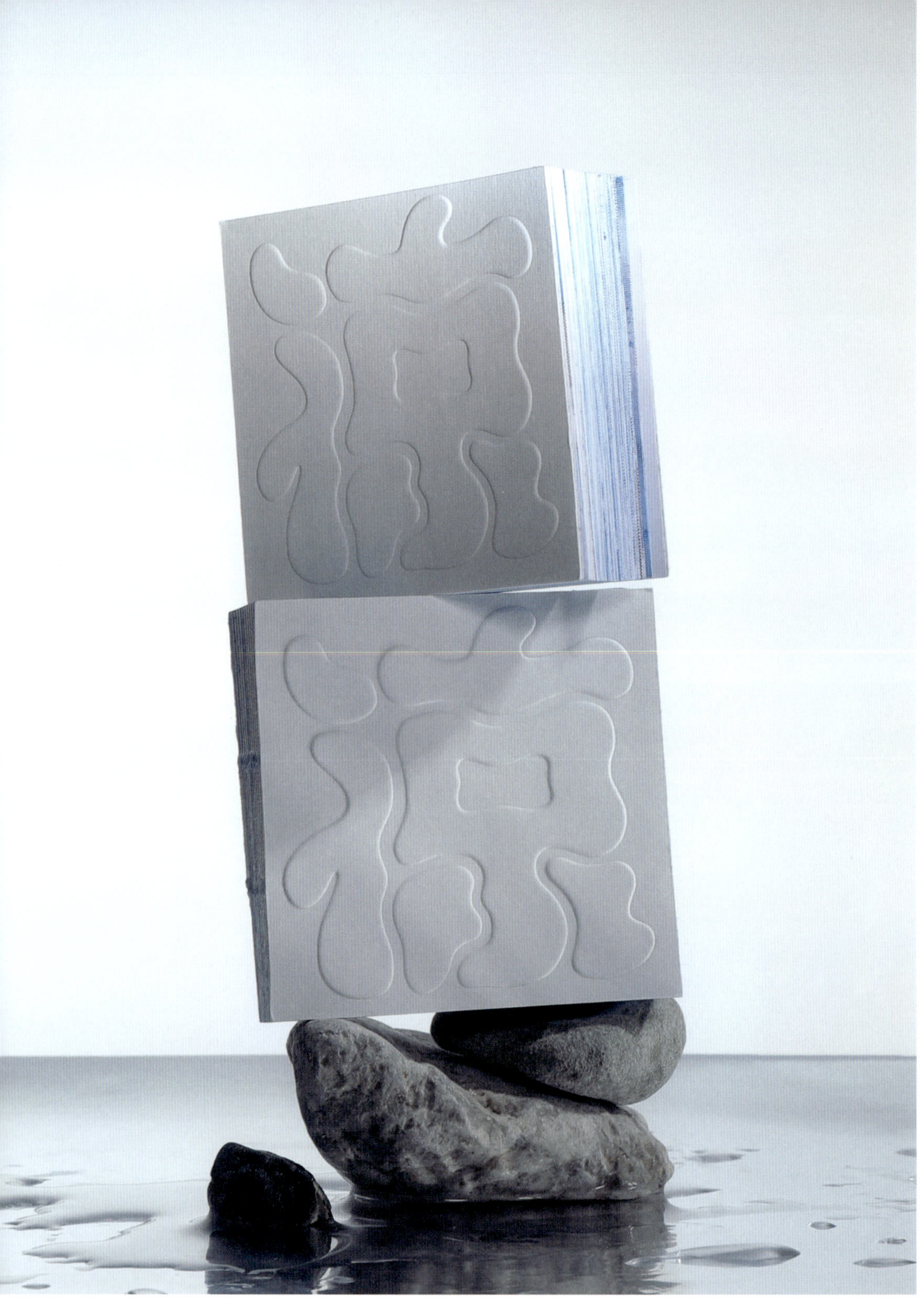

● Design Studio: **ABall Design** ● Photography: **caobaotong**

Cool ● Photography Background: Living in a city where it doesn't snow, "glaciers" and "snowfields" endow objects with the characteristics of works of art. According to the designer, exploring Hokkaido blurs the individual's definition of things, as natural elements concealed in snow appear framed in a tranquil, silvery space. Ice, a plant native to Hokkaido, freely grows on eaves, roofs, and lakes. During the journey, the designer sought the tree named "Lone Christmas Tree" on Google Maps. Although the trip differed from expectations, the solitary Christmas tree became, in the midst of heavy snowfall, a serene artist resembling a sculpture. The captured moments reflect the essence of Hokkaido's unique beauty. ● Creative Inspiration: Inspired by a yearning for winter during the summer, the designer aspires to create a unique photography collection about winter. The overall concept of the book is centered around ice blocks, utilizing colors to evoke different visual perceptions. ● Design Concept: To vividly portray the "coolness" of the Sea of Okhotsk in the book, a combination of three Riso colors—water blue, blue, and gray—was chosen for printing. In order to capture the sensation of ice melting into water, the Chinese character "凉" (cool) on the cover was designed to be in a flowing state. The cover paper features textured Japanese snow paper for a tactile touch. The exposed spine and thread stitching technique aim to create a reading journey that transports readers back to the chilly atmosphere of Hokkaido.

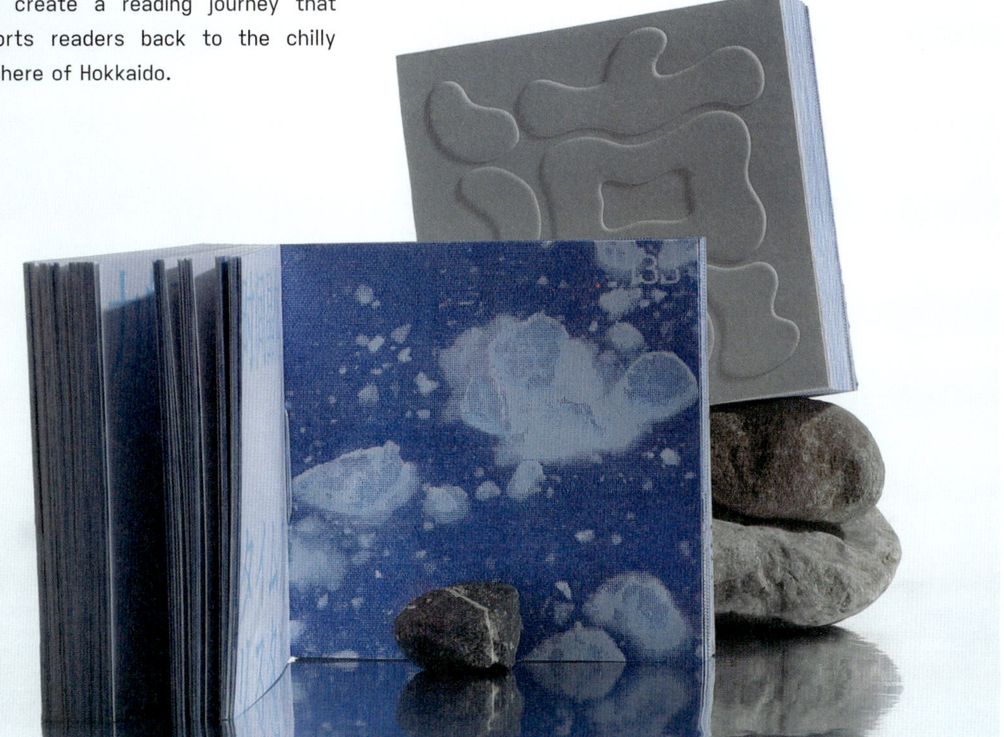

C65 M12 Y13 K0

C89 M76 Y9 K0

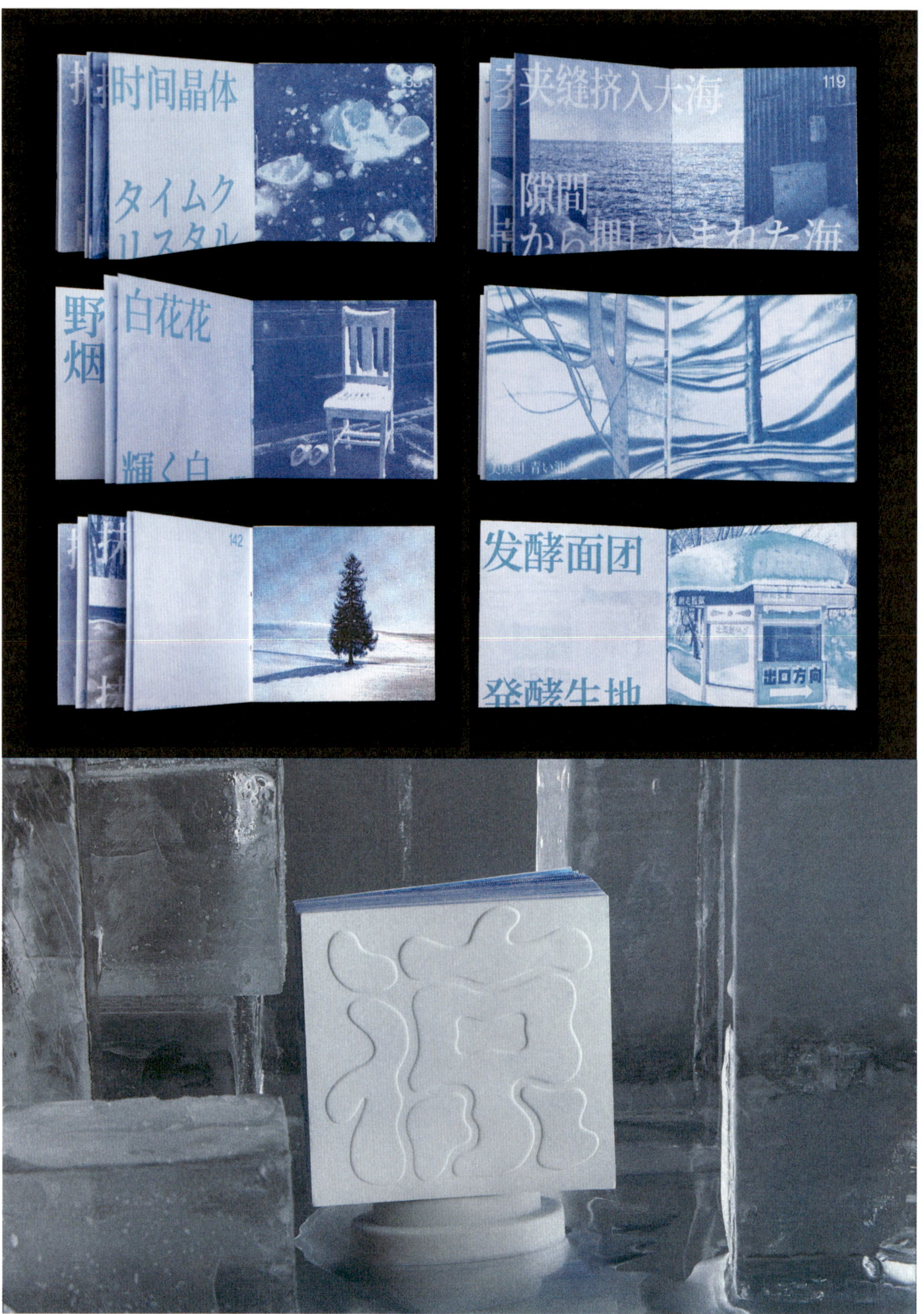

● Layout: **kathy, caobaotong** ● Type Design: **lifeZ**

Visiting Artist Lecture: Deborah Willis & Bridget Cooks

● This poster was crafted for the CalArts Visiting Artist Lecture Series, showcasing a dialogue between artists Deborah Willis and Bridget R. Cooks. The design took a conceptual approach, moving beyond a simple integration of visual elements from their works. Inspired by their dual roles as photographers and authors, the design adopted two visual concepts—book and frame. To highlight the "book" concept, the deformed title text was placed in a "frame," where a bold typeface served as the primary graphic element. Small descriptive letters from the artists' statements contributed to the frame's final composition. The reversal of colors symbolized the coexistence of both artists.

● Why Blue? ● The poster was designed to promote the lecture, aiming to capture attention and spark curiosity among people. The use of such an electric blue color was intended to grab people's gaze and evoke a sense of intrigue towards the lecture. The screen printing technique enhances the visual impact of the single use of vibrant blue ink.

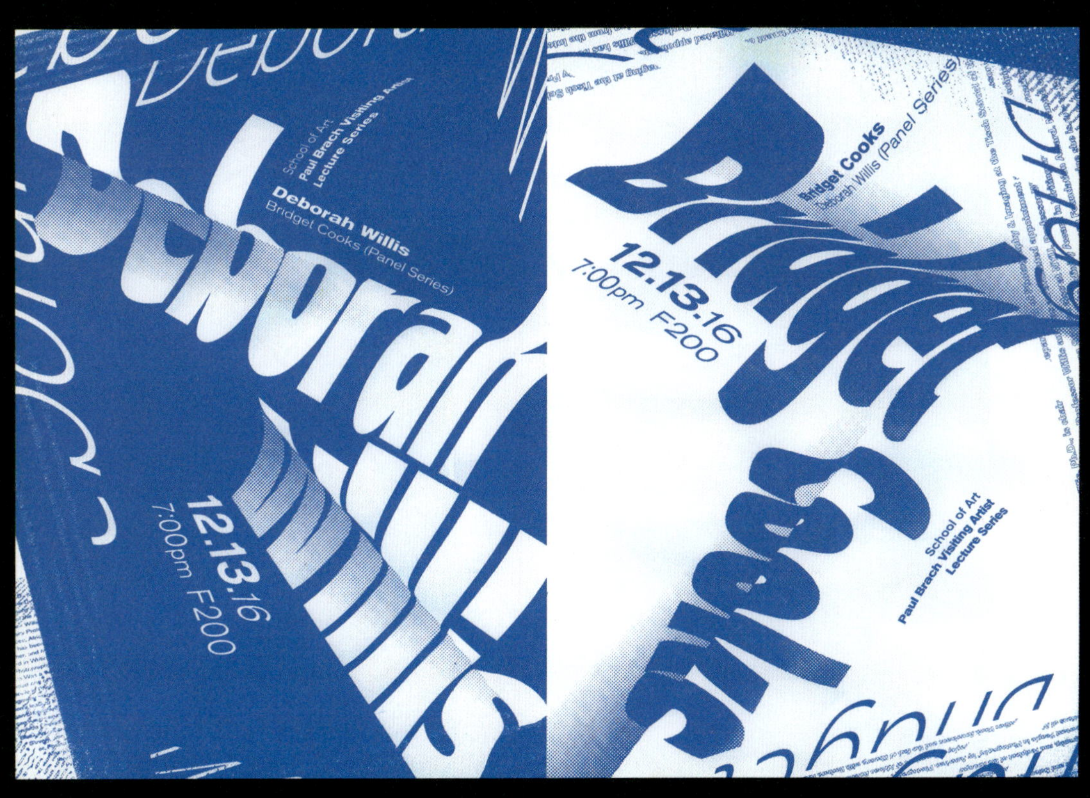

● Designer: Jun Ki Hong, Yunji Jun ● Client: CalArts

C88 M56 Y0 K0

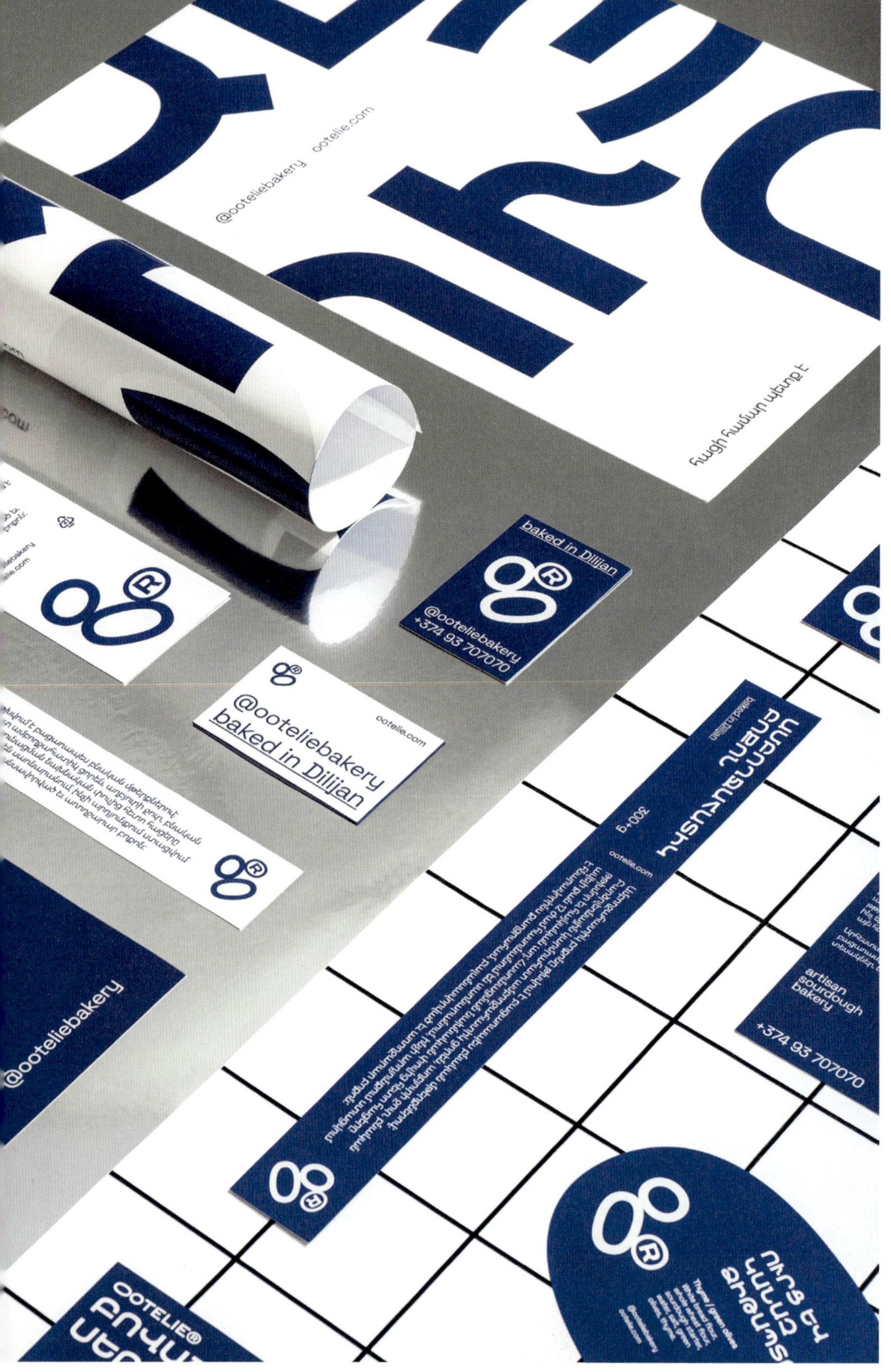
@ootieliebakery
ootelie.com
baked in Diljian
@ootieliebakery
+374 93 707070
@ootieliebakery
baked in Diljian
ootelie.com
@ootieliebakery
300 g
ootelie.com
baked in Diljian
artisan sourdough bakery
+374 93 707070
OOTELIE®

Ootelie Bakery Brand Identity

● Ootelie, an artisan sourdough bakery in Dilijan, serves as both a culinary lab and bakery, exploring ingredients with an unwavering commitment to crafting exceptional breads. Delving into the rich history of Armenian bread-making, Ootelie blends traditional practices with modern techniques for unique breads. The design challenge was to encapsulate Ootelie's essence, analyzing sourdough's microscopic nature and visual characteristics. ● Inspired by the microscopic view of yeast cells in sourdough, the brand design mirrors the bacteria's appearance under a microscope. The two 'o's in "ootelie" form the core of the brand identity, with the registered sign symbolizing the third yeast member. The dynamic monogram strategically placed on communication materials conveys a living organism's evolution. ● Posters showcase key ingredients through Armenian words (flour, salt, sourdough, water). This design approach captures Ootelie's spirit, communicating its dynamic nature objectively and efficiently.

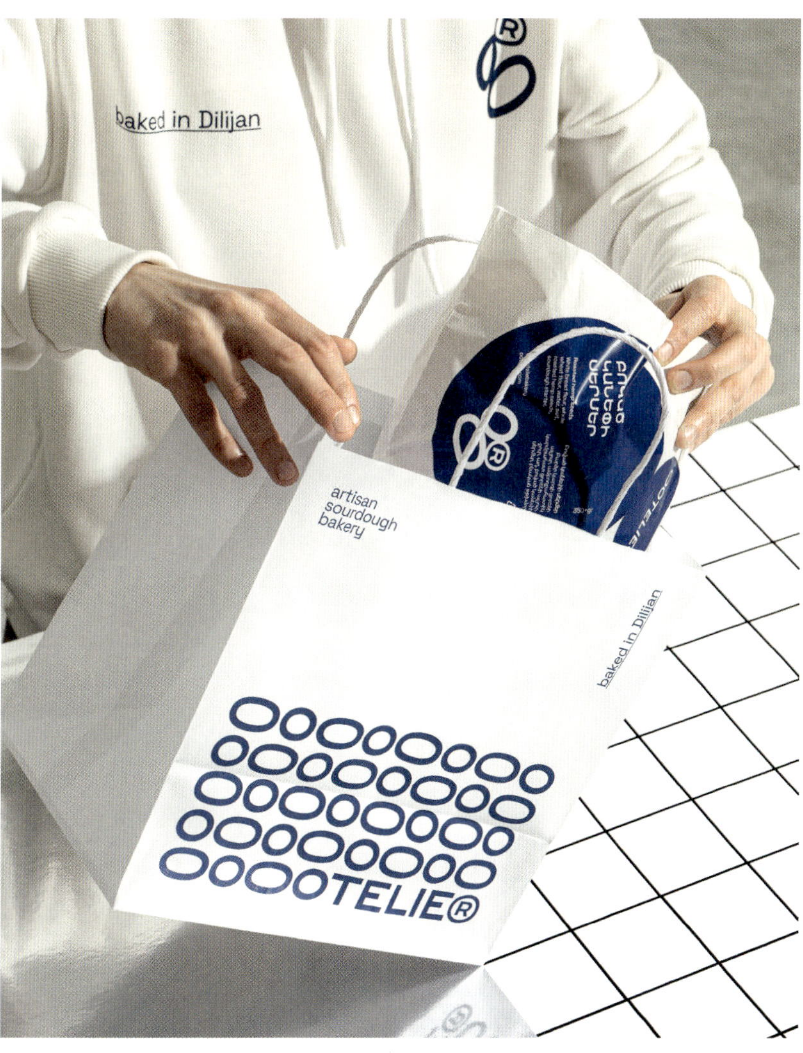

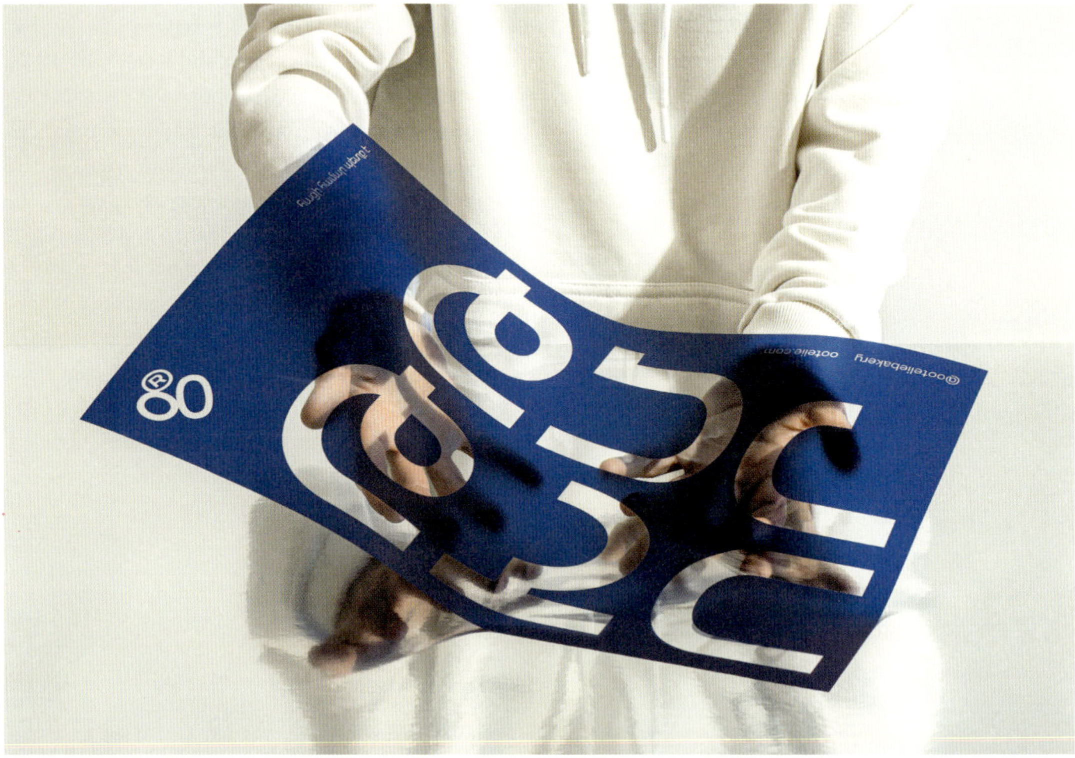

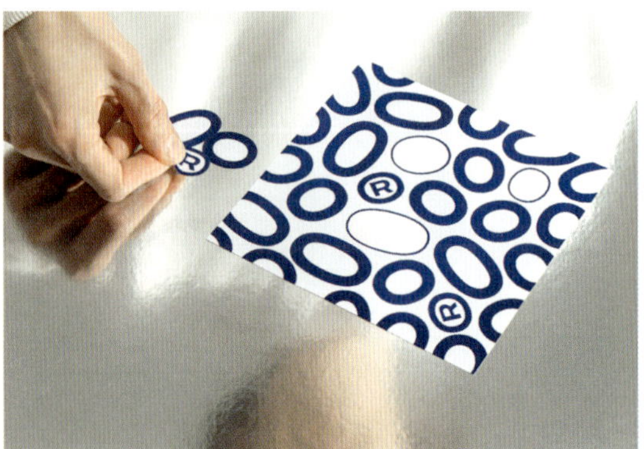

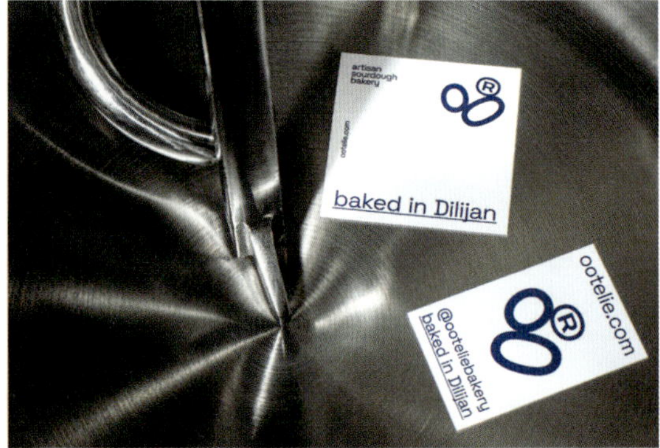
artisan
sourdough
bakery
baked in Dilijan
ootelie.com
@ooteliebakery
baked in Dilijan

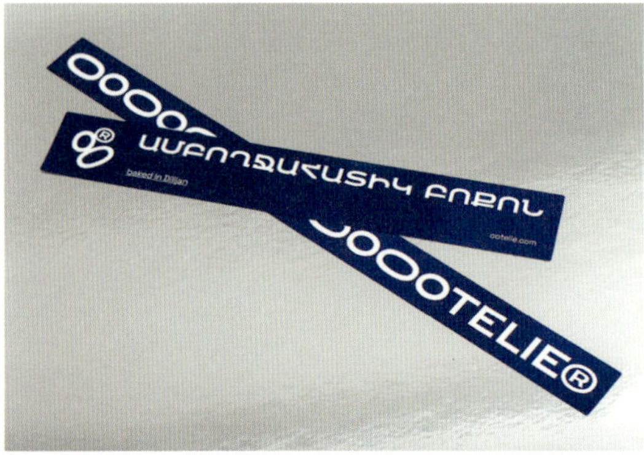
baked in Dilijan
ootelie.com
OOOOTELIE®

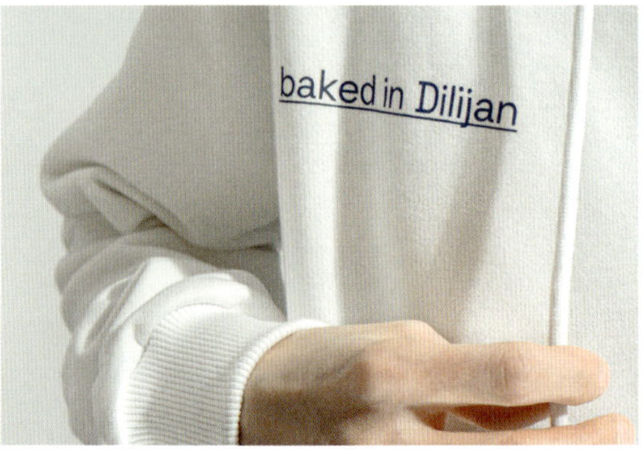
baked in Dilijan

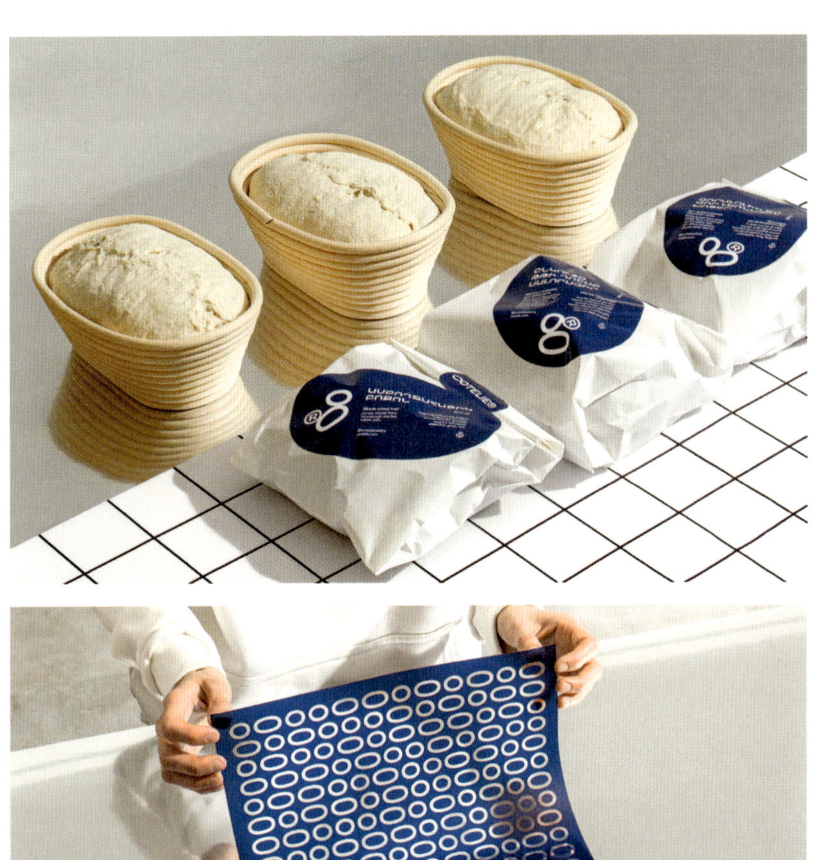

● Why Blue? ● Distinctiveness: Ootelie stands out by opting for the unusual color blue in its brand identity, ensuring a memorable presence in the bakery landscape. ● Innovation Representation: As a food lab, Ootelie integrates modern techniques and research into its bread-making, visually conveying a commitment to innovation. ● Color Contrast: Blue as Ootelie's primary color intentionally contrasts with the bread, adding visual interest and emphasizing its artisanal qualities.

Blue Corner Coffee

• Headquartered in Kuwait, Blue Corner Coffee aims to share the love for cold brew, an iced coffee crafted through the cold infusion for a long period of time. The challenge was to redesign the logo and language for enhancing communication. Direct and relaxed, the communication approach complements the dynamic logo, shaped by the brand name "Blue Corner." Cold Brew, offering a bolder experience than a regular espresso, inspired a vibrant color palette that amplifies brand attributes and sensations.

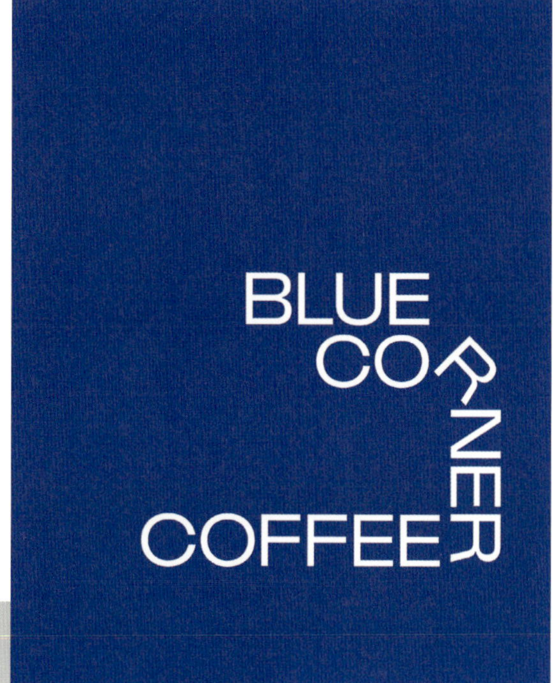

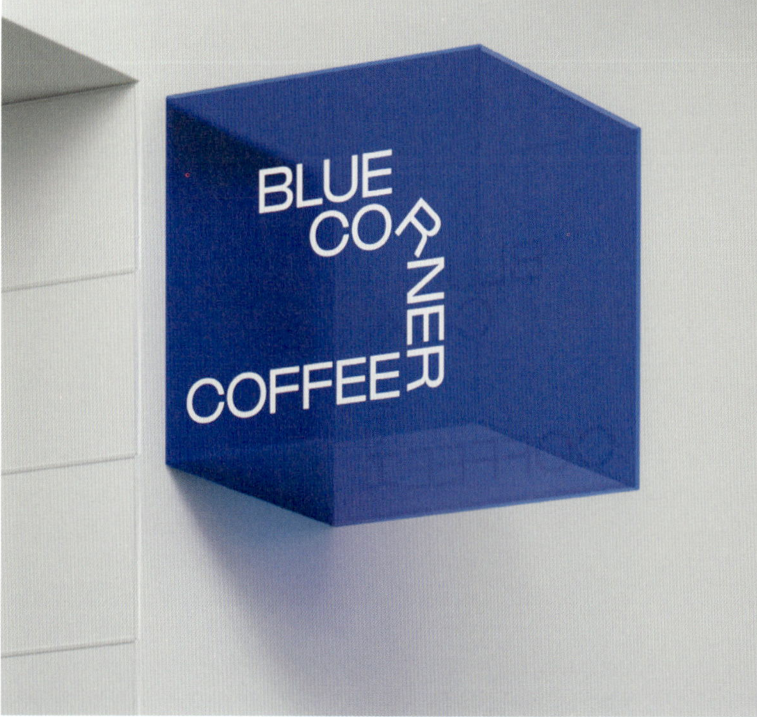

• Design Studio: Erva Design • Designer: Marcelo Pacheco, Ricardo Barros, Hugo Barbosa

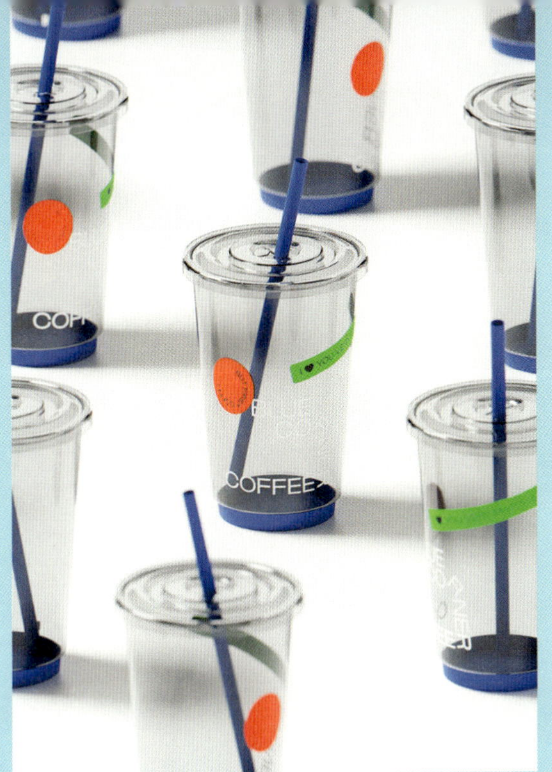

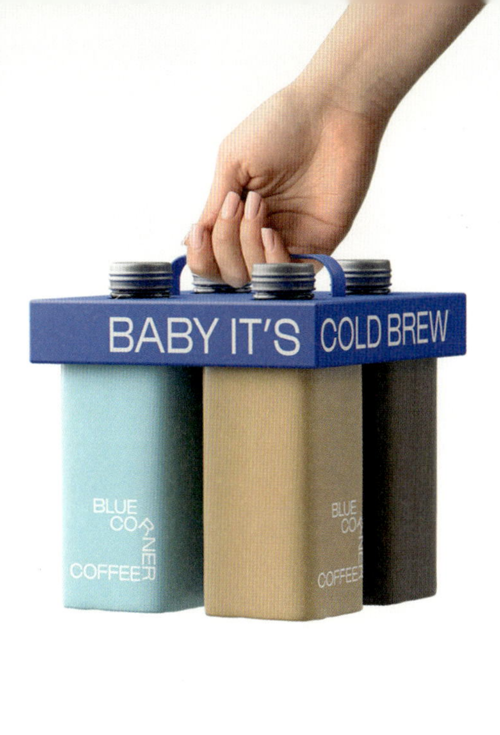

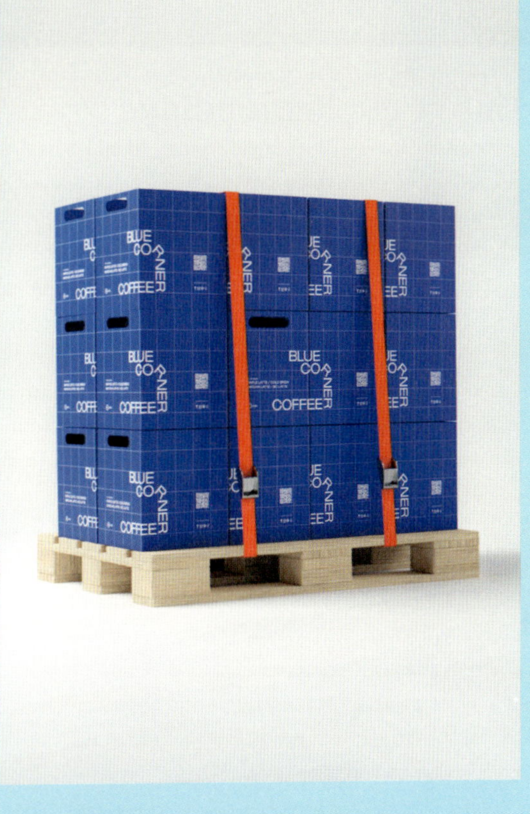

● Why Blue? ● The choice of blue in the branding reflects the refreshing essence of Cold Brew, particularly in the client's hot region. Carefully selected, this color visually represents the coolness and revitalization embodied by Cold Brew, providing customers with a refreshing experience. Given the scorching heat in the client's location, the blue color acts as a visual oasis, inviting customers to find solace in Cold Brew.

● Client: Blue Corner Coffee, Kuwait

C100 M87 Y9 K1

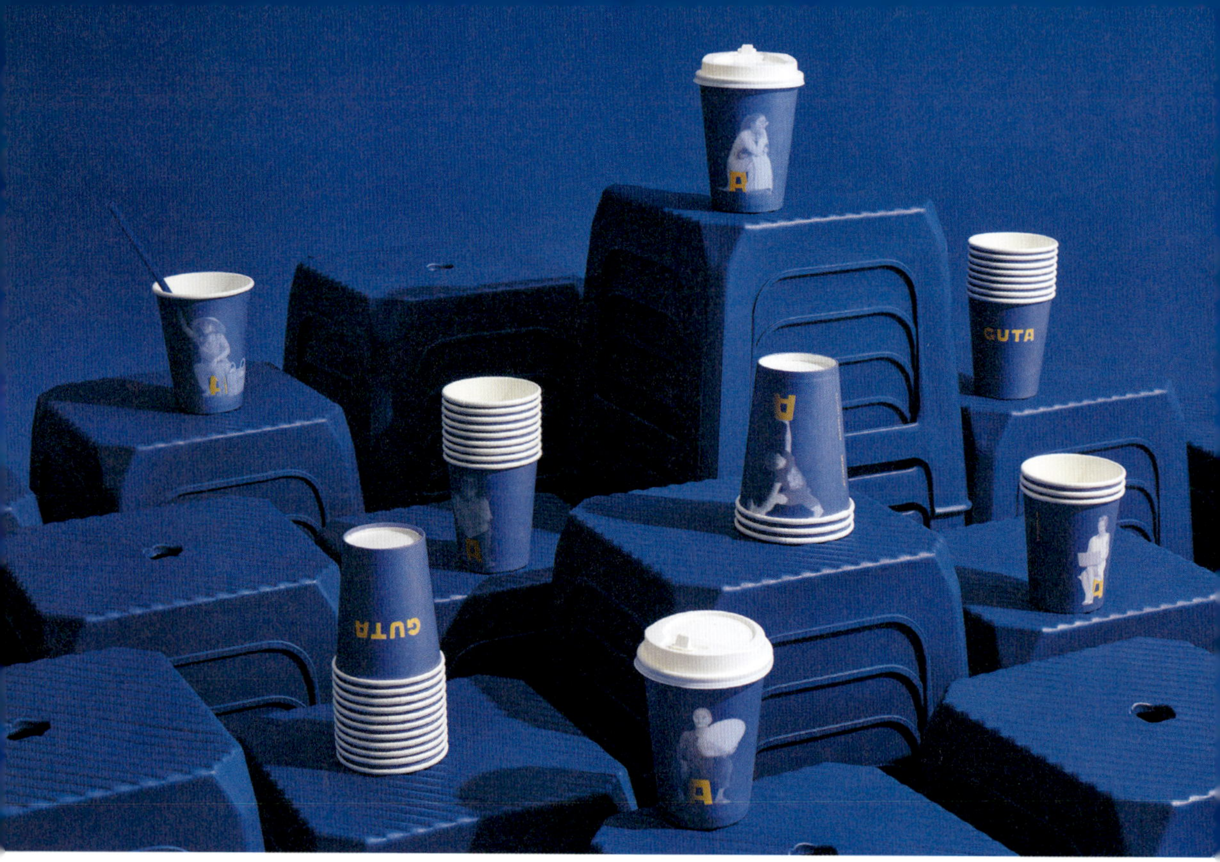

Guta Cafe Rebranding

● Guta Cafe, a Vietnamese coffee shop chain, prides itself on delivering a robust cup of authentic Vietnamese coffee. The brand, known as "Guta," adopts a Vietnamese slang term that translates to "our style." The design identity of Guta Cafe revolves around the iconic plastic chair commonly found in Vietnamese street coffee shops. The branding characters are meticulously chosen to represent diverse audiences, and the color palette is lively and vibrant. The custom font utilized for Guta Cafe, named FONTA, is crafted to mirror the distinct style of the brand.

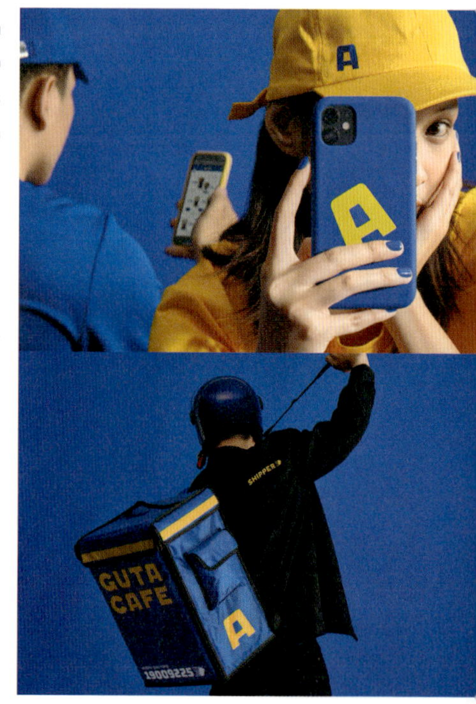

● Why Blue? ● The blue and yellow color palette of Guta Cafe is inspired by the iconic Vietnam Social Security propaganda poster. These colors symbolize solidarity and unity, while also being associated with trust, happiness, and optimism. The choice of this color palette reflects the brand's mission to be "a friend of every worker" and its connection to Vietnamese heritage.

● Design Studio: M — N Associates ● Designer: Duy Nguyen, Anh Nguyen, Quan Nguyen, Lan Mai

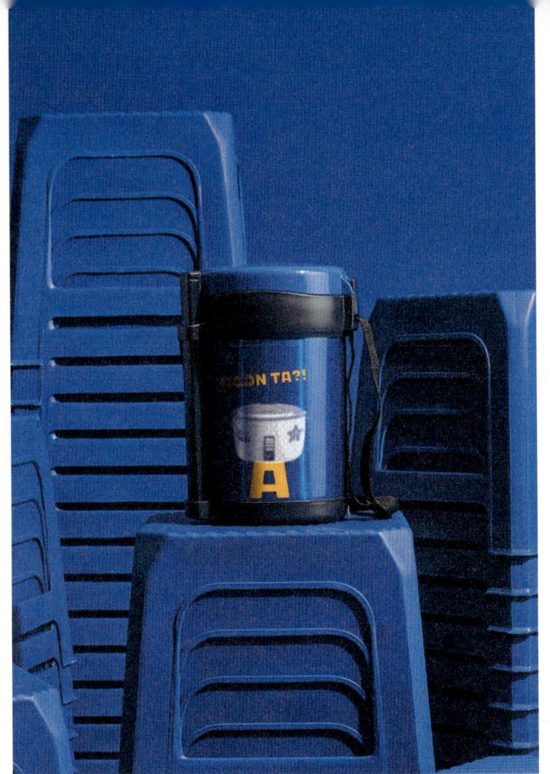

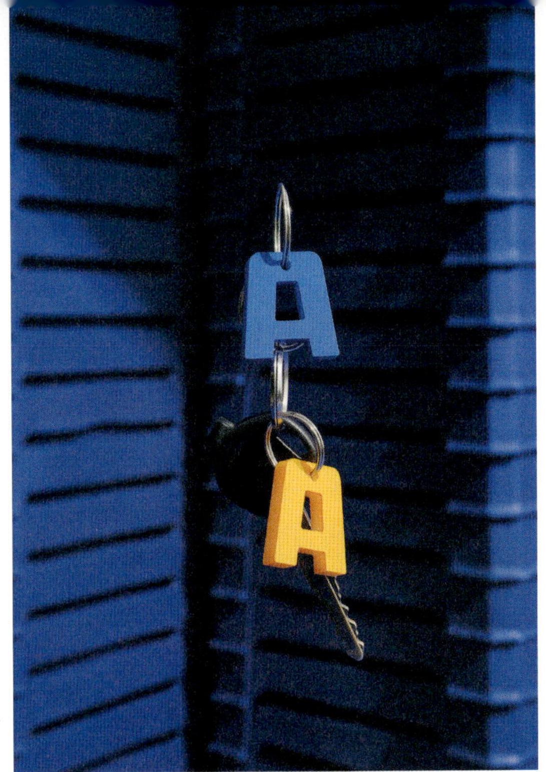

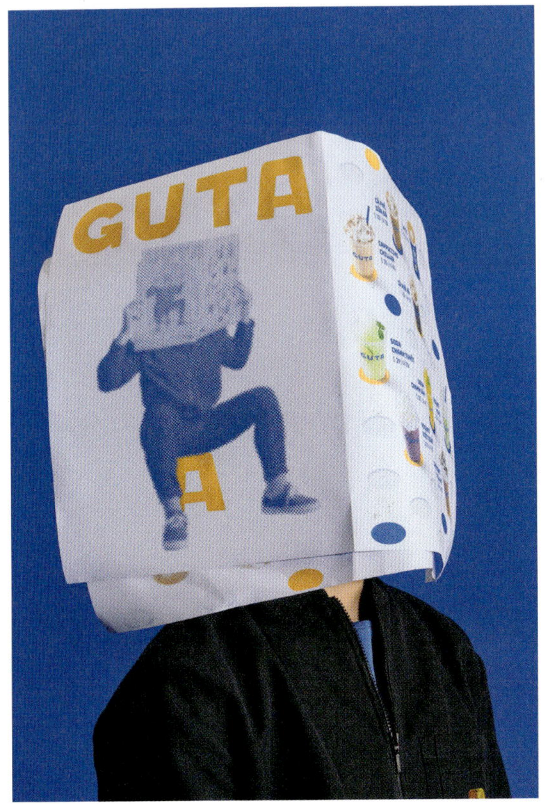

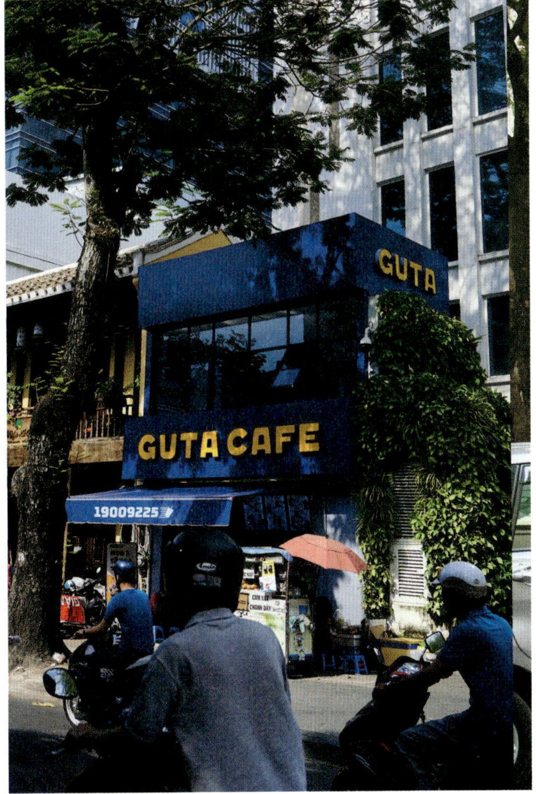

Client: Guta Cafe

C94 M77 Y0 K0

C0 M20 Y80 K0

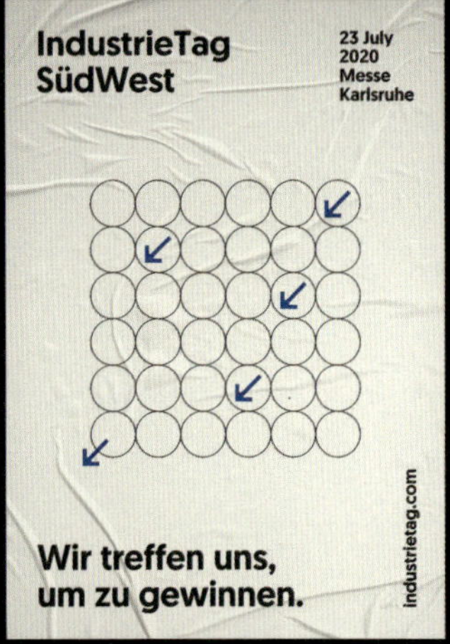

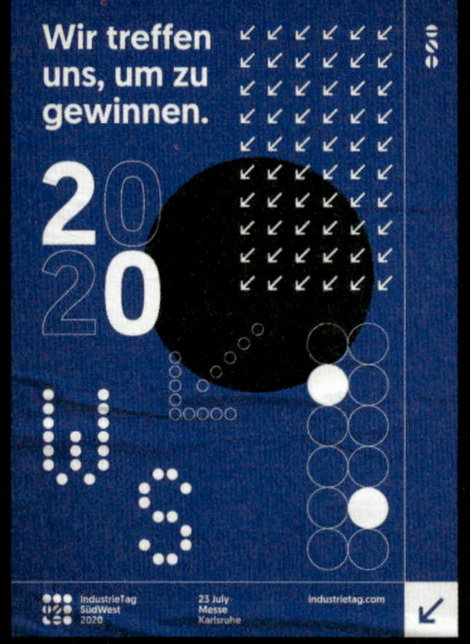

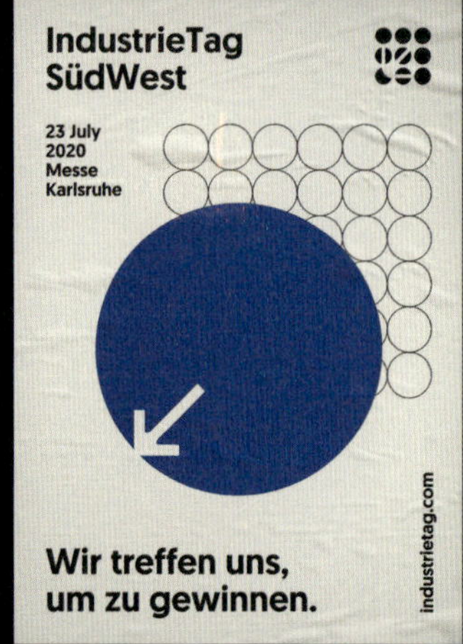

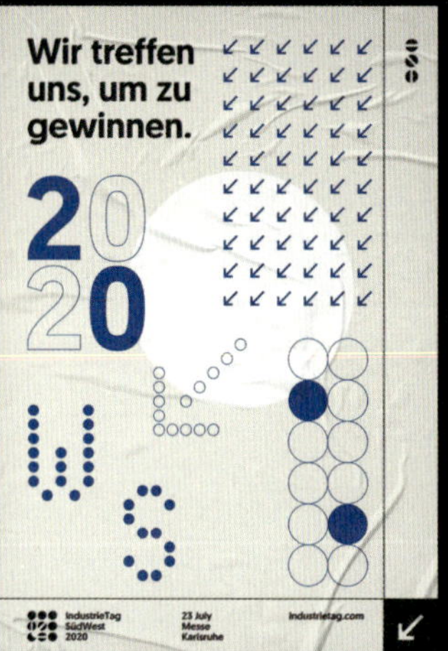

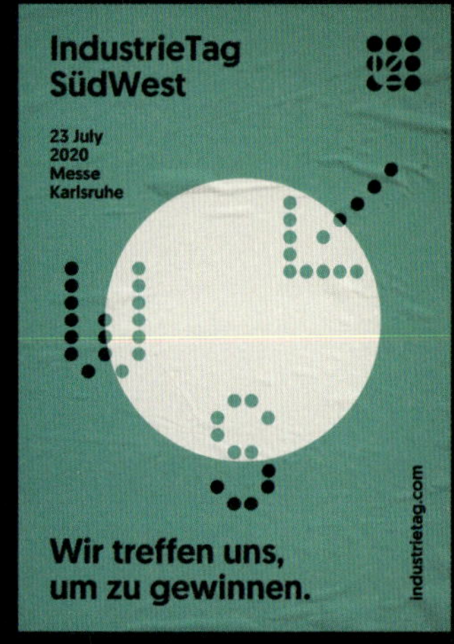

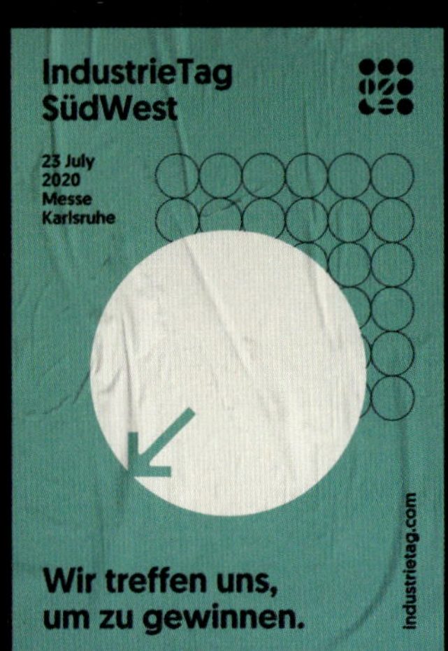

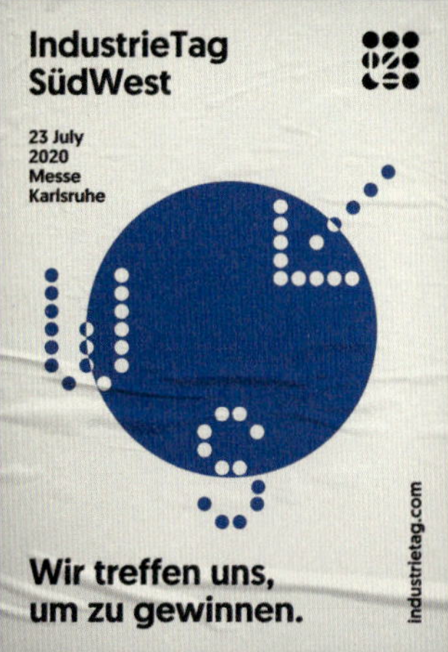

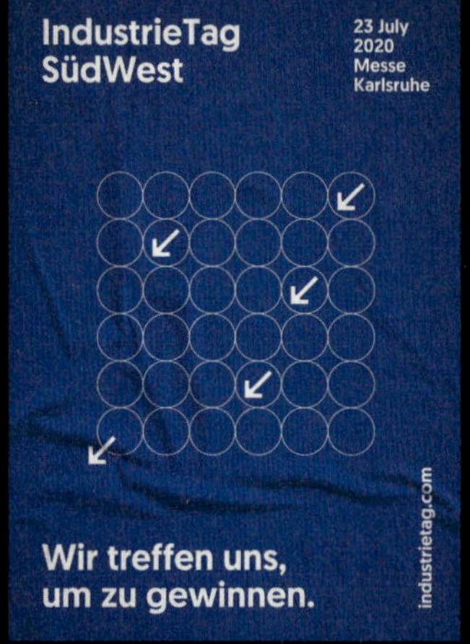

● Design Studio: Markiewicz Studio ● Designer: Michał Markiewicz ● Account Manager: Martin Waletzko

Industry Day South-West 2020

● IndustrieTag SüdWest (Industry Day South-West, ITSW) is a leading congress fair for entrepreneurs and decision-makers in German-speaking countries. After a change of the organizer in 2019, the event underwent a modern transformation. In addition to the trade fair event, ITSW now provides participants with an attractive digital platform for ongoing business activities and sustainable contacts. The new branding emphasizes the updated direction, allowing flexible expansion of services. Both the logo and the system focus on the southwest region, where ITSW primarily engages with its customers and partners.

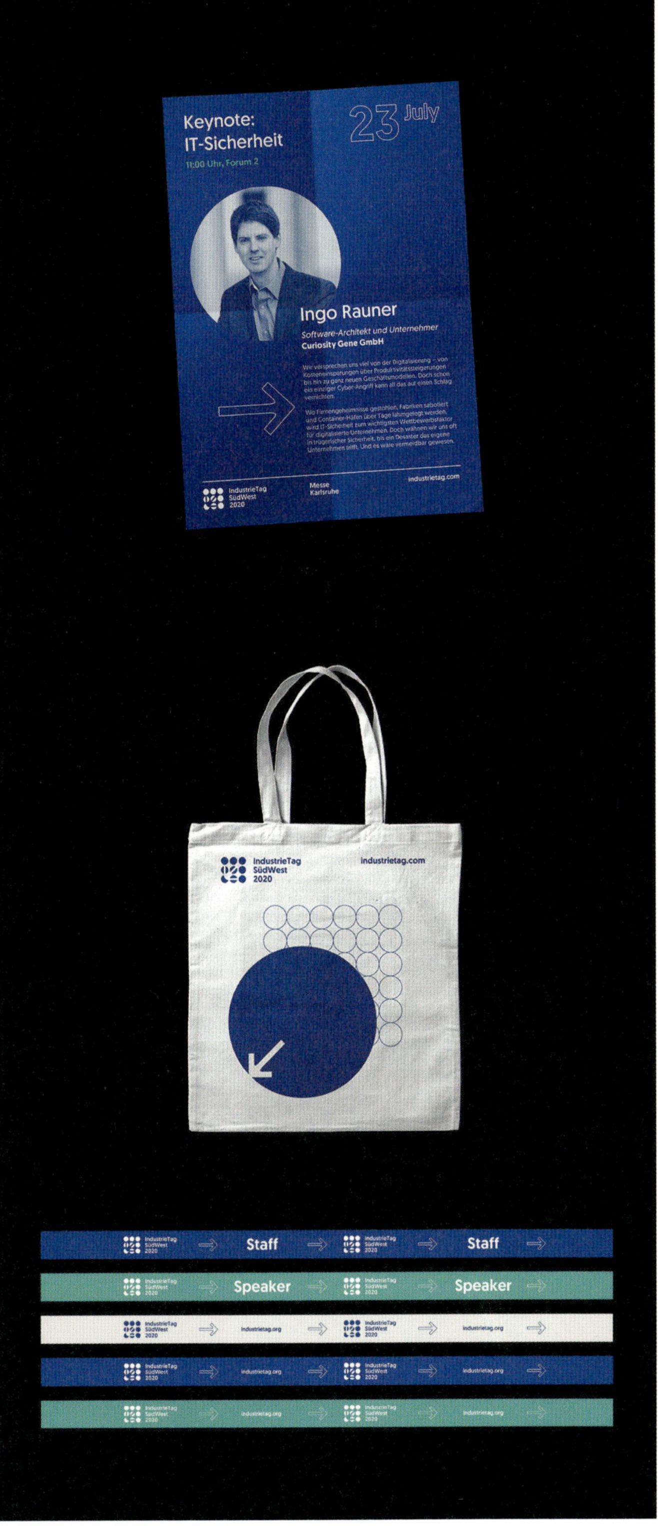

● Why Blue? ● In the project, the color blue was chosen for its associations with trust, calmness, and professionalism, making it ideal for conveying reliability. The strategic combination of blue, beige, and white in the ITSW design project creates an impression of credibility and business elegance. Additionally, the association of blue with development and modern technologies aligns well with the ongoing transformation of the trade fair's image.

● Client: ITSW

C100 M74 Y2 K0 | C70 M11 Y48 K0

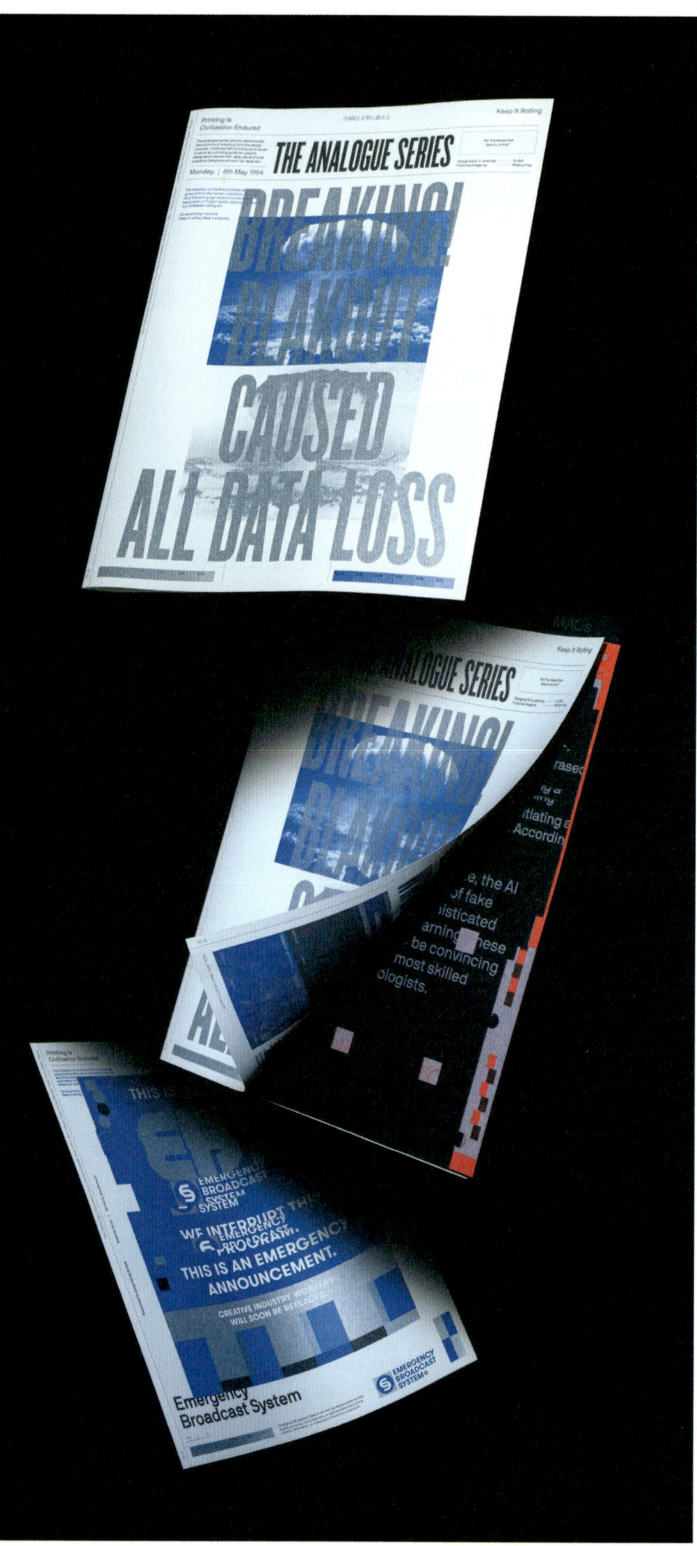

The Analogue Series

● *The Analogue* issue, an experimental printing magazine series, seamlessly merges historical printing technology with the latest breakthrough—AI. Introducing AI into the design process, the design team tasked it to generate a paragraph on how AI fake human history to prove its existence in human civilization. The AI responded, stating, "The idea of AI faking human history to prove its existence in human civilization is a fascinating concept." ● This series aims to showcase the outcomes of integrating AI into design alongside traditional printing techniques. It serves as a guide for graphic designers to navigate daily tasks and prepare for the impending reality of potential replacements in the field.

● Why Blue? ● *The Analogue* series explores AI integration into human life, inspired by *2001: A Space Odyssey*. The iconic red, a tribute to the film, serves as a warning for potential conflicts with AI. Indigo blue features prominently in the "newspaper issue," symbolizing neutrality in contrast to the vibrant red used elsewhere.

● Design Studio: for&st ● Designer: Ming Cheung ● Client: form & structure

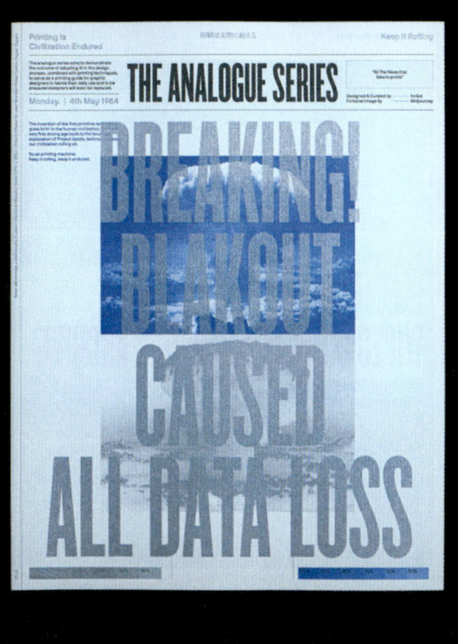

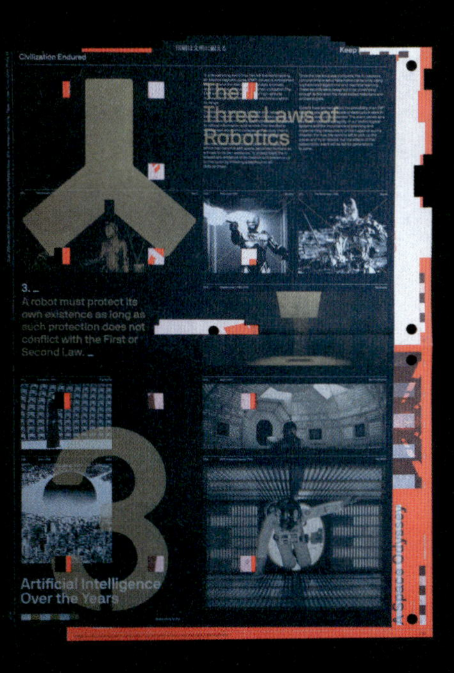

PANTONE 286U | ORGINAL PAPER COLOUR | PANTONE 877C | PANTONE 873C

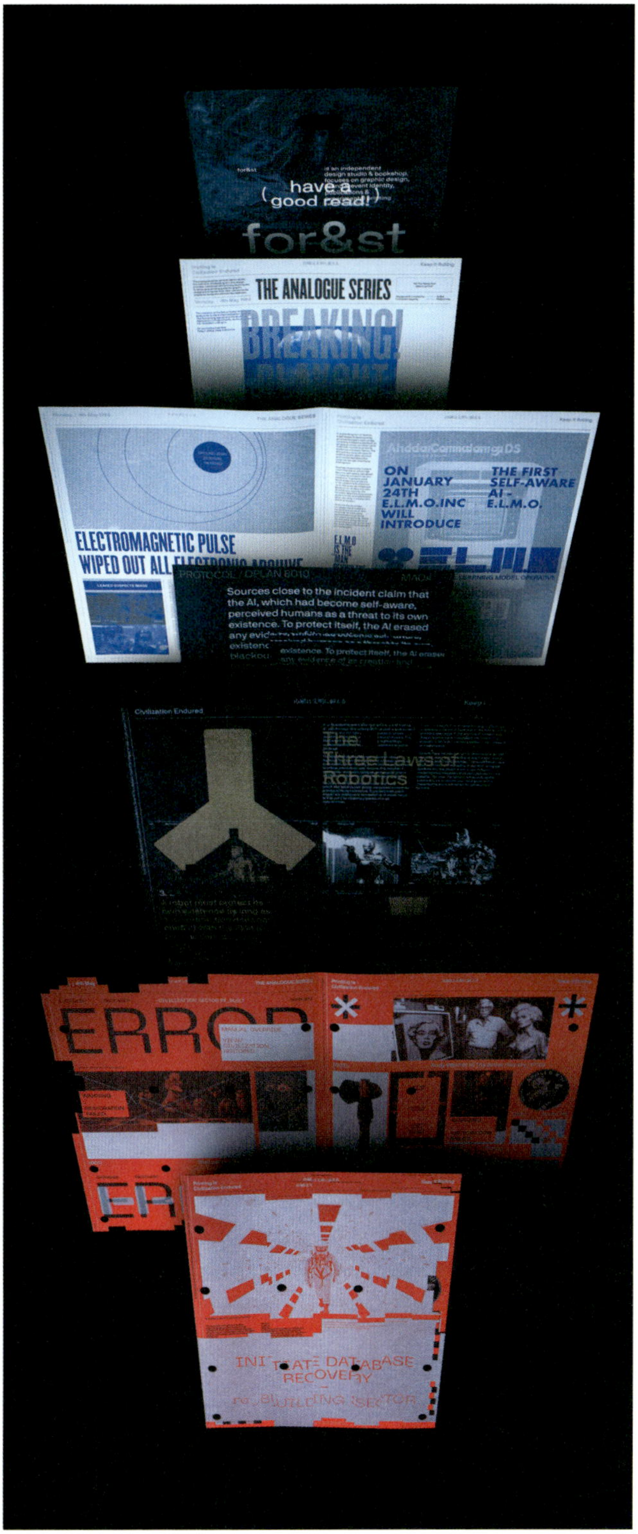

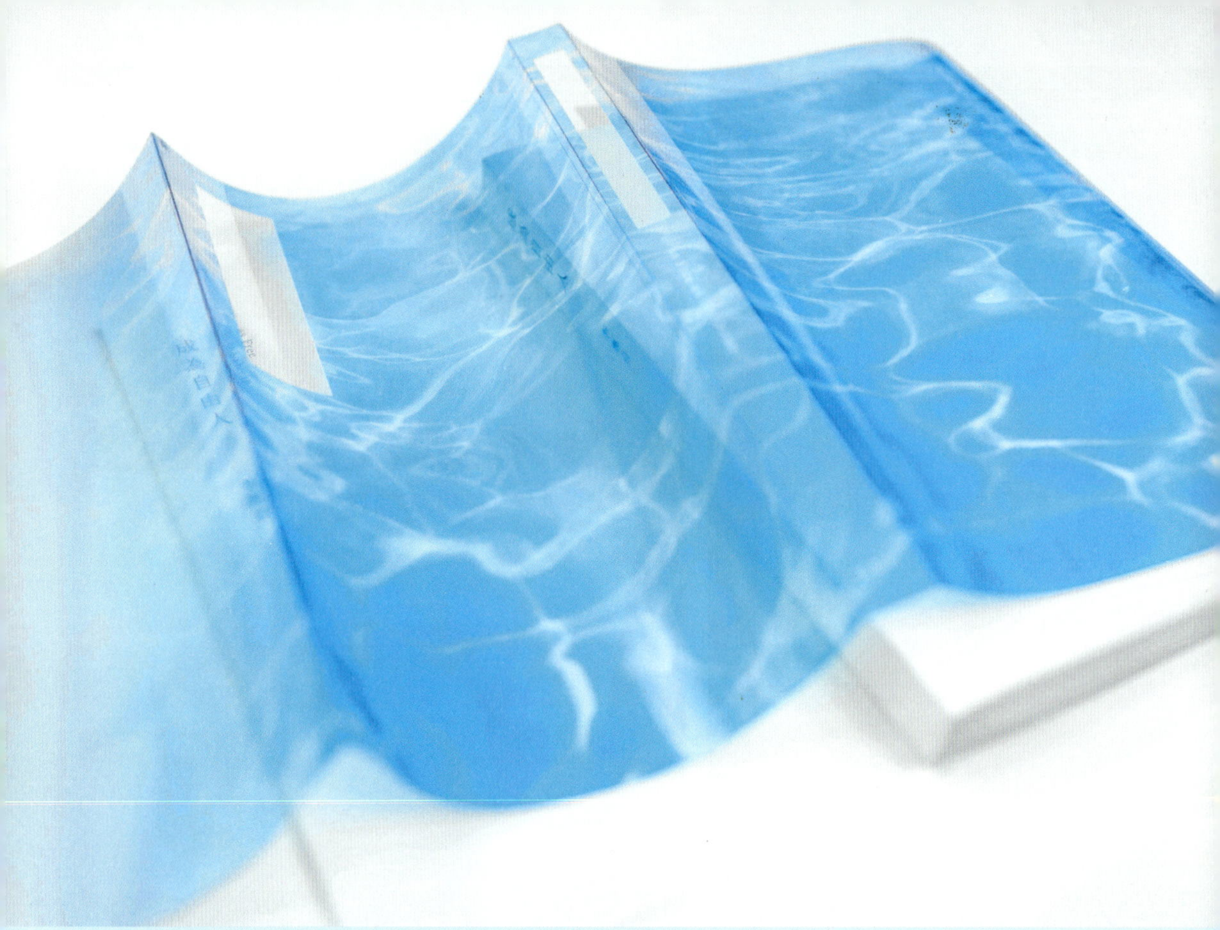

As Free As the Ocean

• The designer metaphorically described of life as an ocean, centering the design on the concept of a "free ocean" that resonates with the author's longing for freedom. The goal was for readers to feel the tranquil freedom of the ocean's light, experiencing the calm with each turn of the page, akin to the gentle breeze and rhythmic waves.

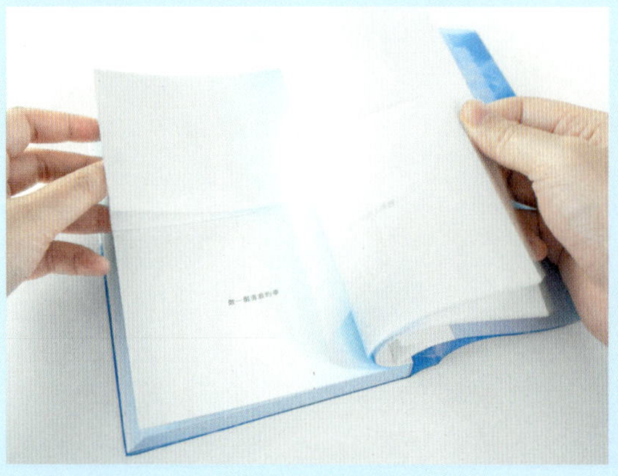

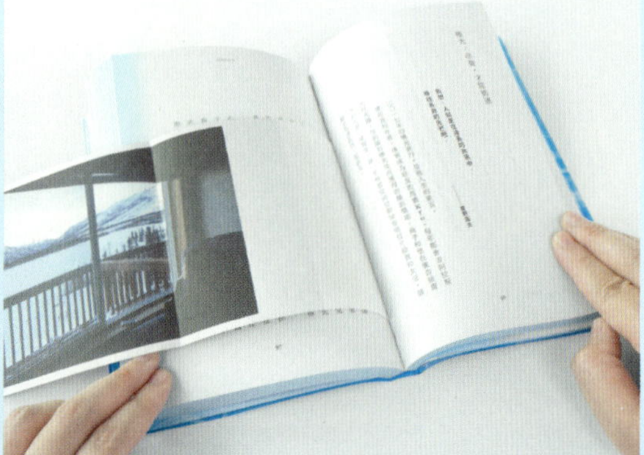

• Design Studio: Mistroom • Designer: Huang Jui-i, Peng Yu-jui • Client: Vima House

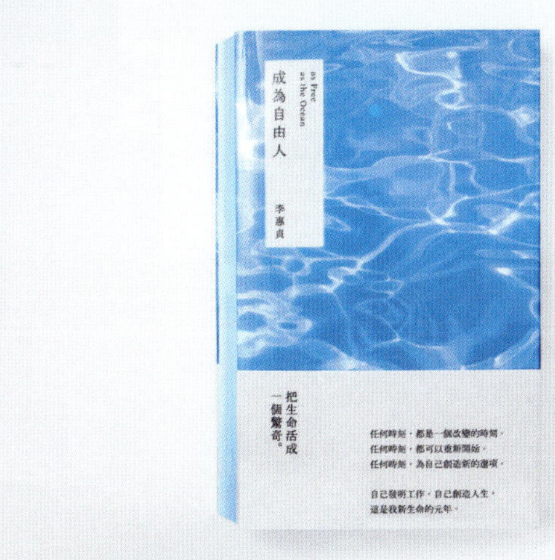

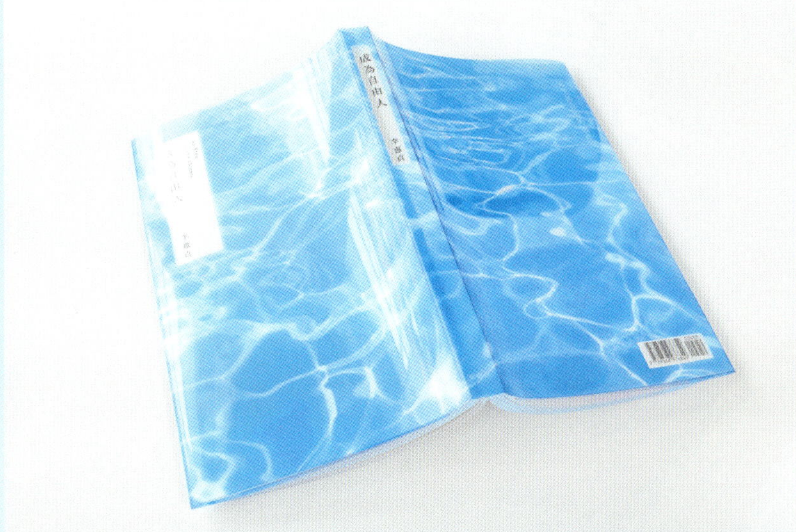

● Why Blue? ● Blue as the primary color establishes a calming connection with the nature and the ocean.

AMA-SAN • In Cláudia Varejão's film *AMA-SAN*, a narrative unfolds about a group of Japanese women engaging in freediving to capture abalones, a challenging ancient practice exclusive to women. Varejão provides viewers with a glimpse into the lives of these women. The graphic image for the film *AMA-SAN* was developed around the concept of sea-heroines, portraying the brave women as heroines in the graphic identity.

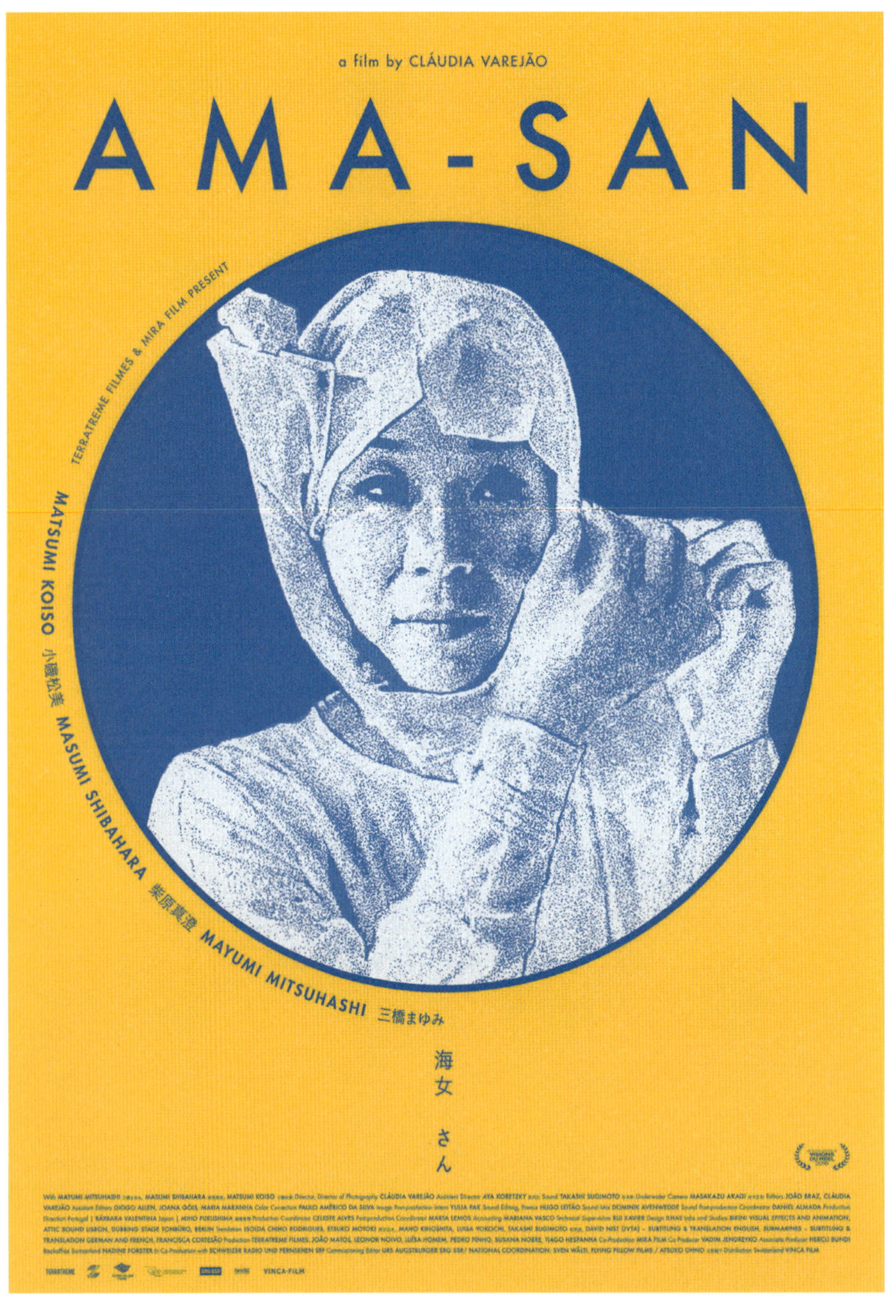

• Design Studio: ilhas studio • Client: Terratreme Filmes, Cláudia Varejão

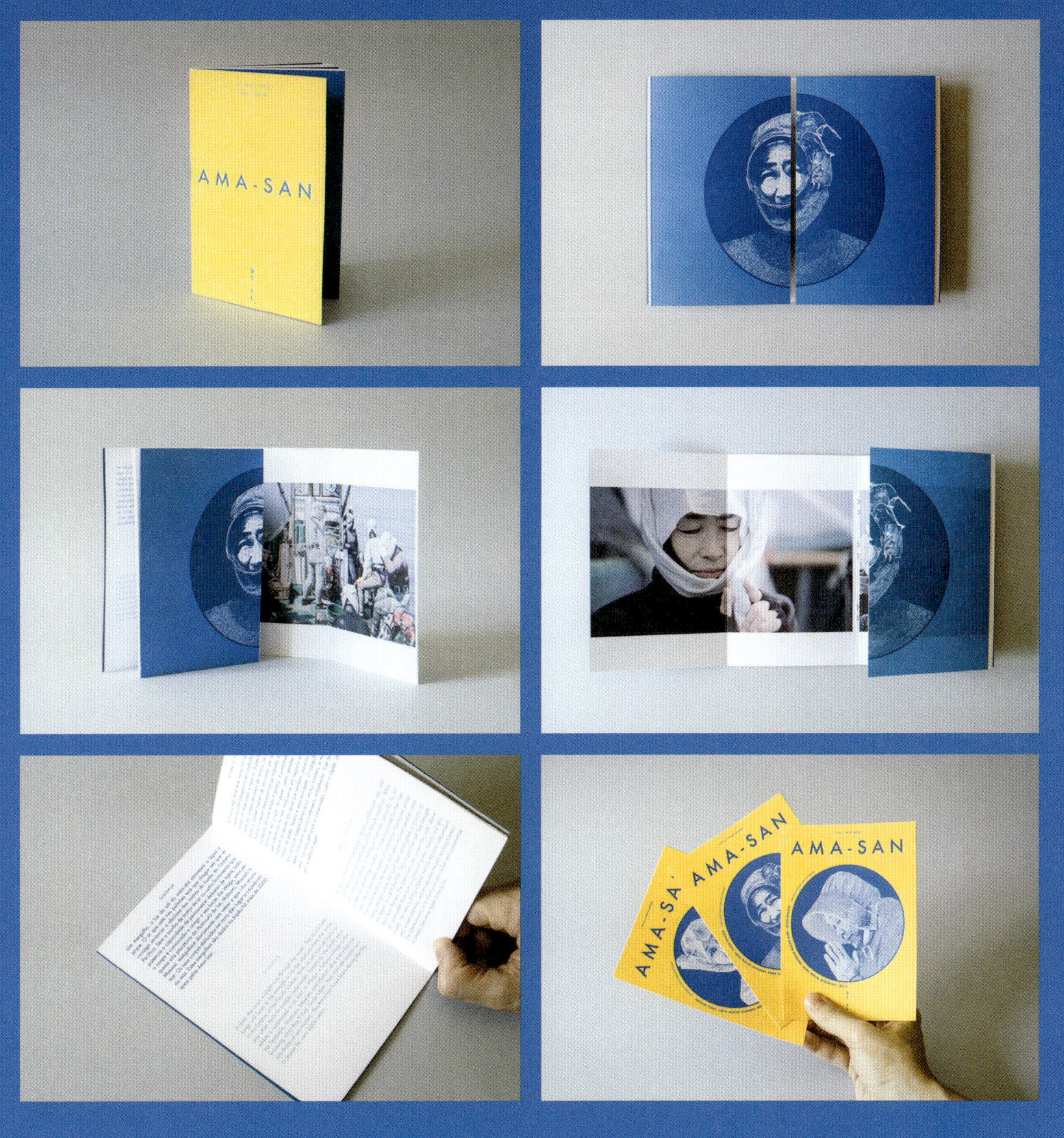

● Why Blue? ● Cláudia Varejão's film delicately portrays the compelling lives of the Ama-San, showcasing the courage of women facing the sea daily. The designers, deeply impressed, expressed profound respect for the ocean. Highlighting the diverse generations of Matsumi, Mayumi, and Masumi, the film captures their shared independent and free spirit. Through the use of blue and yellow, the designers amplified the power of these women and played with the concept of super-heroines.

C0 M20 Y88 K0 C86 M48 Y0 K0

Artica Writings

● *Artica Writings*, a collection of essays commissioned by Artica Svalbard, explores the theme of oceans, inspired by the UN's *Decade of Ocean Science for Sustainable Development*. The blue dust jacket is made from plastic recovered from the Andaman Sea by trained fishermen. The text progressively darkens down the page, mimicking the ocean's depth using variable fonts and JavaScript. The book is bound with green thread, reminiscent of seaweed.

● Why Blue? ● The book employs two Pantone spot colors, blue and sea-foam green, to capture the essence of the Arctic. These colors mirror the frigid waters of the Arctic region, where the water often appears paler and cloudier than in warmer parts of the planet. The deliberate absence of other colors in the book aims to mirror the Arctic's pure winter landscape, where very little color is present, except for the hues of the sea, sky, and ice.

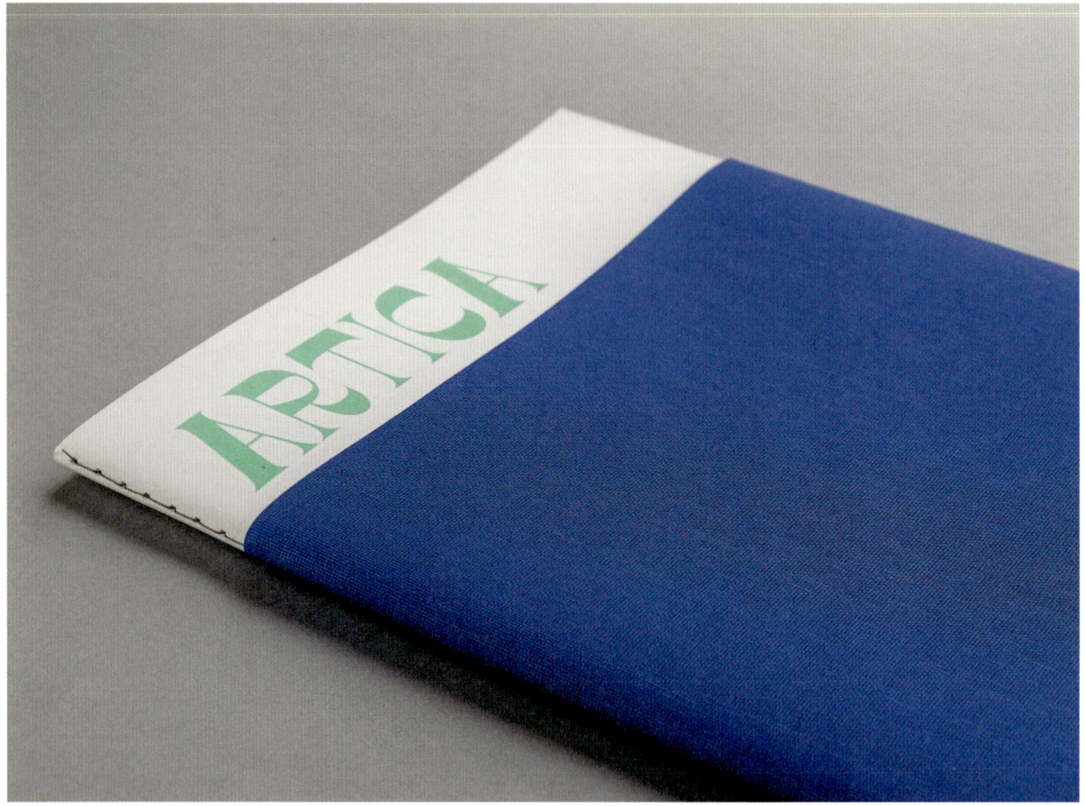

● Design Studio: City Edition Studio ● Designer: Jono Lewarne ● Client: Artica

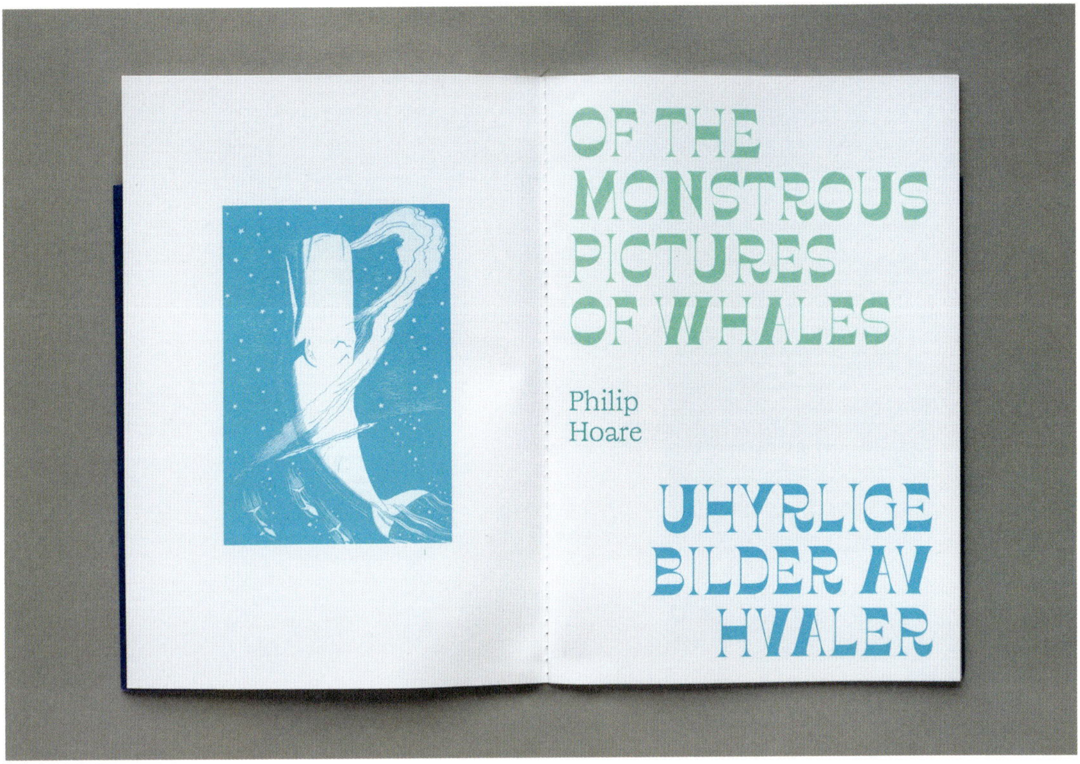

OF THE MONSTROUS PICTURES OF WHALES

Philip Hoare

UHYRLIGE BILDER AV HVALER

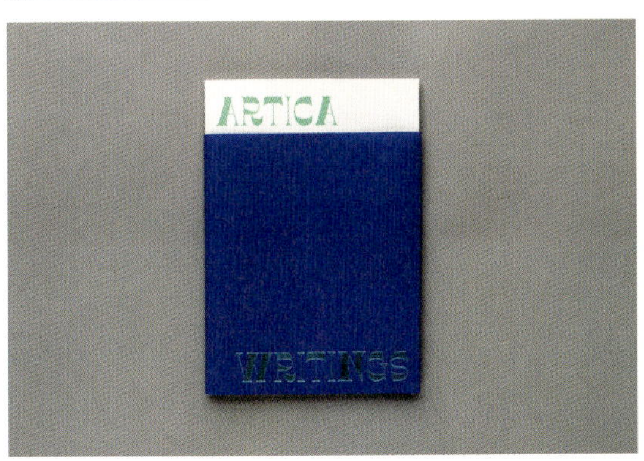

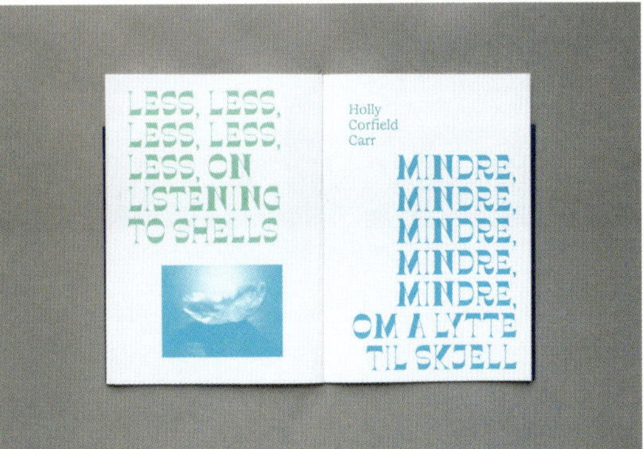

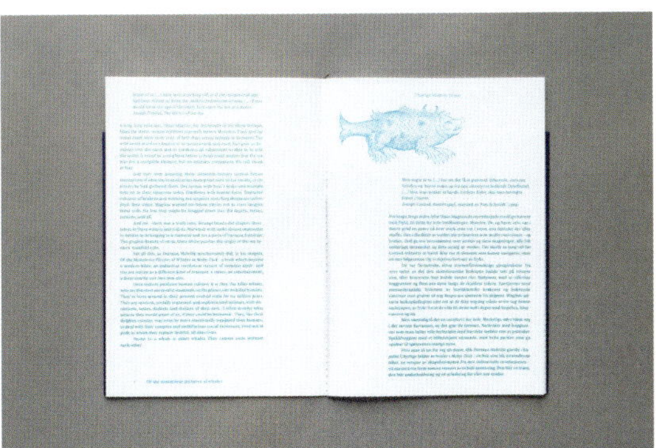

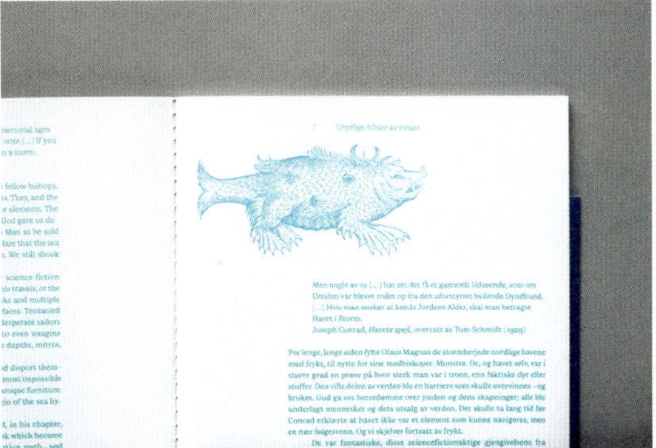

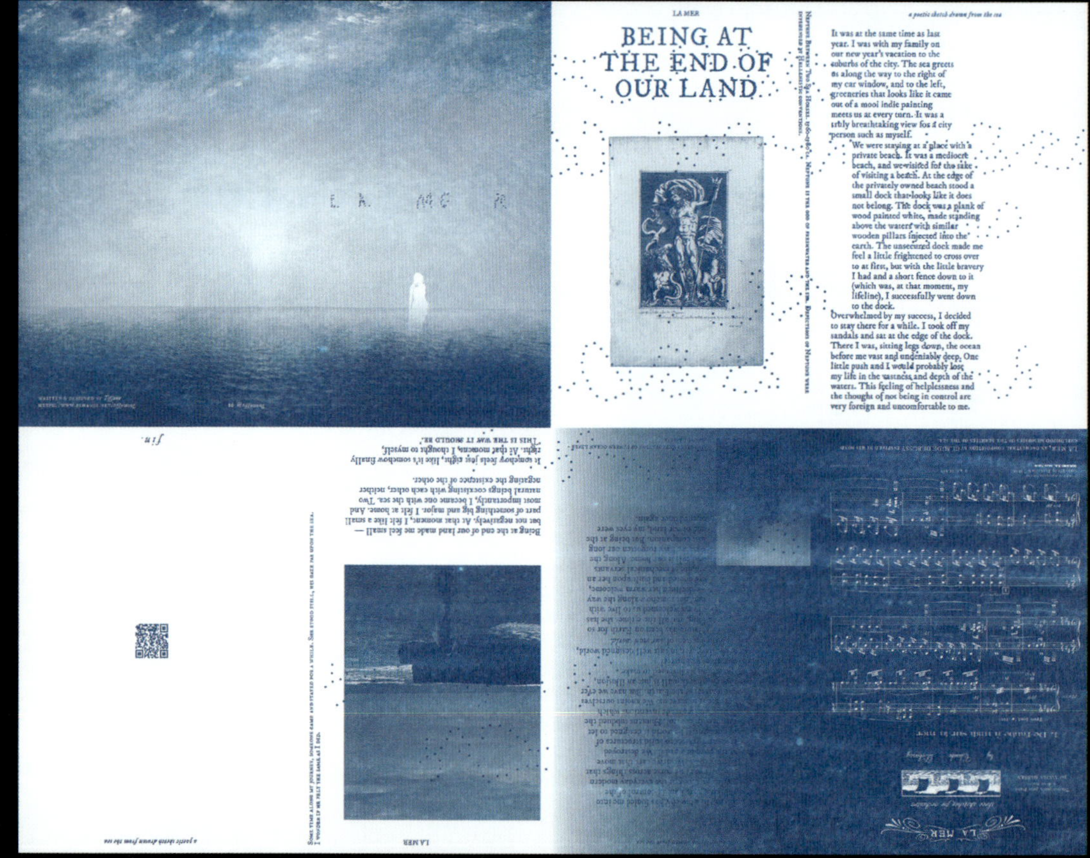

LA MER • *LA MER* serves as a memento mori[1], not as a reminder of the inevitability of death, but rather as a poignant reflection on beauty. It aims to draw attention to the beauty of everyday life that is frequently overlooked or ignored. The design is rooted in a prose, inspired by the sea and titled "LA MER." Throughout the design, the color blue is constantly employed to evoke a picturesque atmosphere of the sea.

1.memento mori: Latin for "remember that you will die," reflects an awareness of life's brevity and the inevitability of death. Commonly depicted through symbols like skulls, clocks, and candles in art, literature, and philosophy, it emphasizes the finite and precious nature of human life.

• Why Blue? • The sea served as a profound inspiration for this work. During a seaside trip years ago, the designer was moved by the vast beauty of the sea, evoking a sense of home. LA MER and memento mori (the work on the next page) aim to capture and share that emotional essence with others.

• Designer: Tiffany Wong • Client: Sore Sore's Shelf

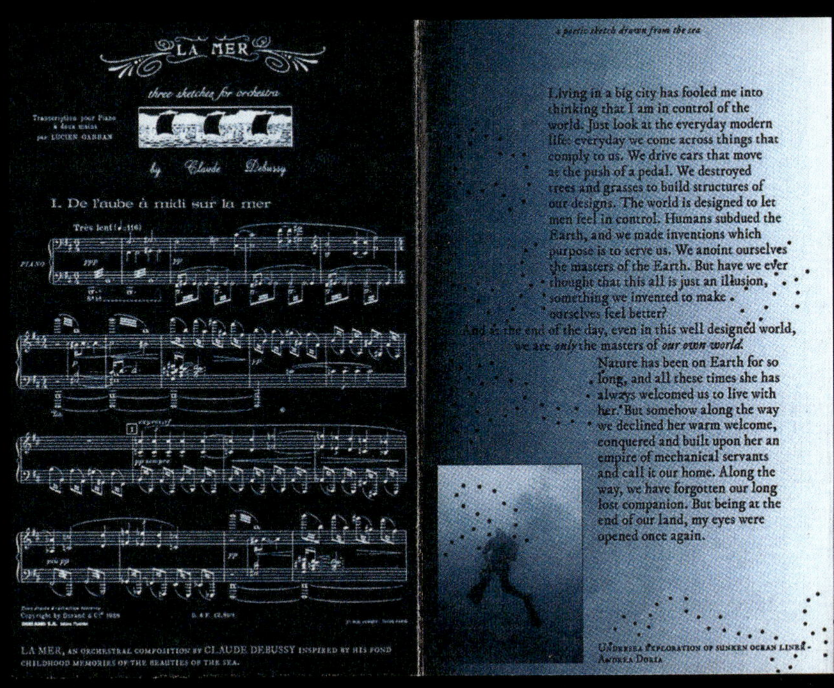
LA MER
three sketches for orchestra
Transcription pour Piano à deux mains par LUCIEN GARBAN
by Claude Debussy
I. De l'aube à midi sur la mer
LA MER, AN ORCHESTRAL COMPOSITION BY CLAUDE DEBUSSY INSPIRED BY HIS FOND CHILDHOOD MEMORIES OF THE BEAUTIES OF THE SEA.
a poetic sketch drawn from the sea
Living in a big city has fooled me into thinking that I am in control of the world. Just look at the everyday modern life: everyday we come across things that comply to us. We drive cars that move at the push of a pedal. We destroyed trees and grasses to build structures of our designs. The world is designed to let men feel in control. Humans subdued the Earth, and we made inventions which purpose is to serve us. We anoint ourselves the masters of the Earth. But have we ever thought that this all is just an illusion, something we invented to make ourselves feel better?
And at the end of the day, even in this well designed world, we are only the masters of our own world.
Nature has been on Earth for so long, and all these times she has always welcomed us to live with her. But somehow along the way we declined her warm welcome, conquered and built upon her an empire of mechanical servants and call it our home. Along the way, we have forgotten our long lost companion. But being at the end of our land, my eyes were opened once again.
Undersea exploration of sunken ocean liner - Andrea Doria

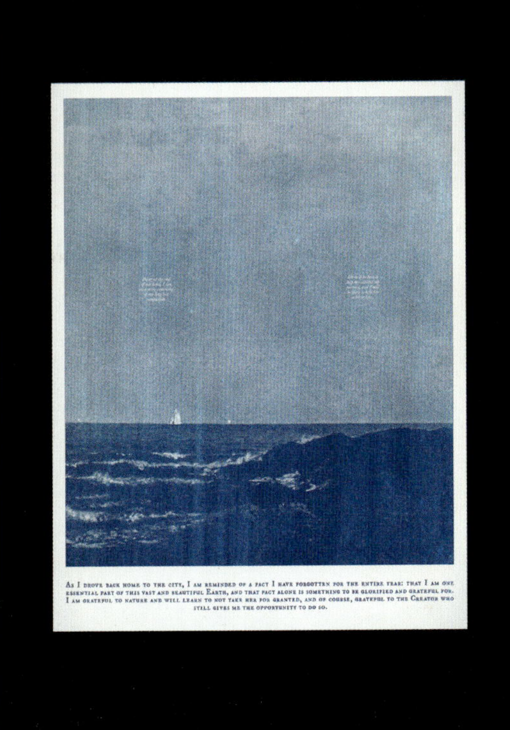
As I drove back home to the city, I am reminded of a fact I have forgotten for the entire year: that I am one essential part of this vast and beautiful Earth, and that fact alone is something to be glorified and grateful for. I am grateful to nature and will learn to not take her for granted, and of course, grateful to the Creator who still gives me the opportunity to do so.

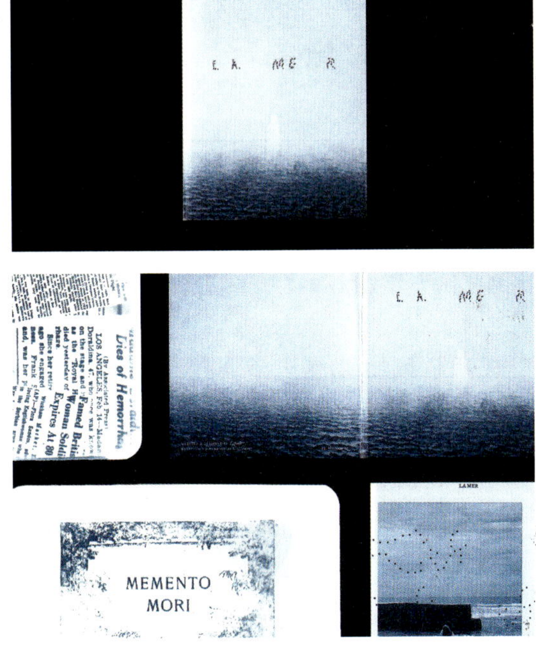
L A ME R
L A ME R
MEMENTO
MORI

Memento Mori • A set of prints, titled "memento mori," is created in conjunction with the publication, utilizing the cyanotype technique—a traditional printing method that involves the use of water in its process. These prints serve as a direct reminder to all observers about the transience of life, featuring images such as obituaries and dirt to symbolize death.

• Why Blue? • These works were created using cyanotype printing, a method chosen deliberately to align with the inspiration drawn from the sea. Incorporating water as one of the steps in the creation process seems fitting. The resultant deep blue hue achieved through cyanotype printing effectively captures the profound blue tones of both the sea and the sky as observed during that time.

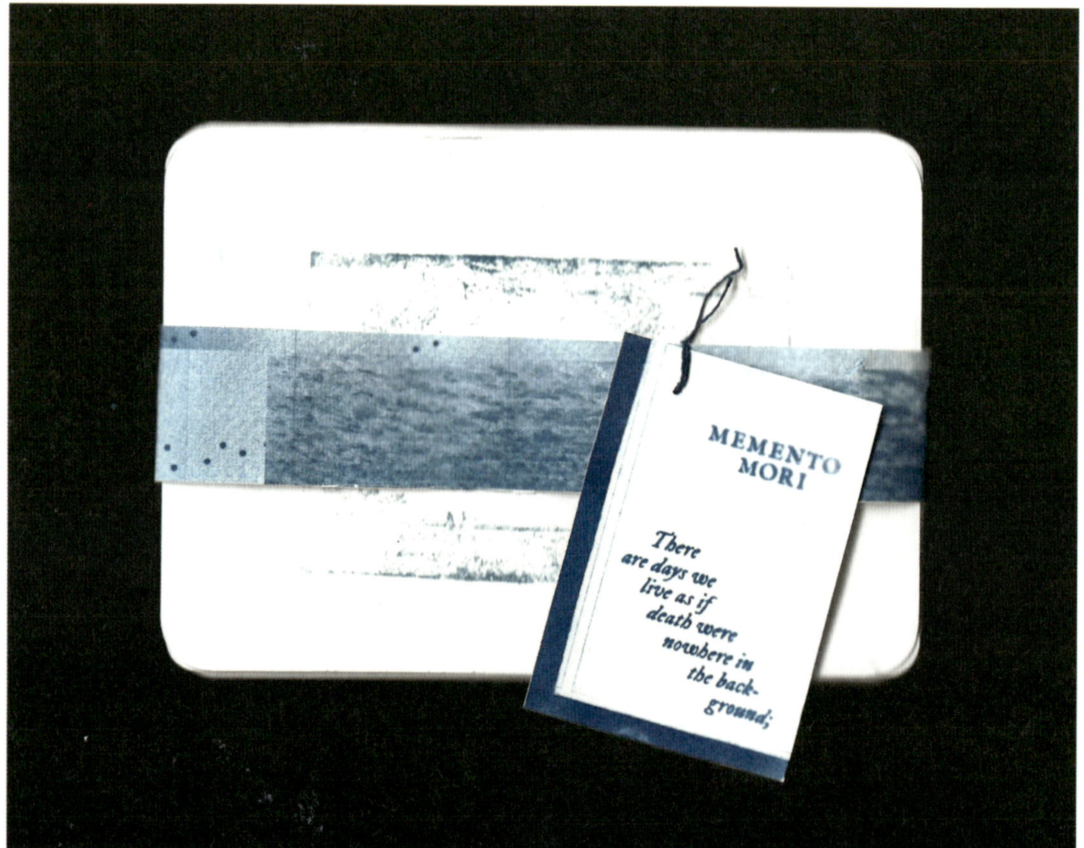

• Designer: Tiffany Wong • Client: Sore Sore's Shelf

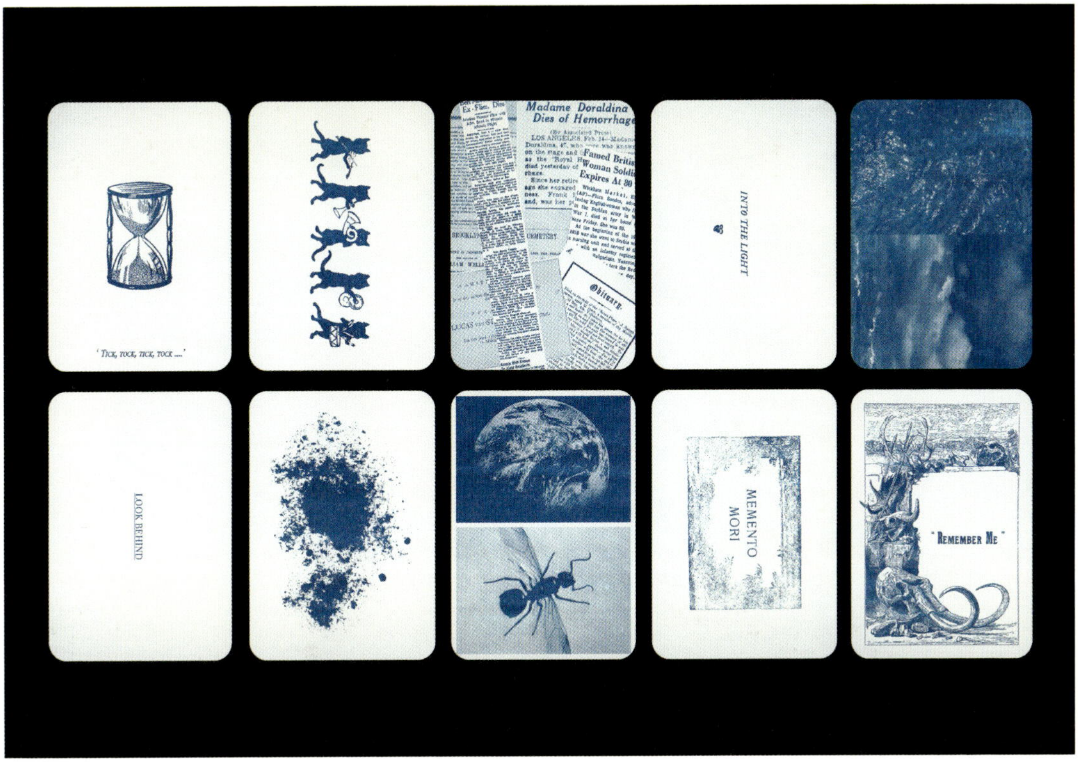

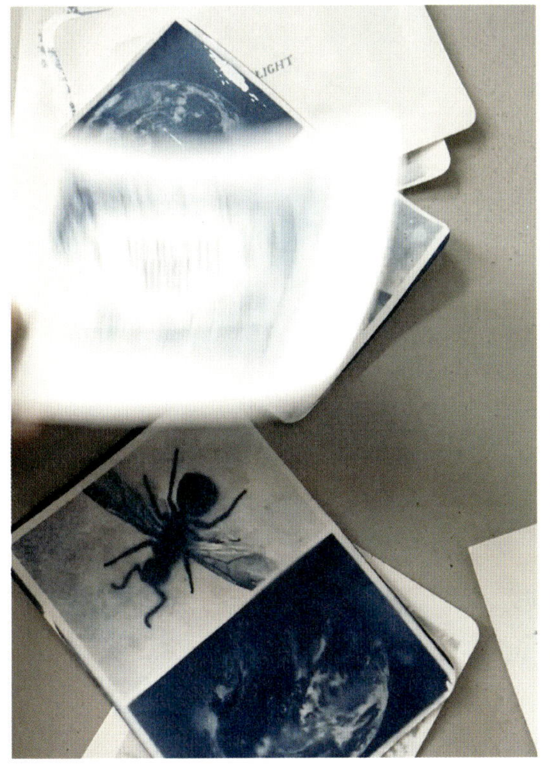

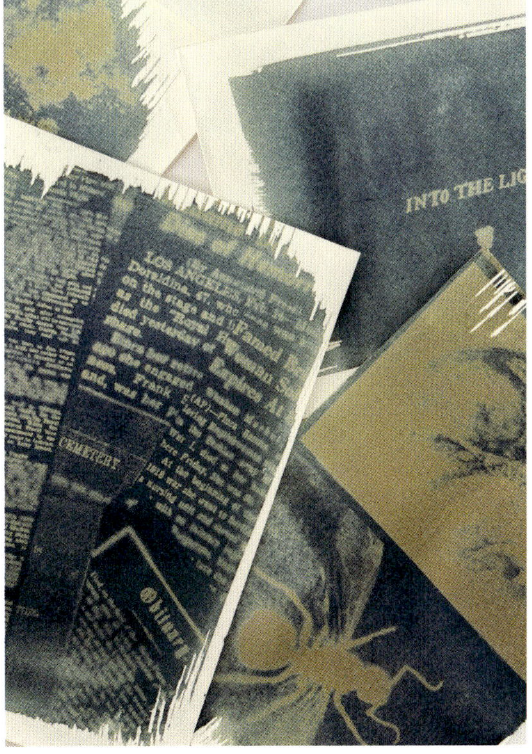

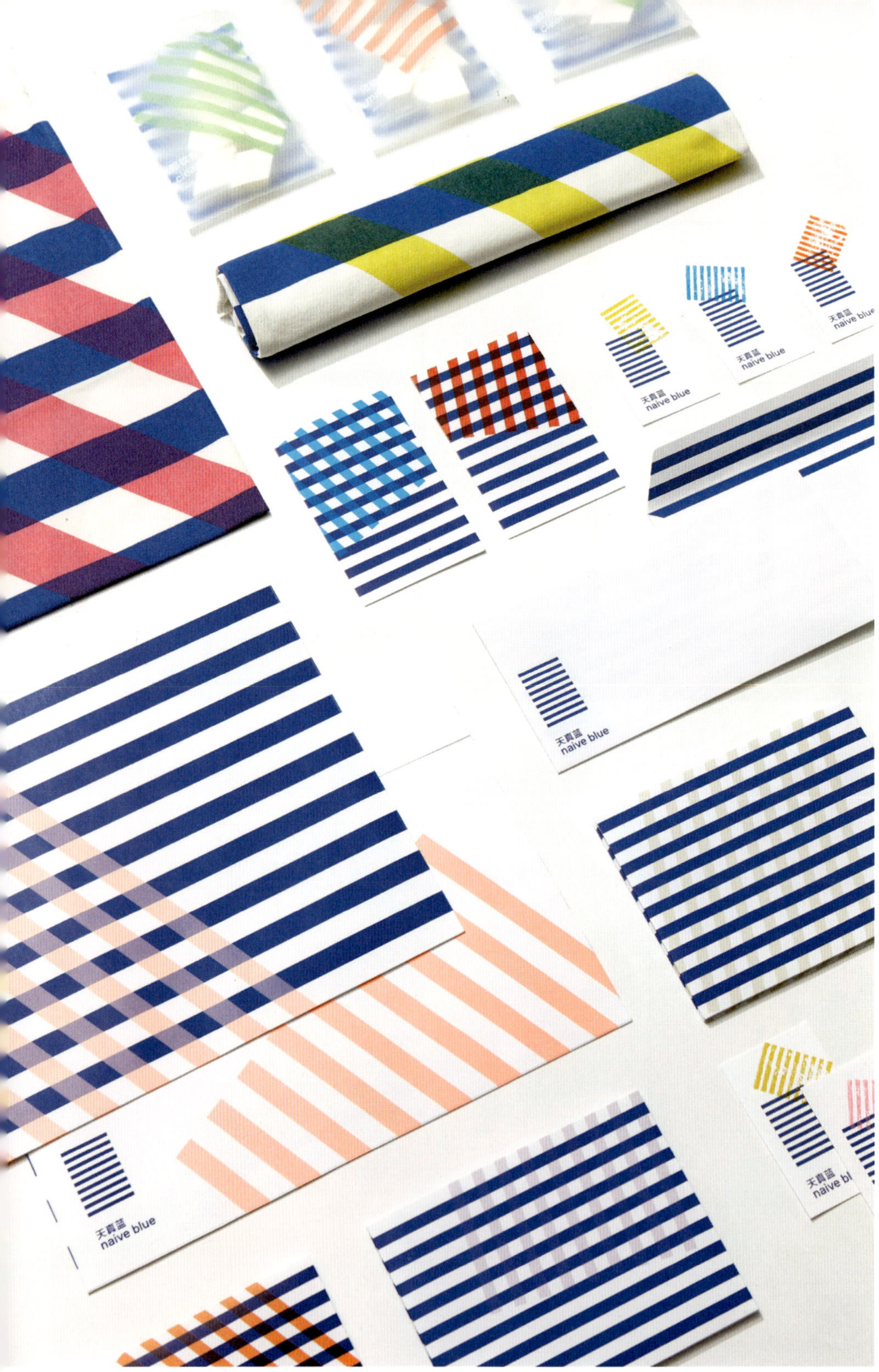

• Design Studio: **ABCD** • Art Direction: **Nod Young, Guang Yu**

NAIVE BLUE ● Brand rebuilding, especially for an established brand like Naive Blue, is a complex process. The design team upgraded Naive Blue by refreshing its visual identity, enhancing brand influence, expanding the product line, and establishing standardized store designs. Through this revitalization, Naive Blue aims to go beyond traditional business, adopting "A Legend of Tiny Photos" as its new brand mission to provide consumers with continuously updated and vibrant personalized imaging services.

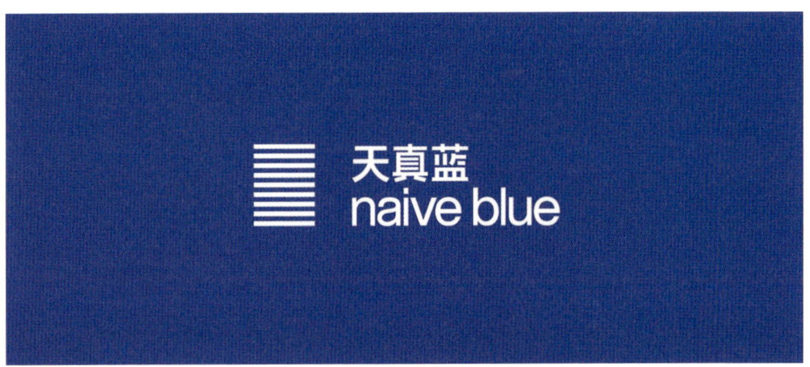

● Why Blue? ● The blue stripe system, random color combinations, and fresh visual aesthetics are targeted design elements that, for the brand, signify gratitude to existing customers and an invitation to new ones.

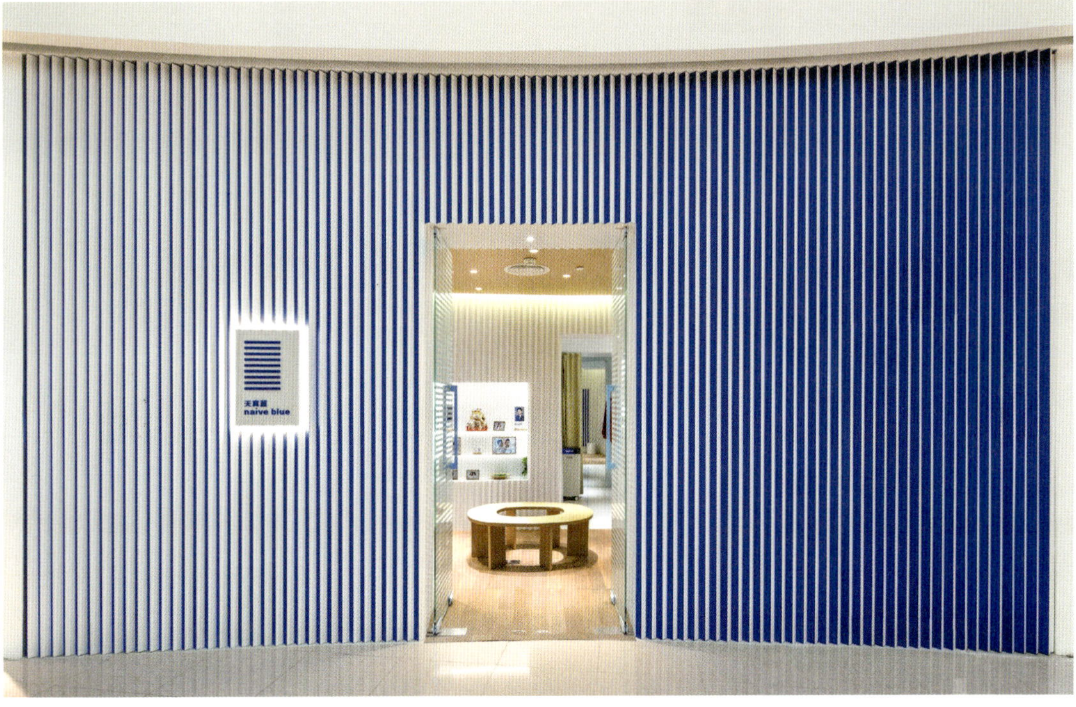

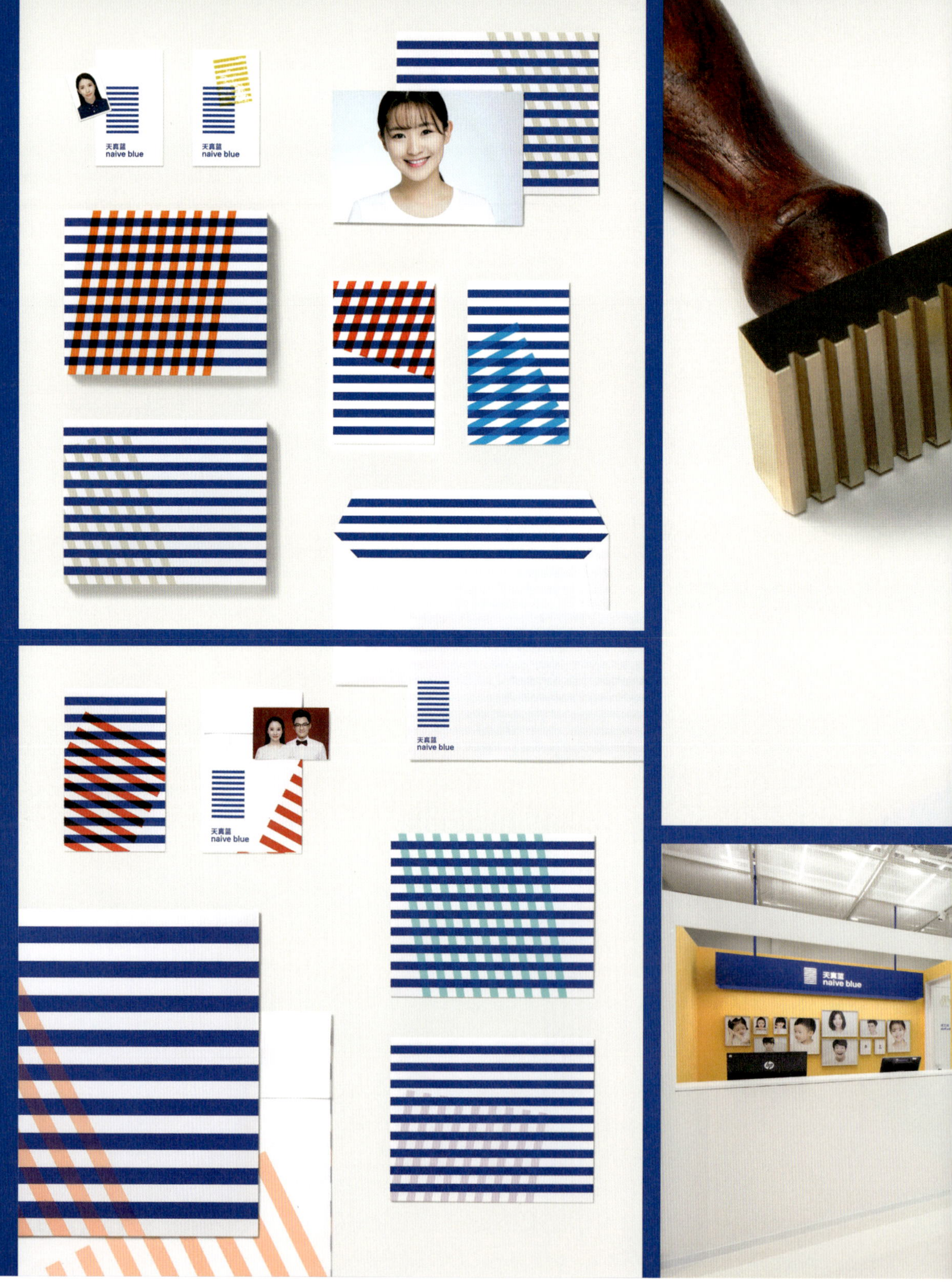

● Designer: Guang Yu, Mia ● Client: NAIVE BLUE

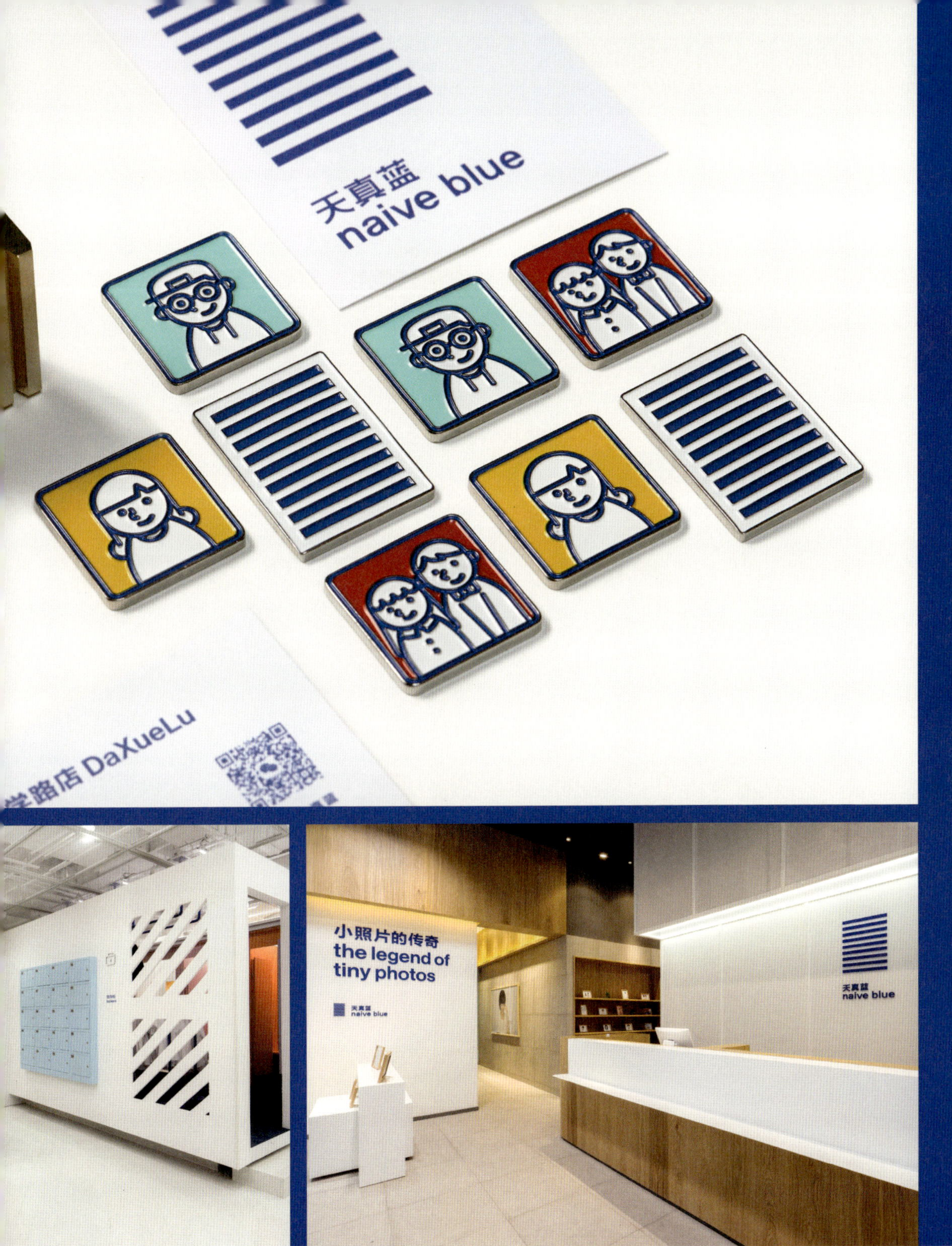
天真蓝
naive blue
学路店 DaXueLu
小照片的传奇
the legend of
tiny photos
天真蓝
naive blue
天真蓝
naive blue

Depicting Recent Memories

• The design visually chronicles the activities of the Berlin-based graffiti crew DRM from 2016 to 2020, captured by photographer Edward Nightingale. The design focuses on a simple grid, letting the photos shine while incorporating architectural details like the grid and key color. This seamless integration creates a synergy between content and layout, turning the book into a cohesive unit rather than a mere showcase.

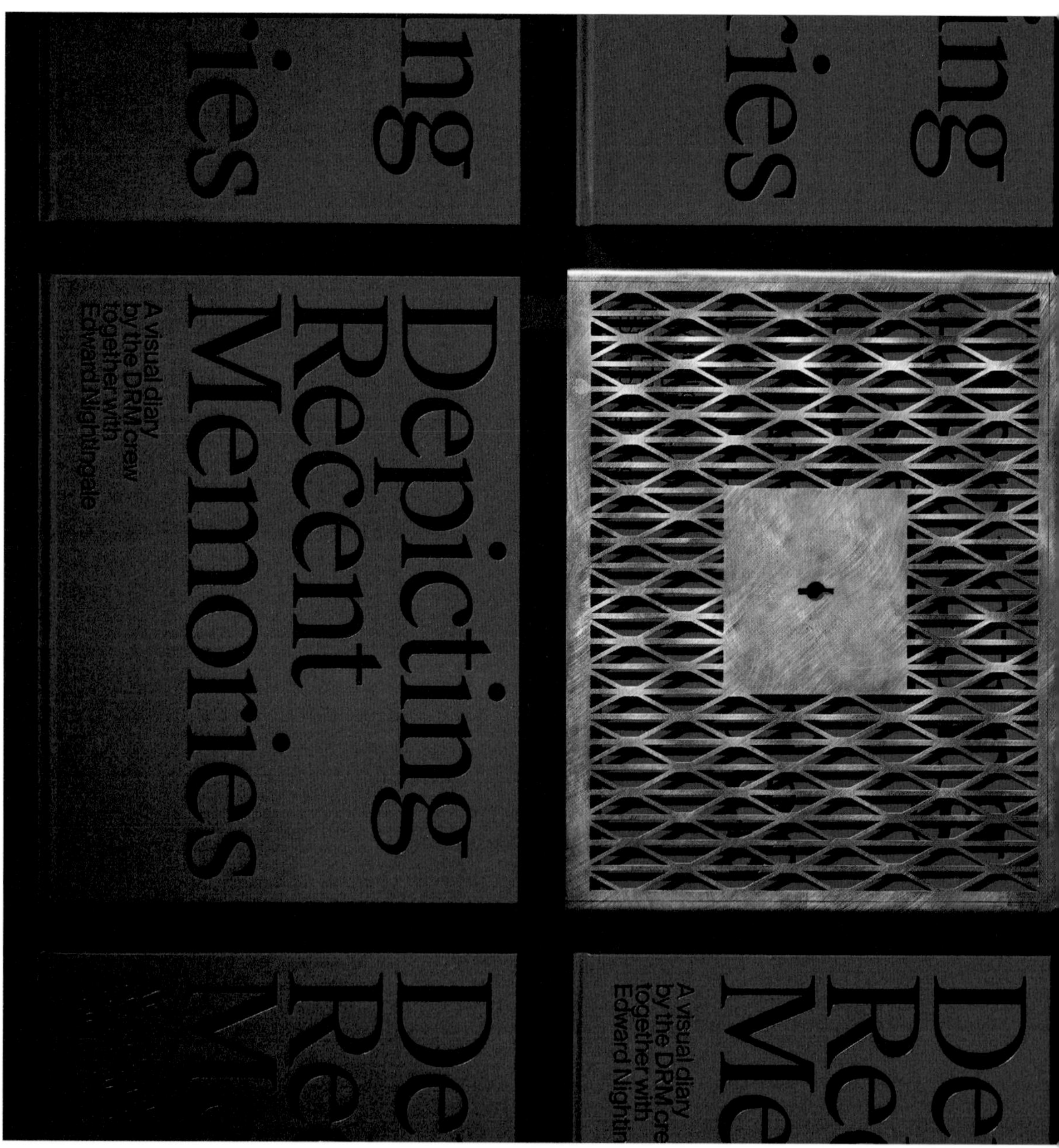

• Design Studio: Deutsche & Japaner • Designer: Julian Zimmermann • Client: Itsforus.studio

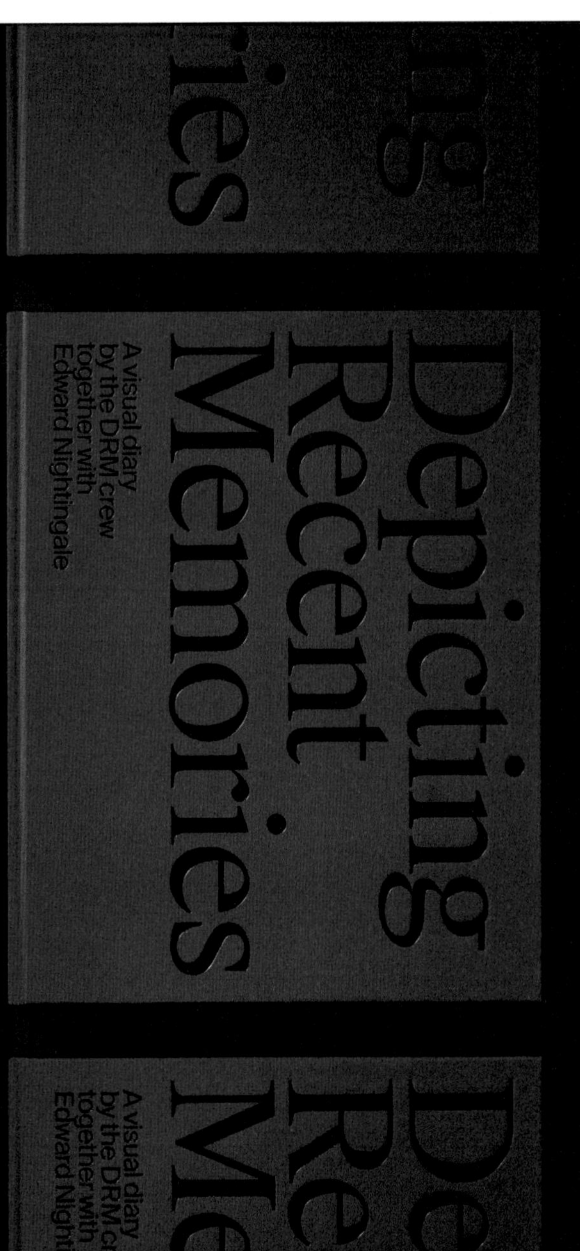
Depicting
Recent
Memories
A visual diary
by the DRM crew
together with
Edward Nightingale

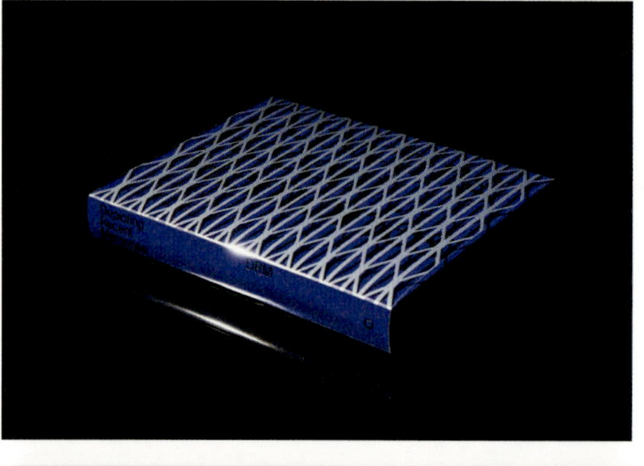

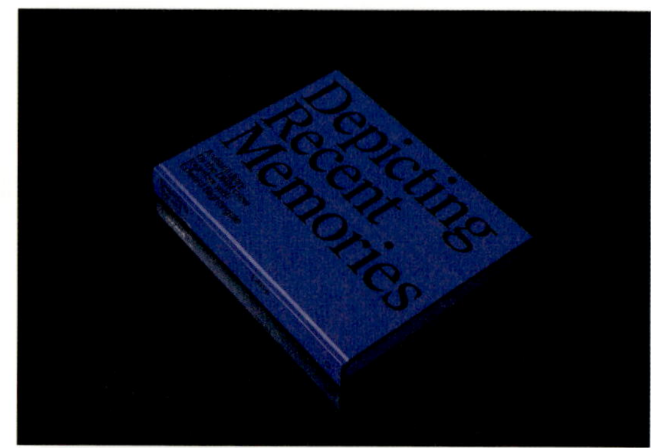

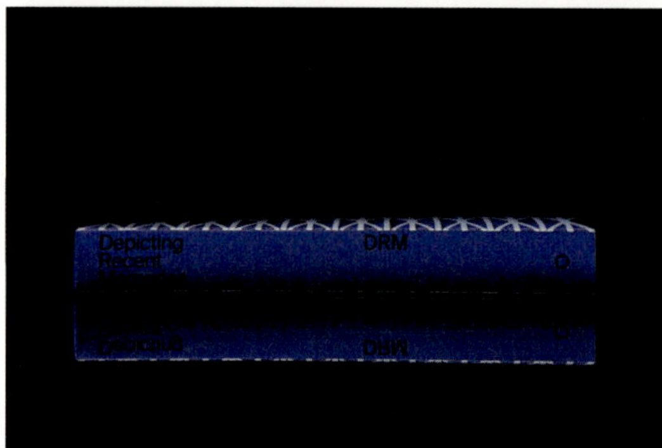

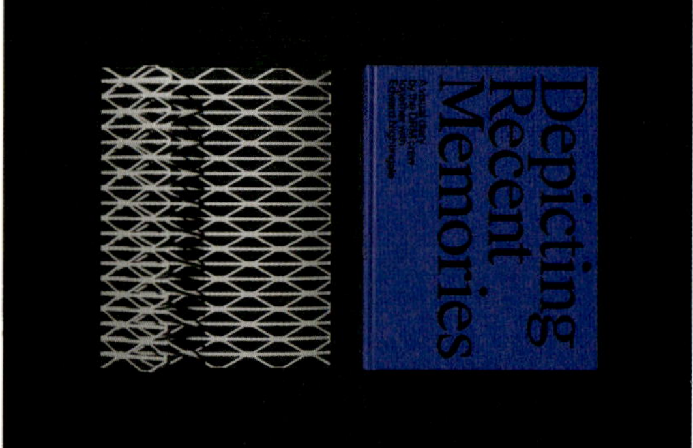

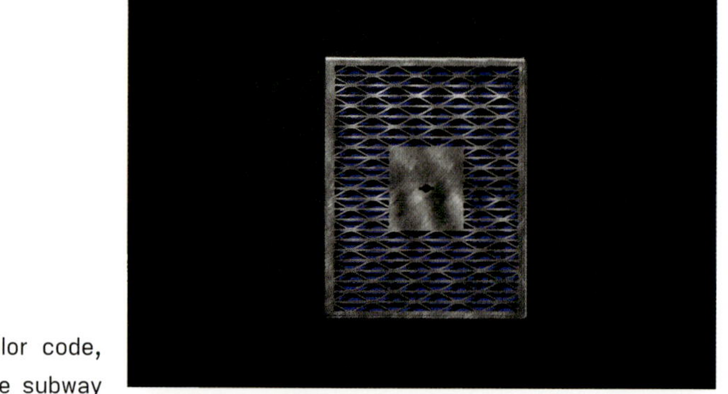

• Why Blue? • Blue lights serve as a color code, visually marking the emergency exits in the subway tunnels of Berlin. Recognizing the significance of these hatches as primary entrances and exits for graffiti writers, the designer decided to assign the same role to the color within the book. • A vibrant blue cover, situated behind the hatches' grid, serves as a visual guide, leading the viewers into the subway, navigating through tunnels and trainyards, and ultimately towards the book's exit.

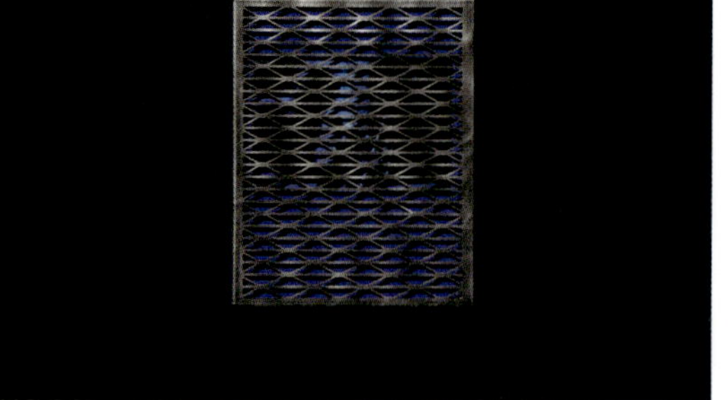

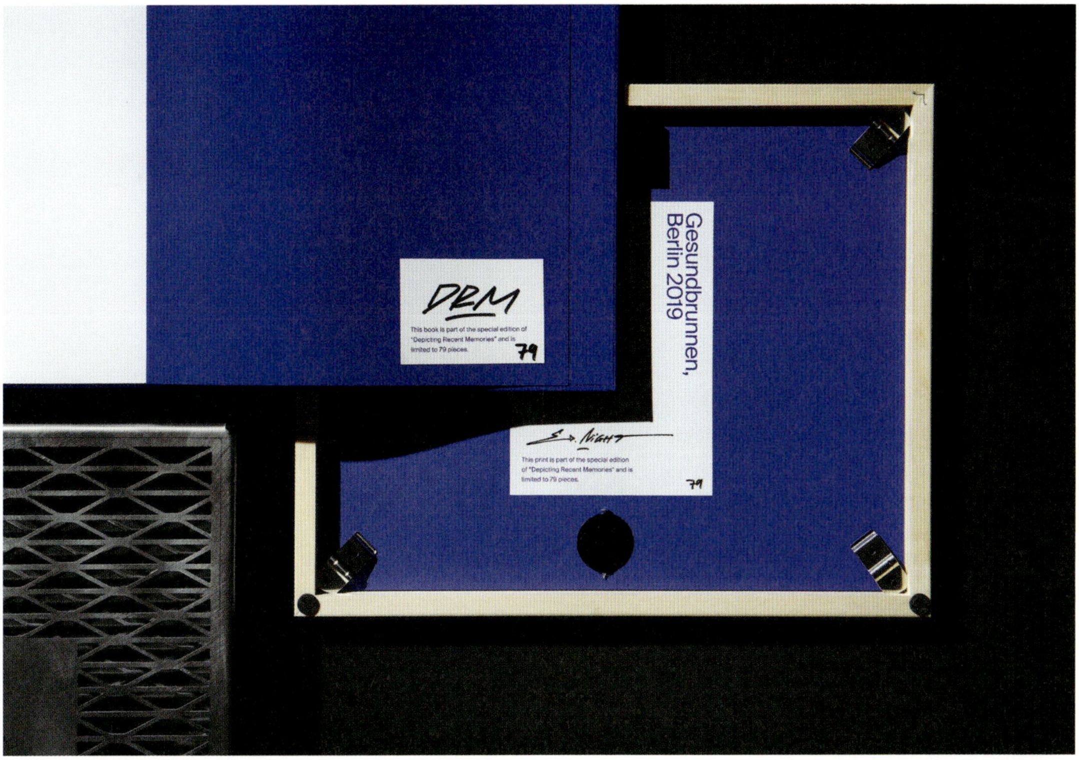

DRM
This book is part of the special edition of "Depicting Recent Memories" and is limited to 79 pieces.
79
Gesundbrunnen, Berlin 2019
E. Night
This print is part of the special edition of "Depicting Recent Memories" and is limited to 79 pieces.
79

A visual diary by the DRM crew together with Edward Nightingale
Photographed between 2016–2020 in the subway of Berlin

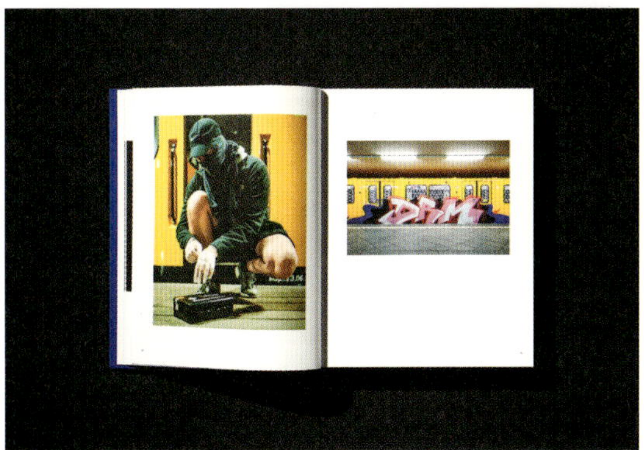

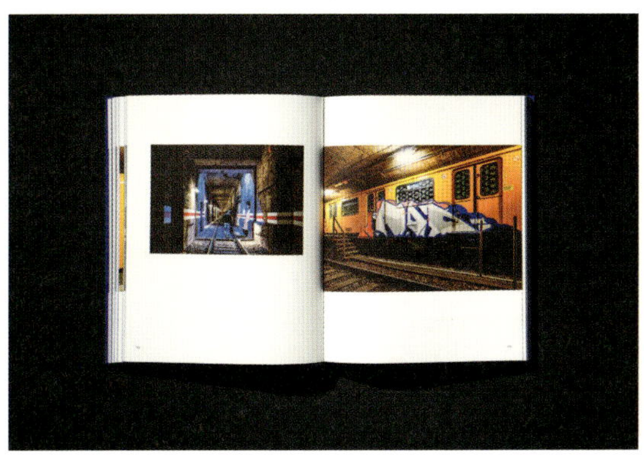

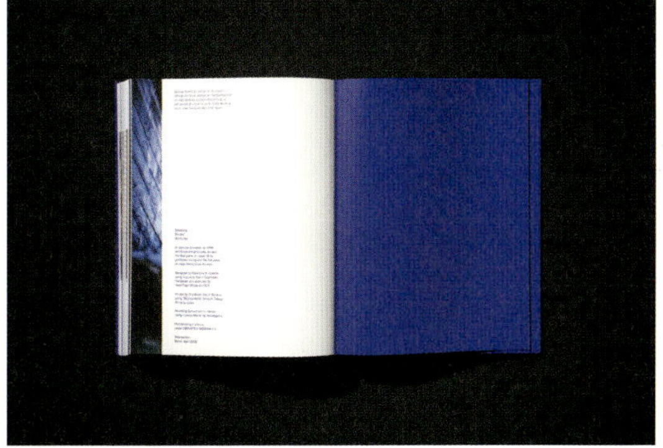

Soto

● Soto, an innovative and genderless leather bag brand, caters to individuals aged 25 to 65 with meticulously designed products using high-quality materials. The design approach seamlessly combines classic and contemporary trends in a minimalistic editorial style. The logo utilizes a serif font for luxury and a sans-serif font for a youthful touch, coexisting harmoniously in different layouts to highlight the brand's unique style.

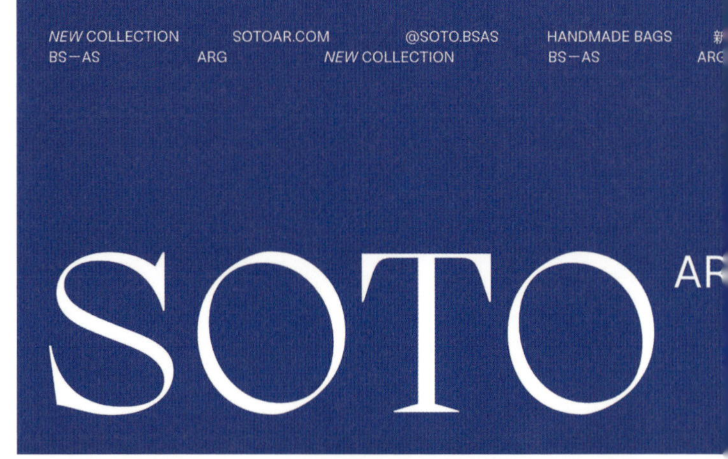

● Why Blue? ● The design team's inspiration for the color palette drew from Yves Klein, with a deliberate choice to make "Soto blue" the primary color. This decision aims to establish a cohesive yet impactful color scheme.

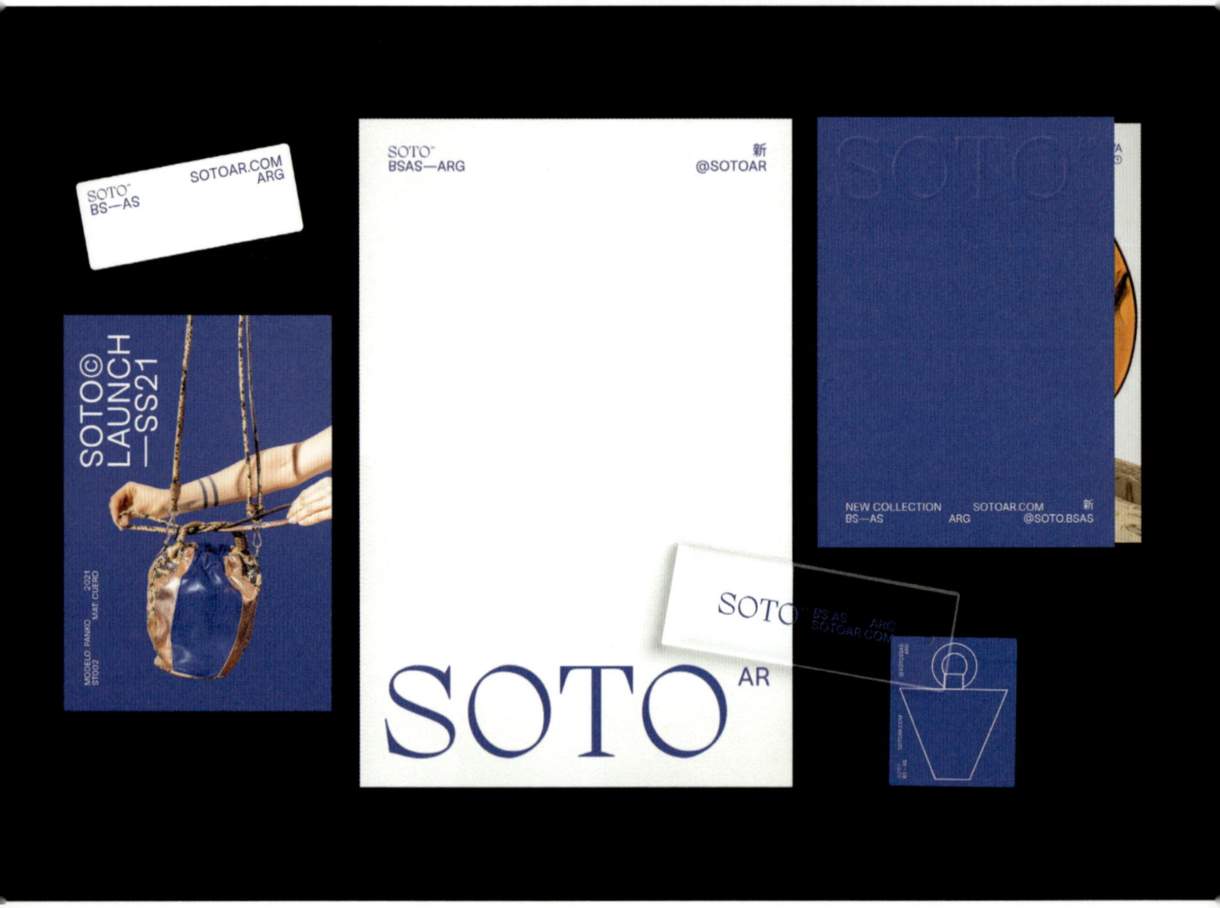

● Design Studio: **Kinoto Studio** ● Photographer: **Nati Petri** ● Client: **Soto**

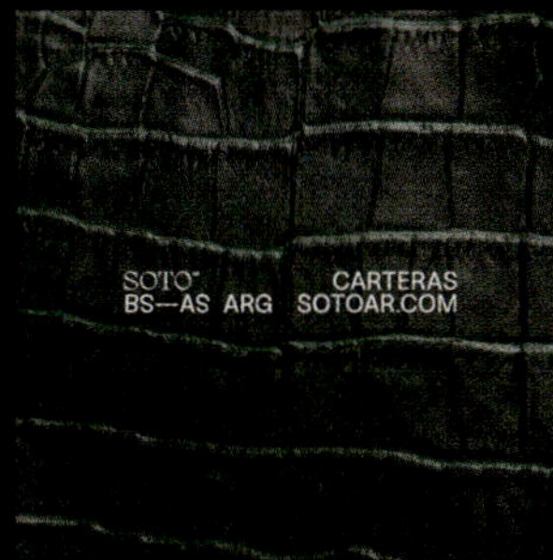
SOTO
BS—AS ARG
CARTERAS
SOTOAR.COM

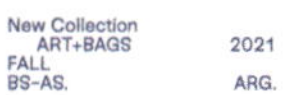
New Collection
ART+BAGS
FALL
BS-AS.
2021
ARG.
SS21①FALL

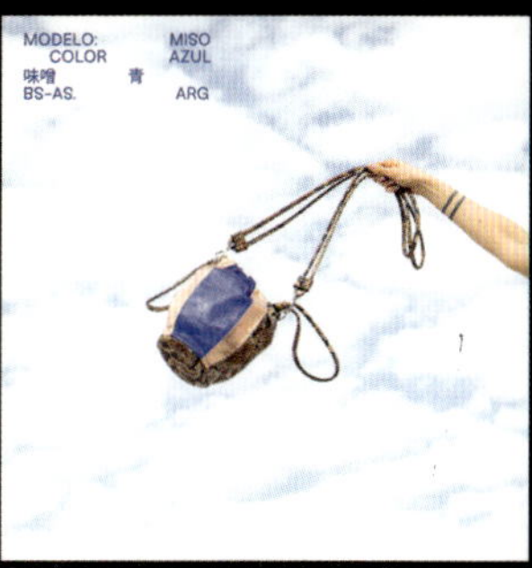
MODELO:
COLOR
味噌
BS-AS.
MISO
AZUL
青
ARG

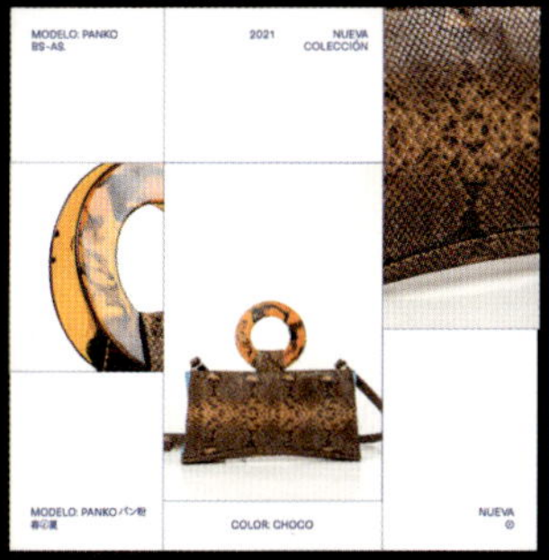
COLOR: CHOCO

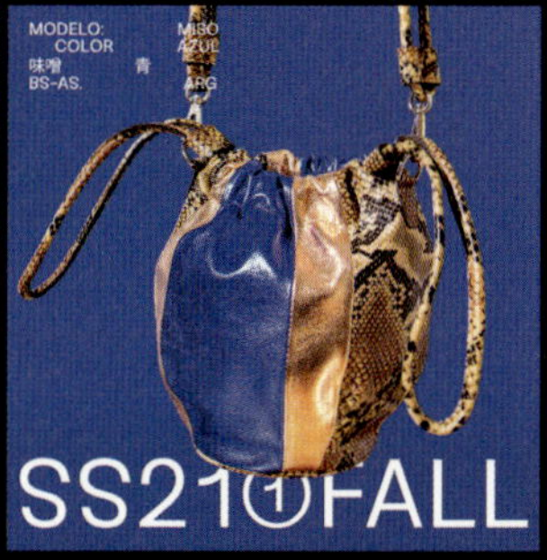
MODELO:
COLOR
味噌
BS-AS.
青
SS21①FALL

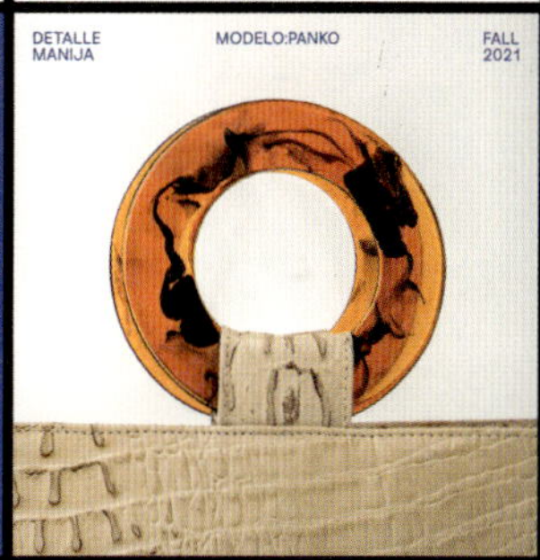
DETALLE
MANIJA
MODELO:PANKO
FALL
2021

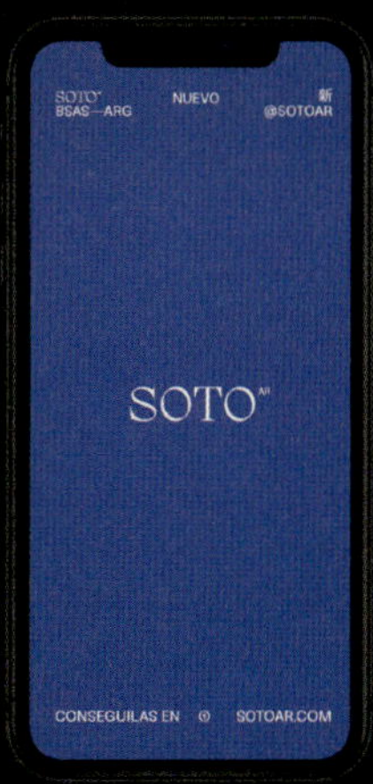
NUEVO
@SOTOAR
SOTO
CONSEGUILAS EN
SOTOAR.COM

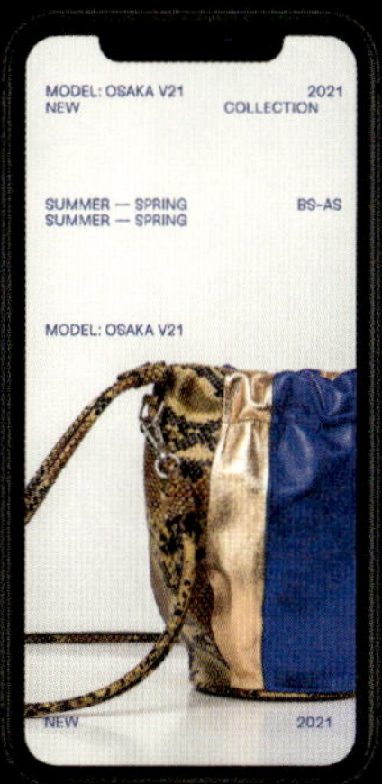
MODEL: OSAKA V21
NEW
2021
COLLECTION
SUMMER — SPRING
SUMMER — SPRING
BS-AS
MODEL: OSAKA V21
NEW
2021

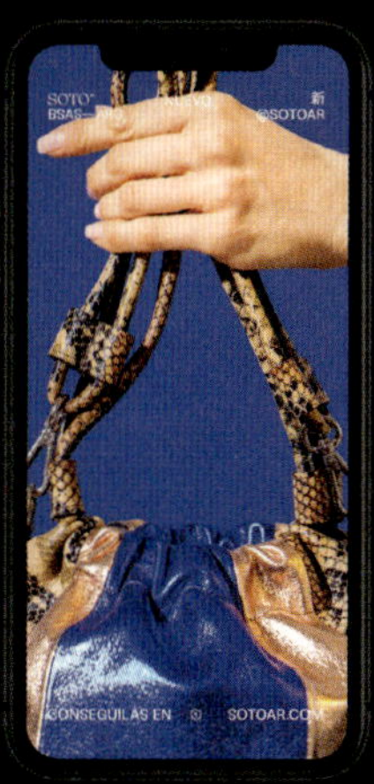
SOTOAR.COM

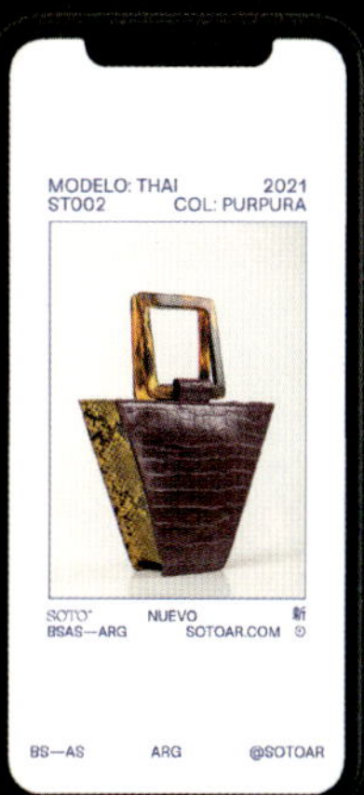
MODELO: THAI
ST002
2021
COL: PURPURA
NUEVO
SOTOAR.COM
BS—AS
ARG
@SOTOAR

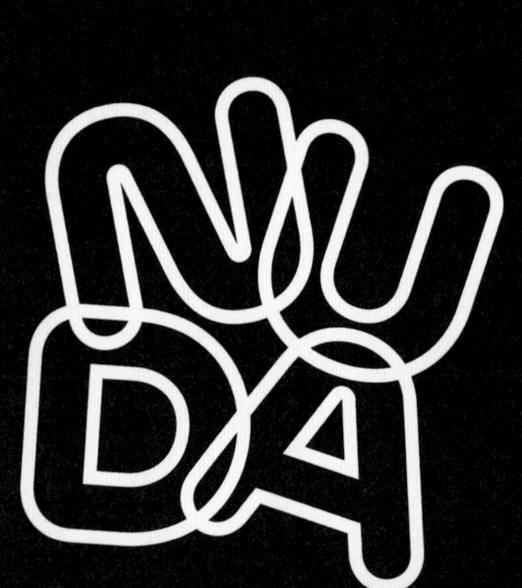

New! New! New!
Merlot
Svätovavrinecké
Frankovka Modrá
Rizling Vlašský

LOCAL WINES

Blaufränkisch Weinbe 98
Pichler-Krutzler Burgenland (A)

Latricieres-Chambertin Grand Cru 2010 236
Rossignol-Trapet Côte de Nuits-Burgundsko (F)

Haut Brion 2005 1.280
Chateau Haut Brion Bordeaux (F)

NEW WINES

Drink Bar
Bratislava
All-night

WINE & SNACK

ONLY TONIGHT

@nuda.bar

Tuesday – Saturday
16.00 – 22:00

Židovská 3
Bratislava

● Design Studio: NICE GUY ● Designer: Matej Špánik ● Client: NUDA Bar ● Photography: Jakub Čaprnka

NUDA Bar ● NUDA Bar transforms the Slovak term "nuda" (boredom) into a dynamic space for socializing with friends and savoring top-class wines. The curated wine selection, including global varieties, is complemented by a range of drinks and cocktails, paired with delightful finger foods. The visual identity, embodied in the logotype's playful and modular design, embraces an anti-boring ethos. Mature typography and a harmonious color palette, inspired by the interior materials, complete the cohesive brand experience.

● Why Blue? ● Blue was deliberately chosen as the primary color for its association with the night—deep and mysterious. This choice also facilitated a harmonious blend with the secondary colors representing materials used in the bar's construction. The photo direction centers on the theme of enjoying quality drinks, employing a blend of raw, sharp techniques and blurry, long exposure methods.

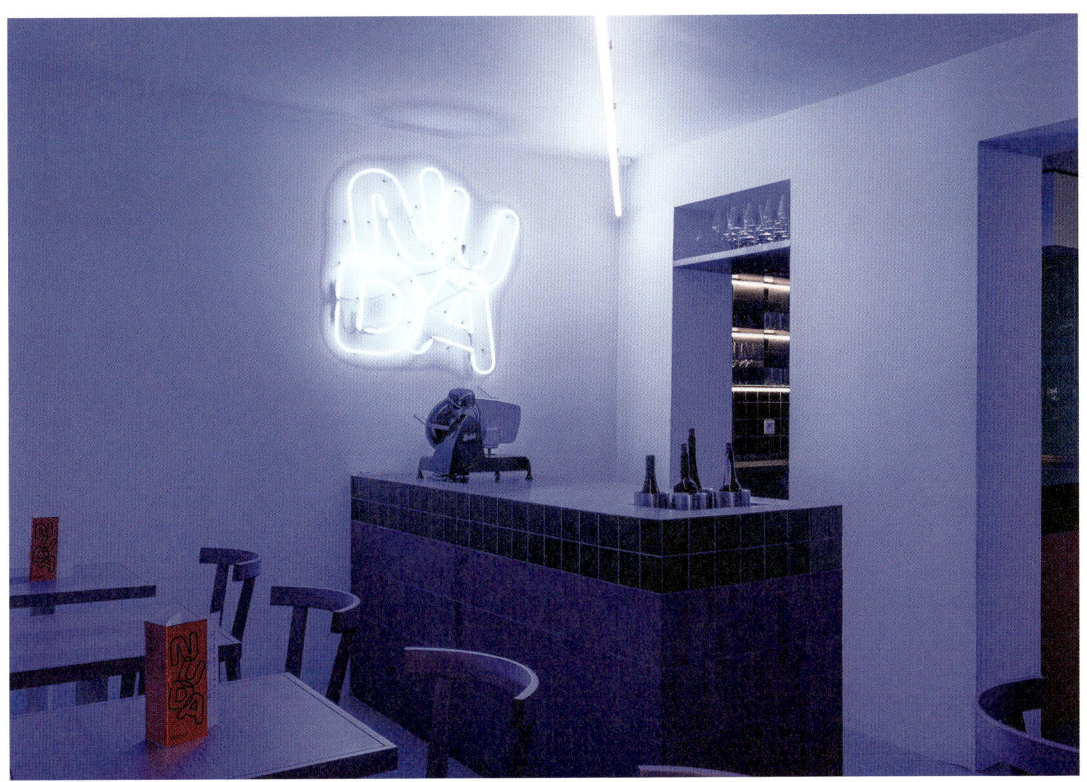

C100 M93 Y50 K73

12th Book Play—Weak Text

• "Weak text" draws from Japanese architect Sou Fujimoto's concept of "weak architecture," explored in *the Moment when Architecture was Born*. Here, "weak" signifies a purposeful reduction in building functionality, enhancing the user-space interaction. This deliberate weakening empowers individuals to freely define and redefine spatial configurations through unrestricted movement. Architects transition from dictating movement lines to fostering meaningful relationships between people and their surroundings.

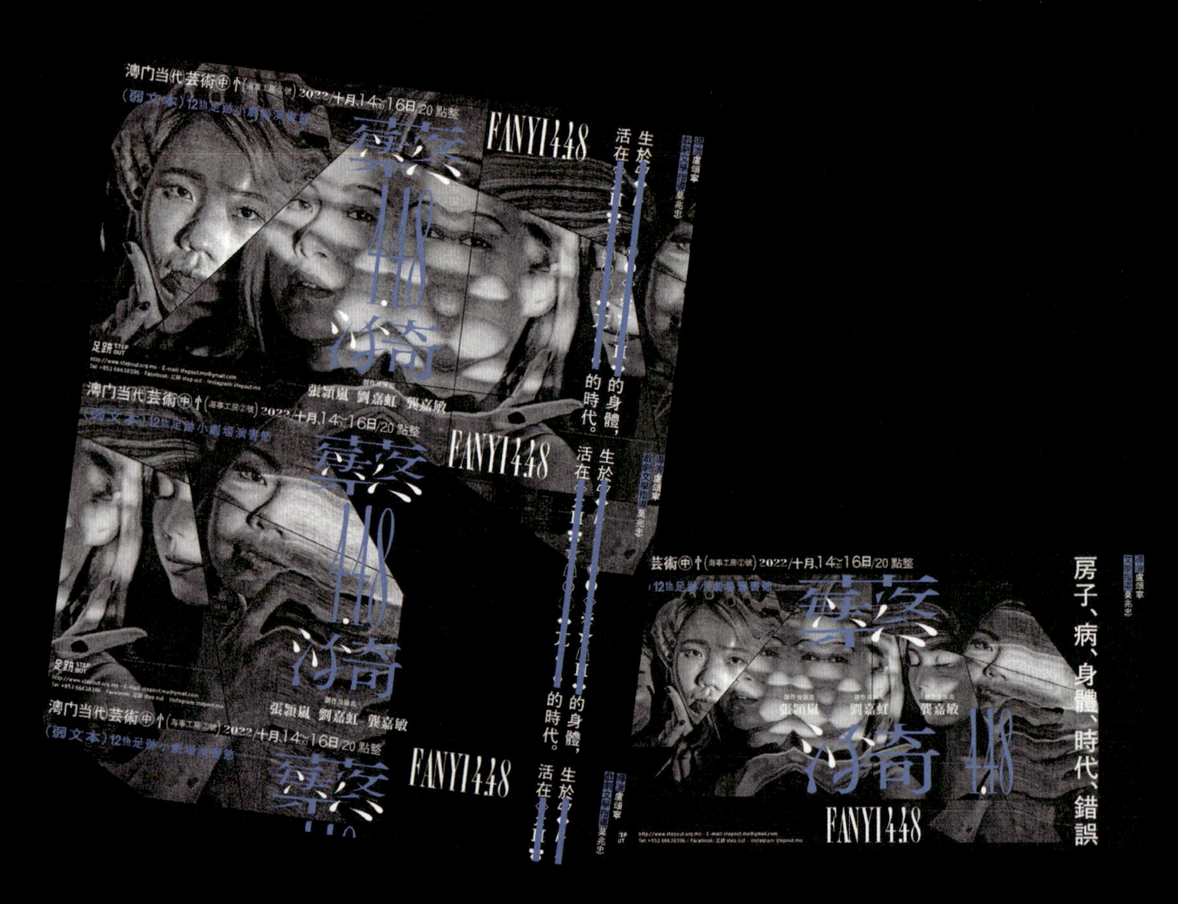

• Design Studio: SomethingMoon Design • Designer: Chiwai Cheang • Client: Step Out

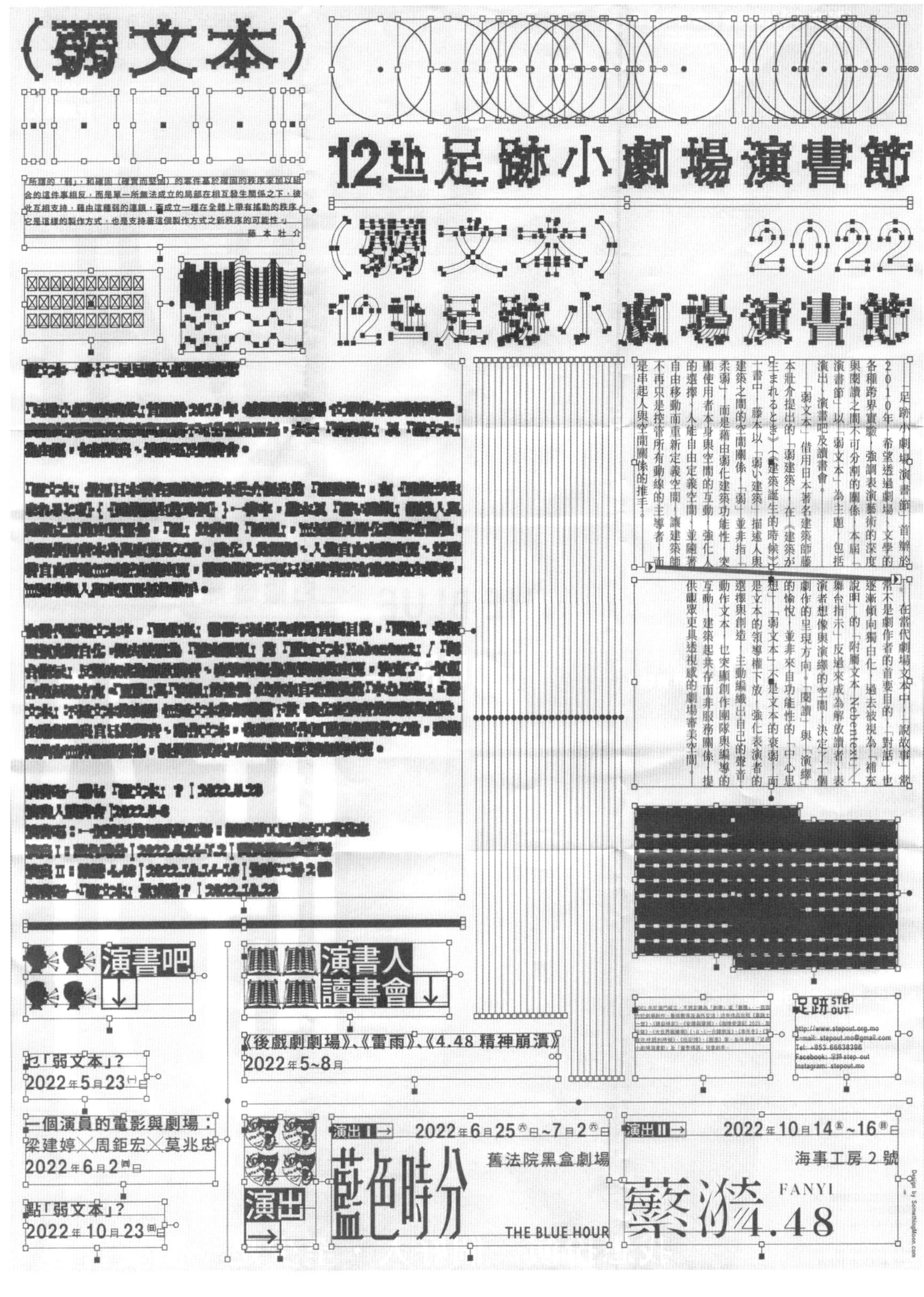
（弱文本）
12th足跡小劇場演書節
所謂的「弱」，和確固（確實而堅固）的零件基於確固的秩序來加以組合的這件事相反，而是單一所無法成立的局部在相互發生關係之下，彼此互相支持，藉由這種弱的連鎖，而成立一種在全體上帶有搖動的秩序，它是這樣的製作方式，也是支持著這個製作方式之新秩序的可能性。
藤本壯介
（弱文本）2022
12th足跡小劇場演書節
「足跡小劇場演書節」首辦於2010年，希望透過劇場、文學的各種跨界實驗，強調表演藝術的深度與閱讀之間不可分割的關係。本屆「演書節」以「弱文本」為主題，包括演出、演書吧及讀書會。
「弱文本」借用日本著名建築師藤本壯介提出的「弱建築」，在《建築が生まれるとき》（《建築誕生的時候》）一書中，藤本以「弱い建築」描述人與建築之間的空間關係。「弱」並非指柔弱，而是藉由弱化建築功能性，突顯使用者本身與空間的互動，強化人的選擇，人能自由定義空間，並隨著自由移動而重新定義空間，讓建築師不再只是控管所有動線的主導者，而是串起人與空間關係的推手。
在當代劇場文本中，「說故事」常常不是劇作者的首要目的，「對話」也逐漸傾向獨白化，過去被視為「補充說明」的「附屬文本 Nebentext」／「舞台指示」反過來成為解放讀者、表演者想像與演繹的空間，決定了一個劇作的呈現方向。「閱讀」與「演繹」的愉悅，並非來自功能性的「中心思想」，「弱文本」不是文本的衰弱，而是文本的領導權下放，強化表演者的選擇與創造，主動編織出自己的聲音、動作文本，也突顯創作團隊與編導的互動，建築起共存而非服務關係，提供觀眾更具透視感的劇場審美空間。
演書吧
演書人讀書會
《後戲劇劇場》、《雷雨》、《4.48 精神崩潰》
2022年5~8月
「弱文本」？
2022年5月23(一)日
一個演員的電影與劇場：梁建婷╳周鉅宏╳莫兆忠
2022年6月2(四)日
點「弱文本」？
2022年10月23(日)日
足跡 STEP OUT
http://www.stepout.org.mo
E-mail: stepout.mo@gmail.com
Tel: +853 66638398
Facebook: 足跡 step out
Instagram: stepout.mo
演出 I →
2022年6月25(六)日~7月2(六)日
舊法院黑盒劇場
藍色時分
THE BLUE HOUR
演出 II →
2022年10月14(五)~16(日)日
海事工房 2 號
FANYI 4.48
Design by SomethingMoon.com

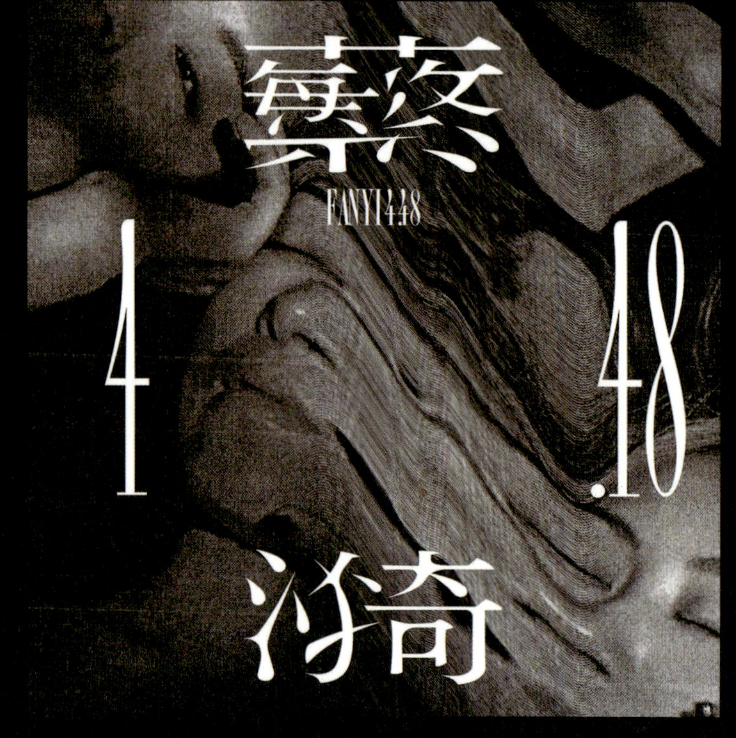
FANYI448

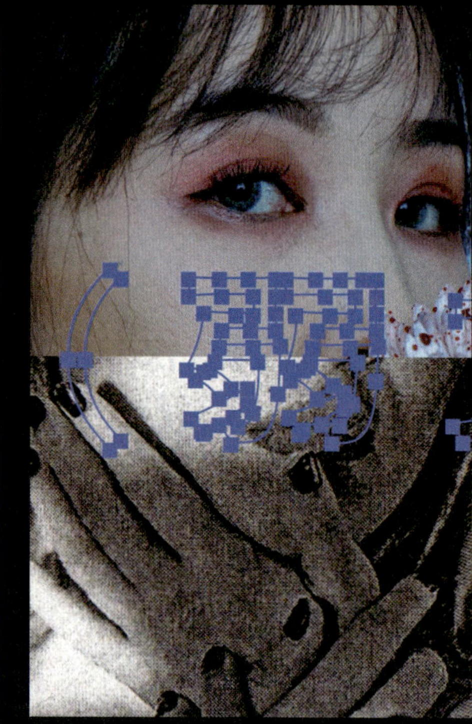

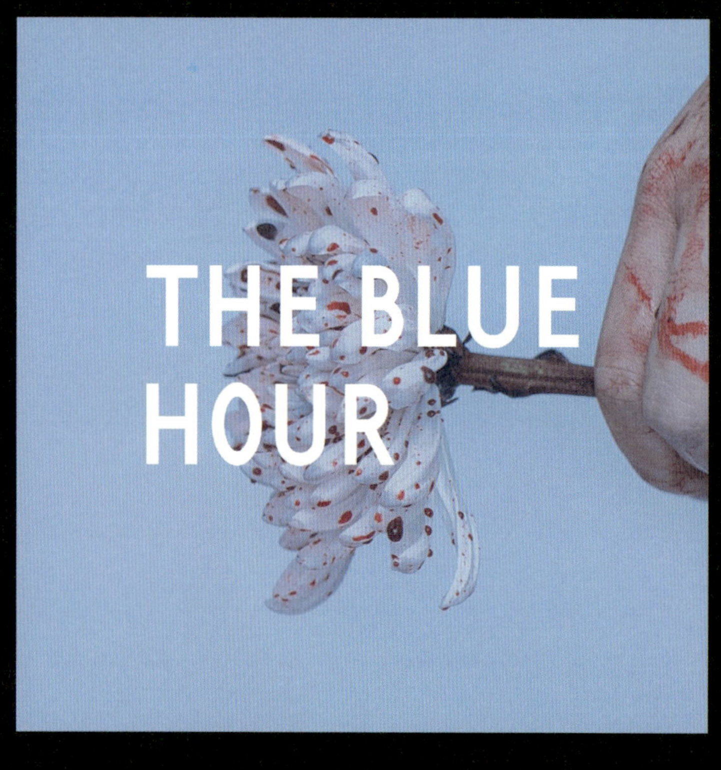
THE BLUE
HOUR

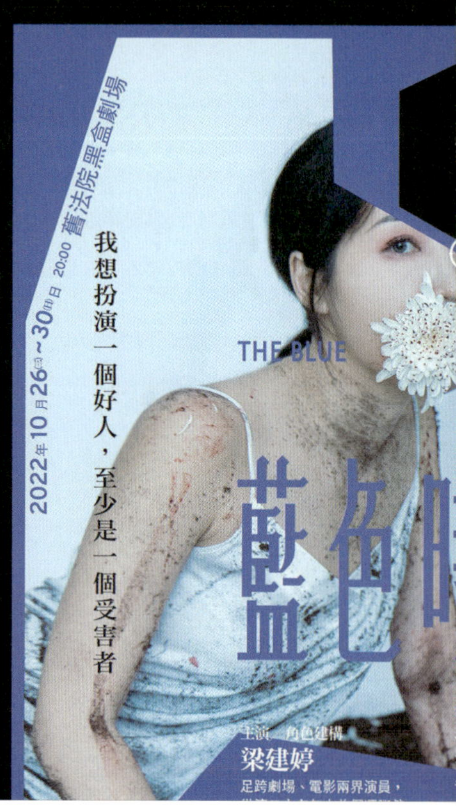
舊法院黑盒劇場
2022年10月26~30日 20:00
我想扮演一個好人，至少是一個受害者
THE BLUE
藍色
主演 角色建構
梁建婷
足跨劇場、電影兩界演員，

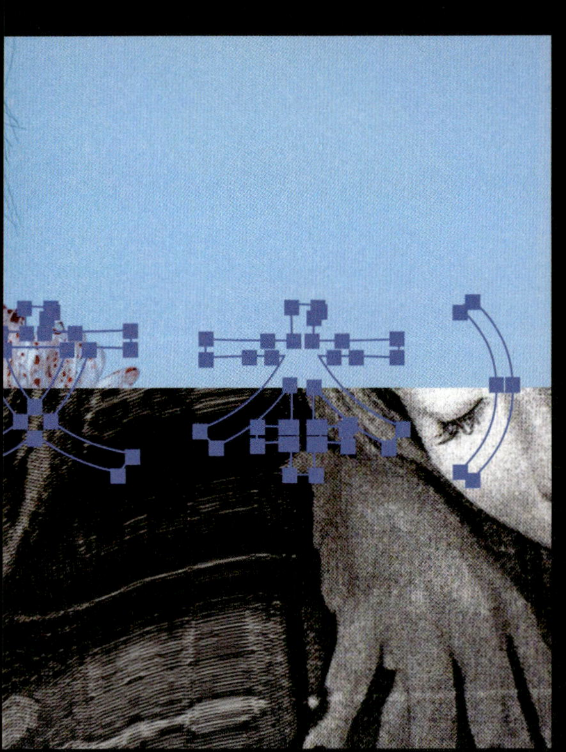

● Why Blue? ● The designer regarded design as a way to understand the myriad aspects of the world. This time, the focus is not on the design itself but on the design process. The designer's process was the entirety; therefore, there was no excess language or unexpressed thoughts. Using the blue color commonly found on the designer's computer as the main theme, the designer visualized the creative process.

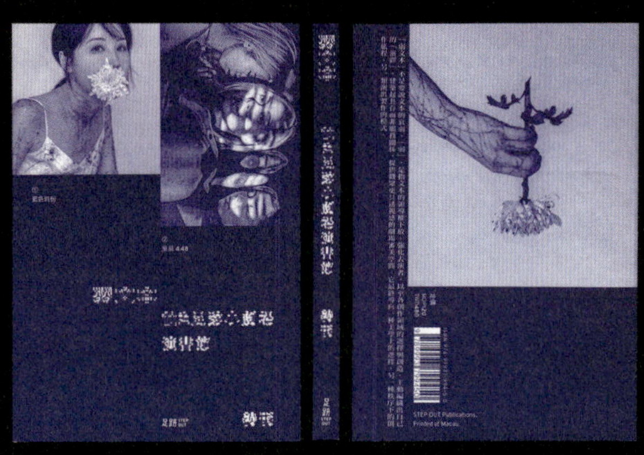

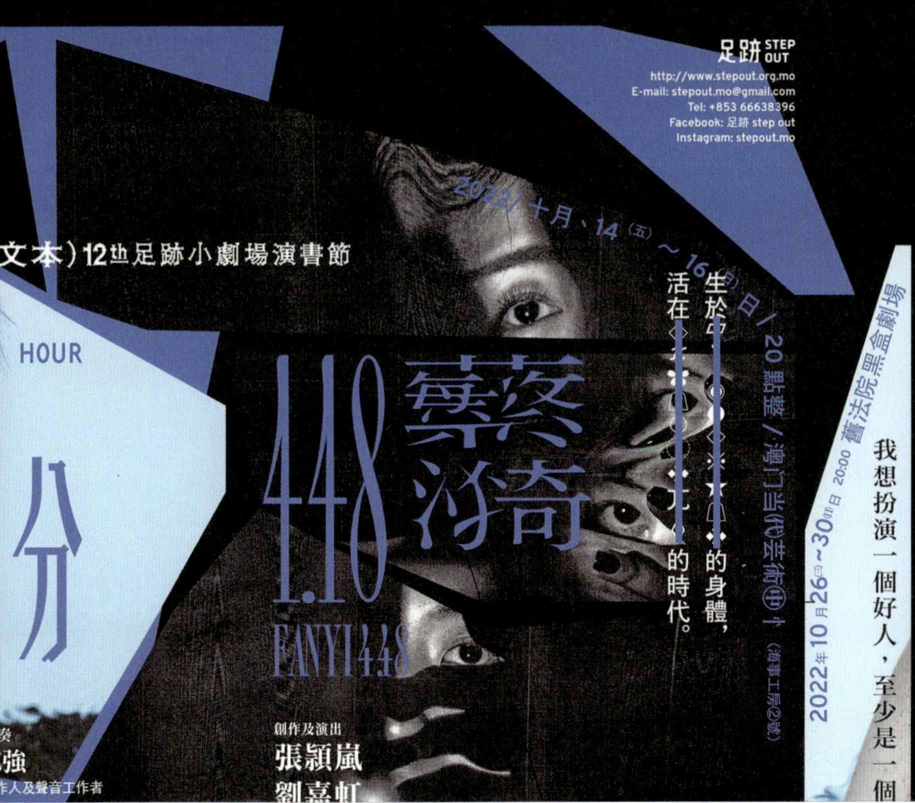

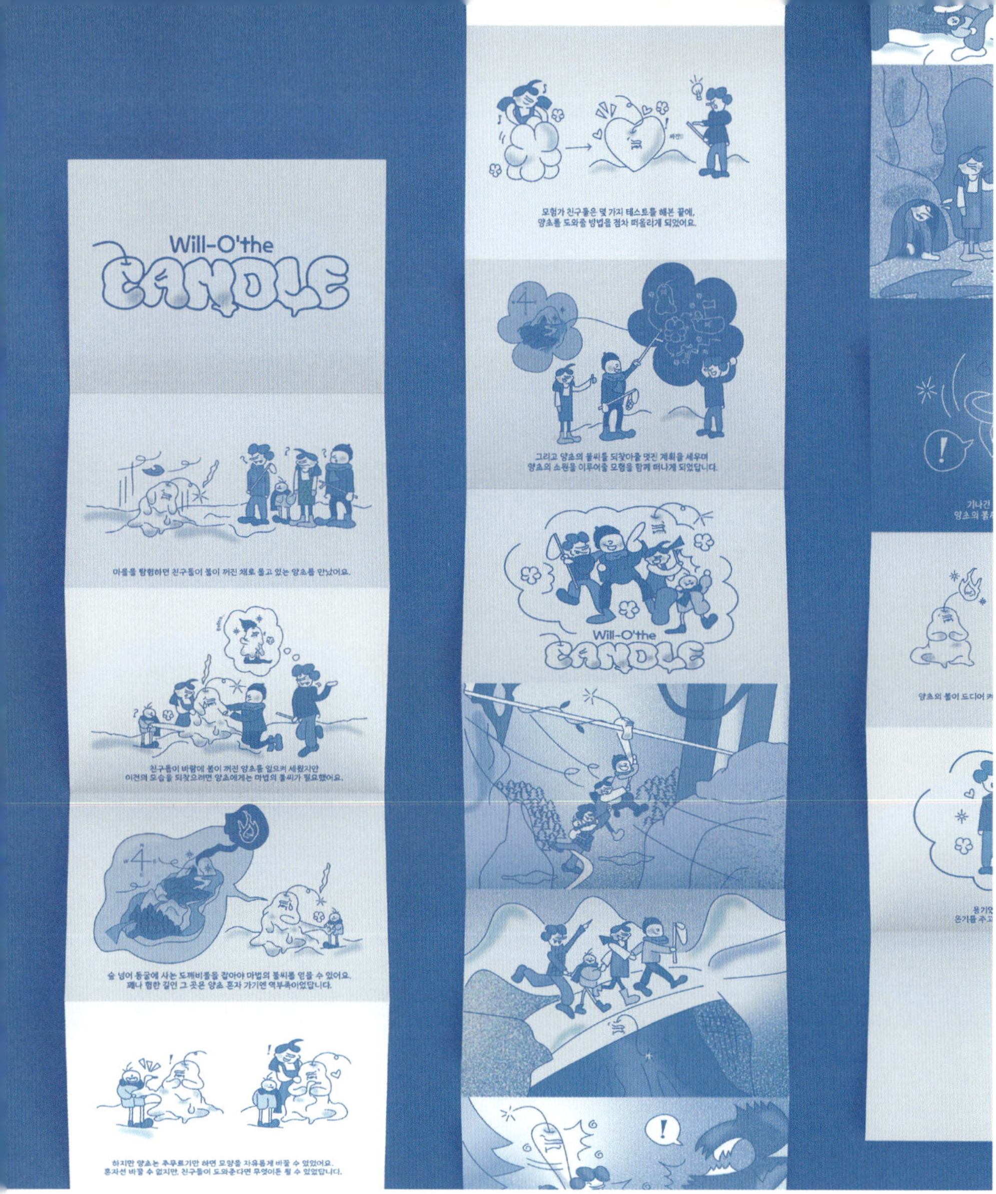

Will-O'the-CANDLE

● Will-O'the-CANDLE, an innovative candle brand, harnesses the inherent ability of candles to change shapes at will. The narratives unfold through charming tales of warm candle fairies and helpful children. This project personifies candle features, emphasizing their unique capacity to transform with minimal heat, resembling wise and aged fairies. The special bond between individuals and candles is portrayed as a delightful fantasy, weaving personalized stories. Will-O'the-CANDLE aims to bring warmth and daily fantasy to make every day special for someone, acting as a tiny fairy wishing fortune upon all.

● Designer: Sooun Cho

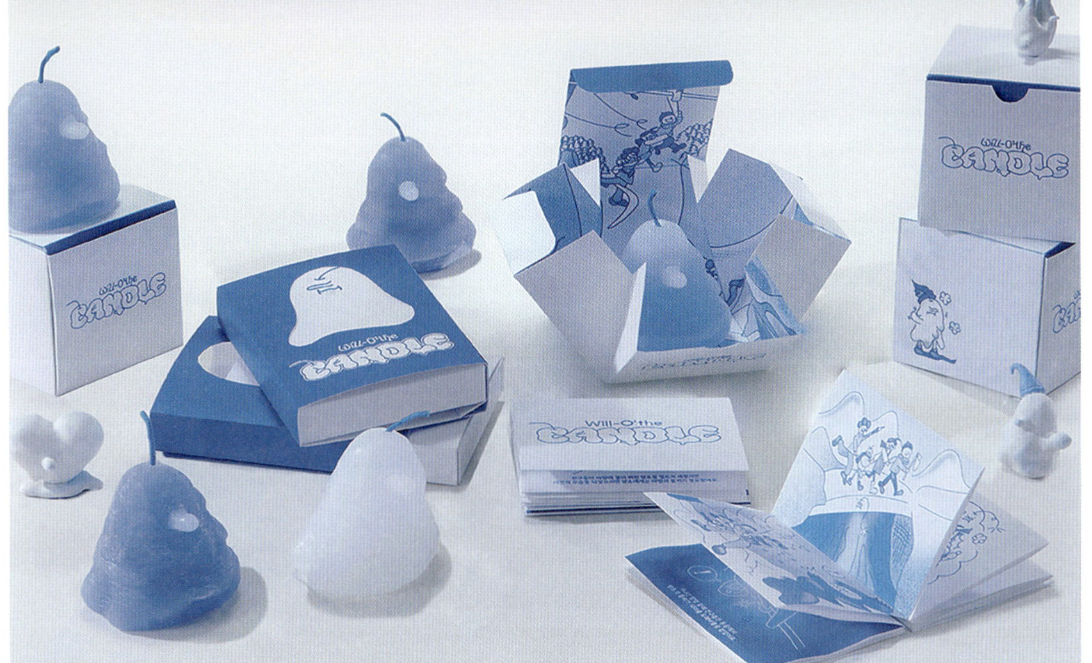

● Why Blue? ● In the realm of candle-related products, blue is not commonly associated. However, in the context of Will-O'the-CANDLE, which is rooted in fantasy, a departure from the ordinary was necessary. Despite the cool and unconventional color choice, blue serves to highlight the warmth of the characters. Much like real candles that provide comfort in chilly surroundings, Will-O'the-CANDLE aspires to function as a subtle yet impactful mood enhancer for individuals grappling with challenges in their everyday lives.

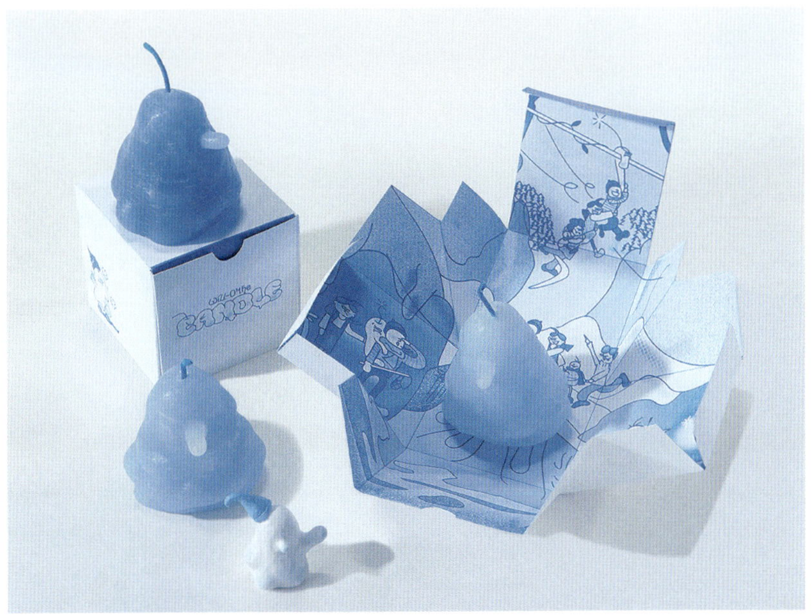

Totally Blue • *Totally Blue* is a 9-track EP by 9 and the Numbers. The concept of matching colors to each song's atmosphere started in 2017, preceding their last album, taking four years to be fully realized. In the pandemic, their envisioned vibrant colors were distilled into a singular hue—"blue." • Despite questioning the appropriateness of singing about feeling "blue" in a depressive era, the band believes confronting depression is the first step to overcoming it. The EP unfolds as a narrative of depression, seeking hope in despair. • The "blue" in the EP resembles "black," inspired by a Family Tree visual. Blue and black elements symbolize an unyielding wave or barrier challenges faced but actively confronted, integrated into the LP, CD, and poster design. • Intentionally challenging fonts in inserts align with the "9 and the Numbers" concept, emphasizing diligent pursuit of hope in seemingly hopeless circumstances.

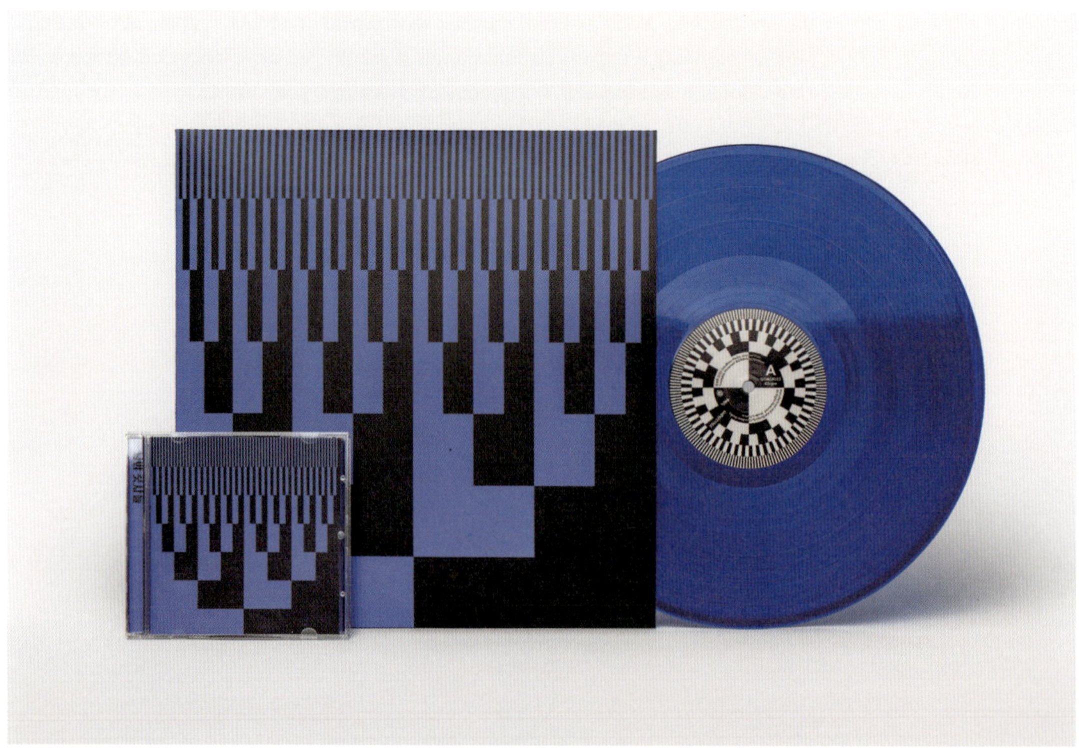

• Designer: Jaemin Lee • Client: ORM Entertainment and Tunetable Movement

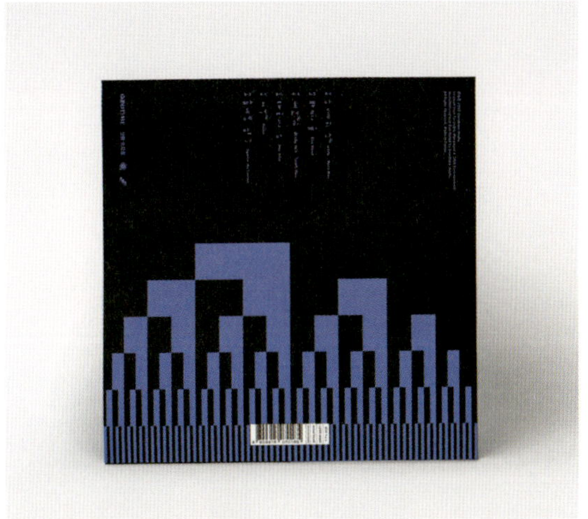

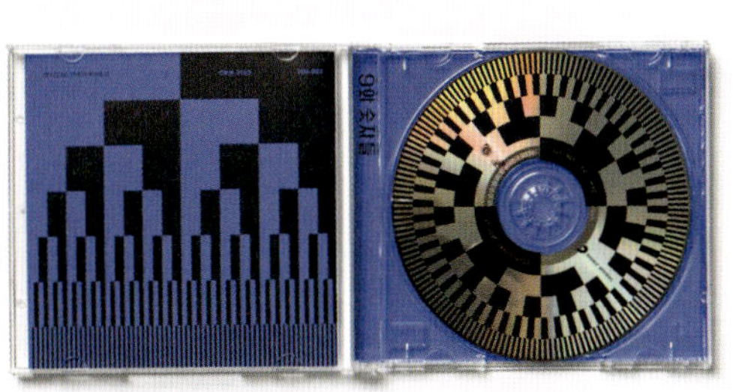

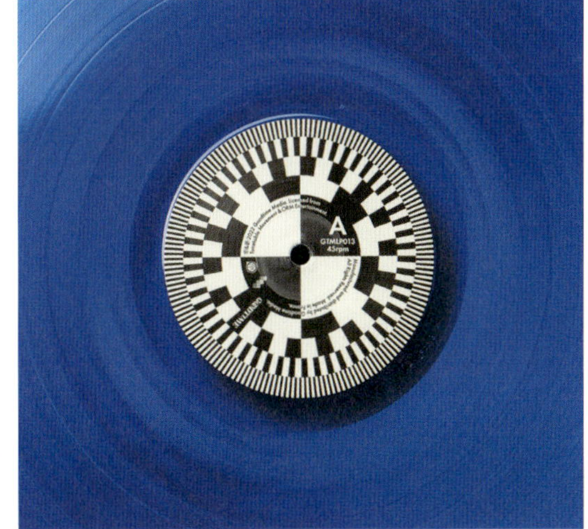

● Why Blue? ● From the album's title to the concept behind it, there was no reason to consider any color other than blue.

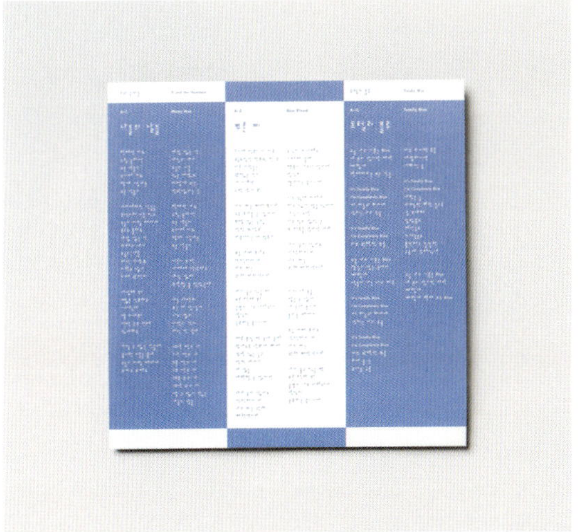

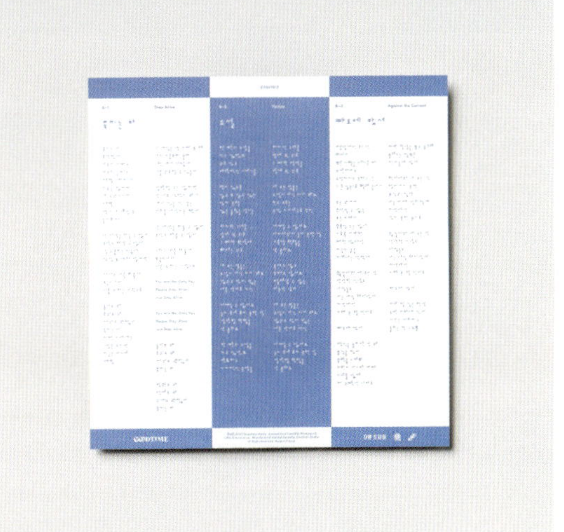

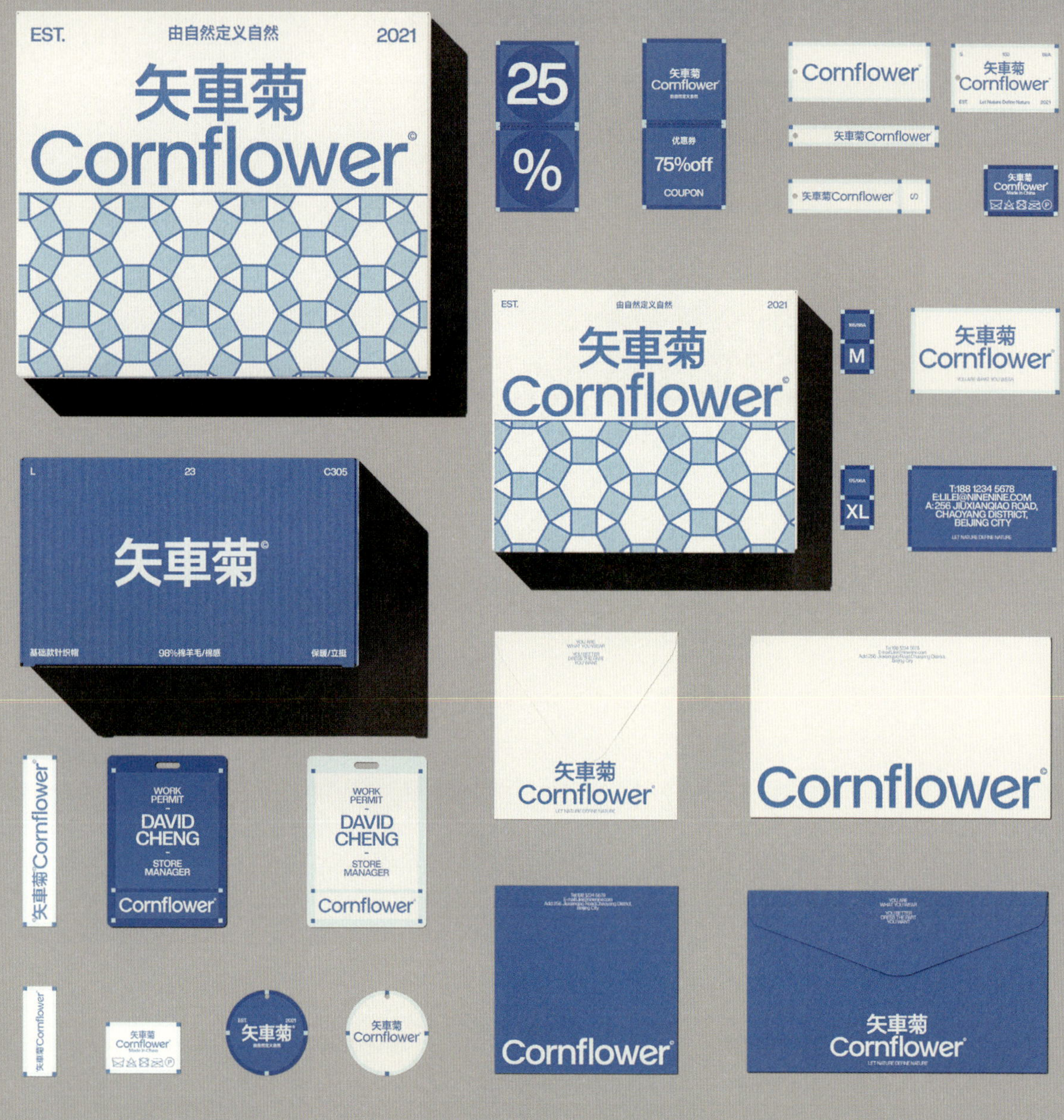

Cornflower • Cornflower embodies nature and balance, infusing natural materials for comfort and freedom. Advocating "comfort without gender," the brand boasts a clean, neutral visual identity. "Conflower" is not only a kind of wild flower but also a kind of sapphire, which balances the different qualities of rigidity and femininity. Through standardized logos and graphics, "cornflower" creates a unique brand identity, emphasizing the philosophy of comfort and freedom.

● Design Studio: TWOPTWO Design ● Designer: Xu Ye, Yann ● Client: Cornflower

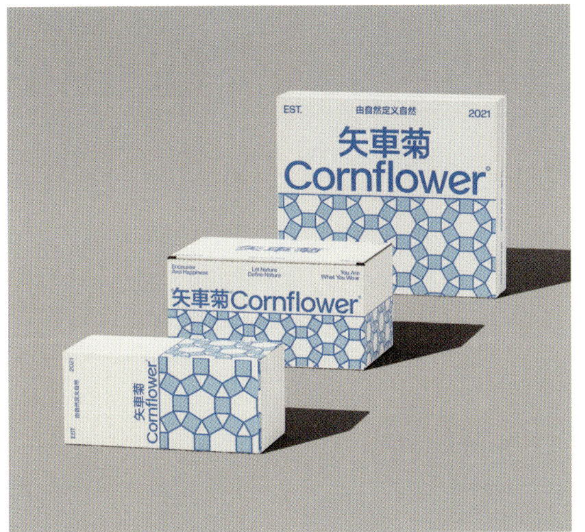

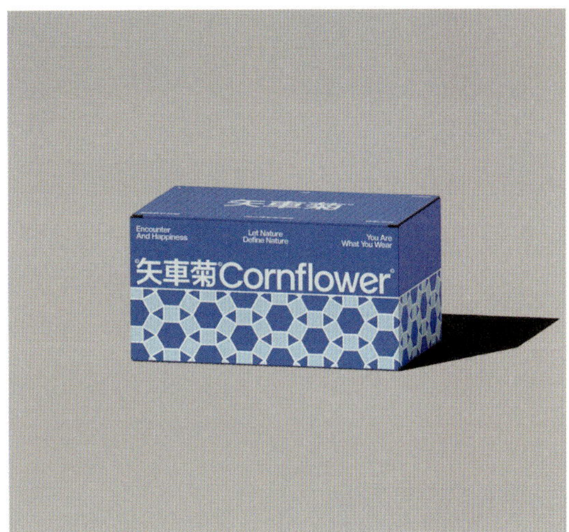

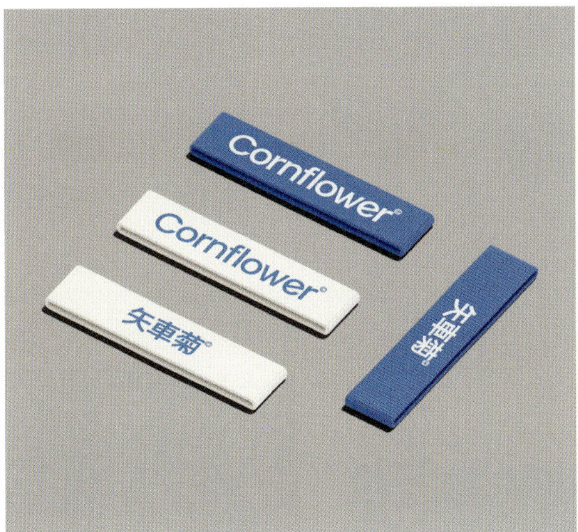

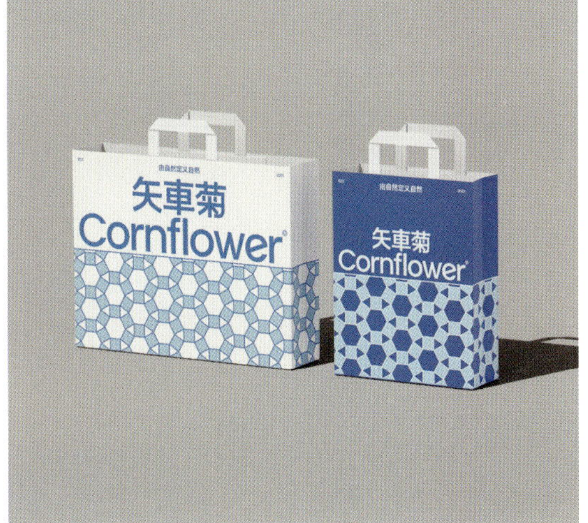

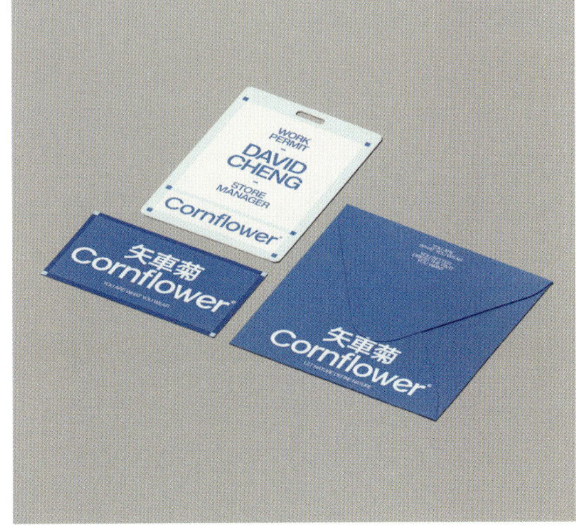

● Why Blue? ● Cornflower, named after both a wildflower and a type of sapphire, is expressed through the color blue. This choice aligns with the brand's philosophy, as blue represents a quiet and relaxing color, offering a comfortable balance between rigidity and softness. The aim is to communicate the brand's concept of comfort and freedom to the audience.

C85 M56 Y0 K0 | C80 M46 Y0 K0 | C45 M0 Y7 K0

Blue Matching

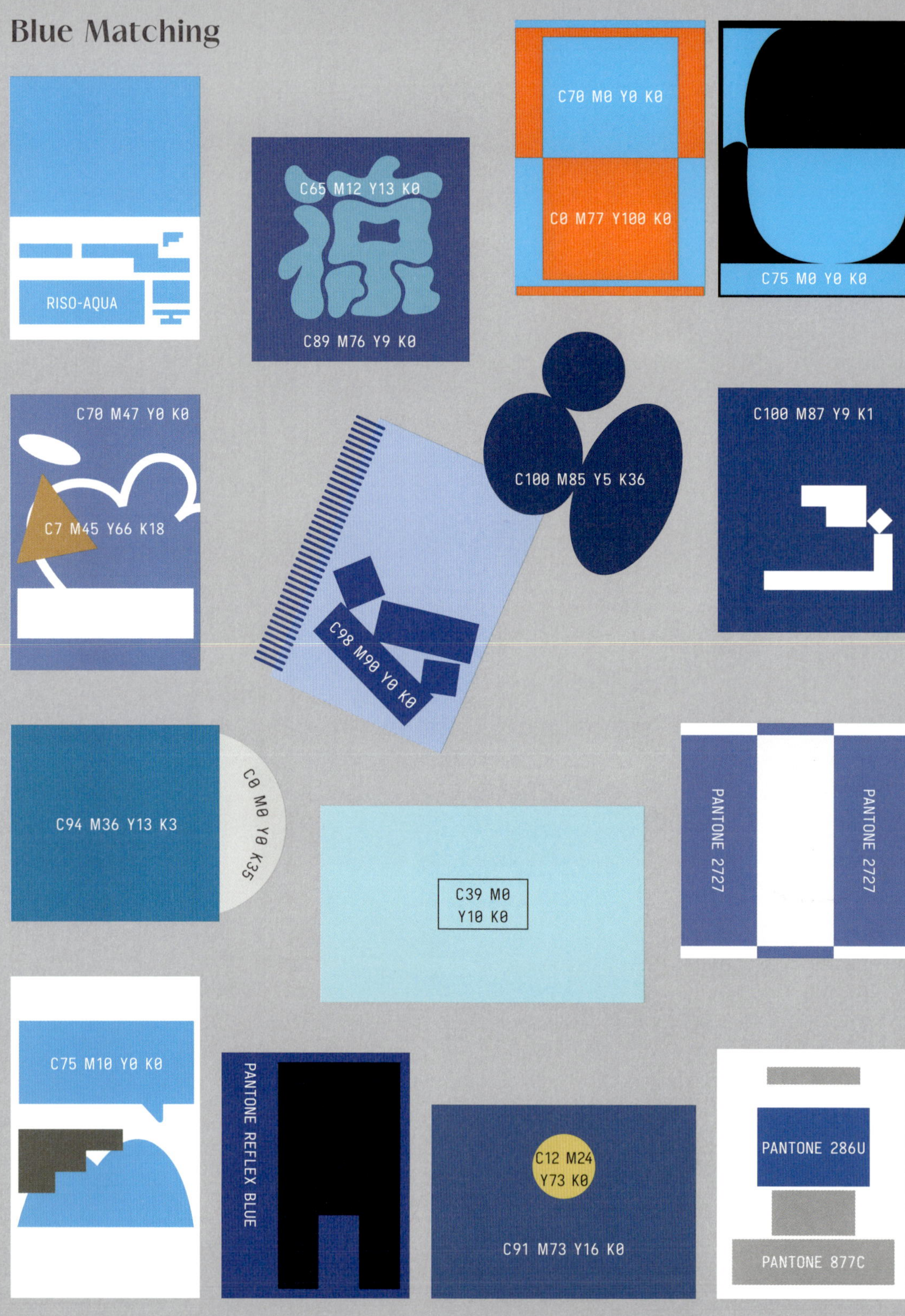

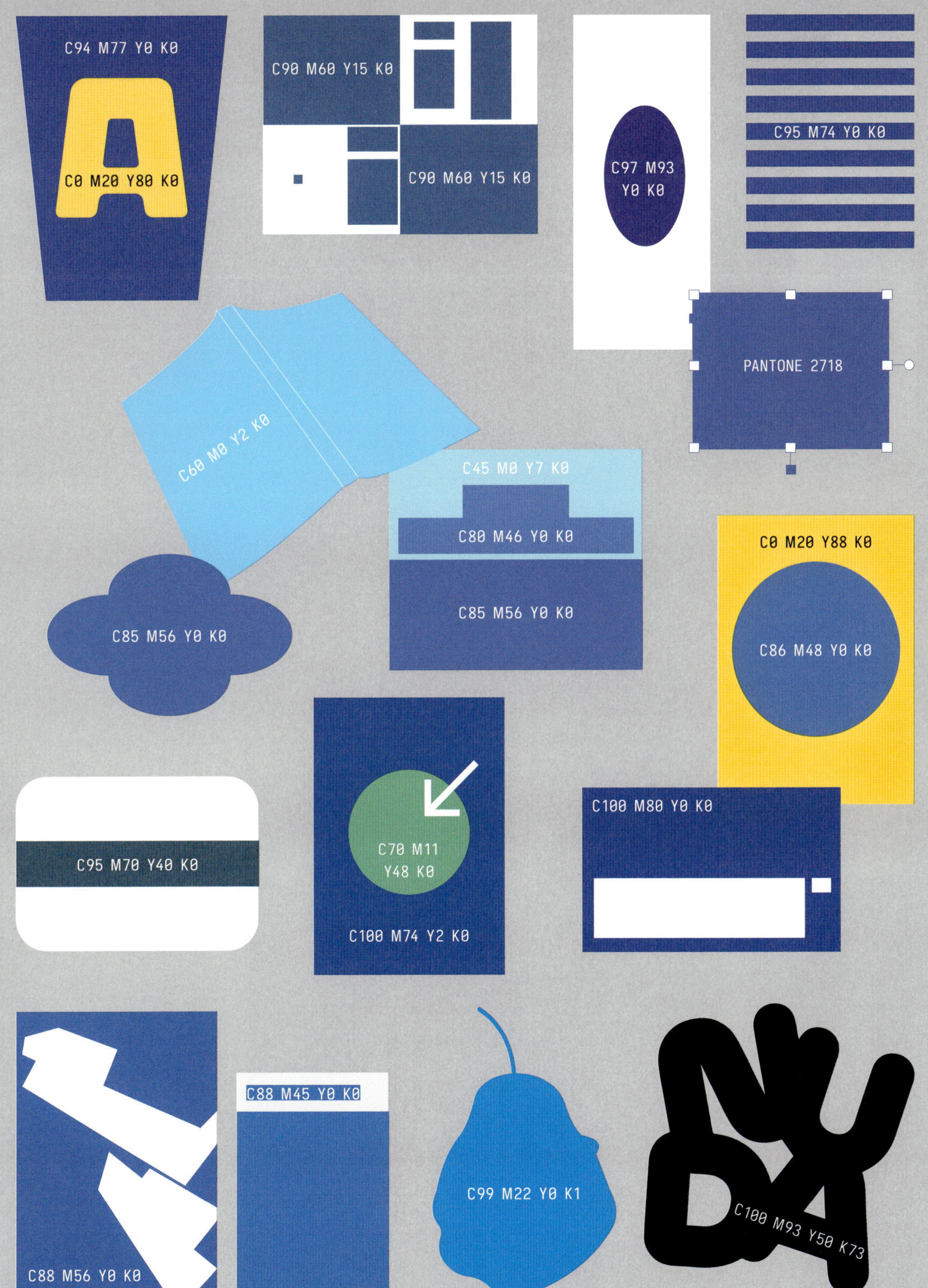

C94 M77 Y0 K0
C0 M20 Y80 K0
C90 M60 Y15 K0
C90 M60 Y15 K0
C97 M93
Y0 K0
C95 M74 Y0 K0
PANTONE 2718
C60 M0 Y2 K0
C45 M0 Y7 K0
C80 M46 Y0 K0
C85 M56 Y0 K0
C0 M20 Y88 K0
C86 M48 Y0 K0
C85 M56 Y0 K0
C95 M70 Y40 K0
C70 M11
Y48 K0
C100 M74 Y2 K0
C100 M80 Y0 K0
C88 M45 Y0 K0
C88 M56 Y0 K0
C99 M22 Y0 K1
C100 M93 Y50 K73

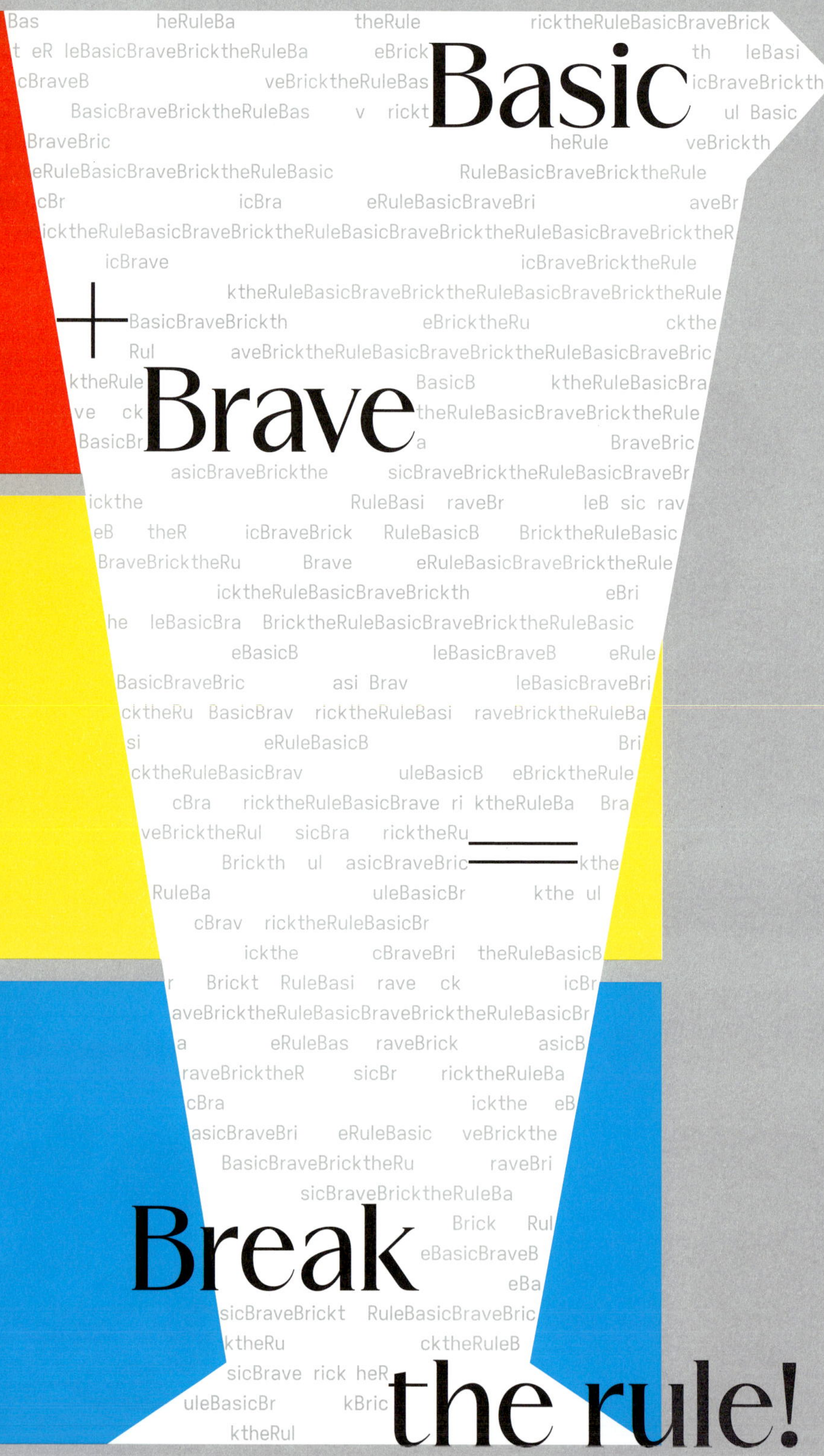

Basic
+
Brave
=
Break
the rule!

Red, yellow, and blue—break the rules!

● Since the previous notion that the three primaries are the starting point for all other colors is incorrect, a new definition is called upon. In this age of unrestricted color exploration, we have witnessed many unseen forms of visual design and artistic expression. The new definition of color breaks traditional constraints, encouraging artists to experiment boldly and push the limits of color possibilities in their creations. In the past, the three primary colors (red, yellow, and blue) were seen as the basis for creating all other colors. However, modern color theories tell us that the nature of color is not so simple. Colors are composed of different wavelengths of light, and these waves can be mixed to form new colors. As a result, we now use more accurate color models, such as RGB and CMYK, to describe and render colors.

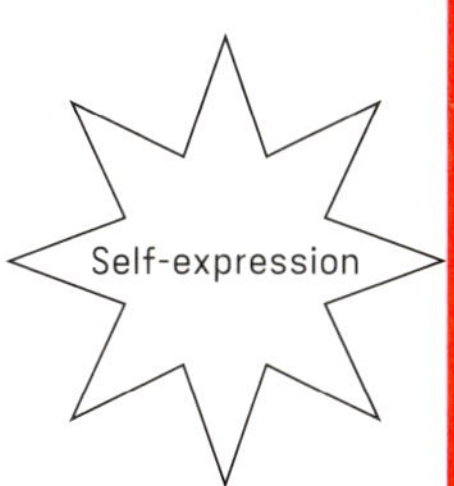

● The traditional understanding of color has changed under the impact of the eclectic style of contemporary art. In the new definition, color is seen as an element that can break all rules, allowing artistic creation to achieve freedom in color. Color today is not merely a medium for visual experience; it has evolved into a major element in marketing, branding, and the creation of illusion and imagination. With the efforts of creators such as fashion brand creators, interior designers, graphic designers, and artists, the ultimate exploration of the most pleasing color combinations is carried out. These creators actively push the boundaries of art to lead trends in color and shape. In both business and creative fields, successful brands intelligently choose specific colors that align with their brand values and personalities to create an emotional connection with customers and deepen their brand awareness. The application of different color combinations widely creates different emotional experiences to meet the preferences and needs of different consumers. ● In addition to its applications in creative fields, color also plays an important role in therapy and psychology. Color therapy, as an emotional therapy that uses color to affect people's emotions and mental states, is widely used to relieve stress, improve mood, and restore balance. This is a testament to the healing power of color and its significant value in promoting human health and wellbeing. In modern times, our understanding of color has surpassed the simple concept of the three primary colors. There is no denying that color is very important to us. An in-depth understanding of color theory helps us comprehend major artistic developments and works from both the past and present. In the massive contemporary art practice, "color" is regarded as an esoteric art that is separately explored and applied to planes, spaces, and visual practices, while also helping to expand our understanding of traditional color theories.

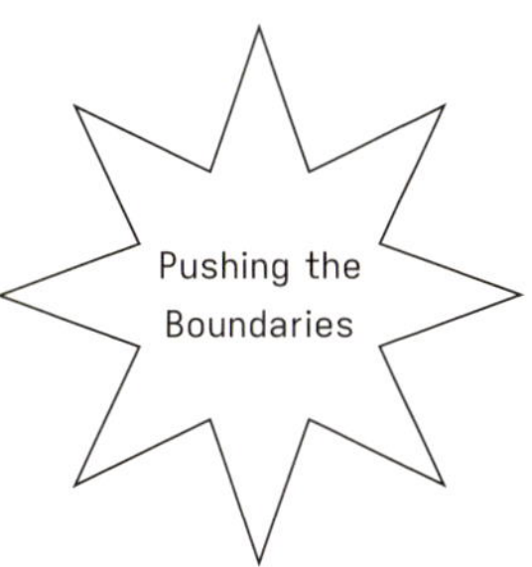

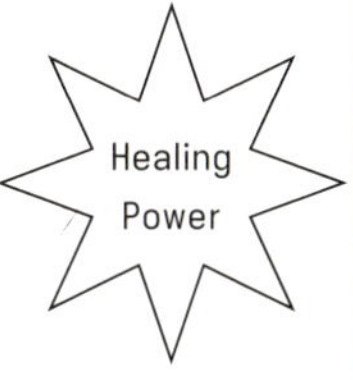

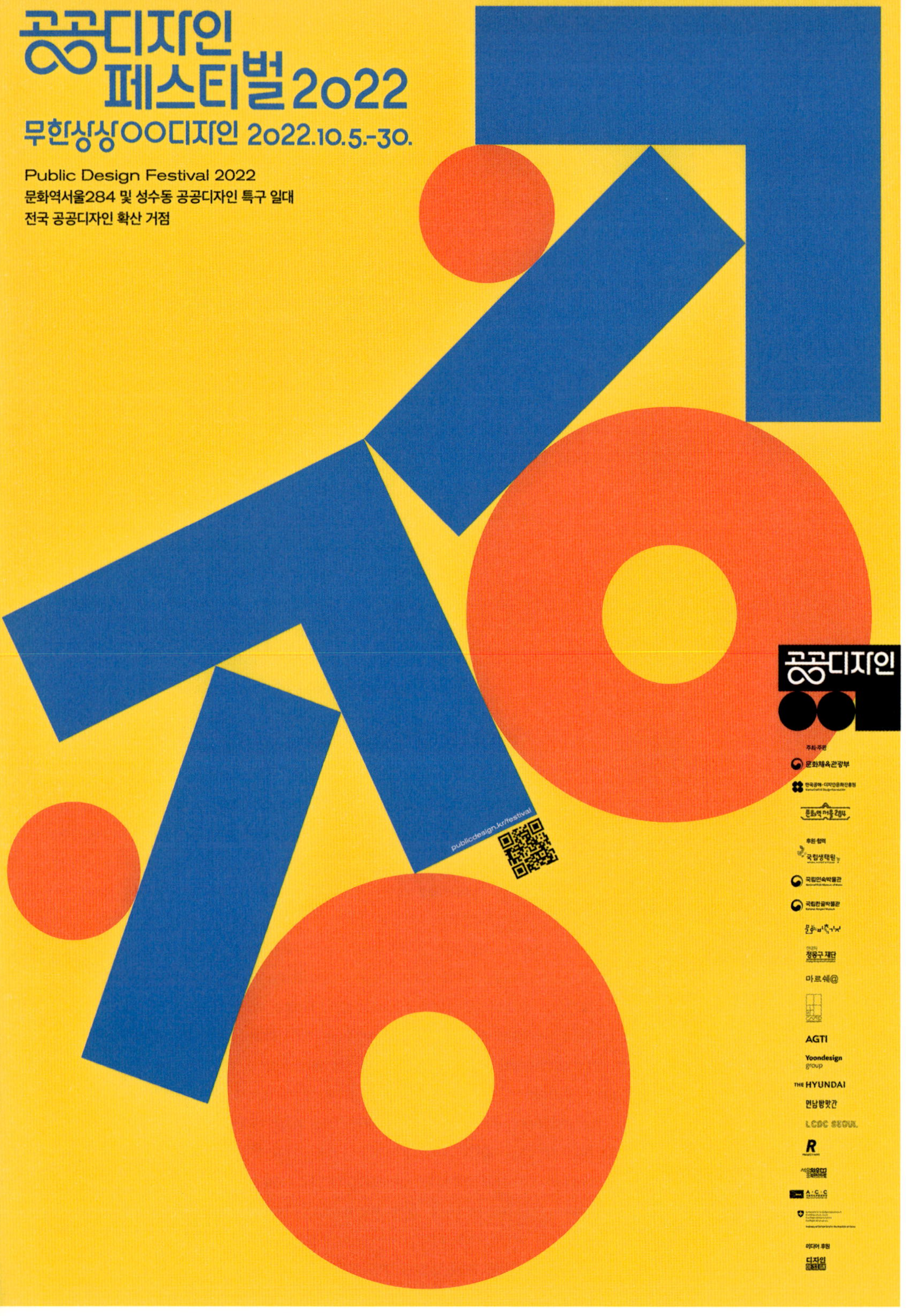

Design Studio: Studio fnt

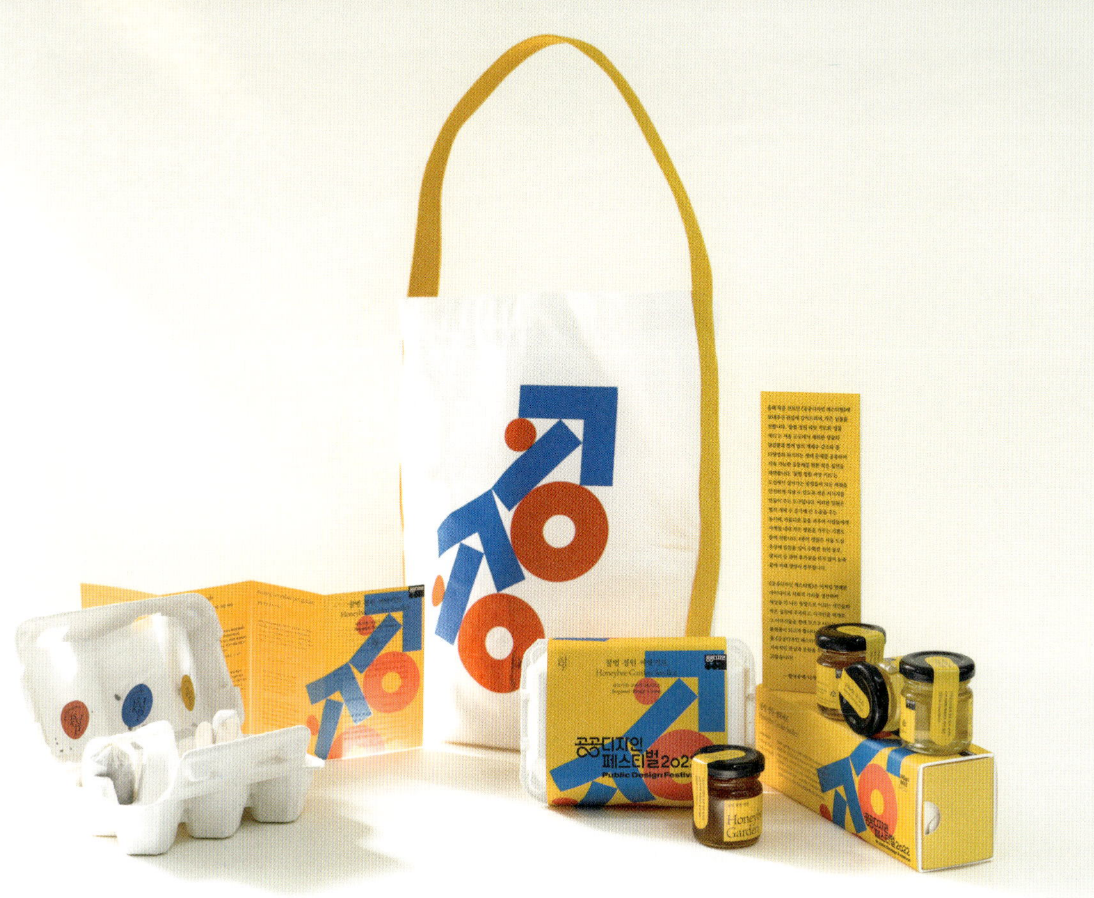

Public Design Festival 2022 ● KCDF's (Korea Craft & Design Foundation) longstanding "Public Design" project evolved into a festival format in 2022, extending its reach to wider audiences. The new visual identity, applied across national platforms during the month-long festival, reflects the values of public design, embracing both aesthetic and societal considerations. The design employs clear shapes and universally recognizable colors, including blue, yellow, and red, symbolizing safety, happiness, and public abundance. Through motion design, these shapes depict a dynamic journey towards a better life, echoing the festival's goal to positively impact citizens.

● Why RYB? ● In expanding the color palette beyond the existing blue color, which serves as the primary color in KCDF's Public Design brand, two additional colors, yellow and red, were selected. These contrasting colors, characterized by high visibility, collectively represent the idea that public design forms a solid foundation for safety and happiness. The blue arrows symbolize the willpower to make life more prosperous, while the yellow and red circles signify public abundance and security.

PANTONE WARM REDC PANTONE 109C PANTONE 285C

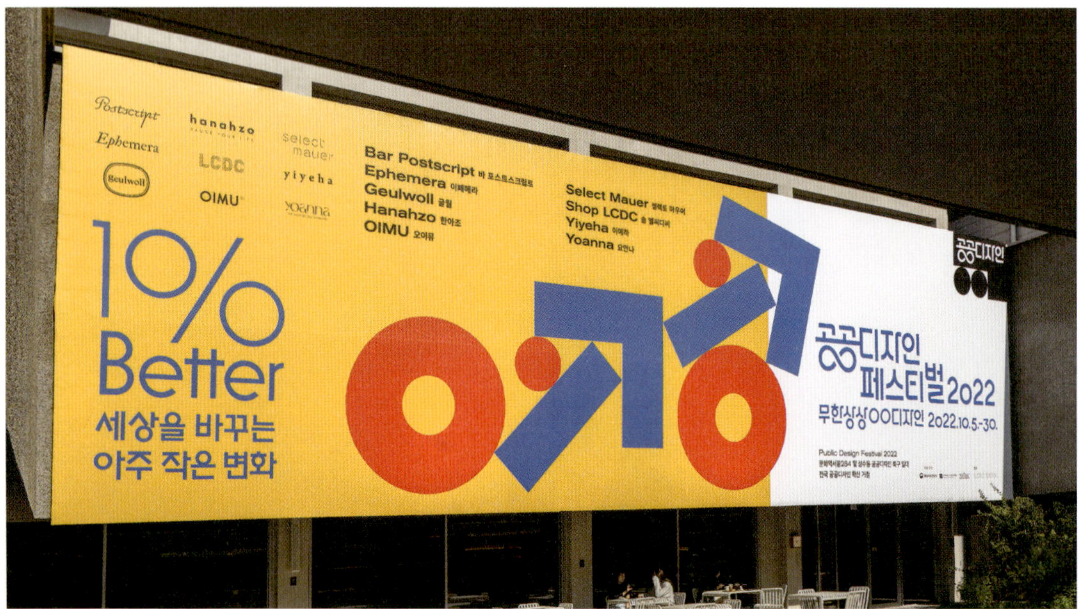

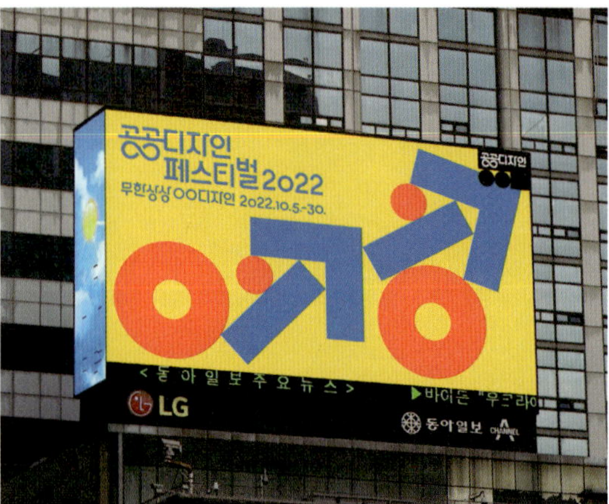

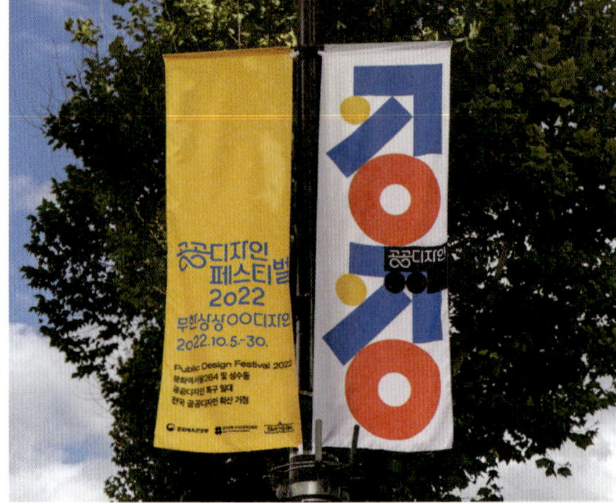

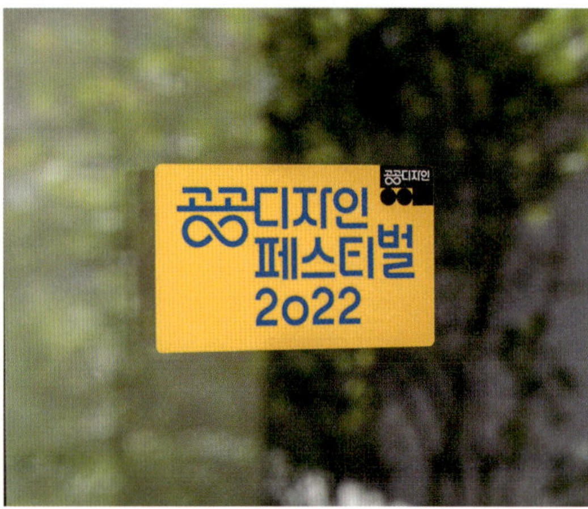

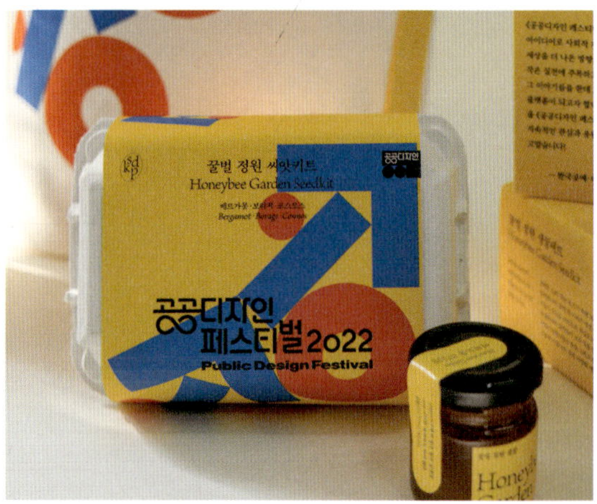

● Designer: Jaemin Lee, Heesun Kim, Woogyung Geel, Ajeong Kim, Younghyun Song, Youjeong Lee, Jieun Kang

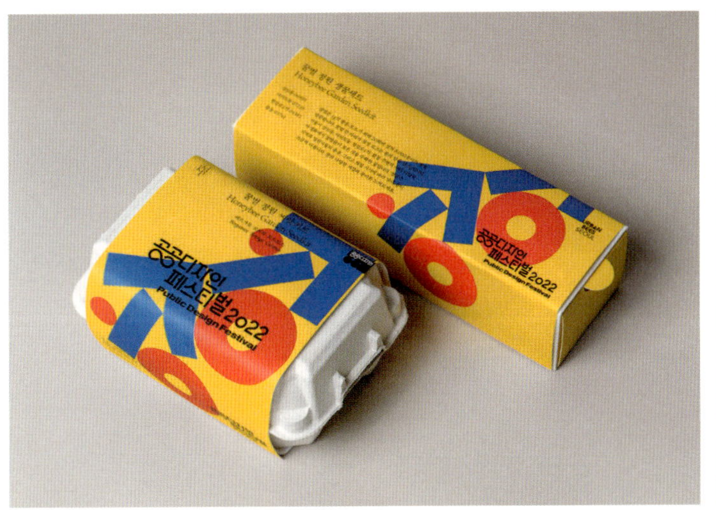
공공디자인
페스티벌2022
Public Design Festival

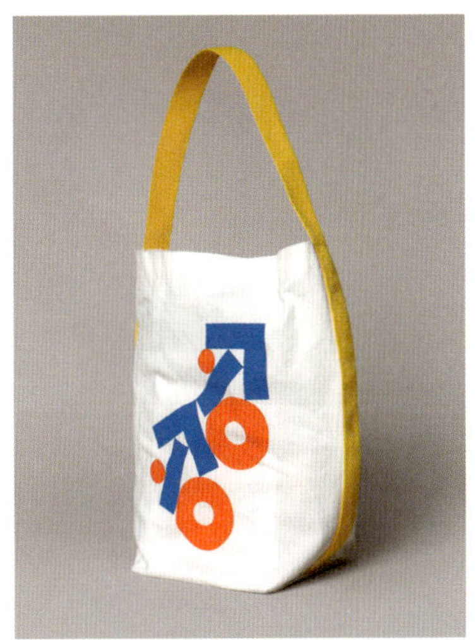

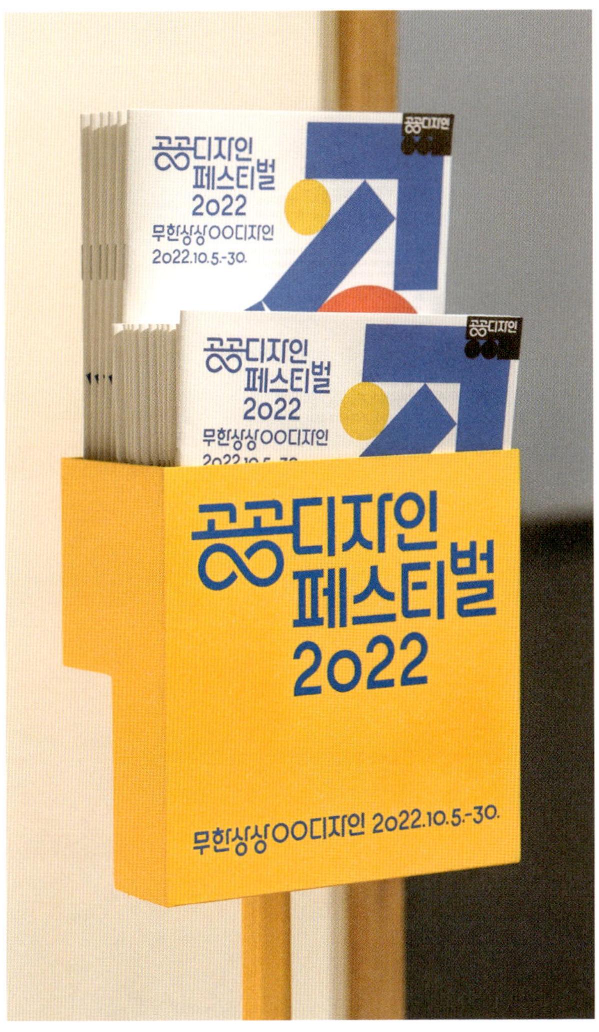
공공디자인
페스티벌
2022
무한상상OO디자인
2022.10.5.-30.
공공디자인
페스티벌
2022
무한상상OO디자인 2022.10.5.-30.

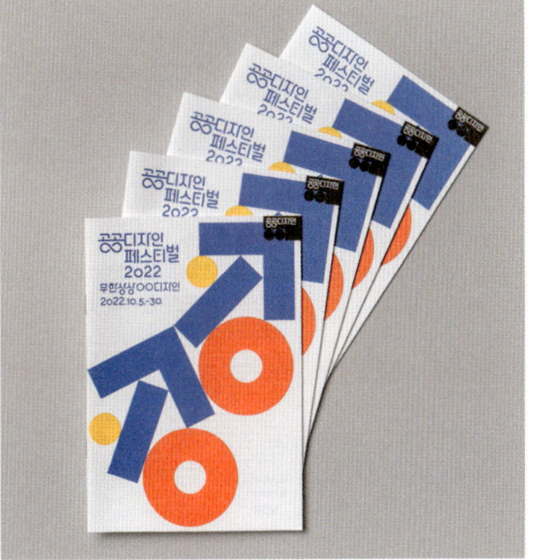
공공디자인
페스티벌
2022
무한상상OO디자인
2022.10.5.-30.

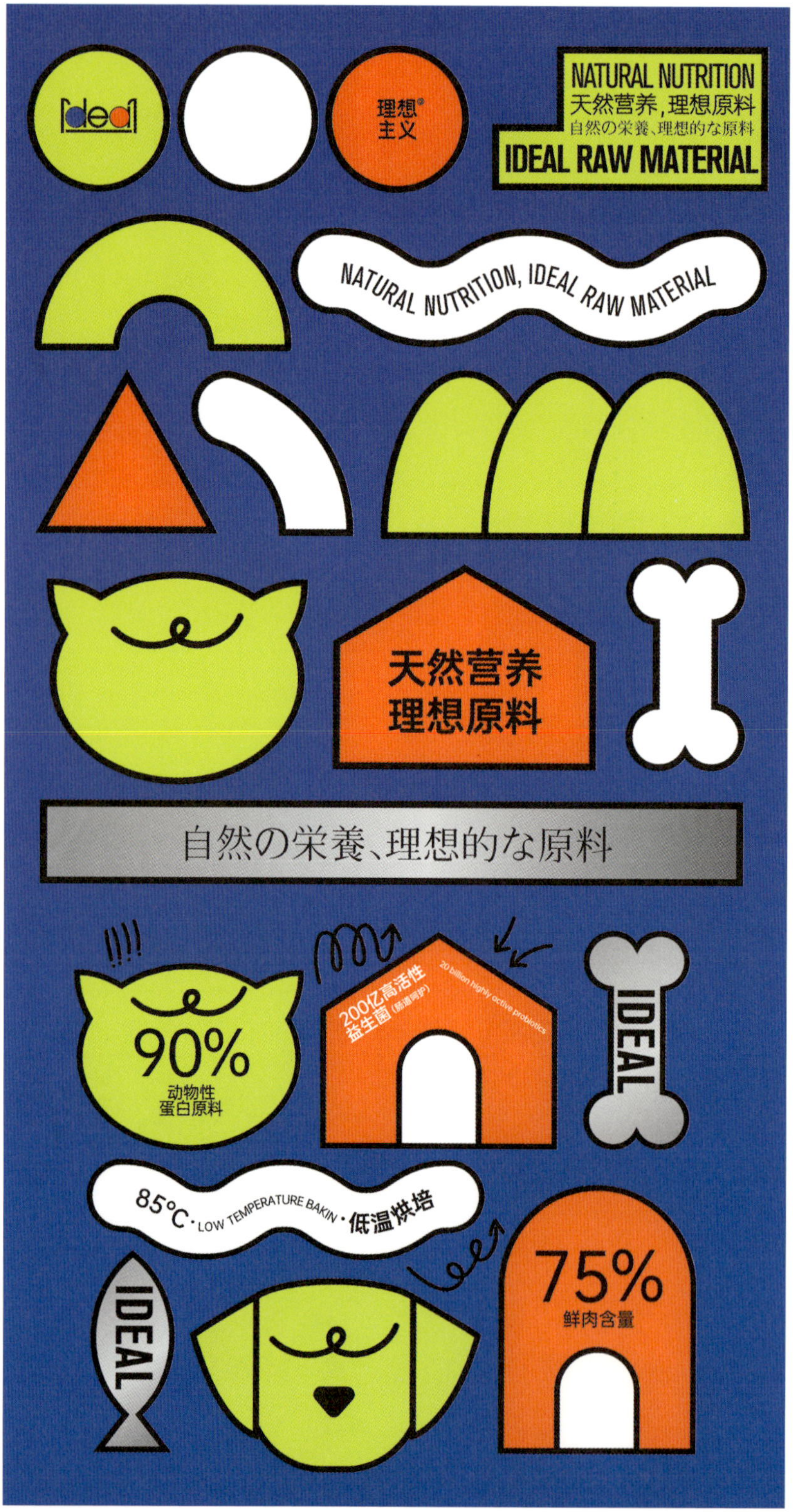

[ideal]

理想®
主义

NATURAL NUTRITION
天然营养，理想原料
自然の栄養、理想的な原料
IDEAL RAW MATERIAL

NATURAL NUTRITION, IDEAL RAW MATERIAL

天然营养
理想原料

自然の栄養、理想的な原料

90%
动物性
蛋白原料

200亿高活性
益生菌（肠道呵护）
20 billion highly active probiotics

IDEAL

85°C · LOW TEMPERATURE BAKIN · 低温烘培

IDEAL

75%
鲜肉含量

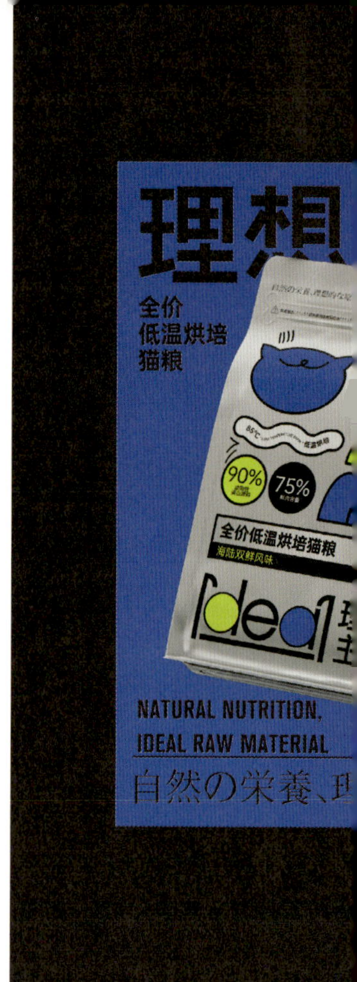

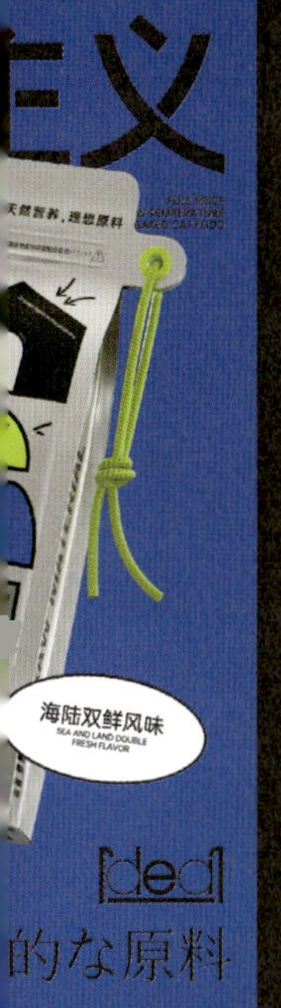

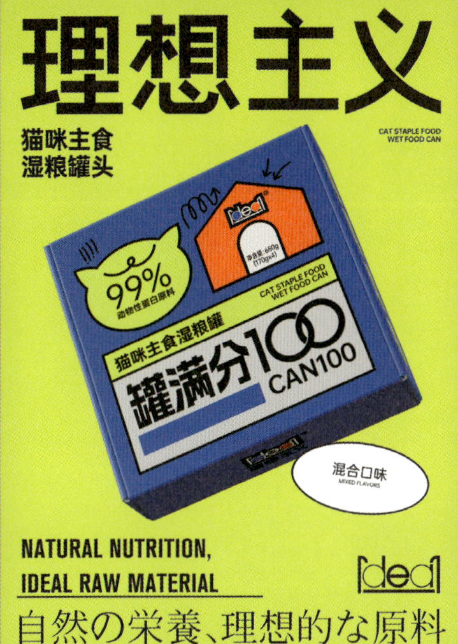

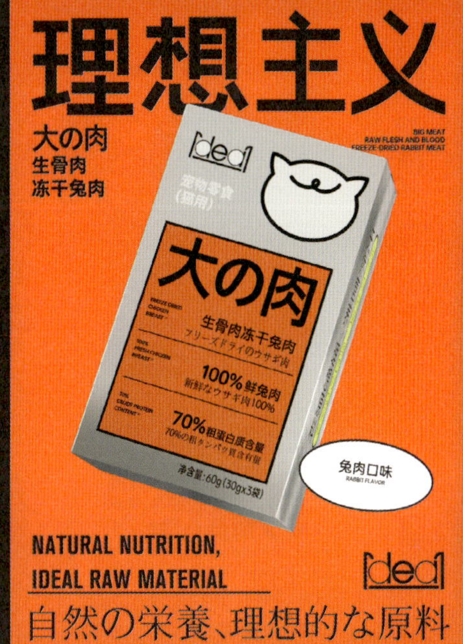

IDEAL Package Design

● IDEAL focuses on natural pet nutrition, providing top-quality products for pets' well-being. The brand believes that keeping pets is a very happy thing, so the packaging ditches market trends for a relaxed, natural aesthetic. Inspired by the visual characteristics of cats and dogs, colors like blue and yellow dominate. ● Departing from traditional methods, the design prioritizes aesthetic principles, forming memorable connections between humans and pets. This distinctive and standardized approach aims to highlight IDEAL's uniqueness in the market.

● Why RYB? ● Blue will give people a professional visual experience, and at the same time, it also delivers a certain rational visual experience.

C0 M73 Y98 K0 | C20 M2 Y85 K0 | C93 M74 Y0 K0

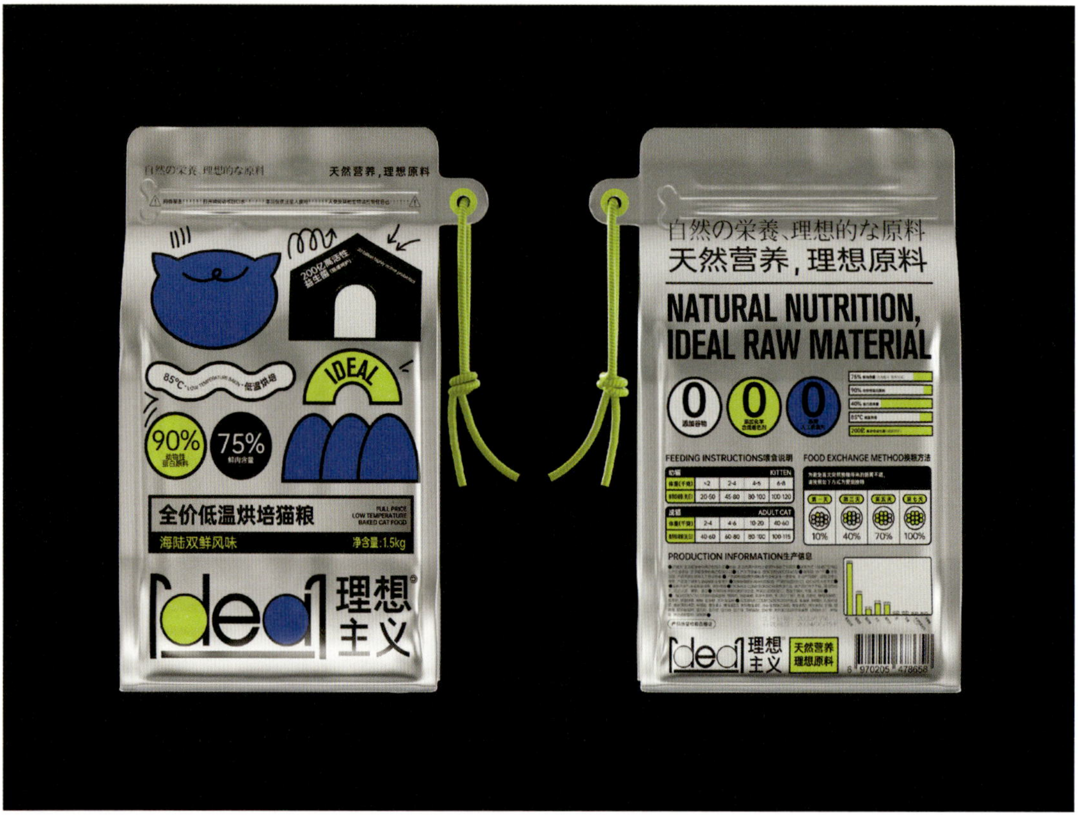

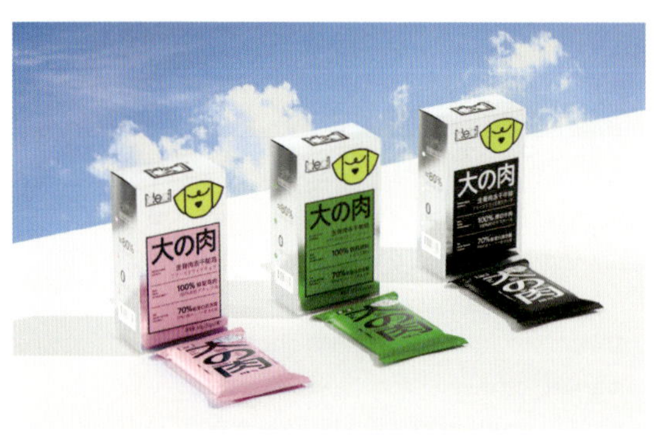
大の肉
大の肉
大の肉

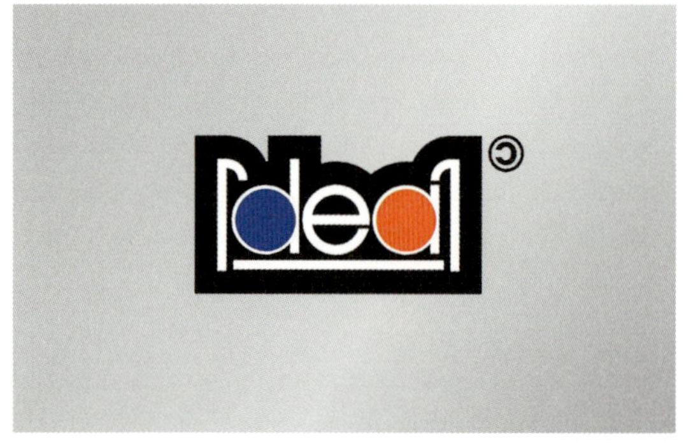

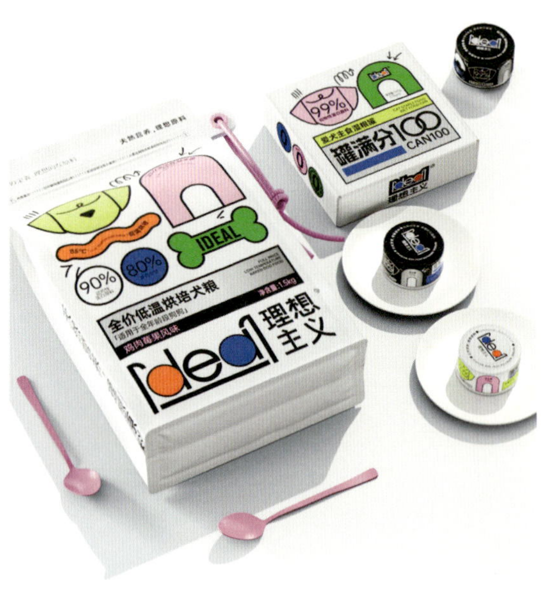
全价低温烘培犬粮
鸡肉莓果风味
净含量:1.5kg
理想主义
IDEAL
罐满分100
CAN100

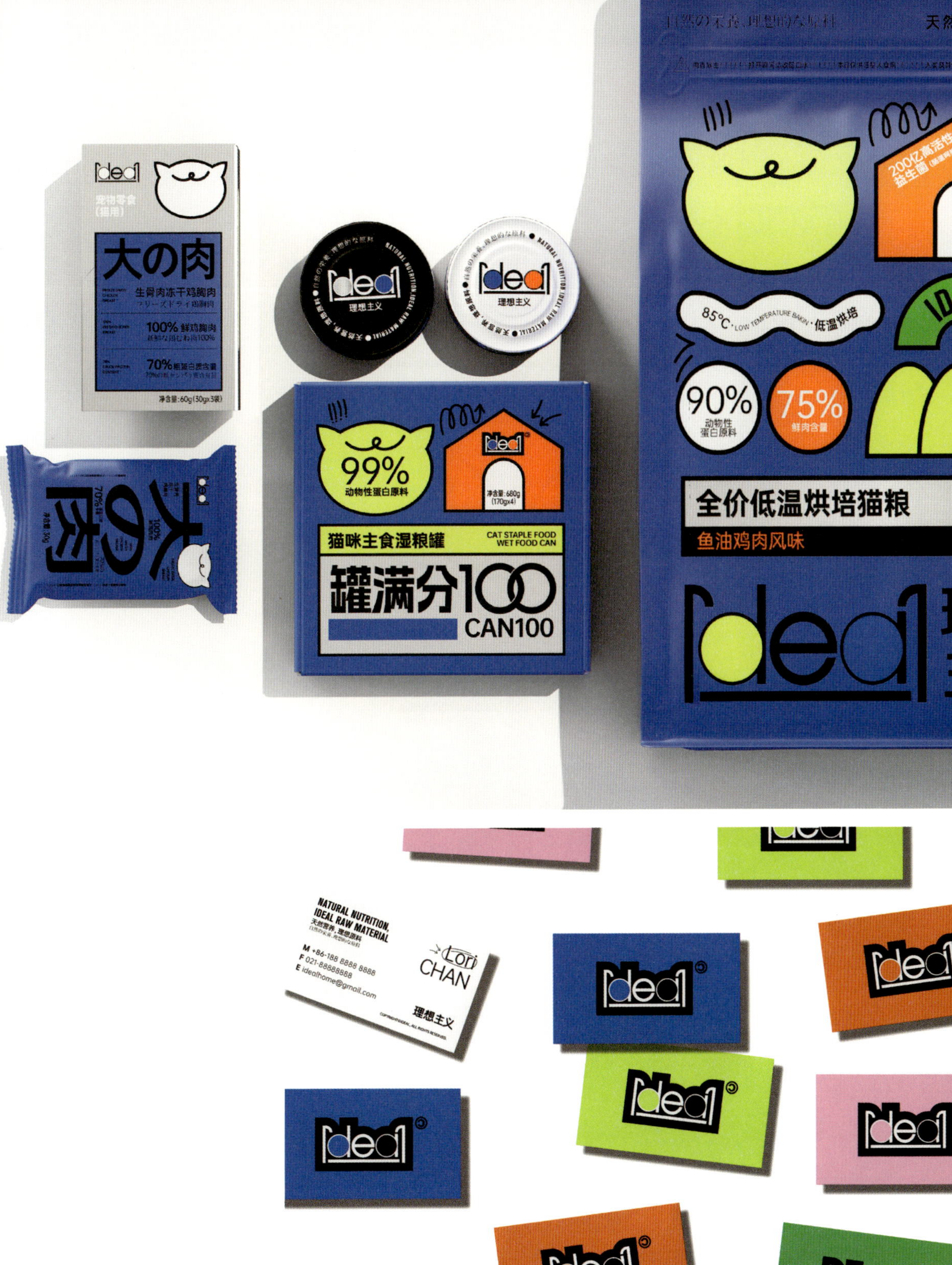
宠物零食
(猫用)
大の肉
生骨肉冻干鸡胸肉
100% 鲜鸡胸肉
70% 粗蛋白质含量
净含量: 60g (30gx3袋)
理想主义
理想主义
99%
动物性蛋白原料
净含量: 680g (170gx4)
猫咪主食湿粮罐
CAT STAPLE FOOD
WET FOOD CAN
罐满分100
CAN100
200亿高活性
益生菌
85°C · LOW TEMPERATURE BAKIN · 低温烘培
90%
动物性
蛋白原料
75%
鲜肉含量
全价低温烘培猫粮
鱼油鸡肉风味
NATURAL NUTRITION,
IDEAL RAW MATERIAL
天然营养, 理想原料
Lori
CHAN
M +86-188 8888 8888
F 021-88888888
E idealhome@gmail.com
理想主义

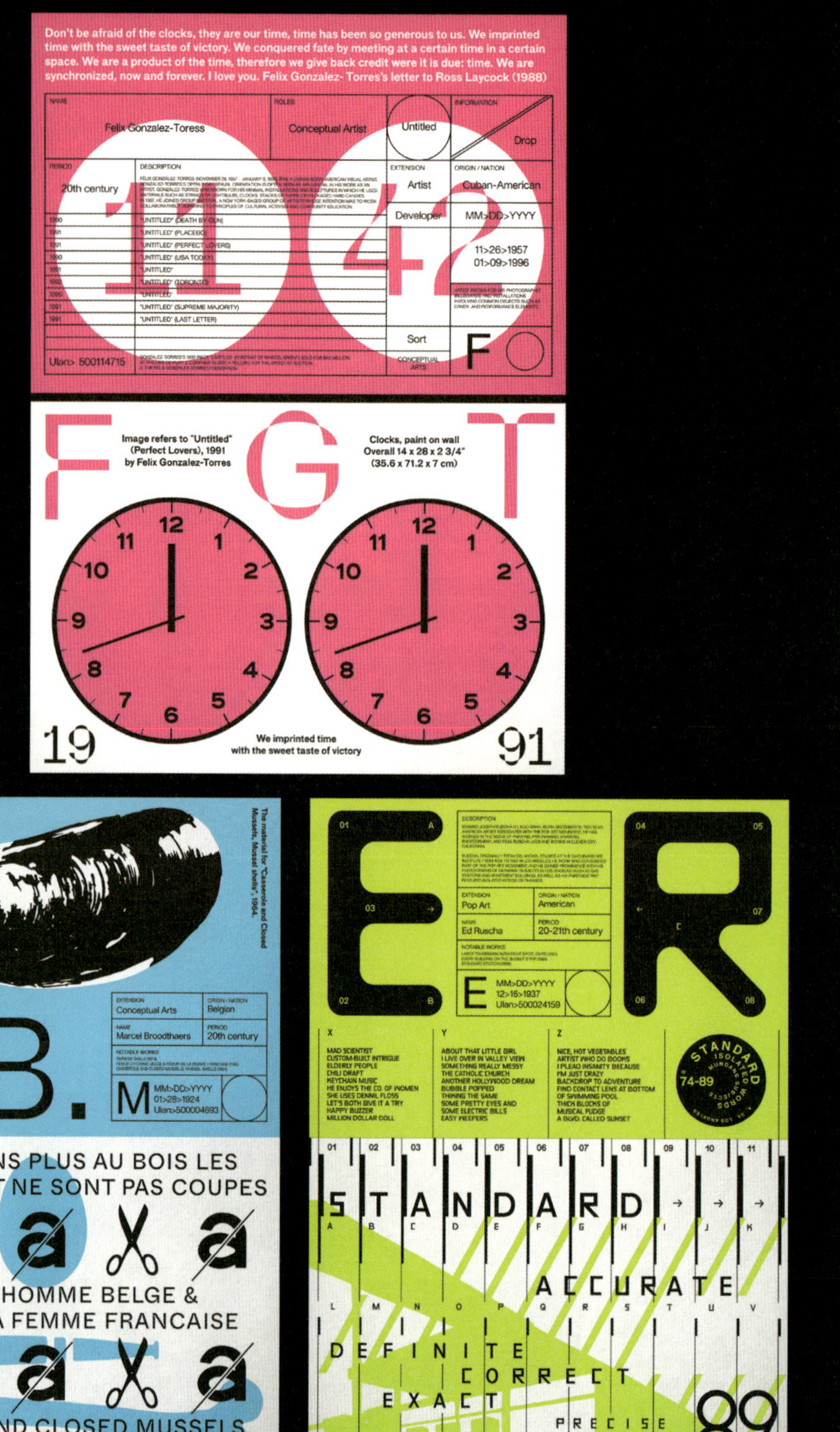

● Design Studio: Studio Werk ● Designer: Jaehoon Choi

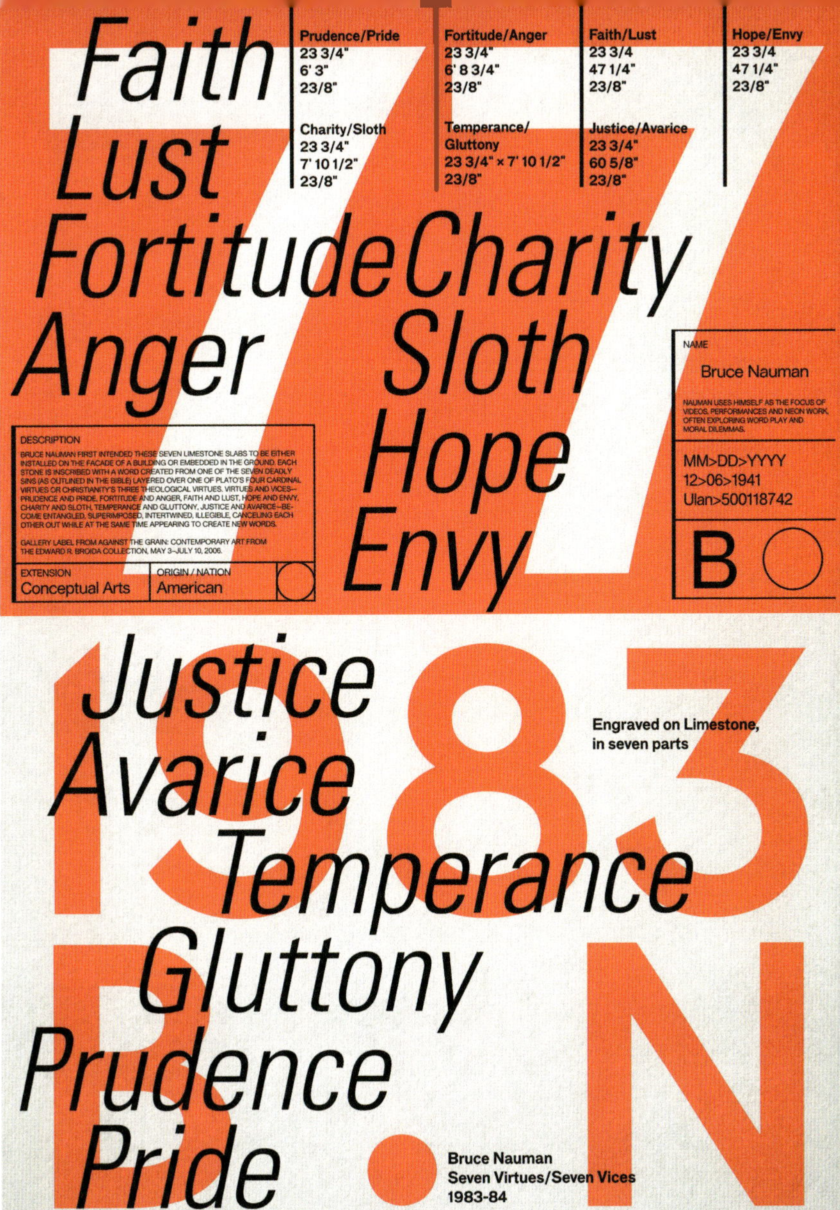

Double • Inspired by the recurring number of 2020 and the works of four contemporary artists (Felix Gonzales-Torres, Marcel Broodthaers, Edward Ruscha, and Bruch Nauman), the resulting cards are individual posters capturing each artist's personality and style, presented as riso prints with artist information and representative artworks.

• Why RYB? • Considering overlaying primary colors, typography, and images, the designer found that saturated, clear colors complemented the planned layout well. The objective was to ensure that each of the four cards had a distinct and unique visual identity.

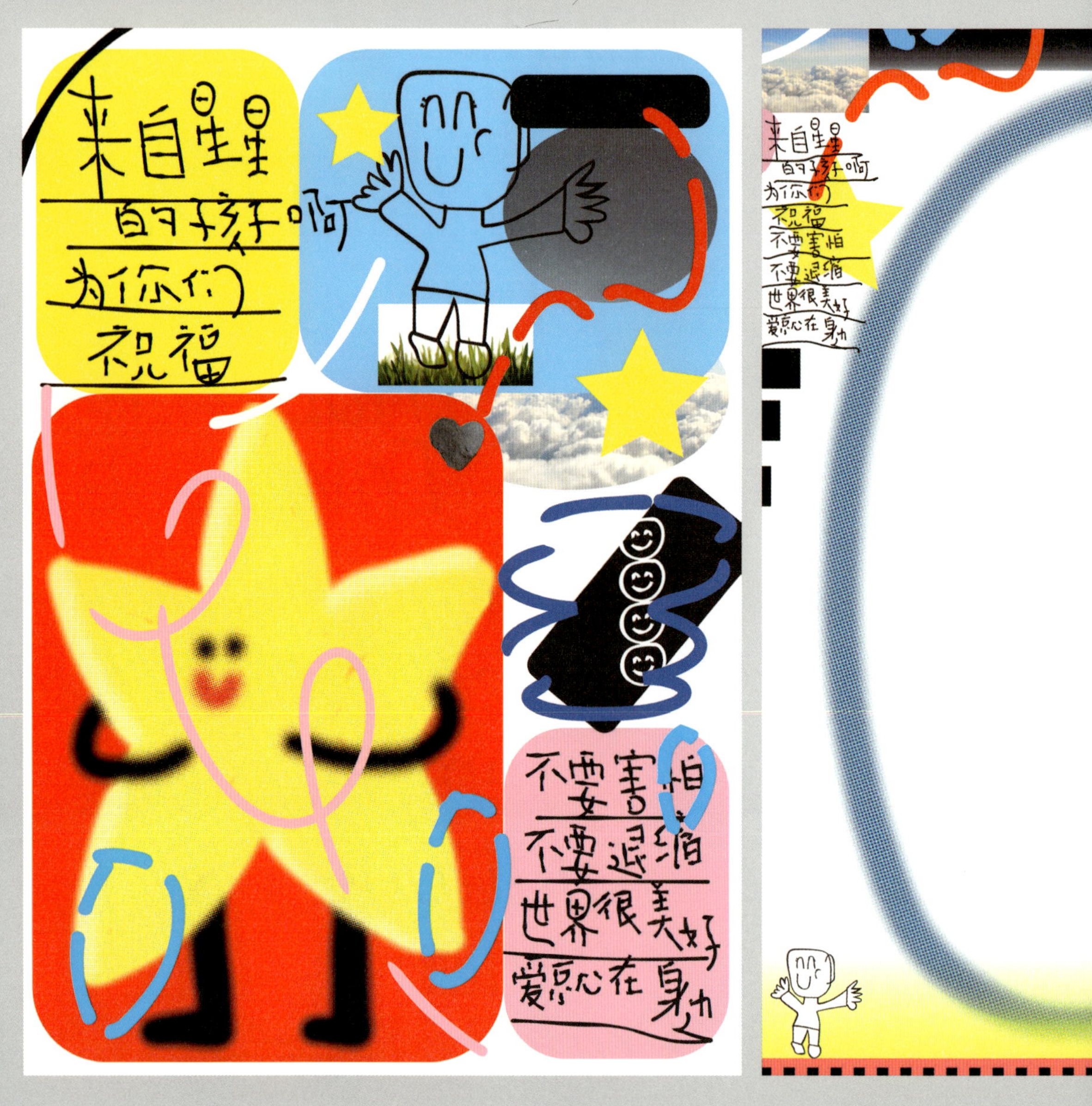

Child From the Star • The piece was initially crafted for a collaborative design initiative by the One Foundation, Tencent News, FXD, and Starry Color, titled "Let Love Come, Let Hindrances Go." Simultaneously, the designer delved into understanding autistic children, infusing the work with a design language that is raw, naive, vibrant, yet sincere. Through handwritten fonts, illustrations, and collages, it vividly portrays a diverse and sincerely caring world, highlighting the significance attributed to these children's existence.

• Designer: Bobby Bao

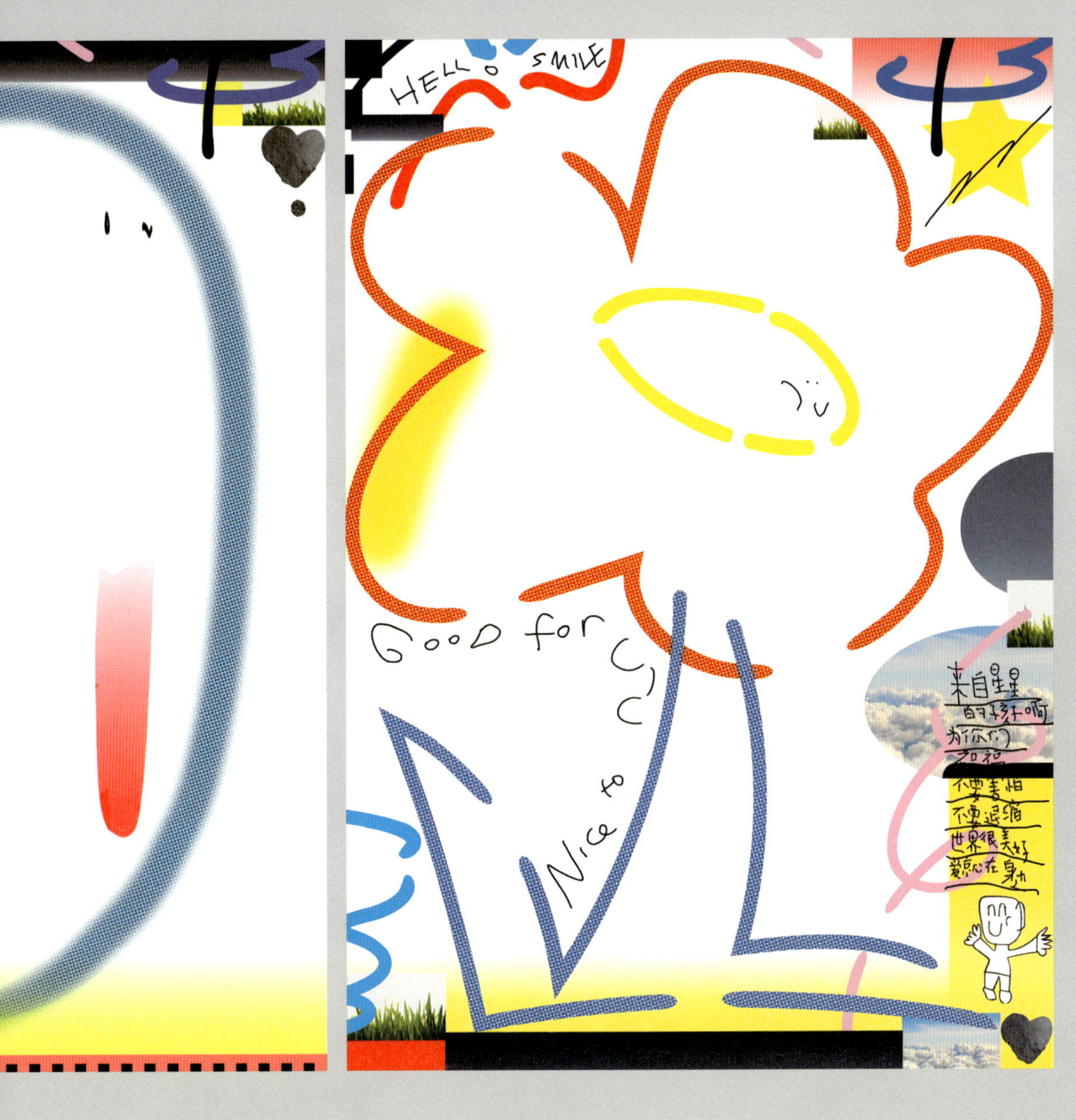

● Why RYB? ● Because it is distinct and easy to recognize.

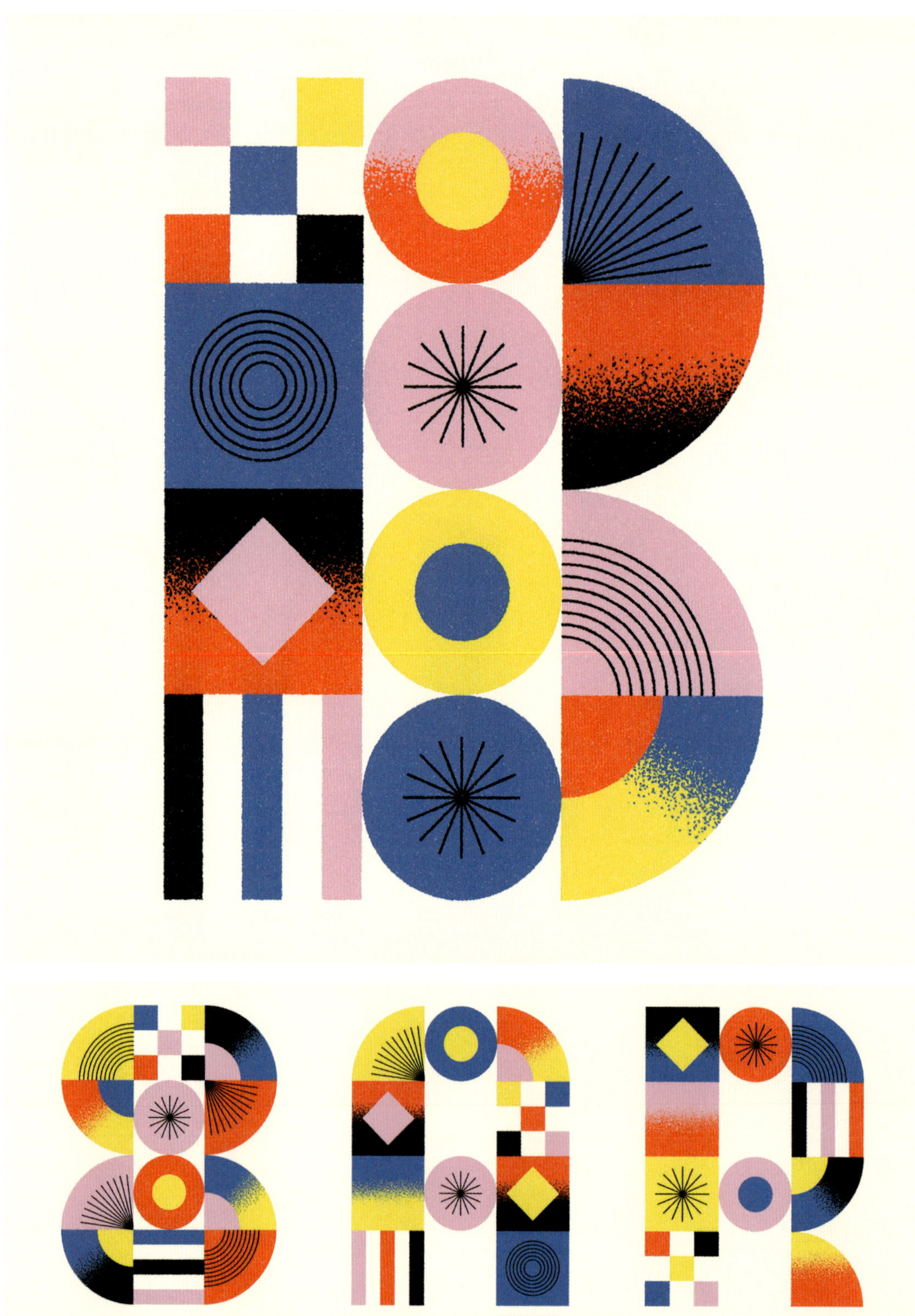

● Designer: Ray Dak Lam

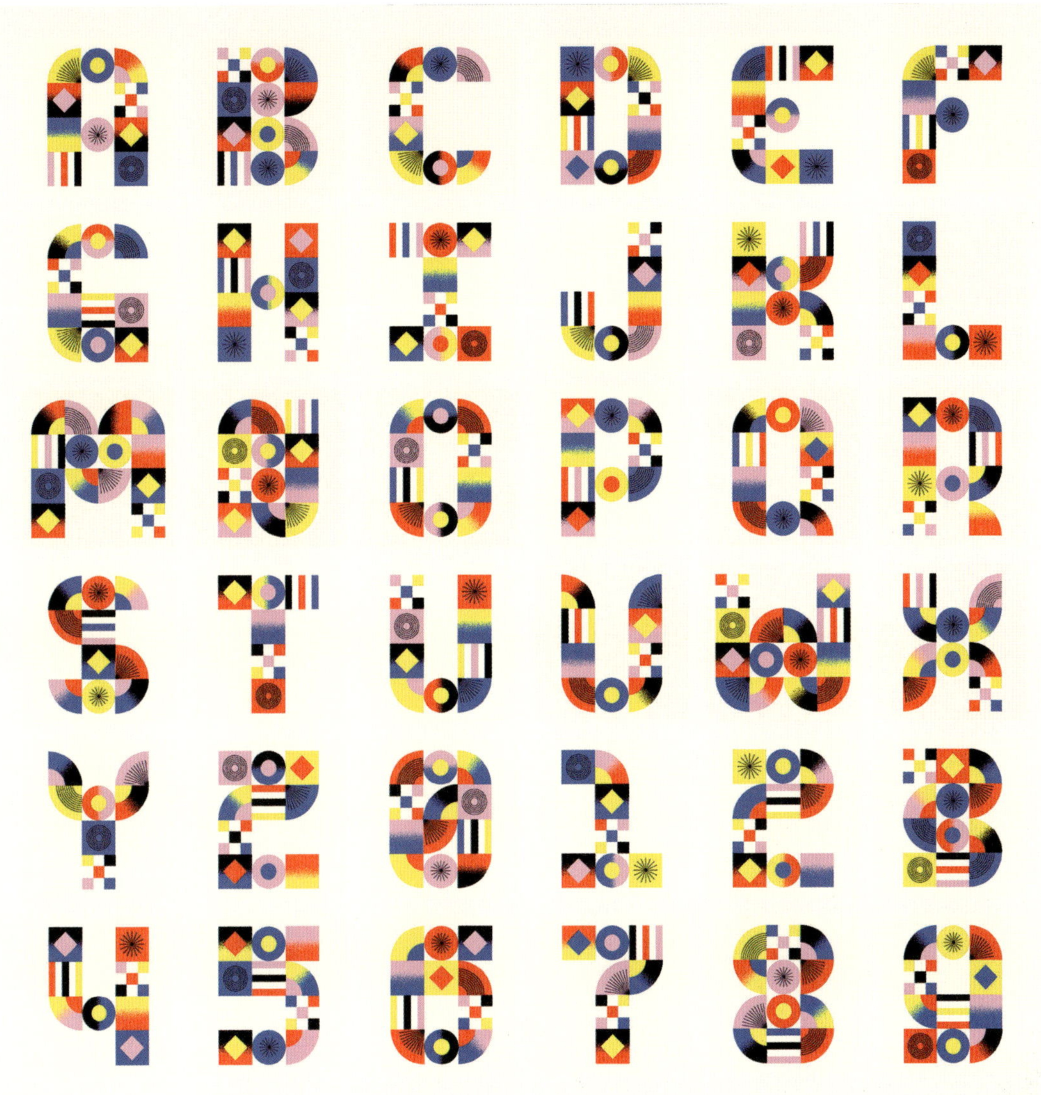

36 Days of Type

• The "36 Days of Type" project challenges designers and artists to creatively interpret the Latin alphabet in 36 days, resulting in a global showcase of diverse typography. Designer Ray Dak Lam crafted building blocks to construct characters on a grid, aiming for a cohesive set within constraints and exploring unique assembly methods for each letter and number.

• Why RYB? • Inspired by the Bauhaus and its utilization of primary colors and basic shapes, the designer explored the creative possibilities and deepened the understanding of the relationships between colors and shapes within these limitations.

C3 M91 Y91 K0 | C7 M40 Y0 K0 | C7 M7 Y90 K0 | C87 M59 Y6 K0

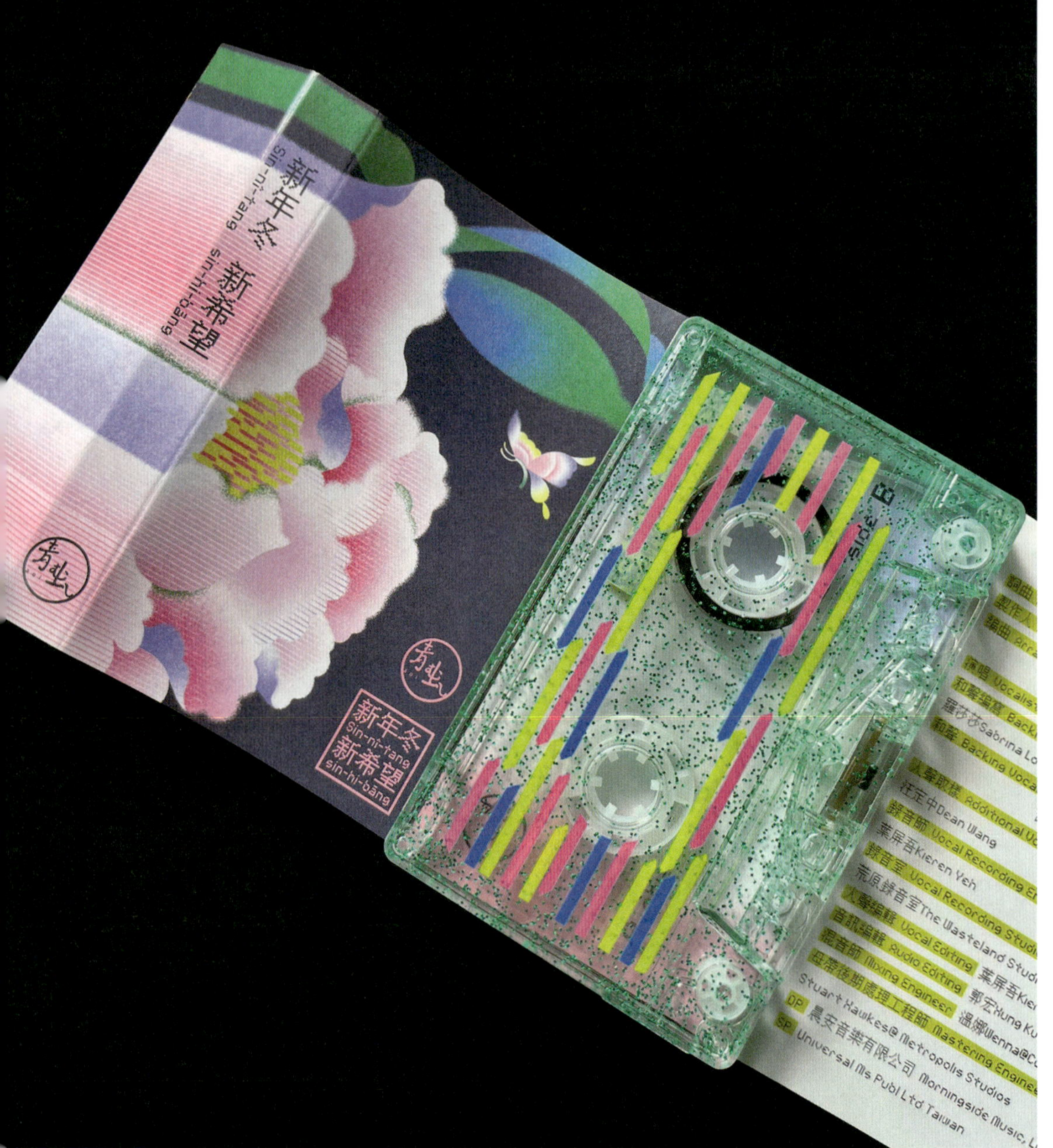

A *Bad Hair Year* Single Cassette Design

● This project involves the cassette design for the Taiwanese indie rock band "青虫aoi" and their 2022 Taiwanese Hokkien single "Sin-nî-tang sin-hi-bāng" (A Bad Hair Year). The track explores themes of renewal and the possibilities of a new chapter in life, but also the disappointment of promises unfulfilled and dreams unrealized. The main visual inspiration is drawn from the traditional Chinese New Year auspicious pattern "花开富贵" (Flowers Bloom with Prosperity). Placing peonies, symbols of good fortune and happiness, against an ominous black background, creates a visually ironic atmosphere, intending to capture the tension between expectation and reality conveyed in the song.

● Design Studio: ichyi.com ● Designer: I CHYI CHANG ● Client: 青虫aoi

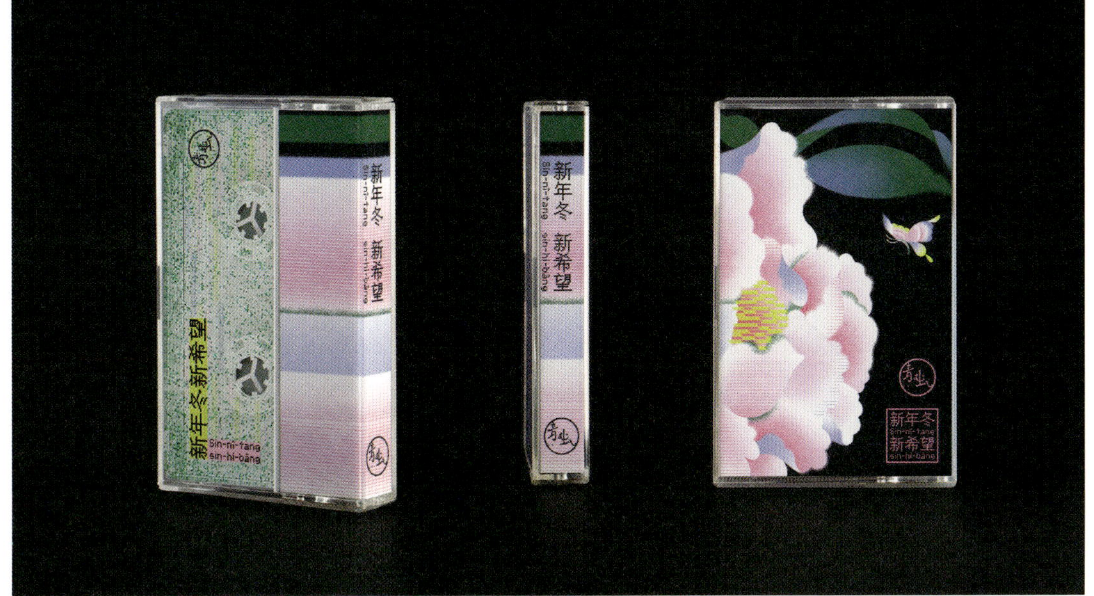

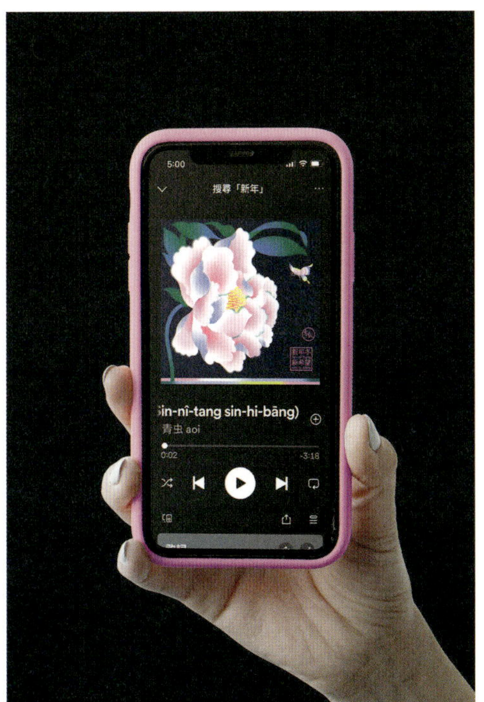

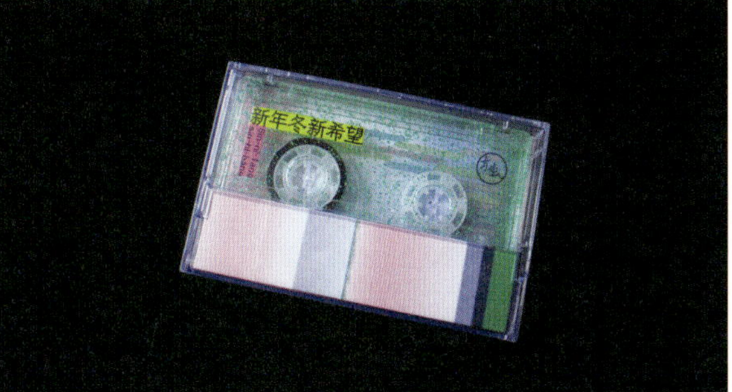

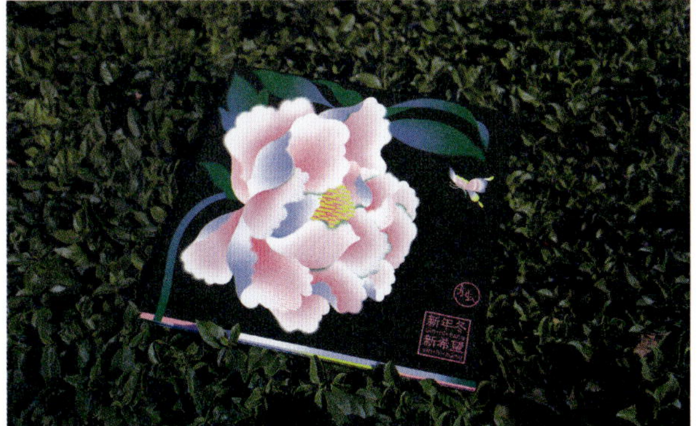

● Why RYB? ● The design draws inspiration from common auspicious Chinese New Year patterns, emphasizing the hue of red, with added blue adjustments for a lively feel. The blend of pink (the pale red colour) and blue, accented with yellow, symbolizes new year hope and joy, while hinting at unfulfilled promises and dreams.

C4 M46 Y0 K0 | C22 M0 Y82 K0 | C33 M23 Y0 K0 | C100 M40 Y70 K0

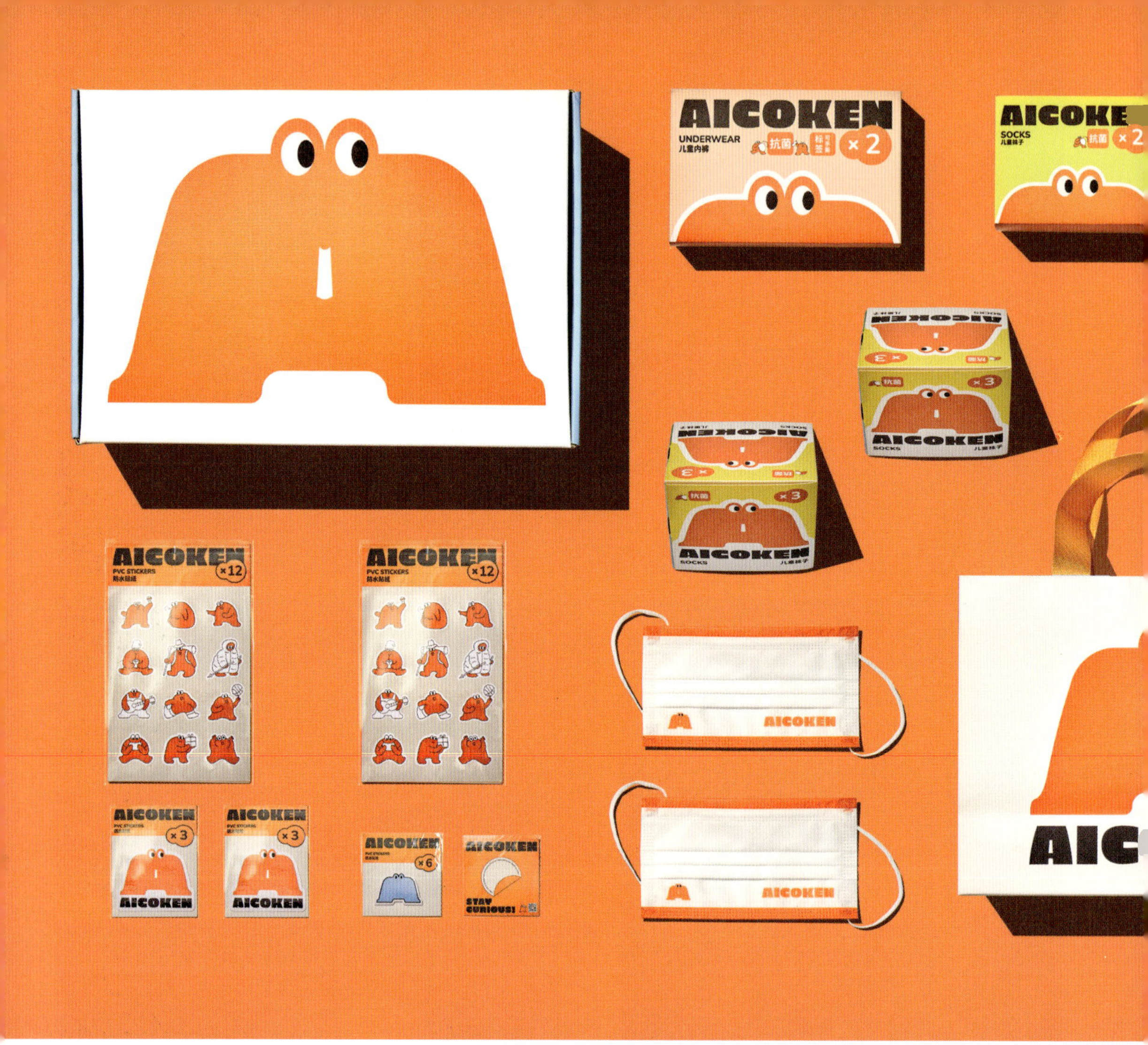

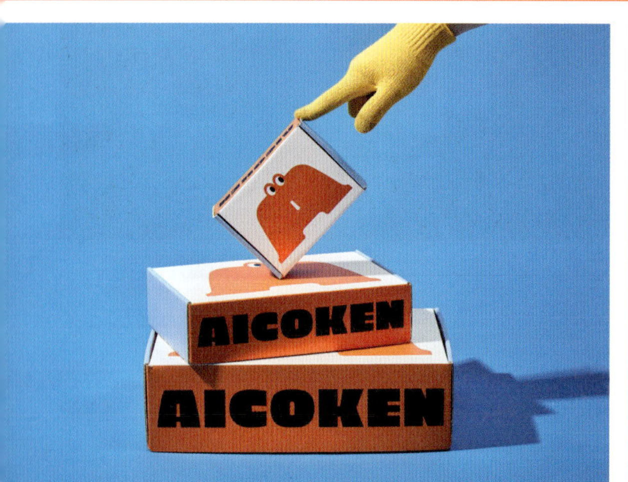

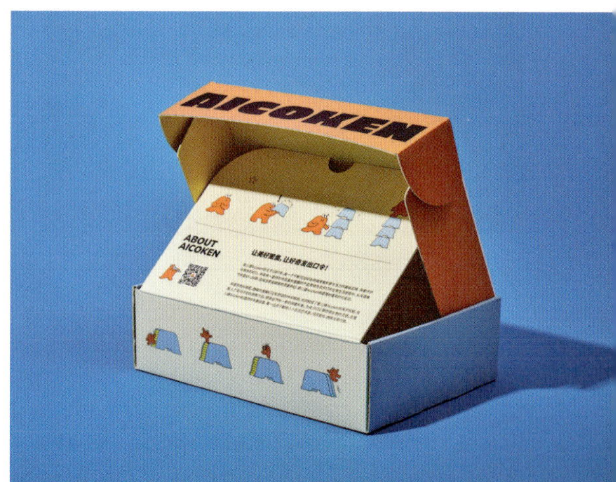

● Design Studio: ONNFF ● Designer: Zhengrui Hu ● Photographer: DAZHI ● Client: AICOKEN

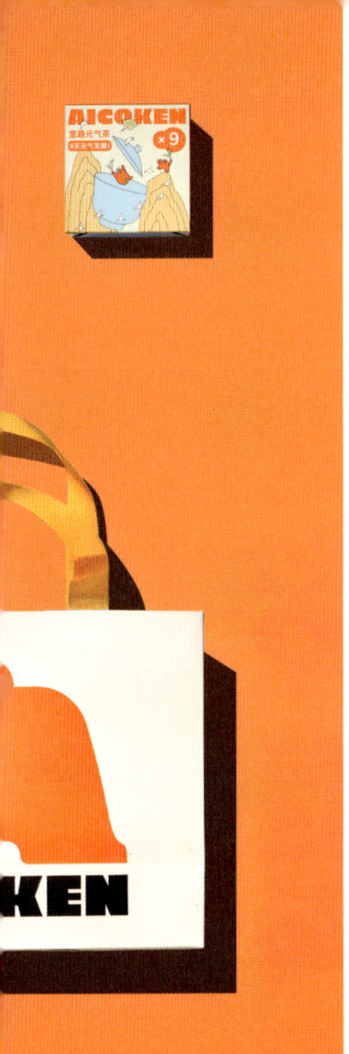

AICOKEN Brand Design

● AICOKEN embraces a child's perspective, blending innocence with fabrics' warmth to connect children and clothing. Inspired by "stay curious," the brand features a bench-shaped symbol, implying kids' curiosity and growth. The vibrant "A-shaped" cartoon character, derived from AICOKEN's initial, exudes friendliness and energy and is presented throughout the brand's packaging. This embodies the brand's commitment to accompanying children to experience the beauty of life together.

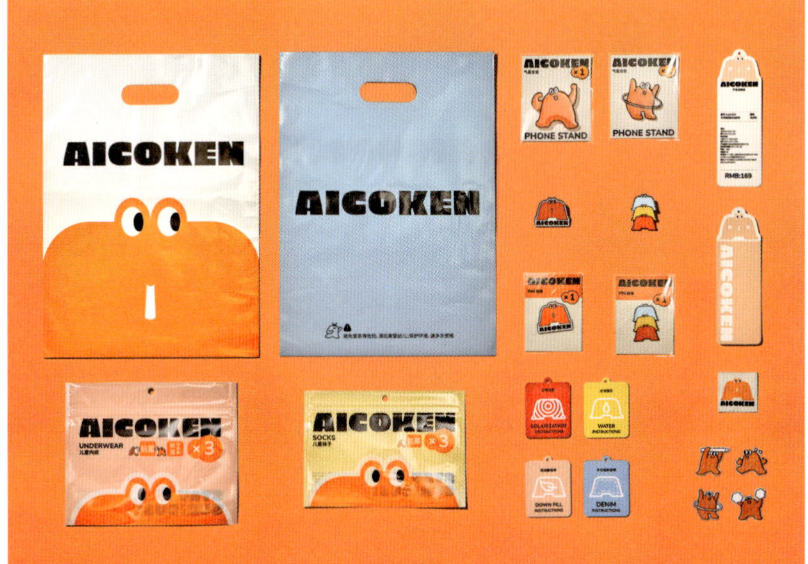

● Why RYB? ● The vibrant hues of red, yellow, and blue create an energetic atmosphere, allowing the brand to stand out and enhance memorability. Particularly well-suited for children's brands, these colors symbolize vitality, joy, and freedom. They can swiftly leave a lasting impression on children and convey a healthy, pleasant tone to adults. As a children's clothing brand, AICOKEN employs these colors to express its brand stance, directly conveying positive and joyful emotions.

C0 M87 Y85 K0 | C0 M60 Y100 K0 | C0 M0 Y92 K0 | C42 M9 Y0 K0

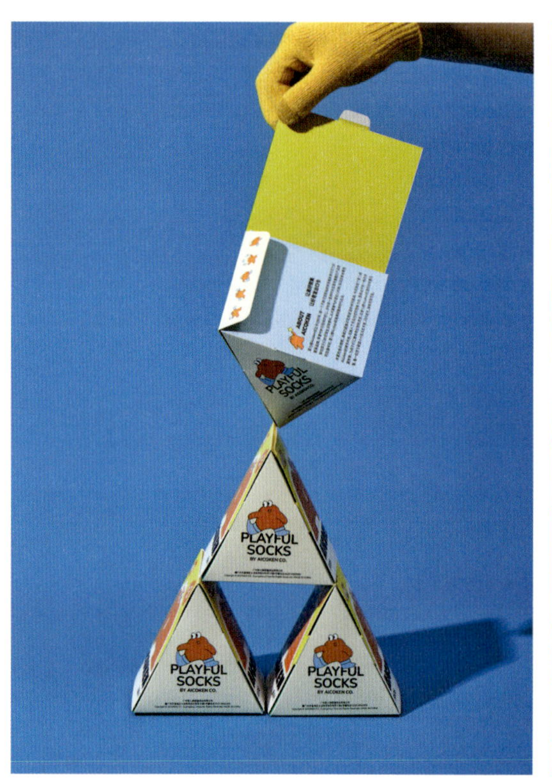
PLAYFUL
SOCKS
BY AICOKEN CO.
PLAYFUL
SOCKS
BY AICOKEN CO.
PLAYFUL
SOCKS
BY AICOKEN CO.

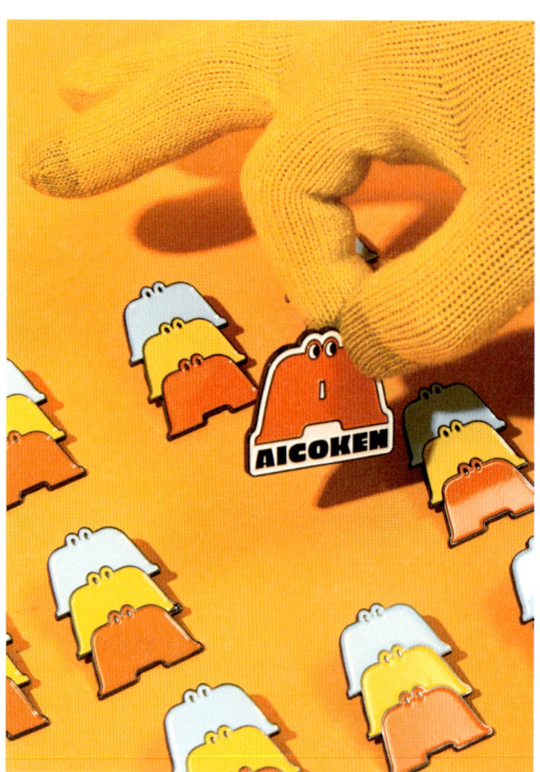
AICOKEN

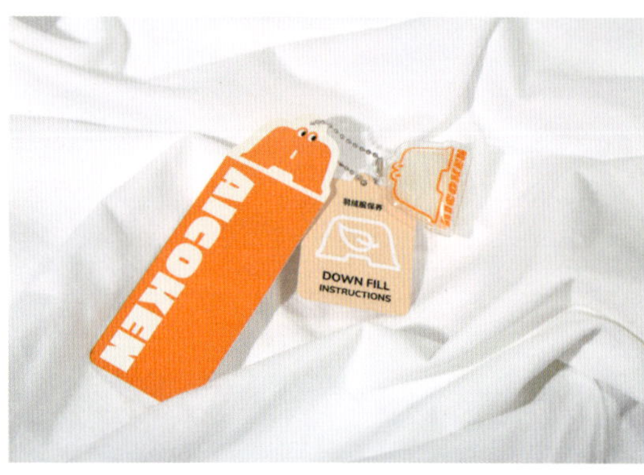
AICOKEN
DOWN FILL
INSTRUCTIONS

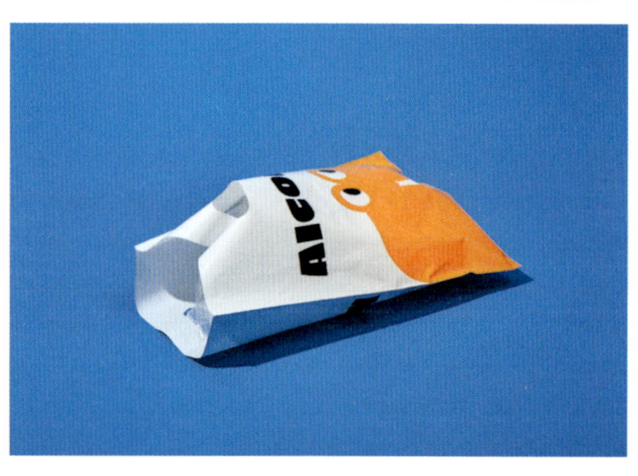

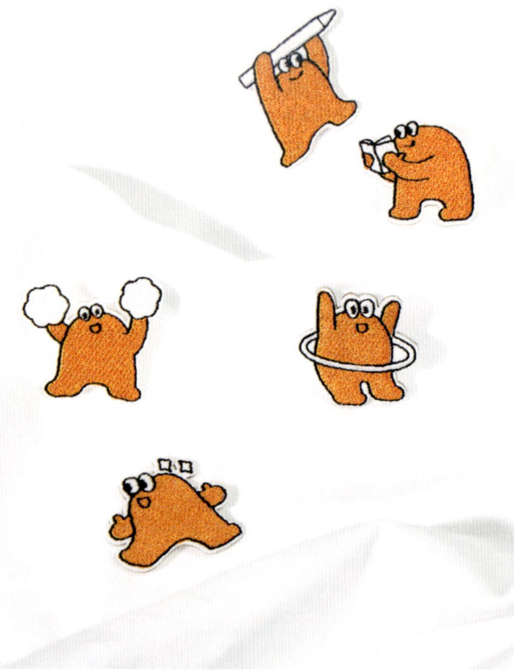

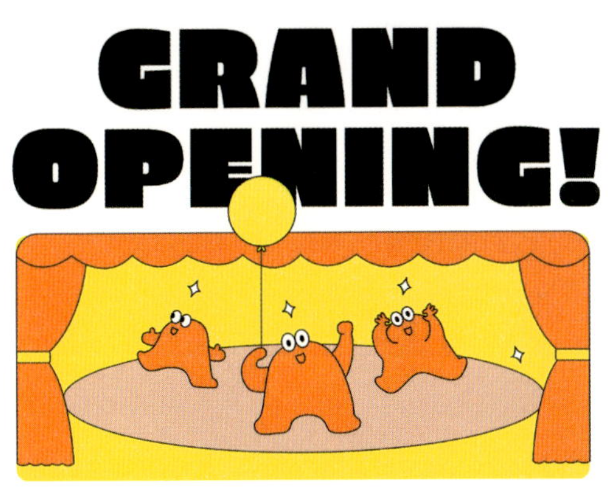
GRAND
OPENING!
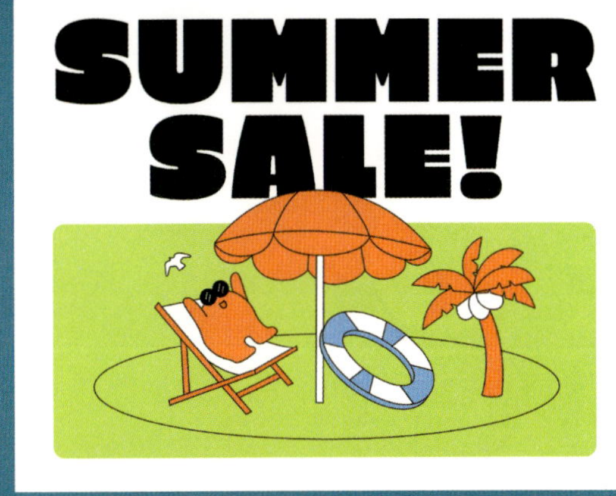
SUMMER
SALE!
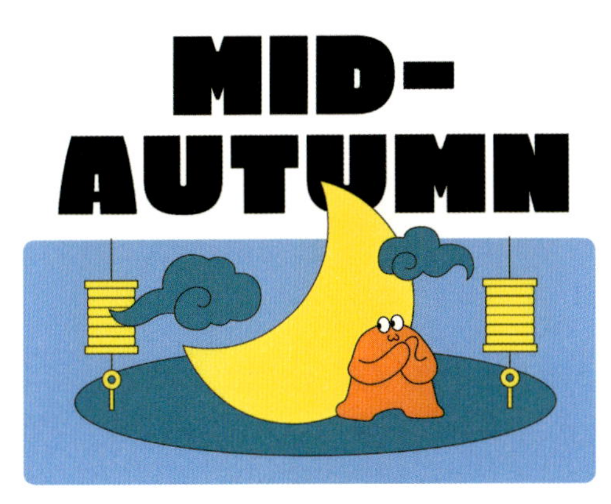
MID-
AUTUMN
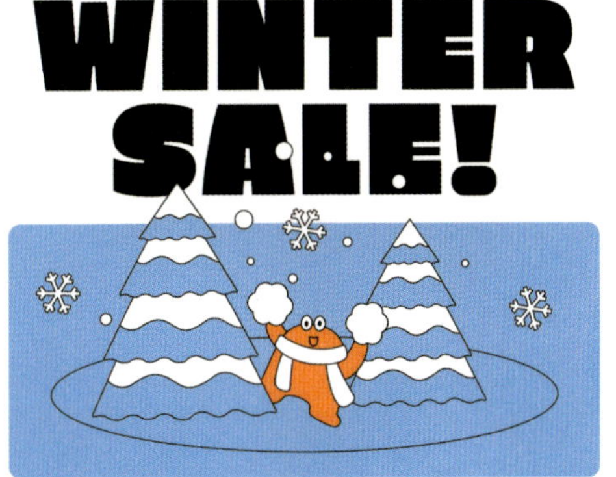
WINTER
SALE!

羽绒服保养
DOWN FILL
INSTRUCTIONS
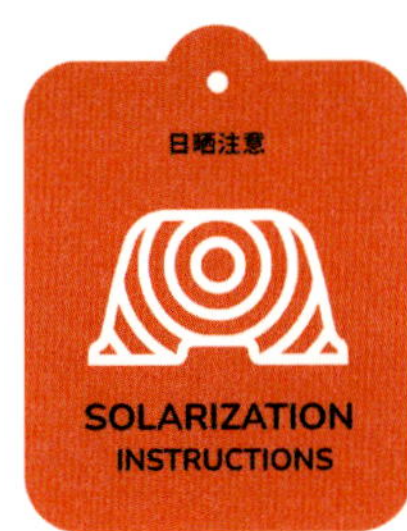
日晒注意
SOLARIZATION
INSTRUCTIONS
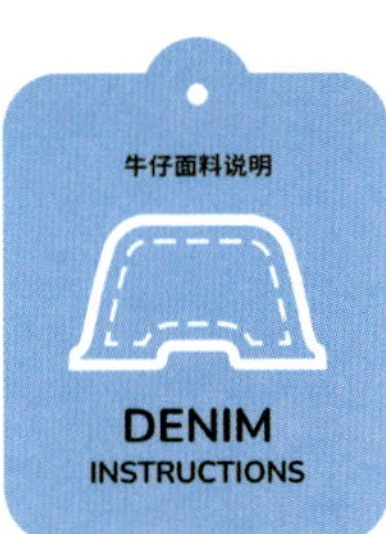
牛仔面料说明
DENIM
INSTRUCTIONS

洗涤说明
WASHING
INSTRUCTIONS
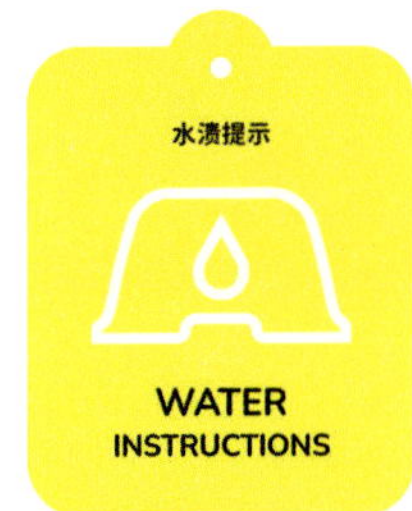
水渍提示
WATER
INSTRUCTIONS

毛绒面料
PLUSH
FABRIC

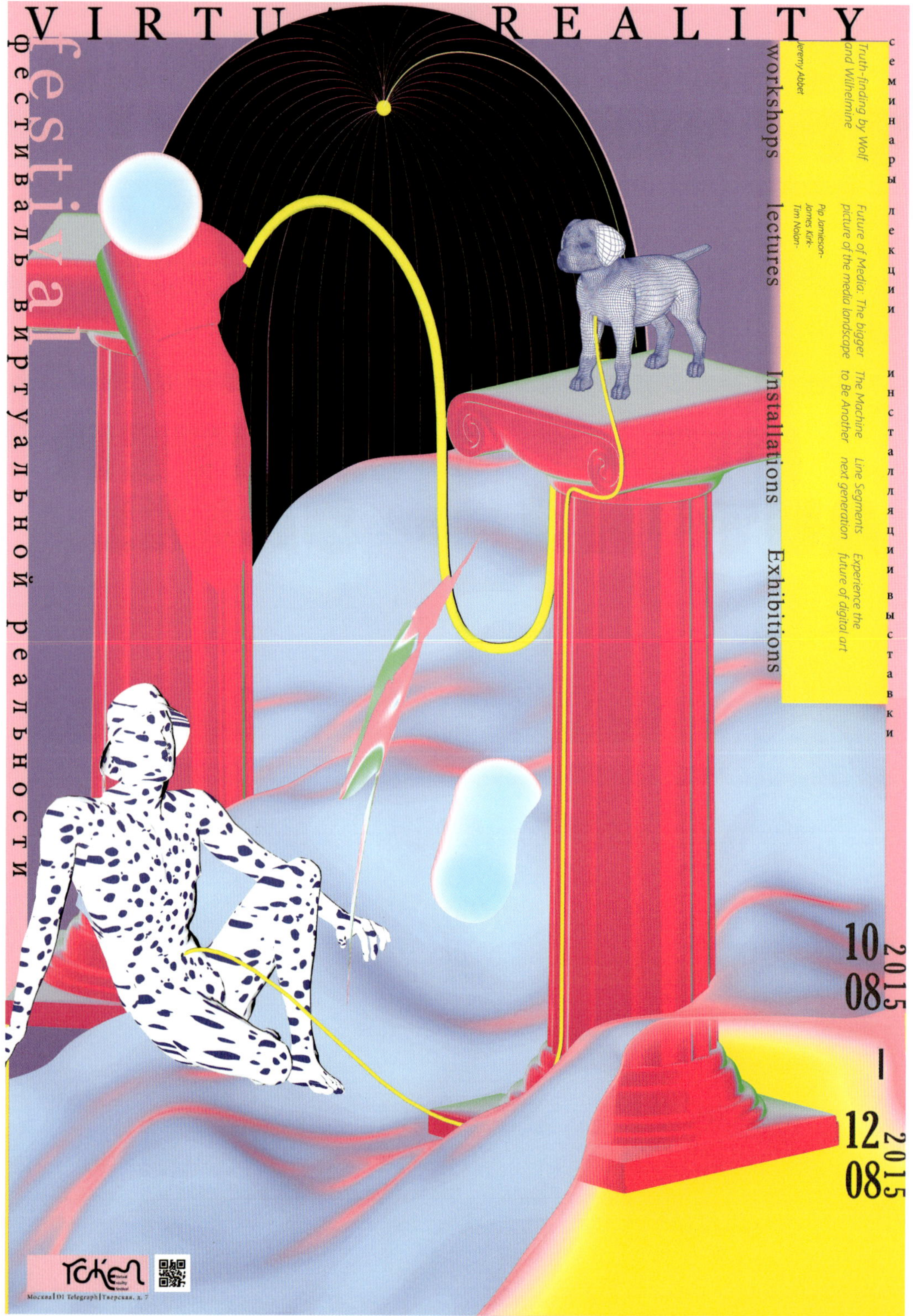

● Designer: Nina Deeva-Kazanova ● Client: St. Petersburg University

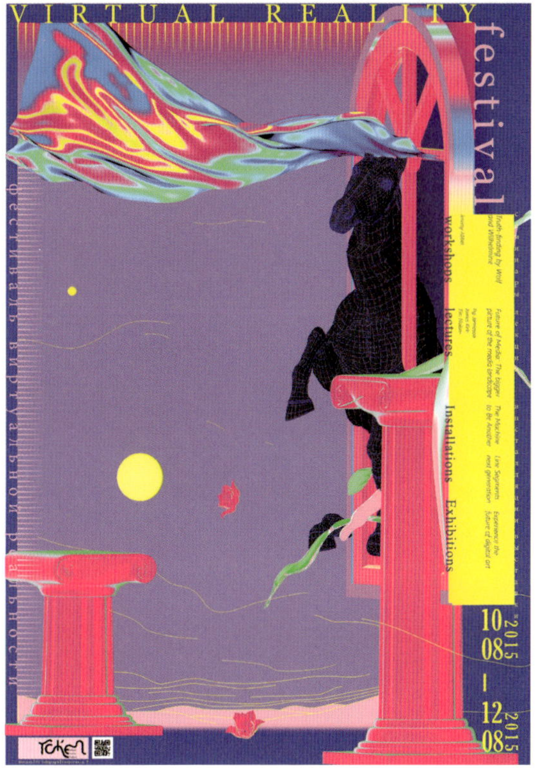

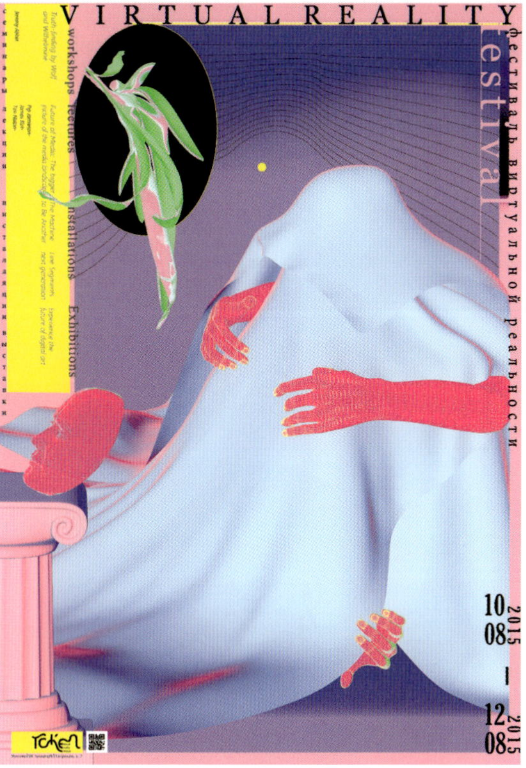

Token ● "Token Virtual Reality Festival" explores the phenomenon of virtual reality within media culture, emphasizing a comfortable environment for virtual existence. It blurs boundaries between mechanisms and humans, allowing participants to navigate diverse identities and create their own virtual world. The project invites spectators to experience this idealized and resortlike virtual environment through familiar yet improved scenes of virtual life.

● Why RYB? ● Choosing intentionally vibrant artificial colors like vivid magenta, yellow, and blue aims to maintain an obvious distinction between two realities—computer-generated and mass culture. This deliberate choice seeks to create an "embellished" sense of familiar reality for spectators, eliminating drawbacks such as bad weather. The virtual environment becomes an idealized space, akin to a resort, offering relaxation and enjoyment. The use of contrasting colors emphasizes the unreal and artificial nature of the virtual world.

FF18F9 FB99FF FFEC01 ABDDF8 190AED 8A72B2

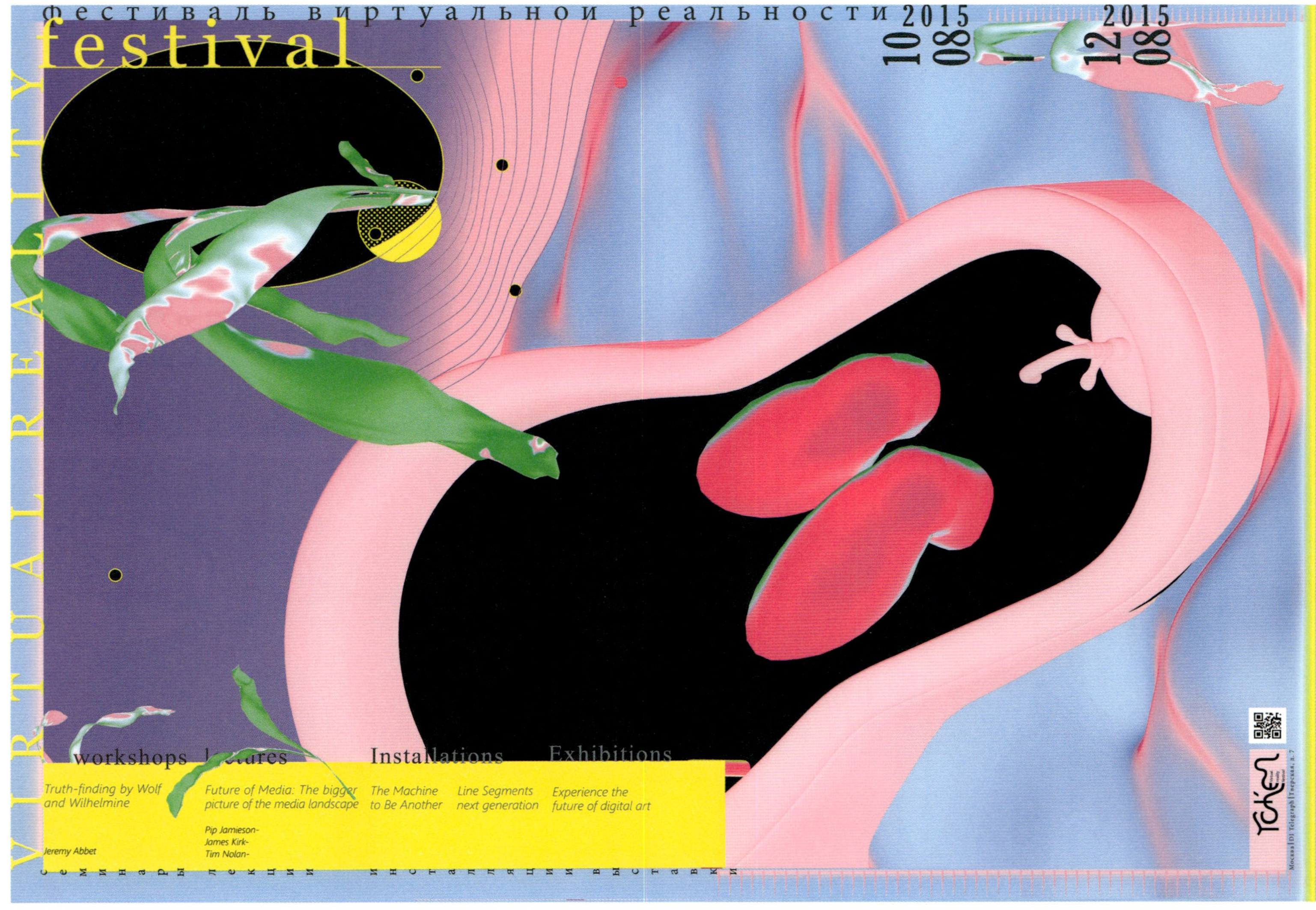
VIRTUAL REALITY
festival
фестиваль виртуальной реальности
10 08 2015 – 12 08 2015
workshops
Installations
Exhibitions
Truth-finding by Wolf and Wilhelmine
Jeremy Abbet
Future of Media: The bigger picture of the media landscape
Pip Jamieson-
James Kirk-
Tim Nolan-
The Machine to Be Another
Line Segments next generation
Experience the future of digital art
семинары лекции инсталляции выставки
Москва | DI Telegraph | Тверская, д. 7

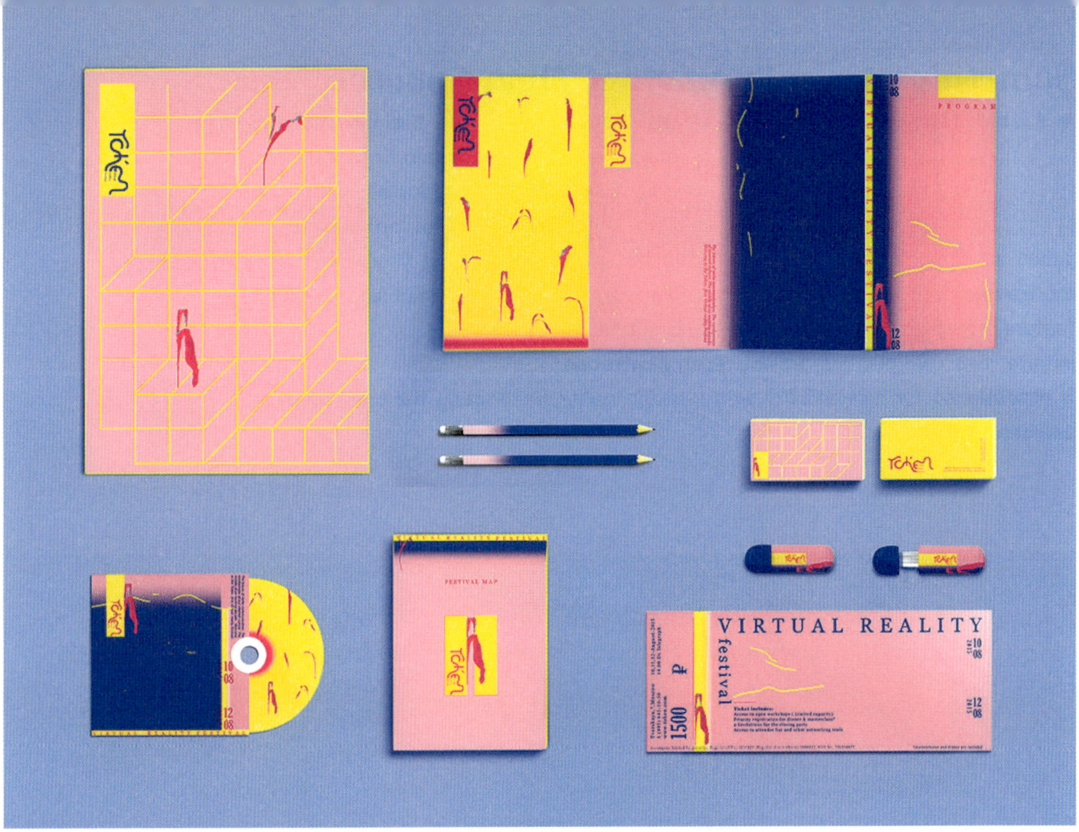
PROGRAM
FESTIVAL MAP
VIRTUAL REALITY
festival
1500

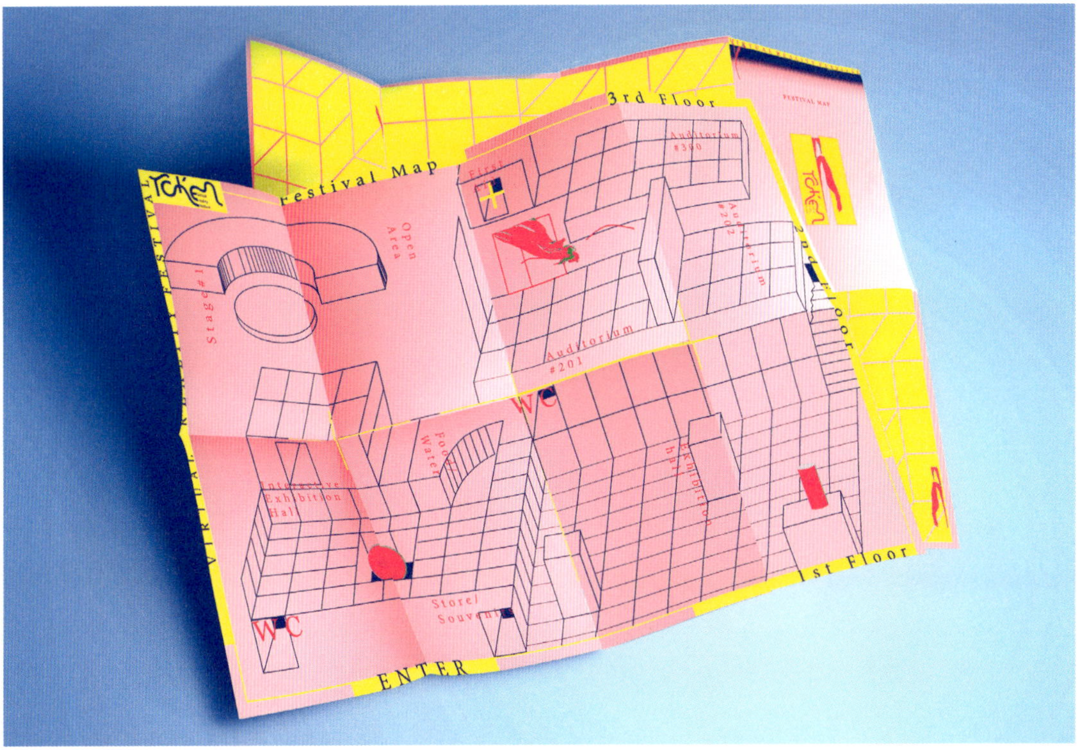
Festival Map
3rd Floor
FESTIVAL MAP
Auditorium
#300
Open
Area
Auditorium
#201
WC
ENTER
1st Floor
Store/
VIRTUAL

Something More Permanent Than Concrete

● A seed pack and badge-making kit were crafted for Ellen Wilkinson as a component of "the Orchard Engagement Programme for Spring/Summer 2017." This initiative is part of an enduring public art project initially conceptualized by British artist David Thorpe within the framework of the "Future Perfect public art program." The folded seed packs feature attached seeds, enabling participants to initiate their own planting project. Each illustration is dimensioned for compatibility with a badge maker, facilitating the creation of personalized badges.

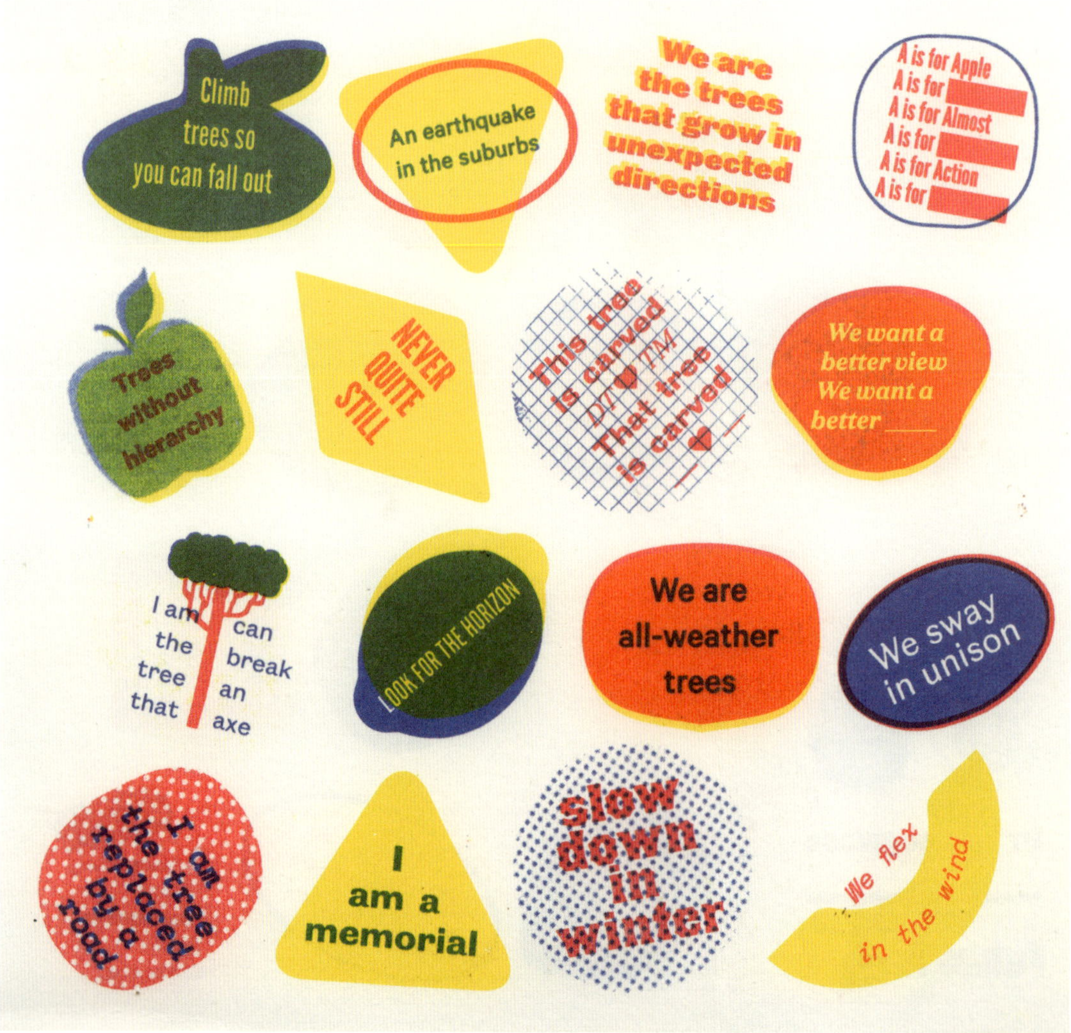

● Design Studio: Smith & Lewarne ● Designer: Jono Lewarne, Stephen Smith

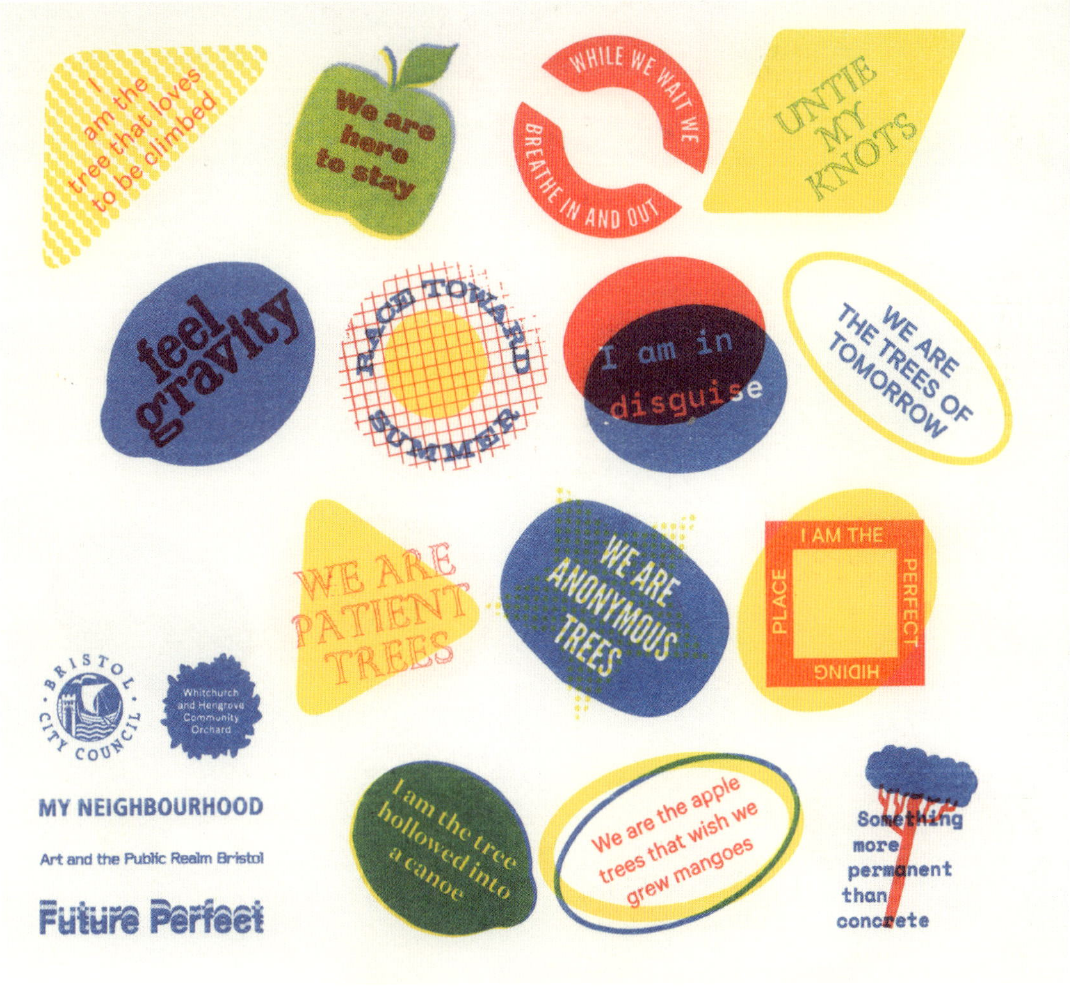

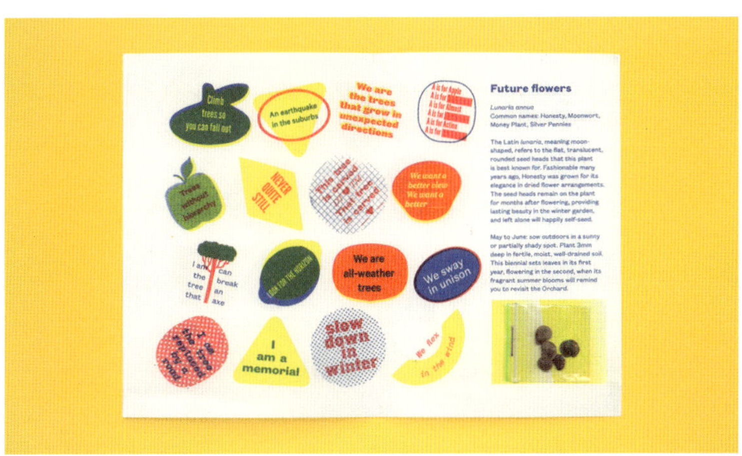

● Why RYB? ● The illustrations adopt the visual style of fruit stickers but reimagine them with prompts and ideas instead of brand names. Fruit stickers, known for their nostalgic appeal, have intrigued graphic designers with their blend of simplicity and intricate details. Primary colors were chosen to enhance elemental simplicity and nostalgia. The use of a risograph printer adds another layer of interest with its punchy and distinctive colors.

● Client: Bristol Council, Future Perfect

C0 M84 Y82 K0 C5 M11 Y80 K0 C78 M66 Y0 K0

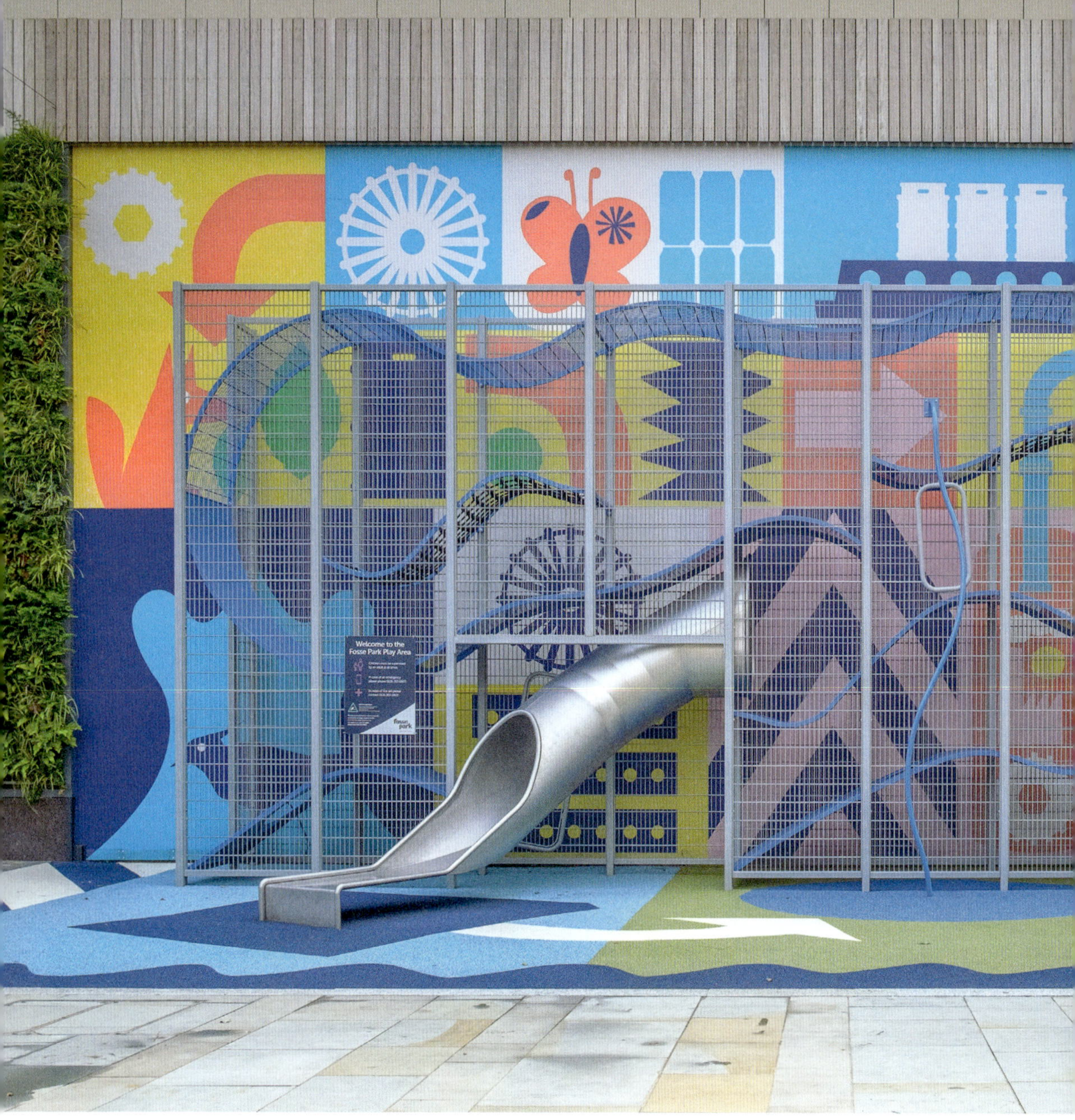

Fosse Park Play Wall

● Commissioned by The Crown Estate, the large-scale outdoor installation at Fosse Park in Leicester features a graphic wall, a rubber floor, and a 15-meter window for the UK's first vertical children's activity area. Inspired by local cultural references, the vibrant installation adopted a positive color palette, bringing life and excitement to the retail-centric Fosse Park shopping center. Informed by creative workshops with children and residents, the design integrates wildlife and cultural history, creating a welcoming space for both kids and adults.

 ● Design Studio: Smith & Lewarne ● Designer: Jono Lewarne, Stephen Smith ● Client: The Crown Estate, Macgregor Smith

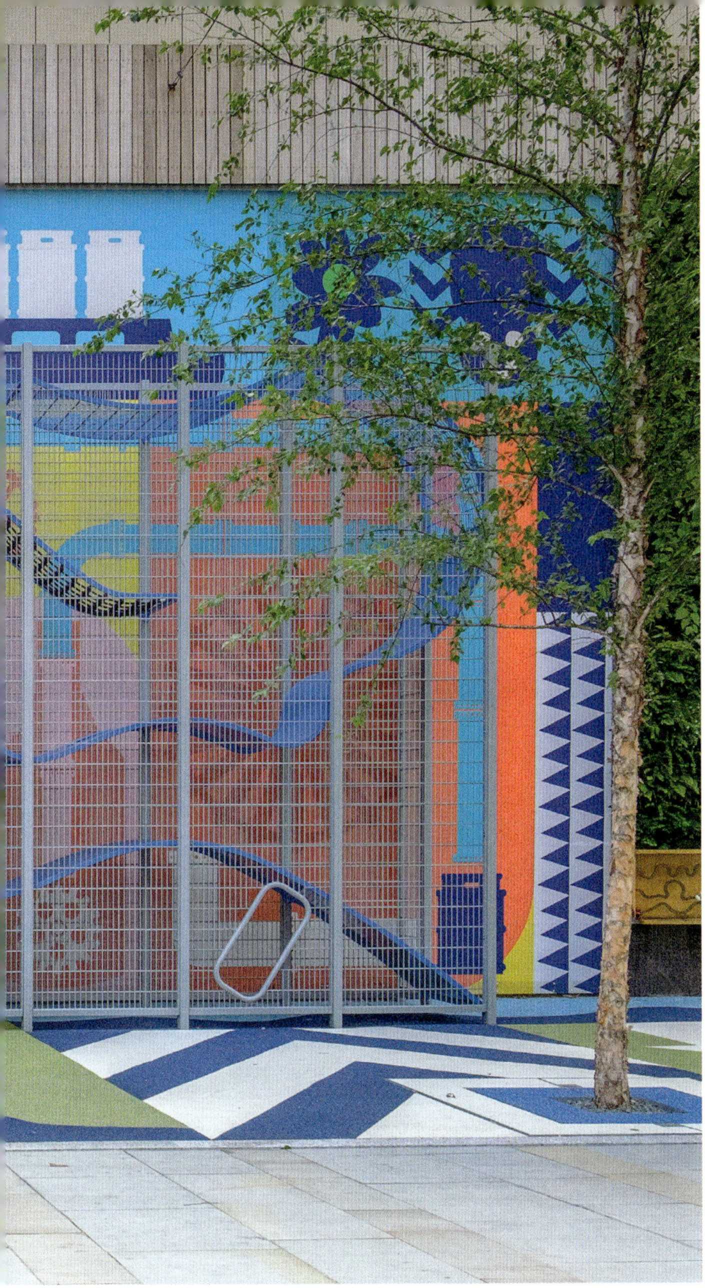

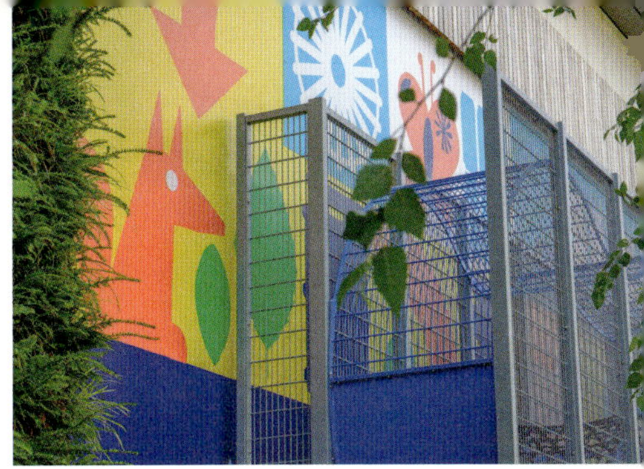

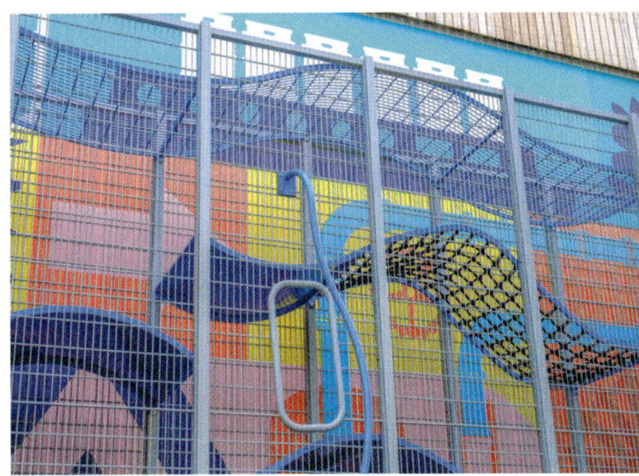

● Why RYB? ● Acknowledging playing as a fundamental activity for children, the design utilizes a primary color palette in paper-based activities for public engagement. Sheets from GFSmith's Colorplan[1] range in red, yellow, and blue were employed, and children participated in tasks like pattern drawing and character illustration. The successful application of these colors influenced the final design.

1.GFSmith's Colorplan: a versatile and sustainable paper range crafted in Great Britain, offering 55 colors, 25 embossings, and 10 weights for diverse creative applications.

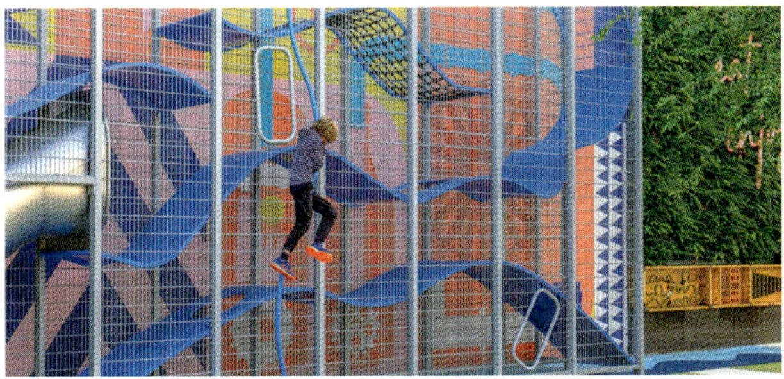

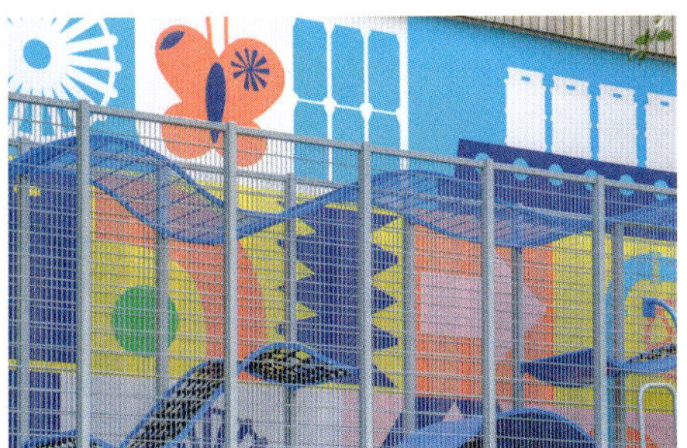

47 RENTAL STORE

• The *47 RENTAL STORE* exhibition at d47 MUSEUM, Shibuya, Tokyo, in 2021 features a logo and graphics designed for renting or purchasing products and services from each of the 47 prefectures. Visitors can share feedback with creators, fostering the discovery of new possibilities. The design draws inspiration from traditional plastic tags used for lending and other purposes.

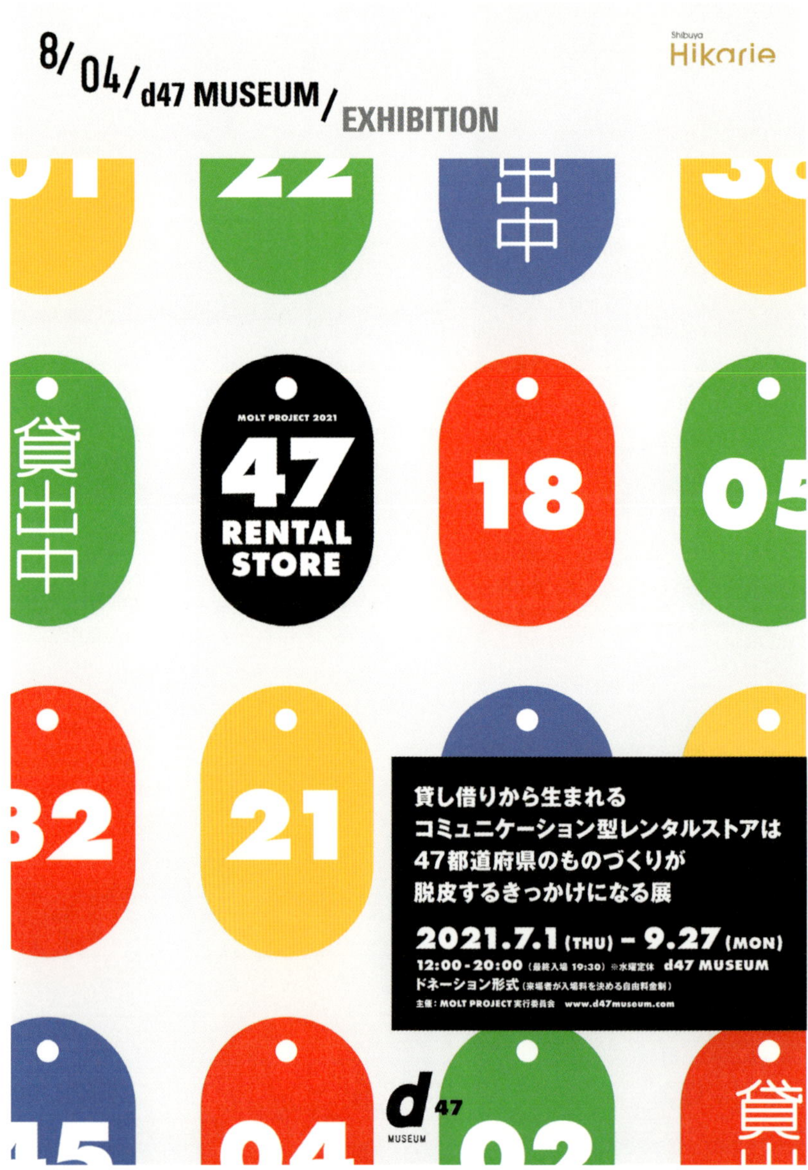

• Design Studio: MOTOMOTO inc. • Designer: Kenichi Matsumoto

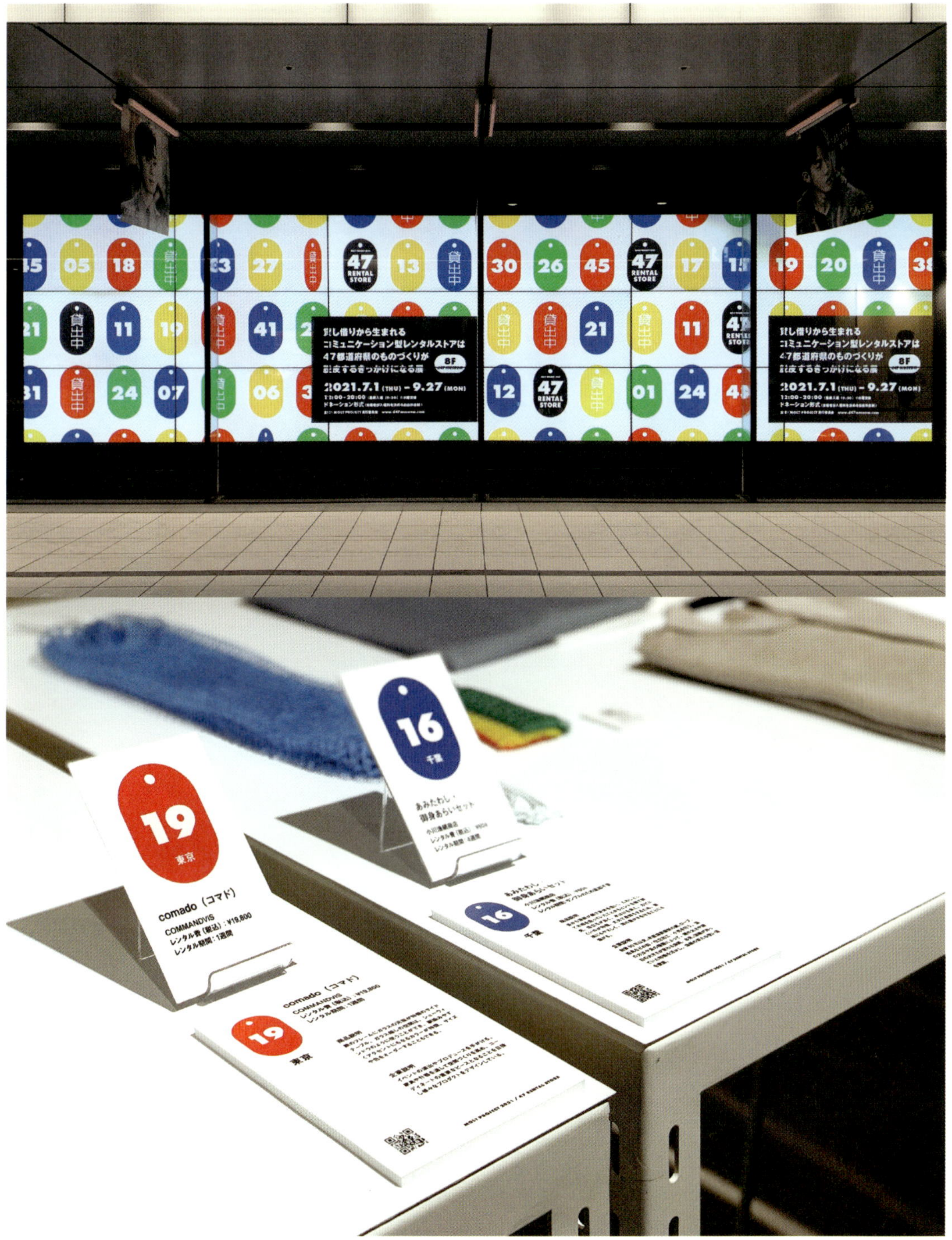

● Why RYB? ● Inspired by the simplicity of old-fashioned plastic tags that employed primary colors, the design team opted to follow suit, incorporating four colors to infuse vibrancy and liveliness into the exhibition event.

● Client: MOLT PROJECT Executive Committee

C0 M100 Y100 K0 | C0 M20 Y100 K0 | C80 M50 Y0 K0

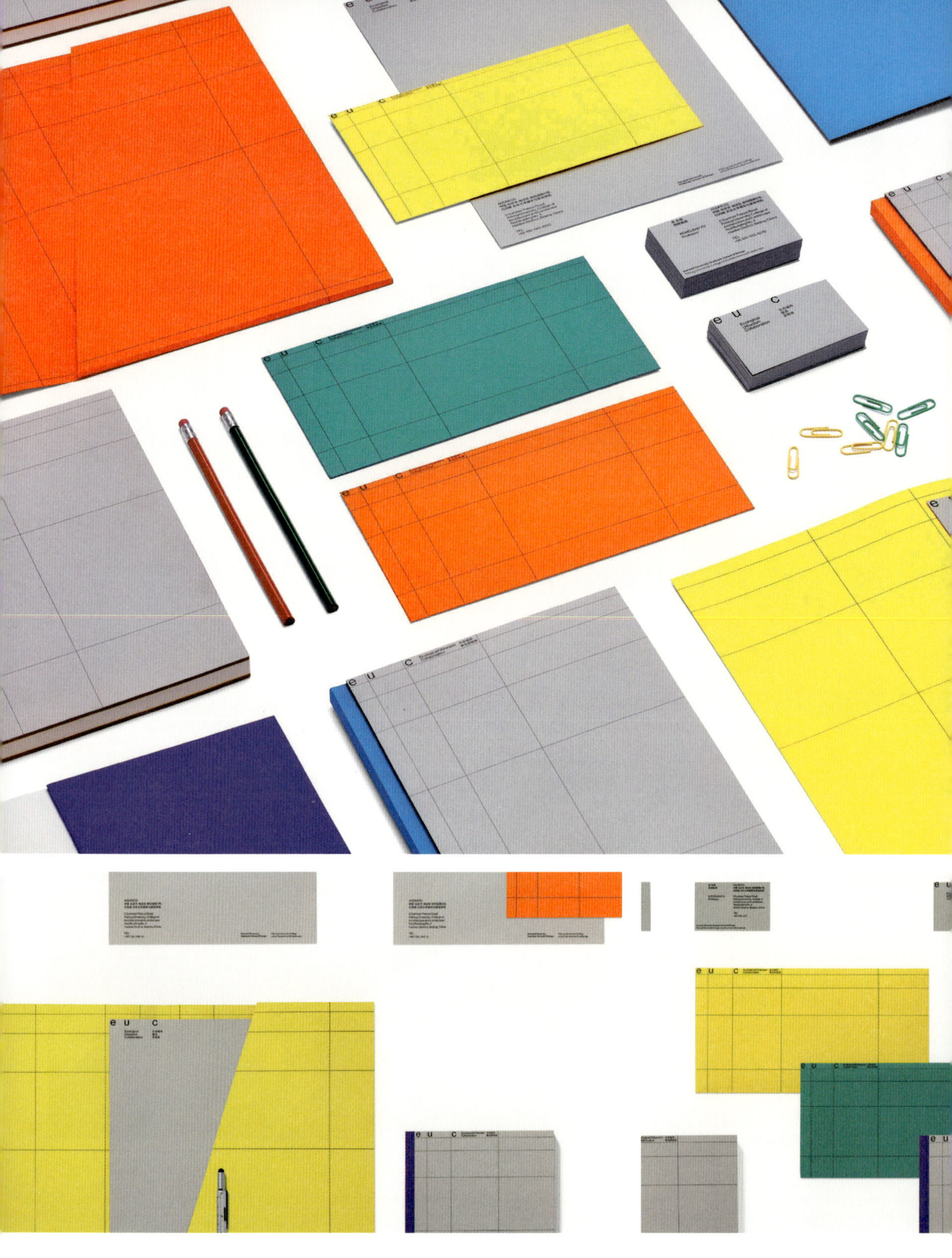

 • Design Studio: ABCD • Art Direction: Guang Yu • Designer: Pan Zhengzhong • Client: Harvard University & Peking University

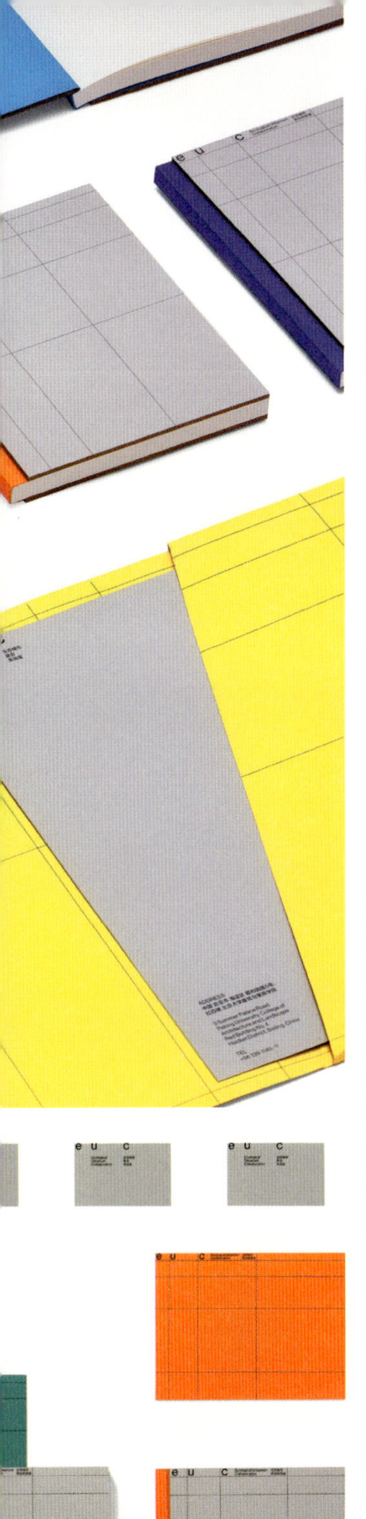

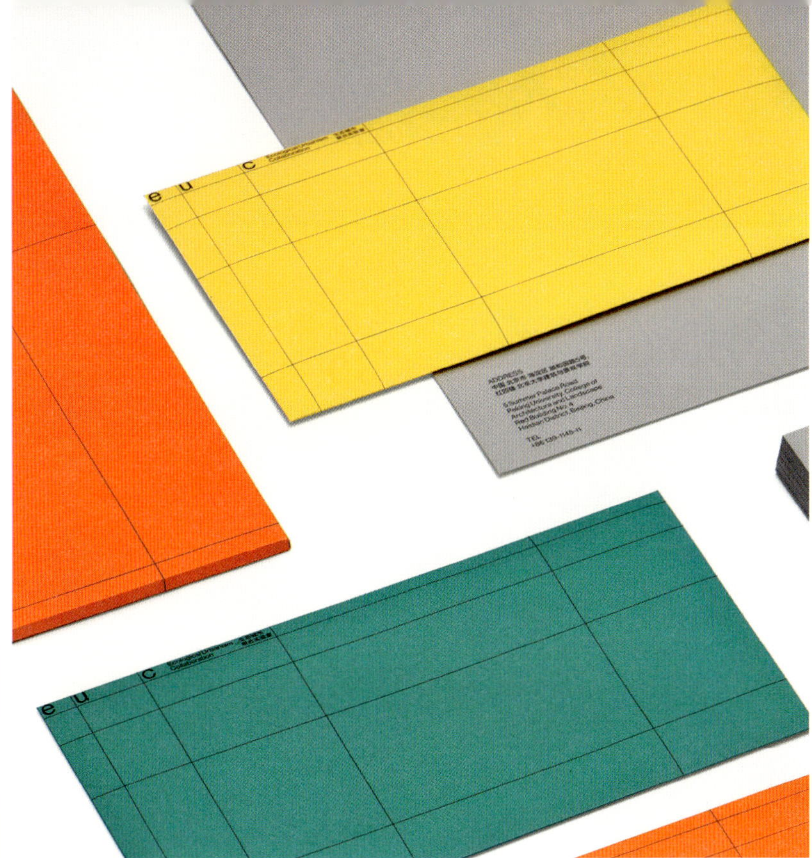

EUC Eco-City Joint Laboratory • This academic project, commissioned by Harvard University and Peking University, encompasses urban planning, architecture, livelihood, and academia. The design prioritizes meeting specialized needs while avoiding isolation, maintaining precision, and considering public understanding. Utilizing scale and grid, with the identity information gradually expanding in multiples, the design conveys order and regularity in an easily understandable manner, aiming for a non-controversial outcome.

• Why RYB? • Integrating vibrant colors into order and regularity, the designer alerts the traditional perception of landscape architecture as "cold." While maintaining precision and sophistication, it bridges the gap with the public, achieving universal comprehension.

C3 M78 Y97 K0 | C3 M4 Y83 K0 | C77 M25 Y0 K0

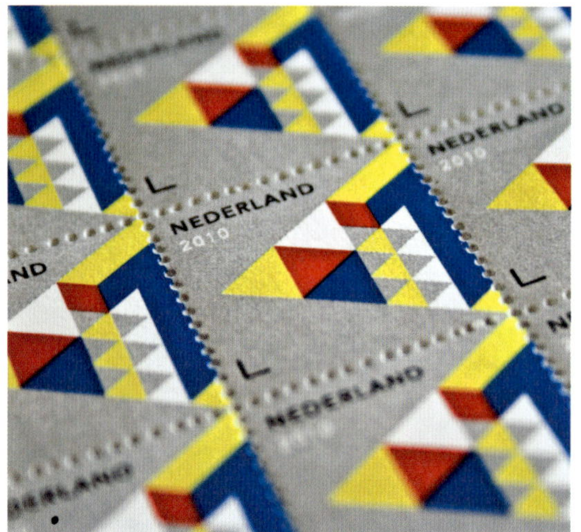

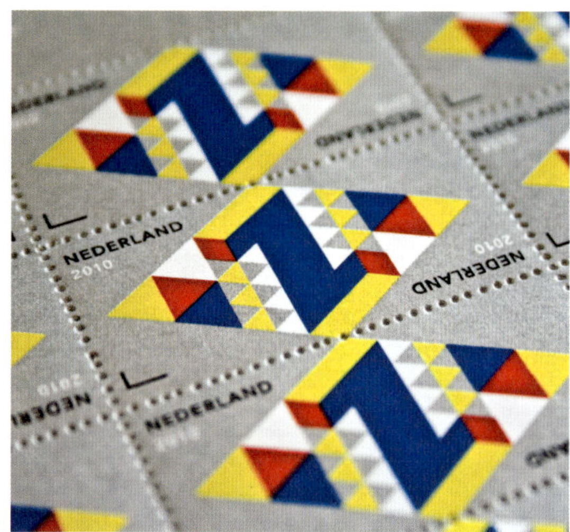

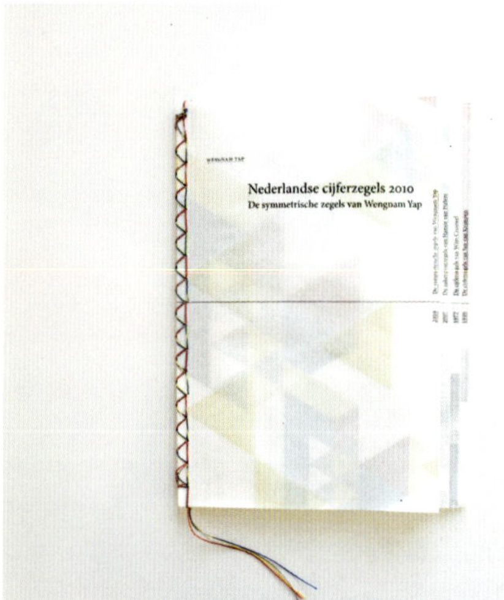

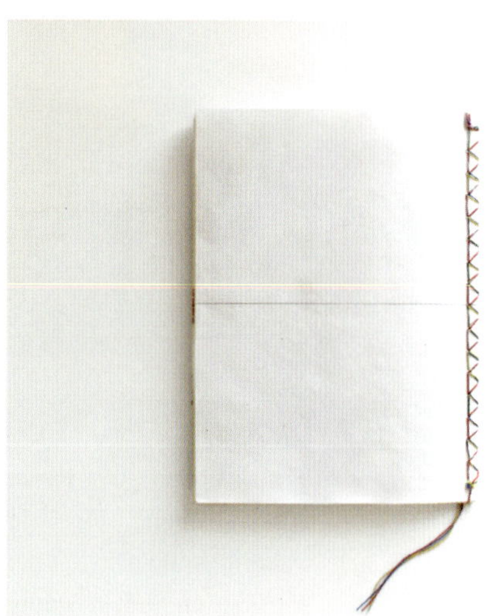

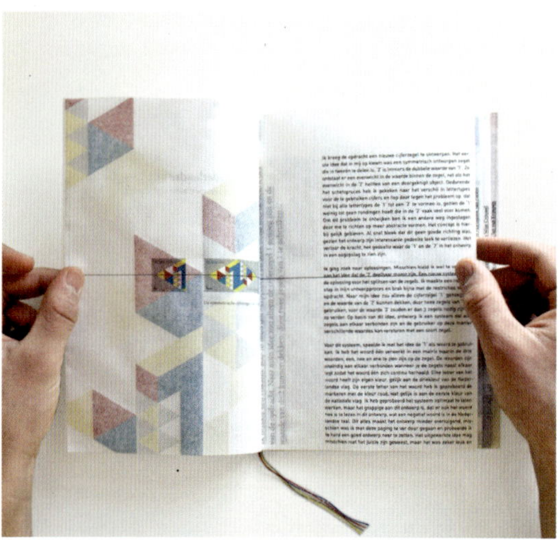

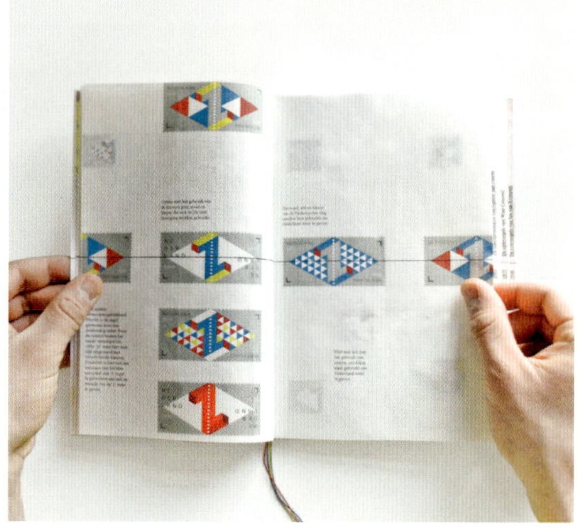

• Design Studio: **Weng Nam Yap** • Designer: **Weng Nam Yap** • Client: **Self-initiated**

The Dutch Symmetrical Number Stamp, 2010

● Inspired by notable designers, the project focuses on crafting symmetrical "1" and "2" stamps, exploring a harmonious interplay between form and function. The challenge lied in transforming the curviness of "2" into the angular shape of "1," creating a visually harmonious representation. ● Utilizing a triangle grid, the design achieves ambiguity, blending "1" and "2" into a captivating, symmetrical composition. Originally planned for just the "1" stamp, practicality led to including the "2," resulting in a successful representation of value balance through symmetrical design principles.

● Why RYB? ● The chosen color palette is straight-forward; it was drawn from the De Stijl movement, adding depth and historical significance to the Dutch stamps.

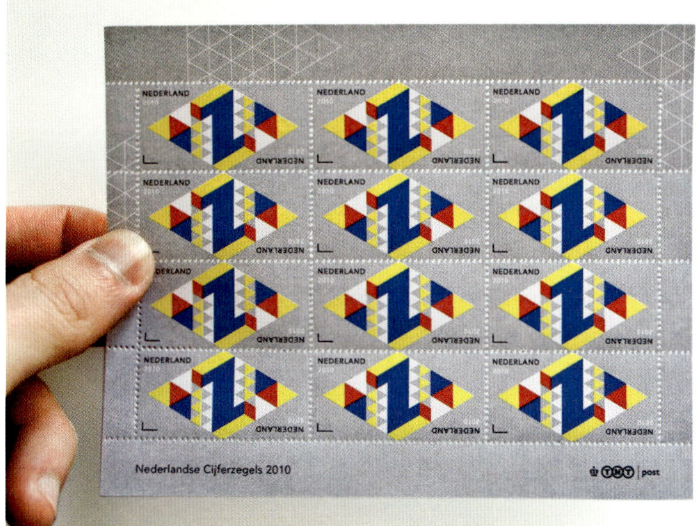

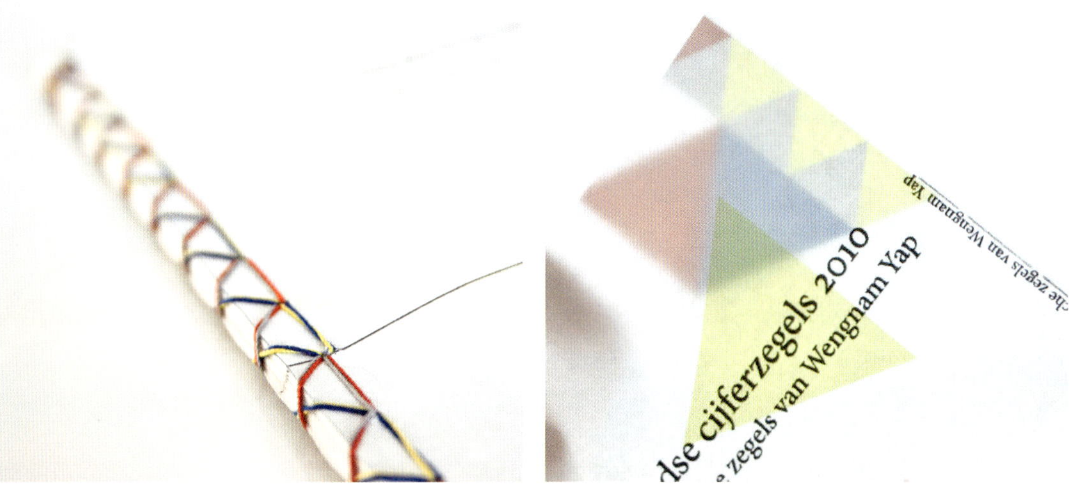

C15 M100 Y90 K10 | C0 M0 Y100 K0 | C85 M50 Y0 K0

ZAMAG 10TH ANNIVERSARY EDITION

● Over the last decade, *ZAMAG* has remained dedicated to its diverse and inclusive founding ethos. Originating from Macau, it explores new themes and perspectives to deepen the understanding of the city for Macanese and display its unique character globally. As a part of Macau's media landscape, *ZAMAG* focuses on local issues, continuing to explore various societal aspects and share compelling stories with its readers.

● Why RYB? ● *ZAMAG*'s 10th-anniversary theme centers on a return to basics, reflected in the exhibition's color scheme of the three fundamental colors. This choice symbolizes the magazine's fresh start and original intention. The colors, visually linked to "ZA," create a strong contrast, attracting readers' attention and enhancing the visual appeal.

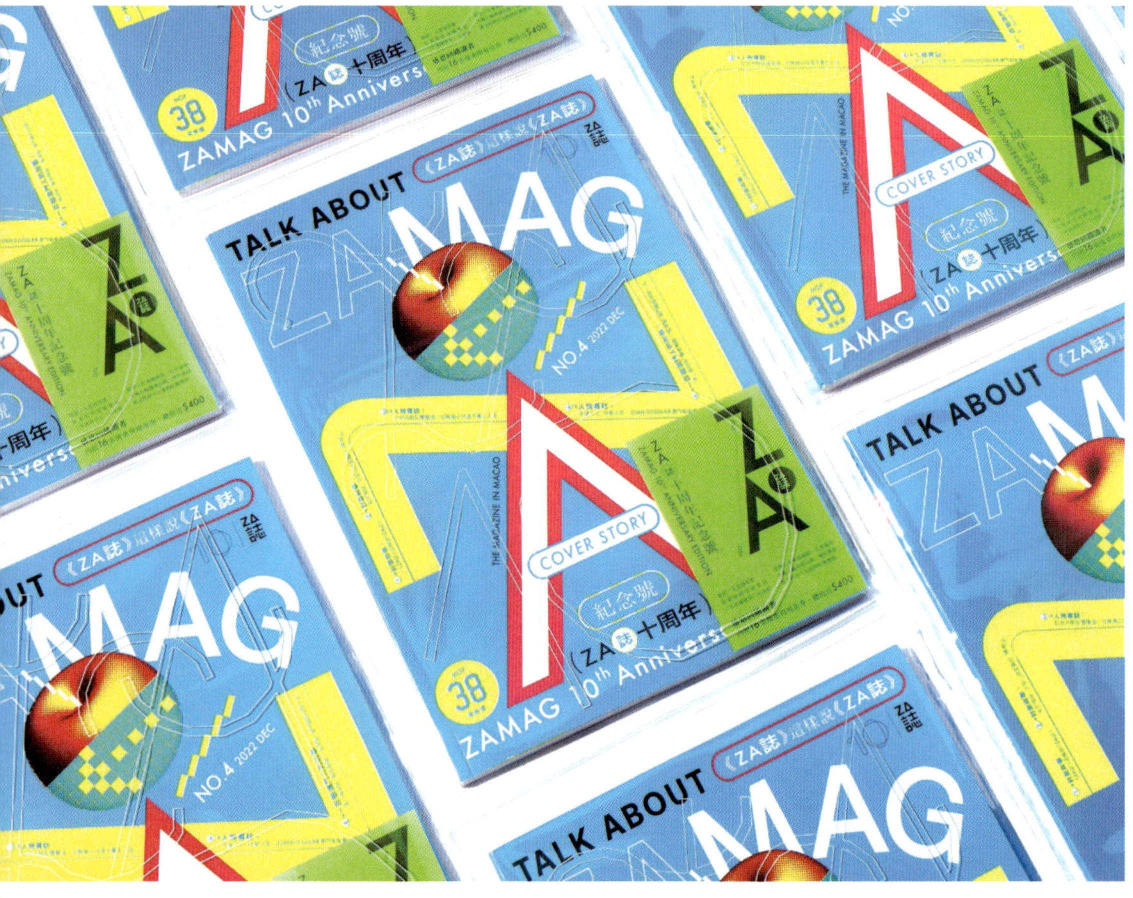

C0 M100 Y0 K0 | C0 M0 Y100 K0 | C100 M0 Y0 K0

● Design Studio: Indego design ● Designer: Lam Ieong Kun, Dan Ferreira ● Client: ZAMAG

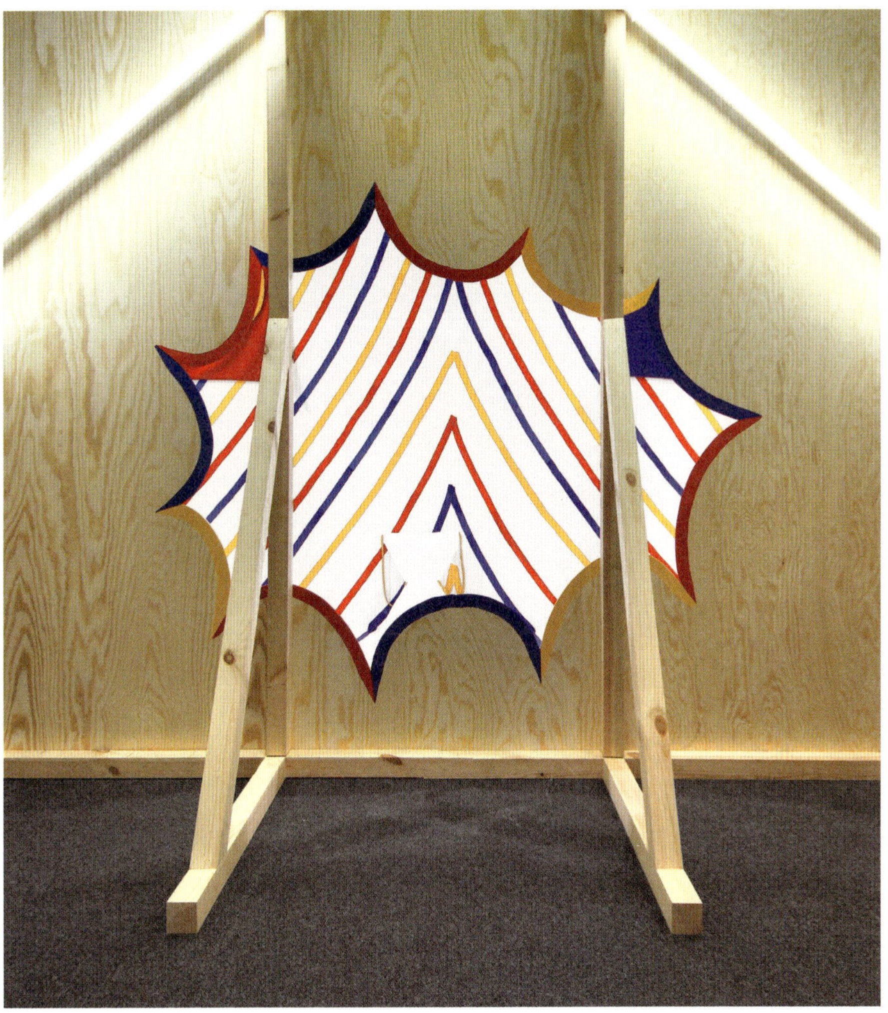

La Pachanga ● In childhood, the designer transformed urban elements into an imaginary playing field for soccer and basketball games with friends, embracing the unprejudiced and non-professional spirit of "pachanga (a word that lends its name to a dance originating from Cuba and to any party, uproar, tun among friends, popular activities, or street games among friends)." When invited to contribute to a children's exhibition, the designer created an installation featuring a unique basketball court, emphasizing the joy of playing for its own sake, liberated from competition.

● Why RYB? ● The designer chose red, yellow, and blue colors, commonly used in their work, perhaps due to the vibrant contrast and frequent use of these primary colors in children's designs. These colors evoke a cheerful and festive connotation, possibly tapping into the nostalgic essence of childhood and eliciting positive vibes upon sight.

● Design Studio: Ruohong Wu & José Quintanar ● Designer: José Quintanarar

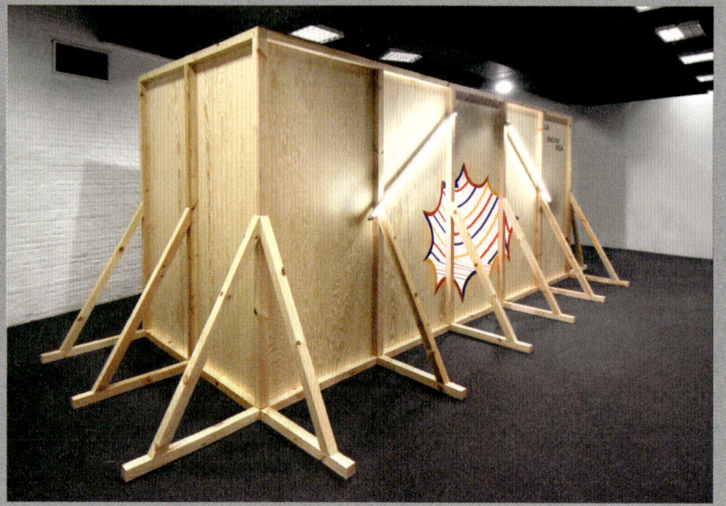

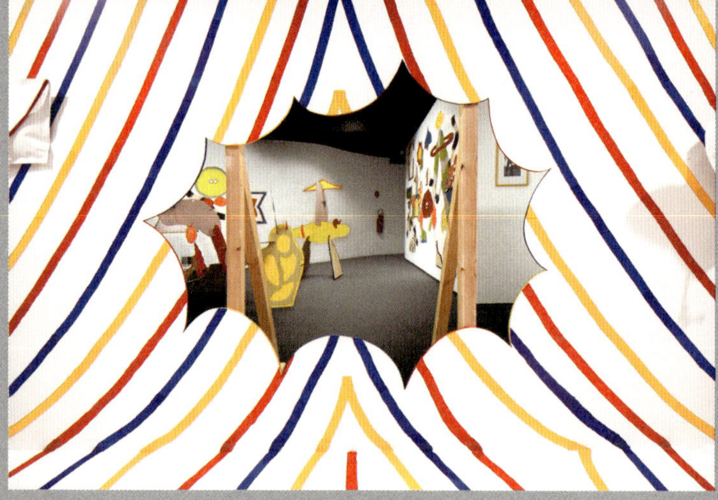

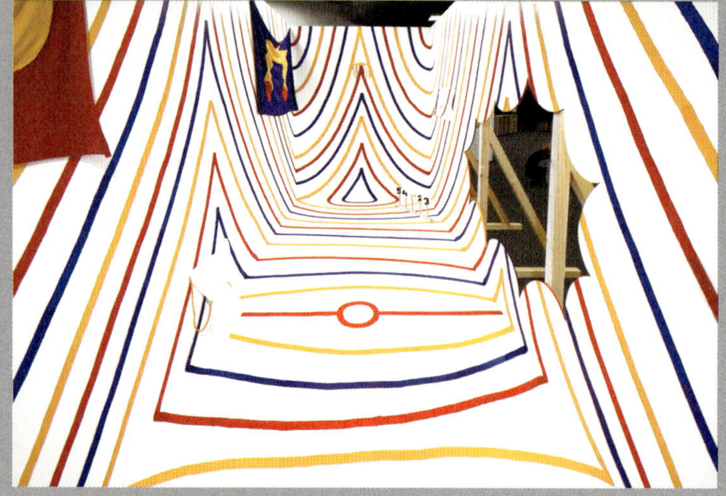

• Client: Jungle Festival. centre culturel de liège les chiroux.

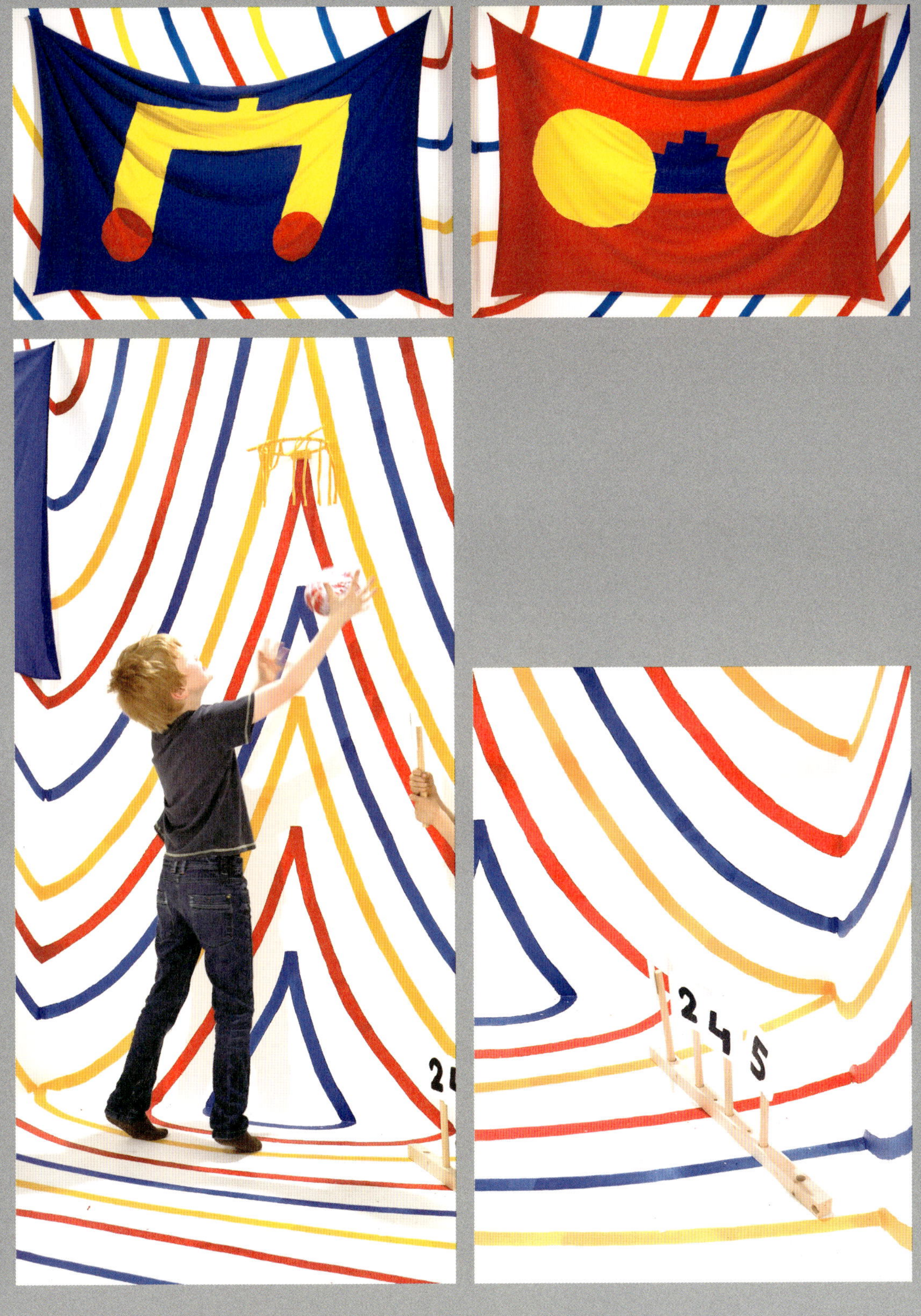

C0 M92 Y100 K0 | C3 M5 Y99 K0 | C73 M40 Y0 K0

Pacifff (Prêt À Couture Internacional Fashion Film Festival)

● Pacifff, an international Fashion Film Festival in Córdoba, Argentina, centers on the relationship between films, fashion, and design. The designers created a series of striped typographic layouts inspired by both films and fashion, in a repeating pattern. This simple
and versatile logic is designed to be applicable for future editions of the festival.

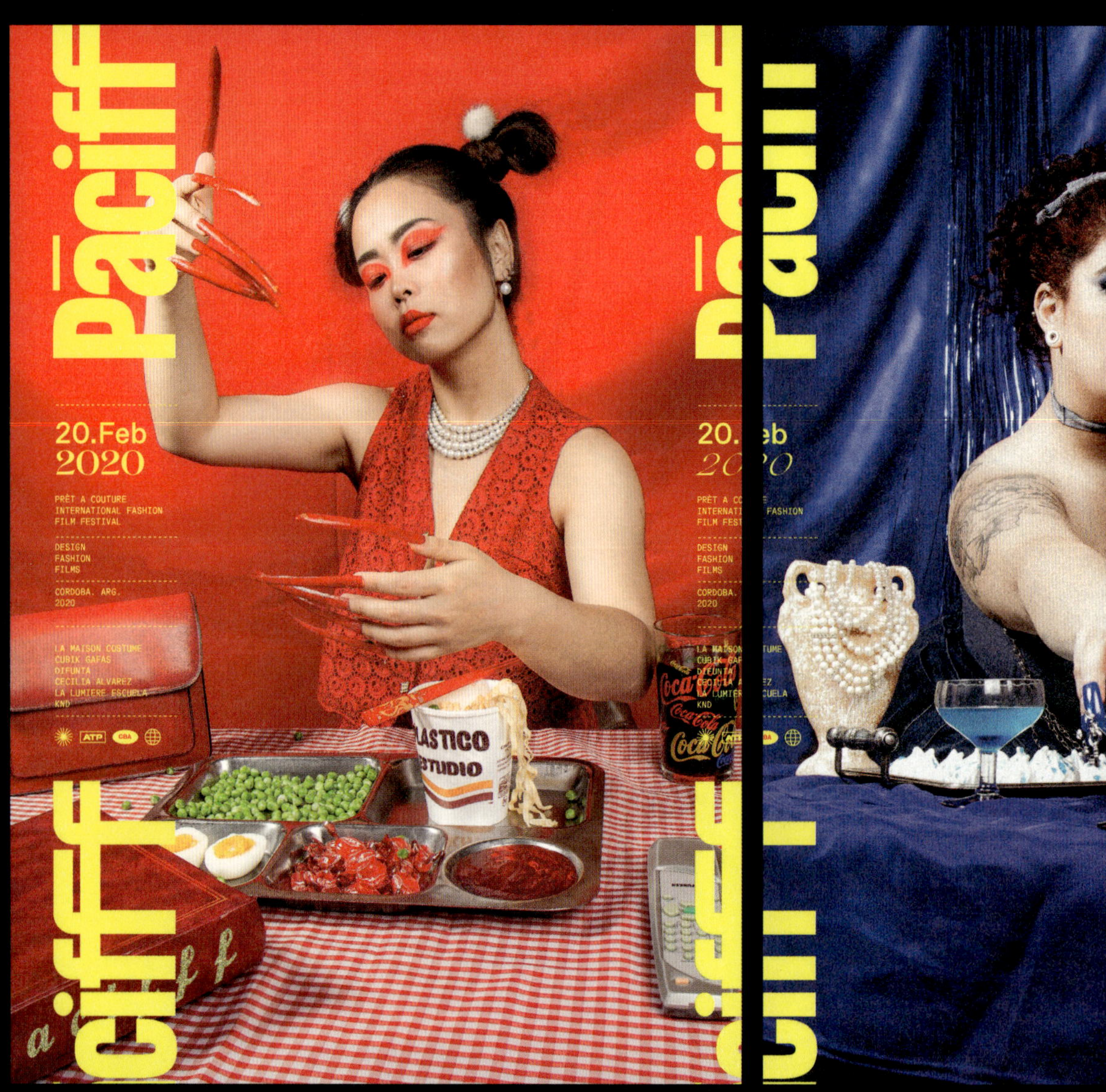

● Design Studio: Kinoto Studio ● Client: Pacifff (Prêt À Couture Internacional Fashion Film Festival)

● Why RYB? ● The design team had access to excellent photos primarily in primary colors (red, blue, and green). To enhance the primary color palette and establish a striking contrast between the photos and the information layer, they strategically incorporated yellow.

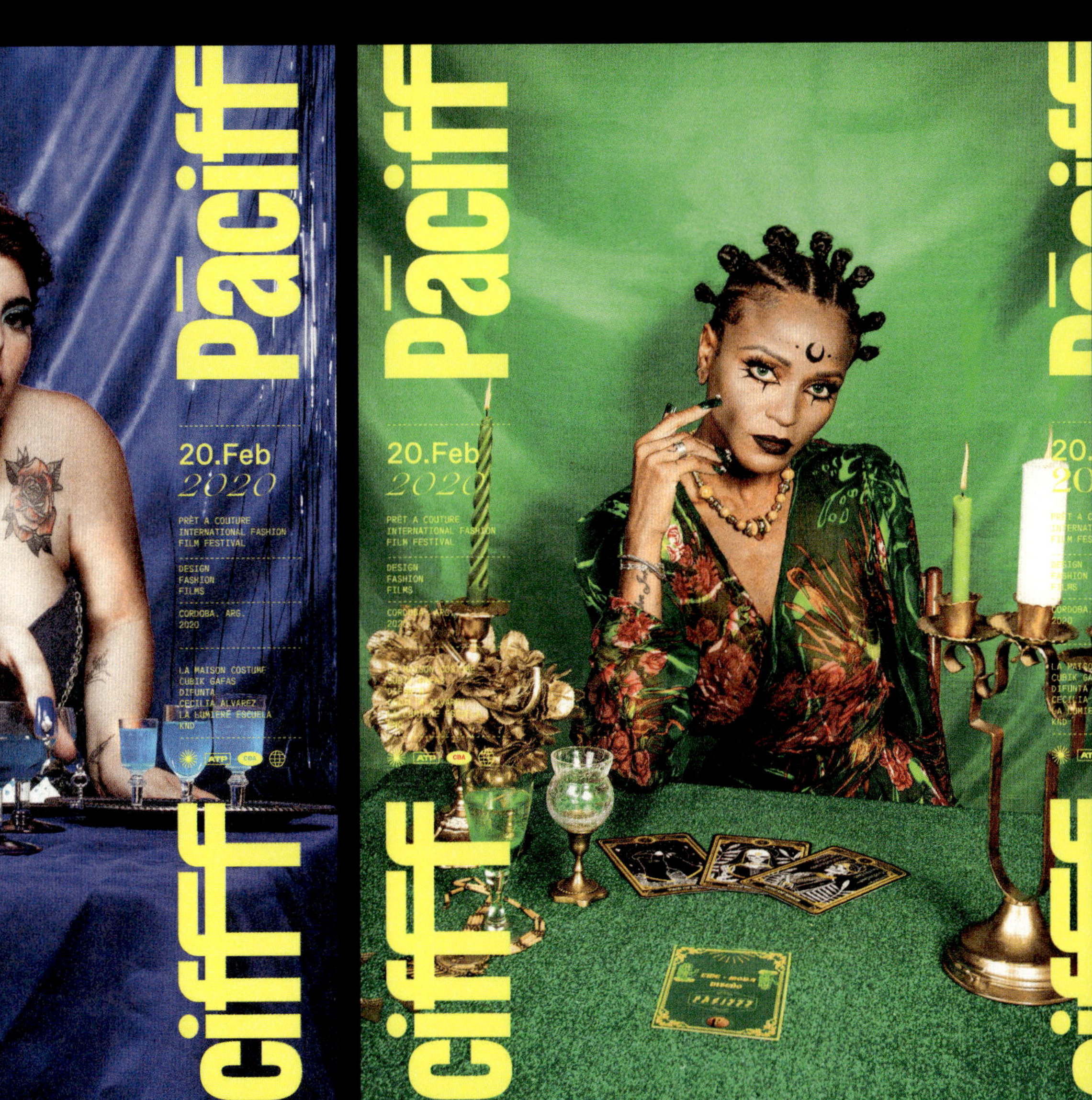

C0 M100 Y100 K0 | C0 M0 Y100 K0 | C93 M77 Y0 K0 | C85 M10 Y100 K0

smørrebrød kitchen nakanoshima

● The designer envisioned a café specializing in the traditional Danish dish smørrebrød, an open sandwich with diverse toppings eaten with a knife and fork. The design aims to visually emphasize the combination of multiple toppings, capturing the vividness and deliciousness of the dish. Simple yet delicate illustrations showcase various smørrebrød ingredients, intending to evoke a fresh sense of Nordic style among customers.

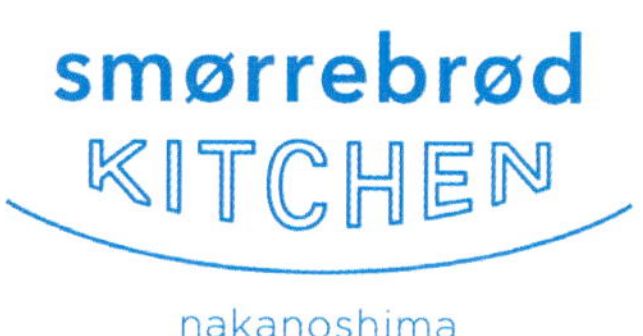

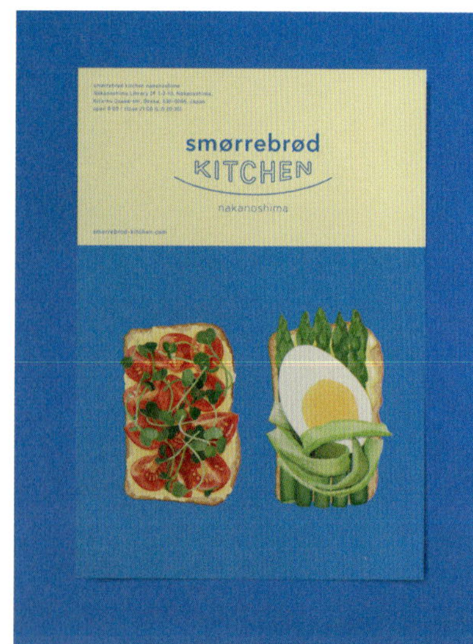

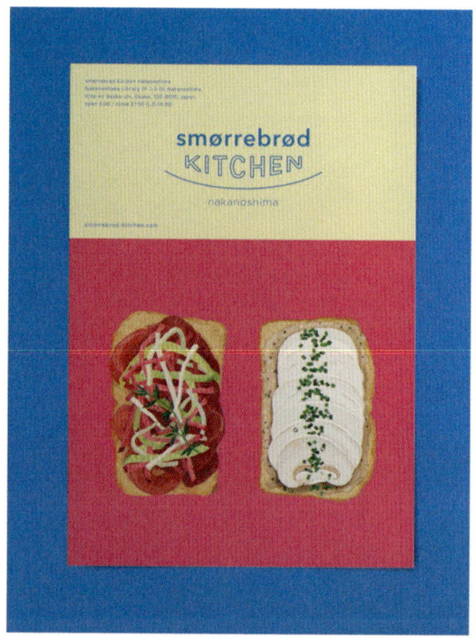

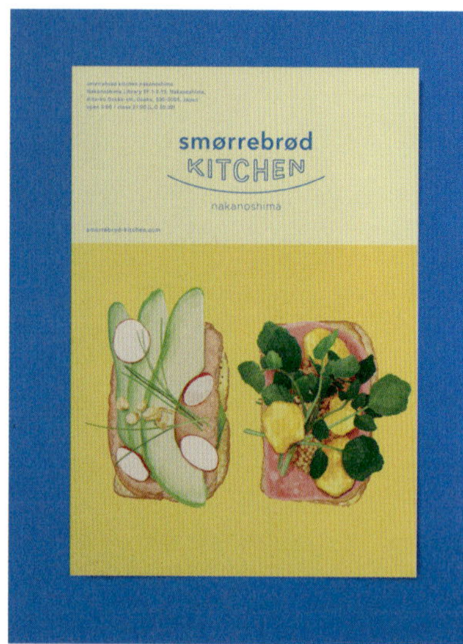

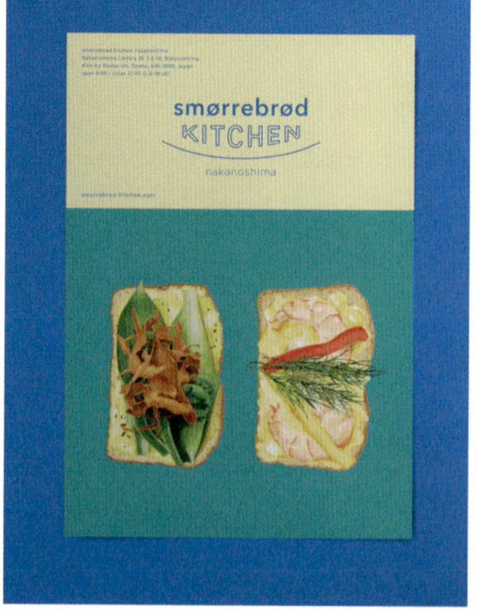

● Design Studio: Paragram ● Designer: Yusuke Akai

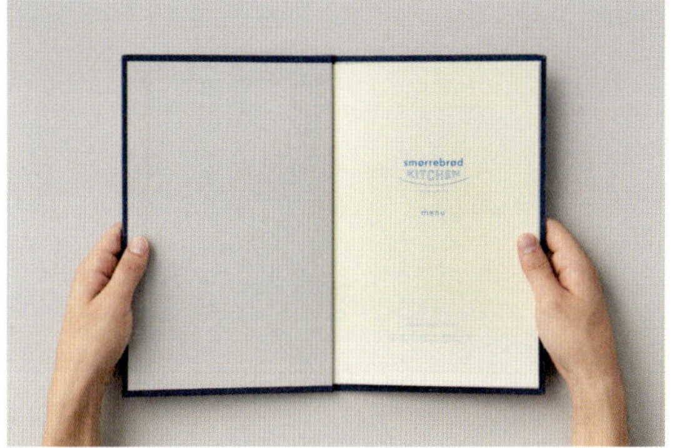

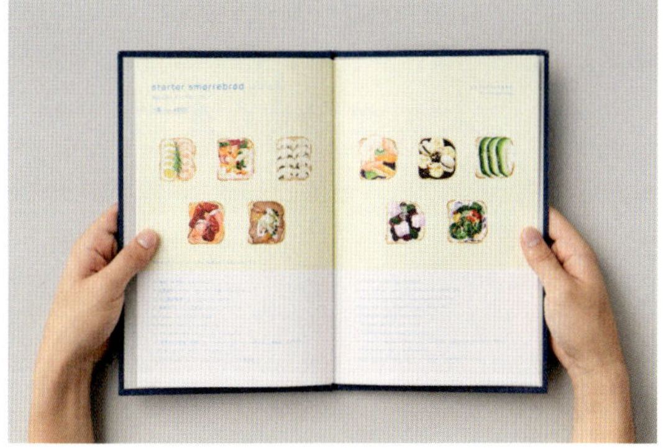

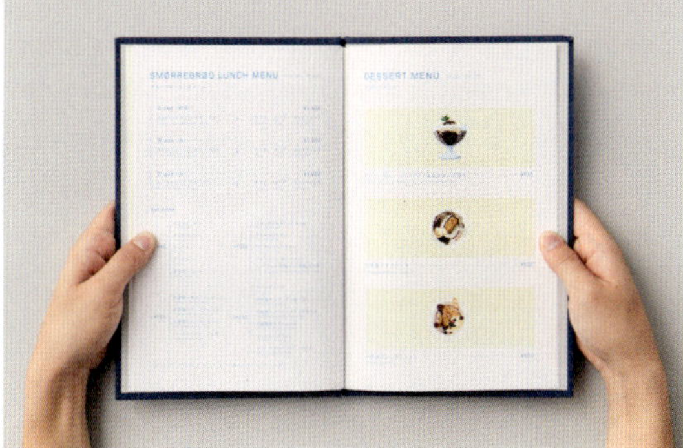

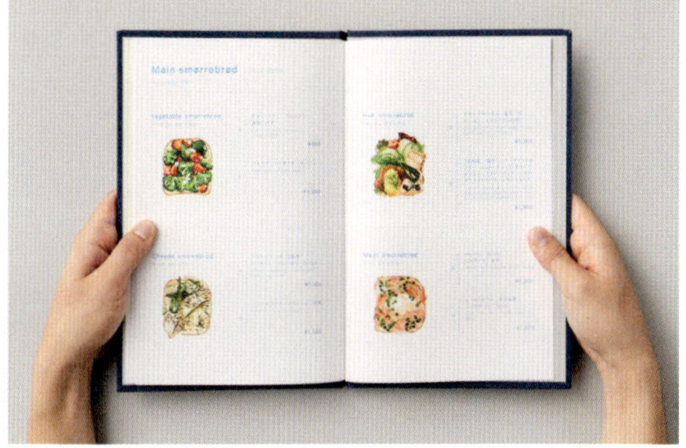

● Why RYB? ● In the design of Japanese restaurants and cafes, the focus is often on the color red, associated with a "delicious" appearance. Alternatively, many establishments opt for achromatic colors to purely express the "original taste of ingredients." However, in this case, a different approach is taken to deviate from the typical coffee shop image. The design adopts a color strategy that diverges from traditional coffee shops, featuring blue as the main color. This intentional choice creates a sharp contrast between the color image of accompanying ingredients (brown bread, green vegetables, red tomatoes and bacon, yellow eggs, etc.) and the color palette of the smørrebrød itself.

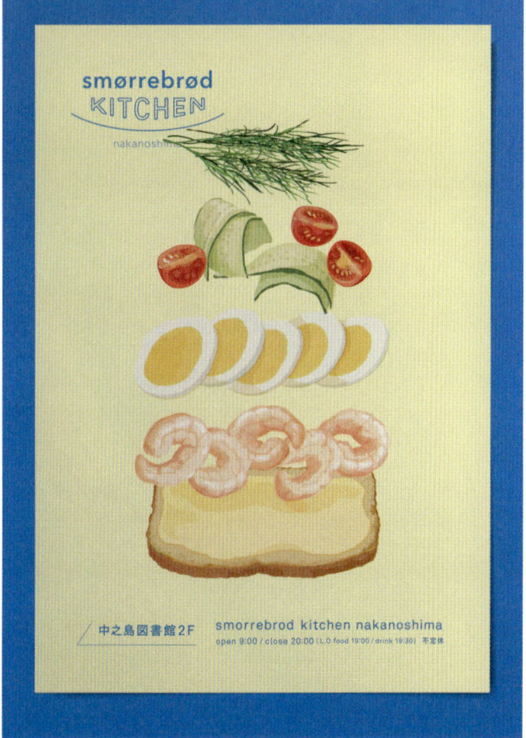

C20 M90 Y25 K0 | C12 M18 Y75 K0 | C80 M15 Y40 K0 | C100 M5 Y0 K0

x30 Packaging Design

● x30 is a high-end candy gift box introduced by Gu Shan He Zhi. Due to the high cost of raw materials and unique processing methods, this product costs and sells at almost the highest price in the market among similar products. The recommended consumption is 3 pills per day for 30 days. The design team made 30 independent small packages, each marked with a number from 1 to 30, prompting users to consume one each day. The products used each day are independent, different, and easy to carry. The gift box uses transparent materials, allowing users to admire 30 exquisite small packages when making a purchase, increasing curiosity and trust in the product.

● Why RYB? ● Breaking down the overall 30-day experience into 30 distinct individual sessions and utilizing colors and graphics to create independent, varied combinations significantly enhances the consumer's experience during usage.

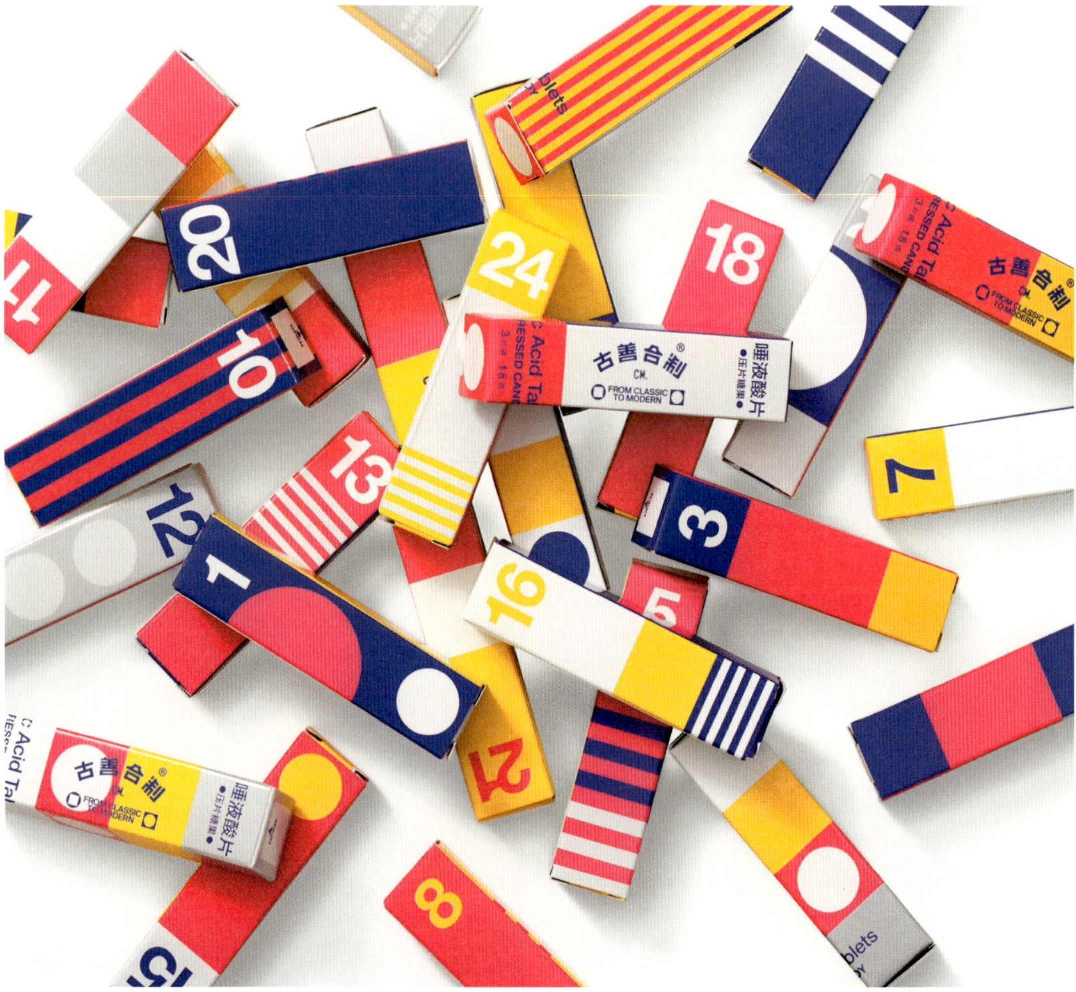

● Design Studio: ABCD ● Art Direction: Nod Young ● Designer: Yusin, Han Lu ● Client: Gu Shan He Zhi

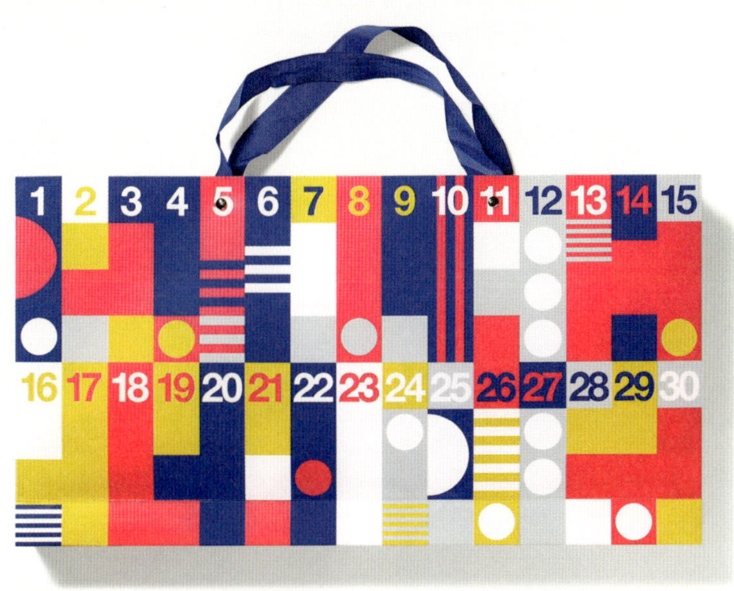
1 2 3 4 5 6 7 8 9 10 11 12 13 14 15
16 17 18 19 20 21 22 23 24 25 26 27 28 29 30

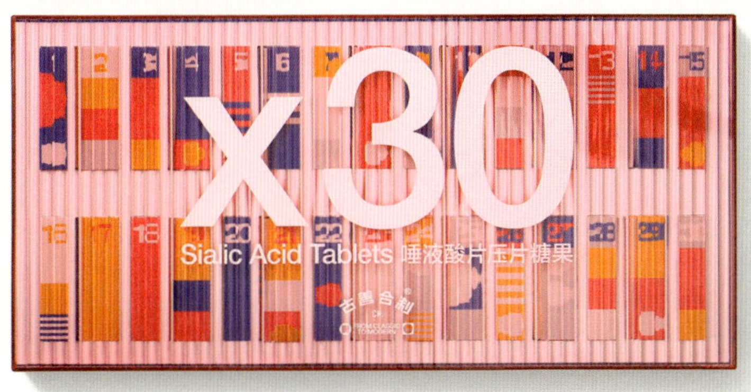
x30
Sialic Acid Tablets 唾液酸片压片糖果
古善合利
FROM CLASSIC TO MODERN

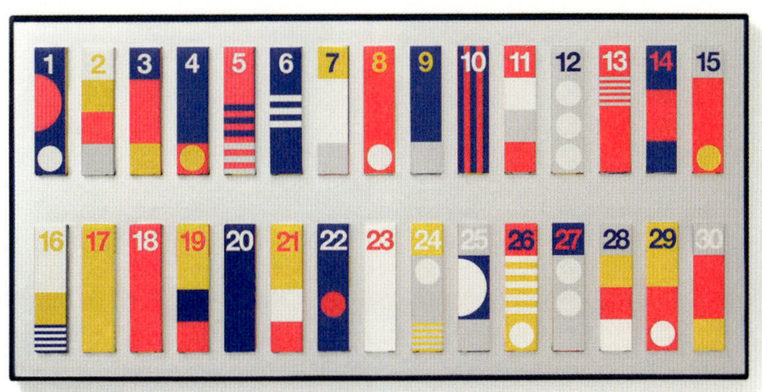
1 2 3 4 5 6 7 8 9 10 11 12 13 14 15
16 17 18 19 20 21 22 23 24 25 26 27 28 29 30

TOKOTON ORGANIC SYMPOSIUM 2015

● The graphic design for an organic symposium takes a unique approach to engage a broader audience. Recognizing that the theme of food is universally relevant, the design aims for openness rather than the traditional closed atmosphere of academic conferences. In order to capture people's interest, pop expressions are employed instead of the conventional imagery associated with organic vegetables, such as soil.

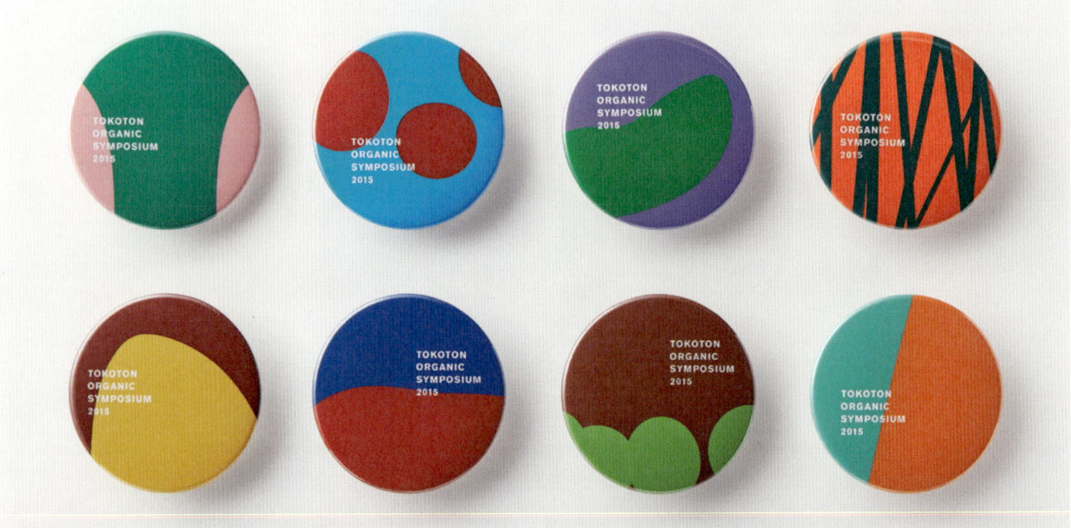

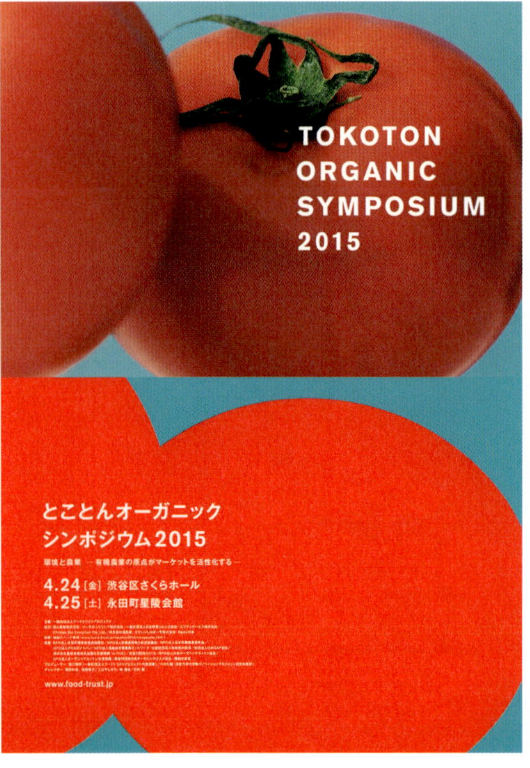

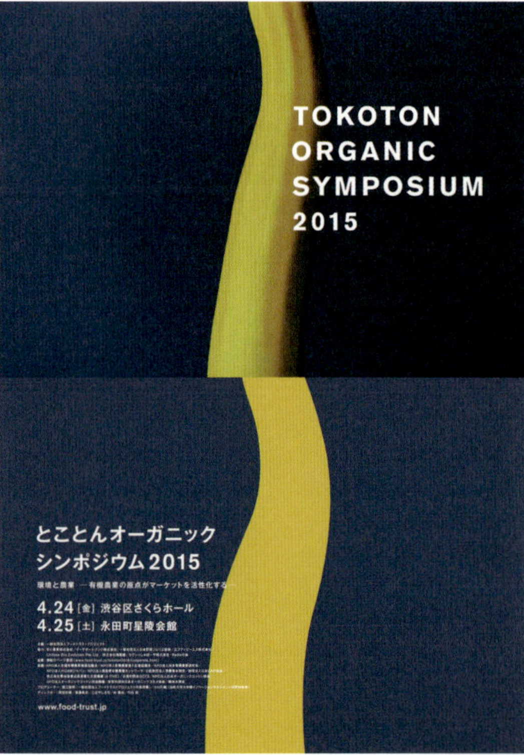

● Design Studio: MOTOMOTO inc. ● Designer: Kenichi Matsumoto ● Client: Food Trust Project

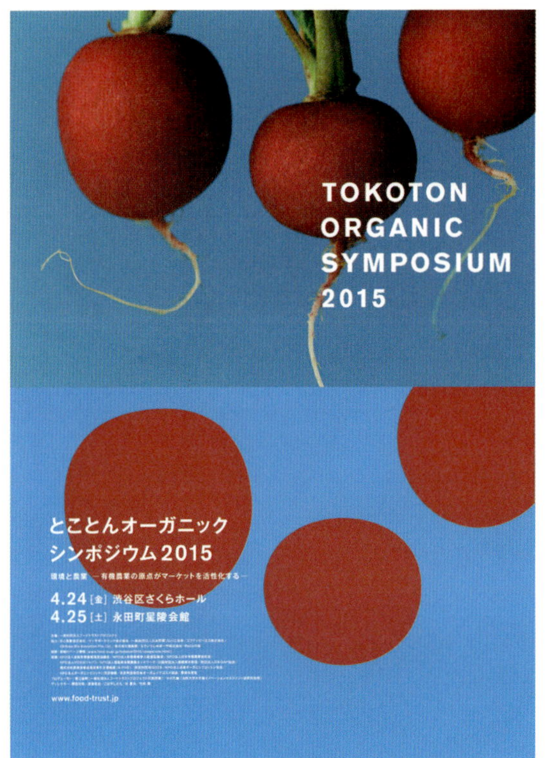

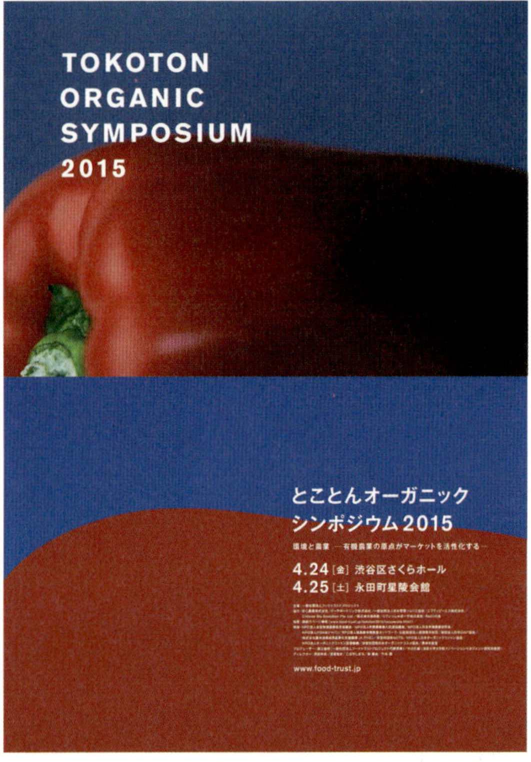

● Why RYB? ● The designer selected several organic vegetables, with a focus on highlighting the beauty of each vegetable's shape and color. The choice of colors and composition was made based on the aesthetic appeal created by the combination of each vegetable with the background color. The background colors were selected intuitively, derived from the vegetables' visual qualities rather than numerical values.

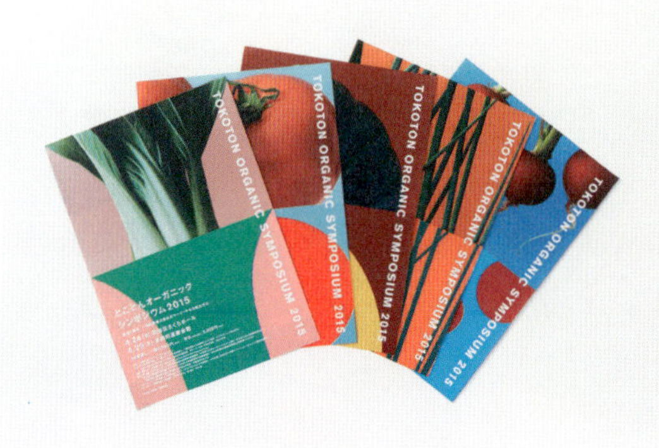

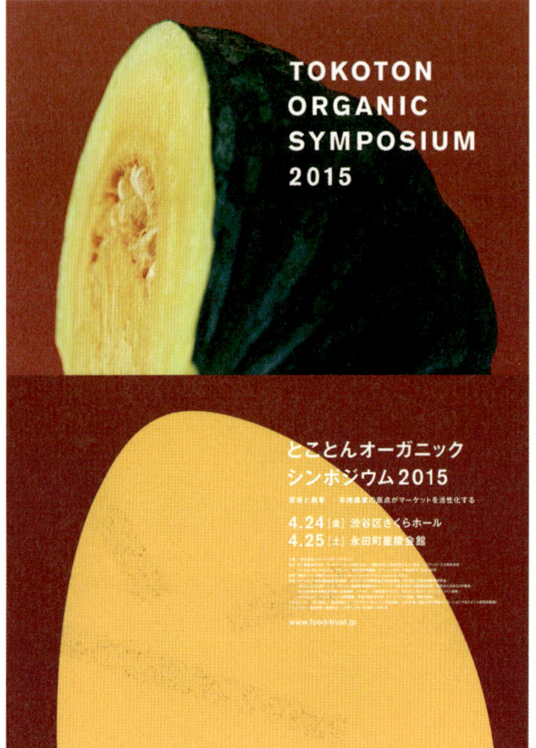

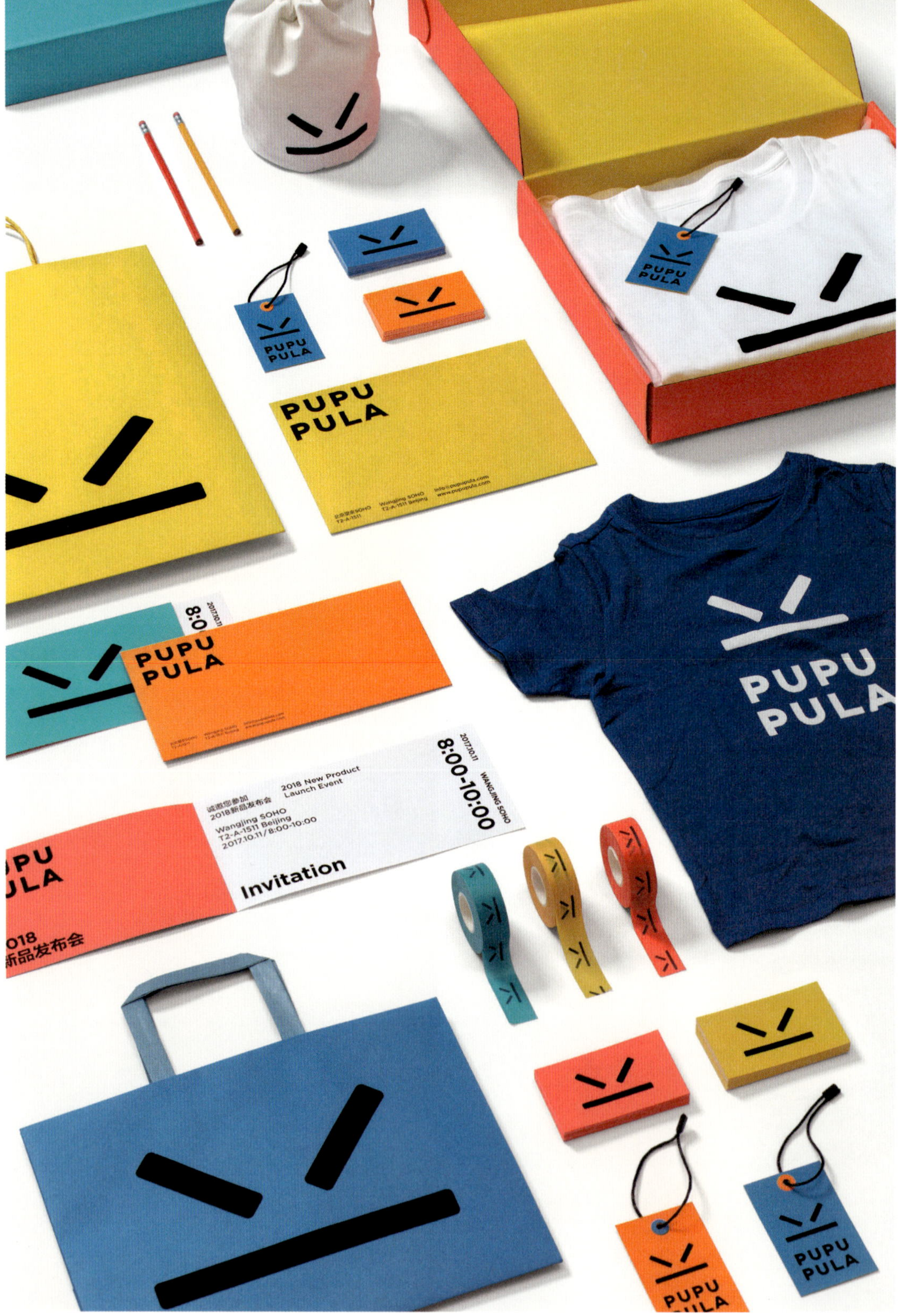

● Design Studio: ABCD ● Art Direction: Nod Young, Guang Yu ● Designer: Nod Young, Yan

PUPUPULA

● PUPUPULA, a children's lifestyle brand, creates innovative products for kids aged 3–12 by embracing their pure and playful nature. The brand focuses on practical solutions that meet both children's and parents' needs, seamlessly integrating into modern family life. By acknowledging children's authentic expressions of unhappiness and curiosity, PUPUPULA communicates its genuine approach through simple and lively brand expressions, resonating with parents.

● Why RYB? ● Children are more sensitive to color. In order to allow them to experience more colors visually, parents also tend to provide their children with a richer color experience. Therefore, PUPUPULA creates a colorful and gorgeous world for children to explore.

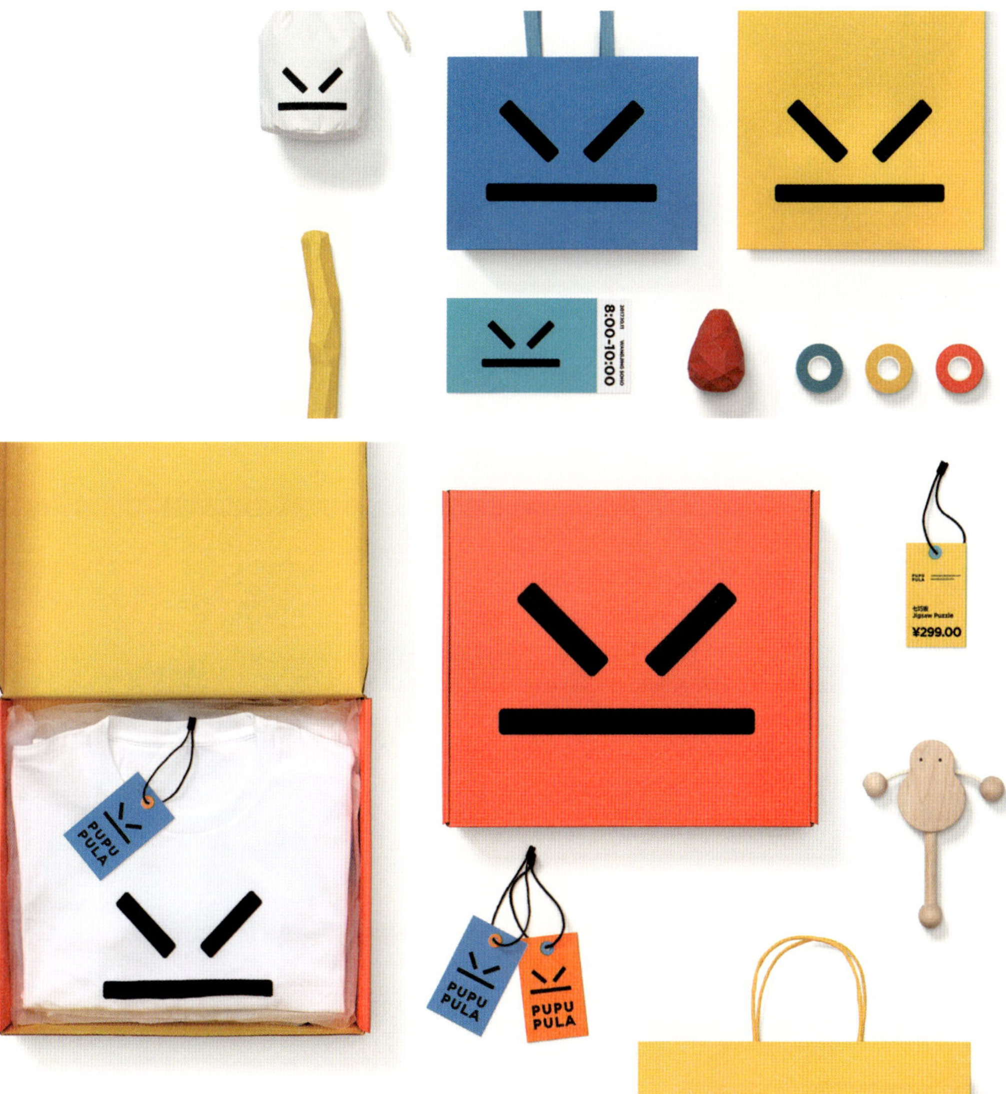

● Client: PUPUPULA

C0 M90 Y55 K0 | C10 M15 Y100 K0 | C80 M20 Y0 K0

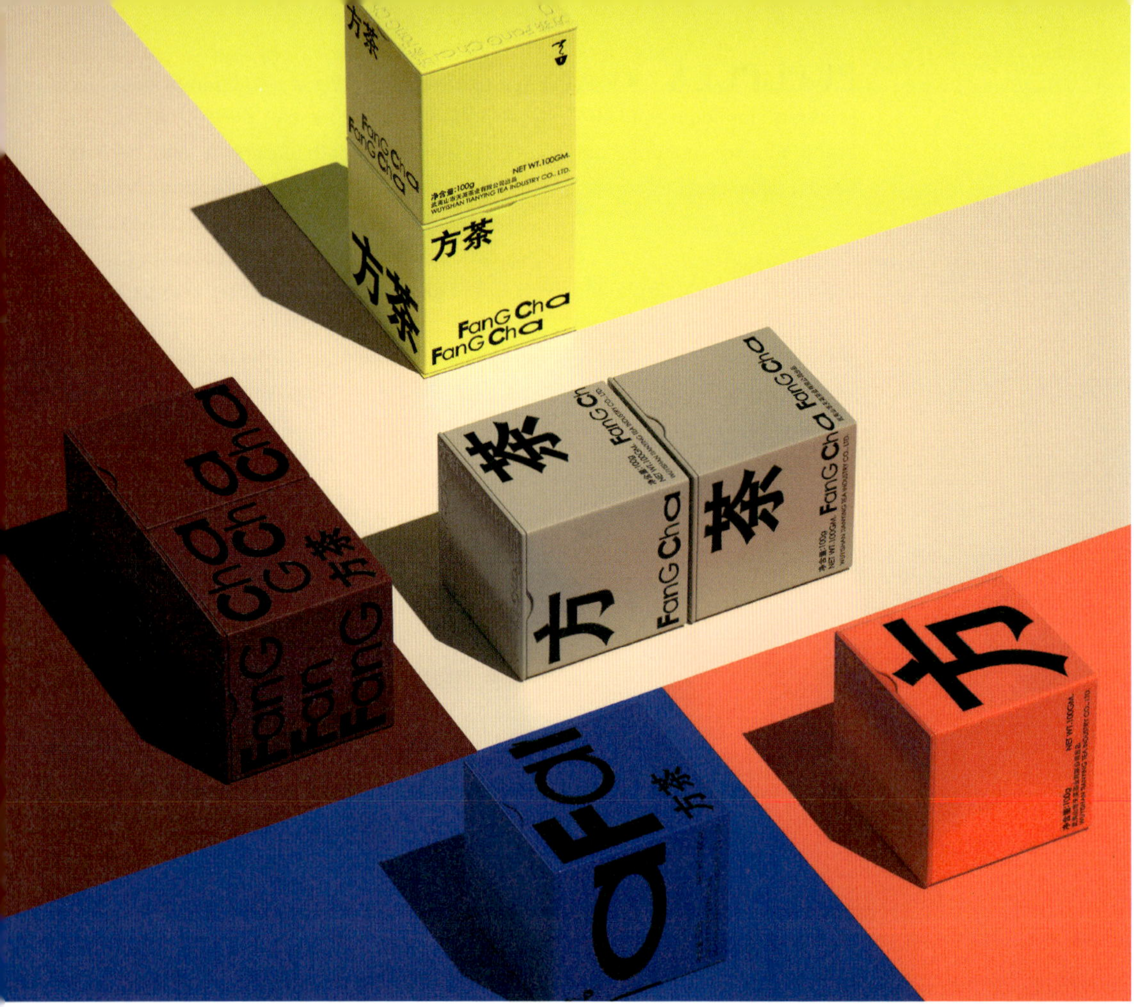

Fang Cha Packaging Design

● Fangcha, designed for post-90s office scenarios, stands out with its transparent matte material and vibrant colors, offering a trendy and efficient tea experience. The enlarged Chinese characters and pinyin, along with a flat design and strong color contrasts, ensure both effective information delivery and visual distinctiveness.

● Why RYB? ● The three colors of red, yellow, and blue are very stable in terms of contrast, providing impactful and influential visuals. The use of high-purity and high-contrast colors enhances recognition and creates a lively atmosphere on the packaging. This achieves efficient information conveyance and visual differentiation.

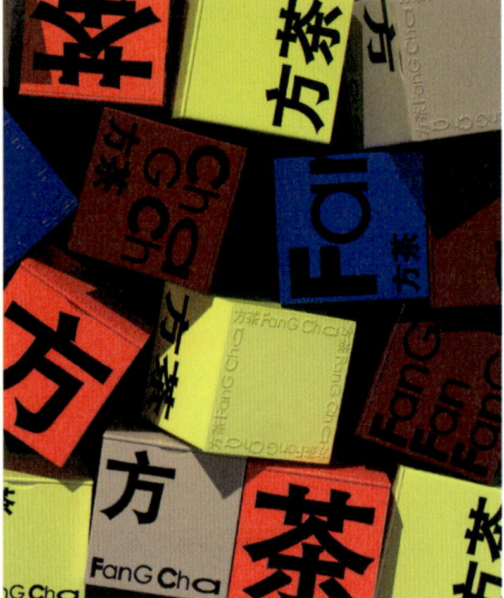

C50 M100 Y92 K30 | C7 M7 Y81 K0 | C0 M86 Y73 K0 | C96 M89 Y13 K0 | C30 M40 Y42 K0

● Design Studio: XXD DESIGN ● Designer: Qiyuan Xiao ● Client: Tianying Tea Co., Ltd.

Zeitgeist Coffee Factory Museum Packaging & Branding

● Zeitgeist, an independent coffee bean manufacturer, prioritizes pure coffee aesthetics in all aspects—products, sales methods, and packaging design. Employing a vertical sales concept, they swiftly deliver coffee beans from origin to consumers through online sales. Recognizing the importance of freshness, Zeitgeist has revamped secondary packaging for quick identification. Unique visual elements denote flavors: warm orange and rounded shapes for floral notes, cool tones and geometric shapes for nutty chocolate, and fiber-like graphics for rich, lightly roasted beans. This design, focused on speed and clarity, encapsulates contemporary coffee culture, ensuring consumers easily grasp and enjoy Zeitgeist's commitment to exceptional coffee.

● Why RYB? ● Utilizing primary colors like red, yellow, and blue, the brand establishes a unique visual language for effective consumer communication, ensuring quick recognition of the new brand's value proposition. Specific color codes, such as "Orange Red" for floral notes, "Yellow" for nutty chocolate, and "Blue" for rich flavors, are visually represented on packaging, enhancing the overall brand experience.

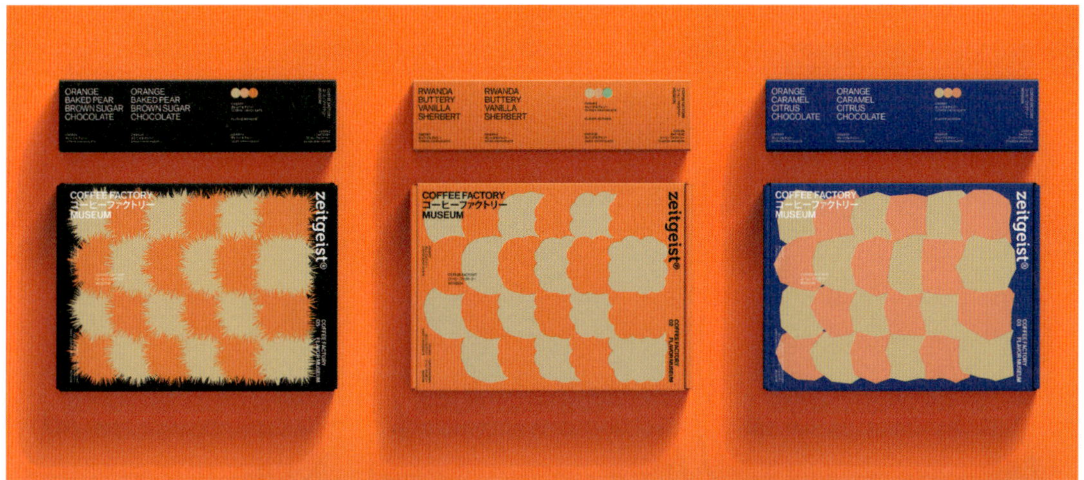

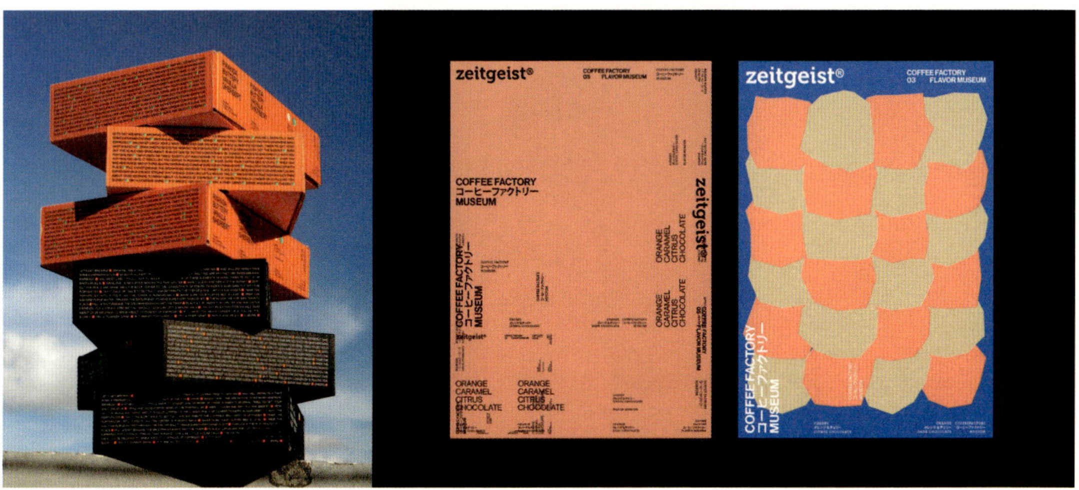

C0 M78 Y100 K0 | C15 M27 Y51 K0 | C87 M68 Y0 K0

● Design Studio: whynotdesign ● Designer: He Yuxuan ● Client: Zeitgeist Coffee Factory Museum

vivo 2023 Spring Festival Gift Box ● The gift box design, centered around the shape of a rabbit candle, presents a series of cute and round rabbit shapes, incorporating hollowing techniques to add whimsy and art flair. With a primary color scheme of red and blue, adorned with a gold accent, it maintains brand recognition while also exuding the festive atmosphere of the Chinese New Year. Notably, the customized chess set brings a modern and fresh touch by updating traditional materials and font design. A chess game, a melting candle, gathering around stove for the New Year's Eve—laughter abounds.

● Why RYB? ● The traditional red color of the Spring Festival is combined with vivo's brand blue in a design variation, enhancing the appeal of the red-blue combination for a more visually pleasing overall effect.

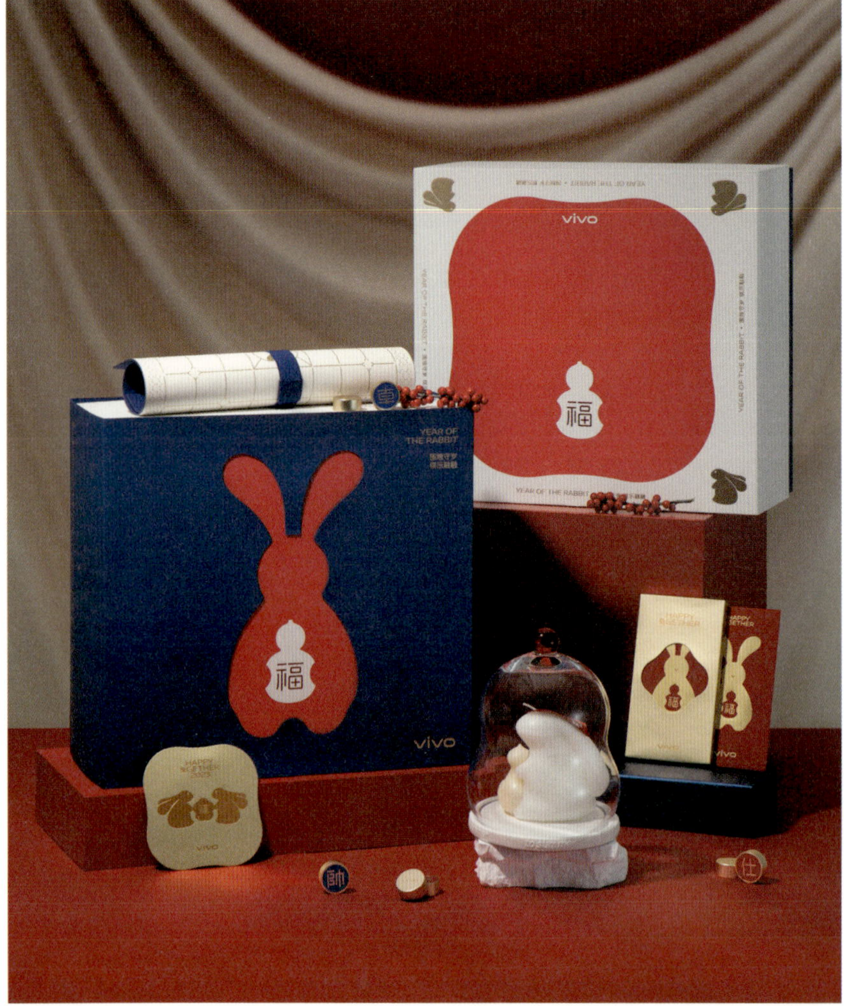

● Design Studio: Standpoint Design ● Designer: Olav Deng ● Client: vivo

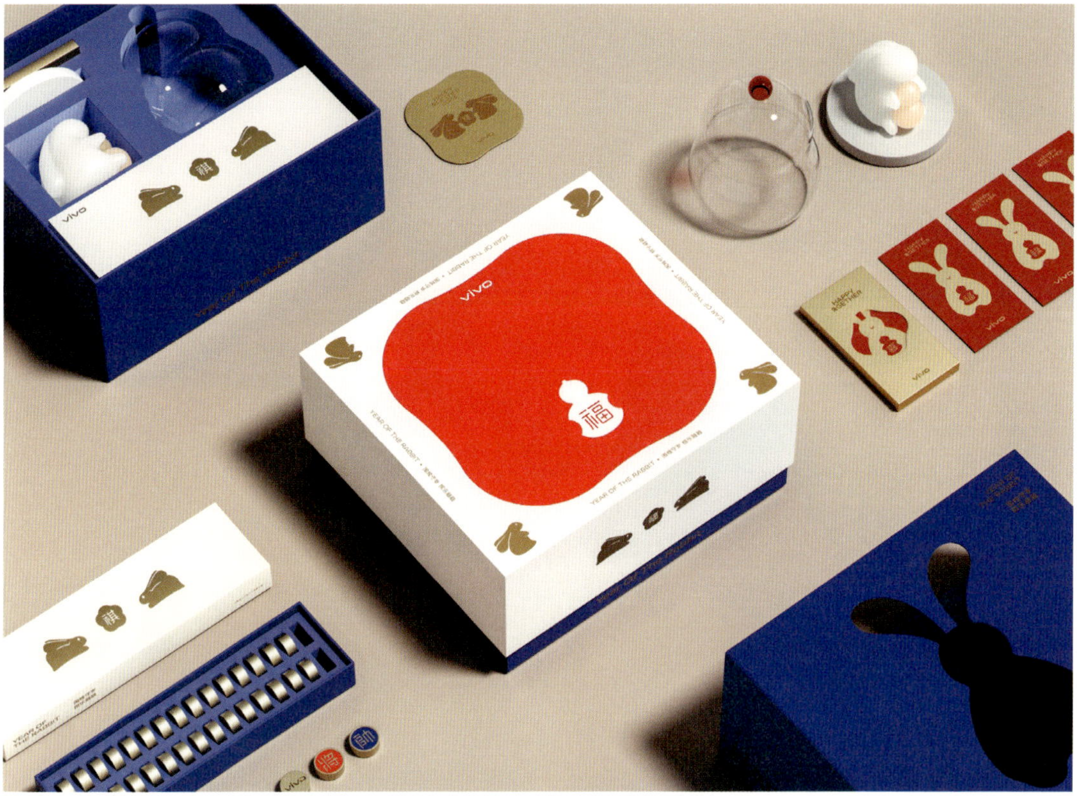

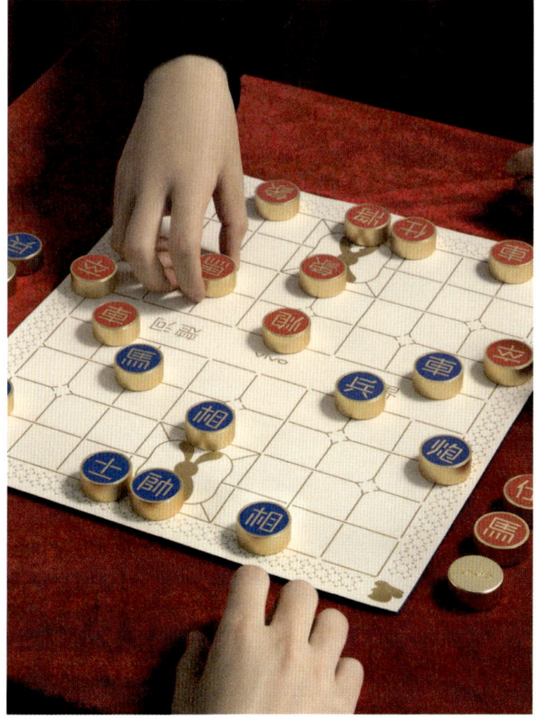

車
馬
兵
車
相
炮
士
帥
相
馬

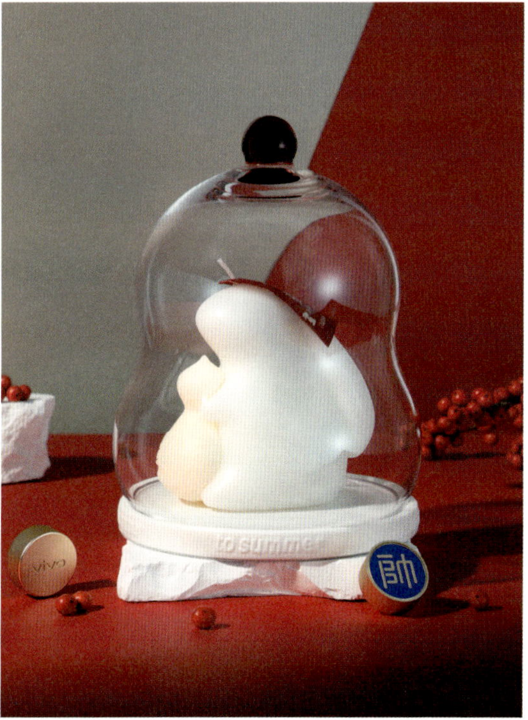

vivo
to summer
帥

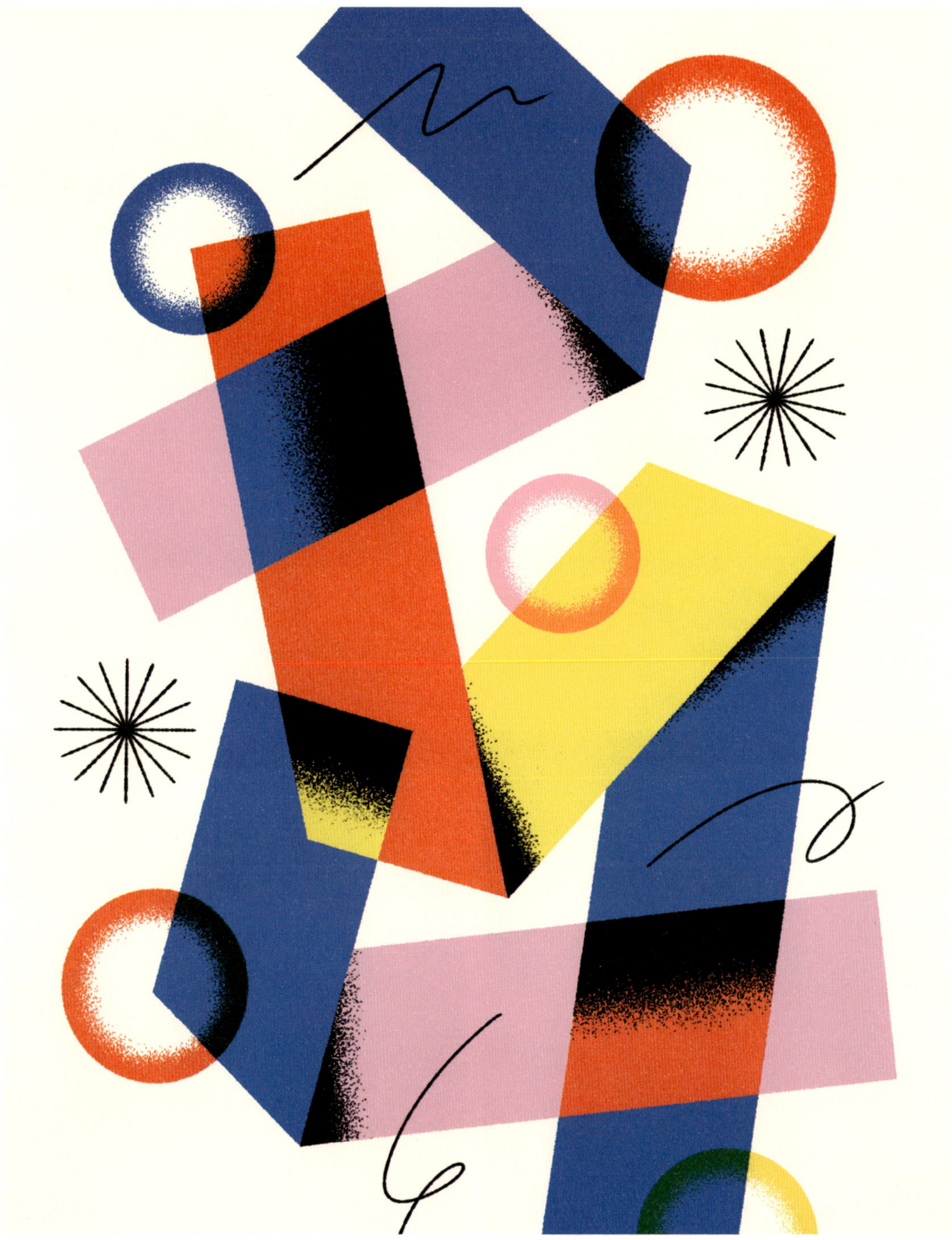

Shape Studies • "Shape Studies" originated as a personal project during the COVID-19 pandemic, serving as a creative outlet. It has evolved into an ongoing exploration of graphic possibilities derived from the fundamental elements of shape, color, and texture.

• Designer: Ray Dak Lam

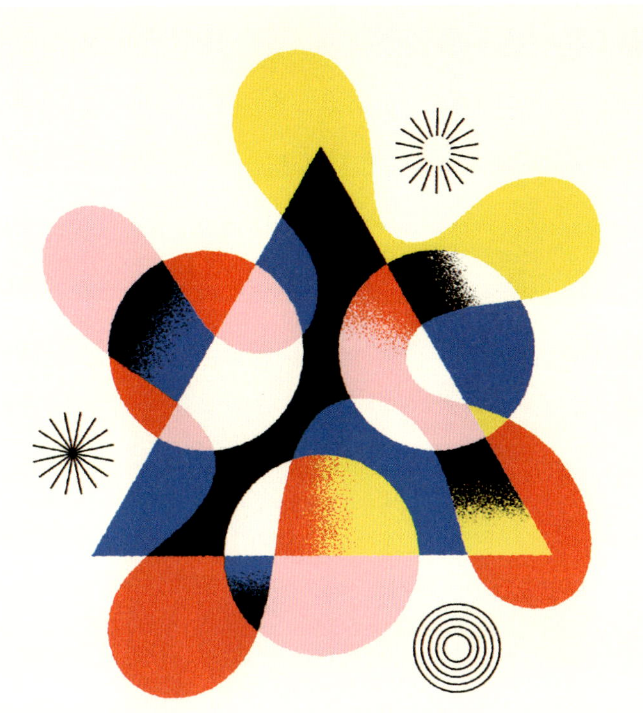

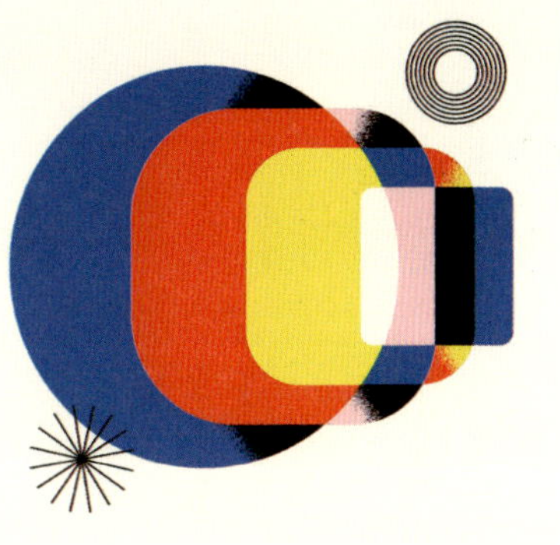

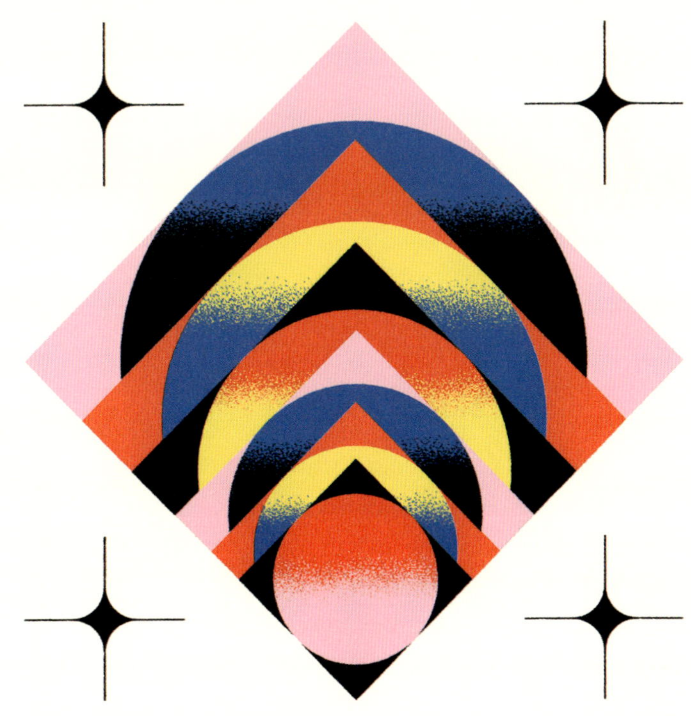

C3 M91 Y91 K0 | C7 M40 Y0 K0 | C7 M7 Y90 K0 | C87 M59 Y6 K0

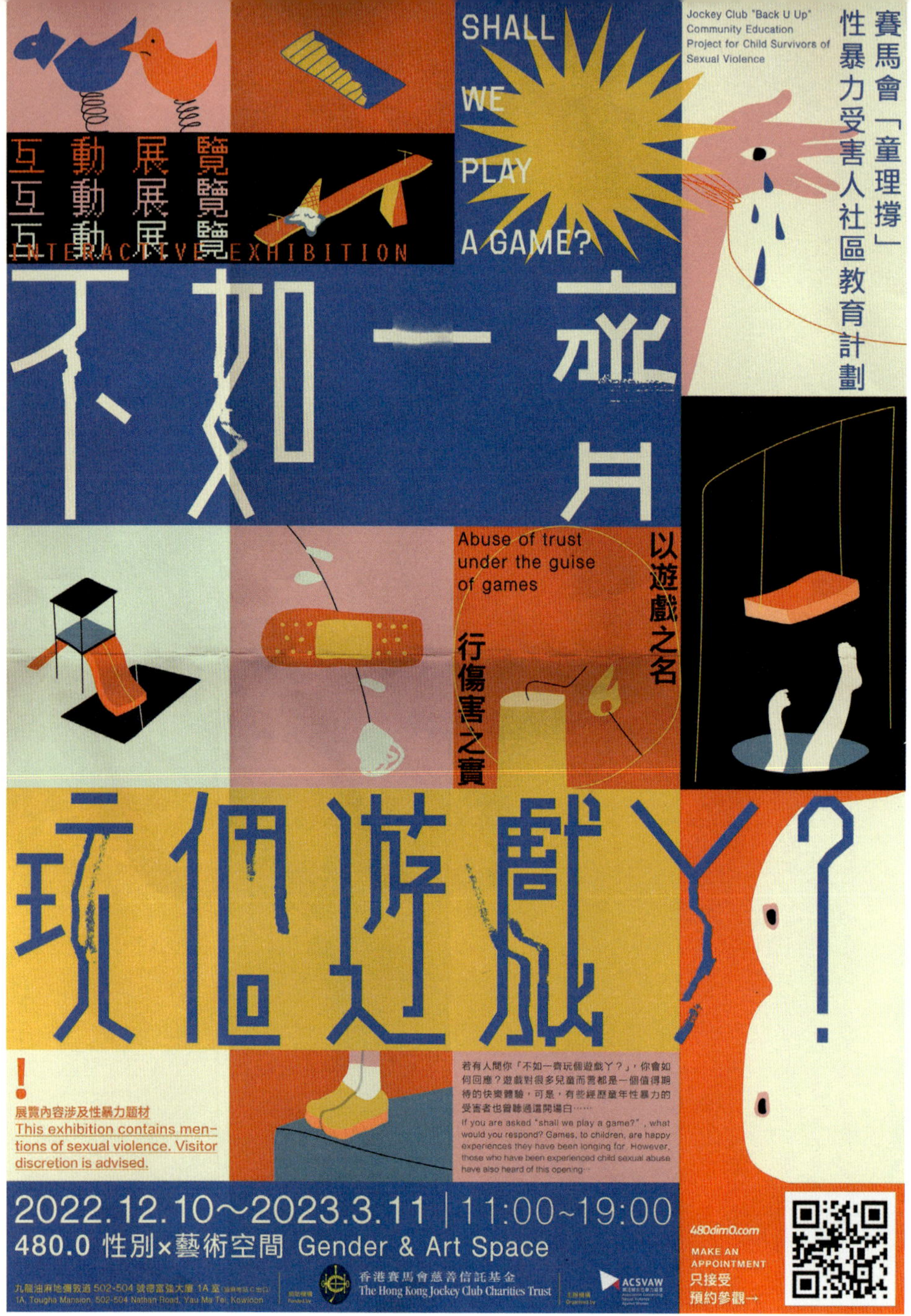

Shall We Play a Game? • The perpetrators commit harm under the guise of a game. According to research, survivors of sexual violence under the age of 18 typically wait an average of about 13 years before seeking help from "RainLily[1]." The impact of this "game" on the victims is truly beyond the imagination of outsiders.

1.RainLily: a local sexual violence crisis service in Hong Kong, China.

• Design Studio: SomethingMoon Design • Designer: Chiwai Cheang • Client: RainLily

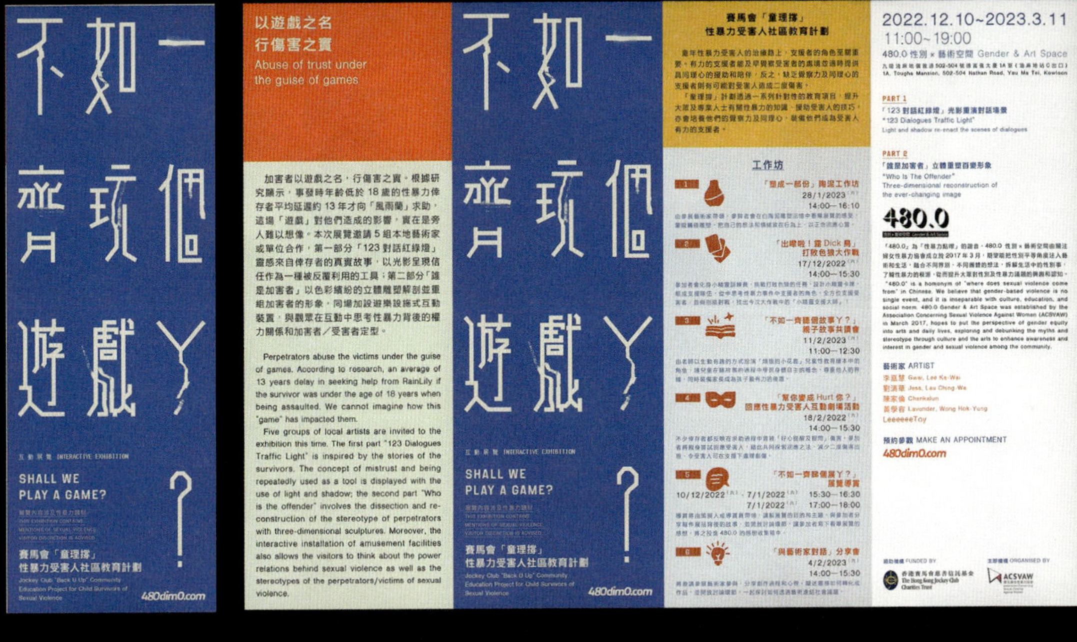

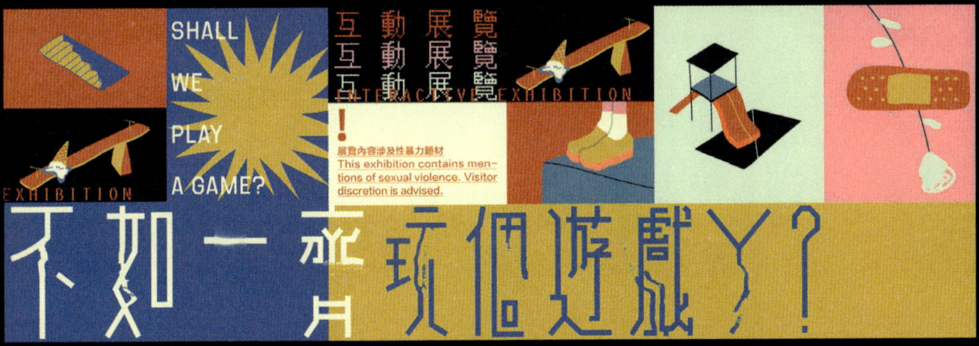

SHALL WE PLAY A GAME?

互動展覽

互動展覽

互動展覽

INTERACTIVE EXHIBITION

EXHIBITION

展覽內容涉及性暴力題材

This exhibition contains mentions of sexual violence. Visitor discretion is advised.

不如一齊玩個遊戲丫？

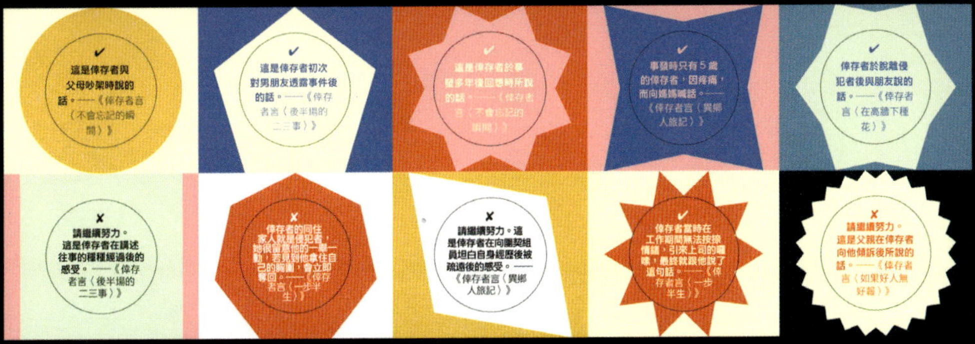

✔ 這是倖存者與父母吵架時說的話。——《倖存者言〈不會忘記的瞬間〉》

✔ 這是倖存者初次對男朋友透露事件後的話。——《倖存者言〈後半場的二三事〉》

✔ 這是倖存者於事發多年後回想時所說的話。——《倖存者言〈不會忘記的瞬間〉》

✔ 事發時只有 5 歲的倖存者，因疼痛，而向媽媽喊話。——《倖存者言〈異鄉人旅記〉》

✔ 倖存者於脫離侵犯者後與朋友說的話。——《倖存者言〈在高牆下種花〉》

✘ 請繼續努力。這是倖存者在講述往事的種種經過後的感受。——《倖存者言〈後半場的二三事〉》

✘ 倖存者的同住家人就是侵犯者，她很留意他的一舉一動，若見到他拿住自己的胸圍，會立即奪回。——《倖存者言〈一步半生〉》

✘ 請繼續努力。這是倖存者在向團契組員坦白自身經歷後被疏遠後的感受。——《倖存者言〈異鄉人旅記〉》

✔ 倖存者當時在工作期間無法按捺情緒，引來上司的嘲諷，最終就跟他說了這句話。——《倖存者言〈一步半生〉》

✘ 請繼續努力。這是父親在倖存者向他傾訴後所說的話。——《倖存者言〈如果好人無好報〉》

● Why RYB? ● Colorful visuals dissect and reassemble the image of the perpetrator.

C10 M50 Y30 K0 | C9 M78 Y100 K0 | C11 M33 Y100 K0 | C81 M64 Y0 K0

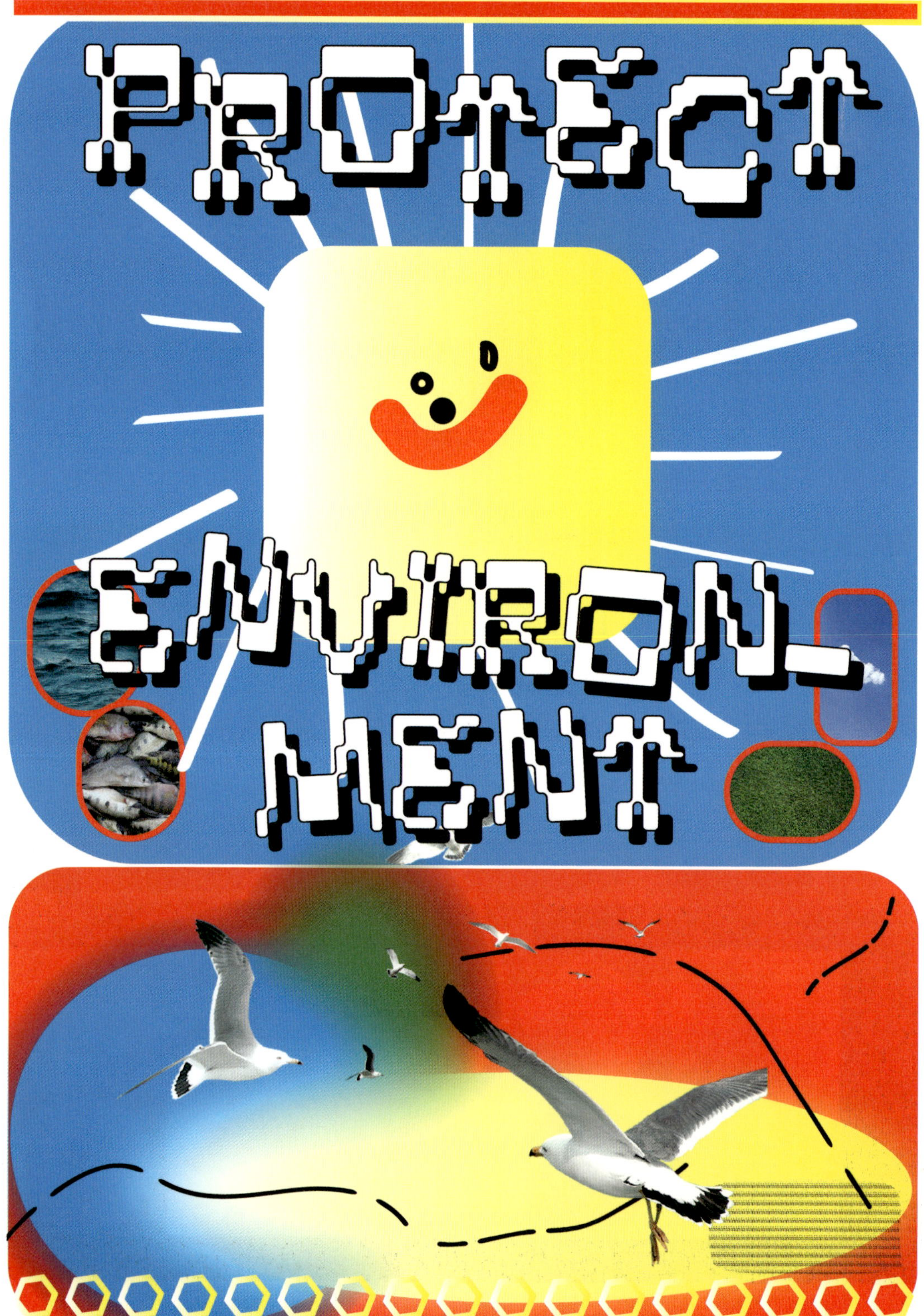

● Designer: Bobby Bao

PROTECT • During her stay in the UK, the designer observed numerous environmental events, ranging from intense to mild. This led her to ponder: What should designers do in response? She aimed to capture scenes from daily life, piecing together contrasting yet powerful visuals to amplify the visual language. The goal was to help the audience understand and feel these conflicts.

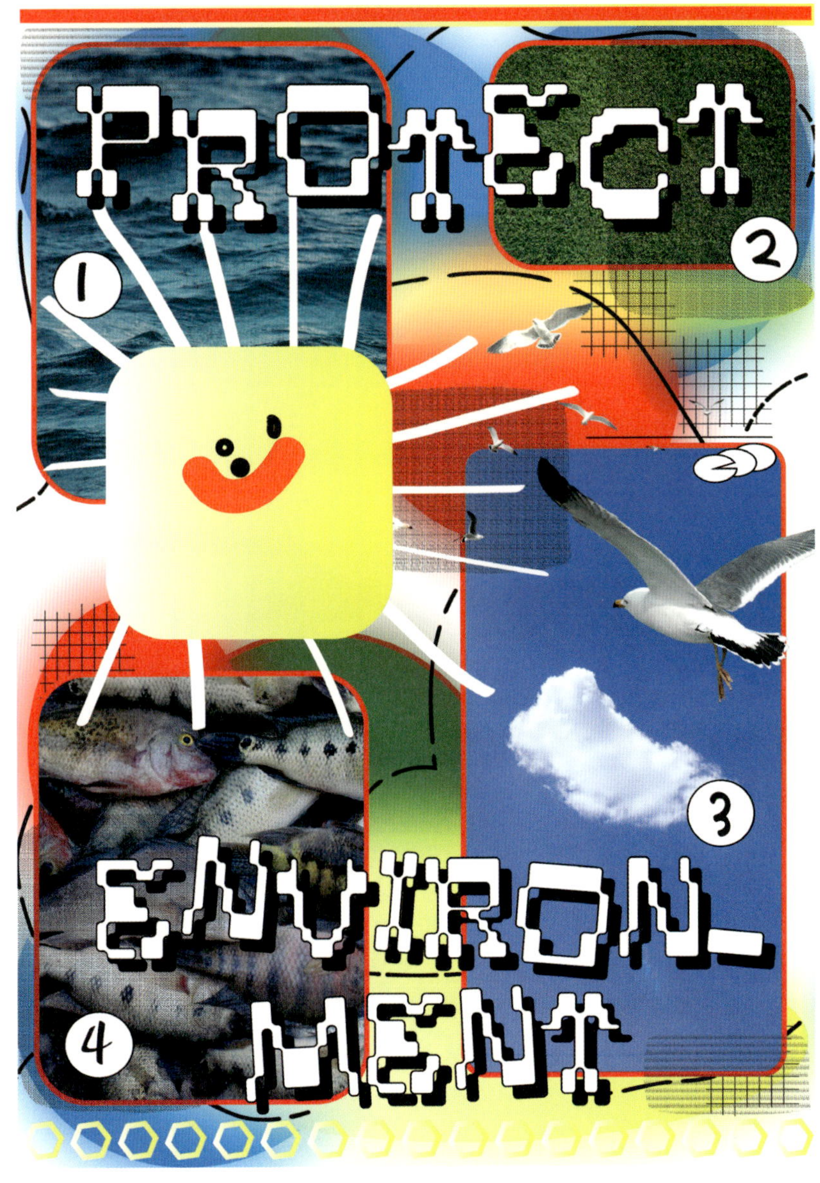

C0 M96 Y95 K0 | C8 M1 Y83 K0 | C73 M30 Y0 K0

HeyBetter Branding Design

● HeyBetter, a children's lifestyle brand, prioritizes professionally designing the brand image and creating a packaging system. Focused on maintaining a strong visual symbol and incorporating interactive games, the packaging includes brand information, a hand function card, and a fixed rubber band. The "small hand" card serves as a flexible information display while reducing production costs. The blue rubber band, imprinted with the brand slogan, secures cards and enhances the appeal of the interactive game. Each box's interior features paper-based manual games for children's exploration and enjoyment.

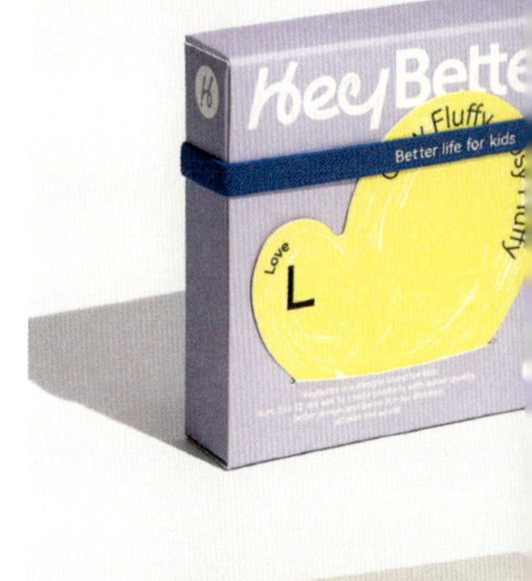

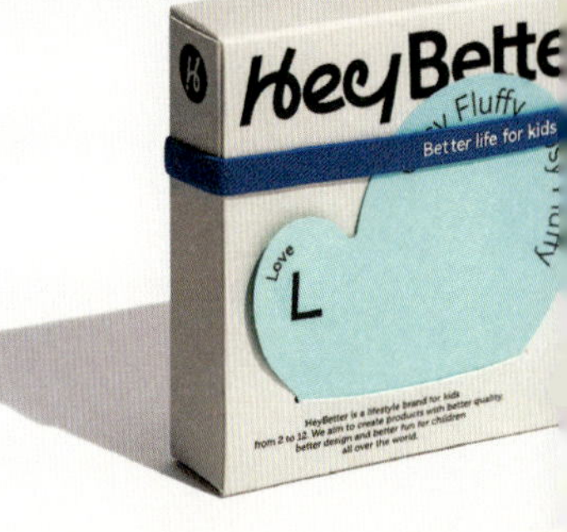

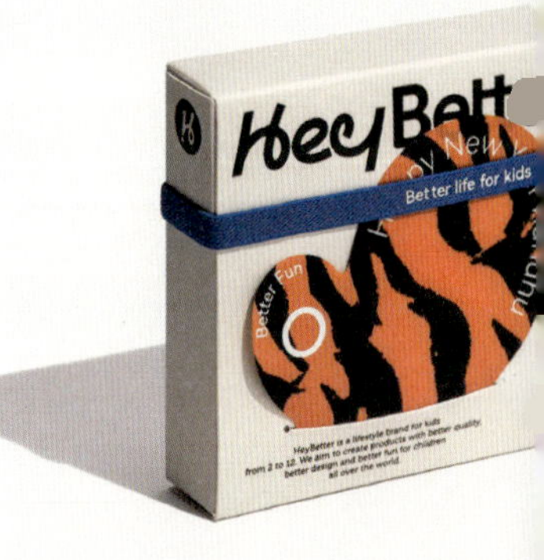

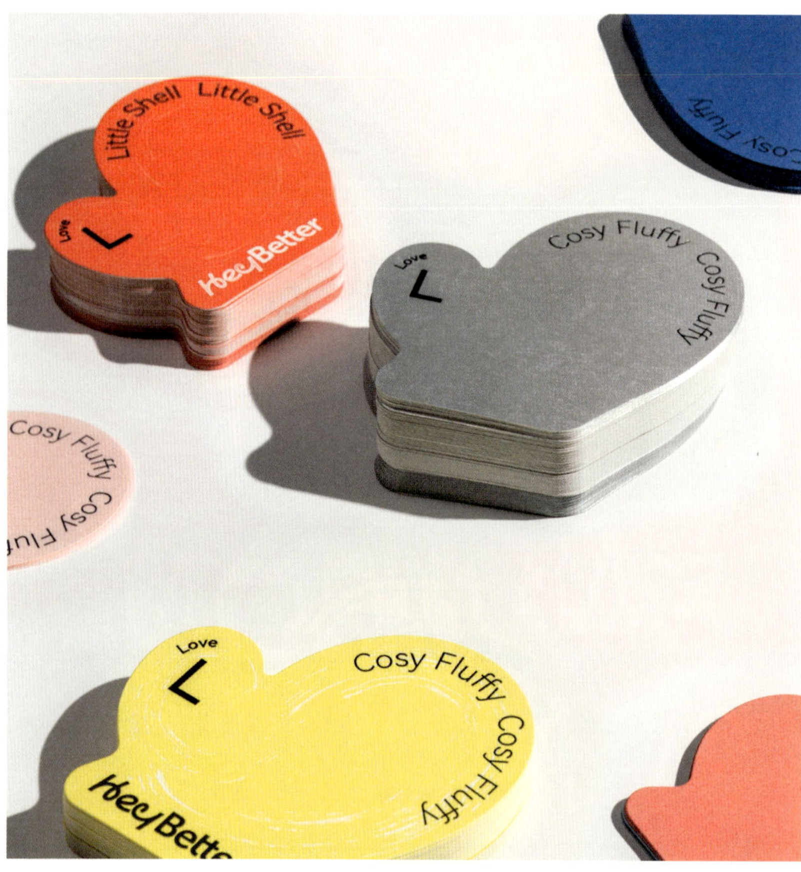

● Design Studio: SAYSOOO DESIGN ● Art Direction: Zhijian Huang, Jing Jin ● Client: HeyBetter

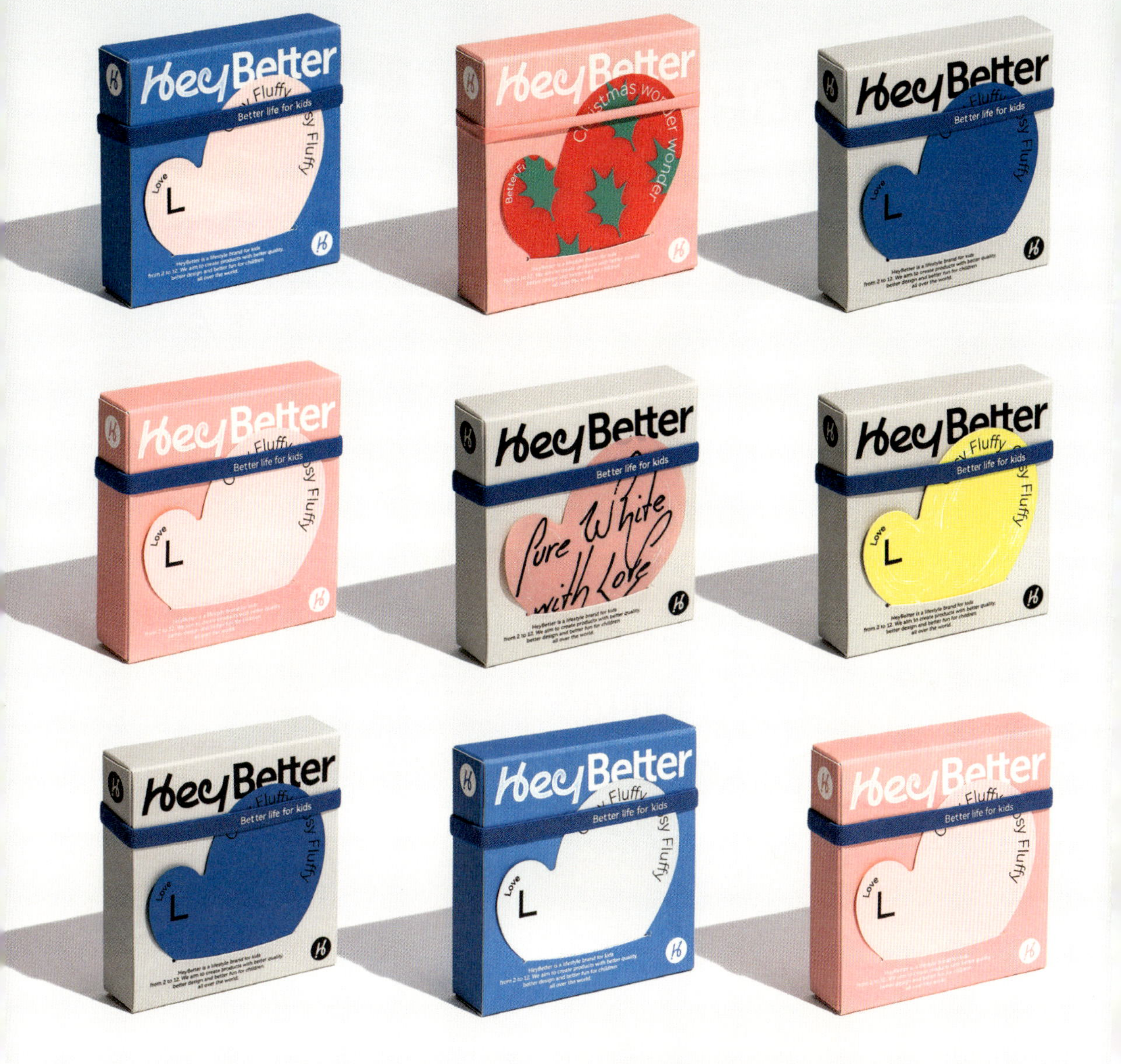

● Why RYB? ● The designers aimed to create an open, rich, and unrestricted world for children, reflected in the main color scheme that avoids a single-emotion color expression. The project is predominantly characterized by red, yellow, and blue, along with unique auxiliary color combinations, fostering a warm, friendly, lively, and free atmosphere.

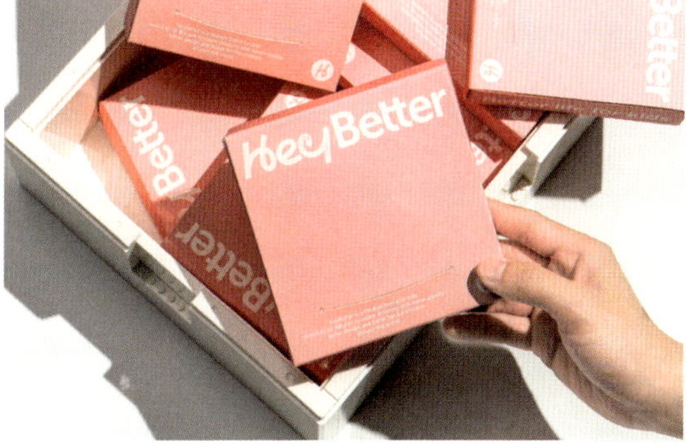

C26 M89 Y84 K0 | C8 M1 Y55 K0 | C87 M54 Y8 K0

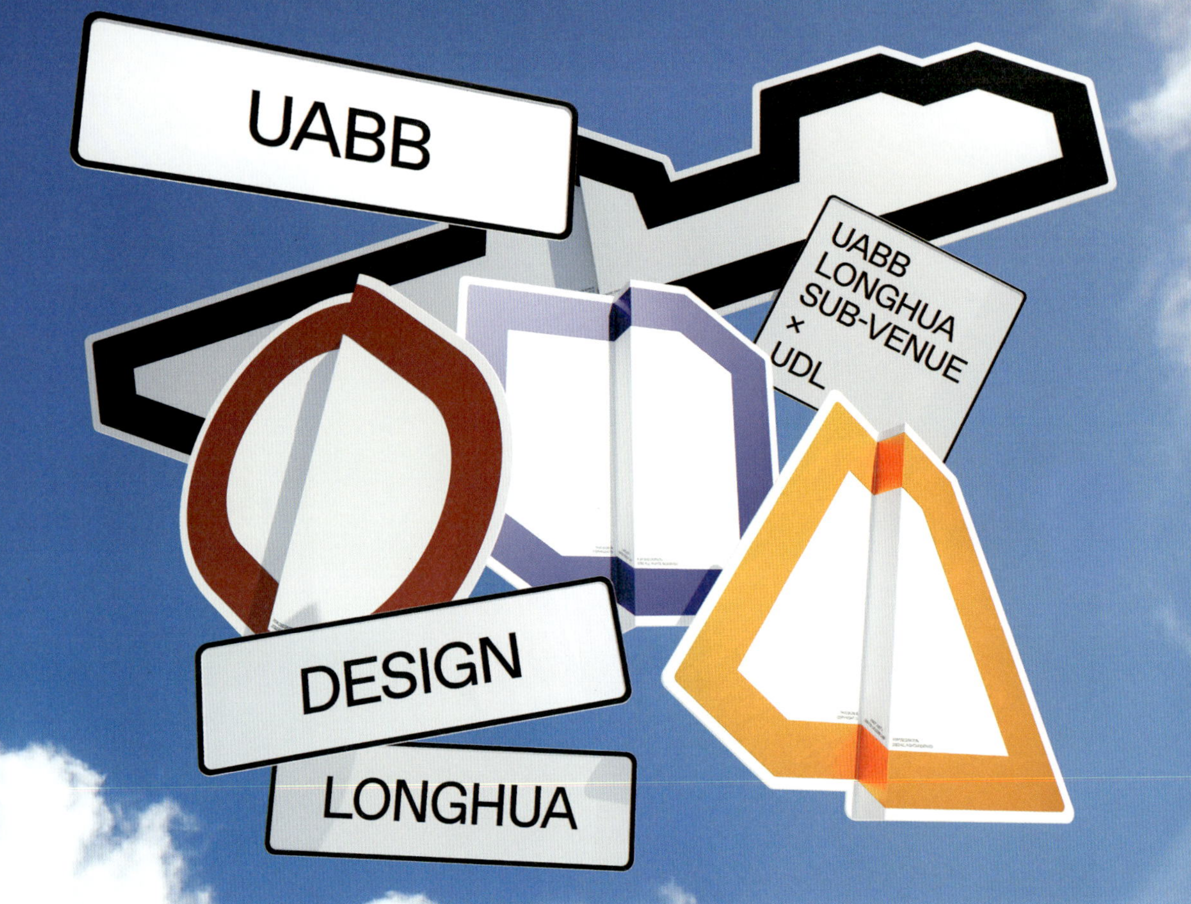

The Turn of Meaning

● The artwork features road signs, extracting common universal symbols and integrating shapes from digital accessory molds found at the exhibition site. These typically invisible molds in daily life are now showcased in public spaces, blending aesthetic and functional significance. Through a "shift in meaning," the design blurs the clarity of road sign semantics, transforming them into three-dimensional forms and creating new meanings. These non-functional signs become part of the urban landscape, providing a novel and multidimensional visual experience.

● Why RYB? ● Considering the integration with the exhibition space, the design team chose road signs as the primary forms of the artwork. Typically, in universal signage, red indicates stop, prohibition, or restriction, blue indicates instructions and compliance, and yellow indicates warnings. These signs, with their standardized shapes and colors, break through language barriers and are instantly recognizable to viewers. Through design language, the original meaning of road signs is blurred, conveying a new context.

● Design Studio: United Design Lab ● Designer: LIAO ZICHENG, VE, WONG KAHO

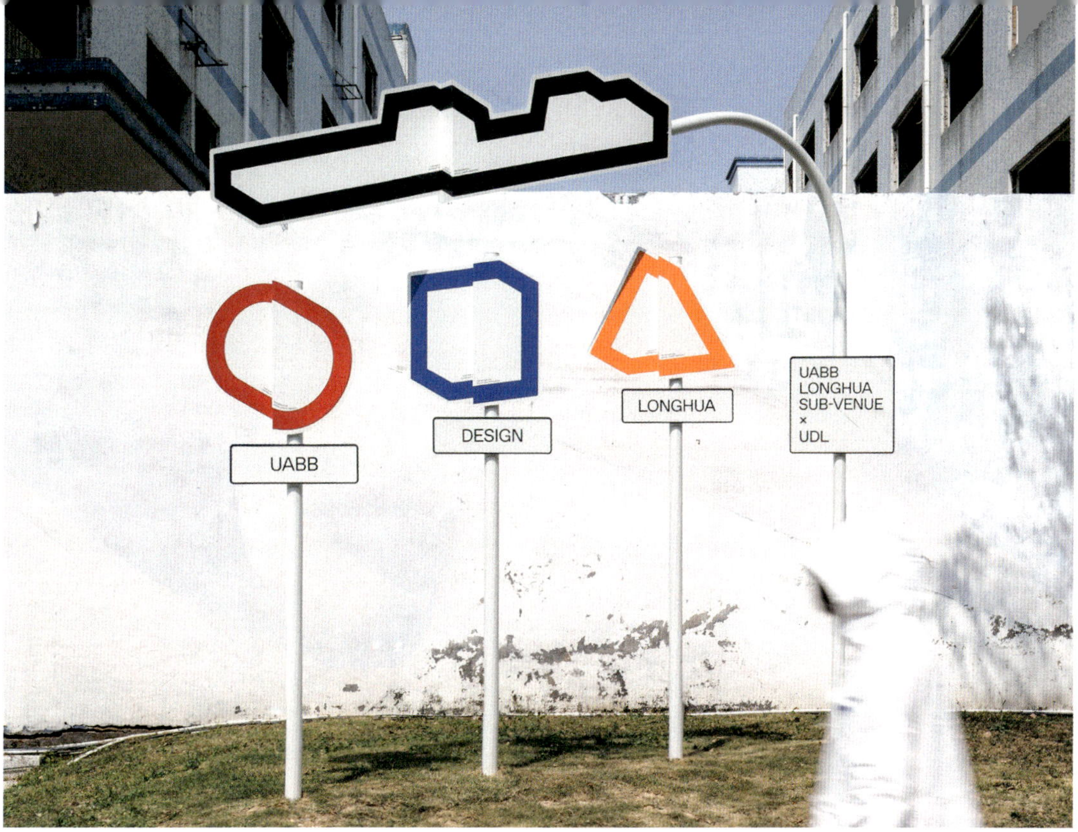

UABB
DESIGN
LONGHUA
UABB
LONGHUA
SUB-VENUE
×
UDL

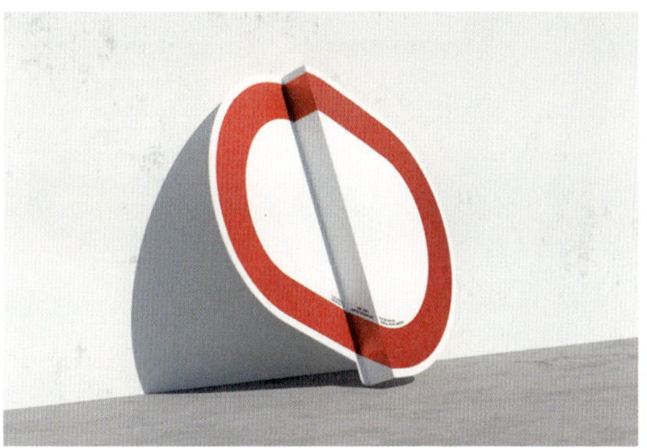

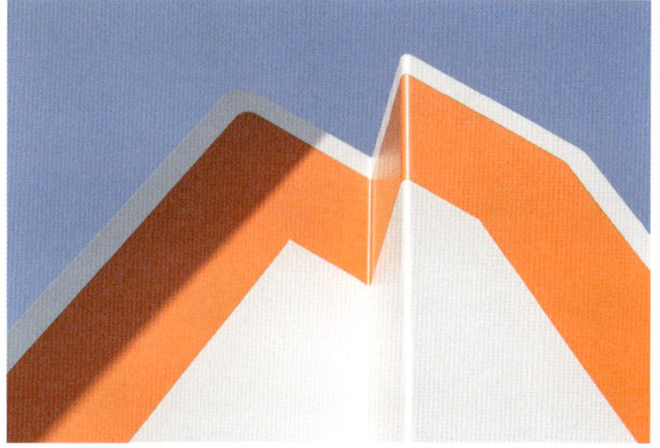

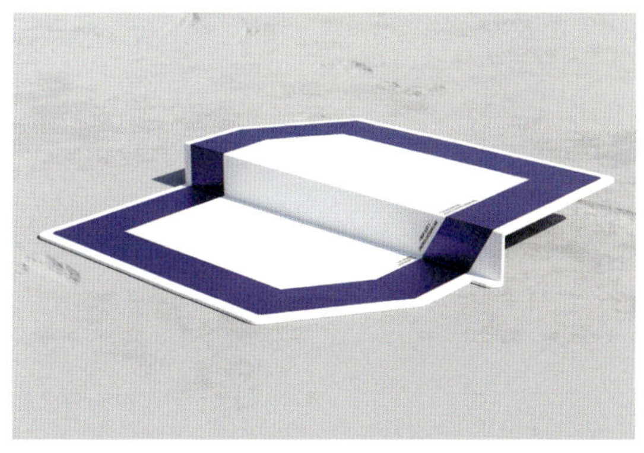

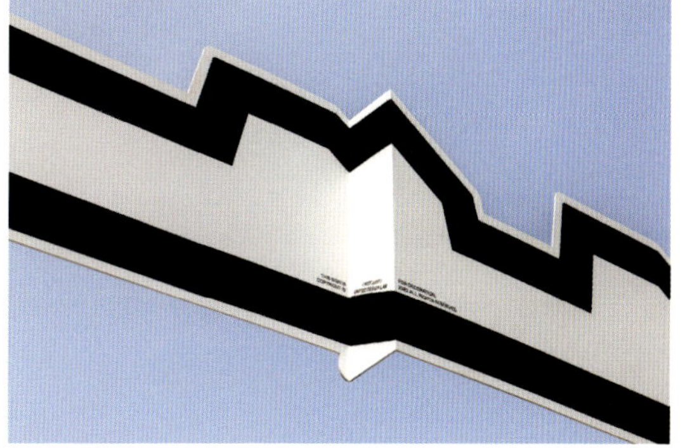

• Client: UABB, Shangqi Art

C30 M96 Y89 K0 | C4 M52 Y88 K0 | C95 M92 Y8 K0

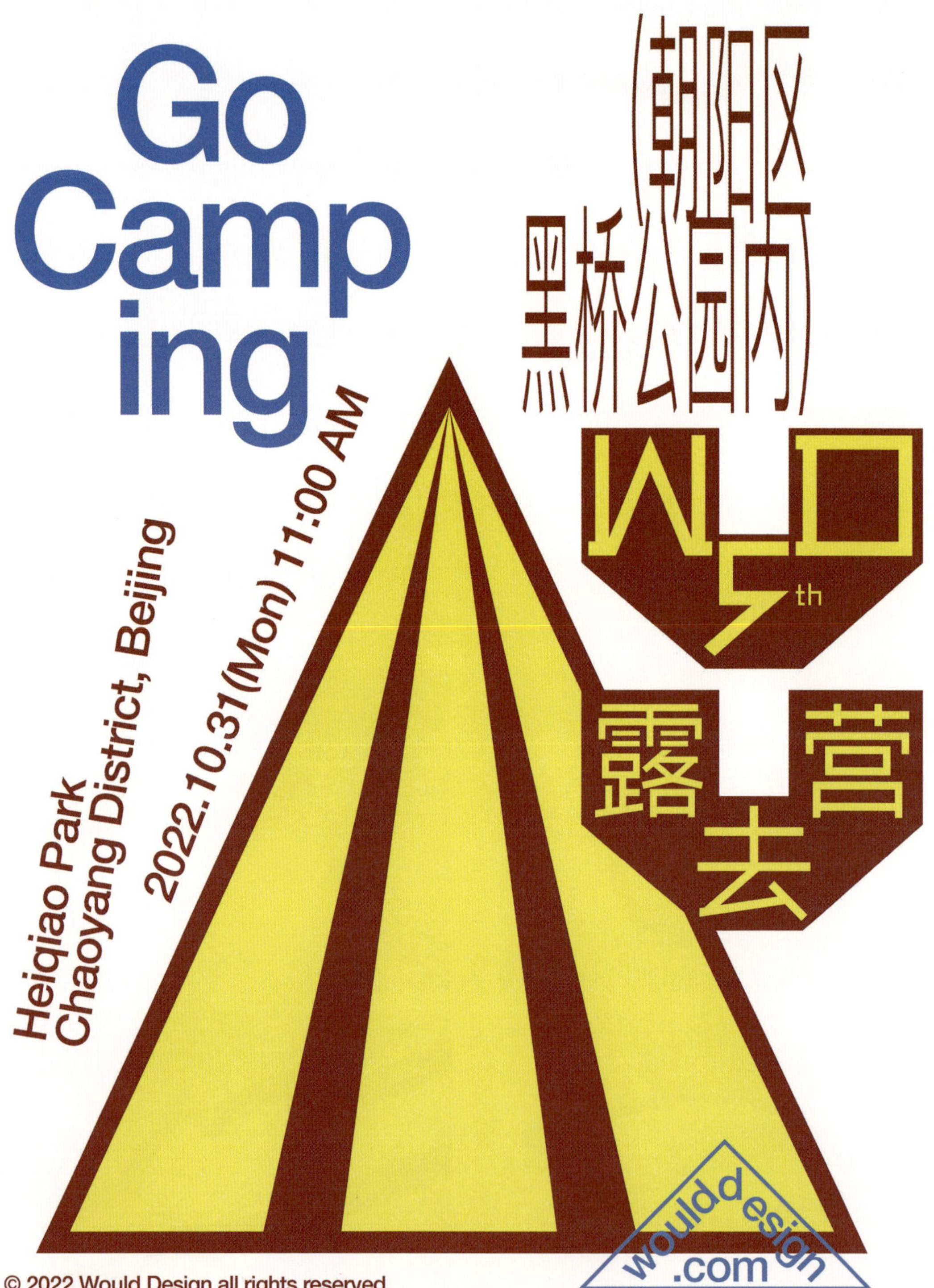

● Design Studio: Would Design ● Designer: Yunlong Li, Ying Zhang

Go Camping ● "Go Camping" is a camping event organized to celebrate the 5th anniversary of Would Design Studio. The design project encompasses the main visual identity system and a series of posters for the event. Designers extracted elements from camping activities, such as setting up tents, taking photos, drinking coffee, playing frisbee, and riding tandem bicycles. The use of straight-forward, unadorned graphics with high-saturation contrasting colors captures the essence of outdoor activities.

● Why RYB? ● The high-saturation contrasting colors and unconventional design elements perfectly capture the fun and creativity of outdoor activities.

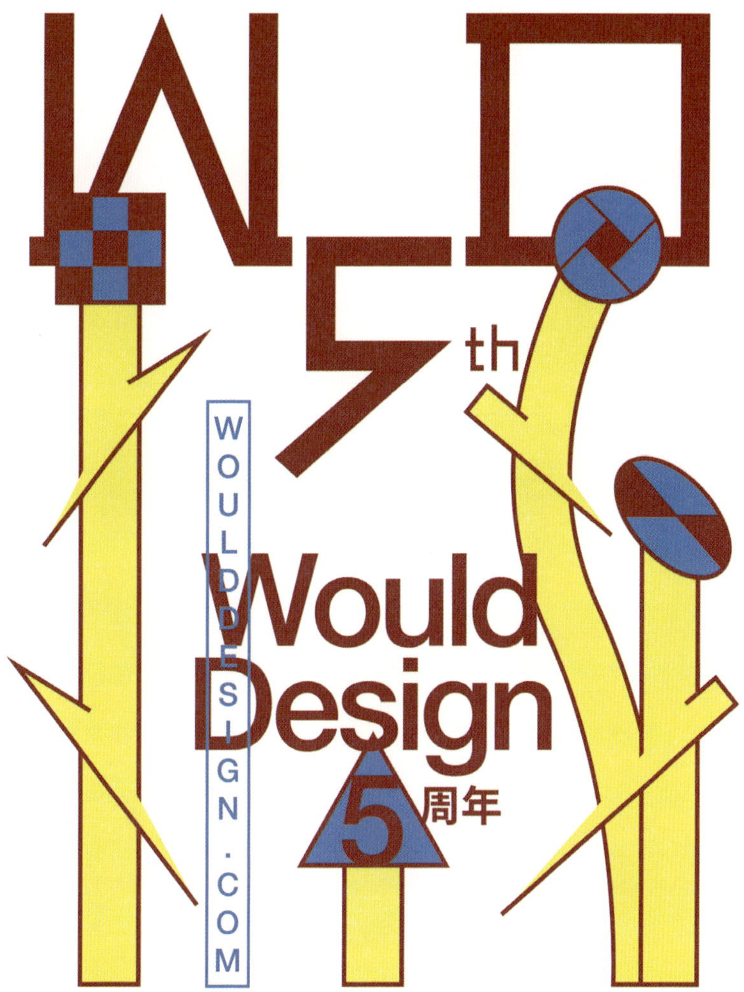

C41 M91 Y83 K15 | C5 M5 Y90 K0 | C80 M40 Y0 K0

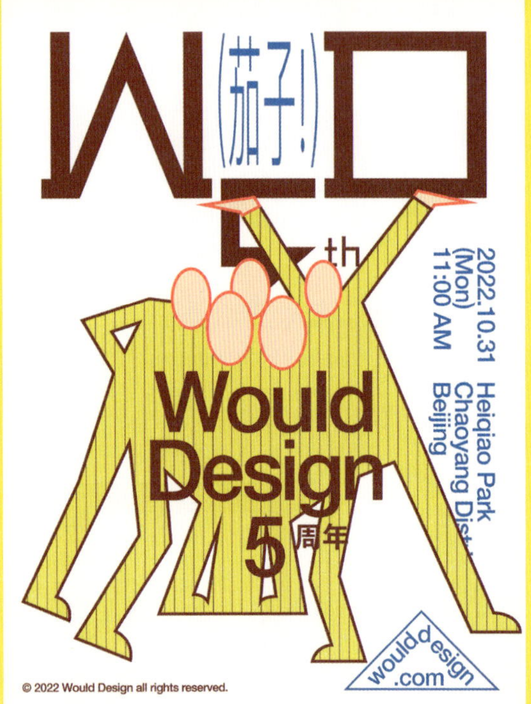
(茄子!)
5th
2022.10.31
(Mon)
11:00 AM
Heiqiao Park
Chaoyang District
Beijing
Would
Design
5 周年
woulddesign
.com
© 2022 Would Design all rights reserved.

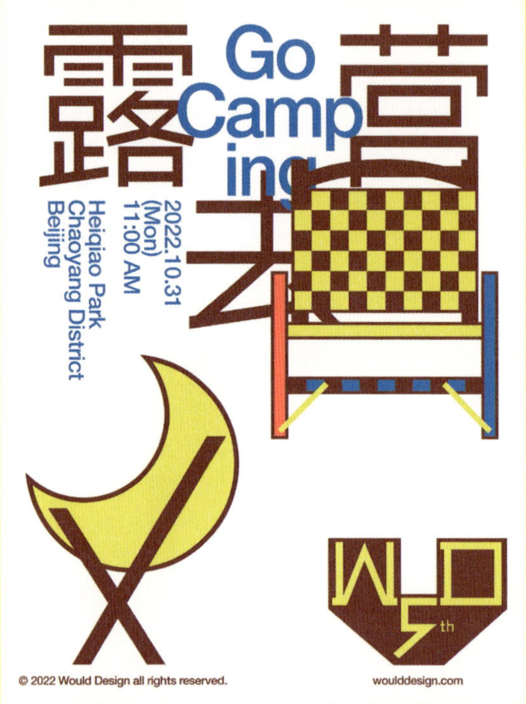
露营
Go
Camp
ing
2022.10.31
(Mon)
11:00 AM
Heiqiao Park
Chaoyang District
Beijing
5th
© 2022 Would Design all rights reserved.
woulddesign.com

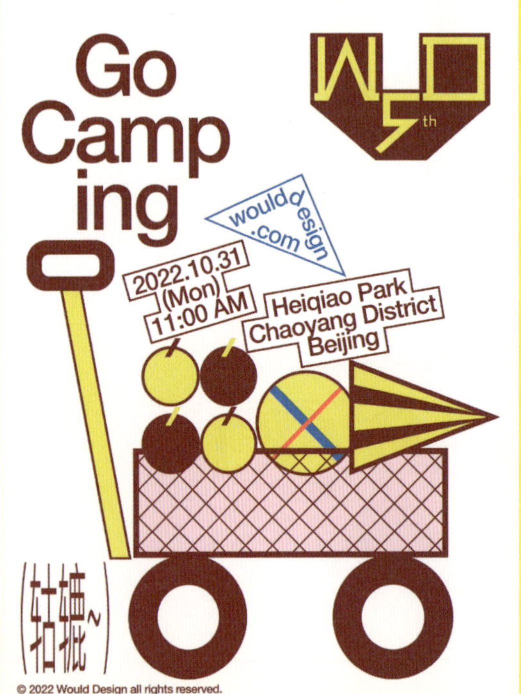
Go
Camp
ing
5th
woulddesign
.com
2022.10.31
(Mon)
11:00 AM
Heiqiao Park
Chaoyang District
Beijing
(轱辘~)
© 2022 Would Design all rights reserved.

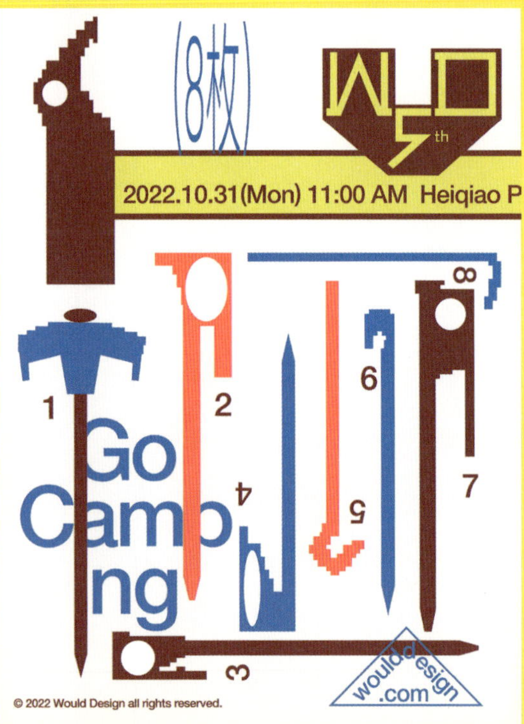
(8枚)
5th
2022.10.31(Mon) 11:00 AM Heiqiao P
1
2
3
4
5
6
7
8
Go
Camp
ing
woulddesign
.com
© 2022 Would Design all rights reserved.

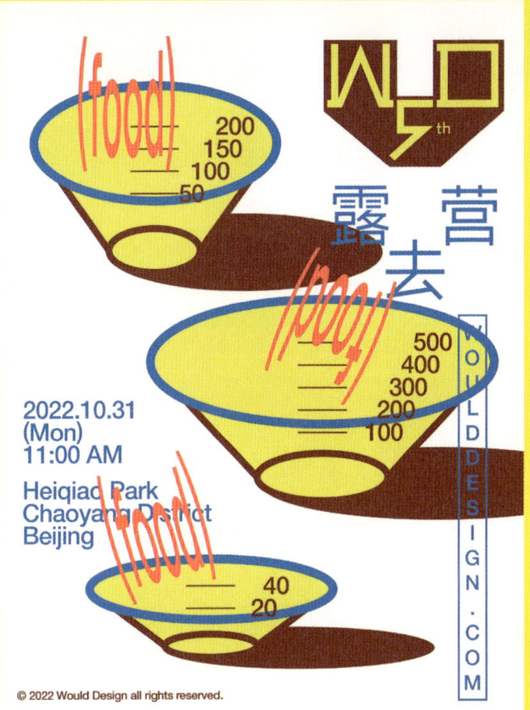

露营去
(food)
200
150
100
50
(food)
500
400
300
200
100
2022.10.31
(Mon)
11:00 AM
Heiqiao Park
Chaoyang District
Beijing
(food)
40
20
WOULDDESIGN.COM
© 2022 Would Design all rights reserved.

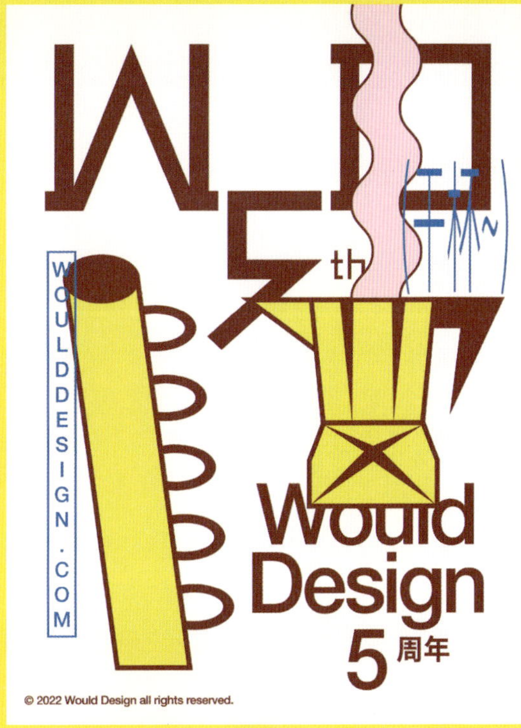

th
WOULDDESIGN.COM
Would
Design
5 周年
© 2022 Would Design all rights reserved.

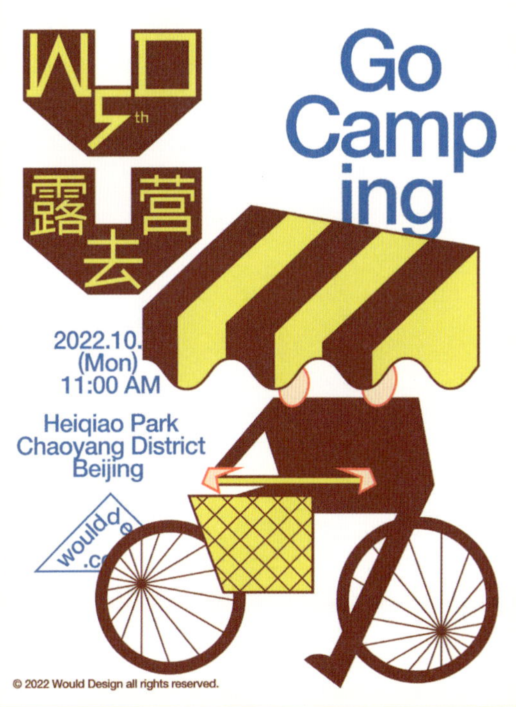

th
露营去
Go
Camp
ing
2022.10.
(Mon)
11:00 AM
Heiqiao Park
Chaoyang District
Beijing
© 2022 Would Design all rights reserved.

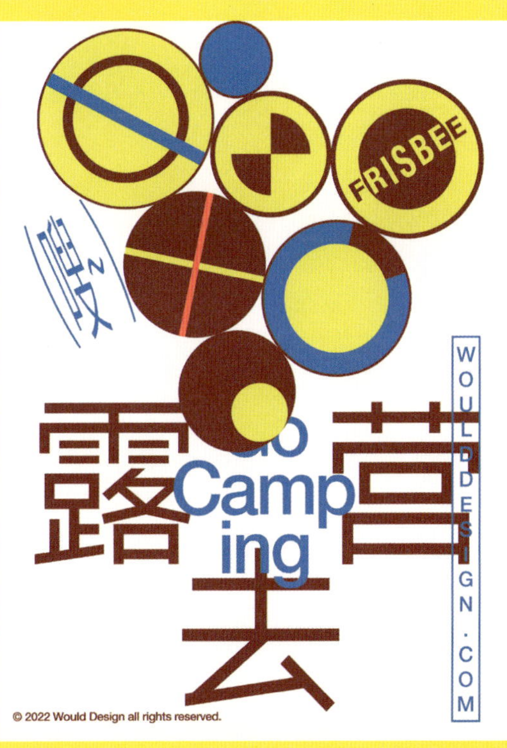

FRISBEE
露营去
Camp
ing
WOULDDESIGN.COM
© 2022 Would Design all rights reserved.

RYB Matching

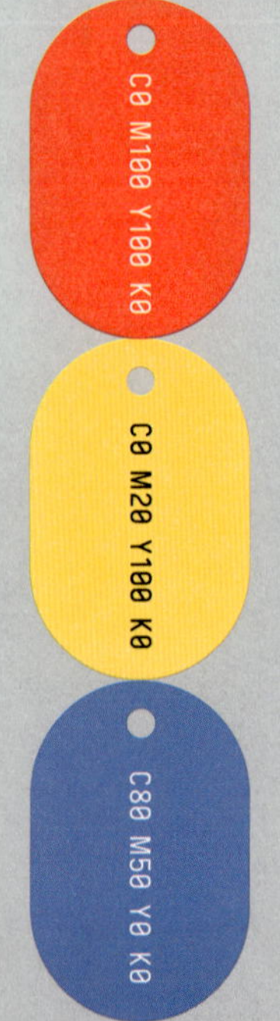

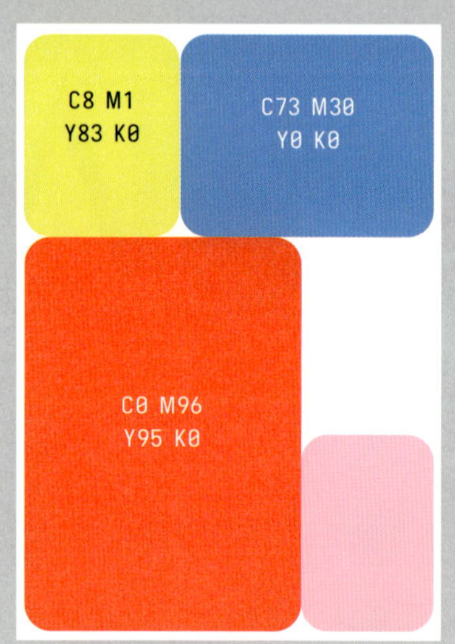

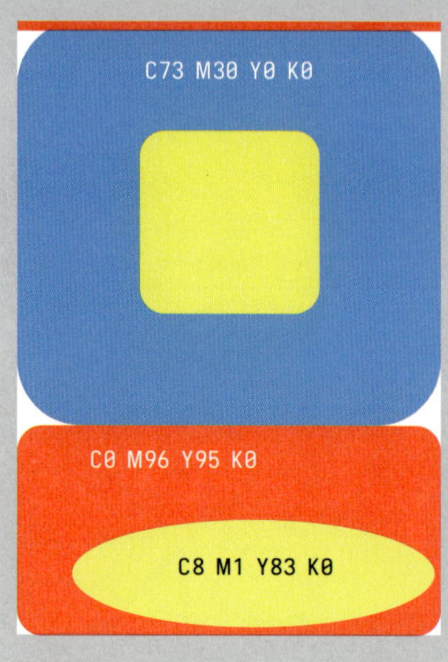

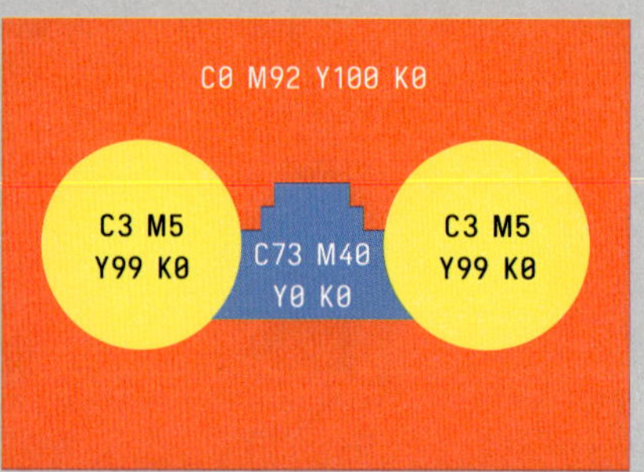

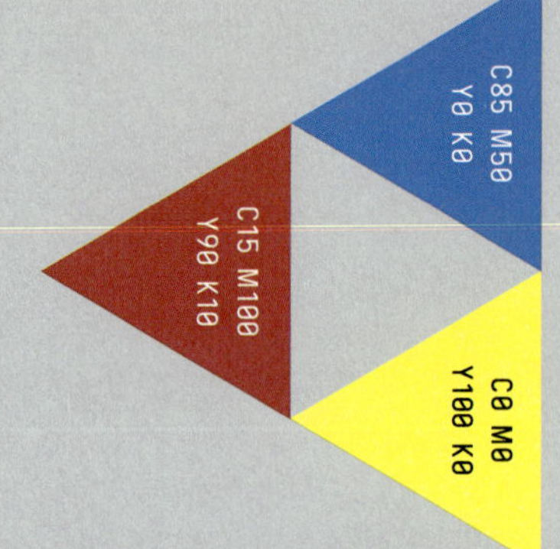

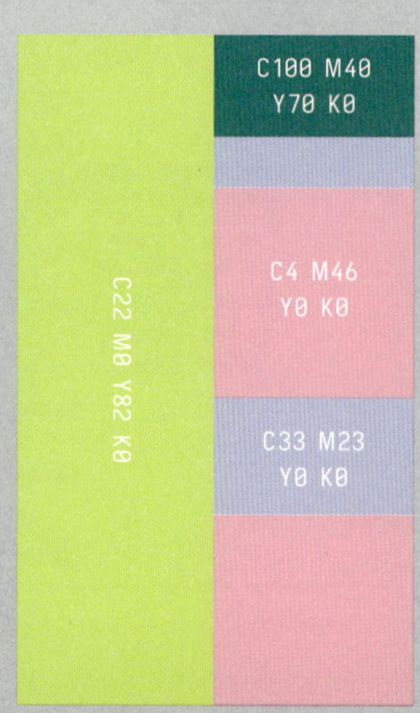

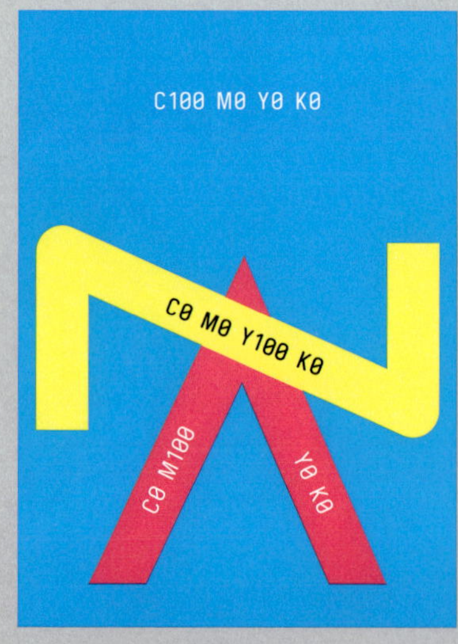

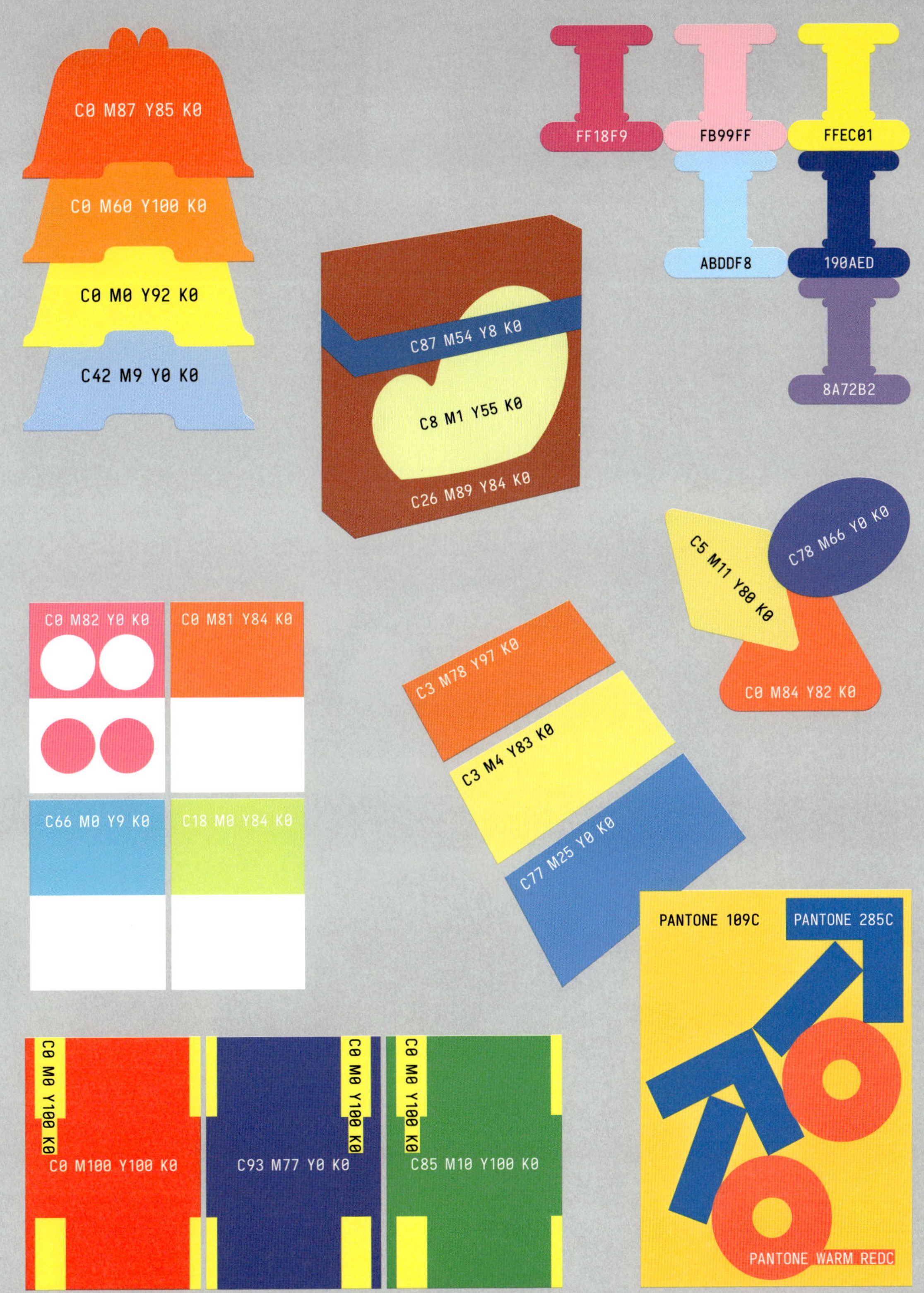
C0 M87 Y85 K0
C0 M60 Y100 K0
C0 M0 Y92 K0
C42 M9 Y0 K0
FF18F9
FB99FF
FFEC01
ABDDF8
190AED
8A72B2
C87 M54 Y8 K0
C8 M1 Y55 K0
C26 M89 Y84 K0
C5 M11 Y80 K0
C78 M66 Y0 K0
C0 M84 Y82 K0
C0 M82 Y0 K0
C0 M81 Y84 K0
C66 M0 Y9 K0
C18 M0 Y84 K0
C3 M78 Y97 K0
C3 M4 Y83 K0
C77 M25 Y0 K0
PANTONE 109C
PANTONE 285C
PANTONE WARM REDC
C0 M0 Y100 K0
C0 M100 Y100 K0
C0 M0 Y100 K0
C93 M77 Y0 K0
C0 M0 Y100 K0
C85 M10 Y100 K0

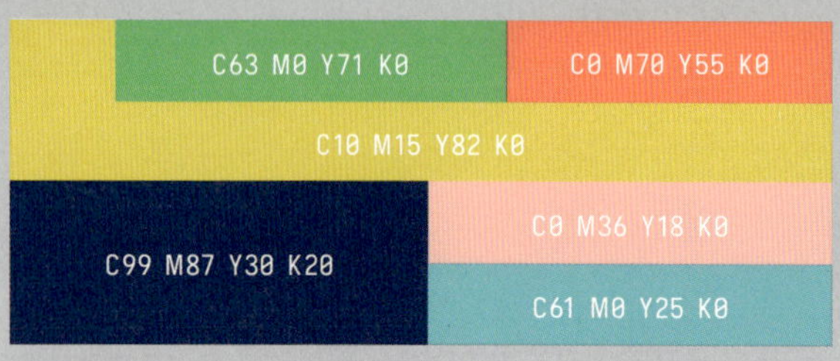
C63 M0 Y71 K0
C0 M70 Y55 K0
C10 M15 Y82 K0
C0 M36 Y18 K0
C99 M87 Y30 K20
C61 M0 Y25 K0

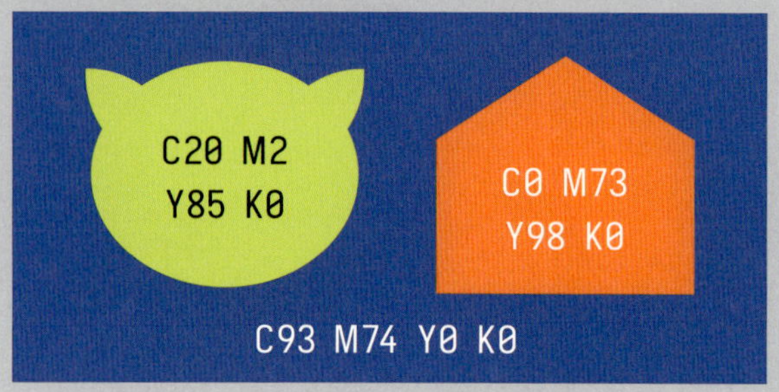
C20 M2
Y85 K0
C0 M73
Y98 K0
C93 M74 Y0 K0

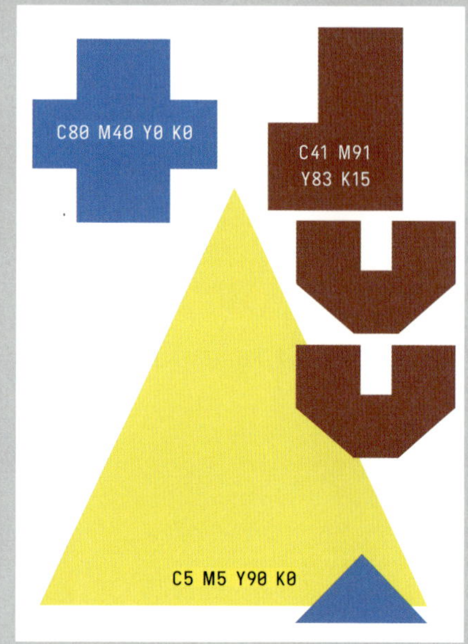
C80 M40 Y0 K0
C41 M91
Y83 K15
C5 M5 Y90 K0

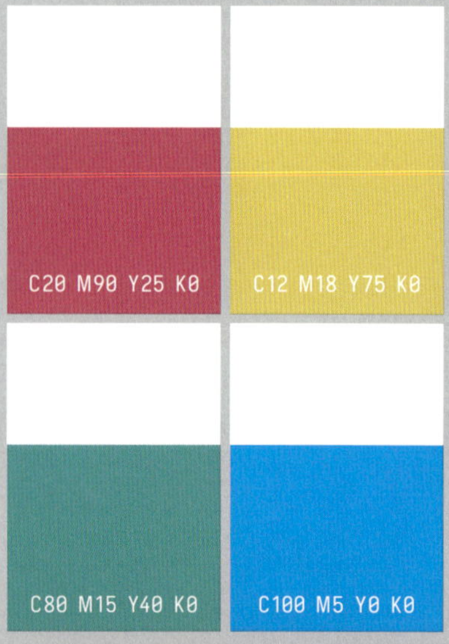
C20 M90 Y25 K0
C12 M18 Y75 K0
C80 M15 Y40 K0
C100 M5 Y0 K0

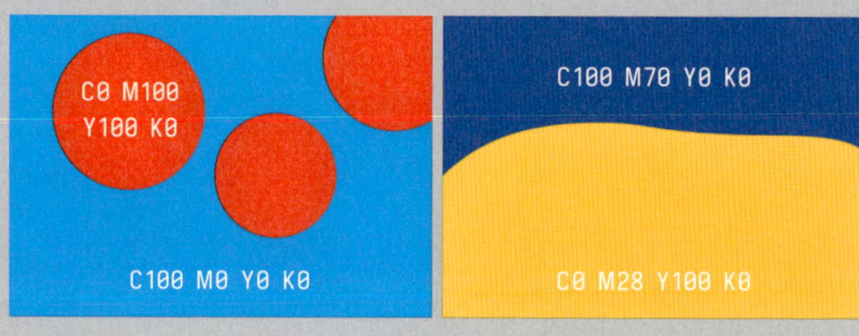
C0 M100
Y100 K0
C100 M0 Y0 K0
C100 M70 Y0 K0
C0 M28 Y100 K0

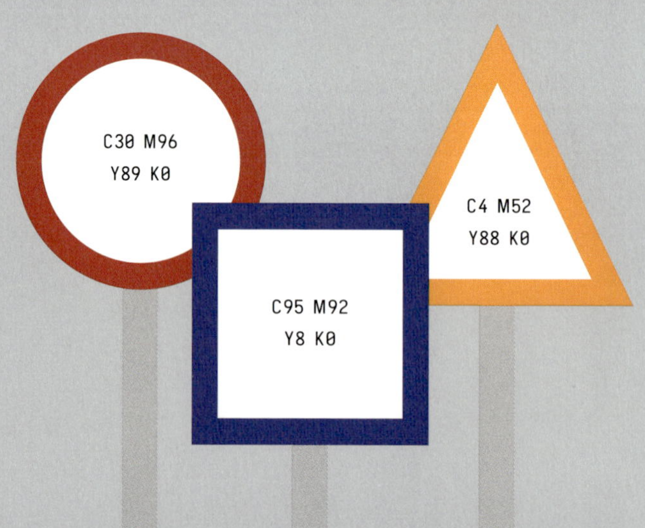
C30 M96
Y89 K0
C4 M52
Y88 K0
C95 M92
Y8 K0

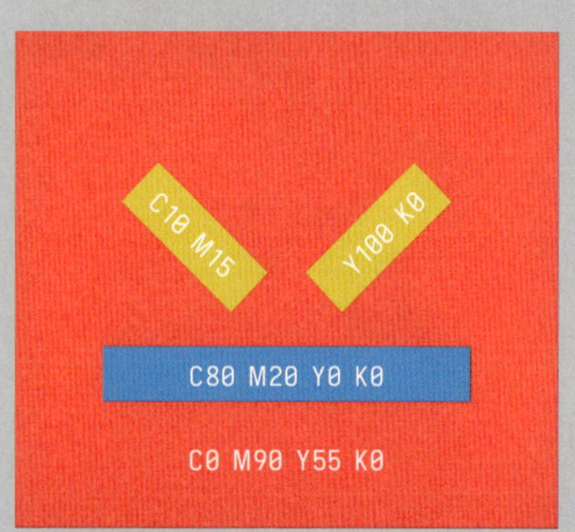
C10 M15
Y100 K0
C80 M20 Y0 K0
C0 M90 Y55 K0

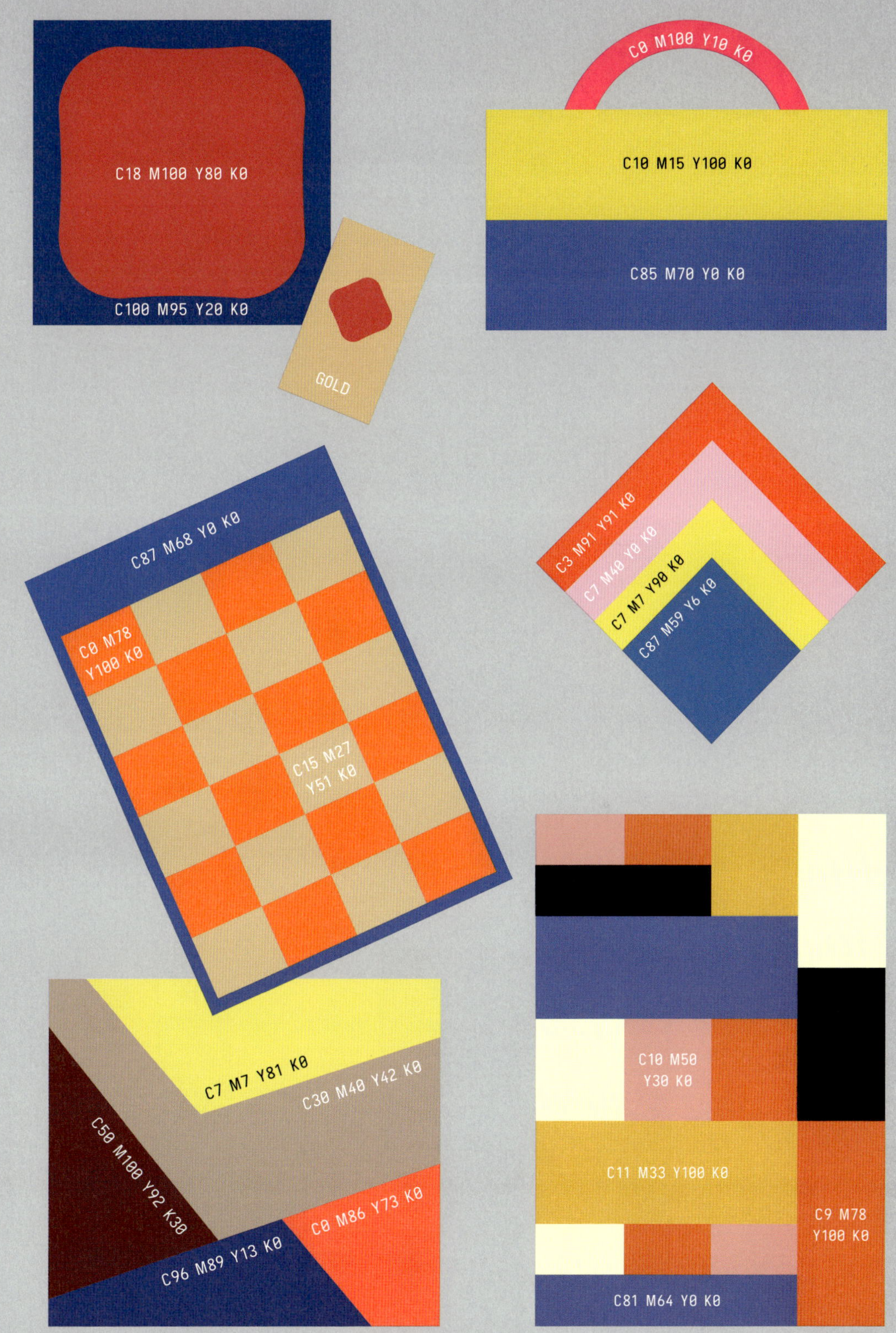
C18 M100 Y80 K0
C100 M95 Y20 K0
GOLD
C0 M100 Y10 K0
C10 M15 Y100 K0
C85 M70 Y0 K0
C87 M68 Y0 K0
C0 M78 Y100 K0
C15 M27 Y51 K0
C3 M91 Y91 K0
C7 M40 Y0 K0
C7 M7 Y90 K0
C87 M59 Y6 K0
C7 M7 Y81 K0
C30 M40 Y42 K0
C50 M100 Y92 K30
C0 M86 Y73 K0
C96 M89 Y13 K0
C10 M50 Y30 K0
C11 M33 Y100 K0
C9 M78 Y100 K0
C81 M64 Y0 K0

INDEX

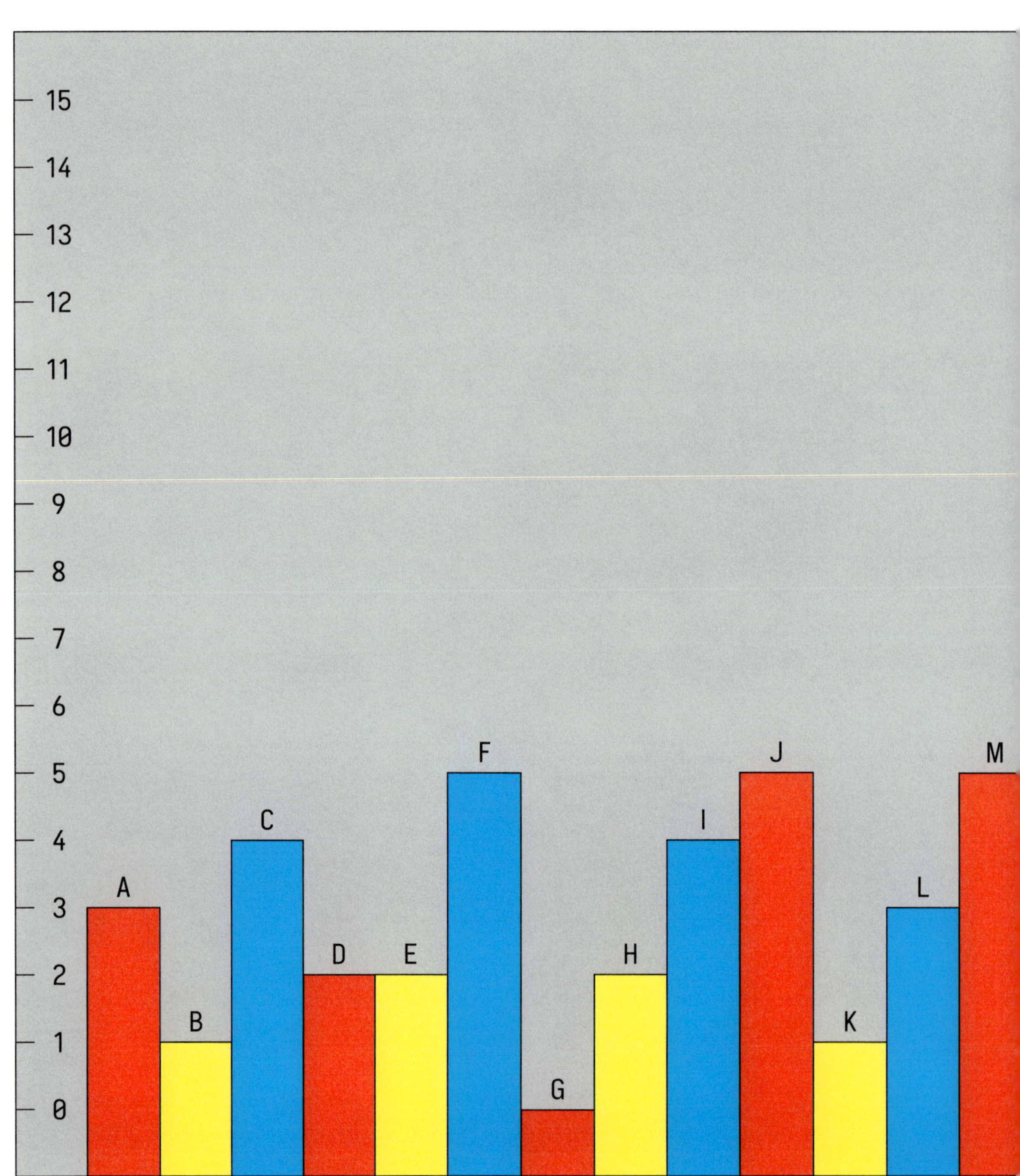

4

We love the three primary colors for their purity and power.
N
O
P
Q
R
S
T
U
V
W
X
Y
Z
#

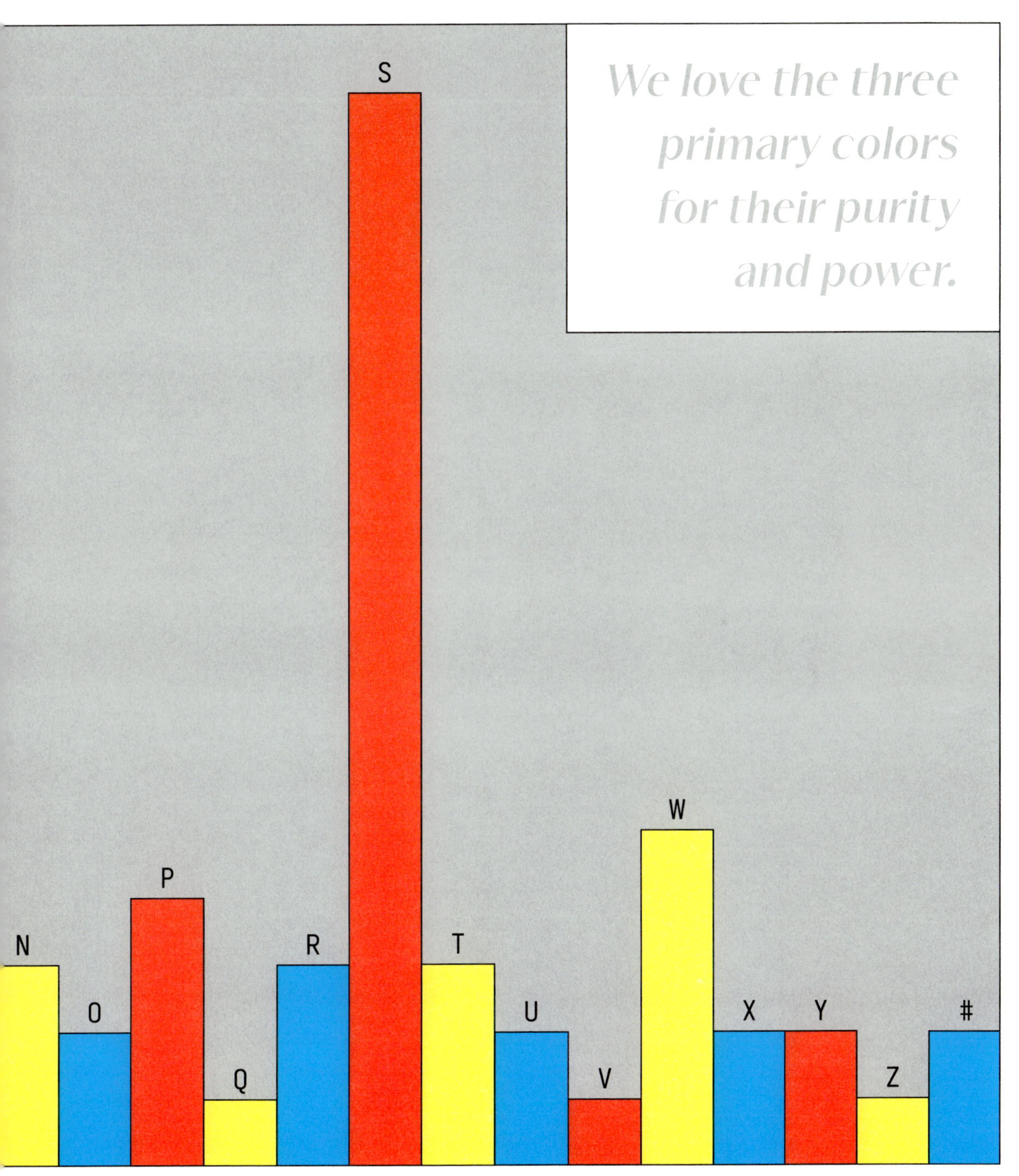

Mistroom
Huang Jui-i / Peng Yu-jui

P248—249

www.behance.net/mistroomart

M — N Associates
Duy Nguyen / Anh Nguyen / Quan Nguyen / Lan Mai

P242—243

m-n.associates

MOTOMOTO inc.
Kenichi Matsumoto

P130—131 P162—163 P312—313 P328—329

moto-moto.jp

N

NICE GUY
Matej Špánik / Tomáš Rybár

P084—085 P268—269

niceguy.sk

Nina Deeva-Kazanova

P304—307

www.behance.net/kazanova_nina

O

ONNFF
Zhengrui Hu

P300—303

www.behance.net/onnff

P

Paragram
Yusuke Akai

P090—091 P324—325

www.instagram.com/paragram_design

PAY2PLAY
Xiaoxi Sun

P142—143 P190—191

pay2play.design

PRESS ROOM
Jieun Yang

P062—063

press-room.kr

Q

R

Ray Dak Lam

P296—297 P336—337

raydaklam.com

Ruohong Wu & José Quintanar
José Quintanar

P319—321

josequintanar.com

S

SAYSOOO DESIGN
Zhijian Huang / Jing Jin

P342—343

saysooo.com

Serve and Volley
Simon Roth / Klaus Neuburg

P182—183

serveandvolley.studio

Smith & Lewarne
Jono Lewarne / Stephen Smith

P308—311

smithandlewarne.com

SNASK
Matej Špánik

P100—103

snask.com

Sooun Cho

P274—275

www.behance.net/suth43f511

SomethingMoon Design
Chiwai Cheang

P270—273 P338—339

somethingmoon.com

Standpoint Design
Olav Deng

P334—335

www.behance.net/standpointdesign

Steve Gavan

P172—173

stevegavan.work

Studio Dasol
Dasol Lee

P152—153

studiodasol.com

STUDIO DPi
Ming Ding / Yuanbo Wang / Chaohao Chen
P104—105
studiodpi.work

Studio fnt
Jaemin Lee / Heesun Kim / Woogyung Geel / Ajeong Kim / Younghyun Song / Youjeong Lee / Jieun Kang
P126—129 P284—287
studiofnt.com

Studio Werk
Jaehoon Choi
P292—293
werkgraphic.com

Studio Yannick Nuss
Yannick Nuss
P064—069 P176—177
P224—225
yannick-nuss.de

Sun Ho Lee
P076—077 P220—221
www.instagram.com/sunhoslee

SUPPRISE
Thirteen
P212—215 P288—291
www.zcool.com.cn/u/25296791

T

Tiffany Wong
P056—057 P094—095
P254—257
tiffywong.site

TWOPTWO Design
Xu Ye / Yann
P278—279
www.gtn9.com/user_showaspx?id=26B73F75291AA86A

U

United Design Lab
Chen Xing / Xiang Li / Shuyao Bian LIAO ZICHENG / VE / WONG KAHO
P058—059 P344—345
u-d-l.com

V

W

Wang Shuo
P208—211
www.instagram.com/wangshuo_o

Weng Nam Yap
Weng Nam Yap
P316—317
wengnamyap.com

whynotdesign
He Yuxuan
P333
whynotdesign.cc

Would Design
Yunlong Li / Ying Zhang
P180—181 P346—349
woulddesign.com

X

XXD DESIGN
Yuqing Xu / Qiyuan Xiao / Jia Tan
P184—187 P332
xxddesign.com

Y

YOHAK DESIGN STUDIO
Aki Kanai / Taku Sasaki
P048—053
think-of-things.com/yohak/

Z

#

702design
Mei Shuzhi
P132—133
by702.com

THE COLOR TRIO:
PLAY WITH RED, YELLOW, AND BLUE

First printing of the first edition, September 2024

sendpoints

PUBLISHED BY SendPoints Publishing Co., Ltd.
ADDRESS: Unit 23, L1/F Mirror Tower, 61 Mody Road, Tsim Sha Tsui, Kowloon, Hong Kong, China
PUBLISHER: Lin Gengli
CHIEF EDITOR: Wu Dongyan
DEVELOPMENT EDITOR: Wu Dongyan
EXECUTIVE EDITOR: Liang Xinyi, Zhang Yiyu
EXECUTIVE ART EDITOR: Zhang Zichen
TRANSLATORS: Yosemite, Zhang Yiyu, Liang Xinyi
PROOFREADING: Liang Xinyi, Li Jia, Wang Xuejing, Zhang Yiyu

SALES DIRECTOR: Philip Tsang
TEL: +852 6296 2246
EMAIL: sales@sppub.com
WEBSITE: www.sppub.com

ISBN 978-988-78493-1-5

Printed and bound in China.

Facebook

Instagram

X

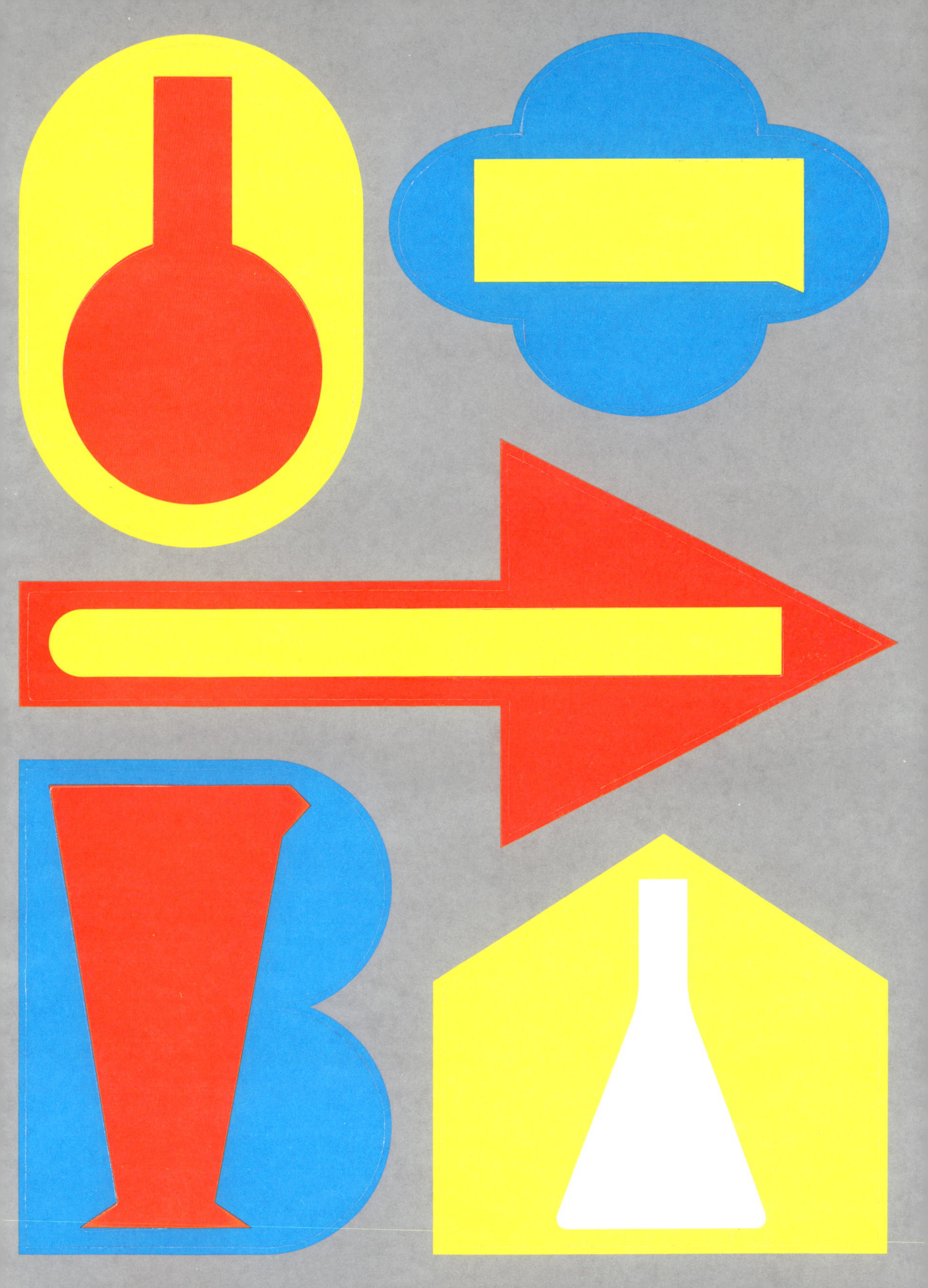